Mastering UML with Rational Rose

Mastering™ UML with Rational Rose®

Wendy Boggs
Michael Boggs

SYBEX®

San Francisco • Paris • Düsseldorf • Soest • London

Associate Publisher: Richard Mills
Contracts and Licensing Manager: Kristine O'Callaghan
Acquisitions & Developmental Editor: Tracy Brown
Editor: Kris Vanberg-Wolff
Project Editor: Rebecca Rider
Technical Editor: Dan Graydon
Book Designers: Patrick Dintino, Catalin Dulfu, Franz Baumhackl
Graphic Illustrators: Tony Jonick, Jerry Williams
Electronic Publishing Specialists: Cyndy Johnsen, Kate Kaminski,
Robin Kibby, Grey Magauran, Nila Nichols, Lesley Rock
Project Team Leader: Lisa Reardon
Proofreader: Carrie Bradley
Indexer: John S. Lewis
Companion CD: Ginger Warner
Cover Designer: Design Site
Cover Illustrator/Photographer: Sergie Loobkoff, Design Site

Library of Congress Card Number: 99-62575
ISBN: 0-7821-2453-4

Manufactured in the United States of America

10 9 8 7 6 5 4 3 2 1

To our parents—Marlene, Jean, Ralph, and John

ACKNOWLEDGMENTS

This book would not have been possible without the efforts of a lot of talented people. First, we'd like to thank the development team at Rational for creating such a good system design tool. Greg Rusnell at METEX Systems, Inc. also deserves our thanks for his help obtaining material for this book's CD-ROM. We'd also like to acknowledge the efforts of the people at Sybex who were dedicated to this project, especially Fred Sloan, Richard Mills, Tracy Brown, Rebecca Rider, Kristen Vanberg-Wolff, Tony Jonick, Jerry Williams, Lisa Reardon, and Carrie Bradley. Your help is greatly appreciated. Thanks to Dan Graydon for spending a great deal of time in the technical review of this book and to Carrie Soltesz for her editorial review. Finally, special thanks to our family and friends for their support during this time. We hope to see more of you now that the project is complete!

CONTENTS AT A GLANCE

TABLE OF CONTENTS

INTRODUCTION

In this ever-changing world of object-oriented application development, it has been getting harder and harder to develop and manage high-quality applications in a reasonable amount of time. As a result of this challenge and a need for a universal object modeling language every company could use, the Unified Modeling Language (UML) was born. UML is the information technology industry's version of a blueprint. It is a method for describing the system's architecture in detail. Using this blueprint, it becomes much easier to build or maintain a system, and to ensure that the system will hold up to requirement changes.

There are a lot of wonderful books out there discussing the processes of rapid application development, object-oriented analysis and design, object modeling, and UML. This book focuses specifically on designing systems with UML and Rational Rose 98 or 98i. Rose is one of a handful of tools that supports rapid application development using UML. It supports Use Case diagrams, Sequence diagrams, Collaboration diagrams, Statechart diagrams, Component diagrams, and Deployment diagrams. Through forward and reverse engineering features, it supports code generation and reverse engineering of C++, Java, Visual Basic, and Oracle8. Add-Ins are also available for PowerBuilder, Forte, and other object-oriented languages, to further extend the functionality provided by Rose.

Who Should Read This Book

This book is intended for beginning and intermediate users of Rational Rose and UML. As we developed the book, we tried to answer three questions: what are each of the diagrams and constructs of UML, why is each type of diagram used, and how do you model each of these diagrams and constructs using Rose?

This book covers the fundamentals of Rose:

◆ How to create actors, use cases, and Use Case diagrams

◆ How to create Sequence and Collaboration diagrams

- How to create classes, attributes, operations, relationships, and Class diagrams

- How to create Statechart diagrams

- How to create components and Component diagrams

- How to create Deployment diagrams

- How to use UML and Rose to create a complete, detailed blueprint of your system

- How to use the new features provided by Rose 98i, including the Web Publisher and integration with Visual C++

- How to generate code from Rose in C++, Java, Visual Basic, and Power-Builder

- How to generate Oracle8 schema with Rose

- How to generate IDL and DDL using Rose

- How to reverse engineer code from C++, Java, Visual Basic and Power-Builder

- How to reverse engineer Oracle8 schema with Rose

This book does not need to be read sequentially. Each chapter was designed to give you a detailed understanding of one piece of Rational Rose. There are exercises provided at the end of most of the chapters to give you some practice using Rose and UML.

If you are new to Rose or UML, you may want to read Chapters 1 through 10 sequentially and complete all of the exercises. The exercises in these chapters will walk you through modeling an order-entry system for a small company. If you are familiar with Rose and UML, this book may be used as a reference for specific Rose or UML questions.

How This Book Is Organized

This book is organzied into four sections described here.

Introduction to UML

Chapters 1 and 2 provide an overview of UML, the object modeling process, and the Rational Rose tool. In Chapter 1, we'll cover the fundamentals of UML and introduce you to Rational Rose. We'll discuss the different types of UML diagrams, what each diagram is used for, and how it is built. In Chapter 2, we'll take a tour of Rose, introducing you to the pieces of the Rose user interface and the functionality Rose provides.

Rose Fundamentals

Chapters 3 through 10 cover all of the basics of Rose. Creating and updating diagrams, adding classes and class details, and generating reports are all covered in these chapters.

Code Generation

Chapters 11 through 18 cover the C++, Java, Visual Basic, PowerBuilder, and Oracle8 code generation capabilities of Rose. In these chapters, we'll examine how each UML construct maps to a particular programming language. You'll see a number of code examples that were generated from Rose. We'll also see how you can generate IDL and DDL directly from your model using Rose.

Reverse Engineering

Chapters 19 through 24 discuss the reverse engineering capabilities of Rose. Rose can reverse engineer code from many different programming languages. In these chapters, we'll look at what is reverse engineered from C++, Java, Visual Basic, PowerBuilder, and Oracle8.

About the CD-ROM

In the book, as we explore the features of Rose, we'll build some Rose models for an ATM system and an order processing system. On the CD-ROM that is packaged with this book, you will find sample UML models for these two systems and examples of the code that can be generated using Rational Rose. You'll also find some sample Rose scripts, which are examples of macros written in the programming language that comes packaged with Rose, and an example of the HTML pages that can be generated using Web Publisher, a new Rose feature. A link to the Rational Web site is included, from which you can find all sorts of information about Rational partners and products, UML, and object modeling. Finally, if you are using PowerBuilder as a development language, you can use the Power-Builder add-in provided on the CD-ROM by METEX Systems, Inc. to generate PowerBuilder code and reverse engineer your PowerBuilder applications. For more information on the CD-ROM, see the "What's on the CD-ROM" page at the end of the book.

How to Contact the Authors

Despite the best efforts of everyone involved, a few errors are bound to slip through in any book. We certainly hope we caught all of them, but if you find any errors or inconsistencies, or anything that just needs clarification, we would appreciate your input.

One of the great things about Rose and UML is that they are both constantly undergoing improvements. However, as with the rest of the information technology industry, it's hard to keep up with all of the changes. If you have any questions at all about Rose or UML, please feel free to contact us. You can contact Wendy at wboggs@jps.net, and Mike at mboggs@jps.net. Please also visit Sybex's Web site at www.sybex.com.

CHAPTER

ONE

1

Introduction to UML

- Learning about the Object-Oriented Paradigm and Visual Modeling

- Exploring Types of Graphical Notation

- Looking at Types of UML Diagrams

- Developing Software Using Visual Modeling

This chapter will provide you with an introduction to UML (Unified Modeling Language), one of the most widely used modeling notations for object-oriented systems. In this chapter, we'll begin by discussing visual modeling and how you can use it to structure your applications. Next, we'll talk about how UML came into being, and where it is used today. Lastly, we'll discuss the development process and how modeling fits into it.

UML is made up of several different types of diagrams. In this chapter, we'll take a brief look at these diagrams. Each one will be explained in detail in the "Rose Fundamentals" section in Chapter 3.

Introduction to the Object-Oriented Paradigm

Object-oriented is the new buzzword for the software industry. Companies are rushing out to adopt this new technology and integrate it into their existing applications. In fact, most applications being developed today are object-oriented. But what does it mean?

The object-oriented paradigm is a different way of viewing applications. With the object-oriented approach, you divide an application into many small chunks, or objects, that are fairly independent of one another. You can then build the application by piecing all of these objects together. Think of it as building a castle out of blocks. The first step is to make or buy some basic objects, the different types of blocks. Once you have these building blocks, you can put them together to make your castle. Once you build or buy some basic objects in the computer world, you can simply put them together to create new applications.

One of the primary advantages of the object-oriented paradigm is the ability to build components once and then use them over and over again. Just as you can reuse a building block in a castle, a house, or a spacecraft, you can reuse a basic piece of object-oriented design and code in an accounting system, an inventory system, or an order-processing system.

So, how is this object-oriented paradigm different from the traditional approach to development? Traditionally, the approach to development has been to concern ourselves with the information that the system will maintain. With this approach, we ask the users what information they will need, design databases to hold the information, provide screens to input the information, and print reports to display the information. In other words, we focus on the information, with less attention paid to what is done with the information, or the behavior of the system. This approach is called *data-centric* and has been used to create thousands of systems over the years.

Data-centric modeling is great for database design and capturing information, but taking this approach when designing business applications presents some problems. One major challenge is that the requirements for the system will change over time. A system that is data-centric can handle a change to the database very easily, but a change to the business rules, or the behavior of the system, is not so easy to implement.

The object-oriented paradigm has been developed in response to this problem. With the object-oriented approach, we focus on both information *and* behavior. Accordingly, we now can develop systems that are resilient and flexible to changes in information and/or behavior.

The benefit of flexibility can only be realized by designing an object-oriented system well. This requires knowledge of some principles of object orientation: encapsulation, inheritance, and polymorphism.

Encapsulation

In object-oriented systems, we combine a piece of information with the specific behavior that acts upon that information. Then we package these into an object. This is referred to as *encapsulation*. Another way to look at encapsulation is that we divide the application into small parts of related functionality. For example, we have information relating to a bank account, such as the account number, balance, customer name, address, account type, interest rate, and opening date. We also have behavior for a bank account: open, close, deposit, withdraw, change type, change customer, and change address. We encapsulate this information and behavior together into an *account* object. As a result, any changes to the banking system regarding accounts can simply be implemented in the account object. It works like a one-stop shop for all account information and behavior.

Another benefit of encapsulation is that it limits the effects of changes to the system. Think of a system as a body of water and the requirement change as a big rock. You drop the rock into the water and—SPLASH!—big waves are created in all directions. They travel throughout the lake, bounce off the shore, reverberate, and collide with other waves. In fact, some of the water may even splash over the shore and out of the lake. In other words, the rock hitting the water caused a huge ripple effect. Now, we encapsulate our lake by dividing it into smaller bodies of water with barriers between them. Then, the requirement change hits the system—SPLASH! As before, waves are created in all directions. But the waves can only go as far as one of the barriers, and then they stop. So, by encapsulating the lake, we have limited the ripple effect of dropping the rock in, as shown in Figure 1.1.

FIGURE 1.1:

Encapsulation: Lake model

Now, let's apply this idea of encapsulation to the banking system. Recently, the bank management decided that if the customer has a credit account at the bank, the credit account could be used as an overdraft for their checking account. In a nonencapsulated system, we begin with a shotgun approach to impact analysis. Basically, we do not know where all of the uses of withdraw functionality are in the system, so we have to look everywhere. When we find it, we have to make some changes to incorporate this new requirement. If we're really good, we probably found about 80% of the uses of withdraw within the system. With an encapsulated system, we do not need to use the shotgun approach to analysis. We look at a model of our system and simply find where the withdrawal behavior was encapsulated. After locating the functionality in the account, we make our requirement change once, only in that object, and our task is complete! As you can see in Figure 1.2, only the Account class needs to change.

A concept similar to encapsulation is *information hiding*. Information hiding is the ability to hide the murky details of an object from the outside world. To an object, the outside world means anything outside of itself, even though that outside world includes the rest of the system. Information hiding provides the same benefit as encapsulation: flexibility. We will discuss this concept more in Chapter 6.

FIGURE 1.2:

Encapsulation: Banking model

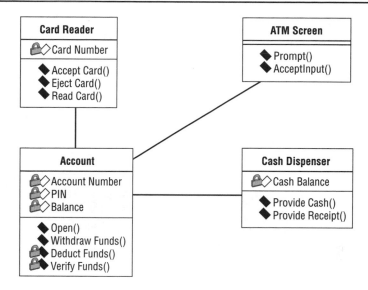

Inheritance

Inheritance is the second of the fundamental object-oriented concepts. No, it has nothing to do with the million dollars you're leaving for little Johnny. It has more to do with the nose you got from your father. In object-oriented systems, inheritance is a mechanism that lets you create new objects based on old ones. The *child* object inherits the qualities of a *parent* object.

You can see examples of inheritance in the natural world. There are hundreds of different types of mammals: dogs, cats, humans, whales, and so on. Each of these has certain characteristics that are unique and certain characteristics that are common to the whole group, such as having hair, being warm-blooded, and nurturing their young. In object-oriented terms, there is a *mammal* object that holds the common characteristics. This object is the parent of the child objects cat, dog, human, whale, etc. The dog object inherits the characteristics of the mammal object, and has some additional *dog* characteristics of its own, such as running in circles and slobbering. The object-oriented paradigm has borrowed this idea of inheritance from the natural world, as shown in Figure 1.3, so we can apply the same concept to our systems.

FIGURE 1.3:

Inheritance: Natural model

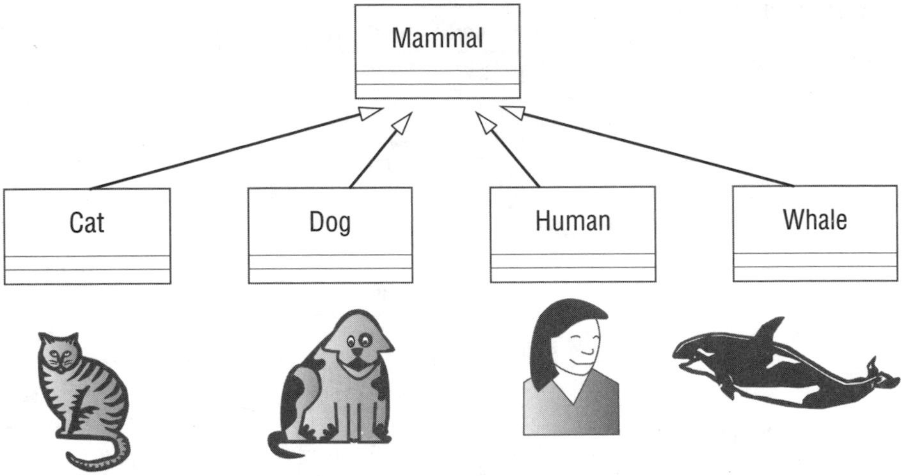

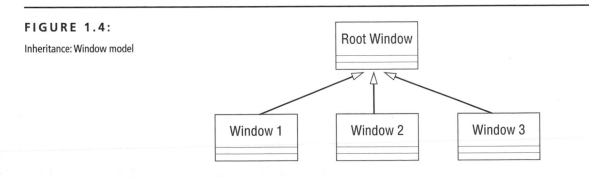

One of the major benefits of inheritance is ease of maintenance. When something changes that affects all mammals, only the parent object needs to change—the child objects will automatically inherit the changes. If mammals were suddenly to become cold-blooded, only the mammal object would need to change. The cat, dog, human, whale, and other child objects would automatically inherit the new, cold-blooded characteristic of mammals.

In an object-oriented system, an example of inheritance might be in the windows. Say we have a large system with 125 windows. One day, a customer requests a disclaimer message on all of the windows. In a system without inheritance, we now have the rather tedious task of going into each one of the 125 windows and making the change. If our system were object-oriented, we would have inherited all of the windows from a common parent. Now, all we need to do is go into the parent and make the change once. All of the windows will automatically inherit the change, as shown in Figure 1.4.

FIGURE 1.4:

Inheritance: Window model

In a banking system, we might use inheritance for the different types of accounts we have. Our hypothetical bank has four different types of accounts: checking, savings, credit card, and certificates of deposit. These different types of accounts have some similarities. Each one has an account number, interest rate, and owner. So, we can create a parent object called *account* to hold the common characteristics of all of the accounts. The child objects can have their own unique characteristics in addition to the inherited ones. The credit account, for example, will also have a credit limit and minimum payment amount. The certificate of deposit will also have a maturity date. Changes to the parent will affect all children, but the children are free to adapt without disturbing each other or their parents.

Polymorphism

The third principle of object orientation is *polymorphism*. The dictionary defines it as the occurrence of different forms, stages, or types. Polymorphism means having many forms or implementations of a particular functionality. As with inheritance, polymorphism can be seen in the natural world. Given the command, or function, of "Speak!" a human may reply, "How do you do?" The dog may reply "Woof!" The cat may reply "Meow!" but will probably just ignore you.

In terms of an object-oriented system, this means that we can have many implementations of a particular functionality. For example, we might be building a graphic drawing system. When the user wants to draw something, be it a line, circle, or rectangle, the system issues a draw command. The system is comprised of many types of shapes, each of which contains the behavior to draw itself. So, when the user wants to draw a circle, the circle object's draw command is invoked. By using polymorphism, the system figures out as it is running which type of shape is being drawn. Without polymorphism, the code for the draw function might look like this:

```
Function Shape.drawMe()
{
    CASE Shape.Type
        Case "Circle"
                Shape.drawCircle();
        Case "Rectangle"
                Shape.drawRectangle();
        Case "Line"
                Shape.drawLine();
    END CASE
}
```

With polymorphism, the code for draw would just call a `drawMe()` function for the object being drawn, as in this example:

```
Function draw()
{
    Shape.drawMe();
}
```

Each shape (circle, line, rectangle, etc.) would then have a `drawMe()` function to draw the particular shape.

One of the benefits of polymorphism, as with the other principles of object orientation, is ease of maintenance. What happens when the application now needs to draw a triangle? In the nonpolymorphic case, a new `drawTriangle()` function has to be added to the Shape object. Also, the `drawMe()` function of the Shape object has to be changed to accommodate the new type of shape. With polymorphism, we create a new triangle object with a `drawMe()` function to draw itself. The `draw()` function that initiates the drawing operation does not have to change at all.

What Is Visual Modeling?

If you are building a new addition to your house, you probably won't start by just buying a bunch of wood and nailing it together until it looks about right. You'll want some blueprints to follow so you can plan and structure the addition before you start working. Odds are the addition will last longer this way. You wouldn't want the whole thing to come crashing down with the slightest rain.

Models do the same thing for us in the software world. They are the blueprints for systems. A blueprint helps you plan an addition before you build it; a model helps you plan a system before you build it. It can help you be sure the design is sound, the requirements have been met, and the system can withstand even a hurricane of requirement changes.

As you gather requirements for your system, you take the business needs of the users and map them into requirements that your team can use and understand. Eventually, you want to take these requirements and generate code from them. By formally mapping the requirements to the code, you can ensure that the requirements were actually met by the code, and that the code can easily be traced back to the requirements. This process is called *modeling*. The result of the modeling process is the ability to trace the business needs to the requirements to the model to the code, and back again, without getting lost along the way.

Visual modeling is the process of taking the information from the model and displaying it graphically using some sort of standard set of graphical elements. A standard is vital to realizing one of the benefits of visual modeling—communication. Communication between users, developers, analysts, testers, managers, and anyone else involved with a project is the primary purpose of visual modeling. You could accomplish this communication using nonvisual (textual) information, but on the whole, humans are visual creatures. We seem to be able to understand complexity better when it is displayed to us visually as opposed to written textually. By producing visual models of a system, we can show how the system works on several levels. We can model the interactions between the users and a system. We can model the interactions of objects within a system. We can even model the interactions between systems, if we so desire.

After creating these models, we can show them to all interested parties and those parties can glean the information they find valuable from the model. For example, users can visualize the interactions they will make with the system from looking at a model. Analysts can visualize the interactions between objects from the models. Developers can visualize the objects that need to be developed and what each one needs to accomplish. Testers can visualize the interactions between objects and prepare test cases based on these interactions. Project managers can see the whole system and how the parts interact. And Chief Information Officers can look at high-level models and see how systems in their organization interact with one another. All in all, visual models provide a powerful tool for showing the proposed system to all of the interested parties.

Booch, OMT, and UML

One important consideration in visual modeling is what graphical notation to use to represent various aspects of a system. This notation needs to be conveyed to all interested parties or the model will not be very useful. Many people have proposed notations for visual modeling. Some of the popular notations that have strong support are Booch, Object Modeling Technology (OMT), and the Unified Modeling Language (UML). Rational Rose 98i supports these three notations; however, UML is a standard that has been adopted by the majority of the industry as well as the standards governing boards such as ANSI and the Object Management Group (OMG).

The *Booch* method is named for its inventor, Grady Booch, the Chief Scientist at Rational Software Corporation. He has written several books discussing the needs and benefits of visual modeling, and has developed a notation of graphical symbols to represent various aspects of a model. For example, objects in this notation are represented by clouds, illustrating the fact that objects can be almost anything. Booch's notation also includes various arrows to represent the types of relationships between objects. We will discuss these types of objects and relationships in the "Rose Fundamentals" section in Chapter 3. Figure 1.5 is a sampling of the objects and relationships represented in the Booch notation.

FIGURE 1.5:

Examples of symbols in the Booch notation

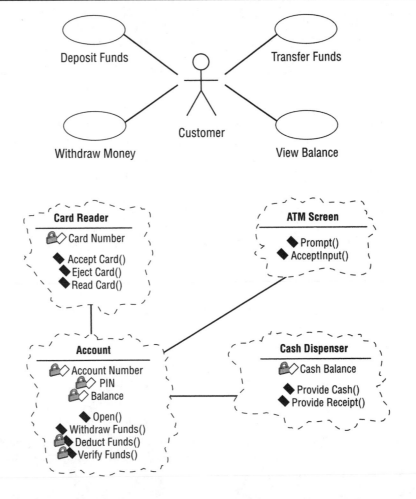

The *OMT (Object Management Technology)* notation comes from Dr. James Rumbaugh, who has written several books about systems analysis and design. In an aptly-titled book, *Systems Analysis and Design*, Rumbaugh discusses the importance of modeling systems in real-world components called objects. The OMT notation he proposes has a strong following, with industry-standard software modeling tools such as Rational Rose and Select OMT supporting it. OMT uses simpler graphics than Booch to illustrate systems. A sampling of the objects and relationships represented in the OMT notation follows in Figure 1.6.

FIGURE 1.6:

Examples of symbols in the OMT notation

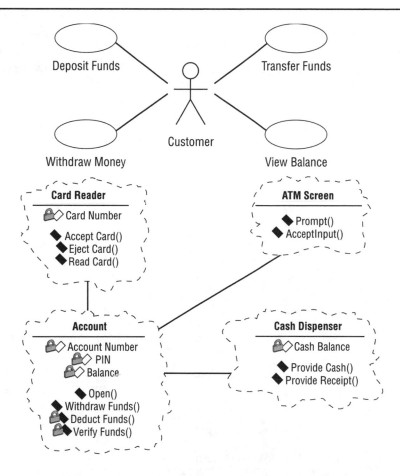

The Unified Modeling Language (UML) notation comes from a collaborative effort of Grady Booch, Dr. James Rumbaugh, Ivar Jacobson, Rebecca Wirfs-Brock, Peter Yourdon, and many others. Jacobson is a scholar who has written about capturing system requirements in packages of transactions called *use cases*. We will discuss use cases in detail later in the "Rose Fundamentals" section in Chapter 3. Jacobson also developed a method for system design called *OOSE (Object Oriented Software Engineering)* that focused on analysis. Booch, Rumbaugh, and Jacobson, commonly referred to as the *three amigos*, all work at Rational Software Corporation and focus on the standardization and refinement of UML. UML symbols closely match those of the Booch and OMT notations, and also include elements from other notations. Figure 1.7 shows a sample of UML notation.

FIGURE 1.7:

Examples of symbols in UML notation

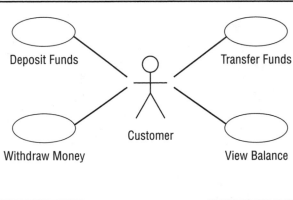

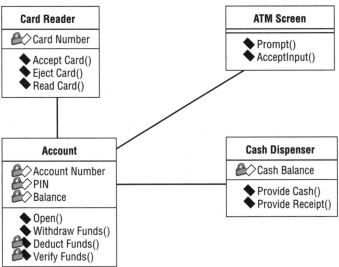

The consolidation of methods that became UML started in 1993. Each of the three *amigos* of UML—Booch, Rumbaugh, and Jacobson—began to incorporate ideas from the other methodologies. Official unification of the methodologies continued until late 1995, when version 0.8 of the Unified Method was introduced. The Unified Method was refined and changed to the Unified Modeling Language in 1996. UML 1.0 was ratified and given to the Object Technology Group in 1997, and many major software development companies began adopting it. Finally, on November 14, 1997, OMG released UML 1.1 as an industry standard.

UML Diagrams

UML allows people to develop several different types of visual diagrams that represent various aspects of the system. Rational Rose supports the development of the majority of these models, as follows:

- Use Case diagram
- Sequence diagram
- Collaboration diagram
- Class diagram
- State Transition diagram
- Component diagram
- Deployment diagram

These model diagrams illustrate different aspects of the system. For example, the Collaboration diagram shows the required interaction between the objects in order to perform some functionality of the system. Each diagram has a purpose and an intended audience.

Use Case Diagrams

Use Case diagrams show the interaction between use cases, which represent system functionality, and actors, which represent the people or systems that provide or receive information from the system. An example Use Case diagram for an Automated Teller Machine (ATM) system is shown in Figure 1.8.

FIGURE 1.8:

Use Case diagram for an ATM (Automated Teller Machine)

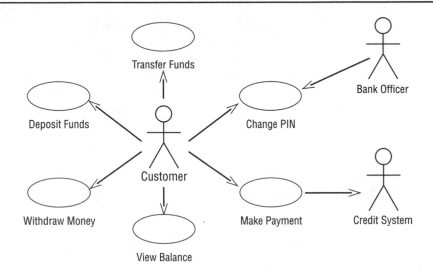

Use Case diagrams show the interactions between use cases and actors. Use cases represent the requirements of the system from the user's perspective. So, use cases are the functionality that the system provides. Actors are the stakeholders of a system. These diagrams show which actors initiate use cases. They also illustrate when an actor receives information from a use case. This Use Case diagram shows the interactions between the use cases and actors of an Automated Teller Machine (ATM) system. In essence, a Use Case diagram can illustrate the requirements of the system. In this example, the bank's customer initiates a number of use cases: Withdraw Money, Deposit Funds, Transfer Funds, Make Payment, View Balance, and Change PIN. A few of the relationships are worthy of further mention. The Bank Officer can also initiate the Change PIN use case. The Make Payment use case shows an arrow going to the Credit System. External systems may be actors and, in this case, the Credit System is shown as an actor because it is external to the ATM system. The arrow going from a use case to an actor illustrates that the use case produces some information that an actor uses. In this case, the Make Payment use case provides credit card payment information to the Credit System.

Much information can be gleaned from viewing Use Case diagrams. This one diagram shows the overall functionality of the system. Users, project managers, analysts, developers, quality assurance engineers, and anyone else interested in the system as a whole can view these diagrams and understand what the system is supposed to accomplish.

Sequence Diagrams

Sequence diagrams are used to show the flow of functionality through a use case. For example, the Withdraw Money use case has several possible sequences, such as withdrawing $, attempting to withdraw without available funds, attempting to withdraw with the wrong PIN, and several others. The normal scenario of withdrawing $20 (without any problems such as entering the wrong PIN or insufficient funds in the account) is shown in Figure 1.9.

FIGURE 1.9:

Sequence diagram for Joe withdrawing $20

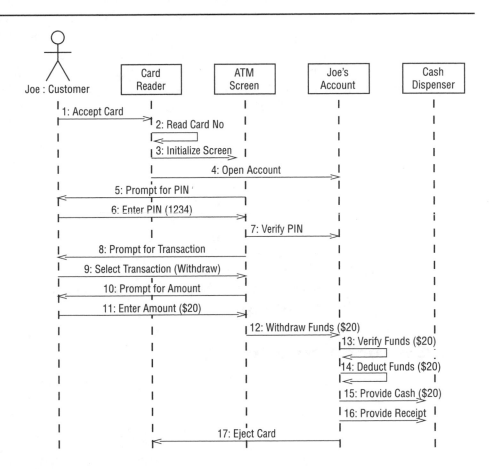

This Sequence diagram shows the flow of processing through the Withdraw Money use case. Any actors involved are shown at the top of the diagram; the customer actor is shown in the above example. The objects that the system needs in order to perform the Withdraw Money use case are also shown at the top of the diagram. Each arrow represents a message passed between actor and object or object and object to perform the needed functionality. One other note about Sequence diagrams—they display objects, not classes. Classes represent types of objects, as we'll discuss later in Chapter 5. Objects are specific; instead of just *customer*, the Sequence diagram shows Joe.

The use case starts with the customer inserting his card into the card reader, an object indicated by the rectangle at the top of the diagram. Then, the card reader reads the card number, opens Joe's account object, and initializes the ATM screen. The screen prompts Joe for his PIN. He enters 1234. The screen verifies the PIN with the account object and they match. The screen presents Joe with his options, and he chooses *Withdraw*. The screen then prompts Joe for the amount to withdraw. He chooses $20. Then, the screen withdraws the funds from the account. This initiates a series of processes that the account object performs. First, Joe's account verifies that the account contains at least $20. Then, it deducts the funds from the account. Next, it instructs the cash dispenser to provide $20 in cash. Joe's account also instructs the dispenser to provide a receipt. Lastly, it instructs the card reader to eject the card.

So, this Sequence diagram illustrated the entire flow of processing for the Withdraw Money use case by showing a specific example of Joe withdrawing $20 from his account. Users can look at these diagrams and see the specifics of their business processing. Analysts see the flow of processing in the Sequence diagrams. Developers see objects that need to be developed and operations for those objects. Quality assurance engineers can see the details of the process and develop test cases based on the processing. Sequence diagrams are useful for all stakeholders in the project.

Collaboration Diagrams

Collaboration diagrams show exactly the same information as the Sequence diagrams. However, Collaboration diagrams show this information in a different way and with a different purpose. The Sequence diagram illustrated in Figure 1.9 is shown in Figure 1.10 as a Collaboration diagram.

In this Collaboration diagram, the objects are represented as rectangles and the actors are stick figures, as before. Whereas the Sequence diagram illustrated the objects and actor interactions over time, the Collaboration diagram shows the objects and actor interactions without reference to time. For example, in this diagram, we see that the card reader instructs Joe's account to open and Joe's account instructs the card reader to eject the card. Also, objects that directly communicate with each other are shown with lines drawn between them. If the ATM screen and card reader directly communicated with one another, a line would be drawn between them. The absence of a line means that no communication occurs directly between those two objects.

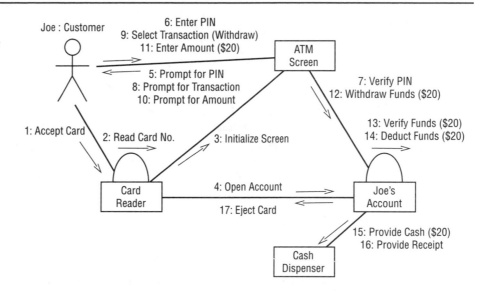

FIGURE 1.10:

Collaboration diagram for Joe withdrawing $20

So, Collaboration diagrams show the same information as Sequence diagrams, but people look at Collaboration diagrams for different reasons. Quality assurance engineers and system architects look at these to see the distribution of processing between objects. Suppose that the Collaboration diagram was shaped like a star, with several objects communicating with a central object. A system architect may conclude that the system is too dependent on the central object and redesign the objects to distribute the processing power more evenly. This type of interaction would have been difficult to see in a Sequence diagram.

Class Diagrams

Class diagrams show the interactions between classes in the system. Classes can be seen as the blueprint for objects, as we'll discuss in Chapter 5. Joe's account, for example, is an object. An account is a blueprint for Joe's checking account; an account is a class. Classes contain information and behavior that acts on that information. The Account class contains the customer's PIN and behavior to check the PIN. A class on a Class diagram is created for each type of object in a

Sequence or Collaboration diagram. The Class diagram for the system's Withdraw Money use case is illustrated in Figure 1.11.

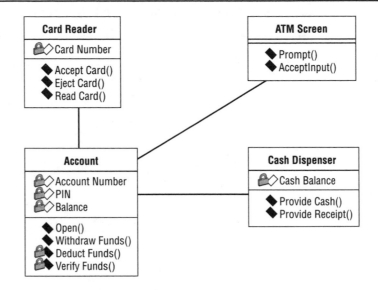

The Class diagram above shows the relationships between the classes that implement the Withdraw Money use case. This is done with four classes: Card Reader, Account, ATM Screen, and Cash Dispenser. Each class on a Class diagram is represented by a rectangle divided into three sections. The first section shows the class name. The second section shows the *attributes* the class contains. An attribute is a piece of information that is associated with a class. For example, the Account class contains three attributes: Account Number, PIN, and Balance. The last section contains the *operations* of the class. An operation is some behavior that the class will provide. The Account class contains four operations: Open, Withdraw Funds, Deduct Funds, and Verify Funds.

The lines connecting classes show the communication relationships between the classes. For instance, the Account class is connected with the ATM Screen class because the two directly communicate with each other. The Card Reader is not connected to the Cash Dispenser because the two do not communicate. Another point of interest is that some attributes and operations have small padlocks to the left of them. The padlock indicates a private attribute or operation. Private attributes and operations can only be accessed from within the class that contains them. The Account Number, PIN, and Balance are all private attributes of the Account class. In addition, the Deduct Funds and Verify Funds operations are private to the Account class.

Developers use Class diagrams to actually develop the classes. Tools such as Rose generate skeletal code for classes, then developers flesh out the details in the language of their choice. Analysts use Class diagrams to show the details of the system. Architects also look at Class diagrams to see the design of the system. If one class contains too much functionality, an architect can see this in the Class diagram and split the functionality out into multiple classes. Should no relationship exist between classes that communicate with each other, an architect or developer can see this too. Class diagrams should be created to show the classes that work together in each use case, and comprehensive diagrams containing whole systems or subsystems can be created as well.

State Transition Diagrams

State Transition diagrams provide a way to model the various states in which an object can exist. While the Class diagrams show a static picture of the classes and their relationships, State Transition diagrams are used to model the more dynamic behavior of a system.

A State Transition diagram shows the behavior of an object. For example, a bank account can exist in several different states. It can be open, closed, or overdrawn. An account may behave differently when it is in each of these states. State Transition diagrams are used to show this information.

Figure 1.12 shows an example of a State Transition diagram for a bank account.

FIGURE 1.12:

State Transition diagram for the account class

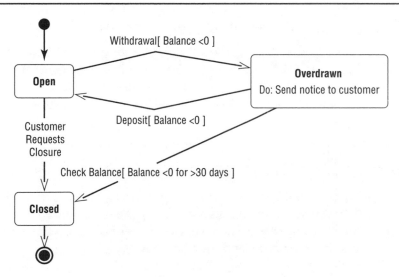

In this diagram, we can see the states in which an account can exist. We can also see how an account moves from one state to another. For example, when an account is open and the customer requests the account's closure, the account moves to the closed state. The customer's request is called the *event* and the event is what causes a transition from one state to another.

If the account is open and the customer makes a withdrawal, the account may move to the overdrawn state. This will only happen if the balance of the account is less than zero. We show this by placing [Balance < 0] on the diagram. A condition enclosed in square brackets is called a *guard condition*, and controls when a transition can or cannot occur.

There are two special states—the *start state* and the *stop state*. The start state is represented by a black dot on the diagram, and indicates what state the object is in when it is first created. The stop state is represented by a bulls-eye, and shows what state the object is in just before it is destroyed. On a State tTansition diagram, there is one and only one start state. You can have no stop state, or there can be as many stop states as you need.

Certain things may happen when the object is inside a particular state. In our example, when an account is overdrawn, a notice is sent to the customer. Processes that occur while an object is in a certain state are called *actions*.

State Transition diagrams aren't created for every class; they are used only for very complex classes. If an object of the class can exist in several states, and behaves very differently in each of the states, you may want to create a State Transition diagram for it. Many projects won't need these diagrams at all. If they are created, developers will use them when developing the classes.

State Transition diagrams are created for documentation only. When you generate code from your Rose model, no code will be generated from the information on the State Transition diagrams. However, Rose add-ins are available for real-time systems that can generate executable code based on State Transition diagrams.

Component Diagrams

Component diagrams show you a physical view of your model. A Component diagram shows you the software components in your system and the relationships between them. There are two types of components on the diagram: executable components and code libraries.

In Rose, each of the classes in the model is mapped to a source code component. Once the components have been created, they are added to the Component diagram. Dependencies are then drawn between the components. Component dependencies show the compile-time and run-time dependencies between the components.

Figure 1.13 illustrates one of the Component diagrams for the ATM system.

FIGURE 1.13:

Component diagram for the ATM client

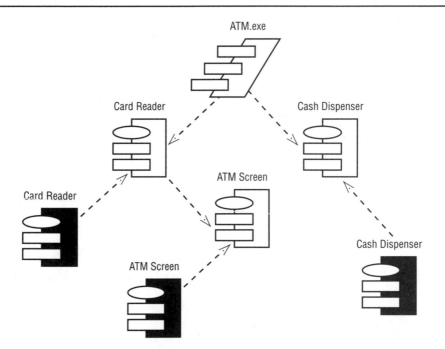

This Component diagram shows the client components in the ATM system. In this case, the team decided to build the system using C++. Each class has its own .CPP and header file, so each class is mapped to its own components in the diagram. For example, the ATM Screen class is mapped to the ATM Screen component. The ATM Screen class is also mapped to a second ATM Screen component. These two components represent the header and body of the ATM Screen class. The shaded component is called a *package specification*. It represents the body file (.CPP) of the ATM Screen class in C++. The unshaded component is also called a package specification. The package specification represents the header (.H) file of the C++ class. The component called ATM.exe is a task specification and represents a thread of processing. In this case, the thread of processing is the executable program.

Components are connected by dashed lines showing the dependency relationships between them. For example, the Card Reader class is dependent upon the ATM Screen class. This means that the ATM Screen class must be available in order for the Card Reader class to compile. Once all of the classes have been compiled, then the executable called ATMClient.exe can be created.

The ATM example has two threads of processing and therefore two executables. One executable comprises the ATM Client, including the Cash Dispenser, Card Reader, and ATM Screen. The second executable comprises the ATM Server, including the Account component. The Component diagram for the ATM Server is shown in Figure 1.14.

FIGURE 1.14:

Component diagram for the ATM server

As this example has shown, there can be multiple Component diagrams for a system depending on the number of subsystems or executables. Each subsystem is a package of components. In general, packages are collections of objects. In this case, packages are collections of components. The ATM example includes two packages: the ATM Client and the ATM Server. Packages will be discussed more in the "Rose Fundamentals" section in Chapter 3.

Component diagrams are used by whoever is responsible for compiling the system. The diagrams will tell this individual in what order the components need to be compiled. The diagrams will also show what run-time components will be created as a result of the compilation. Component diagrams show the mapping of classes to implementation components. These diagrams are also where code generation is initiated.

Deployment Diagrams

Deployment diagrams are the last type of diagram we will discuss. The Deployment diagram shows the physical layout of the network and where the various components will reside. In our ATM example, the ATM is comprised of many subsystems running on separate physical devices, or nodes. The Deployment diagram for the ATM system is illustrated in Figure 1.15.

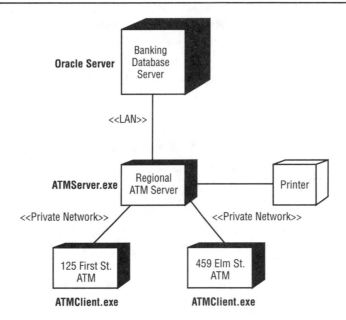

This Deployment diagram tells us much about the layout of the system. The ATM client executable will run on multiple ATMs located at different sites. The ATM client will communicate over a private network with the regional ATM server. The ATM server executable will run on the regional ATM server. The regional ATM server will in turn communicate over the local area network (LAN) with the banking database server running Oracle. Lastly, a printer is connected to the regional ATM server.

So, this one diagram shows us the physical setup for the system. Our ATM system will be following a three-tier architecture with one tier each for the database, regional server, and client.

The Deployment diagram is used by the project manager, users, architect, and deployment staff to understand the physical layout of the system and where the various subsystems will reside. This diagram helps the project manager communicate what the system will be like to the users. It also helps the staff responsible for deployment to plan their deployment efforts.

All of these diagrams together describe the system from several different perspectives. In the "Rose Fundamentals" section in Chapter 3, we will discuss each of these diagrams more closely and show how they are generated in Rational

Rose. You will also be given the opportunity to try creating and using these diagrams in Rational Rose. But before we get into the details of Rose, another aspect of software development projects deserves some attention— the process. While this is not a methodology or process book, we do want to familiarize you with a process for development using UML diagrams we have discussed.

Visual Modeling and the Software Development Process

Software development can be done in many ways. There are several different types of development processes that projects follow, including everything from waterfall to object-oriented processes. Each has its benefits and disadvantages. In this section, we do not plan to tell you which one to use, but we will present an overview of a process that focuses on visual modeling. Again, this is just an overview.

For a long time, software development followed the waterfall model. In this model, we analyzed the requirements, designed a system, developed the system, tested the system, and deployed the system. As its name suggests, we didn't flow back up this chain—water cannot go up. This method has been the documented methodology used on thousands of projects, but we contend that it has not been used as purely as we would like to think. One of the main shortcomings of the waterfall model is that it is necessary to backtrack through the steps. At the outset of a project following the waterfall model, we take on the daunting task of determining *all* of the system requirements. We do this through detailed discussions with the users and detailed examination of business processes. After we're done, we make sure the users sign off on the voluminous requirements we have written, even if they haven't read them yet. If we're really lucky, we might get about 80% of the requirements of the system during this analysis stage.

Then, it's on to design. We sit down and determine the architecture of our system. We address issues such as where programs will reside and what hardware is necessary for acceptable performance. While doing this, we may find out that some new issues have arisen. We then go back to the users and talk about the issues. These result in new requirements. So, we're back in analysis. After going back and forth a few times, we move to development and begin coding the system.

While coding, we discover that a certain design decision is impossible to implement. So, we go back to design and revisit the issue. After coding is done, testing begins. While testing, we learn that a requirement was not detailed enough and the interpretation was incorrect. Now we have to go back to the analysis phase and revisit the requirement.

After some time, we finally get the system done and delivered to the users. Since it took quite awhile and the business has probably changed while we were building the system, the users respond less than enthusiastically with, "That's just what I asked for, but not what I want!" This incantation by the users is a powerful spell that causes the entire project team to age 10 years immediately!

So, after looking at this dismal scenario and wondering if you are in the right industry, what can you do to make it better? Is the problem that the business changes so quickly? Is it that the users don't communicate what they want? Is it that the users don't understand the project team? Is it that the team didn't follow a process? The answers are yes, yes, yes, and no. The business changes very rapidly, and as software professionals we need to keep up. The users do not always communicate what they want because what they do is second nature to them. Asking an accounting clerk who has been on the job for 30 years is roughly like asking someone how you breathe. It becomes so second nature that it is difficult to describe. Another problem is that the users don't always understand the project team. The team shows them flowcharts and produces volumes of requirements text, but the users don't always understand what is being given to them. Can you think of a way around this problem? Visual modeling can help. Lastly, the team did follow a process: the waterfall method. Unfortunately, the plan and the execution of the method were two different things.

So, one of the problems is that the team planned to use the waterfall method, with its neat and orderly passage through the stages of the project, but they had to backtrack throughout the project. Is this due to poor planning? Probably not. Software development is a complex process and trying to do everything in neat stages doesn't always work. If the need for backtracking had been ignored, then the system would have design flaws, missing requirements, and possibly worse. But over the years we have learned to plan the backtracking. With this insight comes *iterative development*. Iterative development just means that we are going to do things over and over. In the object-oriented process, we will go through the steps of analysis, design, development, test, and deployment in small stages many times.

It is impossible to learn all of the requirements during the early part of the project. New things are bound to come out, so we plan for them by planning the project in iterations. With this concept, a project can be seen as a series of small waterfalls. Each one is designed to be big enough to mark the completion of an important part of the project, but small enough to minimize the need for back-tracking. In the project, we go through four phases: Inception, Elaboration, Construction, and Transition. Inception is the beginning of the project. We gather information and do proofs-of-concept. The end of inception is the go/no-go decision for the project. In elaboration, use cases are detailed and architectural decisions are made. Elaboration includes some analysis, design, coding, and test planning. Construction is where the bulk of the coding is done. Transition is the final preparation and deployment of the system to the users. Next, we will discuss what each of these phases means in an object-oriented project.

Inception

The inception phase is the beginning of the project. Inception begins when someone says, "Gee, wouldn't it be great if we had a system to do …." Then, someone researches the idea and management asks how long it would take, how much it will cost, or how feasible the project is. Finding out the answers to these questions is what the inception phase is all about. We discover what the high-level features of the system are and document them. We discover who the actors in the system are and determine use cases. We do not go into details about the use cases here, but just provide a sentence or two. We also provide estimates to upper management. So, using Rose to support our project, we will create actors and use cases and produce use case diagrams. Inception ends when the research is done and management commits the resources to work on the project.

The inception phase of the project is primarily sequential and noniterative. The other phases are iterated multiple times during the project. Because the project can really only start once, inception is only done once on a project. For this reason, one more task remains in inception—the development of an iteration plan. An iteration plan is a plan describing which use cases will be implemented during which iterations. If we find 10 use cases during inception, we may draw up an iteration plan like this:

Iteration One	Use Cases 1, 5, 6
Iteration Two	Use Cases 7, 9

| Iteration Three | Use Cases 2, 4, 8 |
| Iteration Four | Use Cases 3, 10 |

The plan tells us which use cases will be done first. Determining this plan requires looking at dependencies between use cases and planning accordingly. If Use Case 3 is required in order for Use Case 5 to work, then the plan described above is not feasible because Use Case 3 would be implemented during the fourth iteration, far after Use Case 5 is in the first iteration. We may have to adjust our plan to accommodate the dependencies.

Using Rose in Inception

Some inception tasks include determining use cases and actors. Rose can be used to document these use cases and actors, and to create the diagrams to show their relationships. The Use Case diagrams can be presented to the users to validate that the diagrams are a comprehensive view of the system features.

Elaboration

The elaboration phase of the project includes some planning, analysis, and architectural design. Following the iteration plan, elaboration is done for each use case in the current iteration. Elaboration includes several aspects of a project, such as coding proofs-of-concept, developing test cases, and making design decisions.

The major tasks in the elaboration phase are detailing the use cases. In the "Rose Fundamentals" section in Chapter 3, we will discuss what the details of a use case include. The low-level requirements of a use case include the flow of processing through the use case, what actors are involved with the use case, Interaction diagrams to show the flow of processing graphically, and any state changes that may occur during the use case. The requirements, in the form of detailed use cases, are gathered into a document called a Software Requirement Specification (SRS). The SRS contains all of the details of the system requirements.

Other tasks are done in elaboration, such as refining the initial estimates, reviewing the SRS and use case model for quality, and investigating risks. Rational Rose can help with refining the Use Case model and creating the Sequence and

Collaboration diagrams to show the graphical flow of processing. The Class diagrams showing the objects to be built are also designed during the elaboration phase.

The elaboration phase is over when the use cases have been fully detailed and accepted by the users, proofs-of-concept have been completed to mitigate risks, and the Class diagrams are complete. In other words, this phase is complete when the system is designed, reviewed, and ready for the developers to build it.

Using Rose in Elaboration

The elaboration phase presents several opportunities to use Rational Rose. Since elaboration is the detailing of the system requirements, the Use Case model might require updating. As the flow of processing is detailed, Sequence and Collaboration diagrams help illustrate the flow. They also help design the objects that will be required for the system. Elaboration also involves preparing the design for the system so the developers can begin its construction. This can be accomplished by creating Class diagrams and State Transition diagrams in Rose.

Construction

Construction refers to the process of developing and testing the software. As with elaboration, this phase is completed for each set of use cases in an iteration. Tasks in the construction phase include determining any remaining requirements, developing the software, and testing the software. Since the software has been completely designed during the elaboration phase, construction should not involve many design decisions. This helps the project team carry out parallel development. Parallel development means that multiple developers can work on the different objects in the software and know that the whole system will come together when they are through. In elaboration, we design the objects in the system and how they will interact. Construction is just a matter of putting that design into action rather than making new design decisions that could change that interaction.

Another benefit of modeling the system up front is that Rational Rose can generate skeletal code for the system. In order to use this feature, you need to create components and a component diagram as an early part of construction. Once you have created Components and diagrammed their dependencies, code generation can begin. Code generation will provide as much code as possible based on the design. This does not mean that you will get any business-specific code out of Rose. What you will get depends greatly on the language that is chosen, but generally includes class declarations, attribute declarations, scope declarations (public, private, and protected), function prototypes, and inheritance statements. This saves time because this is tedious code to write. After generating code, the developers can focus on the business-specific aspects of the project. As code is completed, it should be reviewed by a peer group of developers to ensure that it meets standards, design conventions, and is functional. After code review, the objects should be subjected to quality assurance review. If any new attributes or functions are added during construction, or if any interactions between objects are altered, then the new code should be updated back into the Rose model through reverse engineering. We will cover this topic further in Chapters 19 through 24 of this book.

Construction is over when the software is complete and tested. It's important to make sure that the model and software are synchronized; the model will be extremely valuable once the software enters maintenance mode.

Using Rose in Construction

Construction is the stage in which the majority of the coding for the project is done. Rose is used to create components according to the object design. Component diagrams are created to show the compile-time dependencies between the components. After languages have been selected for each component, the generation of skeletal code can be done. After code has been created by the developers, the model can be synchronized with the code through reverse engineering.

Transition

The transition phase is when the completed software product is turned over to the user community. Tasks in this phase include completing the final software product, completing final acceptance testing, completing user documentation, and preparing for user training. The Software Requirements Specification, Use Case diagrams, Class diagrams, Component diagrams, and Deployment diagrams must be updated to reflect any final changes. It is important to keep these models synchronized with the software product because the models will be used once the software product goes into maintenance mode. Several months from the completion of the project, the models will be priceless in helping to make enhancements to the software.

Rational Rose is not as helpful in the transition phase as it is in other phases. At this point, the software product has been developed. Rose is designed to aid in the modeling and development of the software, and even helps plan the deployment of the software. However, Rose was not designed as a test tool or to help with the testing plans or deployment procedures. There are other tools that are specifically designed for these purposes. So, Rose will be used in the transition phase primarily to update the models as the software product is completed.

Summary

Visual modeling and Rational Rose are useful at several different stages of the software development process. Toward the beginning of the project, in inception, Rose is used to produce the Use cCse model. During elaboration, Rose is used extensively to develop Sequence and Collaboration diagrams showing the objects that will be developed and how they interact with one another. Class diagrams are developed in Rose, showing how the objects relate to each other. During the initial stages of construction, the Component diagrams are created using Rose. These show the dependencies of the components in the system and allow you to generate skeletal code for the system. Throughout construction, we use Rose to reverse engineer newly developed code back into the model to incorporate any changes that arose during development. After construction, we move into transition, where Rose is used to update any of the models created during the project.

In the next chapter, we'll take a short tour of Rose. We'll examine the different features and capabilities of the Rose tool, take a look at the menu options available in Rose, and talk about how to create and save a Rose model. We'll discuss how to navigate Rose, the four views of the model that Rose provides, and how to publish your Rose model on the Web.

CHAPTER

TWO

2

A Tour of Rose

- Installing Rose 98

- Installing Rose 98i

- Getting around in Rose

- Exploring Four Views in a Rose Model

- Working with Rose

- Setting Global Options

In this chapter, we will take a tour of the Rational Rose product. We'll begin by discussing what Rational Rose is and what a Rational Rose model includes. We'll show how to install Rose on your computer, and then take a visual tour, discussing the various parts of the screen and how to navigate through the product. Then, we'll discuss the four views of a system that are available through Rose and how to work with Rose.

After this, our introduction to UML and to Rose will be complete, and you will be armed with enough information to embark on learning the fundamentals of designing systems with Rose.

What Is Rose?

Rational Rose is a powerful tool to aid in the analysis and design of object-oriented software systems. It helps you model your system *before* you write any code, so you can be sure that the system is architecturally sound from the beginning. Using the model, you can catch design flaws early, while they are still inexpensive to fix.

Rational Rose will help with systems analysis and design by enabling you to design use cases and Use Case diagrams to show the system functionality. It will let you design Interaction diagrams to show how the objects work together to provide the needed functionality. Classes and Class diagrams can be created to show the objects in a system and how they relate to each other. Component diagrams can be developed to illustrate how the classes map to implementation components. Finally, a Deployment diagram can be produced to show the network design for the system.

A Rose *model* is a picture of a system. It includes all of the UML diagrams, actors, use cases, objects, classes, components, and deployment nodes in a system. It describes in great detail what the system will include and how it will work, so developers can use the model as a blueprint for the system being built.

This helps alleviate an age-old problem: The team has talked to the customers and documented the requirements. Now the developers are ready to code. One developer (we'll call him Bob) takes some of the requirements, makes certain design decisions, and writes some code. Jane, on the other hand, takes some requirements, makes completely different design decisions, and writes some more code.

This difference in programming style is perfectly natural; 20 developers given the same requirements may code 20 different systems. The problem comes about when someone needs to understand or maintain the system. Without conducting detailed interviews with each of the developers, it's hard for anyone to see what design decisions were made, what the pieces of the system are, or what the overall structure of the system is. Without a documented design, it's hard to be sure that the system you built is actually the system the users had in mind.

Traditionally, we follow a process that looks like this:

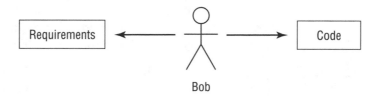

The requirements are documented, but the design is inside Bob's brain, so no one other than Bob has a good idea of the system structure. If Bob leaves, that information leaves with him. If you've ever been the one taking over for Bob, you can appreciate how difficult it can be to understand a system with little documentation.

A Rose model gives us a process that looks like this:

Now, the design is documented. The developers can all gather to discuss the design decisions *before* the code is written. You don't have to worry about everyone going off in a separate direction with the system design.

But the developers aren't the only ones to use the model:

- Customers and project managers will use the Use Case diagrams to get a high-level view of the system and to agree on the project scope.

- Project managers will use the Use Case diagrams and documentation to break the project down into manageable pieces.

- Analysts and customers will look at the use case documentation to see what functionality the system will provide.

- Technical writers will look at the use case documentation to begin to write the user manual and training plans.

- Analysts and developers will look at Sequence and Collaboration diagrams to see how the logic in the system will flow, the objects in the system, and the messages between the objects.

- Quality assurance staff will use the use case documentation and the Sequence and Collaboration diagrams to get the information they need for testing scripts.

- Developers will use the Class diagrams and State Transition diagrams to get a detailed view of the pieces of the system and how they relate.

- Deployment staff will use the Component and Deployment diagrams to see what executable files, DLL files, or other components will be created, and where these components will be deployed on the network.

- The whole team will use the model to be sure the requirements are traced to the code, and that the code can be traced back to the requirements.

So, Rose is a tool meant to be used by the entire project team. It is a repository of scope and design information that each team member can use to get the information they need.

In addition to the above, Rational Rose will help developers by generating skeletal code. It can do this for a number of different languages available on the market, including C++, Java, Visual Basic, and PowerBuilder. Further, Rose can reverse engineer code and create a model based on an existing system. Having a model in Rose for an existing application is very beneficial. When a change occurs to the model, Rose can modify the code to incorporate the change. When a change occurs in the code, you can incorporate that change into the model automatically. These features help you keep the model and the code synchronized, reducing the risk of having an outdated model.

Rose can also be extended using RoseScript, a programming language packaged with Rose. Using this programming language, you can write code to automatically make changes to your model, create a report, or perform other tasks with your Rose model.

There are three different versions of Rose currently available:

- Rose Modeler, which allows you to create a model for your system, but will not support code generation or reverse engineering.

- Rose Professional, which allows you to generate code in one language.

- Rose Enterprise, which allows you to generate code in C++, Java, and Visual Basic, as well as Oracle8 schema.

In addition, Rose 98i, a recent enhancement to Rose, focuses on the integration of Rose with other tools such as Rational RequisitePro, TeamTest, Visual C++, and more. Rose 98i will also allow you to publish your model on the Web. Rose 98i, like Rose 98, is available in the Modeler, Professional, and Enterprise versions. All exercises in this book are available on the CD in both the Rose 98 and Rose 98i versions.

Installing Rose 98

Rational Rose is installed from a CD onto a computer with Windows 95, NT, or Windows 98. To begin the installation process, place the CD in the computer. The setup program should start immediately, but if your computer does not support autostart files on CD, then you will need to run the file `setup.exe` from the root directory on the CD. When the installation process has started, you will be presented with the screen shown in Figure 2.1.

FIGURE 2.1:

Welcome to Rose installation

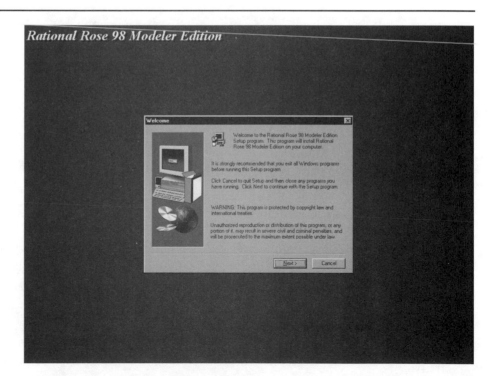

It is recommended that you exit all other Windows applications during the installation process. When you have exited all other applications, click Next to continue.

Next, as you can see in Figure 2.2, the installation program will advise you to remove any previous versions of Rational Rose you may have installed on the computer. Remove any previous versions by using the Add/Remove programs option in the Windows Control Panel, then click Next to continue.

FIGURE 2.2:

Removing other versions of Rose

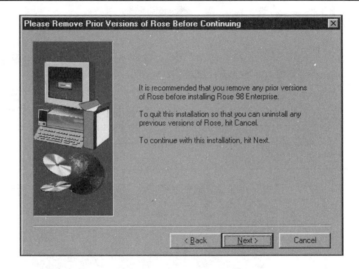

You are then presented with the Rational License Agreement, as shown in Figure 2.3. After reading through the agreement, press Yes to accept the terms. Otherwise, return the package. (Hopefully, you kept the receipt!)

The next installation screen asks you for your name, company, and the individual Rose serial number, as shown in Figure 2.4. You must enter all three to continue. The serial number can be found on the back of the CD case. After entering the name, company, and serial number, the installation process will ask you to verify the information. Click OK if it is correct. If the serial number is valid, the installation process will continue.

After verifying the user information, the installation program asks you for the location where you want Rational Rose installed, as shown in Figure 2.5. The default location is C:\Program Files\Rational\Rational Rose 98 Enterprise Edition. If this directory is acceptable, click Next. If you want to change the destination, click the Browse button to select a different directory.

FIGURE 2.3:

License agreement

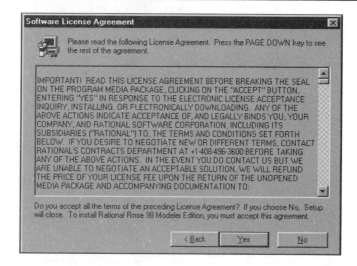

FIGURE 2.4:

User information

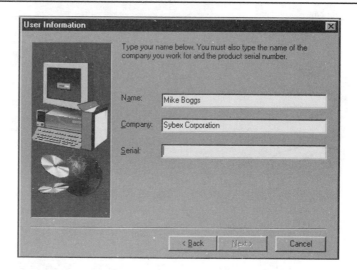

Next, decide which type of setup you prefer. Your options are displayed in the Setup Type box shown in Figure 2.6.

FIGURE 2.5:

Choosing the destination
location

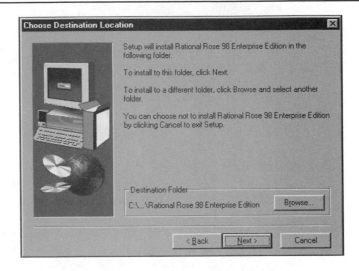

FIGURE 2.6:

Choosing the setup type

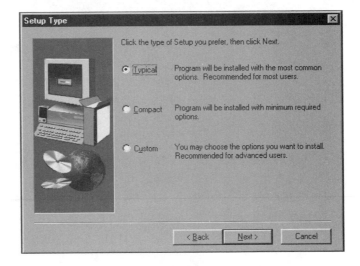

The choices are Typical, Compact, and Custom. The compact option installs Rose with only the Modeler component and help files. The Typical option installs Rose with the commonly used add-ins, as shown below:

- Microsoft Repository Add-In

- SCC Add-In

- Visual Basic Add-In

- C++ Add-In

- Java Add-In

- Oracle8 Add-In

- Framework Add-In

- ERwin Add-In

- TypeLibImporter Add-In

The Custom option allows you to select which add-ins you want to install. We recommend choosing the Typical installation. All exercises in this book assume that you have installed Rational Rose using the Typical option.

After specifying your option, click Next to continue. A short message may appear, advising you that to use the Microsoft Repository Add-In, you must have Visual Studio installed.

Next, you need to select a program folder for the icons, as shown in Figure 2.7. The default folder is Rational Rose 98 Enterprise Edition, but you are free to select a different folder. After making your selection, click Next to continue.

FIGURE 2.7:

Selecting a program folder

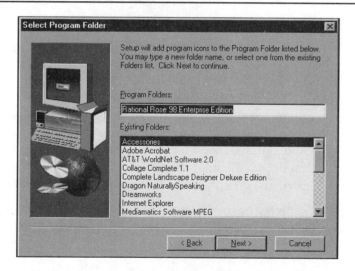

The next option to select is your default language, as shown in Figure 2.8.

When you start Rose, it will be configured to have the object libraries for the language you select. These libraries enable you to generate and reverse engineer code in that language. Your choices are:

- Analysis

- C++

- Java

- Visual Basic

FIGURE 2.8:

Selecting a default language

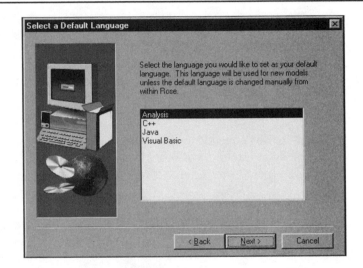

The Analysis option configures Rose to have no default language. The other options configure Rose to use that language as default by including the necessary object libraries in your model. For example, if your development language is Visual Basic, then select this as your default language. When you start a new Rose model, it will automatically include the Visual Basic objects, interfaces, and components. When you have made your selection, click Next to continue.

Before beginning the process of copying files and configuring Rose, you are given one last opportunity to review all of the settings, as shown in Figure 2.9.

You can check the amount of disk space required, which components will be installed, where the files will be installed, in which program group the icons will be installed, and which default language was selected. If everything is correct, click Next to begin copying files and configuring Rose.

FIGURE 2.9:

Checking the setup
information

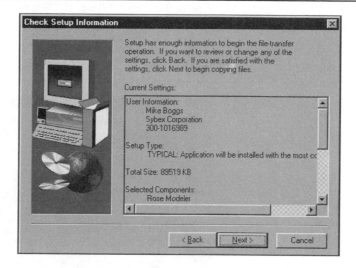

While the installation program is copying files and configuring Rose, the screen
in Figure 2.10 will be displayed to keep you apprised of the progress. If at any
point you wish to cancel the installation, click the Cancel button.

FIGURE 2.10:

Copying files

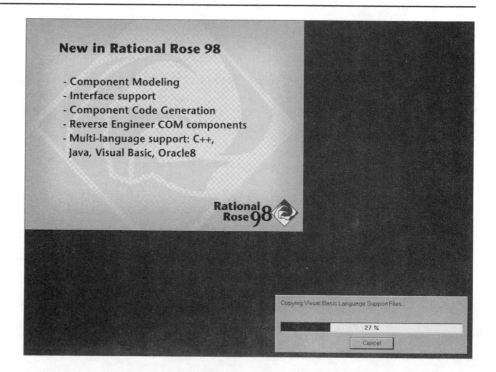

After a few minutes, the setup will be completed. The installation program will display the screen shown in Figure 2.11 and give you the opportunity to read the Readme file or start Rose. If you wish to do either one, click the appropriate checkbox and then click Finish.

FIGURE 2.11:

Choosing to view the release notes or start Rose

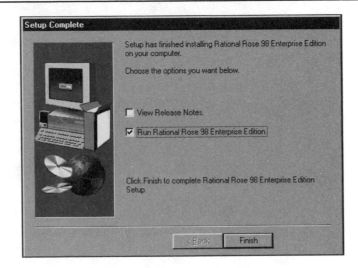

With that, the installation is complete and you can begin modeling your systems in Rational Rose. If you are using the evaluation license, you have a 30-day temporary license to use the product. At that time, the product will no longer be accessible. Also, please be aware that the product will not be accessible if you attempt to re-install or modify the system date on the computer. To use the product after the 30-day evaluation has expired, Rose must be purchased from an authorized Rational reseller.

Installing Rose 98i

Rational Rose 98i is installed from a Rational Software Products CD onto a computer with Windows 95, NT, or Windows 98. To begin the installation process, place the CD in the computer. The setup program should start immediately, but if your computer does not support autostart files on CD, then you will need to run the file setup.exe from the root directory on the CD. When the installation process has started, you will be presented with the screen shown in Figure 2.12.

FIGURE 2.12:

The Rational Software
Setup Wizard

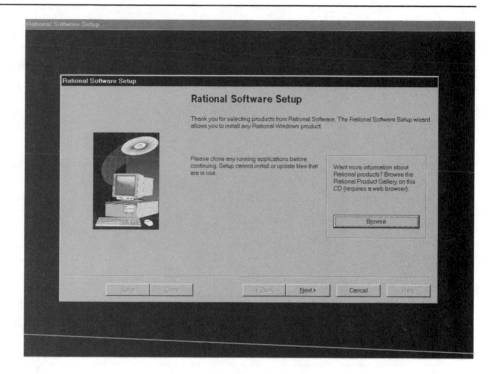

It is recommended that you exit all other Windows applications during the installation process. When you have exited all other applications, click Next to continue.

As you can see in Figure 2.13, the installation program will ask you to choose the product to install. All Rational products, with a few exceptions, come on the CD. Select Rational Rose 98i Enterprise, Professional, or Modeler.

Also, select the location where you want Rational Rose installed. The default location is C:\Program Files\Rational. If this directory is acceptable, click Next. If you want to change the destination, click the Browse button to select a different directory.

You are then presented with the Rational License Agreement, as shown in Figure 2.14. After reading through the agreement, press Yes to accept the terms. Otherwise, return the package. (Hopefully, you kept the receipt!)

FIGURE 2.13:

Choosing which product to install

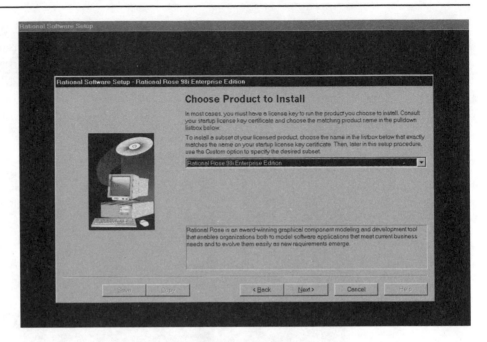

FIGURE 2.14:

License Agreement

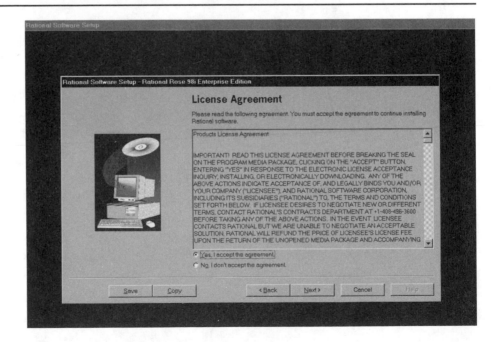

Next, decide which type of setup you prefer. Your options are displayed in the Setup Type box shown in Figure 2.15.

FIGURE 2.15:

Choosing a setup type

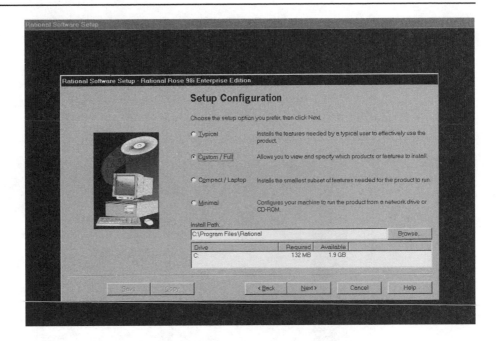

The choices are Typical, Custom/Full, Compact/Laptop, and Minimal. The Compact option installs Rose with only the Modeler and help files. The typical option installs Rose with all the commonly used add-ins. The following add-ins are installed with the Typical option:

- Rational Synchronizer
- Rose C++ Add-In
- Rose CORBA Add-In
- Rose Java Add-In
- Rose Oracle8 Add-In
- Rose Type Library Importer Add-In
- Rose Version Control Add-In
- Rose Visual Basic Add-In

- Rose Visual C++ Add-In

- Rose Web Publisher Add-In

The Custom option allows you to select which add-ins you want to install. We recommend choosing the Typical installation. All exercises in this book assume that you have installed Rational Rose Enterprise edition, using the Typical option.

Next, some components and files will be updated. The installation will not be successful unless the components are updated, so click Next to continue when you see Figure 2.16.

FIGURE 2.16:

Updating shared components

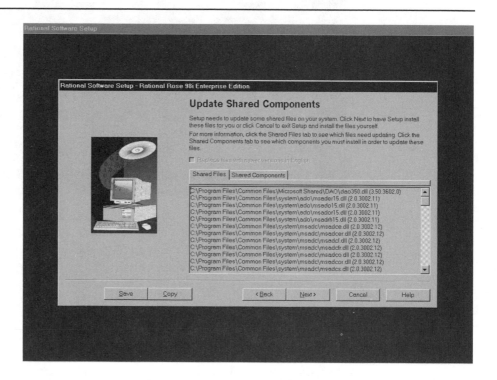

Before beginning the process of copying files and configuring Rose, you are given one last opportunity to review all of the settings, as shown in Figure 2.17. You can check which components will be installed, where the files will be installed, and in which program group the icons will be installed. If everything is correct, click Next to begin copying files and configuring Rose.

FIGURE 2.17:

Confirming your settings

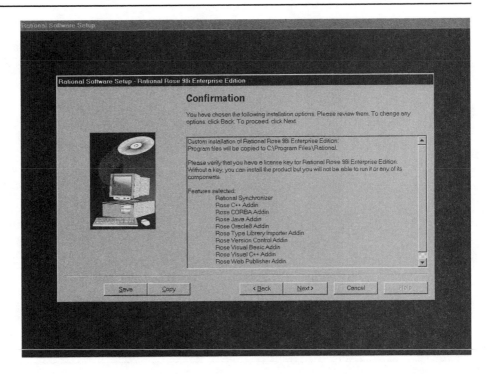

If you are upgrading a Rational Rose 98 installation to Rational Rose 98i, you may see the screen shown in Figure 2.18. This shows a summary of any installation errors. If a file already existed when the installation program attempted to copy it, an error message will be shown. As long as there are no serious errors in the summary, click Next to continue.

After the copying is complete, you will be asked to restart windows from the screen shown in Figure 2.19. In order to complete the installation process, Windows must be restarted. Choose Restart, then click Finish to restart Windows.

After Windows has restarted, Figure 2.20 will be displayed. At this point, the installation process is complete. However, you cannot run Rational Rose until you have entered a valid license key. Ensure the check box for launching the License Key Administrator is checked, then click Finish.

FIGURE 2.18:

If you are upgrading a Rational Rose 98 installation to Rational Rose 98, you may see the Error Summary screen.

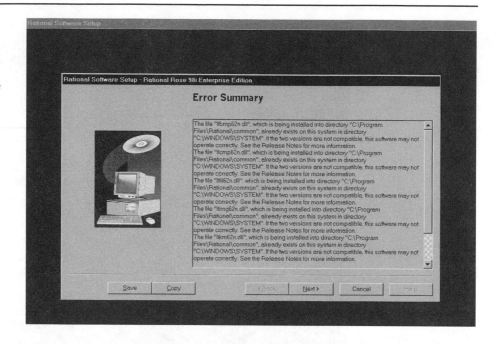

FIGURE 2.19:

Restarting Windows

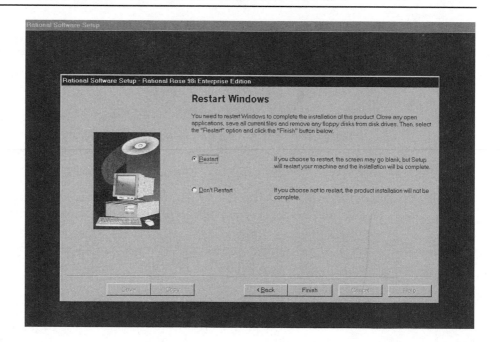

FIGURE 2.20:

Launching the License Key
Administrator

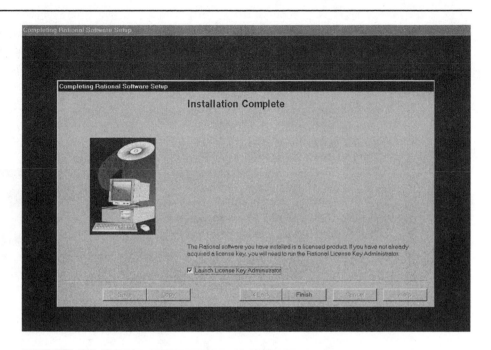

The License Key Administrator will start, as shown in Figure 2.21. Click the
Continue button to begin the licensing process.

FIGURE 2.21:

License Key Administrator

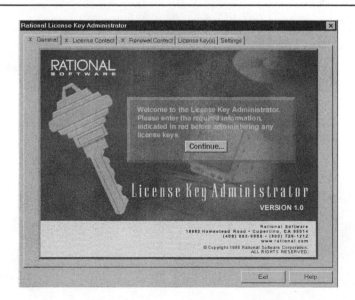

The General tab of the License Key Administrator, as shown in Figure 2.22, will be displayed. Before you can use Rose, you must enter a valid license key. Enter your company name and Rational account number. Your account number is found on the startup license key certificate. Enter the user's name if desired. Select the License Contact tab.

You must enter the contact name of the person responsible for the license. Use the License Contact tab shown in Figure 2.23 to enter this information.

FIGURE 2.22:

The General tab of the License Key Administrator

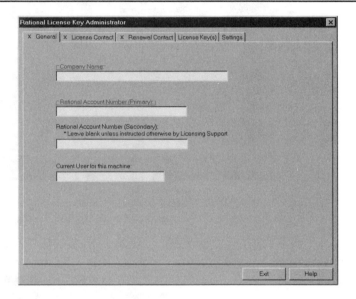

The fields in red are mandatory; those in black are optional. At a minimum, you must enter the following information:

- First name
- Last name
- Country
- Phone number
- E-mail address or fax number
- Complete postal address

FIGURE 2.23:

License Contact tab of the License Key Administrator

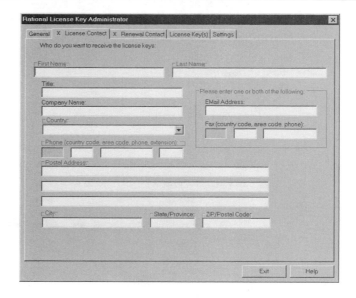

When you have entered the information, select the Renewal Contact tab, as shown in Figure 2.24.

FIGURE 2.24:

Renewal Contact tab of the License Key Administrator

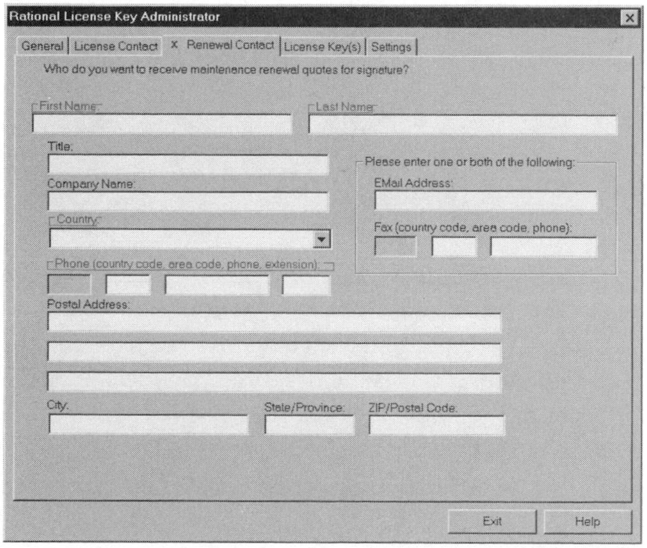

When the time comes to renew your license, Rational will need a person to contact. Enter that person's information on this tab. At a minimum, you must enter the following information:

- First name

- Last name

- Country

- Phone number

When you are ready, select the License Keys tab, as shown in Figure 2.25.

FIGURE 2.25:

License Keys tab of the
License Key Administrator

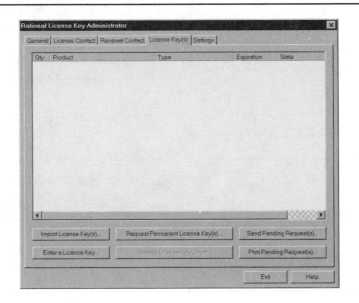

The License Keys tab stores information about the license keys you currently have in use. License keys that will be expiring soon will be highlighted in a different color. If this is the first time you have installed a Rational product on this computer, there will be no license keys in use. Click the Enter a License Key button to set up the license key for Rose.

The wizard shown in Figure 2.26 will initialize. Select the type of license key to enter. A startup license key comes with the Rose product and allows you to use Rose for 30-60 days. A Term License Agreement key allows you to use the product for a specified time. A permanent key allows you to use the product indefinitely. If you downloaded Rose from the Web or received it on CD, a startup license key should be included. Select Startup License Key and click Next.

FIGURE 2.26:

License Key Certificate Wizard

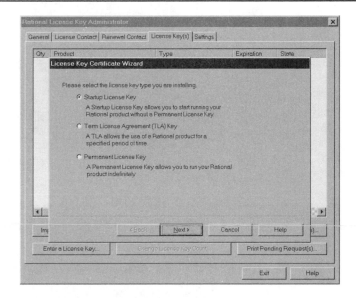

The wizard will ask you for the type of license to enter, as shown in Figure 2.27. A node-locked license can be used on one computer. A floating license can be used across a network. Unless you are installing Rose for a floating license using an established license server, select node-locked. Click Next to continue.

The final screen appears as in Figure 2.28. Enter the product name and version you are licensing, the expiration date, and the license key from the license certificate. Click Finish when you are done.

With that, the installation is complete and you can begin modeling your systems in Rational Rose. If you are using the startup license, you will have a specified amount of time to use the product. After that time, the product will no longer be accessible. To use the product after the evaluation has expired, Rose must be purchased from an authorized Rational reseller.

FIGURE 2.27:

Screen 2 of the License Key
Certificate Wizard

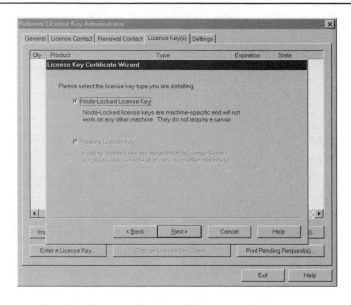

FIGURE 2.28:

Screen 3 of the License Key
Certificate Wizard

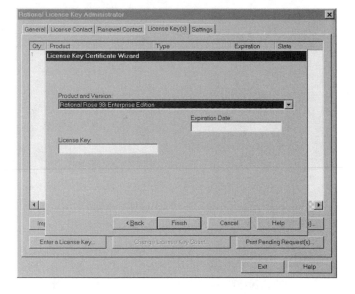

Getting around in Rose

In the next few sections of this chapter, we'll describe each part of the Rose interface. Rose is largely a menu-driven application, with toolbars to help with commonly used features. Rose supports seven different types of UML diagrams: Use Case diagrams, Sequence diagrams, Collaboration diagrams, Class diagrams, State Transition diagrams, Component diagrams, and Deployment diagrams. Rose will present you with a different toolbar for each of these diagrams. In the remaining chapters of this section of the book, we'll show you how to create all of these types of diagrams.

In addition to the toolbars and menus, Rose includes context-sensitive shortcut menus, visible by right-clicking an item. For example, right-clicking a class on a Class diagram will display a menu which includes options for adding attributes or operations to the class, viewing or editing the class specifications, generating code for the class, or viewing the generated code.

One of the easiest ways to get around in Rose is to use the browser. With the browser, you can quickly and easily get to the diagrams and other elements of the model. If you run into trouble while using Rose, press F1 at any time to access the extensive online help file.

Parts of the Screen

The five primary pieces of the Rose interface are the browser, the documentation window, the toolbars, the diagram window, and the log. In this section, we'll look at each of these. Briefly, their purposes are:

Browser   Used to quickly navigate through the model

Documentation window   Used to access documentation of model elements

Toolbars   Used for quick access to commonly used commands

Diagram window   Used to display and edit one or more UML diagrams

Log   Used to view errors and report the results of various commands

Figure 2.29 illustrates the various parts of the Rose interface.

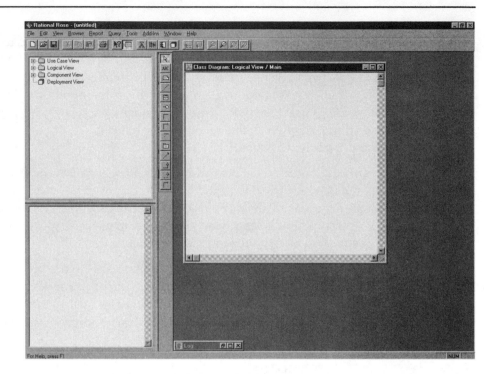

Browser

The browser is a hierarchical structure you can use to easily navigate through your Rose model. Anything you add to the model—actors, use cases, classes, components, and so on—will display in the browser. The browser is shown in Figure 2.30.

Using the browser, you can:

- Add model elements (use cases, actors, classes, components, diagrams, etc.)
- View existing model elements
- View existing relationships between model elements
- Move model elements
- Rename model elements

- Add a model element to a diagram

- Attach a file or URL to an element

- Group elements into packages

- Access the detailed specifications of an element

- Open a diagram

FIGURE 2.30:

Rose Browser

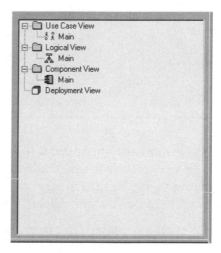

There are four views in the browser: the Use Case view, the Logical view, the Component view, and the Deployment view. Table 2.1 lists each of these views and the model elements found in the views.

TABLE 2.1: Views in Rational Rose

View	Contents
Use Case view	Actors
	Use cases
	Associations (98i)
	Use Case documentation
	Use Case diagrams
	Sequence diagrams
	Collaboration diagrams
	Packages

Continued on next page

TABLE 2.1 CONTINUED: Views in Rational Rose

View	Contents
Logical view	Classes Class diagrams Associations (98i) Interaction diagrams State Transition diagrams Packages
Component view	Components Component diagrams Packages
Deployment view	Processes Processors Devices Deployment diagram

Using the browser, you can view the model elements in each of these four views, move or edit elements, or add new elements. By right-clicking an element in the browser, you can attach files or URLs to the element, access the detailed specifications of the element, delete the element, or rename the element.

The browser is organized in a treeview style. Each model element may contain other elements beneath it in the hierarchy. A minus sign next to a model element means that the branch is fully expanded. A plus sign next to a model element indicates that the branch is collapsed.

By default, the browser will appear in the upper-left area of the screen. You can move the browser to another location, dock the browser or leave it as a floating window, or hide the browser altogether.

To move the browser:

1. Click to select a border of the browser window.

2. Drag the browser from its current location to another area of the screen.

To dock the browser:

1. Right-click a border of the browser window.

2. Select Allow Docking from the shortcut menu. There should be a check mark next to the Allow Docking option. The browser can now be moved, but it will be docked within Rose. That is, the browser window will try to attach itself to another boarder in Rose.

To set the browser to floating:

1. Right-click a border of the browser window.

2. Set the Allow Docking option off. There should not be a check mark next to Allow Docking in the shortcut menu. The browser will now be in a window independent of the Rose window. The browser window can be moved anywhere inside or outside of the Rose window.

To show or hide the browser:

1. Right-click a border of the browser window.

2. Select Hide from the shortcut menu. Rose will show or hide the browser.

OR

Select View ➢ Browser. Rose will show or hide the browser.

Documentation Window

The documentation window is used to document the elements of your Rose model. For example, you may want to write a short definition for each of your actors. You can enter this definition using the documentation window, as shown in Figure 2.31.

When you add documentation to a class, anything you type in the documentation window will appear as a comment in the generated code, reducing the need to go in later and comment on the system's code. The documentation will also appear in the reports you can generate from Rose.

As you select different elements from the browser or on a diagram, the documentation window will automatically be updated to display the documentation for the selected element.

FIGURE 2.31:

The documentation
window

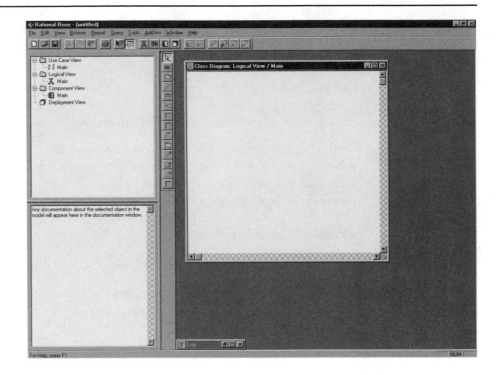

Like the browser, the documentation window can be docked or floating. By default, it appears in the lower-left side of the Rose window, but can be moved or hidden.

To move the documentation window:

1.   Click to select a border of the documentation window.

2.   Drag the documentation window from its current location to another area of the screen.

To dock the documentation window:

1.   Right-click a border of the documentation window.

2.   Select Allow Docking from the shortcut menu. There should be a check mark next to the Allow Docking option. The documentation window can now be moved, but it will be docked within Rose.

To set the documentation window to floating:

1. Right-click a border of the documentation window.

2. Set the Allow Docking option off. There should not be a check mark next to Allow Docking in the shortcut menu. The documentation window will now be in a window independent of the Rose window. The documentation window can be moved anywhere inside or outside of the Rose window.

To show or hide the documentation window:

1. Right-click a border of the documentation window.

2. Select Hide from the shortcut menu. Rose will show or hide the documentation window.

OR

Select view ➣ Documentation. Rose will show or hide the documentation window.

OR

Select the view Documentation toolbar button. Rose will show or hide the documentation window.

Toolbars

Rose toolbars provide you with quick access to commonly used commands. There are two toolbars in Rose: the Standard toolbar and the Diagram toolbar. The standard toolbar is always displayed, and contains options you can use in any diagram. The Diagram toolbar changes for each type of UML diagram. The different diagram toolbars will be discussed in detail in the remainder of this book.

The standard toolbar includes the options shown in Table 2.2.

TABLE 2.2: Icons in Standard Toolbar

Icon	Button	Purpose
	Create New Model	Create a new Rose model (.MDL) file.
	Open Existing Model	Open an existing Rose model (.MDL) file.

Continued on next page

TABLE 2.2 CONTINUED: Icons in Standard Toolbar

Icon	Button	Purpose
	Save Model or Log	Save the Rose model (.MDL) file, or the log for the current model.
	Cut	Move text to the clipboard.
	Copy	Copy text to the clipboard.
	Paste	Paste text from the clipboard.
	Print Diagrams	Print one or more diagrams from the current model.
	Context Sensitive Help	Access the help file.
	View Documentation	View the documentation window.
	Browse Class Diagram	Locate and open a Class diagram.
	Browse Interaction Diagram	Locate and open a Sequence or Collaboration diagram.
	Browse Component Diagram	Locate and open a Component diagram.
	Browse Deployment Diagram	Open the Deployment diagram for the model.
	Browse Parent	Open a diagram's parent diagram.
	Browse Previous Diagram	Open the diagram you were most recently viewing.
	Zoom In	Increase the zoom.
	Zoom Out	Decrease the zoom.
	Fit in Window	Set the zoom so the entire diagram fits within the window.
	Undo Fit in Window	Undo the Fit in Window command.

All of the toolbars can be customized. To customize a toolbar, select Tools ➤ Options, then select the Toolbars tab.

To show or hide the Standard toolbar:

1. Select Tools ➤ Options.

2. Select the Toolbars tab.

3. Use the Show Standard Toolbar check box to show or hide the Standard toolbar.

To show or hide the Diagram toolbar:

1. Select Tools ➤ Options.

2. Select the Toolbars tab.

3. Use the Show Diagram Toolbar check box to show or hide the Diagram toolbar.

To use large buttons on a toolbar:

1. Right-click the desired toolbar.

2. Select the Use Large Buttons option.

To customize a toolbar:

1. Right-click the desired toolbar.

2. Select the Customize option.

3. Add or remove buttons to customize the toolbar by selecting the appropriate button and then clicking the Add or Remove button, as shown in Figure 2.32.

FIGURE 2.32:

Customizing the Standard toolbar

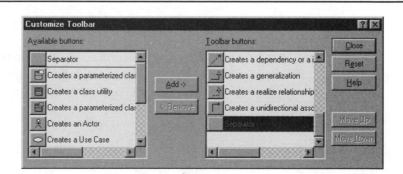

Diagram Window

In the diagram window shown in Figure 2.33, you can view one or more of the UML diagrams in your model. As you make changes to elements in a diagram, Rose will automatically update the browser as necessary. Similarly, when you make changes to an element using the browser, Rose will automatically update the appropriate diagrams. By doing so, Rose helps you maintain a consistent model.

FIGURE 2.33:

Diagram window

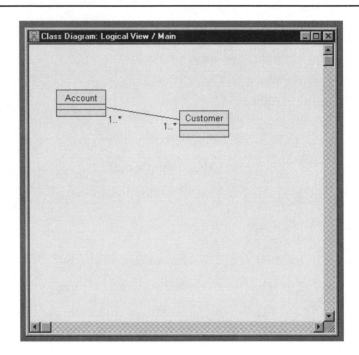

Log

As you work on your Rose model, certain information will be posted to the log window. For example, when you generate code, any errors that are generated are posted in the log window, as shown in Figure 2.34. There is no way to close the log, but it can be minimized.

FIGURE 2.34:

Log window

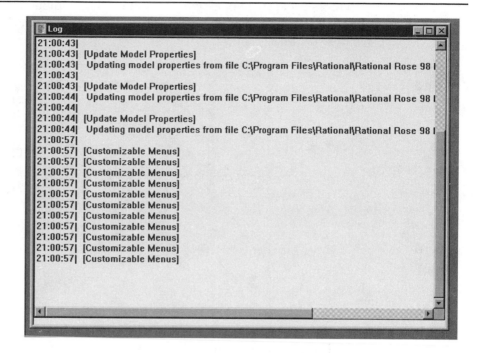

Four Views in a Rose Model

There are four views in a Rose model: the Use Case view, the Logical view, the Component view, and the Deployment view. Each of these four views addresses a different audience and purpose. In the following sections, we'll take a brief look at each of these views. In the remainder of this book, we'll discuss the detailed model elements that appear in each of these views.

Use Case View

The Use Case view includes all of the actors, use cases, and Use Case diagrams in the system. It may also include some Sequence and Collaboration diagrams. The Use Case view is an implementation-independent look at the system. It focuses on a high-level picture of *what* the system will do, without worrying about the details of *how* the system will do it. Figure 2.35 illustrates the Use Case view in the Rose browser.

FIGURE 2.35:

Use Case view

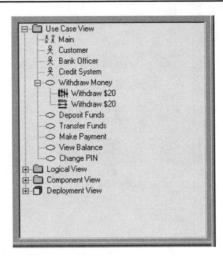

The Use Case view includes:

Actors, which are external entities that interact with the system being built.

Use cases, which are high-level pieces of functionality the system will provide.

Use case documentation, which details the flow through the use case, including any error handling. This icon represents an external file that has been attached to your Rose model. The icon used will depend upon the application you used to document the flow of events. Here, we used Microsoft Word.

Use Case diagrams, which show the actors, the use cases, and the interactions between them. There are typically several Use Case diagrams per system, each showing a subset of the actors and/or use cases.

Interaction diagrams, which display the objects or classes involved in one flow through a use case. There are many Interaction diagrams for each use case. Interaction diagrams can be created in either the Use Case view or the Logical view. Any Interaction diagrams that are language- and implementation-independent are typically created in the Use Case view. These diagrams tend to show objects rather than classes. Any Interaction diagrams that are language-specific are located in the Logical view. These diagrams tend to show classes rather than objects.

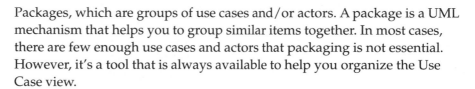

Packages, which are groups of use cases and/or actors. A package is a UML mechanism that helps you to group similar items together. In most cases, there are few enough use cases and actors that packaging is not essential. However, it's a tool that is always available to help you organize the Use Case view.

When the project first begins, the main audience of the Use Case view consists of the customers, analysts, and project managers. These individuals will work with the use cases, Use Case diagrams, and use case documentation to agree on a high-level view of the system. Again, this view focuses only on what the system will do. Implementation details should be left for future discussions.

As the project goes along, all members of the team can look at the Use Case view to get a high-level understanding of the system being built. The use case documentation will describe the flow of events through a use case. With this information, quality assurance staff can begin to write testing scripts. Technical writers can begin the user documentation. Analysts and customers can help ensure that all requirements were captured. Developers can see what high-level pieces of the system will be created, and how the system logic should flow.

Once the customer has agreed to the use cases and actors, they have agreed to the system scope. The development can then continue to the Logical view, which focuses more on how the system will implement the behavior spelled out in the use cases.

Logical View

The Logical view, shown in Figure 2.36, focuses on how the system will implement the behavior in the use cases. It provides a detailed picture of the pieces of the system, and describes how the pieces interrelate. The Logical view includes, among other things, the specific classes that will be needed, the Class diagrams, and the State Transition diagrams. With these detailed elements, developers can construct a detailed design for the system.

The Logical view includes:

Classes, which are the building blocks for a system. A class consists of a little bit of information (its attributes) and a little bit of behavior (its operations), grouped together. For example, an Employee class might store information about the employee's name, address, and social security number, and might include behavior such as hiring or firing an employee.

FIGURE 2.36:

Logical view

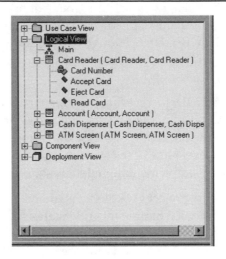

Class diagrams, which are used to view the classes in the system, their attributes and operations, and their relationships to each other. Typically, a system will have several Class diagrams, each showing a subset of all of the classes.

Interaction diagrams, which are used to display the classes that participate in one flow of events through a use case. As we mentioned above, Interaction diagrams can be created in either the Use Case view or the Logical view. Interaction diagrams in the Use Case view tend to display objects, while interaction diagrams in the Logical view focus instead on classes.

State Transition diagrams, which show the dynamic behavior of an object. A State Transition diagram includes all of the states in which a particular object can exist. It also illustrates how the object moves from one state to another, what state the object is in when it is first created, and what state the object is in when it is destroyed.

Packages, which are groups of related classes. Packaging your classes isn't required, but it is certainly recommended. A typical system may have a hundred classes or more. Packaging your classes can help reduce the complexity of your model. To get a general picture of the system, you can look at the packages. To see a more detailed view, you can go into any of the packages and view the classes inside.

Frequently, teams take a two-pass approach to the Logical view. In the first approach, they identify *analysis classes*. Analysis classes are language-independent classes. By focusing first on analysis classes, the team can begin to see the structure of the system without getting bogged down in the language-specific details. In UML, analysis classes can be represented using the following icons:

Boundary   Control   Entity

   The analysis classes might also appear on some Interaction diagrams in the Use Case view. Once the analysis classes have been identified, the team can change each one to a *design class*. A design class is a class that has language-specific detail. For example, we may have an analysis class that's responsible for talking to another system. We don't worry about what language the class will be written in—we focus only on what information and behavior it will have. When we turn it into a design class, however, we look at the language-specific details. We may decide that now we have a Java class. We might even decide that we need two Java classes to actually implement what we uncovered in analysis—that there isn't necessarily a one-to-one mapping between analysis classes and design classes. Design classes are shown on the Interaction diagrams that appear in the Logical view.

   The focus of the Logical view is on the logical structure of the system. In this view, you identify the pieces of the system, examine the information and behavior of the system, and examine the relationships between the pieces. Reuse is one of the main considerations here. By carefully assigning information and behavior to classes, grouping your classes together, and examining the relationships between the classes and the packages, you can identify classes and packages that can be reused. As you complete more and more projects, you can add new classes and packages to a reuse library. Future projects then become more of a process of assembling what you already have, rather than building everything from scratch.

   Nearly everyone on the team will use information from the Logical view, but the primary users will be the developers and architect. Analysts will look at the classes and Class diagrams to help ensure that the business requirements will be implemented in the code. Quality assurance staff will look at the classes, packages, and Class diagrams to see what pieces of the system exist and need to be tested. They will also use the State Transition diagrams to see how a particular class should behave. The project manager will look at the classes and diagrams to ensure the system is well structured, and to get an estimate of how complex the system is.

The primary users, however, will be the developers and the architect. The developers will be concerned with what classes are created, and what information and behavior each class should have. The architect is more concerned with the structure of the overall system. The architect is responsible for ensuring that the system has a stable architecture, that reuse has been considered, and that the system will be flexible enough to change as requirements change.

Once you've identified the classes and diagrammed them, you can move on to the Component view, which focuses more on the physical structure.

Component View

The Component view contains information about the code libraries, executable files, runtime libraries, and other components in your model. A *component* is a physical module of code.

In Rose, components and Component diagrams are displayed in the Component view, as shown in Figure 2.37. The Component view of the system allows you to see the relationships between the modules of code.

FIGURE 2.37:

Component view

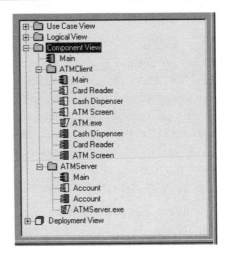

The Component view includes:

Components, which are physical modules of code.

Component diagrams, which show the components and their relationships to each other. Relationships between the components let you know what the compilation dependencies are. With this information, someone can determine the compilation order of the components.

Packages, which are groups of related components. As with packaging classes, reuse is one of the considerations when packaging components. A group of related components may be very easy to pick up and reuse in other applications, so long as the relationships between the group and other groups are carefully monitored. We'll discuss these issues in detail later.

The main users of the Component view are those people responsible for controlling the code, and compiling and deploying the application. Some of the components will be code libraries. Others will be runtime components, such as executable files or dynamic link library (DLL) files. Developers will also use the Component view to see what code libraries have been created, and which classes are contained in each code library.

Deployment View

The final view in Rose is the Deployment view. The Deployment view is concerned with the physical deployment of the system, which may differ from the logical architecture of the system.

For example, the system may have a logical three-tier architecture. In other words, the interface may be separated from the business logic, which is separated from the database logic. However, the deployment may be two-tiered. The interface may be placed on one machine, while the business and database logic are located on another machine.

Other issues, such as fault tolerance, network bandwidth, disaster recovery, and response time, are also handled using the Deployment view. The Deployment view is shown in Figure 2.38.

FIGURE 2.38:

Deployment view

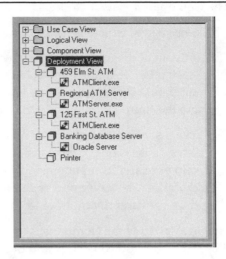

The Deployment view includes:

Processes, which are threads that execute in their own memory space.

Processors, which include any machines with processing power. Each process will run on one or more processors.

Devices, which include any hardware without processing power. Examples are dumb terminals and printers.

A Deployment diagram, which shows the processes and devices on the network and the physical connections between them. The Deployment diagram will also display the processes, and show which processes run on which machines.

Again, the whole team will use the information in the Deployment view to understand how the system will be deployed. However, the primary users will be the staff responsible for distributing the application.

Working with Rose

Everything you do in Rose relates to a model. In this section, we will discuss how to use models. We will first look at how to create and save Rose models. Then, we will discuss team design considerations by using controlled units. Lastly, we will walk through each menu item in Rose.

Creating Models

The first step in working with Rose is to create a model. Models can either be created from scratch or using an existing framework model. A Rose model, including all diagrams, objects, and other model elements are saved in a single file with the extension .MDL (model).

To create a model:

1. Select File ➤ New from the menu.

2. If the Framework Wizard is installed, then the list of available frameworks will be displayed, as in Figure 2.39. Select the framework you want to use and click OK, or click Cancel to use no framework.

FIGURE 2.39:

Framework Wizard

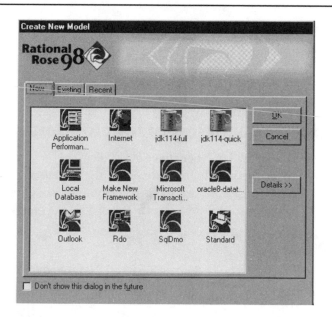

Saving Models

As with any other application, it is good practice to save the file periodically. Rose is no exception. As mentioned above, the entire model is saved in one file. In addition, you can save the log to a file.

To save a model:

> Select File ➤ Save from the menu.

OR

> Click the Save button on the Standard toolbar.

To save the log:

1. Select the log window.

2. Select File ➤ Save Log As from the menu.

3. Enter the filename of the log.

OR

1. Select the log window.

2. Click the Save button on the Standard toolbar.

3. Enter the filename of the log.

Exporting and Importing Models

One of the main benefits of the object-oriented paradigm is reuse. Reuse can apply not only to the code but to the models as well. To fully take advantage of reuse, Rose supports exporting and importing models and model elements. You can export a model or a portion of a model and import it into other models.

To export a model:

1. Select File ➤ Export Model from the menu.

2. Enter the name of the export file.

To export a package of classes:

1. Select the package to export from a Class diagram.

2. Select File ➤ Export <Package> from the menu.

3. Enter the name of the export file.

To export a class:

1. Select the class to export from a Class diagram.

2. Select File ➤ Export <Class> from the menu.

3. Enter the name of the export file.

To import a model, package, or class:

1. Select File ➤ Import Model from the menu.

2. Select the file to import. Allowable file types are model (.MDL), petal (.PTL), category (.CAT), or subsystem (.SUB).

Publishing Models to the Web (98i)

You can easily publish your Rose model to the Web—either to an intranet, Internet, or file system site—using Rational Rose 98i. This way, many people who may need to view the model can do so without having to be Rose users and without printing a ream of model documentation. A model published to the Web is shown in Figure 2.40.

FIGURE 2.40:

ATM model on the Web

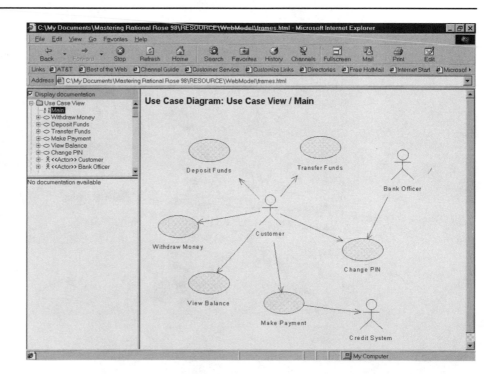

To publish a model to the Web:

1. Select Tools ➤ Web Publisher from the menu.

2. Select the model views and packages to publish from the Web Publisher window shown in Figure 2.41.

3. Select the desired level of detail. Documentation only includes high-level information and none of the properties of the model elements are displayed. Intermediate will display the properties found on the General tab on model element specifications. Full detail will publish all properties, including those listed on the Detail tab on model element specifications.

4. Select the notation to use while publishing. Notation will default to the default notation in Rose.

5. Choose whether or not to publish inherited items.

FIGURE 2.41:

Web Publisher window

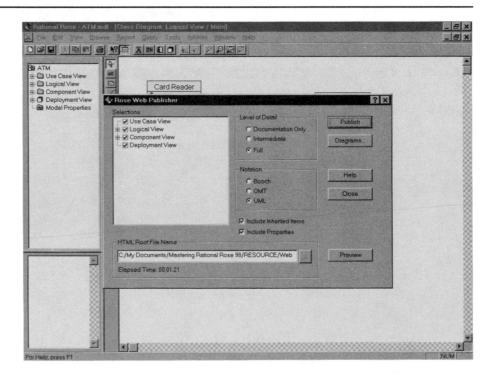

6. Choose whether or not to publish properties.

7. Enter the name of the HTML root filename where the model will be published.

8. If you want to choose the graphic file format for the diagrams, select the Diagrams button. The Diagram Options window will be displayed, as in Figure 2.42.

9. Select the type of graphic format to use while publishing diagrams. Select Windows Bitmap, Portable Network Graphic (PNG), or JPEG. You can also select not to publish any diagrams.

10. When ready, click Publish. Rose will create all of the Web pages to publish your model.

11. If desired, click Preview to see the published model.

FIGURE 2.42:

Diagram Options window

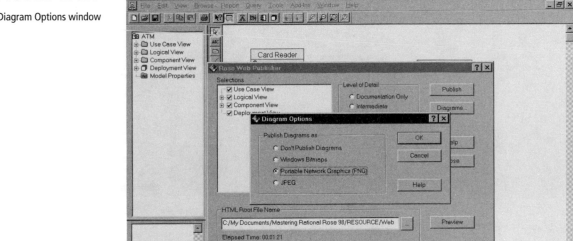

Working with Controlled Units

Rose supports multi-user, parallel development through the use of controlled units. A controlled unit in Rose can be any package within the Use Case view, Logical view, or Component view. In addition, Deployment view and the Model Properties units can also be placed under control. When a unit is controlled, it is stored in a separate file from the rest of the model. This way, the separate file can then be controlled through the use of a SCC-compliant version control tool such as Rational ClearCase, Microsoft SourceSafe, or minimally within Rose directly. Controlled Units can be loaded and unloaded from the model being viewed or Checked In and Out if using a version control tool. In Rose 98, units are managed using the window shown in Figure 2.43. In Rose 98i, units are managed through shortcut menus available by right-clicking a package in the browser.

FIGURE 2.43:

Managing units

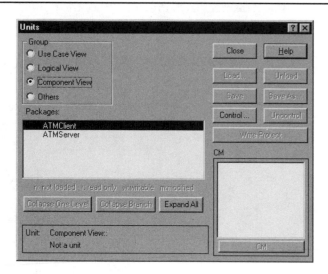

To create a controlled unit in Rose 98:

1. Select Browse ➤ Units from the menu.

2. When the Units window appears, select the package to control.

3. Click the Control button.

To create a controlled unit in Rose 98i:

1. Right-click the Unit to be placed under control.

2. Select Units ➤ Control <package> from the menu.

3. Enter the filename for the controlled unit. Notice that the icon in the browser now has a page symbol on the folder to symbolize that the package is controlled.

In a parallel development environment, you may need to unload a package so that others can work on the package. To unload a controlled unit:

1. Right-click the Unit to be unloaded.

2. Select Units ➤ Unload <package> from the menu. Notice that the items in the package are removed from the browser because they have been removed from the model.

To unload all controlled units in a view:

1. Right-click the view.

2. Select Units ➤ Unload subunits of <View> from the menu.

Periodically, you way want to reload a package that has just been updated by another development team. To load a controlled unit:

1. Right-click the Unit to be reloaded.

2. Select Units ➤ Load <package> from the menu.

3. Click the Load button.

4. Select the controlled unit.

To uncontrol a controlled unit:

1. Make sure the controlled unit is loaded.

2. Right-click the Unit to be uncontrolled.

3. Select Units ➤ Uncontrol <package> from the menu.

At times, you may want to view certain items without modifying them. To protect from modifying controlled units, mark the unit as write-protected.

To write-protect a controlled unit:

1. Right-click the Unit to be write-protected.

2. When the Units window appears, select the package to write-protect. The package must not be already write-protected.

3. Click the Write Protect button.

To write-enable a controlled unit:

1. Select Browse ➤ Units from the menu.

2. When the Units window appears, select the package to write-enable. The package must be write-protected.

3. Click the Write Enable button.

Using Menus

This section includes a listing for each menu item in Rose and a short description about the item. Please note that certain menu options can be accessed only under certain conditions. For example, the Save Log menu option can only be accessed when the log is active. Also, some menu items in Rose 98i have changed locations in the menu. Table 2.3 includes the Rose menu items and their descriptions. Menu items that are only available with Rose 98i are marked (98i). Those only available in Rose 98 are marked (98).

TABLE 2.3: Rose Menu Items

Menu Item	Description
File ➤ New	Create a new Rose model.
File ➤ Open	Open an existing Rose model.
File ➤ Save	Save the current Rose model.
File ➤ Save As	Save the current Rose model with a new filename.
File ➤ Units ➤ Load	Load a controlled unit (package).

Continued on next page

TABLE 2.3 CONTINUED: Rose Menu Items

Menu Item	Description
File ➤ Units ➤ Save	Save a controlled unit.
File ➤ Units ➤ Save As	Save a controlled unit with a new filename.
File ➤ Units ➤ Unload	Unload a controlled unit.
File ➤ Units ➤ Control	Control a package.
File ➤ Units ➤ Uncontrol	Stop controlling a package.
File ➤ Units ➤ Write Protection	Write-protect a controlled unit.
File ➤ Units ➤ CM	Configuration management (only available if a source configuration tool is used).
File ➤ Import	Import a model, subsystem, package, or class.
File ➤ Export Model	Export the model, subsystem, package, or class.
File ➤ Update	Update the model from a reverse-engineered model.
File ➤ Print Diagrams	Print model diagrams.
File ➤ Print Specifications	Specify options for printing diagrams.
File ➤ Print Setup	Setup the printer (Windows printer option).
File ➤ Edit Path Map	Edit the various paths used by Rose.
File ➤ <Recent File>	Open a recent model file.
File ➤ Exit	Exit Rose.
Edit ➤ Undo	Undo the last action.
Edit ➤ Redo	Redo the last action.
Edit ➤ Cut	Cut the selected objects from the diagram (does not delete the object from the model).
Edit ➤ Copy	Copy the selected objects in the diagram.
Edit ➤ Paste	Paste the previously cut or copied objects.
Edit ➤ Delete	Delete the selected objects from the diagram.
Edit ➤ Select All	Select all objects in the current diagram.

Continued on next page

TABLE 2.3 CONTINUED: Rose Menu Items

Menu Item	Description
Edit ➤ Delete From Model	Permanently remove objects from the model (not just the diagram).
Edit ➤ Relocate	Move a class from one package into the current package.
Edit ➤ Diagram Object Properties ➤ Font Size	Change the size of the font for the selected objects.
Edit ➤ Diagram Object Properties ➤ Font	Change the font for the selected objects.
Edit ➤ Diagram Object Properties ➤ Line Color	Change the line color for the selected objects.
Edit ➤ Diagram Object Properties ➤ Fill Color	Change the fill color for the selected objects.
Edit ➤ Diagram Object Properties ➤ Use Fill Color	Toggle the use of the fill color for the selected objects.
Edit ➤ Diagram Object Properties ➤ Automatic Resize	Automatically resize the icon for the selected objects to fit the text.
Edit ➤ Diagram Object Properties ➤ Stereotype Display	Display the stereotype for the selected objects.
Edit ➤ Diagram Object Properties ➤ Stereotype Label	Toggle the display of stereotype labels for the selected relationships.
Edit ➤ Diagram Object Properties ➤ Show Visibility	Toggle the display of icons representing visibility—public/protected/private/package (implementation).
Edit ➤ Diagram Object Properties ➤ Show Compartment Stereotypes	Toggle the display of stereotypes in the current compartment.
Edit ➤ Diagram Object Properties ➤ Show Operation Signature	Toggle the display of operation signatures.
Edit ➤ Diagram Object Properties ➤ Show All Attributes	Display a compartment with all attributes.
Edit ➤ Diagram Object Properties ➤ Show All Operations	Display a compartment with all operations.
Edit ➤ Diagram Object Properties ➤ Suppress Attributes	Do not display the attributes compartment.
Edit ➤ Diagram Object Properties ➤ Suppress Operations	Do not display the operations compartment.
Edit ➤ Find	Find which package an object is in.

Continued on next page

TABLE 2.3 CONTINUED: Rose Menu Items

Menu Item	Description
Edit ➤ Reassign	Change the selected object to another object.
Edit ➤ Compartment	Select which items to display in the current compartment (Overridden with Show All Attributes/Operations and Suppress Attributes/Operations).
Edit ➤ Change Into ➤ Class	Change the selected objects to classes.
Edit ➤ Change Into ➤ Parameterized Class	Change the selected objects to parameterized classes.
Edit ➤ Change Into ➤ Instantiated Class	Change the selected objects to a instantiated classes.
Edit ➤ Change Into ➤ Class Utility	Change the selected objects to class utilities.
Edit ➤ Change Into ➤ Parameterized Class Utility	Change the selected objects to parameterized class utilities.
Edit ➤ Change Into ➤ Instantiated Class Utility	Change the selected objects to instantiated class utilities.
Edit ➤ Change Into ➤ Uses Dependency	Change the selected relationships into dependencies.
Edit ➤ Change Into ➤ Inherits	Change the selected relationships into generalizations.
Edit ➤ Change Into ➤ Instantiates	Change the selected relationships into instantiations.
Edit ➤ Change Into ➤ Association	Change the selected relationships into associations.
Edit ➤ Change Into ➤ Realize	Change the selected relationships into realizations.
Edit ➤ Change Line Style ➤ Rectilinear	Change the line style for the selected relationships to rectilinear (lines with right angles).
Edit ➤ Change Line Style ➤ Oblique	Change the line style for the selected relationships to oblique (straight lines at any angle).
Edit ➤ Change Line Style ➤ Toggle	Toggle the line style for the selected relationships between rectilinear and oblique.
View ➤ Toolbars ➤ Standard	Toggles the display of the Standard toolbar.
View ➤ Toolbars ➤ Toolbox	Toggles the display of the Toolbox toolbar.
View ➤ Toolbars ➤ Configure	Configure the toolbars.
View ➤ Status Bar	Toggle the display of the status bar.
View ➤ Documentation	Toggle the display of the documentation window.
View ➤ Browser	Toggle the display of the browser.

Continued on next page

TABLE 2.3 CONTINUED: Rose Menu Items

Menu Item	Description
View ➤ Zoom to Selection	Zoom to show the selected objects.
View ➤ Zoom In	Zoom in on the current diagram.
View ➤ Zoom Out	Zoom out on the current diagram.
View ➤ Fit in Window	Zoom the current diagram so that all objects fit in the current window.
View ➤ Undo Fit in Window	Undo the last Fit in Window.
View ➤ Page Breaks	Toggle the display of page breaks on the current diagram.
View ➤ Refresh	Redraw the current diagram.
View ➤ As Booch	Show objects on all diagrams using the Booch notation.
View ➤ As OMT	Show objects on all diagrams using the OMT notation.
View ➤ As Unified	Show objects on all diagrams using the Unified Modeling Language notation.
Browse ➤ Class Diagram	Select Class diagrams across all packages.
Browse ➤ Use Case Diagram	Select Use Case diagrams across all packages.
Browse ➤ Interaction Diagram	Select Interaction diagrams across all packages.
Browse ➤ Component Diagram	Select Component diagrams across all packages.
Browse ➤ State Diagram	Select State diagrams across all packages.
Browse ➤ Deployment Diagram	Show the Deployment diagram for the current model.
Browse ➤ Expand	Show the first diagram created for the selected package.
Browse ➤ Parent	Show the selected diagram's parent.
Browse ➤ Specification	Display the selected object's specification window.
Browse ➤ Top Level	Show the top level diagram for the current view.
Browse ➤ Referenced Item	Show the main diagram for the package containing the selected object.
Browse ➤ Previous Diagram	Show the most recent diagram (also Ctrl+Tab).

Continued on next page

TABLE 2.3 CONTINUED: Rose Menu Items

Menu Item	Description
Browse ➤ Create Message Trace Diagram	Create a Sequence diagram from a Collaboration diagram, or vice versa.
Browse ➤ Units (98)	Manage controlled units.
Report ➤ Show Usage	Report every Class diagram on which the selected objects appear.
Report ➤ Show Instances	Report every Interaction diagram on which the selected objects appear.
Report ➤ Show Access Violations	Report usages where relationships have not yet been established.
Report ➤ Show Participants in UC	Report all classes and operations included in diagrams owned by the selected use case.
Report ➤ Documentation Report	Generate a model documentation report in Word format.
Query ➤ Add Classes	Add classes in the model to the current diagram.
Query ➤ Add Use Cases	Add use cases in the model to the current diagram.
Query ➤ Expand Selected Items	Add objects with relationships to the selected object to the current diagram.
Query ➤ Hide Selected Items	Remove objects with relationships to the selected object from the current diagram.
Query ➤ Filter Relationships	Show only selected types of relationships on all diagrams.
Tools ➤ Layout Diagram	Layout the current diagram to minimize overlap of relationship lines.
Tools ➤ Autosize All	Resize all objects on the current diagram.
Tools ➤ Create ➤ Text	Create a text object.
Tools ➤ Create ➤ Note	Create a note object.
Tools ➤ Create ➤ Note Anchor	Anchor a note to an object.
Tools ➤ Create ➤ Class	Create a new class.
Tools ➤ Create ➤ Parameterized Class	Create a new parameterized class.
Tools ➤ Create ➤ Class Utility	Create a new class utility.

Continued on next page

TABLE 2.3 CONTINUED: Rose Menu Items

Menu Item	Description
Tools ➤ Create ➤ Parameterized Class Utility	Create a new parameterized class utility.
Tools ➤ Create ➤ Association	Create a new association.
Tools ➤ Create ➤ Aggregate Association	Create a new aggregation.
Tools ➤ Create ➤ Unidirectional Association	Create a new unidirectional association.
Tools ➤ Create ➤ Unidirectional Aggregate Association (98i)	Create a new unidirectional aggregation.
Tools ➤ Create ➤ Link Attribute	Create a new link attribute.
Tools ➤ Create ➤ Generalization	Create a new generalization.
Tools ➤ Create ➤ Dependency	Create a new dependency.
Tools ➤ Create ➤ Package	Create a new package.
Tools ➤ Create ➤ Instantiated Class	Create a new instantiated class.
Tools ➤ Create ➤ Instantiated Class Utility	Create a new instantiated class utility.
Tools ➤ Create ➤ Instantiates	Create a new instantiates relationship.
Tools ➤ Create ➤ Actor	Create a new actor.
Tools ➤ Create ➤ Use Case	Create a new use case.
Tools ➤ Create ➤ Interface	Create a new interface.
Tools ➤ Create ➤ Realize	Create a new realization.
Tools ➤ Check Model	Check the model for errors.
Tools ➤ Model Properties ➤ Edit	Edit the specifications for the selected object.
Tools ➤ Model Properties ➤ Replace	Replace the current set of model properties with those stored in a file.
Tools ➤ Model Properties➤ Export	Export the current set of model properties to a file.
Tools ➤ Model Properties ➤ Add	Add model properties from a file to the current set of model properties.
Tools ➤ Model Properties ➤ Update	Update a model properties file with the current model properties.
Tools ➤ Options	Display the options window, allowing changes to all options in Rose.

Continued on next page

TABLE 2.3 CONTINUED: Rose Menu Items

Menu Item	Description
Tools ➤ Open Script	Open a RoseScript file.
Tools ➤ New Script	Create a new RoseScript file.
Tools ➤ Synchronize (98i)	Start the Rational Suite Synchronizer (if installed).
Tools ➤ DDL ➤ Generate Code	Generate Data Definition Language (DDL) code for the selected objects.
Tools ➤ DDL ➤ Browse DDL	Browse the generated DDL file.
Tools ➤ IDL ➤ Generate IDL (98)	Generate IDL code for the selected objects.
Tools ➤ IDL ➤ Convert Rose 4.0 IDL to Rose98 IDL (98)	Convert IDL code from Rose 4.0 to Rose98.
Tools ➤ CORBA ➤ Project Specification (98i)	Set up the project specifications, such as the environmental variables, for CORBA generation.
Tools ➤ CORBA ➤ Syntax Check (98i)	Check the model for correct CORBA syntax.
Tools ➤ CORBA ➤ Browse CORBA Source (98i)	Browse the generated CORBA file.
Tools ➤ CORBA ➤ Reverse Engineer CORBA (98i)	Reverse engineer CORBA components into the model.
Tools ➤ CORBA ➤ Generate Code (98i)	Generate CORBA code for the selected objects.
Tools ➤ Java ➤ Project Specification (98i)	Set up the project specifications, such as the environmental variables, for Java generation.
Tools ➤ Java ➤ Syntax Check	Check the syntax of objects for Java code generation.
Tools ➤ Java ➤ Generate Java	Generate Java code for the selected objects.
Tools ➤ Java➤ Browse Java Source	Browse the generated Java code.
Tools ➤ Java➤ Reverse Engineer Java	Reverse engineer Java code into the model.
Tools ➤ Java ➤ Import JDK 1.1.X (98)	Import the Java Developer's Kit (JDK) objects into the current model.
Tools ➤ Oracle8 ➤ Data Type Creation Wizard	Create a new Oracle8 data type using a wizard interface.
Tools ➤ Oracle8 ➤ Ordering Wizard	Change the order of attributes for the selected object.
Tools ➤ Oracle8 ➤ Edit Foreign Keys	Add, edit, or delete foreign keys from a relational table.
Tools ➤ Oracle8 ➤ Analyze Schema	Analyze an Oracle8 schema and import the schema into the current model.

Continued on next page

TABLE 2.3 CONTINUED: Rose Menu Items

Menu Item	Description
Tools ➤ Oracle8 ➤ Schema Generation	Generate an Oracle8 schema from the current model.
Tools ➤ Oracle8 ➤ Syntax Checker	Check the syntax of objects for schema generation.
Tools ➤ Oracle8 ➤ Reports	Create an Oracle8 documentation report.
Tools ➤ Oracle8 ➤ Import Oracle8 Data Types	Import the Oracle8 data types into the current model.
Tools ➤ Publish to Repository (98)	Publish the current model into a Microsoft Repository.
Tools ➤ Import from Repository (98)	Import a model from a Microsoft Repository.
Tools ➤ C++ ➤ Code Generation	Generate C++ code for the selected objects.
Tools ➤ C++➤ Reverse Engineering	Reverse engineer C++ code into the model.
Tools ➤ C++ ➤ Browse Header	Browse the generated C++ header file.
Tools ➤ C++ ➤ Browse Body	Browse the generated C++ body file.
Tools ➤ Web Publisher (98)	Publish the model to the Web.
Tools ➤ Source Control ➤ Add to Source Control (98)	Place the selected objects under source control.
Tools ➤ Source Control ➤ Remove From Source Control (98)	Remove the selected objects from source control.
Tools ➤ Source Control ➤ Start Source Control Explorer (98)	Examine objects currently under source control.
Tools ➤ Source Control ➤ Check In (98)	Check the selected objects back into source control.
Tools ➤ Source Control ➤ Check Out (98)	Check the selected objects out of source control.
Tools ➤ Source Control ➤ Undo Check Out (98)	Undo the previous check out.
Tools ➤ Source Control ➤ Get Latest (98)	Get the latest version of the selected objects from source control.
Tools ➤ Source Control ➤ File Properties (98)	Examine properties of source control file.
Tools ➤ Source Control ➤ File History (98)	Examine history of source control file.
Tools ➤ Source Control ➤ Source Control Options (98)	View source control options.

Continued on next page

TABLE 2.3 CONTINUED: Rose Menu Items

Menu Item	Description
Tools ➤ Source Control ➤ About SCC Provider Integration (98)	View source control integration version information.
Tools ➤ Version Control ➤ Add to Version Control (98)	Place the selected objects under version control.
Tools ➤ Version Control ➤ Remove From Version Control (98)	Remove the selected objects from version control.
Tools ➤ Version Control ➤ Start Version Control Explorer (98)	Examine objects currently under version control.
Tools ➤ Version Control➤ Check In (98)	Check the selected objects back into version control.
Tools ➤ Version Control ➤ Check Out (98)	Check the selected objects out of version control.
Tools ➤ Version Control ➤ Undo Check Out (98)	Undo the previous check out.
Tools ➤ Version Control ➤ Get Latest (98)	Get the latest version of the selected objects from version control.
Tools ➤ Version Control ➤ File Properties (98)	Examine properties of version control file.
Tools ➤ Version Control ➤ File History (98)	Examine history of version control file.
Tools ➤ Version Control ➤ Version Control Options (98)	View version control options.
Tools ➤ Version Control ➤ About Rational Rose Version Control Integration (98)	View version control integration version information.
Tools ➤ Visual Basic ➤ Class Wizard	Create a new class using a wizard.
Tools ➤ Visual Basic ➤ Assign to New Component (98)	Create a new executable or DLL component and assign the selected objects to it.
Tools ➤ Visual Basic ➤ Component Assignment Tool (98)	Create a new executable or DLL component and assign the selected objects to it.
Tools ➤ Visual Basic ➤ Generate Code (98)	Generate Visual Basic code for the selected component.
Tools ➤ Visual Basic ➤ Reverse Engineering Wizard (98)	Reverse engineer Visual Basic code into the model.
Tools ➤ Visual Basic ➤ Update Code (98)	Synchronize Visual Basic code for the selected component.

Continued on next page

TABLE 2.3 CONTINUED: Rose Menu Items

Menu Item	Description
Tools ➤ Visual Basic ➤ Update Model from Code (98)	Reverse engineer Visual Basic code into the model.
Tools ➤ Visual Basic ➤ Revert to Last Saved (98)	Revert the model back to its state at the last successful code generation.
Tools ➤ Visual Basic ➤ Browse Visual Basic Source (98)	Browse the generated Visual Basic source code.
Tools ➤ Visual Basic ➤ Browse Source Code (98)	Browse the generated Visual Basic source code.
Tools ➤ Visual C++ ➤ Model Assistant (98)	Setup model properties for the selected objects.
Tools ➤ Visual C++ ➤ Component Assignment Tool (98)	Create a new component and assign the selected objects to it.
Tools ➤ Visual C++ ➤ Update Code (98)	Synchronize Visual C++ code for the selected component.
Tools ➤ Visual C++ ➤ Update Model from Code (98)	Reverse engineer Visual C++ code into the model.
Tools ➤ Visual C++ ➤ Class Wizard (98)	Create a new class using a wizard.
Tools ➤ Visual C++ ➤ Restore C++ Source Files (98)	Restore the last source files for the selected objects.
Tools ➤ Visual C++ ➤ Quick Import MFC 6.0 (98)	Import the MFC 6.0 classes into the model.
Tools ➤ Visual C++ ➤ Options (98)	Set Visual C++ code generation options.
Tools ➤ Class Wizard	Use the Class Wizard to create a new class.
Tools ➤ Visual Differencing	Check differences between the current model and a saved model.
Tools ➤ ERWin Translation Wizard ➤ Translate Model (98)	Using a wizard, create an ERWin data model from the Rose model, or create a Rose model from an ERWin.
Tools ➤ ERWin Translation Wizard ➤ Select Target Server (98)	Select the target database management system for the ERWin model.
Tools ➤ ERWin Translation Wizard ➤ About ERWin Translation (98)	Display version information about the ERWin Translation Wizard.
Add-Ins ➤ Add-In Manager	Enable or disable the add-ins for Rose.
Window ➤ Cascade	Cascade all open windows in Rose.

Continued on next page

TABLE 2.3 CONTINUED: Rose Menu Items

Menu Item	Description
Window ➤ Tile	Tile all open windows in Rose.
Window ➤ Arrange Icons	Arrange all open icons in Rose.
Window ➤ <Window>	Go to the selected window.
Help ➤ Rational Rose Help Topics	Show help for Rose.
Help ➤ Search for Help On	Search for a particular help topic.
Help ➤ Using Help	Get help on using Windows Help.
Help ➤ Extended Help (98)	Get help using Rational Unified Process (if installed).
Help ➤ About	Display version information about Rose.
Help ➤ Rational on the Web ➤ Online Support	Go to Rational's Online Support page on the Internet.
Help ➤ Rational on the Web ➤ Rose Home Page	Go to the Rational Rose Home Page on the Internet.

Setting Global Options

Options such as the font and color are used for all model objects—classes, use cases, interfaces, packages, and so on. In this section, we discuss how to change the fonts and colors for model objects. The default fonts and colors can be set by using the Tools ➤ Options menu item.

Working with Fonts

In Rose, you can individually change the font of objects on a diagram. This can be done to improve the readability of your model. Here we describe how to set the font or font size for an object on a diagram. Fonts and font sizes are set using the window in Figure 2.44.

To set the font of a object:

1. Select the desired object or objects.

2. Select Edit ➤ Diagram Object Properties ➤ Font from the menu.

3. Select the desired font, style, and size.

FIGURE 2.44:

Font Selection window

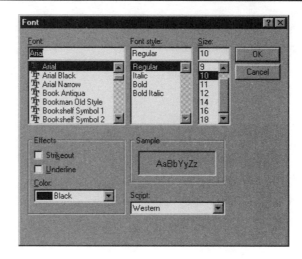

To change the size of the font of an object:

1. Select the desired object or objects.

2. Select Edit ➤ Diagram Object Properties ➤ Font Size from the menu.

3. Select the desired font size from the menu.

Working with Colors

In addition to changing the fonts, the colors of objects can be individually changed. Here we describe how to change the line color and fill color for an object. These options are changed using the window in Figure 2.45.

To change the line color of an object:

1. Select the desired object or objects.

2. Select Edit ➤ Diagram Object Properties ➤ Line Color from the menu.

3. Select the desired line color.

FIGURE 2.45:

Color Selection

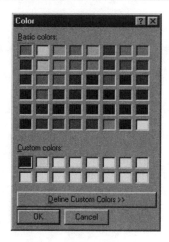

To change the fill color of an object:

1. Select the desired object or objects.
2. Select Edit ➢ Diagram Object Properties ➢ Fill Color from the menu.
3. Select the desired fill color.

Summary

This chapter gave a quick overview of Rational Rose. First, we discussed what Rose is and what it is used for. Next, we looked at how to install the product. Then, we examined various aspects of the Rose environment, including the different parts of the screen and menus. This concludes the introduction to Rose and UML. In the next section, we cover in detail how to create and use the different UML elements and diagrams in Rose.

CHAPTER
THREE

3

Use Cases and Actors

- Using the Use Case View and Use Case Diagrams

- Working with Use Cases, Actors, and Relationships

- Using Notes

- Adding and Deleting Use Case Packages

In this chapter, we will discuss use cases, actors, and Use Case diagrams. The use cases and actors define the scope of the system you are building. Use cases include anything that is within the system; actors include anything that is external to the system. We'll start by discussing how to create Use Case diagrams. Next, we'll add use cases to the diagram and talk about the various options and details you can add to them. Then, we'll add actors to a Use Case diagram and discuss the options available for actors. Finally, we'll take a look at the relationships between use cases and actors, between one actor and another, and between use cases.

At the end of the chapter, we will present the first of a series of exercises in Rose. In these exercises, we'll be building the model for an order processing system. In this chapter, we'll introduce the problem and take you through building a use case model step-by-step.

Use Case View

In this chapter, we'll be talking about some of the items that are created in the Use Case view of Rose. The Use Case view contains all of the following:

- Use cases
- Actors
- Communication relationships between use cases and actors
- Uses and extends relationships between use cases
- Actor generalization relationships
- Use Case diagrams
- Sequence and Collaboration diagrams

We'll talk about all of the above except Sequence and Collaboration diagrams, which we'll cover in Chapter 4.

The Use Case view is largely implementation-independent. The use cases and actors describe the project scope, without getting into implementation details like the programming language that will be used.

Use Case Diagrams

A *Use Case diagram* shows you some of the use cases in your system, some of the actors in your system, and the relationships between them. A *use case* is a high-level piece of functionality that the system will provide. An *actor* is anyone or anything that interacts with the system being built. We'll discuss the details of use cases and actors shortly. An example of a Use Case diagram is shown in Figure 3.1.

FIGURE 3.1:

Sample Use Case diagram

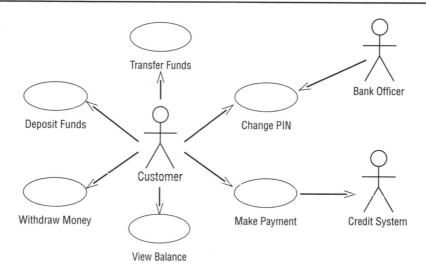

In this diagram, there are three actors: the customer, the bank officer, and the credit system. There are six major pieces of functionality the system will provide: depositing funds, transferring funds, withdrawing money, changing a PIN, viewing a balance, and making a payment.

One of the major benefits of Use Case diagrams is communication. Your customers can look at this diagram and receive a great deal of information. By looking at the use cases, they will know what functionality will be included in the system. By looking at the actors, they will know exactly who will be interfacing with the system. By looking at the set of use cases and actors, they will know exactly what the scope of the project will be. This can help them identify up front any missing functionality. For example, someone could look at the diagram above and say. "That's great, but I also need the ability to view the last 10 transactions for my account."

Frequently, you will want to create several Use Case diagrams for a single system. A high-level diagram, usually called Main in Rational Rose, will show you just the packages, or groupings, of use cases. Other diagrams will show you sets of use cases and actors. You may also want to create a single diagram with all of the use cases and all of the actors. How many Use Case diagrams you create and what you name them is entirely up to you. Be sure that the diagrams have enough information to be useful, but are not so crowded as to be confusing.

Use Case diagrams fulfill a specific purpose—to document the actors (everything outside the system scope), the use cases (everything inside the system scope), and their relationships. Some things to keep in mind as you are creating Use Case diagrams:

- Do not model actor to actor communications. By definition, the actors are outside the scope of the current project. The communication between the actors, therefore, is also outside the scope of what you're building. You can use a workflow diagram to examine the actor communications.

- Do not draw an arrow directly between two use cases (except in a *uses* or *extends* relationship, which we'll describe later). The diagrams show what use cases are available, but don't show what order the use cases will be executed in. An activity diagram can be used for this purpose.

- Every use case must be initiated by an actor. That is, there should be an arrow starting with an actor and ending with the use case. Again, the exception here is a uses or extends relationship, which we'll examine later.

- Think of the database as a layer underneath the entire Use Case diagram. You can enter information in the database using one use case, and then access that information from the database in another use case. You don't have to draw arrows from one use case to another to show information flow.

Creating Use Case Diagrams

In Rose, Use Case diagrams are created in the Use Case view. Rose provides you with one default Use Case diagram called Main. You can create as many additional diagrams as you need to model your system.

To access the Main Use Case diagram, do the following:

1. Click the + next to the Use Case view in the browser to open it.

2.   The Main Use Case diagram will be visible. Note that Use Case diagrams in Rose have the following icon on their left:

3.   Double-click the Main diagram to open it. The title bar will change to include [Use Case Diagram: Use Case view / Main].

To create a new Use Case diagram:

1.   Right-click the package Use Case view in the browser.

2.   Select New ➤ Use Case Diagram from the shortcut menu, as shown in Figure 3.2.

FIGURE 3.2:

Adding a new Use Case diagram

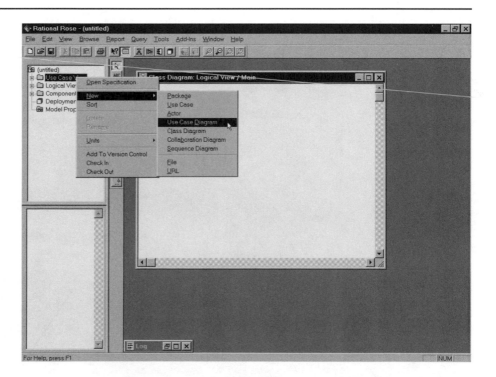

3.   With the new diagram selected, type in the name of your new diagram.

4.   Double-click the name of your new diagram in the browser to open it.

To open an existing Use Case diagram:

1. Locate the Use Case diagram in the Use Case view in the browser.

2. Double-click the Use Case diagram's name to open it.

OR

1. Select Browse ➤ Use Case Diagram. The window displayed in Figure 3.3 will appear.

2. In the Package list box, select the package that contains the diagram you want to open.

3. In the Use Case Diagrams list box, select the diagram you want to open.

4. Press OK.

FIGURE 3.3:

Opening an existing Use Case diagram

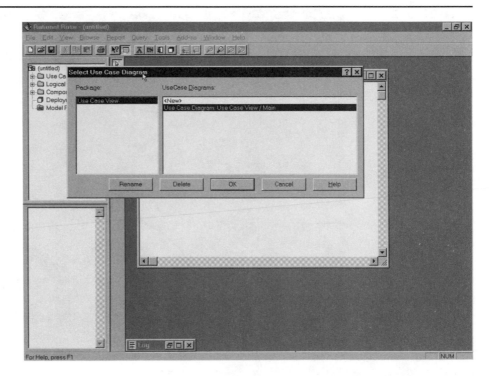

To add an item to a Use Case diagram, use the toolbar buttons as described in the sections below to add use cases, actors, and relationships to the diagram.

There are two ways to remove an item from a Use Case diagram. The first will remove the item from the open diagram, but will leave the item in the browser and on other diagrams. The second method will delete the item from the entire model—from all diagrams as well as the browser.

To remove an item from the current diagram only, highlight the item in the diagram and press the Delete key.

To remove an item from the entire model, highlight the item in the browser and right-click to see the shortcut menu. Select Delete from the shortcut menu. Or, highlight the item in the diagram and press Ctrl+D.

Deleting Use Case Diagrams

You may need to delete some of the Use Case diagrams you've created. Toward the beginning of a project, it's not uncommon to create many Use Case diagrams as you brainstorm the scope. Some of the diagrams may contain the use cases, others will show the actors, and still others will show a subset of the use cases and the actors. As the project goes along, you may find the need to clean up some of these old diagrams. You can delete a Use Case diagram directly in the browser. Be careful, though—once you've deleted a diagram, you cannot undo the deletion.

To delete a Use Case diagram:

1. Right-click the diagram in the browser.

2. Select Delete from the shortcut menu.

NOTE   Rose does not allow you to Undo a deletion of a diagram or to delete the Use Case diagram called Main.

Attaching Files and URLs to a Use Case Diagram

In Rose, you have the ability to attach a file or a URL to a Use Case diagram. Any supplementary documents you have, such as the high-level requirements specifications, the project vision document or business case, or even the project plan, can be attached to a Use Case diagram. You can see any attached files or URLs listed in the browser underneath the Use Case diagram. From the browser, you can double-click the file or URL to automatically launch the appropriate application and load the file or URL.

To attach a file to a Use Case diagram:

1. Right-click the Use Case diagram in the browser.

2. Select New ➢ File.

3. Using the Open dialog box, find the file you wish to attach.

4. Select Open to attach the file to the Use Case diagram.

To attach a URL to a Use Case diagram:

1. Right-click the Use Case diagram in the browser.

2. Select New ➢ URL.

3. Type the name of the URL to attach.

To open an attached file:

1. Locate the file in the browser.

2. Double-click the filename. Rose will open the appropriate application and load the file.

OR

1. Right-click the file in the browser.

2. Select Open from the shortcut menu. Rose will open the appropriate application and load the file.

To open an attached URL:

1. Locate the URL in the browser.

2. Double-click the URL name. Rose will automatically start your Web browser application and load the URL.

OR

1. Right-click the URL in the browser.

2. Select Open from the shortcut menu. Rose will automatically start your Web browser application and load the URL.

To delete an attached file or URL:

1. Right-click the file or URL in the browser.

2. Select Delete from the shortcut menu.

The Use Case Diagram Toolbar

When a Use Case diagram is opened, the diagram toolbar changes to show icons used in Use Case diagrams. In the toolbar, Rose provides shortcuts for all of the commonly used functions for a Use Case diagram. Some of the buttons you will have available are shown in Table 3.1. In the remainder of this chapter, we'll discuss how to use each of these toolbar buttons to add use cases, actors, and other details to your Use Case diagrams.

TABLE 3.1: Icons in the Use Case Diagram Toolbar

Icon	Button	Purpose
	Selects or deselects an item	Return the cursor to an arrow so you can select an item.
	Text Box	Add a text box to the diagram.
	Note	Add a note to the diagram.
	Anchor Note to Item	Connect a note to a use case or actor on the diagram.
	Package	Add a new package to the diagram.
	Use Case	Add a new use case to the diagram.
	Actor	Add a new actor to the diagram.
	Unidirectional Association	Draw a relationship between an actor and a use case.
	Dependency or Instantiates	Draw a dependency between items on the diagram.
	Generalization	Draw a uses or an extends relationship between use cases, or draw an inheritance relationship between actors.

Working with Use Cases

A *use case* is a high-level piece of functionality that the system will provide. In other words, a use case illustrates how someone might use the system. Let's begin by looking at an example. An ATM machine provides some fundamental functionality for a customer. It lets a customer deposit funds, withdraw cash, transfer money from one account to another, view their balance, change their PIN, or make a credit card payment. Each of these transactions is a different way the customer can use the system. Each, therefore, is a different use case. In UML, a use case is represented using the following symbol:

Use Case

The advantage of looking at a system with use cases is the ability to dissociate the implementation of the system from the reason the system is there in the first place. It helps you focus on what is truly important—meeting the customer's needs and expectations without being instantly overwhelmed by implementation details. By looking at the use cases, the customer can see what functionality will be provided, and can agree to the system scope before the project goes any further.

Use cases take a different approach to traditional methods. Splitting the project into use cases is a process-oriented, not an implementation-oriented, way of looking at the system. It is therefore different from the functional decomposition approach that is so often taken. While functional decomposition focuses on how to break the problem down further and further into pieces that the system will handle, the use case approach focuses first on what the user expects from the system.

When you are beginning a project, a natural question is: How do I go about finding the use cases? A good way to begin is to examine any documentation the customers have provided. Frequently, a high-level scope or vision document can help you identify the use cases. Consider also each of the stakeholders of the project. Ask yourself what functionality each stakeholder expects from the system. For each stakeholder, ask questions such as:

- What will the stakeholder need to do with the system?
- Will the stakeholder need to maintain any information (create, read, update, delete)?

- Does the stakeholder need to inform the system about any external events?

- Does the system need to notify the stakeholder about certain changes or events?

As we mentioned before, use cases are an implementation-independent, high-level view of what the user expects from the system. Let's examine each piece of this definition separately.

First, the use cases are implementation-independent. As you are defining the use cases, assume you are building a manual system. Your use cases should be able to be built in Java, C++, Visual Basic, or on paper. Use cases focus on *what* the system should do, not *how* the system will do it. We'll get into the *how* later on in the process.

Secondly, the use cases are a high-level view of the system. If your system has 3000 use cases, you've lost the benefit of simplicity. Your collection of use cases should let the customers easily see, at a very high level, your entire system. There should not be so many use cases that the customer is forced to wade through pages and pages of documentation just to see what the system will do. At the same time, there should be enough use cases to completely describe what the system will do. A typical system will have somewhere between 20 and 50 use cases. As we'll see later, you can use different types of relationships, called uses and extends relationships, to break use cases down a little if you need to. You can also package the use cases together to form groups of use cases to help you organize them better. We'll talk about this a little later.

Finally, the use cases should be focused on what the user will get out of the system. Each use case should represent a complete transaction between the user and the system that results in something of value to the user. The use cases should be named in business terms, not technical terms, and should be meaningful to the customer. In our ATM, we wouldn't have an Interface With The Banking System To Transfer Monies From A Checking To A Credit Card Account use case. Instead, we would have a Make Credit Card Payment use case, which is much more meaningful to the customer. Use cases are typically named with verbs or short verb phrases and describe what the customer sees as the end result. The customer doesn't care how many other systems you have to interface with, what specific steps need to be taken, or how many lines of code you need to make a Visa payment. All they care about is that a payment was made. Again, you focus on the result the user expects from the system—not the steps that were taken to achieve the result.

So, when you have the final list of use cases, how do you know if you've found them all? Some questions to ask are:

- Is each functional requirement in at least one use case? If a requirement is not in a use case, it will not be implemented.

- Have you considered how each stakeholder will be using the system?

- What information will each stakeholder be providing for the system?

- What information will each stakeholder be receiving from the system?

- Have you considered maintenance issues? Someone will need to start the system and shut it down.

- Have you identified all external systems the system will need to interact with?

- What information will each external system be providing to the system and receiving from the system?

Documenting the Flow of Events

The use cases begin to describe what your system will do. To actually build the system, though, you'll need more specific details. These details are written in a document called the *flow of events*. The purpose of the flow of events is to document the flow of logic through the use case. This document will describe in detail what the user of the system will do, and what the system itself will do.

Although it is detailed, the flow of events is still implementation-independent. You can assume as you are writing the flow that there will be an automated system. However, you shouldn't be concerned yet with whether the system will be built in C++, PowerBuilder, or Java. The goal here is describing *what* the system will do, not *how* the system will do it. The flow of events typically includes:

- A brief description

- Preconditions

- Primary flow of events

- Alternate flow of events

- Post-conditions

Let's look at these items one at a time.

Description

Each use case should have a short description associated with it that describes what the use case will do. The Transfer Funds use case from an ATM might have a description like the following:

> The Transfer Funds use case will allow a customer or bank employee to move funds from one checking or savings account to another checking or savings account.

The description should be short and to the point, but should include the different types of users who will be executing the use case and the end result the user expects to achieve through the use case. As the project progresses (especially with a very long project), these use case definitions will help the whole team remember why each use case was included in the project and what the use case is intended to do. They also help reduce confusion among the team members by documenting a clear purpose for the use case.

Pre-conditions

The *preconditions* for a use case list any conditions that have to be met before the use case can start at all. For example, a precondition might be that another use case has been executed or that the user has the necessary access rights to run the current use case. Not all use cases will have preconditions.

We mentioned above that Use Case diagrams aren't intended to show in which order the use cases are executed. Pre-conditions, however, can be used to document some of this type of information. For example, the precondition for one use case may be that another use case has run.

Primary and Alternate Flow of Events

The specific details of the use case are described in the primary and alternate flow of events. The flow of events describes, step-by-step, what will happen to execute the functionality in the use case. The flow of events focuses on *what* the system will do, but not *how* it will do it, and is written from the user's perspective. The primary and alternate flow of events include:

- How the use case starts

- The various paths through the use case

- The normal, or primary, flow through the use case

- Any deviations from the primary flow, known as alternate flows, through the use case

- Any error flows

- How the use case ends

For example, the flow of events for the Withdraw Money use case might look like this:

Primary Flow

1. The use case begins when the bank customer inserts their card into the ATM.

2. The ATM presents a welcome message and prompts the user to enter their personal identification number (PIN).

3. The bank customer enters their PIN.

4. The ATM confirms that the PIN is valid. If the PIN is not valid, Alternate Flow A1 is performed.

5. The ATM presents the options available:

   - Deposit Funds

   - Withdraw Cash

   - Transfer Funds

6. The user selects the Withdraw Cash option.

7. The ATM prompts for the amount to be withdrawn.

8. The user enters the amount to be withdrawn.

9. The ATM determines whether the account has sufficient funds. If there are insufficient funds, Alternate Flow A2 is performed. If there is an error in attempting to verify funds, Error Flow E1 is performed.

10. The ATM deducts the withdrawal amount from the customer's account.

11. The ATM provides the customer with the requested cash.

12. The ATM prints a receipt for the customer.

13. The ATM ejects the customer's card.

14. The use case ends.

Alternate Flow A1: Invalid PIN Entered

1. The ATM notifies the customer that the PIN entered was invalid.

2. The ATM ejects the customer's card.

3. The use case ends.

Alternate Flow A2: Insufficient Funds

1. The ATM notifies the customer that the account has insufficient funds.

2. The ATM ejects the customer's card.

3. The use case ends.

Error Flow E1: Error in Verifying Sufficient Funds

1. The ATM notifies the customer that an error occurred in verifying funds, and provides the customer with the telephone number for the bank's customer service support.

2. The ATM notes the error in the error log. The log entry includes the date and time of the error, the customer's name and account number, and the error code.

3. The ATM ejects the customer's card.

4. The use case ends.

When documenting the flow of events, you can use numbered lists as we have done here, text in paragraph form, bulleted lists, or even flowcharts. The flow of events should be consistent with the collected requirements. When deciding how to document the flow, keep in mind the reviewers of the document. The customers will be reviewing this document to make sure it accurately reflects their expectations. Analysts will review it to be sure it is consistent with the requirements. The project manager will review it to get a better sense of what will be built, and can use it to form or refine project estimates.

As you are writing the flow, be sure to avoid detailed discussions of *how*. Think of writing a recipe. In a recipe, you would say "Add two eggs." You wouldn't say "Go to the refrigerator. Get two eggs from the door. Pick up the first egg. Crack the egg against the side of the bowl...." In a flow of events, you might say "Validate the user ID," but you wouldn't specify that this is done by looking at a particular table in a database. Focus on the information that is exchanged between the user and the system, not on the details of how the system will be implemented.

Postconditions

Postconditions are conditions that must always be true after the use case has finished executing. For example, you may set a flag after the use case has completed. This type of information is included as a postcondition. Like preconditions, postconditions can be used to add information about the order in which the use cases are run. If, for example, one use case must always be run after another use case, you can document this in the postconditions. Not every use case will have postconditions.

Adding Use Cases

There are two ways to add a use case to the model: Add the use case to the active Use Case diagram or add the new use case directly into the browser. From the browser, a use case can then be added to a Use Case diagram.

To add a new use case to a Use Case diagram:

1. Select the Use Case button from the toolbar.

2. Click anywhere inside the Use Case diagram. The new use case will be named NewUseCase.

3. With the new use case selected, type in the name of the new use case.

4. Note that the new use case has been automatically added to the browser, under the Use Case view.

   OR

1. Select Tools ➤ Create ➤ Use Case as shown in Figure 3.4.

2. Click anywhere inside the Use Case diagram to place the new use case. The new use case will be called NewUseCase.

3. With the new use case selected, type in the name of the new use case.

4. Note that the new use case has been automatically added to the browser, under the Use Case view.

FIGURE 3.4:

Adding a use case to a Use Case diagram

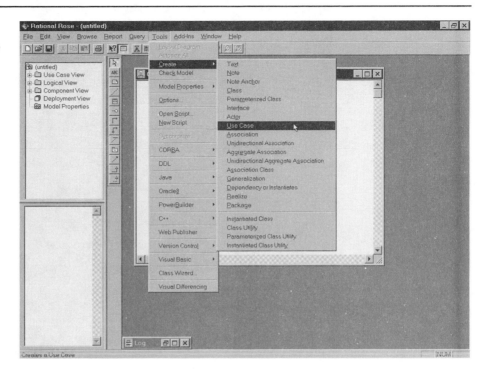

To add an existing use case to a Use Case diagram:

1. Drag the use case from the browser to the open Use Case diagram.

OR

1. Select Query ➤ Add Use Cases. A dialog box will display, as in Figure 3.5, that will allow you to select and add existing use cases.

2. In the Package drop-down list box, select the package that contains the use case(s) you want to add.

3. Move the use case(s) you want to add from the Use Cases list box to the Selected Use Cases list box.

4. Press OK to add the use cases to the diagram.

FIGURE 3.5:

Adding existing use cases to a Use Case diagram

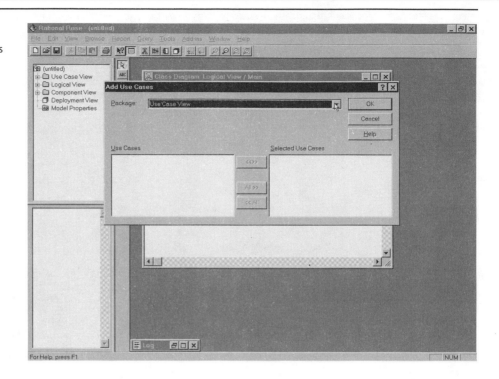

To add a use case to the browser:

1. Right-click the Use Case view package in the browser.

2. From the shortcut menu, select New ➤ Use Case.

3. The new use case, called NewUseCase will appear in the browser. To the left of the new use case will be the UML use case icon.

4. With the new use case selected, type in the name of the new use case.

5. To then add the use case to the diagram, drag the new use case from the browser to the diagram.

Deleting Use Cases

There are two ways to delete a use case. It can be removed from a single diagram or removed from the entire model and all diagrams. As with Use Case diagrams, it's not uncommon to have many extra use cases toward the beginning of a project. They can be very useful for brainstorming the scope of the project. Once the final set of use cases has been agreed upon, however, you will need to go in and delete any extraneous use cases.

To remove a use case from a Use Case diagram:

1. Select the use case on the diagram.

2. Press Delete.

3. Note that the use case has been removed from the Use Case diagram, but still exists in the browser and on other Use Case diagrams.

To remove a use case from the model:

1. Select the use case on the diagram.

2. Select Edit ➤ Delete from Model, or press Ctrl+D.

3. Rose will remove the use case from all Use Case diagrams, as well as the browser.

OR

1. Right-click the use case in the browser.

2. Select Delete from the shortcut menu.

3. Rose will remove the use case from all Use Case diagrams, as well as the browser.

Use Case Specifications

Rose provides detailed specifications for each use case. These specifications can help you document the specific attributes of the use case, such as the use case name, priority, and stereotype. Figure 3.6 shows the use case specification window, which is used to set the use case specifications. In the following sections, we'll take a look at each of the specifications available on the tabs of this window.

To open the use case specifications:

1. Right-click the use case on a Use Case diagram.

2. Select Open Specification from the shortcut menu.

FIGURE 3.6:

Use case specification
window

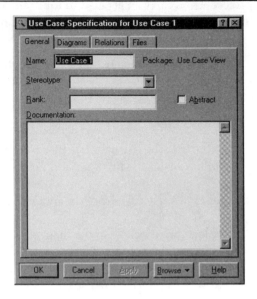

OR

1. Right-click the use case in the browser.

2. Select Open Specification from the shortcut menu.

OR

1. Select the use case on a Use Case diagram.

2. Select Browse ➤ Specification.

OR

1. Select the use case on a Use Case diagram.

2. Press Ctrl+B.

Naming a Use Case

Each use case in the model should be given a unique name. The use case should
be named from the perspective of your customer, as the use cases will help

determine the project scope. The use case name should also be implementation-independent. Try to avoid phrases, such as *Internet*, which tie the use case to a specific implementation. Use cases are typically named with verbs or short verb phrases.

There are two ways to name a use case—you can use the use case specification window or name the use case directly on the diagram.

To name a use case:

1. Select the use case in the browser or on the Use Case diagram.

2. Type the use case name.

OR

1. Right-click the use case in the Use Case diagram or browser.

2. Select Open Specification from the shortcut menu.

3. In the Name field, enter the use case name.

To add documentation to a use case:

1. Select the use case in the browser.

2. In the documentation window, type the use case description.

OR

1. Right-click the use case in the browser or on the Use Case diagram.

2. From the shortcut menu, select Open Specification.

3. In the specification window, type the use case description in the Documentation area.

Viewing Participants of a Use Case

You may want to see a listing of all of the classes and operations that participate in a particular use case. As the project progresses, and you add or change requirements, it can be very helpful to know what classes might be affected by the change. In our ATM example, if we change the requirements for withdrawing cash, we will need to know what classes participate in the Withdraw Money use case.

Even after the system is completed, you may need an inventory of which classes are included in each use case. As the system moves into maintenance mode, you will need to control the scope of upgrades and changes. In Rose, you can view the use case participants using the Report menu.

To view the classes and operations participating in a use case:

1. Select the use case on a Use Case diagram.

2. Select Report ➤ Show Participants in UC.

3. The Participants window will appear, as shown in Figure 3.7.

FIGURE 3.7:

Use case Participants window

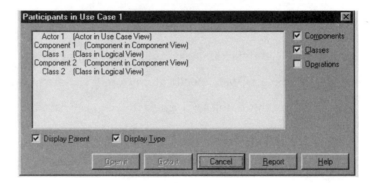

The Display Parent check box will display the package that owns each of the classes participating in the use case. The parent appears in parentheses after the class or operation name.

The Display Type check box will put a notation next to each item in the list box to let you know whether the item is a class or an operation. The type appears in parentheses after the class or operation name.

Use the Components, Classes, and Operations check boxes to control whether components, classes, operations, or all three appear in the list box. Use the Open It button to view the specifications for an item in the list. Use the Goto It button to select the item in the browser.

Assigning a Use Case Stereotype

In UML, *stereotypes* are used to help you categorize your model elements. Say, for example, you had two primary types of use cases, type A and type B. You can create two new use case stereotypes, A and B. Stereotypes aren't used very often for use cases; they are used more for other model elements, such as classes and relationships. However, you do have the option of adding a use case stereotype if you'd like.

To assign a use case stereotype:

1. Right-click the use case in the browser or on the Use Case diagram.

2. Select Open Specification from the shortcut menu.

3. Enter the stereotype in the Stereotype field.

Assigning a Priority to a Use Case

As you define your use cases, you might want to assign a priority to each. With priorities, as the project progresses, you'll know in what order you'll be working on the use cases. In the use case specification in Rose, you can enter the use case priority description using the Rank field.

To assign a priority to a use case:

1. Right-click the use case in the browser or on the Use Case diagram.

2. Select Open Specification from the shortcut menu.

3. On the General tab, enter the priority in the Rank field.

Creating an Abstract Use Case

An *abstract use case* is one that is not started directly by an actor. Instead, an abstract use case provides some additional functionality that can be used by other use cases. Abstract use cases are the use cases that participate in a uses or extends relationship (see the "Viewing Relationships for a Use Case" section later in this chapter). Figure 3.8 includes examples of abstract use cases.

FIGURE 3.8:

Abstract use cases

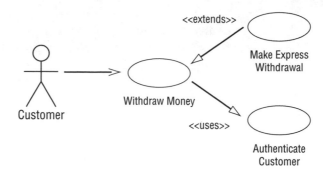

See the relationships section later in this chapter for a description of how to draw the arrows between the use cases.

To create an abstract use case:

1.   Create the use case in the browser or on a Use Case diagram.

2.   Right-click the use case in the browser or on the diagram.

3.   Select Open Specification from the shortcut menu.

4.   Check the Abstract check box.

Viewing Diagrams for a Use Case

In the use case specifications, you can see all of the Sequence diagrams, Collaboration diagrams, Class diagrams, Use Case diagrams, and State Transition diagrams that have been defined under the use case in the browser. Figure 3.9 shows the diagrams tab in the use case specification window. On this tab, you will see the Rose icons that indicate the type of diagram, as well as the diagram name. Double-clicking any of the diagrams will open the diagram in the diagram window.

To view the diagrams for a use case:

1.   Right-click the use case in the browser or on a Use Case diagram.

2.   Select Open Specification from the shortcut menu.

3.   The diagrams will be listed on the Diagrams tab of the specification window.

FIGURE 3.9:

Use case specification Diagrams tab

OR

Look through the browser. The diagrams for the use case will appear underneath the use case in the browser.

To open a diagram for a use case:

Double-click the diagram name on the Diagrams tab of the use case specification window.

OR

1. Right-click the diagram name on the Diagrams tab of the use case specification window.

2. Select Open Diagram from the shortcut menu.

OR

Double-click the diagram in the browser.

To add a diagram to a use case:

1. Right-click anywhere inside the Diagrams tab of the use case specification window.

2. From the shortcut menu, select the type of diagram (Use Case, Sequence, Collaboration, State, or Class) you want to add.

3. Enter the name of the new diagram.

OR

1. Right-click the use case in the browser.

2. Select New ➤ (Collaboration Diagram, Sequence Diagram, Class Diagram, Use Case Diagram) from the shortcut menu.

3. Enter the name of the new diagram.

To delete a diagram for a use case:

1. Right-click the diagram name on the Diagrams tab of the use case specification window.

2. Select Delete from the shortcut menu.

OR

1. Right-click the diagram name in the browser.

2. Select Delete from the shortcut menu.

Viewing Relationships for a Use Case

The Relations tab in the use case specification window will list all of the relationships the use case participates in, either to other use cases or to actors, as shown in Figure 3.10. The list includes the relationship name, and the names of the items joined by the relationship. The relationship name will include any role names or relationship names you have added to the relationship.

To view the relationships for a use case:

1. Right-click the use case in the browser or on a Use Case diagram.

2. Select Open Specification from the shortcut menu.

3. The relationships will be listed on the Relations tab.

FIGURE 3.10:

Use case specification Relations tab

OR

1.   Select the use case on a Use Case diagram.

2.   Select Report ➤ Show Usage.

To view the relationship specifications:

1.   Double-click the relationship in the list.

2.   The relationship specification window will appear. See below for a detailed description of relationship specifications.

OR

1.   Right-click the relationship in the list.

2.   Select Specification from the shortcut menu.

3.   The relationship specification window will appear. See below for a detailed description of relationship specifications.

To delete a relationship:

1. Right-click the relationship in the list.

2. Select Delete from the shortcut menu.

Attaching Files and URLs to a Use Case

The Files tab, as shown in Figure 3.11, will allow you to attach a file to the use case. For example, you may have a document that contains the flow of events for the use case. You may have some additional documents that have scenarios for the use case, requirements specifications for the requirements in the use case, and another file with a rough prototype of the use case. All of these files can be attached to the use case in the Files tab. If you wish, you can also attach a URL to a use case.

To attach a file to a use case:

1. Right-click anywhere inside the white space in the Files tab.

2. Select Insert File from the shortcut menu to insert a file.

FIGURE 3.11:

Use case specification
Files tab

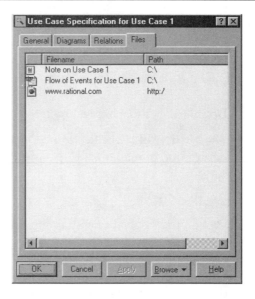

3. Using the Open dialog box, find the file you wish to attach.

4. Select Open to attach the file to the use case.

OR

1. Right-click the use case in the browser.

2. Select New ➤ File.

3. Using the Open dialog box, find the file you wish to attach.

4. Select Open to attach the file to the use case.

To attach a URL to a use case:

1. Right-click anywhere inside the white space in the Files tab.

2. Select Insert URL to insert a URL.

3. Type the name of the URL to attach.

OR

1. Right-click the use case in the browser.

2. Select New ➤ URL.

3. Type the name of the URL to attach.

To open an attached file:

1. Open the use case specification.

2. Double-click the name of the file in the Files tab. Rose will automatically start the appropriate application and load the file.

OR

1. Locate the file in the browser under the appropriate use case.

2. Double-click the filename. Rose will automatically start the appropriate application and load the file.

OR

1. Open the use case specification.

2. Right-click the file in the Files tab.

3. From the shortcut menu, select Open File / URL. Rose will automatically start the appropriate application and load the file.

OR

1. Locate the file in the browser under the appropriate use case.

2. Right-click the file in the browser.

3. From the shortcut menu, select Open. Rose will automatically start the appropriate application and load the file.

To open an attached URL:

1. Open the use case specification.

2. Double-click the name of the URL in the Files tab. Rose will automatically start your Web browser application and load the URL.

OR

1. Locate the URL in the browser under the appropriate use case.

2. Double-click the URL name. Rose will automatically start your Web browser application and load the URL.

OR

1. Open the use case specification.

2. Right-click the URL in the Files tab.

3. From the shortcut menu, select Open File / URL. Rose will automatically start your Web browser application and load the URL.

OR

1. Locate the URL in the browser under the appropriate use case.

2. Right-click the URL in the browser.

3. From the shortcut menu, select Open. Rose will automatically start your Web browser application and load the URL.

To delete an attached file or URL:

1. Right-click the file or URL in the browser.

2. Select Delete from the shortcut menu.

Working with Actors

An *actor* is anyone or anything that interacts with the system being built. While use cases describe anything that is inside the system scope, actors are anything that is outside the system scope. In UML, actors are represented with stick figures:

Actor 1

There are three primary types of actors: users of the system, other systems that will interact with the system being built, and time.

The first type of actor is a physical person, or a user. These are the most common actors, and are present in just about every system. In the ATM example, some users might be the ATM customer, or the ATM maintenance person. When naming these actors, use role names rather than position names. A given individual will play many roles. John Doe may be responsible for maintaining the ATM one morning, playing the ATM maintenance role. Later in the day, he may want to withdraw some money to get lunch, so he may play the ATM customer role. Using role names rather than position names will give you a more stable picture of your actors. Position names change over time; roles and responsibilities are moved from one position to another. By using roles, you won't need to update your model every time a new position is added or a position changes.

The second type of actor is another system. For example, say our bank has a credit system that is used to maintain the information about each customer's credit accounts. Our ATM system must be able to interface with this credit system. If this is the case, the credit system becomes an actor.

Note that by making this system an actor, we are assuming that the credit system will not be changed at all. Remember, actors are outside of the scope of what we're building, and are therefore completely out of our control. If we need to make major modifications to the credit system as well, it is within our project scope and should not be shown as an actor.

The third type of actor that is commonly used is time. Time becomes an actor when the passing of a certain amount of time triggers some event in the system. The ATM system might run some reconciliation processing every midnight, for example. Because time is outside of our control, it is an actor.

Adding Actors

As with use cases, there are two ways to add an actor: to an open Use Case diagram or directly into the browser. An actor in the browser can then be added to one or more Use Case diagrams.

To add an actor to a Use Case diagram:

1. Select the Actor button from the toolbar.
2. Click anywhere inside the Use Case diagram. The new actor will be named NewClass.
3. With the new actor selected, type in the name of the new actor. Note that the new actor has been automatically added to the browser, under the Use Case view.

OR

1. Select Tools ➤ Create ➤ Actor, as shown in Figure 3.12.
2. Click anywhere inside the Use Case diagram to place the new actor. The new actor will be called NewClass.
3. With the new actor selected, type in the name of the new actor. Note that the new actor has been automatically added to the browser, under the Use Case view.

FIGURE 3.12:

Adding an actor to a Use Case diagram

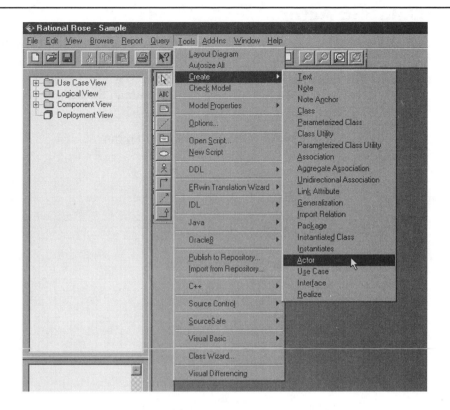

To add an actor to the browser:

1. Right-click the Use Case view package in the browser.

2. Select New ➤ Actor.

3. The new actor, called NewClass, will appear in the browser. To the left of the actor's name will be the UML actor icon.

4. With the new actor selected, type in the name of the new actor.

5. To then add the actor to the diagram, drag the new actor from the browser to the diagram.

Deleting Actors

As with use cases, there are two ways to delete an actor: from a single diagram or from the entire model. If you delete an actor from the entire model, it will be removed from the browser as well as all Use Case diagrams. If you delete an actor from a single diagram, it will remain in the browser and on other Use Case diagrams.

To remove an actor from a Use Case diagram:

1. Select the actor on the diagram.
2. Press Delete.

To remove an actor from the model:

1. Select the actor on the diagram.
2. Select Edit ➤ Delete from Model, or press Ctrl+D.

OR

1. Right-click the actor in the browser.
2. Select Delete from the shortcut menu.

Rose will remove the actor from all Use Case diagrams as well as the browser.

Actor Specifications

Like a use case, each actor has certain detailed specifications in Rose. In the actor specification window, as shown in Figure 3.13, you can specify the actor's name, stereotype, cardinality, and other details. In the next several sections, we'll take a look at each of the specifications you can set for an actor.

As you work with classes later in this book, you may note that the actor specification window and the class specification window are very similar. This is because Rose treats an actor as a specialized form of a class. The actor specification window includes the same fields as the class specification window, but some of these fields are disabled for actors.

FIGURE 3.13:

Actor specification window

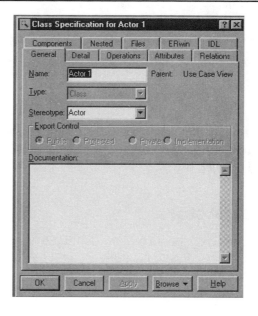

To open the actor specifications:

1. Right-click the actor on the Use Case diagram.

2. Select Open Specification from the shortcut menu. The actor specification window will appear.

    OR

1. Right-click the actor in the browser.

2. Select Open Specification from the shortcut menu. The actor specification window will appear.

    OR

1. Select the actor on the Use Case diagram.

2. Select Browse Specification. The actor specification window will appear.

OR

1. Select the actor on the Use Case diagram.

2. Press Ctrl+B. The actor specification window will appear.

Most of the tab pages in the actor specification will apply to classes, but will not apply to actors. The tab pages that include information about actors are the General tab, the Detail tab, the Relations tab, and the Files tab. Some of the options on these tabs apply only to classes. The options that are available for actors are described below.

Naming Actors

Each actor should be given a unique name. You can name an actor by using the actor specification window or by typing the name directly onto a Use Case diagram or into the browser.

To name an actor:

1. Right-click the actor in the Use Case diagram or browser.

2. Select Open Specification from the shortcut menu.

3. In the Name field, enter the actor name.

OR

1. Select the actor in the browser or on the Use Case diagram.

2. Type the actor name.

To add documentation to an actor:

1. Select the actor in the browser.

2. In the documentation window, type the actor description.

OR

1. Right-click the actor in the browser or on the Use Case diagram.

2. From the shortcut menu, select Open Specification.

3. In the specification window, type the actor description in the Documentation area.

Assigning an Actor Stereotype

As with use cases, you can assign a stereotype to an actor in the specifications window. However, if you change the stereotype of an actor, Rose will change the icon used to represent the actor on a Use Case diagram. Rather than using the actor symbol, Rose will use the standard rectangle that is used to represent a class.

Other than Actor, there are no provided stereotypes available for an actor. However, you can always define your own actor stereotypes and use these in your Rose model.

To assign an actor stereotype:

1. Right-click the actor in the browser or on a Use Case diagram.

2. Select Open Specification from the shortcut menu.

3. In the Stereotype field, enter the actor stereotype.

WARNING If you change the stereotype of an actor, Rose will no longer display the actor using the UML actor symbol. Rose will treat the actor like any other class.

Setting Actor Cardinality

You can specify in Rose how many instances of a particular actor you expect to have. For example, you may want to know that there are many people playing the role of the customer actor, but only one person playing the role of the manager actor. You can use the cardinality field to note this.

Rose provides you with several cardinality options:

Cardinality	Meaning
n (default)	Many
0..0	Zero
0..1	Zero or one
0..n	Zero or more
1..1	Exactly one
1..n	One or more

Or, you can enter your own cardinality, using one of the following formats:

Format	Meaning
\<number\>	Exactly \<number\>
\<number 1\>..\<number 2\>	Between \<number 1\> and \<number 2\>
\<number\>..n	\<number\> or more
\<number 1\>,\<number 2\>	\<number 1\> or \<number 2\>
\<number 1\>, \<number 2\>..\<number 3\>	Exactly \<number 1\> or between \<number 2\> and \<number 3\>
\<number 1\>..\<number 2\>,\<number 3\>..\<number 4\>	Between \<number 1\> and \<number 2\> or between \<number 3\> and \<number 4\>

To set actor cardinality:

1. Right-click the actor in the browser or on a Use Case diagram.

2. Select Open Specification from the shortcut menu.

3. Select the Detail tab.

4. Select from the Cardinality drop-down list box, or type in the actor's cardinality using one of the formats listed above.

Creating an Abstract Actor

An *abstract actor* is an actor that has no instances. In other words, the actor's cardinality is exactly zero. For example, you may have several actors: hourly employee, salaried employee, and temporary employee. All of these are types of a fourth actor, employee. However, no one in the company is just an employee— everyone is either hourly, salaried, or temporary. The employee actor just exists to show that there is some commonality between hourly, salaried, and temporary employees. There are no instances of an employee actor, so it is an abstract actor. Figure 3.14 shows an example of an abstract actor.

See the relationships section later in this chapter for a description of how to draw the arrows between the actors.

FIGURE 3.14:

Abstract actor

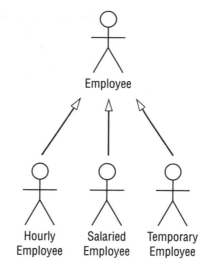

To create an abstract actor:

1. Create the actor in the browser or on a Use Case diagram.

2. Right-click the actor in the browser or on the diagram.

3. Select Open Specification from the shortcut menu.

4. Select the Detail tab.

5. Check the Abstract check box.

Viewing Relationships for an Actor

The Relations tab in the actor specification window lists all of the relationships the actor participates in. Figure 3.15 shows the Relations tab of the window. This tab includes all relationships the actor has with use cases, as well as the relationships to other actors. The list includes the relationship name, and the actors or use cases that participate in the relationship.

FIGURE 3.15:

Actor specification Relations tab

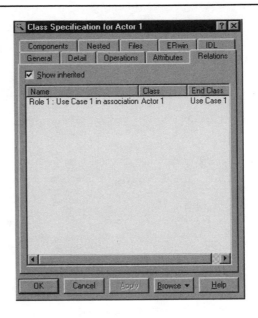

From this tab, you can view, add, or delete relationships. The procedures for viewing, adding, and deleting relationships are listed below.

To view the relationships for an actor:

1. Right-click the actor in the browser or on a Use Case diagram.

2. Select Open Specification from the shortcut menu. The relationships will be listed on the Relations tab.

To view the relationship specifications:

1. Double-click the relationship in the list.

2. The relationship specification window will appear. See below for a detailed description of relationship specifications.

   OR

1. Right-click the relationship in the list.

2. Select Specification from the shortcut menu.

3. The relationship specification window will appear. See below for a detailed description of relationship specifications.

To delete a relationship:

1. Right-click the relationship in the list.

2. Select Delete from the shortcut menu.

Attaching Files and URLs to an Actor

As we did with use cases, we can attach a file or a URL to an actor. This is done using the Files tab of the actor specification window, as shown in Figure 3.16. Files or URLs you attach to an actor should be documents that apply only to that actor. For example, you may have a workflow diagram that illustrates the responsibilities and workflow of an actor. If an actor is another system, you may wish to attach some documentation or specifications related to that external system.

FIGURE 3.16:

Actor specification Files tab

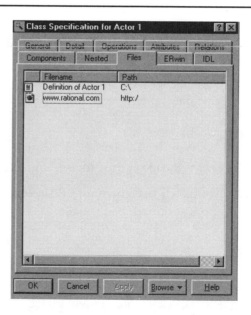

Any files or URLs you attach to an actor will appear in the browser, underneath the actor. Once it has been added, you can double-click a file or URL in the browser to automatically launch the appropriate application and load the file or URL.

To attach a file to an actor:

1. Right-click anywhere inside the white space in the Files tab.

2. Select Insert File to insert a file.

3. Using the dialog box, find the file you wish to attach.

4. Select Open to attach the file to the actor. The name and path of the attached file will appear in the Files tab. It will also appear in the browser, underneath the actor.

To attach a URL to an actor:

1. Right-click anywhere inside the white space in the Files tab.

2. Select Insert URL to insert a URL.

3. Type the name of the URL to attach. The URL name will appear in the browser, underneath the actor.

To open an attached file:

1. Open the actor specification.

2. Double-click the name of the file in the Files tab. Rose will automatically start the appropriate application and load the file.

OR

1. Locate the file in the browser under the appropriate actor.

2. Double-click the filename. Rose will automatically start the appropriate application and load the file.

OR

1. Open the actor specification.

2. Right-click the file in the Files tab.

3. From the shortcut menu, select Open File / URL. Rose will automatically start the appropriate application and load the file.

OR

1. Locate the file in the browser under the appropriate actor.

2. Right-click the file in the browser.

3. From the shortcut menu, select Open. Rose will automatically start the appropriate application and load the file.

To open an attached URL:

1. Open the actor specification.

2. Double-click the name of the URL in the Files tab. Rose will automatically start your Web browser application and load the URL.

OR

1. Locate the URL in the browser underneath the appropriate actor.

2. Double-click the URL name. Rose will automatically start your Web browser application and load the URL.

OR

1. Open the actor specification.

2. Right-click the URL in the Files tab.

3. From the shortcut menu, select Open File / URL. Rose will automatically start your Web browser application and load the URL.

OR

1. Locate the URL in the browser underneath the appropriate actor.

2. Right-click the URL in the browser.

3. From the shortcut menu, select Open. Rose will automatically start your Web browser application and load the URL.

To delete an attached file or URL:

1. Right-click the file or URL in the browser.

2. Select Delete from the shortcut menu.

Viewing an Actor's Instances

As you are modeling the system, you may want to know which Sequence and Collaboration diagrams a particular actor is on. Rose provides this ability through the Report menu.

To view all Sequence and Collaboration diagrams containing the actor:

1. Select the actor on a Use Case diagram.

2. Select Report ➢ Show Instances.

3. Rose will display a list of all Sequence and Collaboration diagrams that contain the actor, as shown in Figure 3.17. To open a diagram, double-click it in the list box or press the Browse button.

FIGURE 3.17:

Viewing instances of an actor

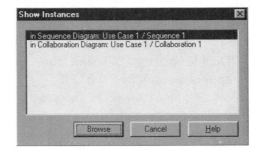

Working with Relationships

UML supports several types of relationships for use cases and actors. These include: communication relationships, uses relationships, extends relationships, and actor generalization relationships. Communication relationships describe the relationships between the actors and the use cases. Uses and extends relationships describe the relationships between the use cases. Actor generalization relationships describe the relationships between actors.

Communicates Relationship

A *communicates relationship* is a relationship between a use case and an actor. In UML, communicates relationships are diagrammed using an arrow:

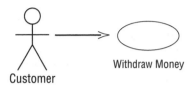

The arrowhead on the relationship indicates who initiates communication. In the example above, the customer actor initiates communication with the system to run the Withdraw Money functionality. A use case can also initiate communication with an actor:

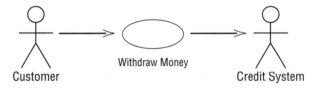

In this example, the use case initiates communication with the Credit System actor. As the Make Payment use case is being run, the ATM system initiates communication with the Credit System to complete the transaction. Information flows in both directions, from the ATM system to the Credit System and back again; the arrow only indicates who initiated the communication.

Every use case must be initiated by an actor, with the exception of use cases in uses and extends relationships, which we will discuss next.

To add a communicates relationship:

1. Select the Unidirectional Association toolbar button.

2. Drag the mouse from the actor to the use case.

3. Rose will draw a relationship between the use case and the actor.

To delete a communicates relationship:

1. Select the relationship on the Use Case diagram.

2. Select Edit ➤ Delete from Model, or press Ctrl+D.

Uses Relationship

A *uses relationship* allows one use case to use the functionality provided by another use case. Uses relationships are typically used to model some reusable functionality that is common to two or more use cases. In the ATM example, both the Withdraw Money and the Deposit Funds use cases need to authenticate the customer and their PIN before allowing the transaction to proceed. Rather than describing in detail the authentication process in both of these use cases, we can move this functionality to its own use case, called Authenticate Customer. Any time another use case needs to authenticate a user, it can use the functionality in Authenticate Customer.

Uses relationships are shown in UML with arrows and the word <<uses>>, as in Figure 3.18.

FIGURE 3.18:

A uses relationship

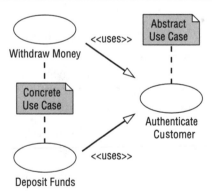

In this example, both the Withdraw Money and Deposit Funds use cases use the functionality in Authenticate Customer. The Authenticate Customer use case is an abstract use case. An abstract use case is one that provides functionality to others through uses or extends relationships. The Withdraw Money and Deposit Funds use cases are concrete use cases.

A uses relationship suggests that one use case *always* uses the functionality provided by another. No matter how you proceed through the Withdraw Money use case, the Authenticate Customer use case is always run. In contrast, an extends relationship allows one use case to *optionally* extend the functionality provided by another.

To add a uses relationship:

1. Select the Generalization toolbar button.

2. Drag from one use case to the use case being used (from the concrete use case to the abstract use case).

3. Rose will draw a generalization between the two use cases.

4. Right-click the relationship's line and select Open Specification, as shown in Figure 3.19.

FIGURE 3.19:

Opening the generalization specification

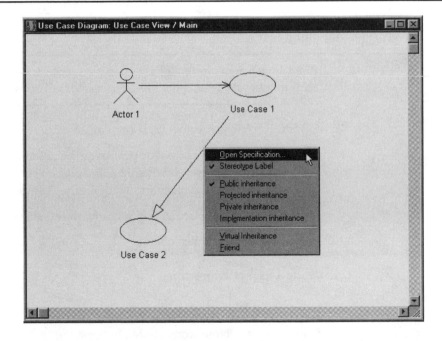

5. Rose will open the generalization specification, as shown in Figure 3.20.

6. In the Stereotype drop-down list box, select uses, or type in **uses** if it is not available. Once you have typed it, it will be available in the drop-down list in the future.

FIGURE 3.20:

Generalization specification

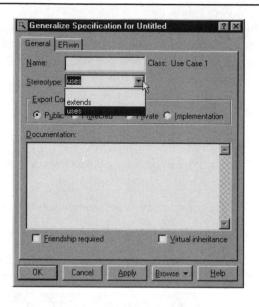

There are a number of other options on the specification window. These don't apply to uses relationships, and will be discussed in Chapter 7.

7. Click OK to close the specification window.

8. The word <<uses>> should appear over the generalization arrow. If it does not, right-click on the relationship's line and be sure there is a check mark next to Stereotype Label, as shown in Figure 3.21.

9. Open the use case specification window of the abstract use case.

10. Check the Abstract check box.

To delete a uses relationship:

1. Select the relationship on the Use Case diagram.

2. Select Edit ➢ Delete from Model, or press Ctrl+D.

FIGURE 3.21:

Stereotype Label with a
check mark next to it

FIGURE 3.21:

Stereotype Label with a
check mark next to it

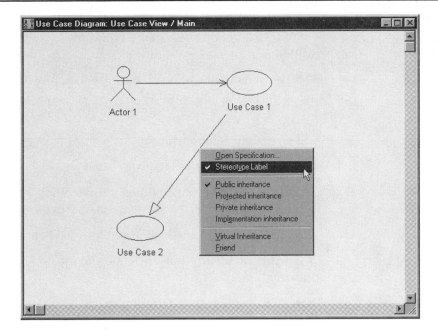

Extends Relationship

An *extends relationship* allows one use case to optionally extend the functionality provided by another use case. It is very similar to a uses relationship. In both of these types of relationships, you separate some common functionality into its own use case.

In UML, the extends relationship is shown as an arrow with the word <<extends>>, as in Figure 3.22.

FIGURE 3.22:

An extends relationship

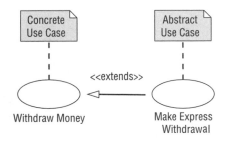

In this example, the Withdraw Money use case *sometimes* uses the functionality in the Make Express Withdrawal use case. If and only if the user selects the $40 quick withdrawal option while in the Withdraw Money use case, the Make Express Withdrawal use case is run.

The Make Express Withdrawal use case, which provides the extending functionality, is the abstract use case. The Withdraw Money use case is a concrete use case.

To add an extends relationship:

1. Select the Generalization toolbar button.

2. Drag from the use case providing the extending functionality to the use case being extended (from the abstract use case to the concrete use case).

3. Rose will draw a generalization between the two use cases.

4. Right-click on the relationship's line and select Open Specification, as shown in Figure 3.19.

5. Rose will open the generalization specification, as shown in Figure 3.23.

FIGURE 3.23:

The generalization specification

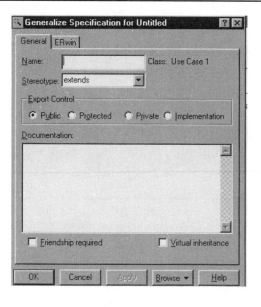

6. In the Stereotype drop-down list box, select extends, or type **extends** if it is not available. Once you have typed it, it will be available in the drop-down list in the future.

NOTE There are a number of other options on the specification window. These don't apply to extends relationships and will be discussed in Chapter 7.

7. Click OK to close the specification window.

8. The word <<extends>> should appear over the generalization arrow. If it does not, right-click on the relationship's line and be sure there is a check mark next to Stereotype Label, as shown in Figure 3.21.

9. Open the use case specification window of the Abstract use case.

10. Check the Abstract check box.

To delete an extends relationship:

1. Select the relationship on the Use Case diagram.

2. Select Edit ➤ Delete from Model, or press Ctrl+D.

Actor Generalization Relationship

An *actor generalization* relationship is used to show that several actors have some commonality. For example, you may have two types of customers: corporate customers and individual customers. You can model this relationship using the notation displayed in Figure 3.24.

This diagram shows that we have two types of customers—individual and corporate. The individual and corporate actors are *concrete* actors. They will be directly instantiated. The customer actor is an *abstract* actor. It is never directly instantiated. It exists only to show that there are two types of customers.

We can break things down further if we need to. Say there are two types of corporate customers—government agencies and private companies. We can modify the diagram to look like Figure 3.25.

FIGURE 3.24:

Actor generalization
relationship

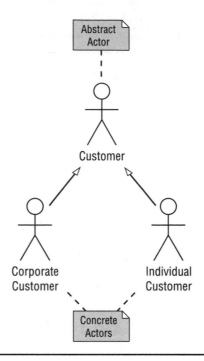

FIGURE 3.25:

Modified actor generalization relationship

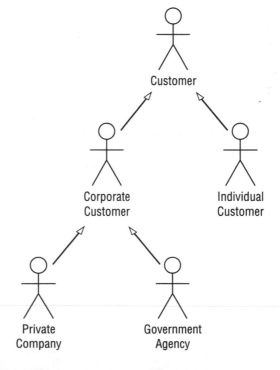

It isn't always necessary to create these types of relationships. In general, they are only needed if one type of actor behaves differently than another type, *as far as the system is concerned*. If the corporate customers will be initiating some use cases that individual customers will not, it's probably worth including the actor generalizations. If both types of customers use the same use cases, it's probably not necessary to show an actor generalization. If both types use the same use cases, but slightly differently, it still probably isn't worth including the generalization. The slight differences are documented in the flow of events for the use cases.

Again, the point of these diagrams is communication. If including an actor generalization would give the team some useful information, then include it. Otherwise, don't clutter up the diagrams with them.

To add an actor generalization:

1. Add the actors to the Use Case diagram.

2. Select the Generalization button from the toolbar.

3. Drag from the concrete actor to the abstract actor.

4. Open the actor specification window for the abstract actor.

5. Select the Detail tab.

6. Check the Abstract check box.

To delete an actor generalization relationship:

1. Select the relationship on the Use Case diagram.

2. Select Edit ➣ Delete from Model, or press Ctrl+D.

Working with Notes

As you create your diagrams, it can be helpful to attach notes to the use cases or actors. For example, you may want to clarify why a particular actor interacts with a particular use case, why one use case participates in a uses or extends relationship, or why one actor inherits from another. Rose provides the ability to add these types of notes through the Note toolbar button.

Adding Notes

There are two types of notes you can add: a note and a text box. In general, notes are used to include a comment that applies to a single item on the diagram. Text boxes are used to place the diagram name or other general information on the diagram.

To add a note to the diagram:

1. Select the Note toolbar button.

2. Click anywhere inside the diagram to place the note.

3. With the new note selected, type the text of the note.

To attach a note to an item:

1. Select the Anchor Note to Item toolbar button.

2. Drag from the note to the use case or actor the note is associated with. Rose will draw a dashed line between the note and the use case or actor, as shown in Figure 3.26.

FIGURE 3.26:

Attaching a note to a use case

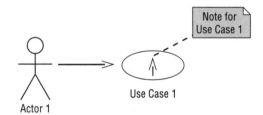

In addition to notes, you can add text boxes to your diagram. These can be used, for example, to add a title to your Use Case diagram.

To add a text box to the diagram:

1. Select the Text Box toolbar button.

2. Click anywhere inside the diagram to place the text box.

3. With the text box selected, type the text.

Deleting Notes

As you change or update your diagram, you may find it necessary to remove some of the notes or text boxes.

To delete a note or text box from the diagram:

1. Select the note or text box on the diagram.

2. Press the Delete key.

Working with Packages

In UML, items such as actors, use cases, classes, and components can be grouped together into *packages* in order to organize them. In the Use Case view, you may want to group your use cases and actors into packages. In UML, a package is represented with the following symbol:

Adding Packages

In Rose, you can add as many packages as you need to organize the items in your model. If you'd like, you can also create one package inside another, nesting packages to further organize your model. When creating a new package, Rose will automatically create a diagram called Package Overview and an Associations list.

To add a package:

1. Right-click Use Case view in the browser. To create a package underneath an existing package, right-click the existing package in the browser.

2. Select New ➤ Package, as shown in Figure 3.27.

3. Type in the name of the new package.

FIGURE 3.27:

Adding a use case package

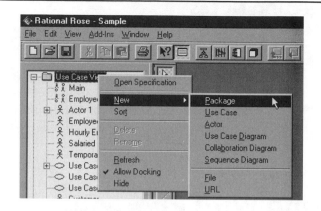

To move an item into a package:

In the browser, drag the item from its existing location to the new package.

Deleting Packages

In Rose, you can delete a package from a single Use Case diagram or from the entire model. If you delete a package from the entire model, the package and everything within it will be removed.

To remove a package from a Use Case diagram:

1. Select the package on the Use Case diagram.

2. Press the Delete key.

3. Note that the package has been removed from the Use Case diagram, but still exists in the browser and on other Use Case diagrams.

To remove a package from the model:

1. Right-click the package in the browser.

2. Select Delete from the shortcut menu.

OR

1. Select the package on a Use Case diagram.

2. Select Edit ➤ Delete from Model, or press Ctrl+D.

WARNING　When you delete a package from the model, all use cases, actors, and other items in the package will also be deleted from the model.

Exercise

These exercises will be provided at the end of every chapter in this section. The exercise for this chapter will walk you through creating a Use Case diagram for an order processing system.

Problem Statement

"I've had it!" said Bob, as he slammed the phone down.

Mary looked up from her computer. "What's the problem?"

"That's the fourth time this month one of our customers has called to complain about not receiving their order. If we keep this up, we'll be out of business."

"Calm down," Mary replied. "We've just been growing too fast. Handling orders on paper worked fine when we were just a five-person operation. We can't expect it to work anymore. Let's talk with Susan to see if we can get a system built that'll help us keep track of things."

Robertson's Cabinets, Inc. is a hypothetical example of a small business that specializes in the manufacturing of standard and custom kitchen cabinets. The company started when a small group of entrepreneurs got together. When they started out three years ago, there were few enough jobs that they could simply keep track of the orders on paper. As their reputation grew, however, they started to receive more and more orders. They began to hire new cabinetmakers, and within three years had grown to a shop with over 50 employees.

Although it was still a relatively small company, Robertson's had just grown too large to continue to rely on manual processes. Bob and Mary Robertson, the company's owners, decided to talk to Susan to resolve the problem. Susan is one of a small number of computer specialists who formed the company's information technology group.

Bob went to talk to Susan.

"It's obvious we need some sort of system to track orders. We've got a serious risk of losing customers."

"I agree."

"Can you build us a Java program that will track orders?"

"Let's not worry about the implementation yet. Why don't we focus on what you want the system to do."

"We need it to track orders."

"Could you be a little more specific? Let's look at the current process."

"Well, when we get calls, we fill out an order form. We give the form to Clint in the warehouse, he fills the orders, and arranges the shipping out to the customers. We give another copy of the form to Don in accounting. He enters it into the accounting system and generates an invoice."

"And you want this new system to support this whole process?"

"Exactly."

From this discussion, Susan was able to determine that the system needed to support adding new orders, modifying existing orders, filling orders, checking current inventory levels, and restocking the inventory. When a new order is added, the system would need to notify the accounting system, so that an invoice could be generated. If an item were out of stock, the system would need to back-order the item. Susan put together a Use Case diagram to model the system.

Create a Use Case Diagram

Create the Use Case diagram for the order processing system. The steps for creating the diagram are outlined below. Your final Use Case diagram should look like Figure 3.28.

FIGURE 3.28:

Order processing system
Use Case diagram

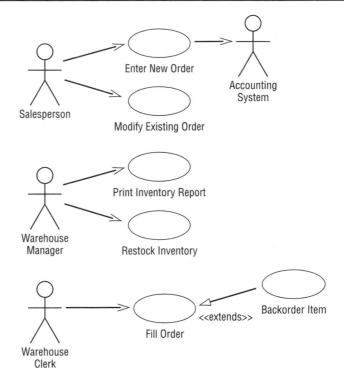

Exercise Steps:

Add the Use Case diagram, Use Cases, and Actors

1. Double-click the Main Use Case diagram in the browser to open the diagram.

2. Use the Use Case toolbar button to add a new use case to the diagram.

3. Name this new use case **Enter New Order.**

4. Repeat steps 2 and 3 to add the remaining use cases to the diagram.

   Modify Existing Order
   Print Inventory Report
   Restock Inventory
   Fill Order
   Backorder Item

5. Use the Actor toolbar button to add a new actor to the diagram.

6. Name this new actor **Salesperson**.

7. Repeat steps 5 and 6 to add the remaining actors to the diagram.

   Warehouse Manager
   Warehouse Clerk
   Accounting System

Mark Abstract Use Case

1. Right-click the Backorder item use case in the diagram.

2. Select the Open Specification option from the shortcut menu.

3. Check the Abstract box to mark this use case as an abstract use case.

Add Associations

1. Use the Unidirectional Association toolbar button to draw the association between the Salesperson actor and the Enter New Order use case.

2. Repeat step 1 to add the rest of the associations to the diagram.

Add Extends Relationship

1. Use the Generalization toolbar button to draw the extends relationship between the Backorder Item use case and the Fill Order use case. When drawing the relationship, start from Backorder Item and drag to Fill Order. The extends relationship suggests that Backorder Item optionally extends the functionality provided by Fill Order.

2. Right-click the new relationship between Backorder Item and Fill Order.

3. From the shortcut menu, select Open Specification.

4. In the stereotype drop-down list box, type **extends** and click OK.

5. The word <<extends>> will appear on the relationship line.

Add Use Case Descriptions

1. Select the Enter New Order use case in the browser.

2. Using the documentation window, add the following description to the Enter New Order use case: **This use case will allow a user to add a new order into the system**.

3. Using the documentation window, add descriptions to the remaining use cases.

Add Actor Descriptions

1. Select the Salesperson actor in the browser.

2. Using the documentation window, add the following description to the Salesperson actor: **A salesperson is an employee who markets and intends to sell products**.

3. Using the documentation window, add descriptions to the remaining actors.

Attach File to Use Case

1. Included on the CD provided with this book is a file called OrderFlow.doc, which contains the primary flow of events for the Enter New Order use case. Use this file, or type the primary flow of events as shown in Figure 3.29 into a file called Order-Flow.doc.

FIGURE 3.29:

Primary flow of events for Enter New Order use case

Primary Flow of Events for 'Enter New Order' Use Case

1. The salesperson selects the 'Create New Order' option from the options menu.

2. System displays the Order Detail form.

3. Salesperson enters the order number, customer, and items ordered.

4. Salesperson saves the order.

5. System creates a new order and saves it to the database.

---

2. Right-click the Enter New Order use case.

3. Select Open Specification from the shortcut menu.

4. Select the Files tab.

5. Right-click inside the white area and select Insert File from the shortcut menu.

6. Find the file OrderFlow.doc and click the Open button to attach it to the use case.

Summary

In this chapter, we have discussed how to work with use cases, actors, and Use Case diagrams. The requirements of the system to be built are the set of all use cases and actors. You begin by creating a Main Use Case diagram to show the overall view of the system. Then, additional diagrams may be created to illustrate the interactions between actors and use cases. Use cases can use or extend other use cases. Otherwise, they cannot directly communicate with each other. One use case uses another when the functionality will always be needed. One use case extends another when the functionality is optionally needed. If a use case is used by or extends another use case, that use case is abstract. Use cases that actors directly participate in are concrete.

Actors can communicate with use cases, illustrating which actors participate in which use cases. Actors can also inherit from one another. For example, a student may be an actor in the system. We may need to further refine the role of student into full-time student and part-time student. We do this by inheriting the full-time and part-time students from the student actor.

Use cases and Use Case diagrams are useful ways to describe system functionality. In the next chapter, we will discuss the use of Sequence and Collaboration diagrams, which are used to show the interactions between objects and actors.

CHAPTER
FOUR

4

Object Interaction

- Looking at Sequence and Collaboration Diagrams

- Adding Objects to Sequence and Collaboration Diagrams

- Using Messages with Sequence and Collaboration Diagrams

- Switching between Sequence and Collaboration Diagrams

- Using the Two-Pass Approach to Create Interaction Diagrams

In this chapter, we will discuss how to model the interactions between the objects in the system. There are two types of Interaction diagrams we'll take a look at: Sequence diagrams and Collaboration diagrams. Both show the objects participating in a flow through a use case and the messages that are sent between the objects. Sequence diagrams are ordered by time; Collaboration diagrams are organized around the objects themselves.

In the exercise at the end of the chapter, we will build a Sequence diagram to support one flow through the Enter New Order use case of our order processing system.

Interaction Diagrams

An *Interaction diagram* shows you, step-by-step, one of the flows through a use case. In the ATM example, we had several alternate flows through the Withdraw Money use case. Therefore, we will have several Interaction diagrams for this use case. We'll have the *happy day* Interaction diagram, which shows what happens when all goes well. We'll have some additional diagrams showing what happens with the alternate flows—what happens when someone enters the wrong PIN, what happens when there isn't enough money in the account to allow the withdrawal, and so on.

There are two types of Interaction diagrams we'll talk about: Sequence diagrams and Collaboration diagrams. A Sequence diagram is ordered by time. Figure 4.1 is an example of a Sequence diagram.

FIGURE 4.1:

Sequence diagram

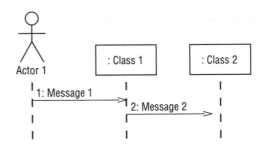

A Collaboration diagram shows the same information, but is organized differently. Figure 4.2 is an example of a Collaboration diagram.

FIGURE 4.2:

Collaboration diagram

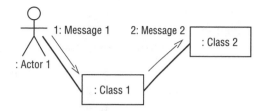

Both a Sequence and a Collaboration diagram will show you the same information; however, there are a couple of differences between Sequence diagrams and Collaboration diagrams. Sequence diagrams can show a focus of control; Collaboration diagrams can show a data flow. We'll talk about these differences when discussing messages below.

Interaction diagrams contain a lot of the same detail spelled out in the flow of events. But here, the information is presented in a way that is more useful to the developers. These diagrams focus on the objects that will be created to implement the functionality spelled out in the use cases. Sequence and Collaboration diagrams can show objects, classes, or both.

What Is an Object?

We see objects all around us. The chair you're sitting in, the book you're reading, and the lightbulb that's helping you see are all examples of objects in the real world. An object in the software world is very much the same.

An *object* is something that encapsulates information and behavior. It's a term that represents some concrete, real-world thing. Examples of objects are:

- Joe's checking account
- The house at 7638 Main Street.
- The yellow flower just outside my kitchen window

In our ATM example, other objects might be the ATM screen, the card reader, Joe's ATM card, and the receipt that printed after Joe withdrew $20.

Every object encapsulates some information and some behavior. Joe's account, for example, has some information: the account number is 123456789, the account belongs to Joe Smith, and the current account balance is $350. Joe's account also has some behavior. It will know how to add money to itself when Joe makes a deposit, how to remove funds from itself when Joe makes a withdrawal, and how to figure out whether it's overdrawn.

The pieces of information held by an object are known as its *attributes*. Although the values of the attributes will change over time (Joe may have $400 in his account next week), the attributes themselves will not change. Joe's account will always have an account number, an owner, and a balance.

The behaviors an object has are known as its *operations*. In this case, the operations for Joe's account include adjusting the balance for a deposit or a withdrawal, and checking to see if the account is overdrawn.

In Rose, objects are added to the Interaction diagrams. When dragging an actor (which is a class stereotype) or some other class onto an Interaction diagram, an object instantiation of that class will automatically be created. Removing an object from a diagram in Rose will not delete the class from the model.

What Is a Class?

A *class* is something that provides a blueprint for an object. In other words, a class defines what information an object can hold and what behavior it can have. For example, classes for Joe's checking account, the house at 7638 Main Street, and the yellow flower just outside my kitchen window would be: Account, House, and Flower. The House *class* would just specify that a house has a height, width, number of rooms, and square footage. The House at 7638 Main Street *object* might have a height of 20 feet, a width of 60 feet, 10 rooms, and 2000 square feet. A class is a more generic term that simply provides a template for objects.

Think of a class as a blueprint for a house, and the objects as the 25 houses that were all built from that blueprint. We'll talk about classes more in the next chapter.

Finding Objects

A good way to find some initial objects is to examine the nouns in your flow of events. Another good place to look is in the scenario documents. A *scenario* is a specific instance of a flow of events. Our flow of events for the Withdraw Money use case talks about a person withdrawing some cash from the ATM. One of the scenarios for this flow would be *Joe withdraws $20*. Another might be *Jane tries to withdraw $20, but she enters the wrong PIN*. Yet another might be *Bob tries to withdraw $20, but there isn't enough money in his account*. There are usually many scenarios for a flow of events. A Sequence or Collaboration diagram illustrates *one* of these scenarios.

As you look at the nouns in your scenarios, some of the nouns will be actors, some will be objects, and some will be attributes of an object. When you're building your Interaction diagrams, the nouns will tell you what the objects will be. If you're looking at a noun and wondering whether it's an object or an attribute, ask whether it has any behavior. If it's information only, it's probably an attribute. If it has some behaviors also, it may be an object.

Not all of the objects will be in the flow of events. Forms, for example, may not appear in the flow of events, but will have to appear on the diagram in order to allow the actor to enter or view information. Other objects that probably won't appear in the flow of events are control objects. These are objects that control the sequencing of the flow through the use case. We'll talk more about control objects and classes in the next chapter.

Using Interaction Diagrams

From the diagrams, designers and developers can determine the classes they will need to develop, the relationships between the classes, and the operations or responsibilities of each class. The Interaction diagrams become the cornerstones upon which the rest of the design is built.

Sequence diagrams are ordered by time. They are useful if someone wants to review the flow of logic through a scenario. Although Collaboration diagrams include sequencing information, it is easier to see on a Sequence diagram.

Collaboration diagrams are useful if you want to assess the impact of a change. It's very easy to see on a Collaboration diagram which objects communicate with which other objects. If you need to change an object, you can easily see which other objects might be affected.

Interaction diagrams contain:

Objects   An Interaction diagram can use object names, class names, or both.

Messages   Through a message, one object or class can request that another carry out some specific function. For example, a form may ask a report object to print itself.

One thing to remember as you create the Interaction diagrams is that you are assigning responsibility to objects. When you add a message to an Interaction diagram, you are assigning a responsibility to the object receiving the message. Be sure to assign the appropriate responsibilities to the appropriate objects. In most applications, screens and forms shouldn't do any business processing. They should only allow the user to enter and view information. By separating the front-end from the business logic, you've created an architecture that reduces the ripple effect of changes. If the business logic needs to change, the interface shouldn't be affected. If you change the format of a screen or two, the business logic won't need to be changed. Other objects should be assigned appropriate responsibilities as well. If we need to print a report of all of the balances of all accounts, Joe's account shouldn't be responsible for that. The responsibilities of Joe's account should focus on Joe and his money. Another object can be responsible for looking at *all* of the accounts to generate a report.

Sequence Diagrams

Let's begin by taking a look at Sequence diagrams. *Sequence diagrams* are Interaction diagrams that are ordered by time; you read the diagram from the top to the bottom. As we mentioned above, each use case will have a number of alternate flows. Each Sequence diagram represents one of the flows through a use case. For example, Figure 4.3 is the Sequence diagram that shows Joe, a bank customer, withdrawing $20 from the ATM.

We can read this diagram by looking at the objects and messages. The objects that participate in the flow are shown in rectangles across the top of the diagram. In this example, there are five objects: Joe, the card reader, the ATM screen, Joe's account, and the cash dispenser. The actor object, Joe, initiating the use case is shown at the upper-left of the diagram.

FIGURE 4.3:

This Sequence diagram shows Joe withdrawing $20 from the ATM.

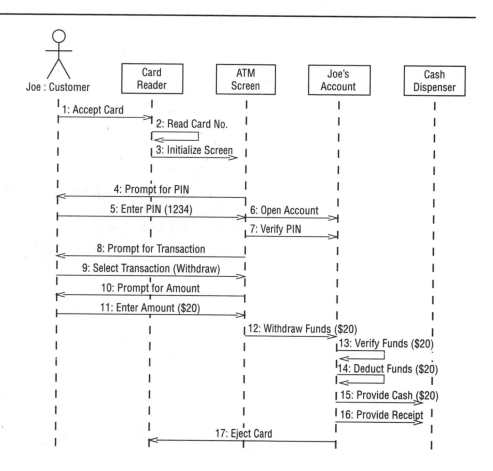

The process begins when Joe inserts his card into the card reader. The card reader reads the number on Joe's card, then tells the ATM screen to initialize itself. The ATM prompts Joe for his PIN. Joe enters his PIN (1234) and the ATM opens his account. Joe's PIN is validated, and the ATM prompts him for a transaction. Joe selects Withdraw. The ATM prompts Joe for the withdrawal amount. Joe enters $20. The ATM verifies that Joe's account has sufficient funds, and subtracts $20 from the account. The ATM dispenses $20 and ejects Joe's card.

Each object has a *lifeline*, drawn as a vertical dashed line below the object. A message is drawn between the lifelines of two objects to show that the objects communicate. Each message represents one object making a function call of another. Later in the process, as we define operations for the classes, each message will become an operation. Messages can also be reflexive, showing that an object is calling one of its own operations. In this example, message two indicates that the card reader asks itself to read the card number.

Creating a Sequence Diagram

Sequence diagrams can be created in either the Use Case view or the Logical view of the browser. Sequence diagrams must reside directly within a use case, as shown in Figure 4.4, or directly within a package.

FIGURE 4.4:

Creating a new Sequence diagram

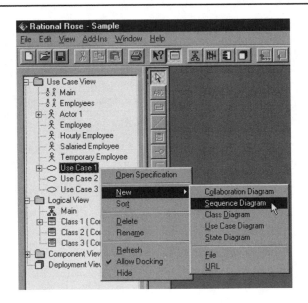

To create a new Sequence diagram:

1. Right-click the appropriate package or use case in the browser.

2. From the shortcut menu, select New ➤ Sequence diagram.

3. Name the new Sequence diagram.

4. Double-click the new Sequence diagram in the browser to open it.

To open an existing Sequence diagram:

1. Locate the Sequence diagram in the Use Case view of the browser.

2. Double-click the Sequence diagram to open it.

OR

1. Select Browse ➤ Interaction diagram. The window shown in Figure 4.5 will appear.

2. In the Package list box, select the package that contains the diagram you want to open.

3. In the Interaction diagrams list box, select the diagram you want to open.

4. Press OK.

FIGURE 4.5:

Opening an existing Sequence diagram

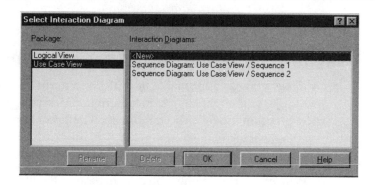

To add an item to a Sequence diagram:

Use the toolbar buttons as described in the sections below to add objects and messages to the diagram.

OR

Drag an actor or class from the browser onto the Sequence diagram.

To remove an item from a Sequence diagram:

1. Select the item on the Sequence diagram.

2. Select Edit ➤ Delete from Model, or press Ctrl+D.

NOTE   Deleting an object from the diagram does not delete the corresponding class from the model.

Deleting a Sequence Diagram

As you continue to work on your project, you may find that some of your Sequence diagrams become outdated or redundant. To keep your model consistent, it's a good idea to delete any Sequence diagrams you are no longer using or that no longer reflect the design of your system. You can delete a Sequence diagram from your model by using the browser in Rose.

To delete a Sequence diagram:

1. Right-click the Sequence diagram in the browser.

2. Select Delete from the shortcut menu.

Attaching Files and URLs to a Sequence Diagram

In Rose, you can attach a file or a URL to a particular Sequence diagram. For example, you might have a document that describes the scenario that the Interaction diagram models. You might attach a file containing some code that implements the logic in the diagram. Or, you might attach a requirement document containing some requirements that are specific to the diagram.

Whichever documents you attach, be sure the information in the file or URL pertains only to the Interaction diagram, not to the entire use case. If it pertains to the entire use case, you may want to attach it to the use case itself.

To attach a file to a Sequence diagram:

1. Right-click the Sequence diagram in the browser.

2. Select New ➤ File.

3. Using the Open dialog box, select the file you wish to attach.

4. Select Open to attach the file.

To attach a URL to a Sequence diagram:

1. Right-click the Sequence diagram in the browser.

2. Select New ➤ URL.

3.   Type the name of the URL to attach.

To open an attached file:

Double-click the file in the browser. Rose will open the appropriate application and load the file.

OR

1.   Right-click the file in the browser.

2.   From the shortcut menu, select Open. Rose will open the appropriate application and load the file.

To open an attached URL:

Double-click the URL in the browser. Rose will automatically start your Web browser application and load the URL.

OR

1.   Right-click the URL in the browser.

2.   From the shortcut menu, select Open. Rose will automatically start your Web browser application and load the URL.

To delete an attached file or URL:

1.   Right-click the file or URL in the browser.

2.   Select Delete from the shortcut menu.

The Sequence Diagram Toolbar

When a Sequence diagram is opened, the Diagram toolbar changes to let you add objects, messages, and other items to the diagram. The options available in the toolbar are described below. In the following sections, we'll discuss adding each of these items. Table 4.1 lists the buttons available in the Sequence diagram toolbar and explains the purpose of each.

TABLE 4.1: Icons in the Sequence Diagram Toolbar

Icon	Button	Purpose
⬆	Selects or deselects an item	Return the cursor to an arrow to select an item.
ABC	Text Box	Add a text box to the diagram.
▤	Note	Add a note to the diagram.
╱	Anchor Note to Item	Connect a note to an item in the diagram.
▤	Object	Add a new object to the diagram.
→	Object Message	Draw a message between two objects.
⮌	Message to Self	Draw a reflexive message.

Collaboration Diagrams

Like Sequence diagrams, *Collaboration diagrams* are used to show the flow through a specific scenario of a use case. Sequence diagrams are ordered by time, Collaboration diagrams focus more on the relationships between the objects. Figure 4.6 is the Collaboration diagram for Joe Withdraws $20.

FIGURE 4.6:

Collaboration diagram for Joe Withdraws $20

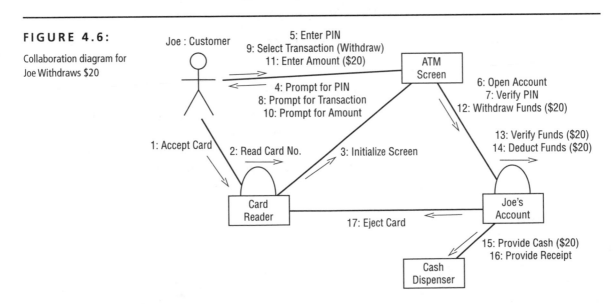

As you can see, the information that was in the Sequence diagram above is still here in the Collaboration diagram, but this diagram gives us a different view of the flow. In this diagram, it's easier to see the relationships between the objects. However, it's a little more difficult to see the sequencing information.

For this reason, you may want to create both a Sequence and a Collaboration diagram for a scenario. Although they serve the same purpose and contain the same information, each gives you a slightly different view. In Rose, you can create a Sequence diagram from a Collaboration diagram (or vice-versa) by pressing F5 or selecting Browse ➢ Create (Sequence / Collaboration) Diagram.

Creating a Collaboration Diagram

Like Sequence diagrams, Collaboration diagrams are usually created in the browser, directly underneath a use case or a package. Figure 4.7 illustrates how to create a new Collaboration diagram to your model. As we mentioned above, an alternate way to create a Collaboration diagram is to create a Sequence diagram and then press F5. Rose will automatically create a Collaboration diagram from the Sequence diagram.

FIGURE 4.7:

Creating a new Collaboration diagram

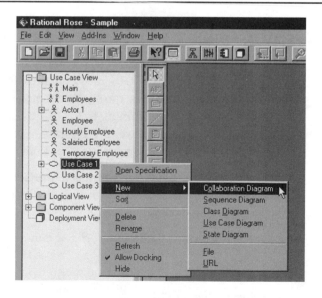

To create a new Collaboration diagram:

1. Right-click the appropriate use case in the browser.

2. From the shortcut menu, select New ➤ Collaboration diagram.

3. Name the new Collaboration diagram.

4. Double-click the new Collaboration diagram in the browser to open it.

Deleting a Collaboration Diagram

As you build your model, you may find that you have some Collaboration diagrams that are no longer accurate or are no longer being used. To clean up the model, you can delete these extra Collaboration diagrams using the browser in Rose.

To delete a Collaboration diagram:

1. Right-click the Collaboration diagram in the browser.

2. Select Delete from the shortcut menu.

Attaching Files and URLs to a Collaboration Diagram

As with Sequence diagrams, you can attach a file or a URL to a Collaboration diagram. The attached file or URL may contain information about the flow of events that the diagram illustrates, the specific requirements the diagram implements, or other documentation pertaining to the diagram. If the attached file or URL contains information about the entire use case, as opposed to a single scenario, it should be attached to the use case rather than the Collaboration diagram.

Once a file or URL has been attached to a Collaboration diagram, you can double-click it in the browser to automatically launch the appropriate application and load the file or URL.

To attach a file to a Collaboration diagram:

1. Right-click the Collaboration diagram in the browser.

2. Select New ➤ File.

3. Using the Open dialog box, select the file you wish to attach.

4. Select Open to attach the file.

To attach a URL to a Collaboration diagram:

1.   Right-click the Collaboration diagram in the browser.

2.   Select New ➤ URL.

3.   Type the name of the URL to attach.

To open an attached file:

Double-click the file in the browser. Rose will open the appropriate application and load the file.

OR

1.   Right-click the file in the browser.

2.   From the shortcut menu, select Open. Rose will open the appropriate application and load the file.

To open an attached URL:

Double-click the URL name in the browser. Rose will automatically start your Web browser application and load the URL.

OR

1.   Right-click the URL in the browser.

2.   From the shortcut menu, select Open. Rose will automatically start your Web browser application and load the URL.

To delete an attached file or URL:

1.   Right-click the file or URL in the browser.

2.   Select Delete from the shortcut menu.

The Collaboration Diagram Toolbar

The Collaboration diagram toolbar is very similar to the Sequence diagram toolbar. There are a few options available here that aren't available in a Sequence diagram, such as an object link and data flow. The following sections describe how to use each of these toolbar buttons to add items to the diagram. Table 4.2 shows the toolbar buttons available on the Collaboration diagram toolbar.

TABLE 4.2: Icons in the Collaboration Diagram Toolbar

Icon	Button	Purpose
	Selects or deselects an item	Return the cursor to an arrow to select an item.
	Text Box	Add a text box to the diagram.
	Note	Add a note to the diagram.
	Anchor Note to Item	Connect a note to an item on the diagram.
	Object	Add a new object to the diagram.
	Class Instance	Add a new class instance to the diagram.
	Object Link	Create a path for communication between two objects.
	Link to Self	Show that an object can call its own operations.
	Link Message	Add a message between two objects or from an object to itself.
	Reverse Link Message	Add a message in the opposite direction between two objects or from an object to itself.
	Data Flow	Show information flow between two objects.
	Reverse Data Flow	Show information flow in the opposite direction between two objects.

Working with Actors on an Interaction Diagram

Every Sequence and Collaboration diagram should have an actor object. The actor object is the external stimulus that tells the system to run some functionality. The actor objects for the Interaction diagram will include the actors that interact with the use case on the Use Case diagram.

To create an actor object on an Interaction diagram:

1. Open the Interaction diagram.

2. Select the actor in the browser.

3. Drag the actor from the browser to the open diagram.

To remove an actor object from an Interaction diagram:

1. Select the actor on the Interaction diagram.

2. Select Edit ➢ Delete from Model, or press Ctrl+D.

NOTE   Deleting an object from the diagram does not delete the corresponding class from the model.

Working with Objects

The Sequence and Collaboration diagrams show you the objects that participate in one flow through a particular use case. Once the actor object has been added to the diagram, the next step is to add other objects. As we discussed above, you can find the objects that participate in a particular Sequence or Collaboration diagram by examining the nouns in the flow of events and scenario documents. After this step, we will go in and add the messages between the objects.

Adding Objects to an Interaction Diagram

One of the first steps in creating a Sequence or a Collaboration diagram is adding the objects. Look at the nouns from your flow of events and scenarios to start finding objects.

To add an object to a Sequence diagram:

1. Select the Object toolbar button.

2. Click in the location on the diagram where you want the object to reside. In a Sequence diagram, objects are arranged in a row near the top.

3. Type the name of the new object.

4. Once you have added the objects, you can rearrange them by dragging and dropping. You can insert an object between two existing objects by clicking between the two existing objects in step two.

To add an object to a Collaboration diagram:

1. Select the Object toolbar button.

2. Click in the location on the diagram where you want the object to reside. In a Collaboration diagram, objects can be located anywhere.

3. Type the name of the new object.

Deleting Objects from an Interaction Diagram

As you build your Interaction diagrams, you may need to delete some of the objects. When you delete an object from the diagram, Rose will automatically delete any messages that start or end with that object. Rose will automatically renumber all of the remaining messages.

When you delete an object from a Sequence diagram, Rose will automatically delete the object from the corresponding Collaboration diagram but will not delete the corresponding class from the model. Similarly, when you delete an object from a Collaboration diagram, Rose will remove it from the Sequence diagram. If you change your mind, you can use the Undo option on the Edit menu. To remove an object from a Sequence or Collaboration diagram:

1. Select the object in the Sequence or Collaboration diagram.

2. Select Edit ➤ Delete from Model, or press Ctrl+D.

NOTE Deleting an object from the diagram does not delete the corresponding class from the model.

Object Specifications

There are a number of different fields Rose provides to add some detail to the objects in your diagram. For example, you can set the object's name, its class, its persistence, and whether there are multiple instances of the object. You can also add documentation to the object in the object specification window, shown in Figure 4.8. In the following sections, we'll take a look at each of the options available on the object specification window.

Object specification
window

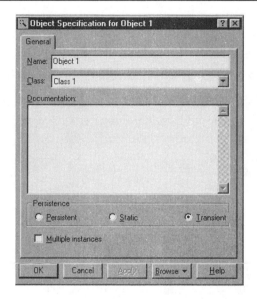

To open the object specifications:

1. Right-click the object in the Sequence or Collaboration diagram.

2. Select Open Specification from the shortcut menu.

   OR

1. Select the object in the Sequence or Collaboration diagram.

2. Select Browse ➢ Specification, or press Ctrl+B.

Naming an Object

Each object on a Sequence or Collaboration diagram should be given a unique name. While class names are very generic (Employee and Company, for example), object names are very specific (John Doe and Rational Software Corporation). On an Interaction diagram, you may have two objects that are instances of the same class. For example, in an inventory system, you may have one instance of a Part class, called Engine, which communicates with another instance of Part, called carburetor. You can enter the name of each object on the diagram in the object specification window, or directly on the diagram.

To name an object:

1. Right-click the object in the Sequence or Collaboration diagram.

2. Select Open Specification from the shortcut menu.

3. In the Name field, enter the object's name. Each object on the diagram should have a unique name. You may also use this field to change the name of the object later on.

OR

1. Select the object in the Sequence or Collaboration diagram.

2. Right-click so that a cursor shows up in the object.

3. Type the object name.

To add documentation to an object:

1. Right-click the object in the Sequence or Collaboration diagram.

2. Select Open Specification from the shortcut menu.

3. In the Documentation field, you can enter documentation for the object.

OR

1. Select the object in the Sequence or Collaboration diagram.

2. Type the object documentation in the documentation window.

NOTE   If the object has already been mapped to a class, the documentation will be added to the class as well. Otherwise, the documentation will stay only with the object. The documentation you enter for an object will not affect code generation; documentation you enter for a class will appear in the code. Documentation for an object will appear in the report generated by using the File ➤ Print Specifications menu option.

Mapping an Object to a Class

On a Sequence or Collaboration diagram, each object may be mapped to a class. For example, Joe's account may be mapped to a class called Account. In the object specification window, you can use the Class field to set the object's class. By default, the class will be set to (Unspecified).

When selecting a class for the object, you can either use an existing class from your model or create a new class for the object. In the procedures below, we describe both of these approaches.

By the time you are ready to generate code, all of the objects should be mapped to classes.

To map an object to an existing class:

1. Right-click the object in the Sequence or Collaboration diagram.

2. Select Open Specification from the shortcut menu.

3. In the Class drop-down list box, type the class name or select an option from the drop-down list box.

4. Once you have mapped the object to a class, the class name will appear with the object name on the diagram, preceded by a colon.

OR

1. Select the class in the Logical view of the browser.

2. Drag the class from the browser to the object in the diagram.

3. Once you have mapped the object to a class, the class name will appear with the object name on the diagram, preceded by a colon:

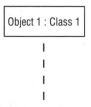

NOTE   If you map the object to a class and then delete the class later, the class name will appear on the diagram, but will be enclosed in parentheses.

To remove an object's class mapping:

1. Right-click the object in the Sequence or Collaboration diagram.

2. Select Open Specification from the shortcut menu.

3. In the Class drop-down list box, select (Unspecified).

To create a new class for the object:

1. Right-click the object in the Sequence or Collaboration diagram.

2. Select Open Specification from the shortcut menu.

3. Select <New> in the Class drop-down list box. Rose will take you to the specification window for the new class.

To ensure all objects have been mapped to classes:

1. Select Report ➤ Show Unresolved Objects.

2. Rose will display a list of all objects that have not yet been mapped to a class.

To show only the object name on the diagram:

1. Right-click the object in the Sequence or Collaboration diagram.

2. Select Open Specification from the shortcut menu.

3. Enter the object name in the Name field.

4. In the Class drop-down list box, select (Unspecified).

To show both the object and class name on the diagram:

1. Right-click the object in the Sequence or Collaboration diagram.

2. Select Open Specification from the shortcut menu.

3. Enter the object name in the Name field.

4. In the Class drop-down list box, type the class name or select an option from the drop-down list box.

To show only the class name on the diagram:

1. If you would rather use only the class name, and not see the object's name at all on the diagram, right-click the object in the Sequence or Collaboration diagram.

2. Select Open Specification from the shortcut menu.

3. Delete the object name from the Name field. Rose will display the object using only the class name. Again, the class name is preceded by a colon.

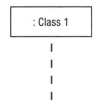

Setting Object Persistence

In Rose, you can set the persistence option for each object in the diagram. Rose provides you with three options:

Persistent   A persistent object is one that will be saved to a database or some other form of persistent storage. The implication here is that the object will continue to exist, even after the program has terminated.

Static   A static object is one that stays in memory until the program is terminated. It lives beyond the execution of this Sequence diagram, but is not saved to persistent storage.

Transient   A transient object is one that stays in memory only for a short time (until the logic in the Sequence diagram has finished, for example).

To set the persistence of an object:

1. Right-click the object in the Sequence or Collaboration diagram.

2. Select Open Specification from the shortcut menu.

3. In the Persistence field, select the appropriate radio button: Persistent, Static, or Transient.

NOTE   If you have set the persistence of the object's class to Persistent, you may set the object's persistence to Persistent, Static, or Transient. If you have set the persistence of the object's class to Transient, you may set the object's Persistence to Static or Transient.

Using Multiple Instances of an Object

Rose provides the option of using one icon to represent multiple instances of the same class. Say, for example, you would like to represent a list of employees on a Sequence or Collaboration diagram. Rather than showing each employee as a separate object, you can use the multiple instances icon to show the employee list. The UML notation for multiple instances looks like this:

To use multiple instances of an object:

1. Right-click the object in the Sequence or Collaboration diagram.

2. Select Open Specification from the shortcut menu.

3. Set the Multiple Instances check box on or off. Rose will use the appropriate icon (single instance or multiple instances) on a Collaboration diagram. Rose will use the single instance icon on a Sequence diagram.

Working with Messages

A *message* is a communication between objects, in which one object (the client) asks another object (the supplier) to do something. By the time you generate code, a message will translate to a function call. In this example, one form is asking another to display itself:

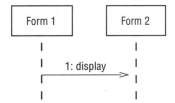

Adding Messages to an Interaction Diagram

Once you have placed the objects on your Sequence or Collaboration diagram, the next step is to add the messages sent between the objects. On a Sequence diagram, messages can be added by drawing an arrow between the lifelines of two objects. On a Collaboration diagram, you must first add a link between two objects. Then, you can add messages between them.

Adding Messages to a Sequence Diagram

In a Sequence diagram, messages are drawn between the lifelines of the objects or from an object's lifeline to itself. Messages are shown in chronological order, from the top of the diagram to the bottom.

To add a message to a Sequence diagram:

1. Select the Object Message button from the toolbar.

2. Drag the mouse from the lifeline of the object or actor sending the message to the object or actor receiving the message, as shown in Figure 4.9.

3. Type in the text of the message.

FIGURE 4.9:

Adding a message to a
Sequence diagram

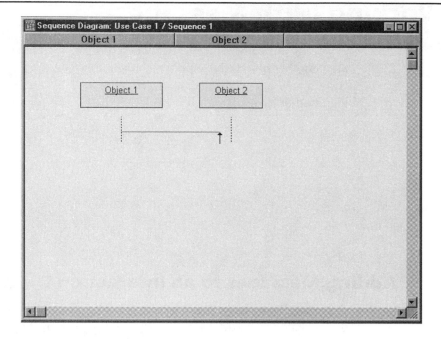

To add a reflexive message to a Sequence diagram:

1.   Select the Message to Self toolbar button.

2.   Click on the lifeline of the object sending and receiving the message, as
     shown in Figure 4.10.

3.   With the new message still selected, type in the text of the message.

Deleting Messages from a Sequence Diagram

As you work on your Sequence diagram, you may need to delete some of the
messages that you've drawn. If you delete a message, Rose will automatically
renumber all of the remaining messages.

To delete a message from a Sequence diagram:

1.   Select the message to be deleted.

2.   Select Edit ➤ Delete from Model, or press Ctrl+D.

FIGURE 4.10:

Adding a reflexive message
to a Sequence diagram

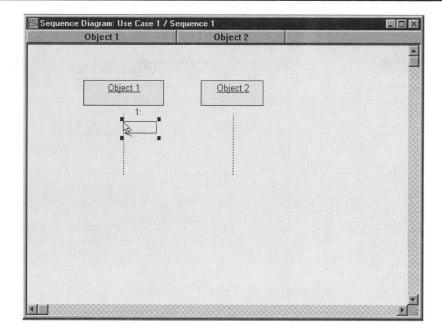

Reordering Messages in a Sequence Diagram

At times, you may want to reorder the messages in your Sequence diagram. In Rose, reordering messages is very easy to do; you simply drag and drop the message into its new location. As the messages are reordered, they will automatically be renumbered.

To reorder the messages in a Sequence diagram:

1. Select the message to be moved.

2. Drag the message up or down in the diagram. Rose will automatically renumber the messages as you reorder them.

Message Numbering in a Sequence Diagram

Although you read the diagram from top to bottom, you have the option of using numbers on each message to display the message order, as shown in Figure 4.11.

Message numbers are optional on Interaction diagrams. By default, numbering is disabled for Sequence diagrams.

FIGURE 4.11:

Message numbering on a
Sequence diagram

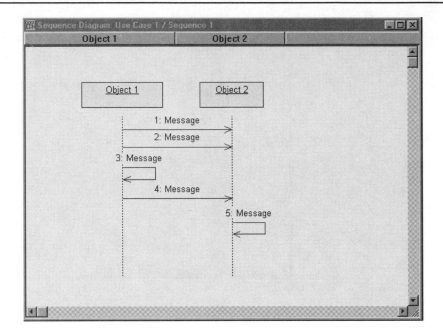

To turn message numbering on or off:

1. Select Tools ➤ Options.

2. Select the Diagram tab.

3. Set the Sequence Numbering check box on or off, as shown in Figure 4.12.

Viewing Focus of Control in a Sequence Diagram

In a Sequence diagram, you have the option of showing the focus of control. The focus of control is a small rectangle, as shown in Figure 4.13, that will let you know which object has control at a particular point in time. This is one of the differences between a Sequence and a Collaboration diagram; the focus of control is shown only on a Sequence diagram.

FIGURE 4.12:

Message numbering
check box

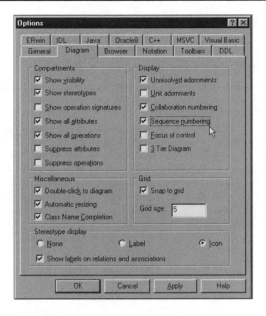

FIGURE 4.13:

Focus of control on a
Sequence diagram

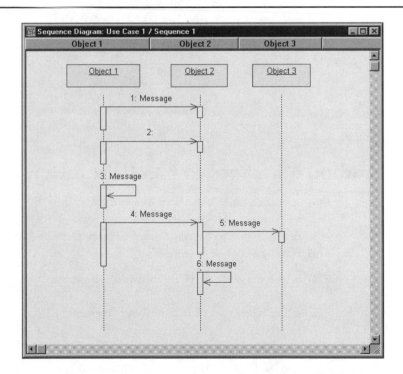

To turn the focus of control on or off:

1. Select Tools ➤ Options.

2. Select the Diagram tab.

3. Set the Focus of Control check box on or off, as shown in Figure 4.14.

FIGURE 4.14:

Focus of Control check box

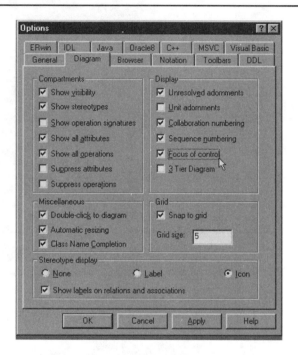

Adding Messages to a Collaboration Diagram

Before you can add messages to a Collaboration diagram, you have to establish a path of communication between two objects. This path is called a *link*, and is created using the Object Link toolbar button. Once the link has been added, you can add messages between the objects.

To add a message to a Collaboration diagram:

1. Select the Object Link toolbar button.

2. Drag from one object to the other to create the link.

3. Select the Link Message or Reverse Link Message toolbar button.

4. Click the link between the two objects. Rose will draw the message arrow, as shown in Figure 4.15.

5. With the new message selected, type the text of the message.

FIGURE 4.15:

Adding a message to a Collaboration diagram

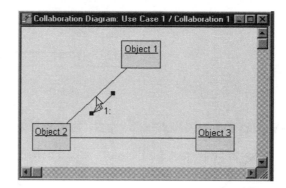

To add a reflexive message to a Collaboration diagram:

1. Select the Link to Self toolbar button.

2. Click the object sending and receiving the message. Rose will draw a reflexive link on the object. It will appear above the object and look like a half-circle.

3. Select the Link Message toolbar button.

4. Click the object's reflexive link. Rose will add the message arrow, as shown in Figure 4.16.

5. With the new message still selected, enter the text of the message.

NOTE

If you are adding more than one reflexive message to an object in a Collaboration diagram, skip steps one and two for each additional message.

FIGURE 4.16:

Adding a reflexive message to a Collaboration diagram

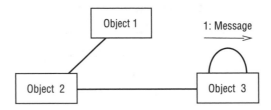

Deleting Messages from a Collaboration Diagram

As with Sequence diagrams, you can delete messages from a Collaboration diagram. When you delete a message, Rose will automatically renumber the remaining messages.

To delete a message from a Collaboration diagram:

1. Select the message to delete.

2. Select Edit ➤ Delete From Model, or press Ctrl+D.

Message Numbering in a Collaboration Diagram

With a Sequence diagram, you know that you read the diagram from top to bottom, so message numbering isn't necessary. A Collaboration diagram, however, loses its sequencing information if you remove the message numbering.

Although it isn't typically recommended, you do have the option in Rose of turning off message numbering in a Collaboration diagram.

To turn message numbering on or off:

1. Select Tools ➤ Options.

2. Select the Diagram tab.

3. Set the Collaboration and Sequence Numbering check box on or off.

Adding Data Flows to a Collaboration Diagram

We mentioned above that one of the differences between a Sequence and a Collaboration diagram is the use of the focus of control. The other difference is in the use of data flow. Collaboration diagrams show data flows; Sequence diagrams do not.

Data flows are used to show the information that is returned when one object sends a message to another. In general, you don't add data flows to every message on a Collaboration diagram—it can clutter the diagram with information that's not really valuable. If a message just returns an *OK, the message was received and everything worked fine* or an *OOPS, there was an error in running the requested function,* it's probably not worth showing on the diagram. But if a message returns a structure, say a list of employees working for the company, this may be significant enough to show on a diagram.

When you eventually map each message to an operation of a class, the information in the data flows will be added to the operation's details. As a general rule, don't waste too much time worrying about data flows now. Add them to the diagram if you think they're significant enough to help the developers. If not, leave them out.

To add a data flow to a Collaboration diagram:

1. Select the Data Flow or Reverse Data Flow toolbar button.

2. Click on the message that will be returning data. Rose will automatically add the data flow arrow to the diagram, as shown in Figure 4.17.

3. With the new data flow still selected, type in the data that will be returned.

FIGURE 4.17:

Adding a data flow to a Collaboration diagram

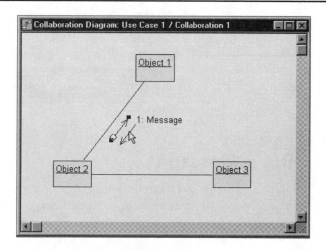

Message Specifications

In Rose, you can set a number of different options to add detail to each message. As with use cases and actors, you can add names and documentation to messages. You can also set synchronization and frequency options. In this section, we'll discuss each of the options you can set for a message.

To open the message specifications:

Double-click the message on the diagram. The Message Specification window will appear, as shown in Figure 4.18.

OR

1. Select the message on the diagram.

2. Select Browse ➤ Specification, or press Ctrl+B.

FIGURE 4.18:

Message Specification window

Naming a Message

In the message specification window, you can name the message or change the name, and add documentation. Each message should have a name that indicates the purpose of the message. Later, as you map each of the messages to operations, the message name will be replaced with the operation name.

To name a message:

1. Double-click the message on the Sequence or Collaboration diagram.

2. If you have mapped the receiving object to a class, the operations of that class will appear in the Name drop-down list box. Select an entry from the list or type in the name of the message.

OR

1. Select the message on the Sequence or Collaboration diagram.

2. Type the message name.

> **NOTE** If you have mapped the receiving object to a class, the name of the receiving class will appear next to the name, in the Class field. This field cannot be modified. To change the receiving class, map the object to another class in the object specification window.

To add documentation to a message:

1. Double-click the message to open the message specification window.

2. In the Documentation area, enter comments for the message. You may, for example, want to enter a little bit of pseudo-code that describes what the message will do.

OR

1. Select the message on the Sequence or Collaboration diagram.

2. Enter comments in the Documentation window.

> **NOTE** If the message has already been mapped to an operation, the documentation will be added to the operation as well. Otherwise, the documentation will stay only with the message. The documentation you enter for a message will not affect code generation. Later in the process, you map each message to an operation of a class. Documentation you enter for an operation will appear as a comment in the generated code.

Mapping a Message to an Operation

Before you generate code, each message on your Sequence and Collaboration diagrams should be mapped to an operation of a class. In this example:

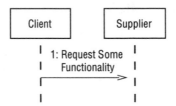

the message *Request some functionality* will be mapped to an operation of the Supplier class.

To map a message to an existing operation:

1. Be sure the receiving object (the supplier) has been mapped to a class.
2. Right-click the message in the Sequence or Collaboration diagram.
3. A list of the supplier's operations will appear.
4. Select the operation from the list, as shown in Figure 4.19.

To remove a message's operation mapping:

1. Double-click the message in the Sequence or Collaboration diagram.
2. In the Name field, delete the operation name and enter the new message name.

To create a new operation for the message:

1. Be sure the receiving object (the supplier) has been mapped to a class.
2. Right-click the message in the Sequence or Collaboration diagram.
3. Select <new operation>.
4. Enter the new operation's name and details. The options available on the operation specification window are discussed in detail in Chapter 6.

FIGURE 4.19:

Mapping a message to an existing operation

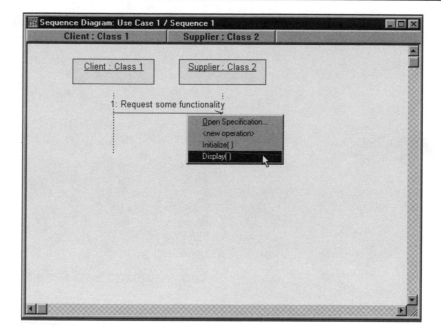

5. Click OK to close the operation specification window and add the new operation.

6. Right-click the message.

7. Select the new operation from the list that appears.

To ensure each message has been mapped to an operation:

1. Select Report ➤ Show Unresolved Messages.

2. Rose will display a list of all messages that have not yet been mapped to operations.

Setting Message Synchronization Options

In the Detail tab of the message specification window, as shown in Figure 4.20, you can specify the concurrency of the message being sent.

FIGURE 4.20:

Setting synchronization
options

FIGURE 4.20:

Setting synchronization
options

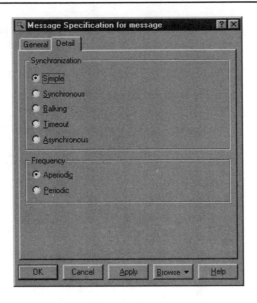

The arrows on the diagram will change if you set the concurrency to balking,
timeout, or asynchronous. You have five synchronization options:

Simple   This is the default value for messages. This option specifies that
the message runs in a single thread of control. On the Sequence or Collaboration diagram, simple messages use this symbol:

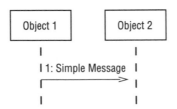

Synchronous   Use this option when the client sends the message and waits
until the supplier has acted upon the message. On the Sequence or Collaboration diagram, synchronous messages will appear this way:

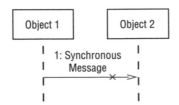

Balking   With this option, the client sends the message to the supplier. If the supplier is not immediately ready to accept the message, the client abandons the message. On the Sequence or Collaboration diagram, balking messages appear like this:

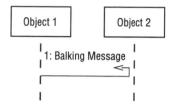

Timeout   Using this option, the client sends the message to the supplier, and waits a specified amount of time. If the supplier isn't ready to receive the message in that time, the client abandons the message. On the Sequence or Collaboration diagram, timeout messages appear using this arrow:

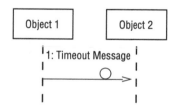

Asynchronous   With this option, the client sends the message to the supplier. The client then continues processing, without waiting to see if the message was received or not. On the Sequence or Collaboration diagram, asynchronous messages look like this:

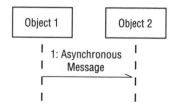

To set the message synchronization:

1.   Double-click the message on the Sequence or Collaboration diagram.

2.   In the message specification window, select the Detail tab.

3. Select the desired synchronization option from the radio buttons on the window.

Setting Message Frequency

Message frequency lets you mark a message that is sent at regular intervals. Say, for example, you have a message that should run once every 30 seconds. You can set that message to be periodic. The frequency options are available in the Detail tab of the message specification window, as shown in Figure 4.21.

FIGURE 4.21:

Setting message frequency

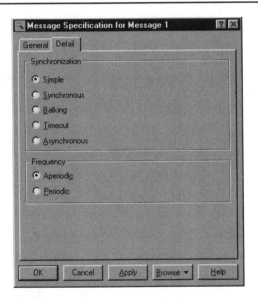

There are two frequency options:

Periodic   This option suggests that the message is sent on a regular, periodic basis.

Aperiodic   This option suggests that the message is not sent on a regular basis. It may be sent only once, or at irregular points in time.

NOTE   Message frequency will not change the appearance of the Sequence or Collaboration diagram.

To set the message frequency:

1. Double-click the message in the Sequence or Collaboration diagram.

2. In the message specification window, select the Detail tab.

3. Select the frequency option from the radio buttons in the window.

Working with Notes

The message names and object names on an Interaction diagram give you a lot of information. However, there may be times when you would like to add some additional information to the diagram. You can do this using notes or scripts.

Notes are used to attach some sort of comment to an object on the diagram. They can be used to clarify the purpose of an object, for example.

Scripts are used to attach a comment to a message. In a Sequence diagram, as you will see, you can use scripts to add some conditional logic.

Adding Notes to an Interaction Diagram

You can attach notes to the objects in an Interaction diagram. A note gives you the opportunity to add a comment directly to the diagram, without affecting any of the code generated. You can use notes to clarify the purpose of an object or to add comments to the diagram.

To add a note to an Interaction diagram:

1. Select the Note button from the toolbar.

2. Click anywhere inside the diagram to add the note.

3. With the note selected, type the text.

To attach a note to an object:

1. Select the Anchor Note to Item button from the toolbar.

2. Drag a line from the note to the object to link the note and object, as shown in Figure 4.22.

FIGURE 4.22:

Attaching a note to an object

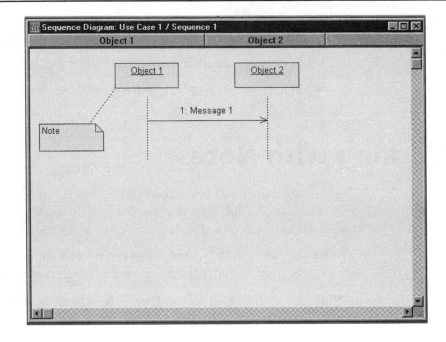

To add a text box to an Interaction diagram:

1. Select the Text Box toolbar button.

2. Click in the location on the diagram where you want the text box to reside.

3. With the text box selected, type the text.

Working with Scripts

In Rose, notes are typically used to add a comment to an object. Scripts, on the other hand, are usually used to add a comment to a message. Scripts are only used on Sequence diagrams. They appear on the left-hand side of the diagram, opposite the message they refer to.

You can use a script to clarify the meaning of a message. You may have a message that reads *Validate User*. In the script, you can expand on the meaning: *Validate the ID to be sure the user exists, and that the password is correct.*

You can also use scripts to enter some conditional logic in your diagram. For example, Figure 4.23 illustrates scripts in a Sequence diagram.

FIGURE 4.23:

Using scripts in a Sequence diagram

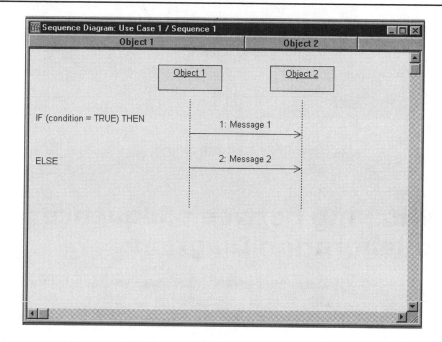

In general, try to avoid putting so much conditional logic on the diagram that the diagram loses its simplicity. By the time you add the details of a nested IF statement inside a nested IF statement inside a nested IF statement, your diagram will probably be cluttered. On the other hand, there are times when you need to show a little bit of conditional logic. Just balance the two extremes. As long as the diagram is *easily* readable and understandable, you should be fine. If the conditional logic gets too complicated, just create additional Sequence diagrams: one to deal with the *if* part, one to deal with the *else* part, and so on.

Besides IF statements, you can use scripts to show loops and other pseudo-code on your diagram. Code won't be generated from any scripts, but they will let the developers know how the logic is intended to flow.

To add a script to a Sequence diagram:

1. Select the Text Box toolbar button.

2. Click in the location on the diagram where you want the script to reside. Usually this is near the left edge of the diagram.

3. With the text box selected, type the text of the script.

4. Select the text box. Press and hold down Shift and select the message.

5. Select Edit ➢ Attach Script.

6. Now, when you move the message up or down in the diagram, the script will move along with it.

To detach a script from a message:

1. Select the script.

2. Select Edit ➢ Detach Script.

Switching between Sequence and Collaboration Diagrams

Typically, you create either a Sequence or a Collaboration diagram for a particular scenario. Without a modeling tool like Rose, it can be too time-consuming to create both, especially because both show you the same information.

In Rose, however, it's very easy to create a Sequence diagram from a Collaboration diagram, or to create a Collaboration diagram from a Sequence diagram. Once you have both a Sequence and a Collaboration diagram for a scenario, it's very easy to switch between the two.

To create a Collaboration diagram from a Sequence diagram:

1. Open the Sequence diagram.

2. Select Browse ➢ Create Collaboration diagram, or press F5.

3. Rose will create a Collaboration diagram with the same name as the open Sequence diagram.

To create a Sequence diagram from a Collaboration diagram:

1. Open the Collaboration diagram.

2. Select Browse ➢ Create Sequence diagram, or press F5.

3. Rose will create a Sequence diagram with the same name as the open Collaboration diagram.

To switch between Sequence and Collaboration diagrams:

1. Open the Sequence or Collaboration diagram.

2. Select Browse ➤ Go to (Sequence or Collaboration) Diagram, or press F5.

3. Rose will look for a Sequence or Collaboration diagram with the same name as the open diagram.

Two-Pass Approach to Interaction Diagrams

Frequently, people use a two-pass approach to creating Interaction diagrams. On the first pass, they focus on higher-level information that the customers will be concerned with. Messages aren't mapped to operations yet, and objects may not be mapped to classes. These diagrams just let the analysts, customers, and anyone else interested in the business flow see how the logic will flow in the system.

The first pass of a Sequence diagram might look like Figure 4.24.

FIGURE 4.24:

First-pass Sequence diagram

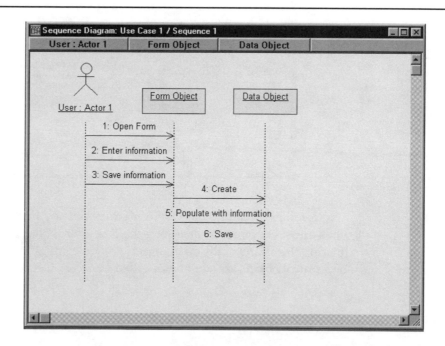

In the second pass, once the customers have agreed to the flow from the first-pass diagram, the team adds more of the detail. The diagram at this point may lose its usefulness to the customer, but will become very useful to the developers, testers, and other members of the project team.

To begin, some additional objects may be added to the diagram. Typically, each Interaction diagram will have a control object, which is responsible for controlling the sequencing through a scenario. All of the Interaction diagrams for a use case may share the same control object, so you have one control object that handles all of the sequencing information for the use case.

If you add a control object, your Sequence diagram will typically look something like Figure 4.25.

FIGURE 4.25:

Sequence diagram with control object

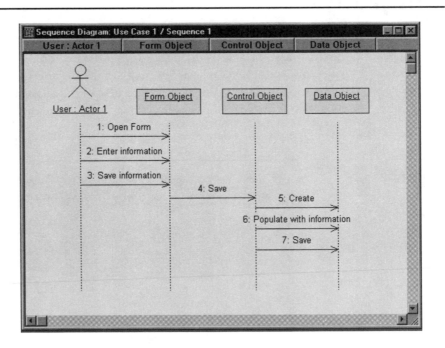

Notice that the control object doesn't carry out any business processing; it just sends messages off to the other objects. The control object is responsible for coordinating the efforts of the other objects and delegating responsibility. For this reason, control objects are sometimes called *manager* objects.

The benefit of using a control object is separating the business logic from the sequencing logic. If the sequencing needs to change, only the control object will be affected.

You may also want to add some objects to handle things like security, error handling, or database connectivity. Many of these objects are generic enough to be built once and reused in many applications. Let's take a look at the database issues, for example.

There are two commonly used options when trying to save information to a database or retrieve information from a database. Say we're trying to save a new employee, John Doe, to the database. The John Doe object can know about the database, in which case it saves itself to the database. Or, John Doe can be completely separated from the database logic, in which case another object has to handle saving John to the database. Let's start with John knowing about the database, as shown in Figure 4.26.

FIGURE 4.26:

Application logic integrated with database logic

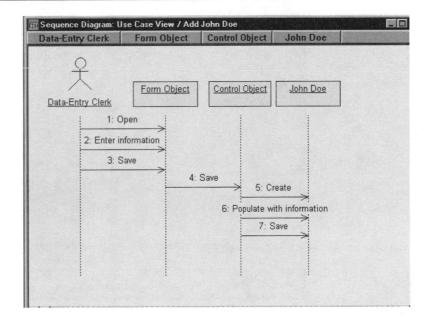

In this situation, there is no separation of application logic and database logic. The John Doe object takes care of application logic, such as hiring and firing John Doe, as well as database logic, including saving John to the database and retrieving him later. Should the database need to change, the change will *ripple* through more of the application this way, because many objects will contain some database logic. On the other hand, this approach can be easy to model and implement.

Another option is to separate the application logic from the database logic. In this situation, you will need to create another object to deal with the database logic. We'll call this new object *Transaction Manager*. John Doe will still hold the business logic. This object will know how to hire or fire John, or how to give him a raise. The Transaction Manager object will know how to retrieve John from the database or save him to the database. The Sequence diagram might look something like Figure 4.27.

FIGURE 4.27:

Application logic separated from database logic

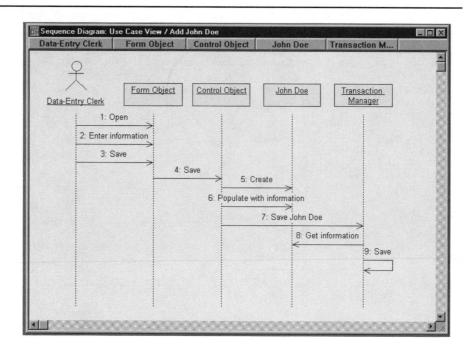

The advantage of this approach is that now it's easier to reuse the John Doe object in another application with a different database, or with no database at all. It also helps minimize the impact of a requirement change. Database changes won't affect the application logic, and application changes won't affect the database logic. The disadvantage here can be that you'll need a little more time to model and implement this solution.

These are two of the more common approaches, although there are some other approaches you can take when dealing with database issues. Whichever decision you make, be sure to keep the approach consistent across Interaction diagrams.

Aside from database issues, you may add objects now for things like error handling, security, or interprocess communication. These details won't interest the customer, but will be critical for the developers.

Once you've added all of the objects, the next step is to map each of the objects to classes. You can map the objects to existing classes or create new classes for the objects (see the above section "Mapping an Object to a Class"). Then, you map each of the messages in the diagram to an operation (see the above section "Mapping a Message to an Operation"). Finally, you go into the object and message specifications if you need to, to set things like object persistence, message synchronization, and message frequency.

Exercise

In this exercise, we'll build a Sequence and a Collaboration diagram to add a new order in our order processing system.

Problem Statement

After talking with Bob, Susan had a good idea which features should be included in the order processing system she was building for Roberton's Cabinets. She created a Use Case diagram. Using this diagram, everyone came to an agreement on the system scope.

Now, Susan set about the task of analyzing a piece of the system. The Enter New Order use case was one with a higher priority to the users, and one with a higher element of risk. To allow plenty of time to deal with the risks of this use case, Susan decided to tackle it first.

She spoke with Carl, the head of the sales department. During this conversation, they spelled out in the flow of events what the use case was supposed to do.

With this information, Susan came up with some scenarios. She documented these:

- Salesperson adds a new order.

- Salesperson tries to add an order, but an item is out of stock.

- Salesperson tries to add an order, but there is an error saving it to the database.

She then set out to create a Sequence and Collaboration diagram for the Adding a New Order scenario.

Create Interaction Diagrams

Create the Sequence diagram and Collaboration diagram to add a new order to the order processing system. Your completed Sequence diagram should look like Figure 4.28.

FIGURE 4.28:

Sequence diagram to add a new order

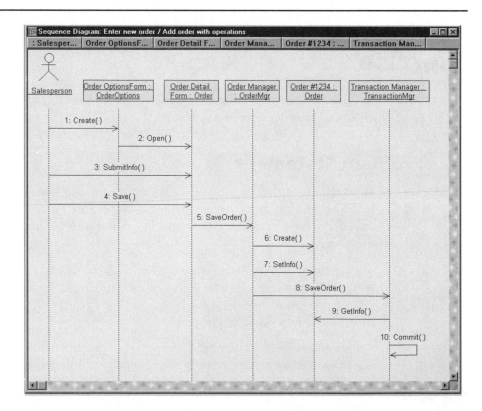

This is just one of the diagrams you would need to model the full Enter New Order use case. This diagram shows what happens when everything goes right. You would need some additional diagrams to model what happens when things go wrong, or when the user selects different options. Each alternate flow in the use case may be modeled in its own Interaction diagram.

Exercise Steps:

Setup

1. Select Tools ➤ Options.

2. Select the Diagram tab.

3. Be sure that Sequence Numbering, Collaboration Numbering, and Focus of Control are all checked.

4. Click OK to exit the Options window.

Create the Sequence Diagram

1. Right-click Logical view in the browser.

2. Select New ➤ Sequence Diagram.

3. Name the new diagram **Add Order**.

4. Double-click the new diagram to open it.

Add Actor and Objects to the Diagram

1. Drag the Salesperson actor from the browser onto the diagram.

2. Select the Object button from the toolbar.

3. Click near the top of the diagram to add the object.

4. Name the new object **Order Options Form**.

5. Repeat steps 3 and 4 to add the other objects to the diagram.

   - Order Detail Form

   - Order #1234

Continued on next page

Add Messages to the Diagram

1. Select the Object Message toolbar button.

2. Drag from the lifeline of the Salesperson actor to the lifeline of the Order Options Form object.

3. With the message selected, type **Create new order**.

4. Repeat steps 2 and 3 to add additional messages to the diagram, as shown below.

   - Open form (between Order Options Form and Order Detail Form)

   - Enter order number, customer, order items (between Salesperson and Order Detail Form)

   - Save the order (between Salesperson and Order Detail Form)

   - Create new, blank order (between Order Detail Form and Order #1234)

   - Set the order number, customer, order items (between Order Detail Form and Order #1234)

   - Save the order (between Order Detail Form and Order #1234)

What we have now, as shown in Figure 4.29, is a completed, first-pass Sequence diagram for adding a new order. We now need to think about things like control objects and database connections. Looking at the diagram now, the Order Detail Form has a lot of sequencing responsibility that's probably better handled by a control object. We also have the new order saving itself to the database. We may want to move this responsibility to another object.

Add Additional Objects to the Diagram

1. Select the Object button from the toolbar.

2. Click between the Order Detail Form object and the Order #1234 object to add a new object.

3. Name the new object **Order Manager**.

Continued on next page

FIGURE 4.29:

First-pass Sequence diagram to Add a New Order

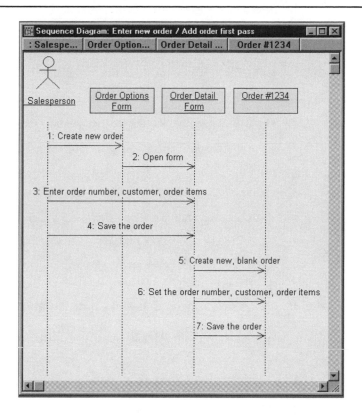

4. Select the Object button from the toolbar.

5. Add a new object to the right of Order #1234.

6. Name the new object **Transaction Manager**.

Assign Responsibilities to the New Objects

1. Select message five: Create new, blank order.

2. Press Ctrl+D to delete the message.

3. Repeat steps 1 and 2 to delete the last two messages.

   - Set the order number, customer, order items.

   - Save the order.

Continued on next page

4. Select the Object Message button from the toolbar.

5. Add a new message, just below message four, from the Order Detail Form to the Order Manager object.

6. Name this new message **Save the order**.

7. Repeat steps 4 through 6 to add messages six through nine, as shown below.

   - Create new, blank order (between Order Manager and Order #1234)

   - Set the order number, customer, order items (between Order Manager and Order #1234)

   - Save the order (between Order Manager and Transaction Manager)

   - Collect order information (between Transaction Manager and Order #1234)

8. Select the Message to Self button from the toolbar.

9. Below message nine, click on the lifeline of the Transaction Manager object to add a reflexive message.

10. Name this new message **Save the order information to the database.**

The Sequence diagram should now look like Figure 4.30.

Map Objects to Classes

1. Right-click the Order Options Form object.

2. Select Open Specification from the shortcut menu.

3. In the Class drop-down list box, select <New>. The class specification window will appear.

4. In the Name field, type **OrderOptions**.

5. Click OK to close the class specification window. You will be returned to the object specification window.

Continued on next page

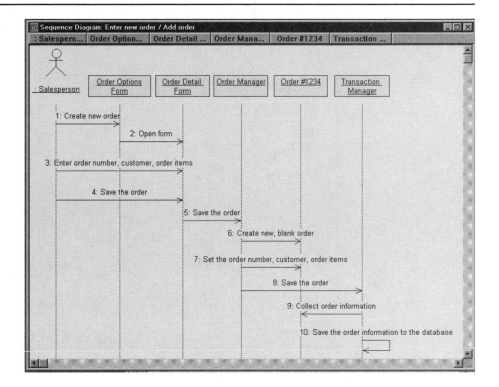

FIGURE 4.30:

Sequence diagram with additional objects

6. In the Class field, select OrderOptions from the drop-down list.

7. Click OK to return to the diagram. The object should now read Order Options Form : OrderOptions.

8. Repeat steps 1 through 7 to map the remaining objects to classes.

   • Create a class called OrderDetail for the Order Detail Form object.

   • Create a class called OrderMgr for the Order Manager object.

   • Create a class called Order for the Order #1234 object.

   • Create a class called TransactionMgr for the Transaction Manager object.

Once these steps are completed, your Sequence diagram should look like the one shown in Figure 4.31.

Continued on next page

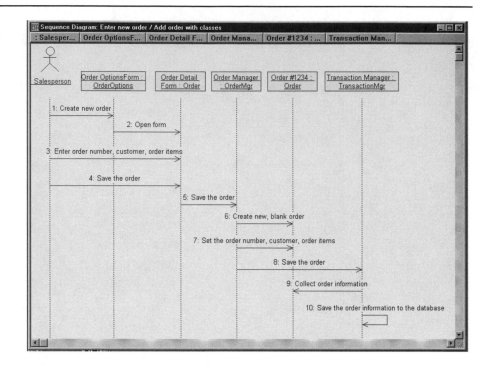

Mapping Messages to Operations

1. Right-click message one, Create new order.

2. From the shortcut menu, select <new operation>. The operation specification window will appear.

3. In the Name field, type the name of the new operation: **Create**.

4. Select OK to close the operation specification window and return to the diagram.

5. Right-click message one.

6. From the shortcut menu, select the new operation: Create().

7. Repeat steps 1 through 6 to map each message to an operation.

   • Map 2: Open form to Open operation

Continued on next page

- Map 3: Enter order number, customer, order items to SubmitInfo operation

- Map 4: Save the order to Save operation

- Map 5: Save the order to SaveOrder operation

- Map 6: Create new, blank order to Create operation

- Map 7: Set the order number, customer, order items to SetInfo operation

- Map 8: Save the order to SaveOrder operation

- Map 9: Collect order information to GetInfo operation

- Map 10: Save the order information to the database to Commit operation

Your diagram should now look like Figure 4.32.

FIGURE 4.32:

Sequence diagram with operations

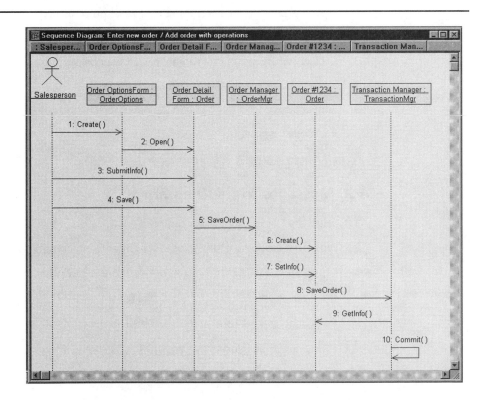

Continued on next page

Create a Collaboration Diagram

To create a Collaboration diagram from the Sequence diagram, you can press F5, or, if you would rather create a Collaboration diagram from scratch, follow the steps outlined here.

Create the Collaboration Diagram

1. Right-click Logical view in the browser.

2. Select New ➤ Collaboration diagram.

3. Name the new diagram **Add order**.

4. Double-click the new diagram to open it.

Add Actor and Objects to the Diagram

1. Drag the Salesperson actor from the browser onto the diagram.

2. Select the Object button from the toolbar.

3. Click anywhere inside the diagram to add the object.

4. Name the new object **Order Options Form**.

5. Repeat steps 2 through 4 to add the other objects to the diagram, as shown below.

    • Order Detail Form

    • Order #1234

Add Messages to the Diagram

1. Select the Object Link toolbar button.

2. Drag from the Salesperson actor to the Order Options Form object.

3. Repeat steps 1 and 2 to add links between the following:

    • Salesperson actor and Order Detail Form

    • Order Options Form and Order Detail Form

    • Order Detail Form and Order #1234 object

4. Select the Link Message toolbar button.

5. Click on the link between Salesperson and Order Options Form.

Continued on next page

6. With the message selected, type **Create new order**.

7. Repeat steps 4 through 6 to add additional messages to the diagram, as shown below.

- Open form (between Order Options Form and Order Detail Form)

- Enter order number, customer, order items (between Salesperson and Order Detail Form)

- Save the order (between Salesperson and Order Detail Form)

- Create new, blank order (between Order Detail Form and Order #1234)

- Set the order number, customer, order items (between Order Detail Form and Order #1234)

- Save the order (between Order Detail Form and Order #1234)

The diagram in Figure 4.33 is the first-pass Collaboration diagram for adding a new order. Now, as we did before, we'll go in and add some additional details and take another look at the responsibilities of the objects.

FIGURE 4.33:

First-pass Collaboration diagram to add a new order

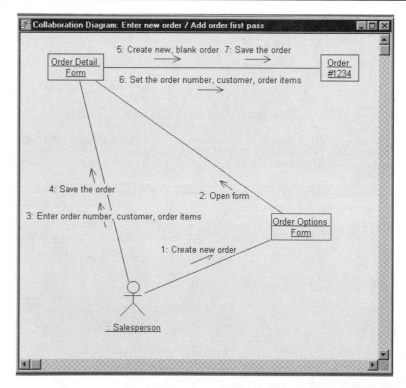

Continued on next page

Add Additional Objects to the Diagram

1. Select the Object button from the toolbar.

2. Click anywhere on the diagram to add a new object.

3. Name the new object **Order Manager**.

4. Select the Object button from the toolbar.

5. Add another new object to the diagram.

6. Name the new object **Transaction Manager**.

Assign Responsibilities to the New Objects

1. Select message five: Create new, blank order. Select the words, not the arrow.

2. Press Ctrl+D to delete the message.

3. Repeat steps 1 and 2 to delete messages six and seven.

   - Set the order number, customer, order items.

   - Save the order.

4. Select the link between the Order Detail Form and Order #1234.

5. Press Ctrl+D to delete the link.

6. Select the Object Link button from the toolbar.

7. Draw a link between the Order Detail Form and the Order Manager object.

8. Select the Object Link button from the toolbar.

9. Draw a link between the Order Manager and the Order #1234 objects.

10. Select the Object Link button from the toolbar.

11. Draw a link between the Order #1234 and the Transaction Manager objects.

12. Select the Object Link button from the toolbar.

13. Draw a link between the Order Manager object and the Transaction Manager object.

14. Select the Link Message button from the toolbar.

Continued on next page

15. Click on the link between the Order Detail Form and the Order Manager object to add a new message.

16. Name this new message **Save the order**.

17. Repeat steps 14 through 16 to add messages six through nine, as shown below.

- Create new, blank order (between Order Manager and Order #1234)

- Set the order number, customer, order items (between Order Manager and Order #1234)

- Save the order (between Order Manager and Transaction Manager)

- Collect order information (between Transaction Manager and Order #1234)

18. Select the Link to Self button from the toolbar.

19. Click on the Transaction Manager object to add the reflexive link.

20. Select the Link Message button from the toolbar.

21. Click on the Transaction Manager's reflexive link to add the message.

22. Name this new message **Save the order information to the database**.

Your Collaboration diagram should now look like Figure 4.34.

Map Objects to Classes (if you already created classes in the Sequence diagram exercise above)

1. Locate the Order Options class in the browser.

2. Drag it over the top of the Order Options Form object in the diagram.

3. Repeat steps 1 and 2 to map each object to the appropriate class.

- Class OrderDetail for the Order Detail Form object

- Class OrderMgr for the Order Manager object

- Class Order for the Order #1234 object

- Class TransactionMgr for the Transaction Manager object

Continued on next page

FIGURE 4.34:

Collaboration diagram with
additional objects

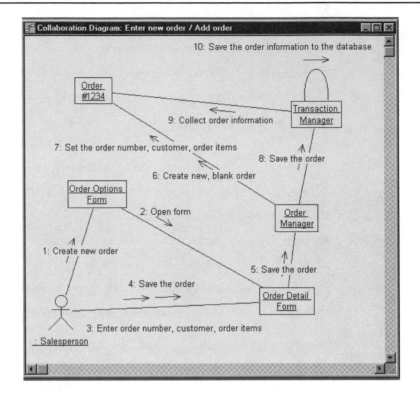

Map Objects to Classes (if you did not complete
the Sequence diagram exercise above)

1. Right-click the Order Options Form object.

2. Select Open Specification from the shortcut menu.

3. In the Class drop-down list box, select <New>. The class specification window will
    appear.

4. In the Name field, enter OrderOptions.

5. Click OK to close the class specification window. You will be returned to the object
    specification window.

Continued on next page

6. In the Class field, select OrderOptions from the drop-down list.

7. Click OK to return to the diagram. The object should now read Order Options Form : OrderOptions.

8. Repeat steps one through seven to map the remaining objects to classes.

   - Create a class called OrderDetail for the Order Detail Form object.

   - Create a class called OrderMgr for the Order Manager object.

   - Create a class called Order for the Order #1234 object.

   - Create a class called TransactionMgr for the Transaction Manager object.

At this point, your Collaboration diagram should look like the one shown in Figure 4.35.

FIGURE 4.35:

Collaboration diagram with class names

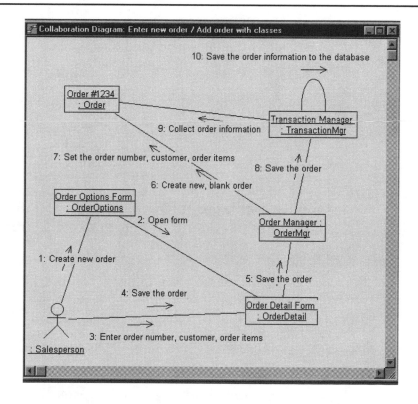

Continued on next page

Mapping Messages to Operations (if you created operations in the Sequence diagram exercise above)

1. Right-click message one: Create new order.

2. Select Open Specification from the shortcut menu.

3. In the Name drop-down list box, select the operation name, Create.

4. Press OK.

5. Repeat steps one through four to map the remaining messages to operations, as shown below.

   - Map 2: Open form to Open operation

   - Map 3: Enter order number, customer, order items to SubmitInfo operation

   - Map 4: Save the order to Save operation

   - Map 5: Save the order to SaveOrder operation

   - Map 6: Create new, blank order to Create operation

   - Map 7: Set the order number, customer, order items to SetInfo operation

   - Map 8: Save the order to SaveOrder operation

   - Map 9: Collect order information to GetInfo operation

   - Map 10: Save the order information to the database to Commit operation

Mapping Messages to Operations (if you did not complete the Sequence diagram exercise above)

1. Right-click message one: the Create new order.

2. From the shortcut menu, select <new operation>. The operation specification window will appear.

3. In the Name field, enter the name of the new operation, **Create**.

4. Select OK to close the operation specification window and return to the diagram.

5. Right-click message one.

6. Select Open Specification from the shortcut menu.

7. In the Name drop-down list box, select the new operation.

8. Click OK.

Continued on next page

9. Repeat steps 1 through 8 to map each message to a new operation, as shown below.

- Map 2: Open form to Open operation

- Map 3: Enter order number, customer, order items to SubmitInfo operation

- Map 4: Save the order to Save operation

- Map 5: Save the order to SaveOrder operation

- Map 6: Create new, blank order to Create operation

- Map 7: Set the order number, customer, order items to SetInfo operation

- Map 8: Save the order to SaveOrder operation

- Map 9: Collect order information to GetInfo operation

- Map 10: Save the order information to the database to Commit operation

Your final Collaboration diagram should look like Figure 4.36.

FIGURE 4.36:

Collaboration diagram with operations

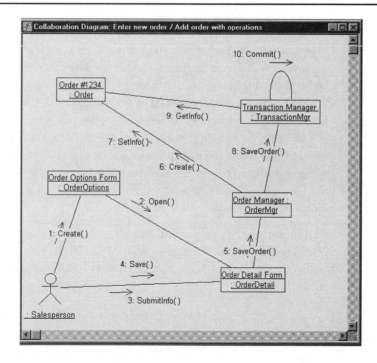

Summary

In this chapter, we have discussed one of the most versatile concepts in UML—Interaction diagrams. Object Interaction diagrams show how objects work together in order to implement the functionality of a use case. There are two types of Interaction diagrams: Sequence diagrams and Collaboration diagrams. Both of these show the same information, just from different perspectives.

Sequence diagrams show the flow of information through time. A Sequence diagram is created for each alternative path through a use case. They are useful for viewing the functionality as a use case progresses. Collaboration diagrams show the flow of information, but not across time. Collaboration diagrams illustrate the relationships between objects and show messages between objects. From a Collaboration diagram, a system designer can see which objects may be bottlenecks or discover which objects need to directly communicate with each other. Collaboration diagrams can also show data flows between objects; Sequence diagrams do not have this capability. Through Rose, Sequence diagrams and Collaboration diagrams are interchangeable. When a change is made on one, the corresponding diagram changes as well.

Typically, each Interaction diagram goes through a two-pass approach. In the first pass, most of the technical details are left off of the diagrams. These diagrams can be shown to the users who can verify that the process is captured correctly. Once the first-pass diagrams have been validated, the second-pass diagrams can be created. The audience of the second-pass diagrams is not the users, but the project team, including the designer, developers, and analysts. The second pass incorporates many details into the Interaction diagrams. Each object of the diagrams is mapped to a class. Each message on the diagrams is mapped to an operation of a class. Model-quality reports can be generated to show any unmapped objects or messages.

After completing the second-pass Interaction diagrams, some classes that the system requires have been created in Rose. In the next chapter, we will discuss how to create the class diagrams that developers use to actually develop classes.

Classes and Packages

- ■ Creating Class Diagrams

- ■ Adding Classes to the Model

- ■ Working with Classes, Notes, and Packages

In the previous chapter, we discussed how objects interact in order to give a system its functionality. Now we will look at the classes themselves and how to organize them into packages. Objects that are modeled in Rose correspond to classes in the Logical view. Classes are the blueprints for creating objects, so an account is the class for creating Joe's savings account object. In this chapter, we will discuss how to create classes and Class diagrams in the Logical view.

Logical View of a Rose Model

In this chapter, we'll discuss some of the items that are stored in the Logical view of a Rose model. As we mentioned in the previous chapter, you can create Sequence and Collaboration diagrams in the Logical view. Other items that you can add to the Logical view include:

- Classes
- Class diagrams
- Use Case diagrams
- Attributes and operations
- Associations
- State Transition diagrams

We'll begin by creating classes and Class diagrams. In the next few chapters, we'll add detail to the Class diagrams, including adding attributes and operations, and relationships between the classes and packages.

Class Diagrams

A *Class diagram* is used to display some of the classes and packages of classes in your system. It gives you a static picture of the pieces in the system, and of the relationships between them. In Rose, a Class diagram has the following symbol next to it:

You will usually create several Class diagrams for a single system. Some will display a subset of the classes and their relationships. Others might display a subset of classes, including their attributes and operations. Still others may display only the packages of classes, and the relationships between the packages. You can create as many Class diagrams as you need to get a full picture of your system.

By default, there is one Class diagram, called Main, directly under the Logical view. This Class diagram displays the packages of classes in your model. Inside each package is another diagram called Main, which includes all of the classes inside that package. In Rose, double-clicking a package in a Class diagram will automatically open its Main Class diagram.

Class diagrams are a good design tool for the team. They help the developers see and plan the structure of the system before the code is written, helping to ensure that the system is well designed from the beginning. An example of a Class diagram is shown in Figure 5.1.

FIGURE 5.1:

Class diagram

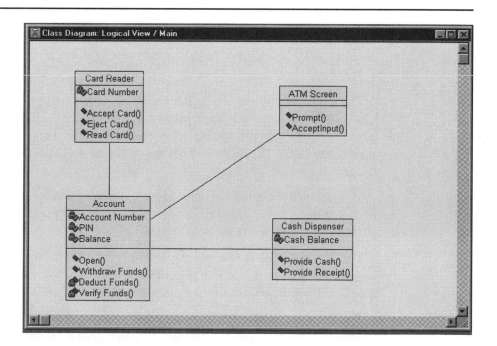

What Is a Class?

A *class* is something that encapsulates information and behavior. Traditionally, we've approached systems with the idea that we have the information over here on the database side, and the behavior over there on the application side. One of the differences with the object-oriented approach is the joining of a little bit of information with the behavior that affects the information. We take a little bit of information and a little bit of behavior, and encapsulate them into something called a class.

For example, in a personnel system, we may have a class called Employee. This class will contain some information, such as an employee ID, name, address, and phone number. The Employee class will also have some behavior. An Employee class will know how to hire or fire an employee, or give an employee a raise.

In UML, a class is shown using the following notation:

The top section of the class holds the class name and, optionally, its stereotype. The middle section holds the attributes, or the information that a class holds. The lower section holds the operations, or the behavior of a class. If you would like, you can hide the attributes and/or the operations of the class to clarify your diagrams.

You can also show the visibility of each attribute and operation, the data type of each attribute, and the signature of each operation on these diagrams. We will discuss these options in the next chapter.

This Employee class will become a template for employee objects. An object is an instance of a class. For example, objects of the employee class might be John Doe, Fred Smith, and the other employees of the company.

The Employee class dictates what information and behavior the employee objects will have. Continuing the above example, a John Doe object can hold the following information: John Doe's name, his address, his phone number, and his salary. The John Doe object will also know how to hire John Doe, fire John Doe, and give John Doe a raise. The object has the information and behavior specified in its class.

Finding Classes

A good place to start when finding classes is the flow of events for your use cases. Looking at the nouns in the flow of events will let you know what some of the classes are. When looking at the nouns, they will be one of four things:

- An actor
- A class
- An attribute of a class
- An expression that is not an actor, class, or attribute

By filtering out all of the nouns except for the classes, you will have many of the classes identified for your system.

Alternatively, you can examine the objects in your Sequence and Collaboration diagrams. Look for commonality between the objects to find classes. For example, you may have created a Sequence diagram that shows the payroll process. In this diagram, you may have illustrated how John Doe and Fred Smith were paid. Now, you examine the John Doe and Fred Smith objects. Both have similar attributes: each holds the appropriate employee's name, address, and telephone number. Both have similar operations: each knows how to hire and fire the appropriate employee. So at this point, an *Employee* class is created, which will become the template for the John Doe and Fred Smith objects.

Each object in your Sequence and Collaboration diagrams should be mapped to the appropriate class. Please refer to the previous chapter for details about mapping objects to classes in Interaction diagrams.

The flow of events and Interaction diagrams are a great place to start when looking for classes. However, there are some classes you may not find in these places. There are three different stereotypes to consider when looking for classes: Entity, Boundary, and Control. Not all of these will be found in the flow of events and the Interaction diagrams. We'll talk about Entity, Boundary, and Control classes in the stereotypes section below.

Creating Class Diagrams

In Rose, Class diagrams are created in the Logical view. Again, you can create as many Class diagrams as you need to provide a complete picture of your system.

When you create a new model, Rose automatically creates a Main Class diagram under the Logical view. Typically, you use this diagram to display the packages of classes in your model. You can create additional Class diagrams directly underneath the Logical view, or within any existing package.

To access the Main Class diagram:

1. Click the + next to the Logical view in the browser to open it.

2. The Main Class diagram will be visible. Note that Class diagrams in Rose have the following icon on their right: 🔀

3. Double-click the Main Class diagram to open it.

NOTE   When you first start Rose and load a model, the Main Class diagram will automatically open.

To create a new Class diagram:

1. Right-click Logical View in the browser.

2. Select New ➢ Class diagram from the shortcut menu.

3. Enter the name of the new diagram.

4. Double-click the diagram in the browser to open it.

To open an existing Class diagram:

1. Locate the Class diagram in the Logical view of the browser.

2. Double-click the diagram to open it.

   OR

1. Select Browse ➢ Class Diagram. The window displayed in Figure 5.2 will appear.

2. In the Package list box, select the package that contains the diagram you want to open.

3. In the Class Diagrams list box, select the diagram you want to open.

4. Press OK.

Opening an existing Class
diagram

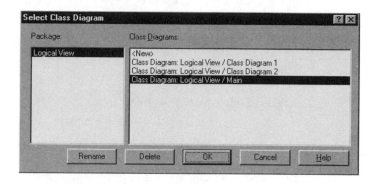

To add an item to a Class diagram:

Use the Class Diagram toolbar buttons to add items to the diagram. Or, you can select Tools ➤ Create, and select the item you wish to create. In the following sections, we'll describe how to add the various items to a Class diagram.

There are two ways to remove an item from the diagram. To remove an item from the current diagram only:

1. Select the item on the diagram.

2. Press Delete.

To remove an item from the model:

1. Select the item on the diagram.

2. Select Edit ➤ Delete from Model, or press Ctrl+D.

 OR

1. Right-click the item in the browser.

2. Select Delete from the shortcut menu.

Deleting Class Diagrams

As you add and remove classes from your model, you may need to delete some of the Class diagrams you have created. In Rose, you can delete Class diagrams using the browser. When you delete a diagram, the classes contained on the diagram will not be deleted. They will still exist in the browser and on other diagrams.

To delete a Class diagram:

1. Right-click the Class diagram in the browser.

2. Select Delete from the shortcut menu.

Organizing Items on a Class Diagram

As more and more classes and relationships are added to a diagram, it can become very cluttered and difficult to read. Rose provides the option of automatically arranging all of the classes on the diagram.

As you add attributes and operations to a class, or resize the classes on the diagram, you may end up with a class that is too large or too small. Rose can also automatically resize all of the classes to fit the text within them. Using these two options, you can turn a diagram that looks like Figure 5.3 into a diagram that looks like Figure 5.4.

FIGURE 5.3:

Class diagram without resizing and automatic layout

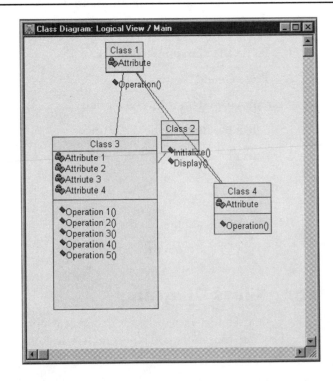

FIGURE 5.4:

Class diagram with resizing
and automatic layout

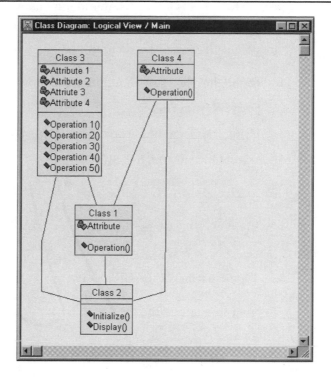

To layout the items on a Class diagram:

Select Tools ➤ Layout Diagram. Rose will automatically align the classes in the diagram.

To resize the items on a Class diagram:

Select Tools ➤ Autosize All. Rose will automatically resize each class on the diagram to fit the class name, attributes, and operations within the class.

Attaching Files and URLs to a Class Diagram

If you have some supplemental information about the classes on a Class diagram, you can attach either a file or a URL to a Class diagram.

Files and URLs you add using this method should apply to all of the classes on the diagram. If you have a file or URL that applies to only one class, it should be attached to the class instead. Later in this chapter, we describe how to attach a file or URL to a class.

To attach a file to a Class diagram:

1.   Right-click the Class diagram in the browser.

2.   Select New ➤ File.

3.   Using the Open dialog box, find the file you wish to attach.

4.   Select Open to attach the file.

To attach a URL to a Class diagram:

1.   Right-click the Class diagram in the browser.

2.   Select New ➤ URL.

3.   Type the name of the URL to attach.

To open an attached file:

Double-click the file in the browser. Rose will open the appropriate application and load the file.

OR

1.   Right-click the file in the browser.

2.   Select Open from the shortcut menu. Rose will open the appropriate application and load the file.

To open an attached URL:

Double-click the URL in the browser. Rose will automatically start your Web browser application and load the URL.

OR

1.   Right-click the URL in the browser.

2.   Select Open from the shortcut menu. Rose will automatically start your Web browser application and load the URL.

To delete an attached file or URL:

1. Right-click the file or URL in the browser.

2. Select Delete from the shortcut menu.

The Class Diagram Toolbar

In this chapter, we'll discuss how to add classes to the model and to a diagram. In the following sections, we'll talk about the options provided by each of these toolbar buttons, with the exception of those dealing with relationships. We will discuss the relationship toolbar buttons in Chapter 7.

If you don't see all of these buttons on the toolbar, right-click the toolbar and select Customize. From this dialog box, you can add each of the buttons listed in Table 5.1.

TABLE 5.1: Icons Used in Class Diagram Toolbar

Icon	Button	Purpose
	Selects or deselects an item	Return the cursor to an arrow to select an item.
	Text Box	Add a text box to the diagram.
	Note	Add a note to the diagram.
	Anchor Note to Item	Connect a note to an item on the diagram.
	Class	Add a new class to the diagram.
	Interface	Add a new interface class to the diagram.
	Association	Draw an association relationship.
	Aggregation	Draw an aggregation relationship.
	Link Attribute	Link an association class to an association relationship.

Continued on next page

TABLE 5.1 CONTINUED: Icons Used in Class Diagram Toolbar

Icon	Button	Purpose
	Package	Add a new package to the diagram.
	Dependency or instantiates	Draw a dependency relationship.
	Generalization	Draw a generalization relationship.
	Realize	Draw a realizes relationship.
	Unidirectional Association	Draw a unidirectional association.
	Parameterized Class	Add a new parameterized class to the diagram.
	Class Utility	Add a new class utility to the diagram.
	Parameterized Class Utility	Add a new parameterized class utility to the diagram.
	Instantiated Class	Add a new instantiated class to the diagram.
	Instantiated Class Utility	Add a new instantiated class utility to the diagram.

Working with Classes

Once you've created your Class diagrams, the next step is to add classes to the model. There are several types of classes you can add: regular classes, parameterized classes, instantiated classes, class utilities, parameterized class utilities, instantiated class utilities, and metaclasses. We'll talk about each of these types of classes in the sections that follow.

We'll also discuss the options Rose provides to add detail to your classes. You can name each class, assign it a stereotype, set its visibility, and set a number of other options. We'll discuss each of these options below.

In this chapter, we'll also cover how to view the attributes, operations, and relationships for your classes. In the next few chapters, we'll discuss the details of adding and maintaining attributes, operations, and relationships.

Adding Classes

To begin, let's add a standard class. There are several ways to add a class, using the toolbar, the browser, or the menu.

You can add a new class to the browser only. In this case, it will be available to add to any diagram, but won't exist on a diagram to start with. Alternatively, you can add a new class to a diagram. If you add a new class to a diagram, it will be automatically added to the browser as well.

To add a new class to a Class diagram:

1. Select the Class button from the toolbar.

2. Click anywhere inside the Class diagram. The new class will be named NewClass.

3. Rose will display a list of all existing classes. To place an existing class on the diagram, double-click the existing class in the list, as shown in Figure 5.5. To create a new class, replace the word NewClass with the new class name. Note that the new class has also been automatically added to the browser, in the Logical view.

FIGURE 5.5:

Adding a new class

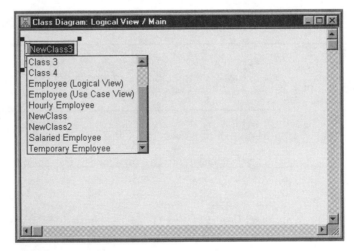

OR

1. Select Tools ➤ Create ➤ Class.

2. Click anywhere inside the Class diagram to place the new class. The new class will be named NewClass.

3. Rose will display a list of all existing classes. To place an existing class on the diagram, double-click the existing class in the list. To create a new class, replace the word NewClass with the new class name. Note that the new class has automatically been added to the browser, in the Logical view.

NOTE   You may also create new parameterized classes, class utilities, parameterized class utilities, instantiated classes, and instantiated class utilities using the Tools ➤ Create menu. See below for a detailed discussion of these types of classes.

To add a new class using an Interaction diagram:

1. Open a Sequence or Collaboration diagram.

2. Right-click an object in the diagram.

3. Select Open Specification from the shortcut menu.

4. Select <New> in the Class drop-down list box. Rose will take you to the specification window for the new class.

5. In the class specification window, enter the class name in the Name field.

NOTE   Because Interaction diagrams are in the Use Case view of the browser, new classes created with this method are created in the Use Case view. To move them to the Logical view, drag and drop the classes in the browser.

To add an existing class to a Class diagram:

Drag the class from the browser to the open Class diagram.

OR

1. Select Query ➤ Add Classes. The Add Classes dialog box will appear, as shown in Figure 5.6.

2. In the Package drop-down list box, select the package that contains the class(es) you want to add to the diagram.

3. Move the class(es) you want to add from the Classes list box to the Selected Classes list box. To add all the classes, press the All button.

4. Press the OK button.

5. Rose will add the selected class(es) to the open diagram.

FIGURE 5.6:

Adding existing classes to a
Class diagram

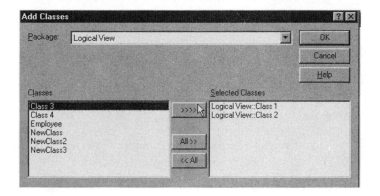

To add a class to the browser:

1. Right-click Logical View in the browser. To add a class to a package, right-click the package name.

2. From the shortcut menu, select New ➤ Class. To add a class utility or an interface, select New ➤ Class Utility or New ➤ Interface. The new class, called NewClass, will appear in the browser.

3. Select the new class and type its name.

4. To then add the new class to a Class diagram, drag it from the browser to the open diagram.

Deleting Classes

As with other model elements, there are two ways of deleting classes. You can delete a class from a diagram, but keep it on other diagrams. Or, you can remove a class from the entire model. Both methods are described here.

To remove a class from a Class diagram:

1. Select the class in the diagram.

2. Press Delete.

3. Note that the class has been removed from the diagram, but still exists in the browser and on other Class diagrams.

To remove a class from the model:

1. Select the class on a Class diagram.

2. Select Edit ➤ Delete from Model, or press Ctrl+D.

OR

1. Right-click the class in the browser.

2. Select Delete from the shortcut menu. Rose will remove the class from all Class diagrams, as well as from the browser.

Class Specifications

Most of the options that you can set for a class are available on the class specification window, as shown in Figure 5.7. For example, this window allows you to set the class stereotype, visibility, and persistence. In the following sections, we'll talk about each of the options available on the tabs of this window.

FIGURE 5.7:

Class specification window

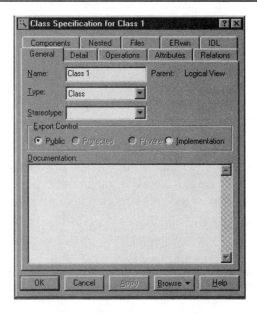

If you are using Rose 98i and examining the specifications for a Java or CORBA class, the specification window that appears is slightly different, as shown below. All of the options on this window are also available through the standard specification.

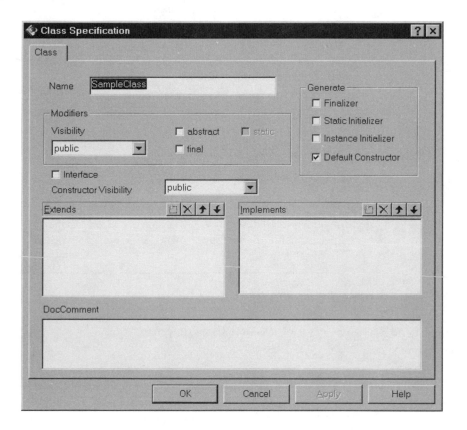

To open the class specifications:

1. Right-click the class on a Class diagram.

2. Select Open Specification from the shortcut menu.

NOTE   If you are using Rose 98i, and the class is a Java or CORBA class, select Open Standard Specification from the shortcut menu. Selecting Open Specification will open a different specification window.

OR

1.   Right-click the class in the browser.

2.   Select Open Specification from the shortcut menu.

NOTE   If you are using Rose 98i, and the class is a Java or CORBA class, select Open Standard Specification from the shortcut menu. Selecting Open Specification will open a different specification window.

OR

1.   Select the class on a Class diagram.

2.   Select Browse ➤ Specification.

NOTE   If you are using Rose 98i, and the class is a Java or CORBA class, select Standard Specification from the Browse menu. Selecting Specification will open a different specification window.

OR

1.   Select the class on a Class diagram.

2.   Press Ctrl+B.

NOTE   If you are using Rose 98i, and the class is a Java or CORBA class, this alternative will open a different specification window.

Adding a Parameterized Class

A parameterized class is the first of the special types of classes we'll discuss. A *parameterized class* is a class that is used to create a family of other classes. Typically, a parameterized class is some sort of container, and is also known as a template. For example, you may have a parameterized class called List. Using instances of the parameterized class, you can create some classes called EmployeeList, OrderList, or AccountList, as described below.

In UML, a parameterized class is displayed using this notation:

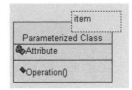

To add a parameterized class:

1. Select the Parameterized Class button from the toolbar.

2. Click anywhere inside the diagram to place the new class.

3. Type the name of the class.

OR

1. Add a class to a Class diagram or to the browser using one of the methods listed above.

2. Open the class specification window.

3. In the Type field, select ParameterizedClass.

4. Press OK.

OR

1. Select Tools ➤ Create ➤ Parameterized Class.

2. Click anywhere inside the diagram to place the new class.

3. Type the name of the class.

Setting Arguments for a Parameterized Class

The arguments for the class are displayed in the dashed-line box. The arguments are placeholders for the items the parameterized class will contain. In the above example, we can replace the parameter "item" with a specific thing, such as Employee, to instantiate an EmployeeList class.

The argument can be another class, a data type, or a constant expression. You can add as many arguments as you need.

To add an argument:

1. Open the class specification window.

2. Select the Detail tab.

3. Right-click anywhere inside the white space in the Formal Arguments area.

4. Select Insert from the shortcut menu.

5. Type the argument name.

6. Click below the Type column header to display a drop-down list of argument types, as shown in Figure 5.8. Select one of the types in the list or enter your own.

7. Click below the Default Value column header to enter a default value for the argument. A default value is not required.

FIGURE 5.8:

Adding an argument to a parameterized class

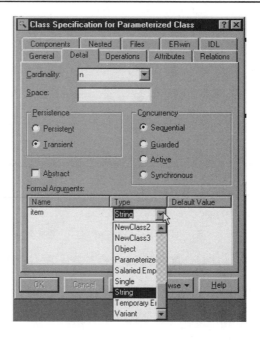

To delete an argument:

1. Open the class specification window.

2. Select the Detail tab.

3. Right-click on the argument you wish to delete.

4. Select Delete from the shortcut menu.

Adding an Instantiated Class

An *instantiated class* is a parameterized class that has actual values for the arguments. From the example above, we know that we have a list of items. Now, we can supply a value for the items argument, to see that we have a list of employees. The UML notation for an instantiated class is a class with the argument name enclosed in < >:

To add an instantiated class:

1. Select the Instantiated Class button from the toolbar.

2. Click anywhere inside the diagram to place the new class.

3. Type the name of the class with the arguments in <>.

OR

1. Add a class to a Class diagram or to the browser using one of the methods listed above.

2. Open the class specification window.

3. In the Type field, select InstantiatedClass.

4. Click OK.

OR

1. Select Tools ➤ Create ➤ Instantiated Class.

2. Click anywhere inside the diagram to place the new class.

3. Type the name of the class.

Adding a Class Utility

A *class utility* is a collection of operations. For example, you may have some mathematical functions—squareroot(), cuberoot(), and so on, that are used throughout your system and don't fit well into any particular class. These functions can be gathered together and encapsulated into a class utility for use by the other classes in the system.

Utility classes are frequently used to extend the functionality provided by the programming language or to hold collections of generic, reusable pieces of functionality that are used in many systems.

A class utility will appear as a shadowed class on the diagram with this symbol:

To add a class utility:

1. Select the Class Utility button from the toolbar.

2. Click anywhere inside the diagram to place the new class.

3. Type the name of the class.

OR

1. Add a class to a Class diagram or to the browser using one of the methods listed above.

2. Open the class specification window.

3. In the Type field, select ClassUtility.

4. Press OK.

OR

1. Select Tools ➤ Create ➤ Class Utility.

2. Click anywhere inside the diagram to place the new class.

3. Type the name of the class.

Adding a Parameterized Class Utility

A *parameterized class utility* is a parameterized class that contains a set of operations. It is the template that is used to create class utilites. It appears on a Class diagram with the following symbol:

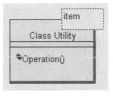

To add a parameterized class utility:

1. Select the Parameterized Class Utility button from the toolbar.

2. Click anywhere inside the diagram to place the new class.

3. Type the name of the class.

OR

1. Add a class to a Class diagram or to the browser using one of the methods listed above.

2. Open the class specification window.

3. In the Type field, select ParameterizedClassUtility.

4. Press OK.

OR

1.   Select Tools ➤ Create ➤ Parameterized Class Utility.

2.   Click anywhere inside the diagram to place the new class.

3.   Type the name of the class.

Adding an Instantiated Class Utility

An *instantiated class utility* is a parameterized class utility that has values set for the parameters. It appears on a Class diagram as follows:

To add an instantiated class utility:

1.   Select the Instantiated Class Utility button from the toolbar.

2.   Click anywhere inside the diagram to place the new class.

3.   Type the name of the class.

OR

1.   Add a class to a Class diagram or to the browser using one of the methods listed above.

2.   Open the class specification window.

3.   In the Type field, select InstantiatedClassUtility.

4.   Click OK.

OR

1.   Select Tools ➤ Create ➤ Instantiated Class Utility.

2.   Click anywhere inside the diagram to place the new class.

3.   Type the name of the class.

Adding a Metaclass

A *metaclass* is a class whose instances are classes rather than objects. Parameterized classes and parameterized class utilities are examples of metaclasses. In UML, metaclasses are displayed as follows:

To add a metaclass:

1. Add a class to a Class diagram or to the browser using one of the methods listed above.

2. Open the class specification window.

3. In the Type field, select MetaClass.

4. Click OK.

Naming a Class

Each class in your Rose model should be given a unique name. Most organizations have a naming convention to follow when naming a class. In general, however, classes are named using a singular noun. In our employee tracking system, for example, we may have a class called employee, and another called position. We would not call them employees and positions.

Class names typically do not include spaces. This is for practical reasons as well as readability—many programming languages do not support spaces in class names. Try to keep your class names relatively short. While ListOfEmployeesThatAreOnProbation is a very good description of what that class does, it can make the code rather unreadable. EmployeeList might be a better class name in this case.

Whether to use uppercase or lowercase letters really depends on your organization. If we have a class that is a list of employees, it could be called employeelist, Employeelist, EmployeeList, or EMPLOYEELIST. Again, each company typically has a naming convention. Just be sure that whichever approach is decided upon is used for all classes.

To name a class:

1. Select the class in the browser or on the Class diagram.

2. Type the class name.

OR

1. Open the class specification window.

2. In the Name field, enter the class name.

To add documentation to a class:

1. Select the class in the browser.

2. In the documentation window, type the class documentation.

OR

1. Open the class specification window.

2. In the specification window, type the information in the Documentation area.

Assigning a Class Stereotype

A stereotype is a mechanism you can use to categorize your classes. Say, for example, you wanted to quickly find all of the forms in the model. You could create a stereotype called *form*, and assign all of your windows this stereotype. To find your forms later, you would just need to look for the classes with that stereotype.

There are three primary class stereotypes in the UML: Boundary, Entity, and Control.

Boundary Classes

Boundary classes are those classes that lie on the boundary between your system and the rest of the world. These would include all of your forms, reports, interfaces to hardware such as printers or scanners, and interfaces to other systems. The UML representation of a Boundary class is:

To find Boundary classes, you can examine your Use Case diagram. At a minimum, there must be one Boundary class for every actor–use case interaction. The Boundary class is what allows the actor to interact with the system.

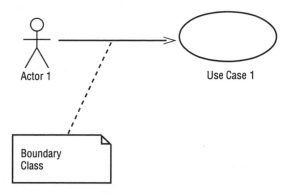

Note that we don't necessarily have to create a unique Boundary class for every actor–use case pair. For example, here we have two actors that both initiate the same use case. They might both use the same Boundary class to communicate with the system.

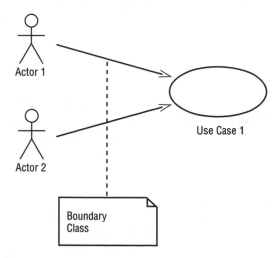

Looking at your Use Case diagram can help you identify the Boundary classes you will need.

Entity Classes

Entity classes hold information that you will save to persistent storage. In our employee tracking system, the Employee class is a good example of an Entity class. Entity classes are usually found in the flow of events and Interaction diagrams. They are the classes that have the most meaning to the user and are typically named using business-domain terminology.

In UML, Entity classes are represented with the following symbol:

Frequently, you create a table in your database for each Entity class. Here we have another deviation from a typical approach to systems development. Rather than defining the database structure first, we have the option of developing our database structure from information gathered in our object model. This allows us to trace all of the fields in the database back to a requirement. The requirements determine the flow of events. The flow of events determines the objects and classes, and the attributes of the classes. Each attribute in an Entity class will become a field in the database. Using this approach, we can trace each database field back to a requirement and reduce the risk of collecting information no one uses.

Control Classes

Finally, let's take a look at Control classes. *Control classes* are responsible for coordinating the efforts of other classes. There is typically one Control class per use case, which controls the sequencing of events through the use case. On an Interaction diagram, a Control class has coordinating responsibilities, as you can see in Figure 5.9.

Notice that the Control class doesn't carry out any functionality itself—other classes don't send many messages to it. Instead, it sends out a lot of messages. The Control class simply delegates responsibility to the other classes. For this reason, Control classes are sometimes called Manager classes. In UML, Control classes are drawn using the following symbol:

FIGURE 5.9:

Control class on a
Sequence diagram

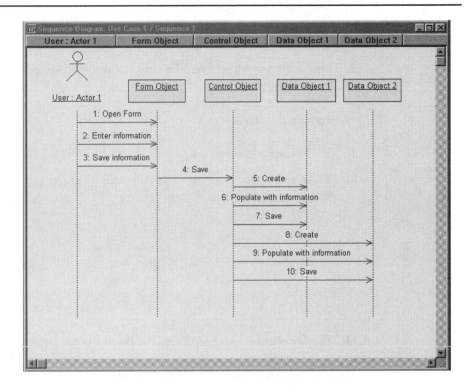

There may be other Control classes that are shared among several use cases. For example, we may have a SecurityManager class that is responsible for controlling events related to security. We may have a TransactionManager class that is responsible for coordinating messages related to database transactions. We may have other managers to deal with other common functionality, such as resource contention, distributed processing, or error handling.

These types of Control classes can be a good way to isolate functionality that is used across the system. Encapsulating security coordination, for example, into a security manager can help minimize the impact of change. If the sequencing of the security logic needs to change, only the security manager will be affected.

In addition to the stereotypes mentioned above, you can add your own stereotypes to the model. In the Stereotype field, you can enter the new stereotype. After this point, it will be available in your current Rose model. If you'd like, you can also add a new stereotype for use in all of your Rose models. You can create toolbar buttons and stereotype icons for the new stereotype as well. These procedures are described below.

To assign a class stereotype:

1. Open the class specification window.

2. Select a stereotype from the drop-down list box or type in the stereotype name.

To display the stereotype name on the diagram:

1. Right-click a class on a Class diagram.

2. From the shortcut menu, select Options ➤ Stereotype Display ➤ Label. The stereotype name will appear, enclosed in << >>, just above the class name.

To display the stereotype icon on the diagram:

1. Right-click a class on a Class diagram.

2. From the shortcut menu, select Options ➤ Stereotype Display ➤ Icon.

3. The representation of the class will change to the appropriate icon. For example, here is the icon for an Interface class:

NOTE   Not all of the stereotypes have icons. If there is no icon for a stereotype, only the stereotype name will appear on the diagram.

To turn off the stereotype display on the diagram:

1. Right-click a class on a Class diagram.

2. From the shortcut menu, select Options ➢ Stereotype Display ➢ None. The class will still have a stereotype, visible in the class specification window, but the stereotype will not display on the diagram.

To change the default stereotype display option:

1. Select Tools ➢ Options.

2. Select the Diagram tab.

3. In the Compartments area, as shown in Figure 5.10, select or deselect the Show Stereotypes check box to control whether or not the stereotype will display.

4. In the Stereotype Display area, select the default display type (None, Label, or Icon).

FIGURE 5.10:

Changing the default stereotype display

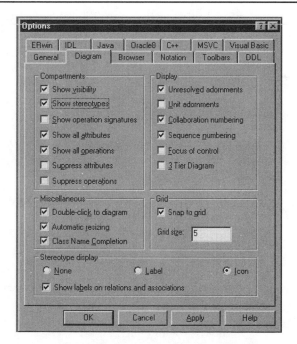

To add a new stereotype to the current Rose model:

1. Open the class specification window.

2. Type in a new stereotype in the Stereotype field. The new stereotype will now be available in the drop-down list box as you add more classes, but only in the current Rose model.

To add a new stereotype for use in all Rose models:

1. Exit Rose.

2. In the file `DefaultStereotypes.ini`, look for the section called [Stereotyped Items].

3. In the [Stereotyped Items] section, add a new line for the new stereotype. For example, to add the Boundary stereotype, you would add:

```
[Stereotyped Items]
Class:Boundary
```

4. Add a new section to the `DefaultStereotypes.ini` file for the new stereotype. In this section, you'll let Rose know what the stereotype is for (classes, use cases, etc.), and the name of the stereotype. For the Boundary stereotype, you would add:

```
[Class:Boundary]
Item=Class
Stereotype=Boundary
```

To add a new diagram icon for a stereotype:

1. Exit Rose.

2. Create a diagram icon using either the Windows metafile (`.WMF`) format or the extended metafile (`.EMF`) format.

3. Open the file `DefaultStereotypes.ini`.

4. Go to the section for the stereotype. For example, to add an icon for the Boundary stereotype, go to the section called [Class:Boundary].

5. Add a line to this section, specifying the name of the metafile that holds the icon. For example:

```
[Class:Boundary]
Item=Class
```

➔
```
Stereotype=Boundary
Metafile=c:\program files\rational rose 98\boundary.emf
```

You can use either standard Windows metafile (.WMF) files, or extended metafile (.EMF) files. If the metafile is in the same directory as the `Default-Stereotypes.ini` file, you can use an & rather than the full path name. For example,

```
Metafile=&\boundary.emf
```

6. If you are using a standard Windows metafile (.WMF) file rather than an extended metafile, add two additional lines, ExtentX and ExtentY, to the section. These lines will let Rose know the width and height of the icon. For example, the Boundary stereotype section would look like this:

```
[Class:Boundary]
Item=Class
Stereotype=Boundary
Metafile=c:\program files\rational rose 98\boundary.wmf
```
➔
```
ExtentX=20
```
➔
```
ExtentY=20
```

7. Now, when you use the stereotype in a Rose model, you can display the stereotype icon. For example, we added the UML boundary icon to the Boundary stereotype in Rose:

8. To display the stereotype icon by default, add the following lines. Otherwise the stereotype display will depend on the model default settings.

```
[Class:Boundary]
Item=Class
Stereotype=Boundary
Metafile=c:\program files\rational rose 98\boundary.wmf
```
➔
```
ExtentX=20
```
➔
```
ExtentY=20
```
➔
```
StereotypeIconStyle=Icon
```

To add a small toolbar button for a stereotype:

1. Exit Rose.

2. Create the small toolbar icon using a graphics application. Save the icon in bitmap (.BMP) format. The icon should be 15 pixels high and 16 pixels wide, using a gray background (which is RGB = 192, 192, 192 in Rational Rose).

3. Open the file DefaultStereotypes.ini.

4. Go to the section for the stereotype. For example, to add a small toolbar button for the Boundary stereotype, go to the section called [Class:Boundary].

5. Add a line for the small toolbar icon. Again, you can use an & for the path if the .BMP file is in the same directory as the DefaultStereotypes.ini file:

```
       [Class:Boundary]
       Item=Class
       Stereotype=Boundary
       Metafile=c:\program files\rational rose 98\boundary.wmf
       ExtentX=20
       ExtentY=20
→      SmallPaletteImages=&\smalltoolbar.bmp
```

6. If the icon you'd like to use is one of several in a .BMP file, add another line to the DefaultStereotypes.ini file to tell Rose the location of the icon in the .BMP file:

```
       [Class:Boundary]
       Item=Class
       Stereotype=Boundary
       Metafile=c:\program files\rational rose 98\boundary.wmf
       ExtentX=20
       ExtentY=20
       SmallPaletteImages=&\smalltoolbar.bmp
→      SmallPaletteIndex=1
```

NOTE   There is a 512KB limit on the size of bitmap files. If your file is larger than 512K, break it into smaller files.

---

7. Select Tools ➢ Options.

8. Select the Toolbars tab.

9. Press the ... button next to the toolbar you want to customize in the Customize toolbars area.

10. Add the new toolbar button to the Class diagram toolbar.

To add a large toolbar button for a stereotype:

1. Exit Rose.

2. Create the large toolbar icon using a graphics application. Save the icon in bitmap (.BMP) format. The icon should be 24 pixels high and 24 pixels wide, using a gray background (which is RGB = 192, 192, 192 in Rational Rose).

3. Open the file DefaultStereotypes.ini.

4. Go to the section for the stereotype. For example, to add a large toolbar button for the Boundary stereotype, go to the section called [Class:Boundary].

5. Add a line for the large toolbar icon. Again, you can use an & for the path if the .BMP file is in the same directory as the DefaultStereotypes.ini file:

```
[Class:Boundary]
Item=Class
Stereotype=Boundary
Metafile=c:\program files\rational rose 98\boundary.wmf
ExtentX=20
ExtentY=20
MediumPaletteImages=&\largetoolbar.bmp
```

6. If the icon you'd like to use is one of several in a .BMP file, add another line to the DefaultStereotypes.ini file to tell Rose the location of the icon in the .BMP file:

```
[Class:Boundary]
Item=Class
Stereotype=Boundary
Metafile=c:\program files\rational rose 98\boundary.wmf
ExtentX=20
ExtentY=20
MediumPaletteImages=&\largetoolbar.bmp
MediumPaletteIndex=1
```

7. Select Tools ➤ Options.

8. Select the Toolbars tab.

9. Press the … button next to the toolbar you want to customize in the Customize toolbars area.

10. Add the new toolbar button to the Class diagram toolbar.

To add a browser icon for a stereotype:

1. Exit Rose.

2. Create the icon using a graphics application. Save the icon in bitmap (.BMP) format. The icon should be 16 pixels high and 16 pixels wide, using a white background.

3. Open the file DefaultStereotypes.ini.

4. Go to the section for the stereotype. For example, to add a browser icon for the Boundary stereotype, go to the section called [Class:Boundary].

5. Add a line for the icon. Again, you can use an & for the path if the .BMP file is in the same directory as the DefaultStereotypes.ini file:

```
[Class:Boundary]
Item=Class
Stereotype=Boundary
Metafile=c:\program files\rational rose 98\boundary.wmf
ExtentX=20
ExtentY=20
ListImages=&\listimages.bmp
```

6. If the icon you'd like to use is one of several in a .BMP file, add another line to the DefaultStereotypes.ini file to tell Rose the location of the icon in the .BMP file:

```
[Class:Boundary]
Item=Class
Stereotype=Boundary
Metafile=c:\program files\rational rose 98\boundary.wmf
ExtentX=20
ExtentY=20
ListImages=&\listimages.bmp
ListIndex=3
```

7. When you create a new item with this stereotype, it will display in the browser using the new icon.

Setting Class Visibility

The Visibility option determines whether or not a class can be seen outside of its package. There are three visibility options for a class:

Public   Suggests that the class can be seen by all of the other classes in the system.

(98i) Protected, Private   Suggests that the class can be seen in nested classes, friends, or within the same class.

Package or Implementation   Suggests that the class can only be seen by other classes in the same package.

To set class visibility:

1. Right-click the class in the browser or on a Class diagram.
2. Select Open Specification from the shortcut menu.
3. Set the export control to Public; Protected, Private; or Implementation.

Setting Class Cardinality

The Cardinality field gives you a place to set the number of instances of the class you expect to have. In the employee tracking system, we can probably expect to have many instances of the employee class—one for John Doe, one for Bill Smith, and so on. The cardinality for the Employee class, then, would be n.

Control classes, however, frequently have a cardinality of one. As you're running the application, you probably only need one instance of a security manager.

In Rose, the following cardinality options are available in the drop-down list box:

Cardinality	Meaning
n (default)	Many
0..0	Zero
0..1	Zero or one

Cardinality	Meaning
0..n	Zero or more
1..1	Exactly one
1..n	One or more

Or, you can enter your own cardinality, using one of the following formats:

Format	Meaning
<number>	Exactly <number>
<number 1>..<number 2>	Between <number 1> and <number 2>
<number>..n	<number> or more
<number 1>,<number 2>	<number 1> or <number 2>
<number 1>, <number 2>..<number 3>	Exactly <number 1> or between <number 2> and <number 3>
<number 1>..<number 2>,<number 3>..<number 4>	Between <number 1> and <number 2> or between <number 3> and <number 4>

To set class cardinality:

1. Open the class specification window.

2. Select the Detail tab.

3. In the cardinality drop-down list box, select the cardinality. Or, type in a cardinality option that is not available in the drop-down list box.

Setting Storage Requirements for a Class

As you are building your model, you may want to note the amount of relative or absolute memory you expect each object of the class to require. The Space field in the class specification window is used for this purpose.

You cannot use the Space field for class utilities, instantiated class utilities, or parameterized class utilities.

To set class space:

1. Open the class specification window.

2. Select the Detail tab.

3. Enter the storage requirements for the class in the Space field.

Setting Class Persistence

In Rose, you can generate DDL (Data Definition Language) from your model. The DDL defines the structure of your database.

When you generate DDL, Rose will look for classes that have been set to persistent. The Persistence field in the class specification window is used to specify whether a class is:

Persistent   Suggests that the class will live beyond the execution of the application. In other words, the information in objects of the class will be saved to a database or some other form of persistent storage.

Transient   Suggests that information in objects of the class will not be saved to persistent storage.

You cannot use the Persistence field for class utilities, instantiated class utilities, or parameterized class utilities.

To set the persistence of a class:

1. Open the class specification window.

2. Select the Detail tab.

3. Select Persistent or Transient in the Persistence area.

Setting Class Concurrency

Concurrency is used to describe how the class behaves in the presence of multiple threads of control. There are four concurrency options:

Sequential   This is the default setting, and suggests that the class will behave normally (i.e. the operations will perform as expected) when there is only one thread of control, but the behavior of the class is not guaranteed in the presence of multiple threads of control.

Guarded   Suggests that the class will behave as expected when there are multiple threads of control, but the classes in the different threads will need to collaborate with each other to ensure that they don't interfere with each other.

Active   Suggests that the class will have its own thread of control.

Synchronous   Suggests that the class will behave as expected, with multiple threads of control. There won't be any collaboration required with other classes, because the class will deal with the mutual exclusion on its own.

To set the concurrency of a class:

1.   Open the class specification window.

2.   Select the Detail tab.

3.   Select a concurrency radio button in the concurrency area.

Creating an Abstract Class

An *abstract class* is a class that will not be instantiated. In other words, if Class A is abstract, there will never be any objects of Type A in memory.

Abstract classes are typically used in inheritance structures. They hold some information and behavior that is common to some other classes. For example, we may have an Animal class, which has some attributes called height, color, and species. From this class, we inherit three other classes—Cat, Dog, and Bird. Each of these will inherit height, color, and species from the Animal class, and will have their own unique attributes and operations as well.

When the application is run, there are no animal objects created—all of the objects are cats, dogs, or birds. The Animal class is an abstract class that just holds the commonality between cats, dogs, and birds.

In UML, an abstract class is shown on a Class diagram with its name in italics:

To create an abstract class:

1. Create a class using one of the methods described above.

2. Open the class specification window.

3. Select the Detail tab.

4. Check the Abstract check box.

Viewing Class Attributes

In the next chapter, we'll talk in detail about adding, deleting, and working with attributes for a class. Part of the class specification window allows you to see the attributes that have already been created for a class. For additional information about attributes and operations, please refer to Chapter 6.

To view the class attributes:

1. Open the class specification window.

2. Select the Attributes tab. The attributes for the class, including the attribute visibility, stereotype, name, data type, and default value, will be listed on this tab.

Viewing Class Operations

In the next chapter, we'll discuss the details of adding, deleting, and maintaining the operations for a class. Here, in the class specification window, you can view the operations for a class. For additional information about operations, please refer to the next chapter.

To view the class operations:

1. Open the class specification window.

2. Select the Operations tab. The operations for the class, including the operation visibility, stereotype, signature, and return type, will be listed on this tab.

Viewing Class Relationships

In Chapter 7, we will discuss in detail the different types of relationships you can add to classes. We'll talk about adding and deleting relationships, and setting the detailed information about each relationship. In the class specification window, you can view all of the relationships that have been added to a class. For additional information about relationships between classes, please refer to Chapter 7.

To view the class relationships:

1. Open the class specification window.

2. Select the Relations tab. All of the relationships the class participates in will be listed on this tab.

Using Nested Classes

In Rose, you can nest one class inside another. You can also nest additional classes inside the nested class, to as many levels of depth as necessary.

To create a nested class:

1. Open the class specification window for the parent class.

2. Select the Nested tab.

3. Right-click anywhere inside the white space on the Nested tab.

4. Select Insert from the shortcut menu.

5. Type the name of the nested class.

To display a nested class on a Class diagram:

1. Open a Class diagram.

2. Select Query ➢ Add Classes.

3. Move the nested class from the Classes list box to the Selected Classes list box. The nested class will display with the format ParentClass::NestedClass.

4. Click OK. The nested class will appear on the diagram, with the parent class name in parentheses.

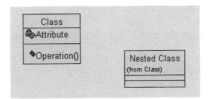

To delete a nested class from the model:

1. Open the class specification window for the parent class.

2. Select the Nested tab.

3. Right-click on the name of the nested class you wish to delete.

4. Select Delete from the shortcut menu. The nested class will be removed from all Class diagrams.

Attaching Files and URLs to a Class

We mentioned above that you can attach a file or a URL to a Class diagram. You can also attach a file or a URL directly to a class. For example, you may want to attach the source code file to a class in your model. Or you may want to attach a testing script that will test the functionality provided by the class. Rose allows you to attach a file or URL through the browser or the class specification window.

To attach a file to a class:

1. Open the class specification window.

2. Select the Files tab.

3. Right-click anywhere inside the white space in the Files tab.

4. Select Insert File from the shortcut menu.

5. Using the Open dialog box, find the file you wish to attach.

6. Select Open to attach the file to the class.

OR

1. Right-click the class in the browser.

2. Select New ➤ File.

3. Using the Open dialog box, find the file you wish to attach.

4. Select Open to attach the file to the class.

To attach a URL to a class:

1. Open the class specification window.

2. Select the Files tab.

3. Right-click anywhere inside the white space in the Files tab.

4. Select Insert URL from the shortcut menu.

5. Type the name of the URL to attach.

OR

1. Right-click the class in the browser.

2. Select New ➤ URL.

3. Type the name of the URL to attach.

To open an attached file:

1. Locate the file in the browser.

2. Double-click the filename. Rose will automatically start the appropriate application and load the file.

OR

1. Right-click the file in the browser.

2. Select Open from the shortcut menu. Rose will automatically start the appropriate application and load the file.

OR

1. Open the class specification window.

2. Select the Files tab.

3. Double-click the file you wish to open. Rose will automatically start the appropriate application and load the file.

OR

1. Open the class specification window.

2. Select the Files tab.

3. Right-click the file you wish to open.

4. Select Open File/URL from the shortcut menu. Rose will automatically start the appropriate application and load the file.

To open an attached URL:

1. Locate the URL in the browser.

2. Double-click the URL. Rose will automatically start your Web browser application and load the URL.

OR

1. Right-click the URL in the browser.

2. Select Open from the shortcut menu. Rose will automatically start your Web browser application and load the URL.

OR

1. Open the class specification window.

2. Select the Files tab.

3. Double-click the URL you wish to open. Rose will automatically start your Web browser application and load the URL.

OR

1. Open the class specification window.

2. Select the Files tab.

3. Right-click the URL you wish to open.

4. Select Open File/URL from the shortcut menu. Rose will automatically start your Web browser application and load the URL.

To delete an attached file or URL:

1. Right-click the file or URL in the browser.

2. Select Delete from the shortcut menu.

Viewing the Interaction Diagrams That Contain a Class

When you need to change a class, it can be helpful to know exactly where in the system the class is being used. The two types of Interaction diagrams, Sequence diagrams and Collaboration diagrams, will let you know exactly where and how each class is being used. You can use the Report menu to see which Sequence and Collaboration diagrams contain objects of a particular class.

To view all Sequence and Collaboration diagrams that contain a certain class:

1. Select the class on a Class diagram.

2. Select Report ➤ Show Instances.

3. Rose will display a list of all Sequence and Collaboration diagrams that contain objects of that class, as shown in Figure 5.11. To open a diagram, double-click it in the list, or click the Browse button.

FIGURE 5.11:

Viewing class instances

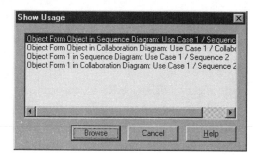

Working with Notes

You can add a note to a Class diagram to provide a little more information about a particular class, package, attribute, operation, or relationship. Although these notes don't affect code generation, they can help the developers and other members of the project team gain a clearer understanding of the model.

Adding Notes

There are two tools you can use to add documentation to a Class diagram. A note is a comment you can attach to a class or other item on the diagram. A text box can be used to add a comment that applies to the whole diagram. For example, you can use a text box to add a title to your diagram.

To add a note to the diagram:

1. Select the Note toolbar button.
2. Click anywhere inside the diagram to place the note.
3. Type the text of the note.

To attach a note to an item:

1. Select the Anchor Note to Item toolbar button.
2. Drag the mouse from the note to the item.
3. Rose will draw a dashed line between the note and the item.

To add a text box to the diagram:

1. Select the Text Box toolbar button.
2. Click anywhere inside the diagram to place the text box.
3. Type the text.

Deleting Notes

You may need to delete some of the notes you've added to your diagram. In Rose, you can delete the notes directly on the Class diagram.

To delete a note or text box from the diagram:

1. Select the note or text box on the diagram.
2. Press the Delete key.

Working with Packages

A package is used to group classes together that have some commonality. In UML, a package is displayed with this symbol:

There are a few common approaches when packaging classes, but you can group the classes together however you'd like. One approach is to group the classes together by stereotype. With this approach, you have one package with your Entity classes, one with your Boundary classes, one with your Control classes, and so on. This can be a helpful approach to take for deployment's sake—all the Boundary classes that will go on the client machine are already packaged together.

Another approach is to group the classes together by functionality. For example, you might have a package called Security, which holds all of the classes that deal with application security. You might have some other packages called Employee Maintenance, Reporting, or Error Handling. The advantage of this approach is in reuse. If you carefully group your classes together, you end up with packages that are fairly independent of one another. In this example, you can just pick up the Security package and reuse it in other applications.

Finally, you can use a combination of these approaches. Packages can be nested inside each other to further organize your classes. At a high level, you may group your classes by functionality to create your Security package. Within this package, you can have some other packages, grouping the security classes by functionality or stereotype.

Adding Packages

The next step in creating your model is adding some packages. Class packages are created in the Logical view of the browser.

To add an existing package to a Class diagram:

Drag the package from the browser onto the Class diagram.

To add a new package to a Class diagram:

1. Select the Package toolbar button.

2. Click anywhere inside the Class diagram to place the package.

3. Type the package name.

To add a package to the browser:

1. Right-click Logical View in the browser. To create a package inside an existing package, right-click the existing package in the browser.

2. Select New ➤ Package.

3. Type the name of the new package.

To move an item into a package:

In the browser, drag the item from its existing location to the new package.

Deleting Packages

You can delete a package from a Class diagram or from the entire model. If you delete a package from the model, the package and all of its contents will be removed.

To remove a package from a Class diagram:

1. Select the package on the Class diagram.

2. Press the Delete key.

3. Note that the package has been removed from the Class diagram, but still exists in the browser and on other Class diagrams.

To remove a package from the model:

1. Right-click the package in the browser.

2. Select Delete from the shortcut menu.

OR

1. Select the package on a Class diagram.

2. Select Edit ➤ Delete from Model, or press Ctrl+D.

WARNING   When you delete a package from the model, all classes and diagrams within the package will also be deleted.

Exercise

In this exercise, we'll take the classes we created last time and group them into packages. Then we'll create some Class diagrams to show the classes in the system and the packages.

Problem Statement

From the Interaction diagrams, Bob could see that the system met the business needs of the company. So Susan spoke with Karen, the lead developer.

"Here are the Interaction diagrams for adding a new order."

"Great! I'll get going on development."

Karen took a look at the classes in the Rose model. She decided to group them together by stereotype. So, she created packages called Entities, Boundaries, and Control, and moved each class into the appropriate package. Then, she created a Class diagram in each package: a Main Class diagram to display the packages and an Enter New Order Class diagram to show all of the classes for that use case.

Creating a Class Diagram

Group the classes that we've identified so far into packages. Create a Class diagram to display the packages, Class diagrams to display the classes in each package, and a Class diagram to display all of the classes in the Enter New Order use case.

Exercise Steps:

Setup

1. Select Tools ➤ Options.

2. Select the Diagram tab.

3. Be sure the Show Stereotypes check box is selected.

4. Be sure the Show All Attributes and Show All Operations check boxes are selected.

5. Be sure the Suppress Attributes and Suppress Operations check boxes are *not* checked.

Create Packages

1. Right-click Logical View in the browser.

2. Select New ➤ Package.

3. Name the new package **Entities**.

4. Repeat steps 1-3 to create a **Boundaries** package and a **Control** package.

At this point, the browser should look like Figure 5.12.

FIGURE 5.12:

Packages for the order processing system

Continued on next page

Create Main Class Diagram

1. Double-click the Main Class diagram, directly underneath the Logical view in the browser, to open the diagram.

2. Drag the Entities package from the browser to the diagram.

3. Drag the Boundaries and Control packages from the browser to the diagram.

The Main Class diagram should look like Figure 5.13.

FIGURE 5.13:

Main Class diagram for the order processing system

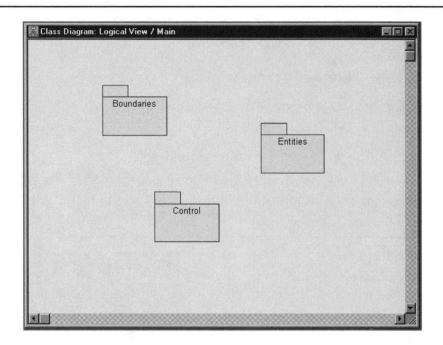

Create Class Diagram with All Classes in the Enter New Order Use Case

1. Right-click Logical View in the browser.

2. Select New ➢ Class Diagram.

3. Name the new Class diagram **Add New Order**.

4. Double-click the Add New Order Class diagram in the browser to open it.

Continued on next page

5. Drag each of the classes (OrderOptions, OrderDetail, Order, OrderMgr, and TransactionMgr) from the browser to the diagram.

The Class diagram should look like Figure 5.14.

FIGURE 5.14:

Add New Order Class diagram

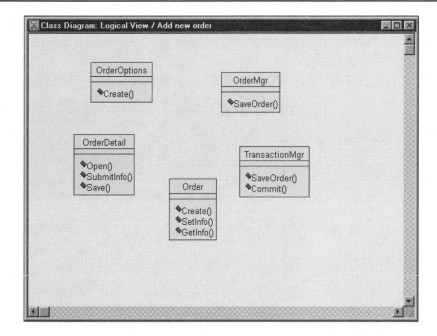

Add Stereotypes to the Classes

1. Right-click the OrderOptions class in the diagram.

2. Select Open Specification from the shortcut menu.

3. In the stereotype field, type **Boundary**.

4. Click OK.

5. Right-click the OrderDetail class in the diagram.

6. Select Open Specification from the shortcut menu.

7. The Boundary stereotype will be available in the drop-down list box of the stereotype field. Select Boundary.

8. Click OK.

Continued on next page

9. Repeat steps one through four to assign the OrderMgr and TransactionMgr classes the Control stereotype, and the Order class the Entity stereotype.

The Class diagram should look like Figure 5.15.

FIGURE 5.15:

Stereotypes for classes in Add New Order use case

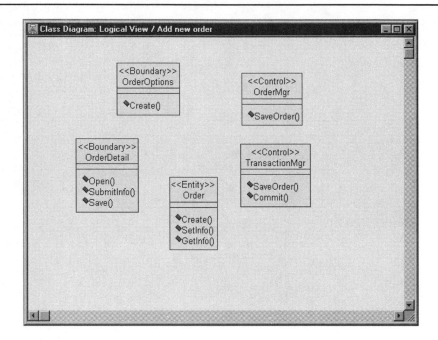

Group Classes into Packages

1. In the browser, drag the OrderOptions class to the Boundaries package.

2. Drag the OrderDetail class to the Boundaries package.

3. Drag the OrderMgr and TransactionMgr classes to the Control package.

4. Drag the Order class to the Entities package.

The classes and packages in the browser are shown in Figure 5.16.

Continued on next page

FIGURE 5.16:

Classes and packages
in the Add New Order
use case

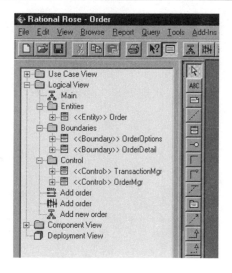

Add Class Diagrams to Each Package

1. In the browser, right-click the Boundaries package.

2. Select New ➤ Class Diagram.

3. Name the new diagram **Main**.

4. Double-click the new diagram to open it.

5. Drag the OrderOptions and OrderDetail classes from the browser to the diagram.

The Main Class diagram for the Boundaries package should look like Figure 5.17.

6. Close the diagram.

7. Right-click the Entities package in the browser.

8. Select New ➤ Class Diagram.

9. Name the new diagram **Main**.

Continued on next page

FIGURE 5.17:

Main Class diagram for
Boundaries package

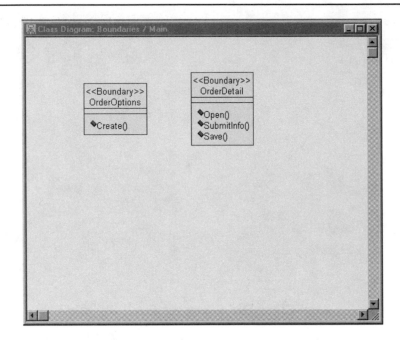

10. Double-click the new diagram to open it.

11. Drag the Order class from the browser to the diagram.

The Main Class diagram for the Entities package should look like Figure 5.18.

12. Close the diagram.

13. Right-click the Control package in the browser.

14. Select New ➤ Class Diagram.

15. Name the new diagram **Main**.

16. Double-click the new diagram to open it.

17. Drag the OrderMgr and TransactionMgr classes from the browser to the diagram.

18. Close the diagram.

Continued on next page

FIGURE 5.18:

Main Class diagram for
Entities package

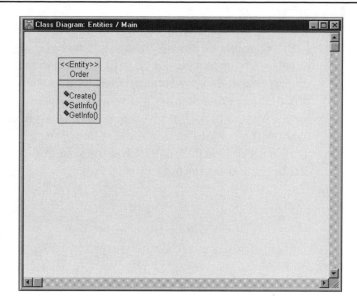

The Main Class diagram for the Control package should look like Figure 5.19.

FIGURE 5.19:

Main Class diagram for
Control package

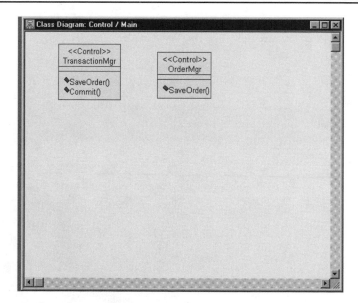

Summary

In this chapter, we discussed classes, Class diagrams, and packages. By now, we have greatly improved our view of the system that is being built. By the end of the last chapter, we had created Object Interaction diagrams such as Collaboration diagrams and Sequence diagrams. These illustrate the interactions required for the system to perform its functions. In this chapter, we created Class diagrams to show the static behavior in the system. We also organized the classes into packages in order to better understand the system. Next, we will look in detail at the attributes and operations of the classes.

CHAPTER
SIX

6

Attributes and Operations

- ■ Working with Attributes

- ■ Working with Operations

- ■ Displaying Attribute and Operations on Class Diagrams

- ■ Mapping Operations to Messages

In the previous chapter, we looked at classes and packages. Remember that classes are encapsulated attributes (data) and the operations (behavior) that act on those attributes. Now we will discuss working with attributes and operations. We will begin by talking about how to find attributes, add them to the Rose model, and add details about the attributes. We will then look at finding operations, adding them to the model, and adding details to the operations. Next, we will look at displaying attributes and operations on Class diagrams. Lastly, we will discuss how to map operations to messages on Interaction diagrams.

Working with Attributes

An *attribute* is a piece of information associated with a class. For example, a Company class might have attributes called Name, Address, and NumberOfEmployees.

In Rose, you may add one or more attributes to each of the classes in the model. The following sections describe how to find attributes, add them to the model, delete them from the model, and set the detailed specifications for each attribute.

Finding Attributes

There are a number of sources of attributes. To begin, you can take a look at the use case documentation. Look for nouns in your flow of events. Some of the nouns will be objects or classes, some will be actors, and others will be attributes. For example, your flow of events may read: *The user enters the employee's name, address, social security number, and phone number,* letting you know that the Employee class has attributes called Name, Address, SSN, and Phone.

Another good place to look is the requirements document. There may be requirements that outline what information should be collected by the system. Any piece of information that is collected should be an attribute in a class.

Finally, you can check the database structure. If your database structure has already been defined, the fields in the tables will give you a good idea of what your attributes are. Frequently, there's a one-to-one mapping between database tables and entity classes. Going back to our previous example, an Employee table may have fields called Name, Address, SSN, and Phone. The corresponding class, called Employee, will have attributes called Name, Address, SSN, and Phone. It's important to note that there isn't always a one-to-one mapping between the database tables and the classes. There are different considerations when designing your database and designing your classes. Relational databases, for example, don't directly support inheritance.

However, when you identify attributes, be sure that each one can be traced back to a requirement. This can help solve the classic problem of an application capturing a great deal of information that nobody uses. Each requirement should be traced back to the flow of events of a use case, to a particular requirement, or to an existing database table. If you cannot trace the requirement, you cannot be sure it is needed by the customer. This can be a bit of a deviation from some older methodologies—rather than create the database structure first and then *wrap* the system around it, you're building the system and the database at the same time, to conform to the same requirements.

As you identify attributes, carefully assign them to the appropriate classes. An attribute should be a piece of information related to the class. For example, an Employee class might have name and address, but shouldn't include information about the products the employee's company manufactures. A Product class would be a better place to store information about products.

Be cautious of classes with too many attributes. If you find that a particular class has a large number of attributes, it might be an indication that the class should be split into two smaller classes. If you have a class with more than about 10 or 15 attributes, be sure to take a close look at it. The class may be perfectly legitimate—just be sure all of the attributes are needed, and truly belong to that class. Similarly, be cautious of classes with too few attributes. Again, it may be perfectly legitimate. Control classes, for example, tend to have very few attributes. However, it may also be a sign that two or more classes should be combined. If you have a class with only one or two attributes, it may be worth a closer look.

Sometimes you may run into a piece of information and wonder whether it's an attribute or a class. For example, let's look at an attribute like Company Name. The question you face might be: Is the company name an attribute of a Person class, or should Company be its own class? The answer really depends on the application you are writing. If you need to keep information about the company, and there is some behavior associated with a company, it may be its own class. For example, you may be building a system to keep track of your customers. In this case, you'll want to keep some information about the companies you sell products or services to. You may want to know how many employees the company has, the company's name and address, the name of your contact with the company, and so on.

On the other hand, you may not need to know specific information about the company. You may be writing an application that will generate letters to your contacts in other organizations. When generating the letters, you will need to know a company name. However, you don't need to know any more information about the company. In this case, you could consider the company name to be an attribute of a Contact class.

Another thing to consider is whether the piece of information in question has behavior. If the Company has some behavior in your application, it is better modeled as a class. If the company has no behavior, it may be better modeled as an attribute.

Once you've identified the attributes, the next step is to add them to your Rose model. In the following sections, we'll discuss how to add attributes and add details to the attributes, such as the data type and default value.

Adding Attributes

As you identify attributes, you can add them to the appropriate class in your Rose model. There are three main pieces of information you can supply for each attribute: the attribute name, the data type, and the initial value. Before you can generate code for your model, you must supply a name and data type for each attribute. Initial values are optional.

There are three ways to add an attribute. You may type the attribute directly onto a Class diagram, add the attribute using the browser, or add the attribute using the class specification window.

Once you've added an attribute, you can add documentation for it. Typically, attribute documentation would include a short description or definition of the attribute. Any attribute documentation will be included as a comment in the code generated from the model. By documenting the attributes as you go along, you are beginning to document the code as well.

To add an attribute to a class:

1. Right-click the class on a Class diagram.

2. Select New ➤ Attribute.

3. Type the attribute name, using the format Name : Data Type = Initial value. For example:

    Address : String

    IDNumber : Integer = 0

The data type is required in order to generate code, but the initial value is optional.

4. To add more attributes, press Enter and type the new attributes directly on the Class diagram.

OR

1. Right-click the class in the browser.

2. Select New ➢ Attribute.

3. A new attribute called *name* will appear under the class in the browser. Type the name of the new attribute. Attribute data types and default values cannot be assigned in the browser; you can enter them on the Class diagram, as we'll discuss shortly.

OR

1. Open the class specification window for the attribute's class.

2. Select the Attributes tab. If the class has some attributes already, they will be listed here.

3. Right-click anywhere inside the attributes area, as in Figure 6.1.

FIGURE 6.1:

Adding a new attribute in the class specification window

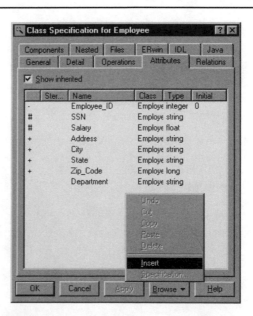

4. Select Insert from the shortcut menu.

5. Type the name of the new attribute.

6. Enter the visibility, stereotype, data type, and initial value in the appropriate columns. We'll discuss each of these in detail in the sections below.

To add documentation to an attribute:

1. Select the attribute in the browser.

2. Type the attribute documentation in the documentation window.

OR

1. Select the attribute on a Class diagram.

2. Type the attribute documentation in the documentation window.

OR

1. Right-click the attribute in the browser.

2. Select Open Specification from the shortcut menu.

3. Enter the attribute documentation in the Documentation area of the class attribute specification window.

OR

1. Open the class specification window for the attribute's class.

2. Select the Attributes tab.

3. Select the attribute.

4. Type the attribute documentation in the documentation window.

Deleting Attributes

At times, you may find that you need to delete an attribute you have created. This is most common when the system requirements change, removing the need for a particular attribute. In Rose, the quickest way to delete an attribute is typically through the browser. However, you can also use a Class diagram to delete an attribute. When an attribute is deleted from one Class diagram, Rose will automatically remove it from the model, including any other Class diagrams it was on.

To delete an attribute from a class:

1. Right-click the attribute in the browser.

2. Select Delete from the shortcut menu.

OR

1. Select the attribute on a Class diagram.

2. Use the Backspace key to erase the attribute name, data type, and initial value from the diagram.

3. Single-click anywhere on the diagram.

4. Rose will confirm the deletion before the attribute is removed.

OR

1. Open the class specification window for the attribute's class.

2. Select the Attributes tab.

3. Right-click the attribute you want to delete.

4. Select Delete from the shortcut menu.

5. Rose will confirm the deletion before the attribute is removed.

Attribute Specifications

As with other Rose model elements, there are a number of detailed specifications you can add to an attribute. These include, among other things, the attribute data type, initial value, stereotype, and visibility. In the next several sections, we'll take a look at each specification.

All of the specifications are viewed or changed on the attribute specification window, as shown in Figure 6.2.

FIGURE 6.2:

Attribute specification
window

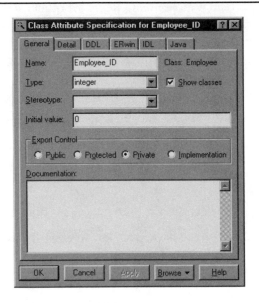

To open the attribute specifications:

1.   Right-click the attribute in the browser.

2.   Select Open Specification from the shortcut menu.

    OR

1.   Open the class specification window for the attribute's class.

2.   Select the Attributes tab.

3.   Double-click the appropriate attribute.

NOTE   In Rose 98i, following these procedures will open a different specification window. To open the specification window shown in Figure 6.2, right-click the attribute in the browser, and select Open Standard Specification from the shortcut menu.

Setting the Attribute Data Type

One of the main pieces of information you specify about an attribute is its data type. The data type is the language-specific type, such as string, integer, long, or boolean. Before you can generate code, you must enter a data type for each attribute.

When you are entering the data type, you can either use built-in data types (string, integer, long, etc.) for your programming language, or the names of classes that you have defined in your Rose model. To see the classes you have defined in the drop-down list box, select the Show Classes check box.

To set the attribute data type:

1. Right-click the attribute in the browser.

2. Select Open Specification from the shortcut menu. Rose will open the class attribute specification window.

3. Select a data type from the Type drop-down list box or enter a new data type.

OR

1. Select the attribute on a Class diagram.

2. Type a colon and the data type after the attribute name. For example, if you have an attribute called Address that you want to set as a string, type **Address : String**.

Setting the Attribute Stereotype

Like actors, use cases, and classes, attributes can be stereotyped. An attribute stereotype is a way to classify the attribute. For example, you may have some attributes that map to fields in your database, and other attributes that do not. You can define two stereotypes, one for each of these types of attributes.

In Rose, you are not required to assign stereotypes to attributes. You can generate code without using attribute stereotypes. Stereotypes can, however, improve the readability and comprehensibility of your model.

To set the attribute stereotype:

1. Right-click the attribute in the browser.

2. Select Open Specification from the shortcut menu. Rose will open the Class Attribute Specification window.

3. Select a stereotype from the drop-down list box or enter a new stereotype.

OR

1. Select the attribute in the browser.

2. Single-click the attribute again to edit the name. Before the name, the characters << >> will appear:

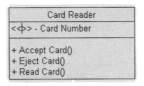

3. Type the stereotype between the << >>:

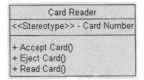

Setting the Attribute Initial Value

Many attributes will have some sort of a default value associated with them. For example, you may have a class called Order, which holds information and behavior about purchase orders for your company. The Order class may have an attribute called TaxRate for the sales tax rate of the purchase. In your city, the tax rate is 7.5%, so most of your orders will be at the 7.5% rate. You can assign an initial value of .075 to the TaxRate attribute.

Like attribute stereotypes, initial values aren't required in order to generate code. However, if an initial value is present, Rose will generate the code necessary to initialize the attribute.

To set the attribute initial value:

1. Right-click the attribute in the browser.

2. Select Open Specification from the shortcut menu. The class attribute specification window will appear.

3. In the Initial Value field, enter the attribute's default value.

OR

1. Select the attribute on a Class diagram.

2. After the attribute data type, enter an equal sign, followed by the default value. For example, if you have an integer attribute called EmployeeID, and you wish to set its default value to 0, your Class diagram would look like this:

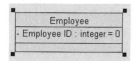

Setting the Attribute Visibility

One of the central concepts of Object Oriented programming is that of encapsulation. Each class, by having attributes and operations, encapsulates a little bit of information and a little bit of behavior. One of the benefits of this approach is the ability to have small, self-contained pieces of code. The Employee class, for example, has all of the information and behavior related to an employee.

You can view a class like this:

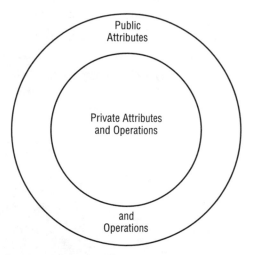

The attributes are contained inside the class, hidden away from other classes. Because the attributes are encapsulated within a class, you will need to define which classes have access to view and change the attribute. This is known as the *attribute visibility*.

There are four visibility options for an attribute. Let's look at each in the context of an example. We have an Employee class with an attribute called Address, and a Company class.

Public   Suggests that the attribute is visible to all other classes. Any other class can view or modify the value of the attribute. In this case, the Company class could view or modify the value of the Address attribute of the Employee class. The UML notation for a public attribute is a plus sign.

Private   Means that the attribute is not visible to any other class. The Employee class would know what the value of the Address attribute is, and would be able to change the value, but the Company class wouldn't be able to view or edit the Address attribute. If the Company class needed to view or edit Address, it would have to ask the Employee class to view or edit the attribute. This is typically done through public operations. We'll talk more about this in the operations part of this chapter. The UML notation for a private attribute is a minus sign.

Protected   Suggests that the class and any of its descendants have access to the attribute. In our example, assume we have two different types of employees, hourly employees and salaried employees. The classes HourlyEmp and SalariedEmp are inherited from the Employee class. If the Address attribute has protected visibility, it can be viewed or changed by the Employee class, the HourlyEmp class, or the SalariedEmp class, but not by the Company class. The UML notation for a protected attribute is a pound sign.

Package or Implementation   Indicates that the attribute is public, but only to classes in the same package. In our example, assume the Address attribute of the Employee class has package visibility. Address could be modified by Company only if Company and Employee are in the same package. With implementation visability, no icon appears next to the attribute.

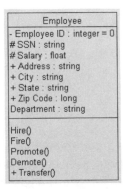

In general, private or protected visibility is recommended for attributes. Using these options helps you maintain better control of your code and the attribute. By using private or protected attributes, you won't have a situation where an attribute is being modified by all sorts of classes throughout the system. Instead, the logic for modifying an attribute is encapsulated in a single class, along with the attribute. The visibility options you select will affect the generated code. For example, Figure 6.3 is the Java code generated for the class above.

FIGURE 6.3:

Attribute visibility in generated code

```
// Source file: Employee.java

public class Employee {
    private integer Employee_ID = 0;
    protected string SSN;
    protected float Salary;
    public string Address;
    public string City;
    public string State;
    public long Zip_Code;
    string Department;

    Employee() {
    }
    /**
        @roseuid 36A95C440186
     */
    integer Hire() {
    }

    /**
        @roseuid 36A95C5C0118
     */
    void Fire() {
    }

    /**
        @roseuid 36A95C61003C
     */
    void Promote() {
    }

    /**
        @roseuid 36A95C6302BC
     */
    void Demote() {
    }

    /**
        @roseuid 36A95C66003C
     */
    public void Transfer() {
    }
}
```

Rose supports two sets of visibility notations. The first is UML notation (+, -, #) for public, private, and protected attributes, respectively. The second notation includes four Rose icons, as shown in Table 6.1.

TABLE 6.1: Rose Visibility Icons

Icon	Description
	Public
	Private
	Protected
	Package or Implementation

On a Class diagram, you can use either of these notations. See below for a description of how to switch between these two notations. Figure 6.4 shows an example of a class using UML visibility notation. Figure 6.5 shows the same class using Rose visibility notation. Rose and UML visibility notations are summarized in Table 6.2.

FIGURE 6.4:

UML visibility notation

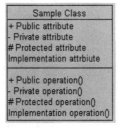

FIGURE 6.5:

Rose visibility notation

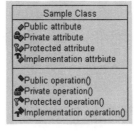

TABLE 6.2: Rose and UML Visibility Notations

If you want to	Use	UML Notation	Rose Notation
Make an attribute visible to all classes	Public visibility	+	![public icon]
Make an attribute visible to only one class	Private visibility	-	![private icon]
Make an attribute visible to a class and its descendants	Protected visibility	#	![protected icon]
Make an attribute visible to all classes in the same package	Package or Implementation visibility	<no icon>	![package icon]

To set the attribute visibility:

1. Right-click the attribute in the browser.

2. Select Open Specification from the shortcut menu. The Class Attribute Specification window will appear.

3. In the Export Control field, select the attribute's visibility: Public, Protected, Private, or Implementation. By default, all attributes have Private visibility.

OR

1. Select the attribute on a Class diagram.

2. If you are using UML notation for visibility, single-click the +, -, or # next to the attribute. Select a visibility option from the list of Rose visibility icons that appears.

3. If you are using Rose notation for visibility, single-click the Rose visibility icon to the left of the attribute name. Select a visibility option from the list of icons that appears.

To change the visibility notation:

1. Select Tools ➢ Options.

2. Select the Notation tab.

3. Set the Visibility as Icons check box on to use Rose notation, or off to use UML notation.

NOTE   Changing this option will change the notation used on new diagrams only. Existing diagrams will not be changed.

Setting the Attribute Containment

The attribute's containment describes how the attribute is *stored* within the class. There are three containment options:

By value   Suggests that the attribute is contained within the class. For example, if you have an attribute of type string, the string is contained within the class definition.

By reference   Suggests that the attribute is located outside the class, but the class has a pointer to it. For example, you may have an attribute of type Employee within a Timecard class. The employee object itself is located outside of the timecard. The attribute inside the timecard is simply a pointer to this external object.

Unspecified   Suggests that the containment has not yet been specified. When generating code, Rose will assume *by value* if the containment is unspecified.

To set the attribute containment:

1.   Right-click the attribute in the browser.

2.   Select Open Specification (or Open Standard Specification in 98i) from the shortcut menu. The class attribute specification window will appear.

3.   Select the Detail tab.

4.   Select the attribute's containment: By Value, By Reference, or Unspecified. By default, all attributes are set to an Unspecified containment.

Making an Attribute Static

When an attribute is added to a class, each instance of the class will receive its own copy of the attribute. For example, let's look at our Employee class. At runtime, we may instantiate three employees: John Doe, Bill Jones, and Jane Smith. Each of these three objects has its own copy of the attribute Salary.

A *static* attribute is one that is shared by all instances of a class. Returning to the above example, if Salary was a static attribute, it would be shared by John, Bill and Jane. The UML representation of a static attribute is a $ before the attribute name. In our example, Salary would become $Salary.

To make an attribute static:

1. Right-click the attribute in the browser.

2. Select Open Specification (or Open Standard Specification in 98i) from the shortcut menu. The Class Attribute Specification window will appear.

3. Select the Detail tab.

4. Select the Static check box to mark the attribute as static. Rose will place a $ before the attribute name on the Class diagram.

Specifying a Derived Attribute

A *derived attribute* is one that is created from one or more other attributes. For example, a Rectangle class might have attributes called Width and Height. It might also have an attribute called Area, which is calculated from the width and height. Because Area is derived from the Width and Height, two other attributes, it is considered a derived attribute.

In UML, derived attributes are marked with a / before the attribute name. In the above example, area would be written as /area.

To specify a derived attribute:

1. Right-click the attribute in the browser.

2. Select Open Specification (or Open Standard Specification in 98i) from the shortcut menu. The class attribute specification window will appear.

3. Select the Detail tab.

4. Select the Derived check box to mark the attribute as derived. Rose will place a / before the attribute name on the Class diagram.

Working with Operations

An *operation* is a behavior associated with a class. An operation has three parts: the operation name, the operation parameters, and the operation return type. The parameters are arguments the operation receives as input. The return type is the output of the operation.

On a Class diagram, you can view either the operation name or the operation name followed by the parameters and return type. To reduce clutter on Class diagrams, it can be helpful to have some Class diagrams with operation names only, and others with the full operation signature, including parameters and the return type.

In UML, operations are displayed using the following notation:

Operation Name (argument1 : argument1 data type, argument2 : argument2 data type, ...) : return type

Operations define the responsibilities of your classes. As you identify operations and examine your classes, keep a few things in mind:

- Be suspicious of any classes with only one or two operations. It may be perfectly legitimate, but it may also indicate that the class should be combined with another.

- Be very suspicious of classes with no operations. A class typically encapsulates both behavior and information. A class with no behavior might be better modeled as an attribute or two.

- Be wary of classes with too many operations. A class should have a manageable set of responsibilities. If you have a class with too many operations, it may be difficult to maintain. Dividing it instead into two smaller classes may ease maintenance.

In this section, we'll talk about finding operations, adding them to your Rose model, and adding the operation details. We'll also take a look at how operations can be displayed on the Class diagrams.

Finding Operations

Finding operations is fairly straightforward. As you created your Sequence and Collaboration diagrams, you did most of the work necessary to find operations.

There are four different types of operations to consider:

Implementor Operations

Implementor operations implement some business functionality. Implementor operations are found by examining interaction diagrams. The Interaction diagrams focus on business functionality, and each message on the diagram will most likely be mapped to an implementor operation.

Each implementor operation should be able to be traced back to a requirement. This is achieved through the various pieces of the model. Each operation comes from a message on an interaction diagram, which comes from the details in the flow of events, which comes from the use case, which comes from the requirements. This ability to trace can help you ensure that each requirement was implemented in the code and that each piece of code can be traced back to a requirement.

Manager Operations

Manager operations manage the creation and destruction of objects. For example, the constructor and destructor operations of a class fall into this category.

In Rose, you don't need to manually create constructor and destructor operations for each of your classes. When you generate code, Rose gives you the option of automatically generating constructors and destructors.

Access Operations

Attributes are typically private or protected. However, other classes may need to view or change the attributes of a particular class. This can be accomplished through *access operations*.

For example, if we have an attribute called Salary in an Employee class, we wouldn't want all of the other classes to be able to go in and change the Salary. Instead, we add two access operations to the Employee class—GetSalary and Set-Salary. The GetSalary operation, which is public, can be called by other classes. It will go in and get the value of the Salary attribute, and return this value to the calling class. The SetSalary operation, which is also public, will help another class set the value of the Salary attribute. SetSalary can contain any validation rules for the salary that must be checked before the value in Salary is changed.

This approach keeps the attributes safely encapsulated inside a class, and protected from other classes, but still allows controlled access to the attributes. The industry standard has been to create a Get and Set operation for each attribute in a class.

As with manager operations, you don't have to manually enter each access operation. When you generate code, Rose can automatically create Get and Set operations for each of the attributes in the class.

Helper Operations

Helper operations are those operations that a class needs to carry out its responsibilities, but that other classes don't need to know about. These are the private and protected operations of a class.

Like implementor operations, helper operations are found by examining the Sequence and Collaboration diagrams. Frequently, helper operations appear as reflexive messages on a Sequence or Collaboration diagram.

To identify operations, you can perform the following series of steps:

1. Examine Sequence and Collaboration diagrams. Most messages will become implementor operations. Reflexive messages may become helper operations.

2. Consider manager operations. You may want to add constructors and destructors. Again, this isn't required—Rose can generate these for you when code is generated.

3. Consider access operations. Create a Get and Set operation for any attribute that will need to be viewed or changed by another class. As with manager operations, these don't need to be manually added—Rose can generate them for you when code is generated.

Adding Operations

Like attributes, operations can be added to your Rose model through a Class diagram or through the browser. You can also add operations to a class through the class specification window.

Once you've added an operation, you can add documentation to it. Any documentation you add to an operation will be included as a comment in the generated code. Documentation for operations typically includes information like the purpose of the operation, a short description of the operation's parameters, and the operation return type.

To add an operation to a class:

1. Right-click the class on a Class diagram.

2. Select New ➤ Operation.

3. Type the operation name, using the format

   Name(Argument1 : Argument1 data type): Operation Return Type

   For example:

   ```
   Add(X : Integer, Y: Integer) : Integer
   Print(EmployeeID : Long) : Boolean
   Delete() : Long
   ```

4. To add more operations, press Enter and type the new operations directly on the Class diagram.

OR

1. Right-click the class in the browser.

2. Select New ➤ Operation.

3. A new operation called opname will appear under the class in the browser. Type the name of the new operation. Rose does not allow you to enter the operation arguments or return type value in the browser; as with attributes, you can enter these details on the Class diagram.

OR

1. Open the class specification window (or standard specification window in 98i) for the operation's class.

2. Select the Operations tab. If the class has some operations already, they will be listed here.

3. Right-click anywhere inside the operations area, as shown in Figure 6.6.

FIGURE 6.6:

Adding a new operation in the class specification window

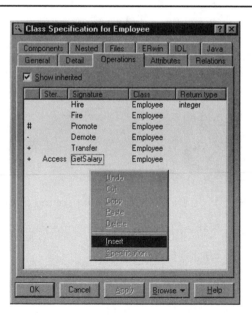

4. Select Insert from the shortcut menu.

5. Type the name of the new operation in the Operation column.

6. Enter the visibility, stereotype, and return type in the appropriate columns.

To add documentation to an operation:

1. Select the operation in the browser.

2. Type the operation documentation in the documentation window.

OR

1. Select the operation on a Class diagram.

2. Type the operation documentation in the documentation window.

OR

1. Right-click the operation in the browser.

2. Select Open Specification from the shortcut menu.

3. Enter the operation documentation in the DocComment area of the operation specification window.

OR

1. Open the class specification window (or standard specification window in 98i) for the operation's class.

2. Select the Operations tab.

3. Select the operation.

4. Type the operation documentation in the documentation window.

Deleting Operations

If you need to delete an operation, you can do so through a Class diagram or the browser. When an operation is deleted from one diagram, it is automatically removed from the entire model, including any other diagrams it was on.

When deleting an operation, be sure to keep the model consistent. You may have used the operation in a Sequence or Collaboration diagram. If you delete the operation, it will be automatically converted into a message on all Sequence and

Collaboration diagrams. Be sure to update the Sequence or Collaboration diagram appropriately.

To determine which diagrams reference an operation:

1. Open the class specification window (or standard specification window in 98i) for the operation's class.

2. Select Browse ➤ Show Usage… at the bottom of the dialogue box.

To delete an operation from a class:

1. Right-click the operation in the browser.

2. Select Delete from the shortcut menu.

OR

1. Select the operation on a Class diagram.

2. Use the backspace key to erase the operation name and signature from the diagram.

3. Single-click anywhere on the diagram.

4. Rose will confirm the deletion before the operation is removed.

OR

1. Open the class specification window (or standard specification window in 98i) for the operation's class.

2. Select the Operations tab.

3. Right-click the operation you want to delete.

4. Select Delete from the shortcut menu.

5. Rose will confirm the deletion before the operation is removed.

Operation Specifications

In the operation specifications, you can set details such as the operation parameters, return type, and visibility. In the next several sections, we'll take a look at each specification.

All of the specifications are viewed or changed on the operation specification window, as shown in Figure 6.7.

FIGURE 6.7:

Operation specification window

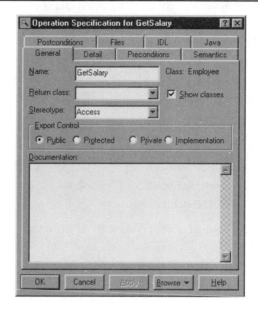

To open the operation specifications:

1. Right-click the operation in the browser.

2. Select Open Specification from the shortcut menu.

OR

1. Open the class specification window for the operation's class.

2. Select the Operations tab.

3. Double-click the appropriate operation.

NOTE   In Rose 98i, following these procedures will open a different specification window. To open the specification window shown in Figure 6.7, right-click the operation in the browser and select Open Standard Specification from the shortcut menu.

Setting the Operation Return Class

The return class of an operation is the data type of the operation's result. For example, say we have an operation called Add, which takes as parameters two strings, X and Y. The operation will convert X and Y to integers, add them, and return the result as an integer. The return class of Add will be integer.

When specifying the return class, you can either use built-in data types of your programming language, such as string, char, or integer, or use classes that you have defined in your Rose model.

To set the operation return class:

1. Right-click the operation in the browser.

2. Select Open Specification (or Open Standard Specification in 98i) from the shortcut menu.

3. Select a return class from the drop-down list box, or enter a new return type.

    OR

1. Select the operation on a Class diagram.

2. After the operation name, enter a colon, followed by the return type. For example, if you have an operation called Print that should return an Integer, your Class diagram will look like this:

Setting the Operation Stereotype

As with other model elements, operations can be stereotyped to classify them. As discussed above, there are four commonly used operation stereotypes:

Implementor   Operations that implement some business logic.

Manager   Constructors, destructors, and memory management operations.

Access   Operations that allow other classes to view or edit attributes. Typically, these are named Get<attribute name> and Set<attribute name>.

Helper   Private or protected operations used by the class but not seen by other classes.

Setting stereotypes for operations isn't required to generate code. However, stereotypes can help improve the understandability of the model. Also, they can help you to be sure you haven't missed any operations.

To set the operation stereotype.

1. Right-click the operation in the browser.

2. Select Open Specification (or Open Standard Specification in 98i) from the shortcut menu. Rose will open the operation specification window.

3. Select a stereotype from the drop-down list box or enter a new stereotype.

OR

1. Select the operation in the browser.

2. Single-click the operation again to edit the name. Before the name, the characters <<>> will appear:

3. Type the stereotype between the <<>>.

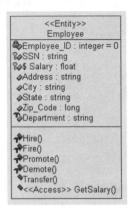

Setting the Operation Visibility

As we discussed before, visibility has to do with how information and behavior is encapsulated in a class. There are four visibility options for operations. (To familiarize yourself with the way these are represented visually, see Table 6.2.)

Public   Suggests that the operation is visible to all other classes. Any other class can request that the operation be executed.

Private   Means that the operation is not visible to any other class.

Protected   Suggests that the class and any of its descendants have access to the operation.

Package or Implementation   Indicates that the operation is public, but only to classes in the same package.

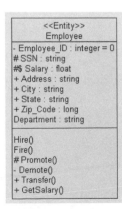

While attributes are typically private or protected, operations may be public, private, protected, or package. When making this decision, think about what other classes, if any, will need to know that the operation exists. When you generate code, Rose will generate the appropriate visibility. For example, the code generated for the class above is shown in Figure 6.8.

As mentioned earlier in this chapter, you can use either UML or Rose notation on a Class diagram. See below for a description of how to switch between these two notations. Refer to Figure 6.4 to see a class using UML visibility notation and to Figure 6.5 to see the same class using Rose visibility notation. To revisit a summary of the possible visibility options, including their Rose and UML notations, see Table 6.2.

FIGURE 6.8:

Operation visibility in generated code

```
public class Employee {
    private integer Employee_ID = 0;
    protected string SSN;
    protected static float Salary;
    public string Address;
    public string City;
    public string State;
    public long Zip_Code;
    string Department;

    Employee() {
    }
    /**
       @roseuid 36A95C440186
     */
    integer Hire() {
    }

    /**
       @roseuid 36A95C5C0118
     */
    void Fire() {
    }

    /**
       @roseuid 36A95C61003C
     */
    protected void Promote() {
    }

    /**
       @roseuid 36A95C6302BC
     */
    private void Demote() {
    }

    /**
       @roseuid 36A95C66003C
     */
    public void Transfer() {
    }

    /**
       @roseuid 36A96B620334
     */
    public void GetSalary() {
    } }|
```

To set the operation visibility:

1. Right-click the operation in the browser.

2. Select Open Specification (or Open Standard Specification in 98i) from the shortcut menu. The Operation Specification window will appear.

3. In the Export Control field, select the operation's visibility: Public, Protected, Private, or Implementation. By default, all operations have Public visibility.

OR

1. Select the operation on a Class diagram.

2. If you are using UML notation for visibility, single-click the +, -, or # next to the operation. Select a visibility option from the list of Rose visibility icons that appears.

3. If you are using Rose notation for visibility, single-click the Rose visibility icon to the left of the operation name. Select a visibility option from the list of icons that appears.

Adding Arguments to an Operation

Operation arguments, or parameters, are the input data the operation receives. An Add operation, for example, may take two arguments, X and Y, and add them together.

There are two pieces of information to supply for each argument. The first is the argument name. The second is its data type. On a Class diagram, the arguments and data types appear in parentheses after the operation name:

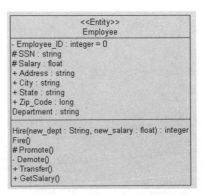

If you'd like, you can also specify a default value for each argument. If you include a default value, the UML notation is:

Operation name(argument1 : argument1 data type = argument1 default value) : operation return type

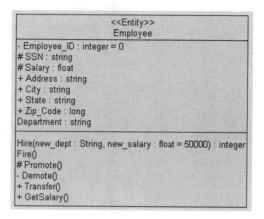

When you generate code, Rose will generate the operation name, arguments, argument data types, argument default values, and return type. Rose will also create comments if any documentation was added to the operation.

To add an argument to an operation:

1. Open the operation specification window (or standard specification window in 98i).

2. Select the Detail tab.

3. Right-click in the arguments box, then select Insert from the menu.

4. Enter the name of the argument, as shown in Figure 6.9.

5. Click on the data type column and enter the data type of the argument.

6. Click on the default column and enter the default for the argument if desired.

To delete an argument from an operation:

1. Open the operation specification window (or standard specification window in 98i).

2. Select the Detail tab.

FIGURE 6.9:

Operation arguments

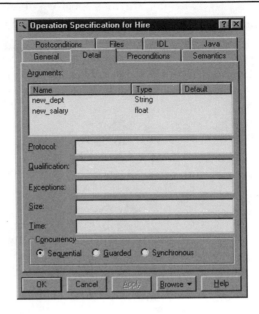

3. Right-click the argument to delete in the arguments box, then select Delete from the menu.

4. Confirm the deletion.

Specifying the Operation Protocol

The operation protocol describes what operations a client may perform on the object, and in which order the operations must be executed. For example, if operation A should not be executed until operation B has been executed, you can note this in the protocol field of operation A.

The information you enter here will be included as a comment when you generate code; however, it will not have an impact on what code is generated for the operation. The operation protocol screen is shown in Figure 6.10.

To specify the operation protocol:

1. Open the operation specification window (or standard specification window in 98i).

2. Select the Detail tab.

3. Enter the protocol in the Protocol field.

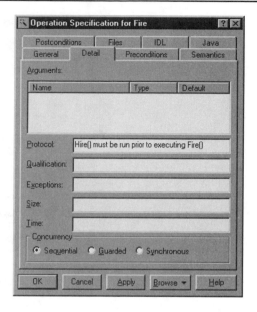

Specifying the Operation Qualifications

This field lets you identify any language-specific qualifications for the operation. Anything you enter here will be included as a comment when you generate code. However, it will not affect the code generated for the operation.

To specify the operation qualifications:

1. Open the Operation Specifications window (or Standard Specification window in 98i).

2. Select the Detail tab.

3. Enter the qualifications in the Qualification field.

Specifying the Operation Exceptions

The operation Exceptions field gives you a place to list the exceptions that the operation may throw. As with the protocol and qualifications, the exception information is generated as a comment in the code. The exception information will also affect the code generated for the operation. For example, Figure 6.11 is some C++ code generated with exception information.

FIGURE 6.11:

Operation exceptions in
generated code

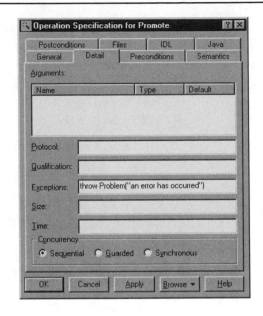

To specify the operation exceptions:

1. Open the operation specification window (or standard specification window in 98i).

2. Select the Detail tab.

3. Enter the exceptions in the Exceptions field.

Specifying the Operation Size

The Size field is a place to note how much memory you expect the operation to require at runtime. This information will be generated as a comment in the code.

To specify the operation size:

1. Open the operation specifications window (or standard specification window in 98i).

2. Select the Detail tab.

3. Enter the size in the Size field.

Specifying the Operation Time

The operation time is the approximate amount of time you expect this operation to require as it executes. Any information you enter here will be generated as a comment in the code.

To specify the operation time:

1. Open the operation specifications window (or standard specification window in 98i).

2. Select the Detail tab.

3. Enter the time in the Time field.

Specifying the Operation Concurrency

The Concurrency field specifies how the operation will behave in the presence of multiple threads of control. There are three concurrency options:

Sequential   Suggests that the operation will only run properly if there is a single thread of control. The operation must run to completion before another operation may be run.

Guarded   Suggests that the operation will run properly with multiple threads of control, but only if the classes collaborate to ensure that mutual exclusion of running operations is achieved.

Synchronous   Suggests that the operation will run properly with multiple threads of control. When called, the operation will run to completion in one thread. However, other operations can run in other threads at the same time. The class will take care of mutual exclusion issues, so collaboration with other classes is not required.

The operation concurrency will appear as a comment in the generated code.

To specify the operation concurrency:

1. Open the operation specifications window (or standard specification window in 98i).

2. Select the Detail tab.

3. Select the desired concurrency from the concurrency box.

Specifying the Operation PreConditions

A precondition is some condition that must be true before the operation can run. You can enter any preconditions for the operation on the Preconditions tab of the operation specification window, as shown in Figure 6.12.

FIGURE 6.12:

Operation preconditions

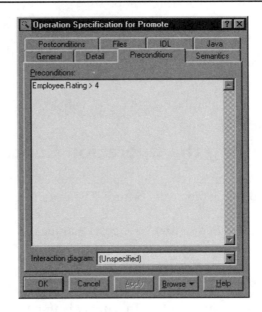

Preconditions will not affect the code that is generated for the operation; however, the preconditions will appear as a comment in the generated code. If you have an Interaction diagram that illustrates the operation preconditions, you can enter the Interaction diagram name at the bottom of the Preconditions tab.

To specify the operation preconditions:

1. Open the operation specification window (or standard specification window in 98i).

2. Select the Preconditions tab.

3. Enter the preconditions in the Preconditions field.

Specifying the Operation PostConditions

Postconditions are conditions that must always be true after the operation has finished executing. Postconditions are entered on the Postconditions tab of the Operation Specification window, as shown in Figure 6.13.

FIGURE 6.13:

Operation postconditions

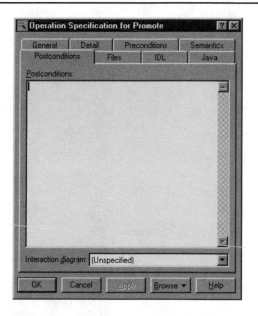

Like preconditions, the postconditions will not affect the code generated for an operation, but will appear as a comment in the generated code. If you have an Interaction diagram that includes information about the postconditions, you can enter its name at the bottom of the Postconditions tab.

To specify the operation postconditions:

1. Open the operation specification window (or standard specification window in 98i).

2. Select the Postconditions tab.

3. Enter the postconditions in the Postconditions field.

Specifying the Operation Semantics

The Semantics field of the operation specification window gives you a place to describe what the operation will do, as shown in Figure 6.14. You can use pseudo-code here, or just a description, to spell out the operation logic. Anything you enter in the Semantics field will be generated as a comment in the code. If you have an Interaction diagram related to the operation's semantics, you can enter it at the bottom of this tab page.

FIGURE 6.14:

Operation semantics

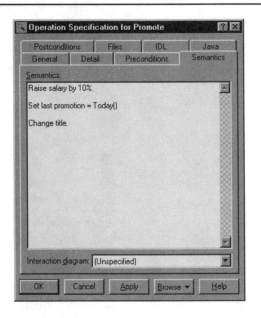

To specify the operation semantics:

1. Open the operation specification window (or standard specification window in 98i).

2. Select the Semantics tab.

3. Enter the semantics in the Semantics field.

Attaching Files and URLs to an Operation

You may have an external file or URL that contains some information relevant to a particular operation. For example, you may have a requirements document that contains requirements justifying the need for a particular operation, or describing what the operation should do.

In your Rose model, you can attach a file or URL to an operation. Once you've attached a file or URL, you can open the attached file or URL directly from the browser.

To attach a file to an operation:

1. Open the operation specification window (or standard specification window in 98i).

2. Right-click anywhere inside the white space in the Files tab.

3. Select Insert File from the shortcut menu to insert a file.

4. Using the Open dialog box, find the file you wish to attach.

5. Select Open to attach the file to the operation.

OR

1. Right-click the operation in the browser.

2. Select New ➢ File.

3. Using the Open dialog box, find the file you wish to attach.

4. Select Open to attach the file to the operation.

To attach a URL to an operation:

1. Open the operation specification window (or standard specification window in 98i).

2. Right-click anywhere inside the white space in the Files tab.

3. Select Insert URL to insert a URL.

4. Type the name of the URL to attach.

OR

1. Right-click the operation in the browser.

2. Select New ➢ URL.

3. Type the name of the URL to attach.

To open an attached file:

1. Open the operation specification window (or standard specification window in 98i).

2. Double-click the name of the file in the Files tab. Rose will automatically start the appropriate application and load the file.

OR

1. Locate the file in the browser under the appropriate operation.

2. Double-click the filename. Rose will automatically start the appropriate application and load the file.

OR

1. Open the operation specification window (or standard specification window in 98i).

2. Right-click the file in the Files tab.

3. From the shortcut menu, select Open File / URL. Rose will automatically start the appropriate application and load the file.

OR

1. Locate the file in the browser under the appropriate operation.

2. Right-click the file in the browser.

3. From the shortcut menu, select Open. Rose will automatically start the appropriate application and load the file.

To open an attached URL:

1. Open the operation specification window (or standard specification window in 98i).

2. Double-click the name of the URL in the Files tab. Rose will automatically start your Web browser application and load the URL.

OR

1. Locate the URL in the browser under the appropriate operation.

2. Double-click URL name. Rose will automatically start your Web browser application and load the URL.

OR

1. Open the operation specification window (or standard specification window in 98i).

2. Right-click the URL in the Files tab.

3. From the shortcut menu, select Open File / URL. Rose will automatically start your Web browser application and load the URL.

OR

1. Locate the URL in the browser under the appropriate operation.

2. Right-click the URL in the browser.

3. From the shortcut menu, select Open. Rose will automatically start your Web browser application and load the URL.

Displaying Attributes and Operations on Class Diagrams

UML is very flexible; it allows for all details to be shown on a Class diagram, or only those details you'd like to see. In Rose, you can customize your Class diagrams to:

- Show all attributes and operations
- Hide the attributes
- Hide the operations

- Show selected attributes and operations

- Show operation signatures or operation names only

- Show or hide attribute and operation visibility

- Show or hide operation and attribute stereotypes

In the following sections, we'll take a look at each of these options. In a typical project, you'll have many Class diagrams. Some will focus on the relationships, and will show little attribute and operation detail. Others may focus on the classes, and may not show attributes and operations at all. Still others may focus on the attributes and operations, showing all of the detailed information. In Rose, you can place a class on as many Class diagrams as you'd like. You can then use the following options to show or hide the attribute and operation detail.

You can set the defaults for each of these options using the Tools ➢ Options window. The specific instructions for setting the defaults are listed in the sections below.

Showing Attributes

For a given class on a Class diagram, you can:

- Show all attributes

- Hide all attributes

- Show selected attributes

- Suppress attributes

Suppressing the attributes will not only hide the attributes on the diagram, but will remove the line indicating where the attributes would be located in the class. To illustrate the difference between hiding and suppressing attributes, let's look at an example. Here we have employee class with hidden attributes:

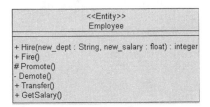

Here, we have the same class, but the attributes have been supressed:

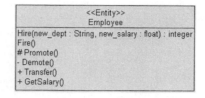

There are two ways to change the attribute display options. You can visit each class individually, setting the appropriate options. Or, you can change the default attribute display options before you create the Class diagram. When you change the defaults, only new diagrams will be affected.

To show all attributes for a class:

1. Select the desired class on a diagram.

2. Right-click on the class to display the shortcut menu.

3. Select Options ➤ Show All Attributes.

   OR

1. Select the desired class on a diagram.

2. Select Edit ➤ Diagram Object Properties ➤ Show All Attributes.

To show selected attributes for a class:

1. Select the desired class on a diagram.

2. Right-click on the class to display the shortcut menu.

3. Select Options ➤ Select Compartment Item.

4. Select the desired attributes in the Edit Compartment window.

   OR

1. Select the desired class on a diagram.

2. Select Edit ➤ Compartment.

3. Select the desired attributes in the Edit Compartment window, as shown in Figure 6.15.

FIGURE 6.15:

Selecting attributes in the Edit Compartment window

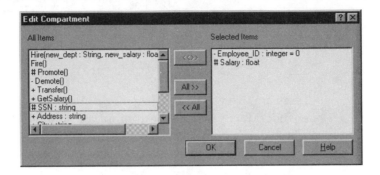

To suppress all attributes for a class on a diagram:

1. Select the desired class.

2. Right-click on the class to display the shortcut menu.

3. Select the Options ➢ Suppress Attributes.

OR

1. Select the desired class on the diagram.

2. Select the Edit ➢ Diagram Object Properties ➢ Suppress Attributes.

To change the default option for showing attributes:

1. Select Tools ➢ Options.

2. Select the Diagram tab.

3. Use the Suppress Attributes and Show All Attributes check boxes to set the default options.

NOTE   When the default is changed, only new diagrams will be affected. Existing Class diagrams will not be changed.

Showing Operations

As with attributes, you have several choices for displaying operations:

- Show all operations
- Show selected operations
- Hide all operations
- Suppress operations

In addition, you have the following options:

- Display operation name only, which will display the operation name on the Class diagram, but hide the operation's arguments and return type.
- Display full operation signature, which will show not only the operation's name, but all of the parameters, parameter data types, and the operation return type.

To show all operations for a class:

1. Select the desired class on a diagram.
2. Right-click on the class to display the shortcut menu.
3. Select the Options ➤ Show All Operations.

OR

1. Select the desired class on a diagram.
2. Select Edit ➤ Diagram Object Properties ➤ Show All Operations.

To show selected operations for a class:

1. Select the desired class on a diagram.
2. Right-click on the class to display the shortcut menu.
3. Select the Options ➤ Select Compartment Items.
4. Select the desired operations in the Edit Compartment window.

OR

1. Select the desired class on a diagram.

2. Select Edit ➤ Compartment.

3. Select the desired operations in the Edit Compartment window, as shown in Figure 6.16.

FIGURE 6.16:

Selecting opertations in the Edit Compartment window

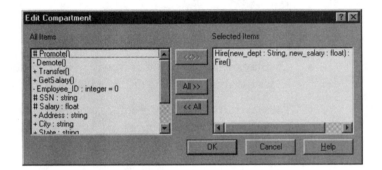

To suppress all operations for a class:

1. Select the desired class on a diagram.

2. Right-click on the class to display the shortcut.

3. Select the Options ➤ Suppress Operations menu.

OR

1. Select the desired class on a diagram.

2. Select the Edit ➤ Diagram Object Properties ➤ Suppress Operations.

To show operation signatures on a Class diagram:

1. Select the desired class on a diagram.

2. Right-click on the class to display the shortcut menu.

3. Select the Options ➤ Show Operation Signature.

OR

1. Select the desired class on a diagram.

2. Select Edit ➤ Diagram Object Properties ➤ Show Operation Signature.

To change the default option for showing operations:

1. Select the Tools ➤ Options.

2. Select the Diagram tab.

3. Use the Suppress Operations, Show All Operations, and Show Operation Signatures check boxes to set the default options.

NOTE   When the default is changed, only new diagrams will be affected. Existing Class diagrams will not be changed.

Showing Visibility

There are four visibility options for attributes and operations: public, private, protected, and package. In UML, these are represented with the +, -, and # for public, private, and protected, and no icon for implementation.

Rather than using UML notation, you can use Rose notation for attribute and operation visibility. The Rose and UML notations for attribute and operation visibility are listed in Table 6.3.

TABLE 6.3: Rose and UML Visibility Notations

Visibility	UML Notation	Rose Notation
Public	+	◈
Private	-	🔒
Protected	#	🔑
Package or Implementation	\<no icon\>	🔖

You can use either UML or Rose notation for visibility, or you can hide the visibility icons altogether.

To show attribute and operation visibility for a class:

1. Select the desired class on a diagram.

2. Right-click on the class to display the shortcut menu.

3. Select the Options ➤ Show Visibility.

OR

1. Select the desired class on a diagram.

2. Select the Edit ➤ Diagram Object Properties ➤ Show Visibility.

To change the default visibility display option:

1. Select the Tools ➤ Options.

2. Select the Diagram tab.

3. Use the Show Visibility check box to set the default option.

To switch between Rose and UML visibility notations:

1. Select the Tools ➤ Options.

2. Select the Notation tab.

3. Use the Visibility as Icons check box to switch between notations. If the check box is selected, Rose notation will be used. If the check box is not selected, UML notation will be used. When you change the default, only new diagrams will be affected. Existing diagrams will not be changed.

Showing Stereotypes

In Rose, you can show or hide the stereotypes of your operations and attributes. If you show the stereotypes, they will be displayed before the attribute and operation names, enclosed in <<>>:

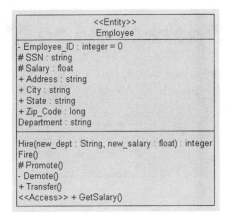

To show attribute and operation stereotypes for a class:

1. Select the desired class on a diagram.

2. Right-click on the class to display the shortcut menu.

3. Select Options ➤ Show Compartment Stereotypes.

OR

1. Select the desired class on the diagram.

2. Select Edit ➤ Diagram Object Properties ➤ Show Compartment Stereotypes.

To change the default stereotype display option:

1. Select the Tools ➤ Options.

2. Select the Diagram tab.

3. Use the Show Stereotypes check box to set the default option.

NOTE   When you change the default, only new diagrams will be affected. Existing diagrams will not be changed.

Mapping Operations to Messages

As we discussed above, each message on a Sequence or Collaboration diagram will be mapped to an operation. If your Sequence diagram looks like this:

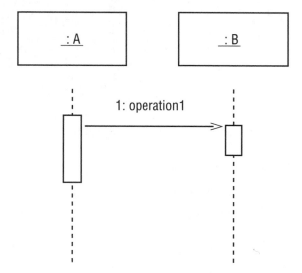

the operation Operation1 will be placed inside Class B. When you first create your Sequence and Collaboration diagrams, you may use message names that are English phrases rather than operation names, as shown in Figure 6.17.

However, as you are identifying operations, you'll want to map each message to the appropriate operation. The Sequence diagram above will be changed to look like Figure 6.18.

Mapping an Operation to a Message on an Interaction Diagram

As you identify operations, go through each message on your Sequence and Collaboration diagrams. Before you generate code, be sure that each message has been mapped to the appropriate operation.

> **NOTE**   Operations can only be mapped to messages if the Interaction Diagram object has been mapped to a class.

FIGURE 6.17:

Sequence diagram with no operation mapping

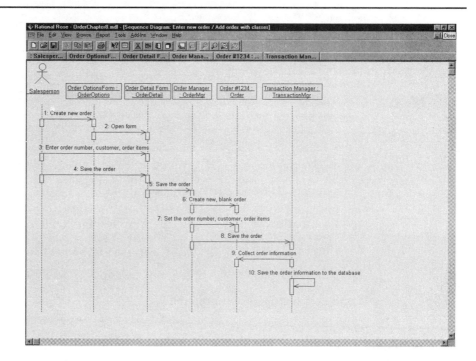

Sequence diagram with operation mapping

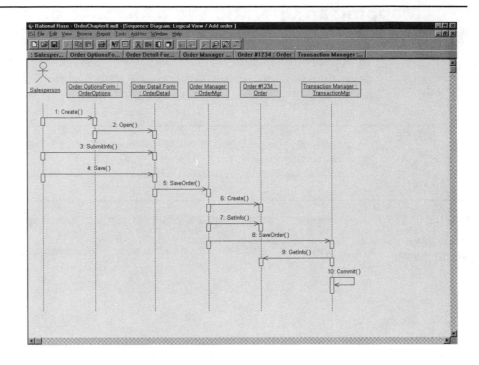

To map a message to an existing operation:

1. Be sure the receiving object (the supplier) has been mapped to a class.

2. Right-click the message in the Sequence or Collaboration diagram.

3. A list of the supplier's operations will appear, as shown in Figure 6.19.

4. Select the operation from the list.

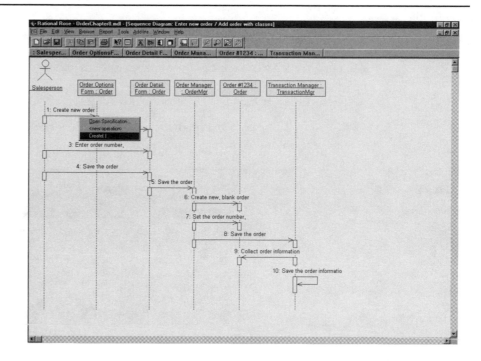

FIGURE 6.19:

Mapping a message to an existing operation

To remove a message's operation mapping:

1. Double-click the message in the sequence or collaboration diagram.

2. In the Name field, delete the operation name and enter the new message name.

To create a new operation for the message:

1. Be sure the receiving object (the supplier) has been mapped to a class.

2. Right-click the message in the Sequence or Collaboration diagram.

3. Select <new operation>.

4. Enter the new operation's name and details. The options available on the operation specification window are discussed in earlier in this chapter.

5. Click OK to close the operation specification window and add the new operation.

6. Right-click the message.

7. Select the new operation from the list that appears.

To ensure each message has been mapped to an operation:

1. Select Report ➤ Show Unresolved Messages.

2. Rose will display a list of all messages that have not yet been mapped to operations, as shown in Figure 6.20.

FIGURE 6.20:

View unresolved messages

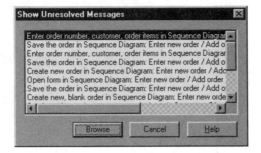

Exercise

In the exercise for Chapter 4, we created some of the operations for the classes in our problem. In the previous exercise, we diagrammed the classes on a Class diagram. In this exercise, we'll add details to the operations, including parameters and return types. We'll also add attributes to the classes.

Problem Statement

Now that Karen had a Class diagram with the classes for the Enter New Order use case, she began to fill in the details. She chose C++ as a programming language, then proceeded to add parameters, data types, and return types to the classes.

She also went back to the flow of events to identify attributes. She added the attributes Order Number and Customer Name to the Order class on the Class diagram. She also took a look at the order items. Because there are many order items on a particular order, and each has some information and behavior, she decided to model order items as a class rather than an attribute of Order.

To keep the model consistent, she updated the Sequence diagram, as shown in Figure 6.21.

FIGURE 6.21:

Updated Sequence diagram

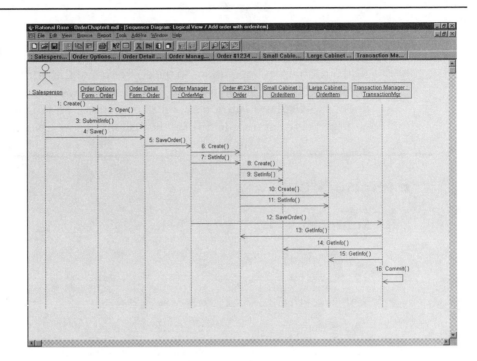

Just then, Bob came in with a requirement change.

"We need to start keeping track of the order date and order fill date. Also, we've got some new suppliers, and the procedure for restocking the inventory has changed quite a bit."

Karen first documented the new date requirements, and took a high-level look at the changes to the restocking procedures. Because she was currently working on the Enter New Order use case, she was primarily concerned with how the procedural changes would affect this use case. She was planning to work on the Restock Inventory use case next month, and would worry about the details of the restocking procedures then. It turned out that the new procedures, while they drastically affected the Restock Inventory use case, didn't affect the Enter New Order use case.

The new date requirements necessitated the addition of a couple of new attributes to the Order class. With these added, the model again reflected the most current requirements.

Add Attributes and Operations

Add attributes and operations to the classes using the Add New Order Class diagram. Add language-specific details to the attributes and operations. Set the options to display all attributes and all operations, and display the operation signatures. Set the options to display the visibility using UML notation.

Exercise Steps:

Setup

1. Select Tools ➤ Options.

2. Select the Diagram tab.

3. Be sure the Show Visibility check box is checked.

4. Be sure the Show Stereotypes check box is checked.

5. Be sure the Show Operation Signatures check box is checked.

6. Be sure the Show All Attributes and Show All Operations check boxes are checked.

7. Be sure the Suppress Attributes and Suppress Operations check boxes are *not* checked.

8. Select the Notation tab.

9. Be sure the Visibility as Icons check box is *not* checked.

Add New Class

1. Locate the Add New Order Class diagram in the browser.

2. Double-click to open the diagram.

3. Select the Class button from the toolbar.

4. Click anywhere inside the diagram to place the new class.

Continued on next page

5. Name the new class **OrderItem**.

6. Set the stereotype of the OrderItem class to **Entity**.

7. Drag the OrderItem class in the browser to the Entities package to move it into that package.

Add Attributes

1. Right-click the Order class.

2. Select New Attribute from the shortcut menu.

3. Enter the new attribute.

OrderNumber : Integer

4. Press Enter.

5. Enter the next attribute.

CustomerName : String

6. Repeat steps 4 and 5 to add these attributes:

OrderDate : Date

OrderFillDate : Date

7. Right-click the OrderItem class.

8. Select New Attribute from the shortcut menu.

9. Enter the new attribute.

ItemID : Integer

10. Press Enter.

11. Enter the next attribute.

ItemDescription : String

Continued on next page

Add Operations to OrderItem Class

1. Right-click the OrderItem class.

2. Select New Operation from the shortcut menu.

3. Enter the new operation.

Create

4. Press Enter.

5. Enter the next operation.

SetInfo

6. Press Enter.

7. Enter the next operation.

GetInfo

Add Operation Details Using the Class Diagram

1. Single-click the Order class to select it.

2. Single-click inside the Order class again to move the cursor inside the class.

3. Edit the Create() operation to read:

Create() : Boolean

4. Edit the SetInfo() operation to read:

SetInfo(OrderNum : Integer, Customer : String, OrderDate : Date, FillDate : Date) : Boolean

5. Edit the GetInfo() operation to read:

GetInfo() : String

Continued on next page

Add Operation Details Using the Browser

1. Locate the OrderItem class in the browser.

2. Click the + next to OrderItem to expand it. The attributes and operations should be visible in the browser.

3. Double-click the GetInfo() operation to open the Operation Specification window, as shown here.

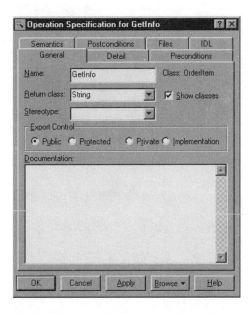

4. In the Return class drop-down list box, select String.

5. Click OK to close the operation specification window.

6. Double-click the SetInfo() operation of the OrderItem class in the browser to open the operation specification window.

7. In the Return class drop-down list box, select Boolean.

8. Select the Detail tab.

Continued on next page

9. Right-click in the white space of the arguments area to add a parameter, as shown below.

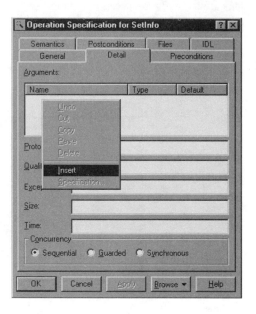

10. Select Insert from the shortcut menu. Rose will add an argument called `argname`.

11. Single-click the word `argname` to select it, and change the argument name to ID.

12. Click in the Type column to open a drop-down list box of types. Select Integer from the drop-down list.

13. Click in the Default column to add a default value. Type 0 in this column.

14. Click OK to close the operation specification window.

15. Double-click the Create() operation of the OrderItem class to open the operation specification window.

16. In the Return class drop-down list box, select Boolean.

17. Click OK to close the operation specification window.

Continued on next page

Add Operation Details Using Either Method

1. Using either the browser or the Class diagram, add details to the operations in the OrderDetail class. The operation signatures should read:

   Open() : Boolean

   SubmitInfo() : Boolean

   Save() : Boolean

2. Using either the browser or the Class diagram, add details to the operations in the OrderOptions class. The operation signatures should read:

   Create() : Boolean

3. Using either the browser or the Class diagram, add details to the operations in the OrderMgr class. The operation signatures should read:

   SaveOrder(OrderID : Integer) : Boolean

4. Using either the browser or the Class diagram, add details to the operations in the TransactionMgr class. The operation signatures should read:

   SaveOrder(OrderID : Integer) : Boolean

   Commit() : Integer

Summary

In this chapter, we looked at the details of classes, including their attributes and operations. We discussed adding attributes, their names, data types, and default values. We also examined operations, including adding them to the model. We looked at operation details such as the arguments, data types, and return types.

So far, we have looked at classes individually. In the next chapter, we will focus on the relationships between the classes. It is this coordination between classes that lets the application do what it needs to do.

Relationships

- Adding association, dependency, aggregation and generalization relationship to a Rose model through a Class diagram

- Adding relationship names, stereotypes, role names, static relationships, friend relationships, qualifiers, link elements, and constraints

- Setting multiplicity, export control, and containment

At this point, we've looked at classes, their attributes, and their operations. In the Interaction diagrams, we began to look at how classes communicate with one another. Now, we'll focus on the relationships between the classes.

A relationship is a semantic connection between classes. It allows one class to know about the attributes, operations, and relationships of another class. In order for one class to send a message to another on a Sequence or Collaboration diagram, there must be a relationship between the two classes.

In this chapter, we'll take a look at the different types of relationships that can be established between classes and between packages. We'll discuss the implications of each type of relationship, and how to add the relationship to your Rose model.

Relationships

This section includes a description of the four types of relationships you can use in a Rose model. We'll also take a look at how to find relationships. Much of the work in finding relationships has already been done by this point in the process. Here, we formally look at relationships and add them to the model. Relationships are shown on Class diagrams.

Types of Relationships

There are four types of relationships you can set up between classes: associations, dependencies, aggregations, and generalizations. We'll take a close look at each of these types of relationships, but let's talk about them briefly here.

Associations are semantic connections between classes. They are drawn on a Class diagram with a single line, as shown in Figure 7.1.

FIGURE 7.1:

Association relationship

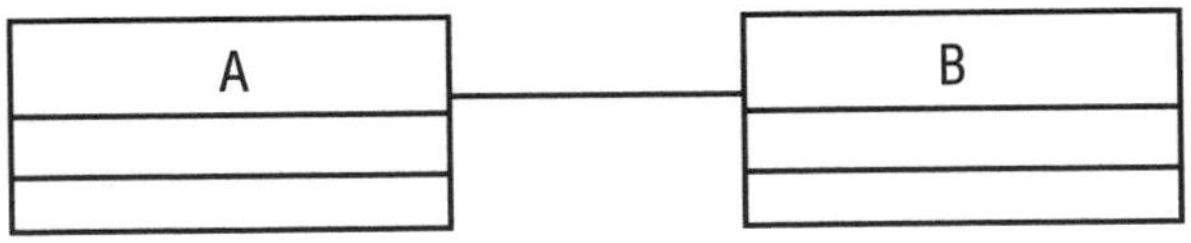

When an association connects two classes, as in the above example, each class can send messages to the other in a Sequence or a Collaboration diagram. Associations can be bi-directional, as shown above, or unidirectional. In UML, bi-directional associations are drawn either with arrowheads on both ends or without arrowheads altogether. Unidirectional associations contain one arrowhead showing the direction of the navigation.

With an association, Rose will place attributes in the classes. For example, if there is an association relationship between a House class and a Person class, Rose would place a person attribute inside House to let the house know who the owner is, and a house attribute inside Person to let the person know which house they own.

Dependencies also connect two classes, but in a slightly different way than associations. Dependencies are always unidirectional and show that one class depends on the definitions in another class. Rose will not generate attributes for the classes in a dependency relationship. Going back to the House example, if there is a dependency from Person to House, rather than an association, Rose will not generate a Person attribute inside House or a House attribute inside Person. However, Person will depend on the definitions in House. Dependencies are shown with dashed arrows, as shown in Figure 7.2.

FIGURE 7.2:

Dependency relationship

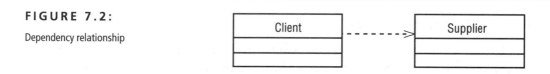

Aggregations are a stronger form of association. An aggregation is a relationship between a whole and its parts. For example, you may have a Car class, as well as an Engine class, a Tire class, and classes for the other parts of a car. In this case, a Car object will be made up of an Engine object, four Tire objects, and so on. Aggregations are shown as a line with a diamond next to the class representing the whole, as shown in Figure 7.3.

FIGURE 7.3:

Aggregation relationship

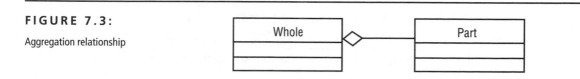

Generalizations are used to show an inheritance relationship between two classes. Most object-oriented languages directly support the concept of inheritance. Inheritance allows one class to inherit all of the attributes, operations, and relationships of another class. In UML, an inheritance relationship is known as a generalization, and is shown as an arrow from the child class to the parent class, as shown in Figure 7.4.

FIGURE 7.4:

Generalization relationship

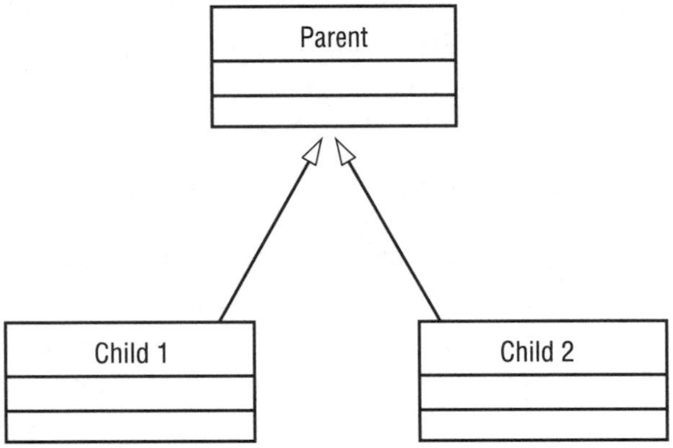

Finding Relationships

To find relationships, you can examine the model elements you've created so far. Much of the relationship information has already been outlined in the Sequence and Collaboration diagrams. Now, you can revisit those diagrams to get association and dependency information. You can then examine your classes to look for aggregations and generalizations.

To find relationships, you can do the following:

1.   Begin by examining your Sequence and Collaboration diagrams. If Class A sends a message to Class B on a Sequence or Collaboration diagram, there must be a relationship between them. Typically, the relationships you find with this method are associations or dependencies.

2.   Examine your classes and look for any whole-part relationships. Any class that is made up of other classes may participate in an aggregation.

3.   Examine your classes to look for generalization relationships. Try to find any class that may have different types. For example, you may have an

Employee class. In your company, there are two different types of employees, hourly and salaried. This may indicate that you should have an HourlyEmp and a SalariedEmp class, each of which inherit from an Employee class. Attributes, operations, and relationships that are common to all employees are placed in the Employee class. Attributes, operations, or relationships that are unique to hourly or salaried employees are placed in the HourlyEmp or SalariedEmp classes.

4. Examine your classes to look for additional generalization relationships. Try to find classes that have a great deal in common. For example, you may have two classes called CheckingAccount and SavingsAccount. Both have similar information and behavior. You can create a third class, called Account, to hold the information and behavior common to a checking and a savings account.

Be cautious of classes with too many relationships. One goal of a well-designed application is to reduce relationships in the system. A class with many relationships may need to know about a great many other classes. It can therefore be harder to reuse and your maintenance effort may also be greater. If any of the other classes change, the original class may be affected.

Associations

An association is a semantic connection between classes. An association allows one class to know about the public attributes and operations of another class. For example, in Figure 7.5, we have a bi-directional association between House and Person.

FIGURE 7.5:

Association relationship

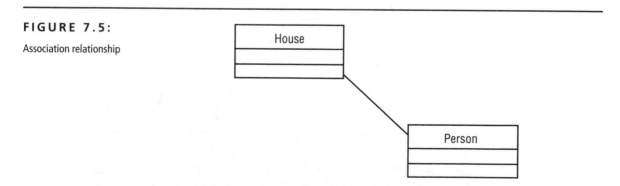

The Person class knows about the public attributes and operations of House, and the House class knows about the public attributes and operations of Person. On a Sequence diagram, therefore, House can send messages to Person, and Person can send messages to House.

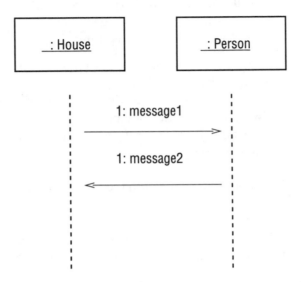

In the example above, the relationship is bi-directional. However, you will want to refine most of your associations to be unidirectional. Unidirectional relationships are easier to build and to maintain, and can help you find classes that can be reused. Let's look at the above example again, but this time the association is unidirectional. Figure 7.6 shows the unidirectional relationship.

FIGURE 7.6:

Unidirectional association relationship

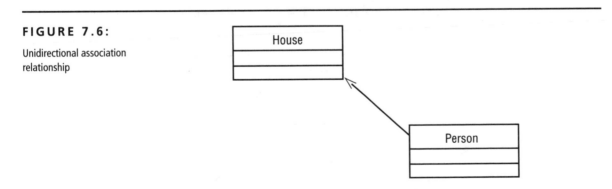

In this case, the Person class knows about the public attributes and operations of House, but House does not know about the public attributes and operations of

Person. Messages on a Sequence or Collaboration diagram can be sent by Person and received by House, but cannot be sent by House.

You can determine the direction of an association by looking at the Sequence and Collaboration diagrams. If every message on the Interaction diagrams is sent by Person and received by House, there is a unidirectional relationship from Person to House. If there is even one relationship from House to Person, you will need a bi-directional relationship.

Unidirectional relationships can help you identify classes that are good candidates for reuse. If the association between Person and House is bi-directional, each class needs to know about the other, so neither can be reused without the other. But assume instead that there is a unidirectional relationship from Person to House. Person needs to know about House, so it can't be reused without House. However, House doesn't need to know about Person, so House can be easily reused. Any class that has a number of unidirectional relationships coming out of it is hard to reuse; any class that has only unidirectional relationships coming into it is easy to reuse, as shown in Figure 7.7.

FIGURE 7.7:

Reuse with unidirectional associations

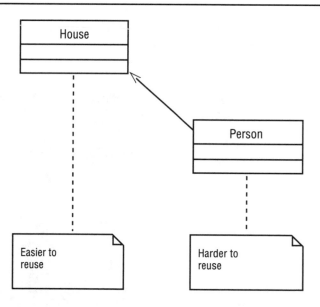

When you generate code for a bi-directional association, Rose will generate attributes in each class. In our Person and House example, Rose will place a Person attribute inside House, and a House attribute inside Person. Figure 7.8 is an example of the code generated for these two classes.

FIGURE 7.8:

Code generated for a bi-directional association

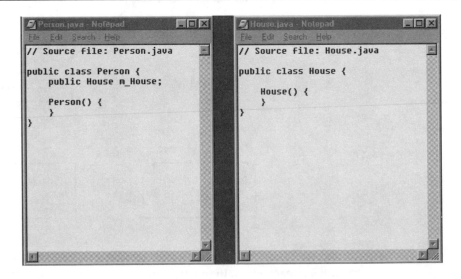

If, instead, we have a unidirectional association, Rose will place a House attribute inside Person, but not a Person attribute inside House. Figure 7.9 is an example of the code generated for a unidirectional association.

FIGURE 7.9:

Code generated for a unidirectional association

```
// Source file: Person.java

public class Person {
    public House m_House;

    Person() {
    }
}
```

```
// Source file: House.java

public class House {

    House() {
    }
}
```

Associations can also be reflexive. A reflexive association suggests that one instance of a class is related to other instances of the same class. For example, we

may have a Person class. One person can be the parent of one or more other people. Because there are separate instances of Person with a relationship to each
other, we have a reflexive association, as shown in Figure 7.10.

FIGURE 7.10:

Reflexive association

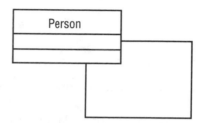

Creating Associations

In Rose, you create associations directly on a Class Diagram. The Diagram toolbar
includes buttons for creating both unidirectional and bi-directional associations.

If you create a bi-directional association, you can later change it to a unidirectional association by changing its navigability. Later in this chapter, in the "Working with Relationships" section, we will discuss the detailed specifications of an
association, including navigability.

To create a bi-directional association on a Class diagram:

1.   Select the Association icon from the toolbox.

2.   Drag the association line from one class to the other class.

   OR

1.   Select Tools ➢ Create ➢ Association.

2.   Drag the association line from one class to the other class.

To create a unidirectional association on a Class diagram:

1. Select the Unidirectional Association icon from the toolbox.

2. Drag the association line from one class to the other class.

OR

1. Select Tools ➢ Create ➢ Unidirectional Association.

2. Drag the association line from one class to the other class.

To set navigability of a relationship:

1. Right-click the desired relationship, at the end to be navigated.

2. Select Navigable from the menu.

OR

1. Open the desired relationship's specification window.

2. Select the Role Detail tab for the end to be navigated.

3. Change the navigability using the Navigable check box.

To create a reflexive association on a Class diagram:

1. Select the Association icon from the toolbox.

2. Drag the association line from the class to somewhere outside of the class.

3. Release the association line.

4. Drag the association line back into the class.

OR

1. Select Tools ➢ Create ➢ Association.

2. Drag the association line from the class to somewhere outside of the class.

3. Release the association line.

4. Drag the association line back into the class.

To add documentation to an association:

1. Double-click the desired association.

2. Select the General tab.

3. Enter documentation in the Documentation field.

   OR

1. Select the desired association.

2. Select Browse ➤ Specification.

3. Select the General tab.

4. Enter documentation in the Documentation field.

To change a relationship to an association:

1. Select the desired relationship.

2. Select Edit ➤ Change Into ➤ Association.

Deleting Associations

There are two ways to delete an association. The first is to delete it from a single diagram. In this case, Rose still knows the association exists, and keeps track of it behind the scenes. Although the association may be deleted from one diagram, it may still exist on other Class diagrams.

The second way to delete an association is to remove it from the entire Rose model. In this case, the relationship is removed from all Class diagrams, and Rose no longer keeps track of it.

To delete an association from the diagram only:

1. Select the desired association.

2. Press the Delete key.

   OR

1. Select the desired association.

2. Select Edit ➤ Delete.

NOTE　　　　Deleting an association from the diagram does not delete it from the model.

To delete an association from the model:

1. Select the desired association.
2. Press Ctrl+D.

OR

1. Select the desired association.
2. Select Edit ➤ Delete from Model.

OR

1. Open the specification window for either class participating in the relationship.
2. Select the Relations tab.
3. Right-click the relationship.
4. Select Delete from the shortcut menu.

Dependencies

A dependency relationship shows that a class references another class. Therefore, a change in the referenced class specification may impact the using class. When there is a dependency between two classes, Rose does not add any attributes to the classes for the relationship. Returning to our example above, assume there is a dependency relationship between Person and House. A dependency relationship is shown as a dashed arrow, as shown in Figure 7.11.

When we generate code for these two classes, attributes will not be added to either class for the relationship, as shown in Figure 7.12. However, any language-specific statements needed to support the relationship will be generated. For example, in C++, the necessary #include statements will be included in the generated code.

FIGURE 7.11:

Dependency relationship

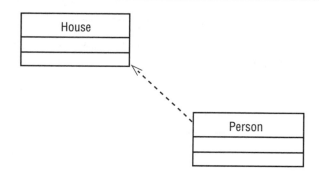

FIGURE 7.12:

Code generated for a
dependency relationship

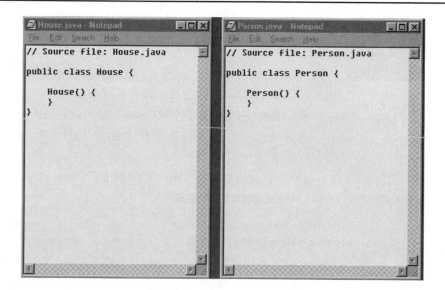

The implication here is that Person will need some other way to know that House exists. The direction of the arrow indicates that Person depends on House. In other words, there is a Sequence or Collaboration diagram in which Person sends a message to House. Had there been a regular association between these two, Person would have a House attribute. To send a message to House, Person would just look at its own House attribute.

With a dependency, however, Person won't have a house attribute. It therefore has to find out about House some other way. There are three ways it can know about House. House could be global, in which case Person would know it exists. Or, House could be instantiated as a local variable inside an operation of Person.

Finally, House could be passed in as a parameter to some operation inside Person. When there is a dependency, one of these three approaches must be taken.

Although we are now at the detailed coding level, this decision may affect the model. We may need to add an argument to an operation of Person.

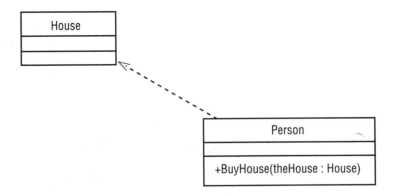

The second difference between an association and a dependency lies in the direction. Associations can be bi-directional, but dependencies are unidirectional. Dependencies are also used for relationships between packages. This will be discussed later in this chapter.

Creating Dependencies

After you've added associations, you may want to revisit them to see if any should be dependencies instead. If so, you can change the relationship from an association to a dependency using the method outlined below.

To create a new dependency, you can use the Dependency icon on the Class diagram toolbar.

To create a dependency on a Class diagram:

1. Select the Dependency icon from the toolbox.

2. Click the class to be dependent.

3. Drag the dependency line to the other class.

OR

1. Select Tools ➤ Create ➤ Dependency.

2. Click the class to be dependent.

3. Drag the dependency line to the other class.

To add documentation to a dependency:

1. Double-click the desired dependency.

2. Select the General tab.

3. Enter documentation in the Documentation field.

OR

1. Select the desired dependency.

2. Select Browse ➤ Specification.

3. Select the General tab.

4. Enter documentation in the Documentation field.

To change a relationship to a dependency on a Class diagram:

1. Select the desired relationship.

2. Select Edit ➤ Change Into ➤ Uses Dependency.

Deleting Dependencies

As with associations, there are two ways to delete a dependency. You can remove it from a single Class diagram, or from the entire model. The following are the procedures for deleting a dependency.

To delete a dependency from the diagram:

1. Select the desired dependency.

2. Press the Delete key.

OR

1.   Select the desired dependency.

2.   Select Edit ➤ Delete.

NOTE   Deleting a dependency from the diagram does not delete it from the model.

To delete a dependency from the model:

1.   Select the desired dependency.

2.   Press Ctrl+D.

OR

1.   Select the desired dependency.

2.   Select Edit ➤ Delete from Model.

OR

1.   Open the specification window for either class participating in the relationship.

2.   Select the Relations tab.

3.   Right-click the relationship.

4.   Select Delete from the shortcut menu.

Package Dependencies

Dependencies can be drawn between packages as well as classes. In fact, a dependency is the only type of relationship drawn between packages. A package dependency, like a class dependency, is drawn as a dashed arrow. Figure 7.13 is an example of a package dependency.

A package dependency from package A to package B suggests that some class in package A has a unidirectional relationship to some class in package B. In other words, some class in A needs to know about some class in B.

FIGURE 7.13:

Package dependency

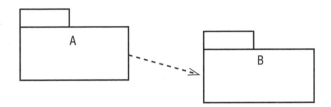

This has reuse implications. If our dependencies look like this, package A depends on package B. Therefore, we can't just pick up package A and reuse it in another application. We would also have to pick up B and reuse it. Package B, on the other hand, is easy to reuse because it doesn't depend on anything else.

You can find package dependencies by examining the relationships on your Class diagram. If two classes from different packages have a relationship, their packages must have a relationship as well.

As you are creating package dependencies, try to avoid circular dependencies whenever possible. A circular dependency looks like Figure 7.14.

FIGURE 7.14:

Circular dependency

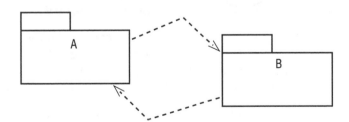

This suggests that some class in A needs to know about some class in B, while some class in B needs to know about some class in A. In this case, neither package can be easily reused, and a change to one package may affect the other. We've lost some of the benefits of packaging classes with this approach—the packages are too interdependent. To break circular dependencies, you can split one package apart into two. In our example, we can take the classes in B that A depended on, and move them to another package we'll call C. Now our package dependencies look like this:

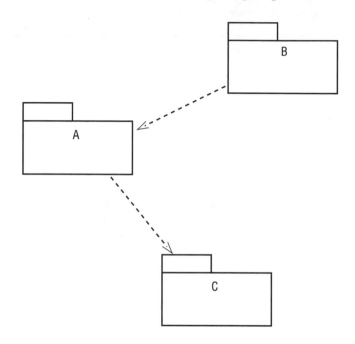

Creating Package Dependencies

As you identify package dependencies, you can add them to your Rose model through a Class diagram. Typically, you will have one Class diagram which displays all of the packages and the relationships between them. As with class dependencies, you use the Dependency toolbar button to draw the relationships.

To create a package dependency on a Class diagram:

1. Select the Dependency icon from the toolbox.

2. Drag the dependency line from the dependent package to the other package.

    OR

1. Select Tools ➤ Create ➤ Dependency.

2. Drag the dependency line from the dependent package to the other package.

Deleting Package Dependencies

As before, there are two ways to delete a package dependency—from a single Class diagram or from the entire model.

If you delete a package dependency, but classes from the two packages still have relationships to each other, you will have difficulty generating code. You can use the Report ➤ Show Access Violations option to see if this has happened.

To delete a package dependency on a Class diagram:

1. Select the desired package dependency.
2. Press the Delete key.

OR

1. Select the desired package dependency.
2. Select Edit ➤ Delete.

Aggregations

An aggregation is a stronger form of association. An aggregation is a relationship between a whole and its parts. For example, an EmployeeList might be made up of Employees. In UML, an aggregation is shown as a line connecting the two classes, with a diamond next to the class representing the whole, as shown in Figure 7.15.

FIGURE 7.15:

Aggregation relationship

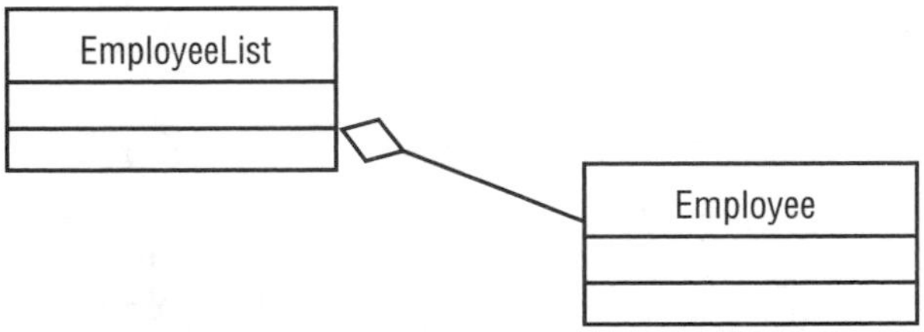

One class may have several aggregation relationships with other classes. For example, a Car class might have relationships to its parts.

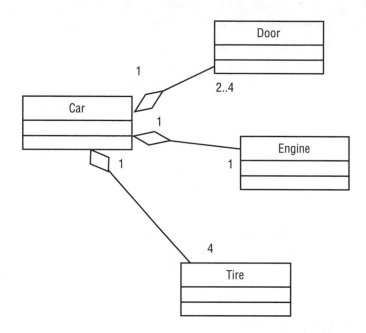

Like associations, aggregations can be reflexive, as shown in Figure 7.16. A reflexive aggregation suggests that one instance of a class is made up of one or more other instances of the same class. For example, when cooking, you may combine some ingredients, which form ingredients for other things. In other words, each ingredient can be made up of other ingredients.

FIGURE 7.16:

Reflexive aggregation relationship

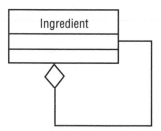

When you generate code for an aggregation, Rose will generate attributes to support the aggregation. In the Car example, the Car class will have attributes for the door, engine, tire, and all of the other parts in the aggregation relationship.

Creating Aggregations

Aggregations are created on the Class diagrams. To create an aggregation, you can use the Aggregation button on the Class diagram toolbar.

To create an aggregation on a Class diagram:

1. Select the Aggregation icon from the toolbox.

2. Drag the aggregation line from the class to the parent class.

OR

1. Select Tools ➤ Create ➤ Aggregation.

2. Drag the aggregation line from the class to the parent class.

To create a reflexive aggregation on a Class diagram:

1. Select the Aggregation icon from the toolbox.

2. Drag the aggregation line from the class to somewhere outside of the class.

3. Release the aggregation line.

4. Drag the aggregation line back into the class.

OR

1. Select Tools ➤ Create ➤ Aggregation.

2. Drag the aggregation line from the class to somewhere outside of the class.

3. Release the aggregation line.

4. Drag the aggregation line back into the class.

To add documentation to the aggregation:

1. Double-click the desired aggregation.

2. Select the General tab.

3. Enter documentation in the Documentation field.

OR

1. Select the desired aggregation.

2. Select Browse ➤ Specification.

3. Select the General tab.

4. Enter documentation in the Documentation field.

To change a relationship to an aggregation on a Class diagram:

1. Select the desired relationship.

2. Select Edit ➤ Change Into ➤ Aggregation.

OR

1. Open the relationship specification window for the desired relationship.

2. Select the Role Detail tab.

3. Select the aggregate check box.

Deleting Aggregations

You can either delete an aggregation from a single Class diagram, or from the entire model. Here we list the procedures for both.

To delete an aggregation from the diagram:

1. Select the desired aggregation.

2. Press the Delete key.

OR

1. Select the desired aggregation.

2. Select Edit ➤ Delete.

Deleting an aggregation from the diagram does not delete it from the model.

To delete an aggregation from the model:

1.   Select the desired aggregation.

2.   Press Ctrl+D.

OR

1.   Select the desired aggregation.

2.   Select Edit ➤ Delete from Model.

OR

1.   Open the Specification window for either class participating in the relationship.

2.   Select the Relations tab.

3.   Right-click the relationship.

4.   Select Delete from the shortcut menu.

Generalizations

A generalization is an inheritance relationship between two classes. It allows one class to inherit the public and protected attributes and operations of another class. For example, we may have the relationship shown in Figure 7.17.

FIGURE 7.17:

Generalization relationship

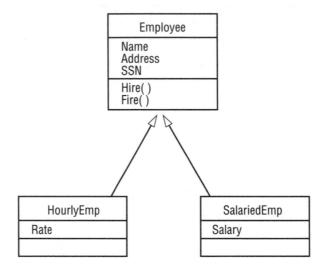

In this example, we have two types of employees: hourly and salaried, both of which inherit from the Employee class. The Employee class is known as the *superclass*, and the HourlyEmp and SalariedEmp classes are known as the *subclasses*. The arrow points from the subclass to the superclass.

The elements that are common to both types are placed in the Employee class. Both HourlyEmp and SalariedEmp inherit the Name, Address, and SSN attributes of the Employee class, and the Hire() and Fire() operations of the Employee class.

Each subclass can have its own unique attributes, operations, and relationships in addition to those it inherits. For example, only hourly employees have an hourly rate, and only salaried employees have a salary.

Generalization relationships can save a great deal of time and effort in both development and maintenance. In the above example, you don't need to program and maintain two separate copies of the Hire() operation—one in HourlyEmp and one in SalariedEmp. Instead, you can create and maintain one copy of the operation. Any changes you make to the operation will be automatically inherited by HourlyEmp and SalariedEmp, and any other subclasses of Employee.

When you are defining your generalizations, you can build your inheritance structure either from the top down or the bottom up. To build the structure from the top down, look for classes that might have different types. For example, you would have started with the Employee class and realized that there are different types of employees. To build the structure from the bottom up, look for classes with commonality. Here, you would have started with the HourlyEmp and SalariedEmp classes, and realized that they were similar. You would then have created an Employee class to hold the common elements.

Be careful not to create an inheritance structure that isn't maintainable. A hierarchy with too many layers can become very difficult to maintain. Every change toward the top of the structure will ripple down through the hierarchy to the classes below. While this can be an advantage, it can make change analysis and control even more essential. In some languages, too many layers can also slow down the application.

Creating Generalizations

As you discover generalization relationships, you can add them to your Rose model using a Class diagram. Frequently, an organization will create a single Class diagram or two that are dedicated to the inheritance structure. These Class diagrams will typically show only limited attribute or operation information.

As you add generalizations, you may need to move some of the attributes and operations. For example, you may have started with the HourlyEmp and SalariedEmp classes, each of which had an attribute called Address. Now, you'll want to move the Address attribute up the structure to the Employee class. In the browser, you can drag the Address attribute from either the HourlyEmp or the SalariedEmp class to the Employee class. Be sure to remember to remove the other copy of Address from HourlyEmp or SalariedEmp.

To create a generalization on a Class diagram:

1. Select the Generalization icon from the toolbox.

2. Drag the generalization line from the subclass to the superclass.

   OR

1. Select Tools ➣ Create ➣ Inherits.

2. Drag the generalization line from the subclass to the superclass.

To add documentation to a generalization:

1. Double-click the desired generalization.

2. Select the General tab.

3. Enter Documentation in the Documentation field.

OR

1. Select the desired generalization.

2. Select Browse ➤ Specification.

3. Select the General tab.

4. Enter documentation in the Documentation field.

To change a relationship to a generalization:

1. Select the desired relationship.

2. Select Edit ➤ Change Into ➤ Inherits.

Deleting Generalizations

As with the other relationships, you can delete a generalization from a single diagram or from the model. If you delete a generalization from the entire model, keep in mind that the attributes, operations, and relationships of the superclass will no longer be inherited by the subclass. Therefore, if the subclass needs those attributes, operations, or relationships, they will have to be added to the subclass.

To delete a generalization from the diagram:

1. Select the desired generalization.

2. Press the Delete key.

OR

1. Select the desired generalization.

2. Select Edit ➤ Delete.

NOTE   Deleting a generalization from the diagram does not delete it from the model.

To delete a generalization from the model:

1. Select the desired generalization.

2. Press Ctrl+D.

OR

1. Select the desired generalization.

2. Select Edit ➤ Delete from Model.

OR

1. Open the specification window for either class participating in the relationship.

2. Select the Relations tab.

3. Right-click the relationship.

4. Select Delete from the shortcut menu.

Working with Relationships

In this section, we'll take a look at the detailed specifications of the relationships in Rose. In your model, you can add things like association names, role names, and qualifiers to specify why the relationship exists.

Before you generate code, you should specify the relationship multiplicity— otherwise Rose will provide a default. Most of the other specifications we present in this section are optional. Rose will notify you if a required specification has not been set when you attempt to generate code.

Setting Multiplicity

Multiplicity indicates how many instances of one class are related to a single instance of another class at a given point in time.

For example, if we're looking at a course registration system for a university, we may have classes called Course and Student. There is a relationship between them; courses have students and students have courses. The questions answered by the multiplicity are "How many courses can a student take at one time?" and "How many students can be enrolled in a single course at one time?"

Because the multiplicity answers both questions, the multiplicity indicators are included at both ends of the relationship. In the course registration example, we decide that each student can be enrolled in zero to four classes, and each course can have 10 to 20 students. On a Class diagram, this would be shown as in Figure 7.18.

FIGURE 7.18:

Relationship multiplicity

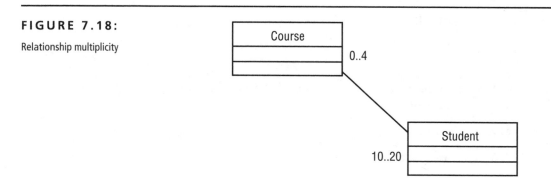

The 0..4 means that each student can be enrolled in zero through four classes, and the 10..20 means that each class can have 10 to 20 students.

UML notations for multiplicity are as follows:

Multiplicity	Meaning
*	Many
0	Zero
1	One
0..*	Zero or more
1..*	One or more
0..1	Zero or one
1..1	Exactly one

Or, you can enter your own multiplicity, using one of the following formats:

Format	Meaning
<number>	Exactly <number>
<number 1>..<number 2>	Between <number 1> and <number 2>
<number>..n	<number> or more
<number 1>,<number 2>	<number 1> or <number 2>
<number 1>, <number 2>..<number 3>	Exactly <number 1> or between <number 2> and <number 3>
<number 1>..<number 2>,<number 3>..<number 4>	Between <number 1> and <number 2> or between <number 3> and <number 4>

Keep in mind that the multiplicity settings will let you know whether the relationship is optional. In our example above, a student can take from zero to four courses at any one time. Therefore, someone is still considered a student if they have taken a semester off. Had the multiplicity been 1..4 instead, every student would be required to take at least one course per semester. The multiplicity, therefore, implements business rules such as "every student must take at least one course per semester."

Typically, multiplicity between forms, screens, or windows will be 0..1 on each side of the relationship. Although this doesn't always hold true, this multiplicity would indicate that each form can exist independently of the other.

To set relationship multiplicity:

1. Right-click the desired relationship, on one end.

2. Select Multiplicity from the shortcut menu.

3. Select the desired multiplicity.

4. Repeat steps 1–3 for the other end of the relationship.

OR

1. Open the desired relationship's specification window.

2. Select the Role Detail tab for one end.

3. Change the multiplicity using the cardinality field.

4. Repeat steps 1–3 for the other end of the relationship.

Using Relationship Names

Relationships can be refined using relationship names or role names. A relationship name is usually a verb or verb phrase that describes why the relationship exists. For example, we may have an association between a Person class and a Company class. From this, though, we might ask the question: why does this relationship exist? Is the person a customer of the company, an employee, or an owner? We can name the relationship *employs* to specify why the relationship exists. Figure 7.19 is an example of a relationship name.

FIGURE 7.19:

Relationship name

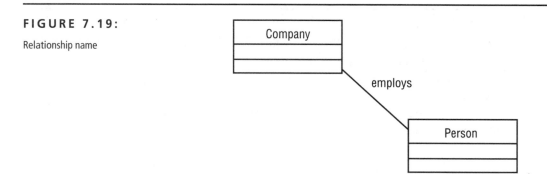

Relationship names are optional, and are typically used only when the reason for the relationship is not obvious. Relationship names are shown along the relationship line.

In Rose, you can also set the relationship direction. In the example above, we can say the company employs the person, but can't say that the person employs the company. In the relationship specification window, you can set the name direction.

To set the relationship name:

1. Select the desired relationship.

2. Type in the desired name.

OR

1. Open the desired relationship's specification window.

2. Select the General tab.

3. Enter the name in the name field.

To set the name direction:

1. Open the desired relationship's specification window.

2. Select the Detail tab.

3. Set the name direction using the name direction field.

Using Stereotypes

Like other model elements, you can assign a stereotype to a relationship. Stereotypes are used to classify relationships. You may, for example, have two types of associations you frequently use. You can create stereotypes for these association types. Stereotypes are shown along the association line enclosed in <<>>. To set the relationship stereotype, you can use the General tab of the relationship specification window, as shown in Figure 7.20.

FIGURE 7.20:

Relationship specification window

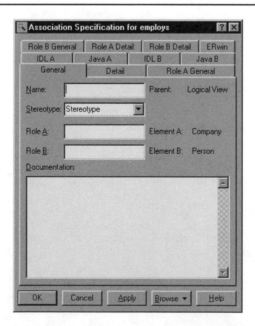

To set a relationship stereotype:

1. Open the desired relationship's specification window.

2. Select the General tab.

3. Enter the stereotype in the stereotype field.

Using Roles

Role names can be used in associations or aggregations instead of relationship names to describe the reason the relationship exists. Returning to our Person and Company example, we can say that a Person playing the role of an employee is related to a Company. Role names are typically nouns or noun phrases, and are shown next to the class playing the role. Typically, you would use a relationship name or a role name, but not both. Like relationship names, role names are optional, and are only used when the purpose of the relationship is not obvious. Figure 7.21 shows an example of roles.

FIGURE 7.21:

Roles in a relationship

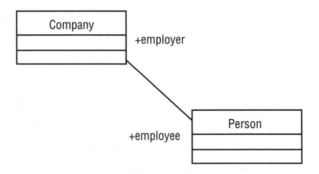

You can add documentation to a role using the relationship specification window. Any documentation you add to a role will be generated as a comment when you generate code. To view the role on the diagram, right-click the relationship and select Role name, as shown in Figure 7.22.

To set a role name:

1. Right-click the desired association, on the end to be named.

2. Select role Name from the shortcut menu.

3. Type in the role name.

Setting role documentation

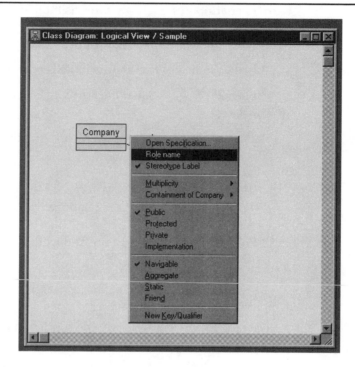

OR

1. Open the desired association's specification window.

2. Select the Role General tab for the role to be named.

3. Enter the role name in the Role field.

To add role documentation:

1. Open the desired association's specification window.

2. Select the Role General tab for the desired role.

3. Enter the documentation in the Documentation field.

Setting Export Control

In an association relationship, Rose will create attributes when you generate code. The visibility of the generated attributes is set through the Export Control field. As with other attributes, there are four visibility options:

Public   Indicates that the attribute will be visible to all other classes

Private   Indicates that the attribute is not visible to any other class

Protected   Suggests that the attribute is visible only to the class and its subclasses

Package or Implementation   Means that the attribute is visible to all other classes in the same package

In a bi-directional relationship, you can set the Export Control of two attributes, one created at each end of the relationship. In a unidirectional relationship, only one will need to be set. The Export Control can be set using the Role A General and Role B General tabs of the relationship specification window.

To set export control for a role:

1.   Right-click the desired role's name.

2.   Select the Export Control from the shortcut menu.

OR

1.   Open the desired relationship's specification window, as shown in Figure 7.23.

2.   Select the Role General tab for the desired role.

3.   Set the Export Control to Public, Protected, Private, or Implementation.

Using Static Relationships

As we mentioned above, Rose will generate attributes for association and aggregation relationships. The Static field determines whether the generated attributes will be static. A static attribute is one that is shared by all instances of a class.

FIGURE 7.23:

Setting export control

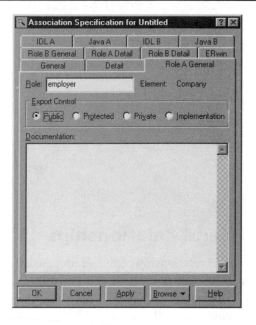

If you set one of the roles to be static, the associated attribute that is generated will be static. On the Class diagram, the static role will appear with a $ in front of it, as shown in Figure 7.24.

To classify an association as static:

1. Right-click the desired end of the association to be static.

2. Select Static from the pop-up menu.

OR

1. Open the desired association's specification window.

2. Select the Detail tab for the role to be static.

3. Select the Static check box.

FIGURE 7.24:

Static role

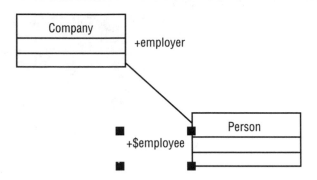

Using Friend Relationships

A friend relationship indicates that the Client class has access to the non-public attributes and operations of the Supplier class. You can set the friend property for an association, aggregation, dependency, or generalization. The source code for the Supplier class will include logic to allow the Client class to have friend visibility.

For example, say we have a unidirectional association from a Person class to a Company class, and we've set the Friend check box for the relationship. When we generate C++ code, the Company .H file will include the line *friend class Person*. This suggests that the Person class has access to the non-public parts of the Company class.

To classify a relationship as a friend:

1. Right-click the appropriate end of the desired relationship.

2. Select Friend from the pop-up menu.

OR

1. Open the desired relationship's specification window.

2. Select the Role Detail tab for the appropriate end.

3. Select the Friend check box.

Setting Containment

The Containment of Button field determines whether the generated attributes of an aggregation will be contained by value or by reference. In an aggregation, the *whole* class will have attributes added for each of the *part* classes. Whether these attributes are *by value* or *by reference* is set here.

A By Value attribute suggests that the whole and the part are created and destroyed at the same time. For example, if there is a by value aggregation between a window and a button, the window and button are created and destroyed at the same time. In UML, a by value aggregation is shown with a filled diamond, as shown in Figure 7.25.

FIGURE 7.25:

By value aggregation

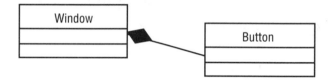

A *by reference* aggregation suggests that the whole and the part are created and destroyed at different times. If we have an EmployeeList class that is made up of Employees, a by reference aggregation would suggest that the Employee may or may not be around in memory, and the EmployeeList may or may not be around in memory. If they are both there, they are related via an aggregation. The Employee and EmployeeList are created and destroyed at different times. A by reference aggregation is shown with a clear diamond, as in Figure 7.26.

To set containment:

1. Right-click the desired end of the association to set containment.

2. Select Containment from the popup menu.

3. Select the containment as By Reference, By Value, or Unspecified.

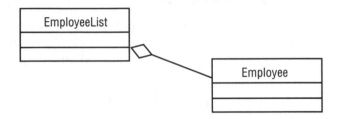

OR

1. Open the desired relationship's specification window.

2. Select the Role Detail tab for the desired role.

3. Select the containment as By Reference, By Value, or Unspecified, as shown in Figure 7.27.

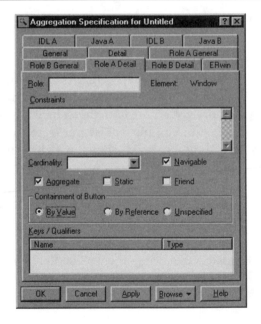

Using Qualifiers

A qualifier is used to reduce the scope of an association. For example, we may have an association between a Person class and a Company class. Suppose we want to say that for a given value of Person ID, there are exactly two related companies. We can add a qualifier called Person ID to the Person class. The diagram would look like Figure 7.28.

FIGURE 7.28:

Using a qualifier

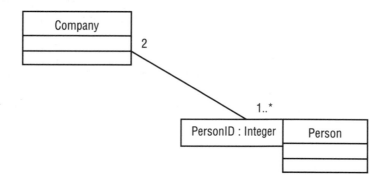

To add a qualifier:

1. Right-click the desired association at the end to add a qualifier.
2. Select New Key/Qualifier from the pop-up menu.
3. Enter the new qualifier's name and type.

OR

1. Open the desired association's specification window.
2. Select the Role Detail tab for the desired role.
3. Right-click the Keys/Qualifiers box.
4. Select Insert from the pop-up menu.
5. Enter the new qualifier's name and type.

To delete a qualifier:

1. Open the desired association's specification window.

2. Select the Role Detail tab for the desired role.

3. Right-click the qualifier to be deleted.

4. Select Delete from the pop-up menu.

Using Link Elements

A *link element*, also known as an Association class, is a place to store attributes related to an association. For example, we may have two classes, Student and Course. Where should the attribute Grade be placed? If it is inside the Student class, we will need to add an attribute to Student for every course the student is enrolled in. This can clutter the Student class. If we put the attribute in Course, we will need an additional attribute for every student enrolled in the course.

To get around this problem, we can create an Association class. The attribute Grade, because it's more related to the link between a student and a course than to each individually, can be placed in this new class. UML notation for an association class is shown in Figure 7.29.

FIGURE 7.29:

Link element (association class)

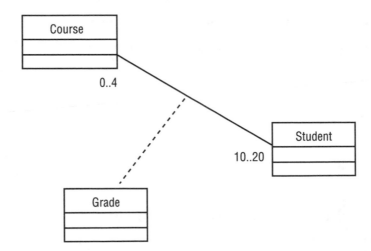

To set a link element for the relationship:

1. Open the desired relationship's specification window.

2. Select the Detail tab.

3. Set the link element using the Link Element field.

Using Constraints

A constraint is some condition that must be true. In Rose, you can set constraints for the relationship or for a single role. Any constraints you enter will be generated as comments in the generated code.

To set a relationship constraint:

1. Open the desired relationship's specification window, as shown in Figure 7.30.

2. Select the Detail tab.

3. Enter constraints in the Constraints field.

FIGURE 7.30:

Relationship constraints

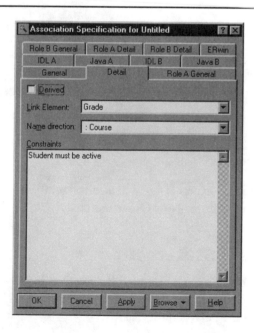

To add constraints to a role:

1. Open the desired relationship's specification window.

2. Select the Role Detail tab for the desired role.

3. Enter the constraints in the Constraints field, as shown in Figure 7.31.

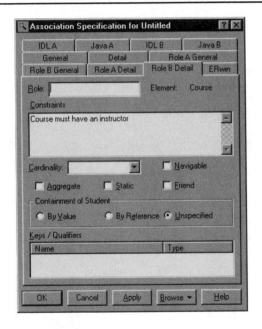

Exercise

In this exercise, we will add the relationships between the classes that participate in the Enter New Order use case.

Problem Statement

Once Karen had added the attributes and operations to the classes, she was nearly ready to generate code. First, though, she had to take a look at the relationships between the classes.

She examined the Sequence diagrams for adding an order to find the relationships. Any classes that communicated in the Sequence diagram needed a relationship on the Class diagram. Once she identified the relationships, she added them to the model.

Adding Relationships

Add relationships to the classes that participate in the Enter New Order use case.

Exercise Steps:

Setup

1. Locate the Add New Order Class diagram in the browser.

2. Double-click to open the diagram.

3. Look for a Unidirectional Association button on the Diagram toolbar. If one does not exist, continue through step 5. Otherwise, skip to the next section of the exercise.

4. Right-click the Diagram toolbar and select Customize from the shortcut menu.

5. Add the button labeled Creates A Unidirectional Association to the toolbar.

Add Associations

1. Select the Unidirectional Association toolbar button.

2. Draw an association from the OrderOptions class to the OrderDetail class.

3. Repeat steps 1 and 2 to draw the following associations:

- From OrderDetail to OrderMgr

- From OrderMgr to Order

- From OrderMgr to TransactionMgr

- From TransactionMgr to Order

- From TransactionMgr to OrderItem

- From Order to OrderItem

4. Right-click the unidirectional association between the OrderOptions class and the OrderDetail class, near the OrderOptions class.

Continued on next page

5. Select Multiplicity ➤ Zero or One from the shortcut menu.

6. Right-click the other end of the unidirectional association.

7. Select Multiplicity ➤ Zero or One from the shortcut menu.

8. Repeat steps 4 through 7 to add the remaining multiplicity to the diagram, as shown in Figure 7.32.

FIGURE 7.32:

Associations for Add New Order use case

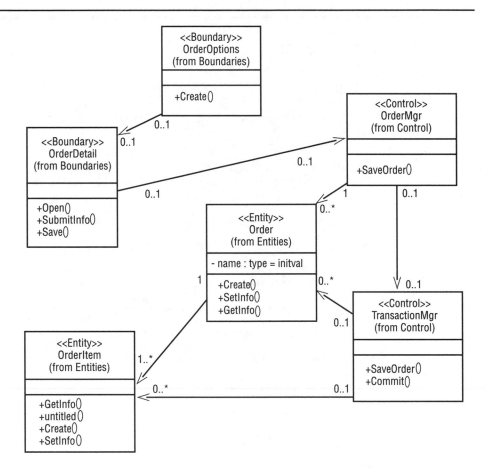

Summary

In this chapter, we discussed the different types of relationships in UML—associations, dependencies, aggregations, and generalizations. Each of these types of relationships can be added to a Rose model through a Class diagram.

Once the relationships have been added, you can add various details, such as relationship names, role names, qualifiers, and multiplicity. In the next chapter, we'll take a look at object behavior. We'll focus in on a single class to examine the various states in which the class can exist, and how the class transitions from one state to another.

CHAPTER

EIGHT

8

Object Behavior

- Creating a State Transition Diagram

- Adding Activities, Entry Actions, Exit Actions, Events, and State Histories to States

- Adding Events Arguments, Guarding Conditions, Actions, and Send Events to Transitions

- Adding Start, Stop, and Nested States

We've looked at classes and their relationships; we'll now examine the life of a single object. A given object can exist in one or more states. For example, an employee can be employed, fired, on probation, on leave, or retired. An Employee object may behave differently in each of these states.

In this chapter, we'll discuss State Transition diagrams, which include information about the various states in which an object can exist, how the object transitions from one state to another, and how the object behaves differently in each of the states.

State Transition Diagrams

A State Transition diagram shows the life cycle of a single object, from the time it is created until it is destroyed. These diagrams are a good way to model the dynamic behavior of a class. In a typical project, you do not create a State Transition diagram for every class. In fact, many projects do not use them at all. Figure 8.1 is an example of a State Transition diagram for a Course class.

FIGURE 8.1:

State Transition diagram for a Course class

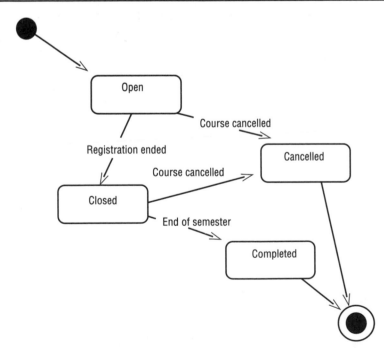

If you have a class that has some significant dynamic behavior, it can be help-ful to create a State Transition diagram for it. A class with significant dynamic behavior is one that can exist in many states. In our Course example above, a Course object can be open, closed, cancelled, or completed. In the exercise for this chapter, we'll look at the Order class. An Order object can exist in several states, including pending, filled, and canceled. An order will behave differently in each of these states.

To decide whether a class has significant dynamic behavior, begin by looking at its attributes. Consider how an instance of the class might behave differently with different values in an attribute. If you have an attribute called Status, this can be a good indicator of various states. How does the object behave differently as differ-ent values are placed in this attribute?

You can also examine the relationships of a class. Look for any relationships with a zero in the multiplicity. Zeroes indicate that the relationship is optional. Does an instance of the class behave differently when the relationship does or does not exist? If it does, you may have multiple states. For example, let's look at a relationship between a person and a company. If there is a relationship, the per-son is in an employed state. If there is no relationship, the person may be fired or retired.

In Rose, no source code is generated from a State Transition diagram. These diagrams serve to document the dynamic behavior of a class so that developers and analysts will have a clear understanding of this behavior. The developers are ultimately responsible for implementing the logic outlined in this diagram. As with the other UML diagrams, State Transition diagrams give the team a chance to discuss and document the logic before it is coded.

Creating a State Transition Diagram

In Rose, you can create one State Transition diagram per class. All of the states and transitions for the class appear on this diagram. In the browser, the State Transition diagram appears underneath the class. The Rose icon for a State Tran-sition diagram in the browser is shown below:

To create a State Transition diagram:

1. Right-click the desired class in the browser.

2. Select Open State Diagram from the pop-up menu.

OR

1. Select the desired class in a Class diagram.

2. Select Browse ➤ State Diagram.

Adding States

A *state* is one of the possible conditions in which an object may exist. As we discussed above, you can examine two areas to determine the state of an object: the values of the attributes and the relationships to other objects. Consider the different values that can be placed in the attributes and the state of the object if a relationship does or does not exist.

As with other Rose elements, you can add documentation to a state. However, because code is not generated from these diagrams, comments will not be inserted into generated code for state documentation.

In UML, a state is shown as a rounded rectangle:

> State

To add a state:

1. Select State from the toolbox toolbar.

2. Click on the State Transition diagram where the state should appear.

OR

1. Select Tools ➤ Create ➤ State.

2. Click on the State Transition diagram where the state should appear.

To add documentation to a state:

1. Double-click the desired state to open the state specification window.

2. Select the General tab.

3. Enter documentation in the Documentation field.

OR

1. Select the desired state.

2. Select Browse ➢ Specification.

3. Select the General tab.

4. Enter documentation in the Documentation field.

Adding State Details

While an object is in a particular state, there may be some activity that it performs. A report may be generated, some calculation may occur, or an event may be sent to another object. In Rose, you can include this type of information in the model through the state specification window.

There are five types of information you can include for a state: an activity, an entry action, an exit action, an event, or state history. Let's look at each of these in the context of an example. Figure 8.2 is the State Transition diagram for an Account class of an ATM system.

Activity

An *activity* is some behavior that an object carries out while it is in a particular state. For example, when an account is in the closed state, the account holder's signature card is pulled. An activity is an interruptible behavior. It may run to completion while the object is in that state, or may be interrupted by the object moving to another state.

An activity is shown inside the state itself, preceded by the word *do* and a colon.

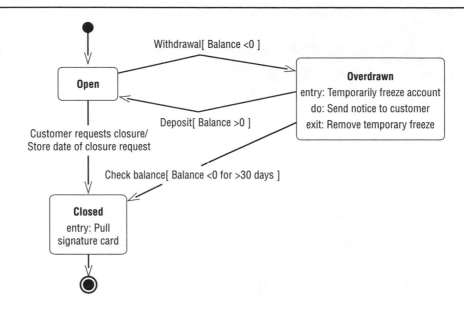

FIGURE 8.2:

Transition diagram for an
Account class of an ATM
system

Entry Action

An *entry action* is a behavior that occurs while the object is transitioning into the state. Let's look at the account example. When an account moves into the overdrawn state, no matter where it came from, the "Temporarily freeze account" entry action occurs. The action, however, doesn't occur after the object has moved to the overdrawn state. Instead, it happens as part of the transition into the state. Unlike an activity, an entry action is considered to be noninterruptible.

An entry action is shown inside the state, preceded by the word *entry* and a colon.

Exit Action

An *exit action* is similar to an entry action. However, an exit action occurs as part of the transition out of a state. In the account example, when an account leaves the overdrawn state, no matter where it goes, the Remove Temporary Freeze exit action occurs as part of the transition. Like an entry action, an exit action is considered to be noninterruptible.

An exit action is shown inside the state, preceded by the word *exit* and a colon.

```
 _____
| State        |
| exit: action |
 ‾‾‾‾‾‾‾
```

The behavior in an activity, entry action, or exit action can include sending an event to some other object. For example, the account object may be sending an event to a card reader object. In this case, the activity, entry action, or exit action is preceded by a ^. The diagram would then read:

Do: ^Target.Event(Arguments)

where Target is the object receiving the event, Event is the message being sent, and Arguments are parameters of the message being sent. In Rose, you can add all of these details to a send event.

An activity may also happen as a result of some event being received. For example, an account may be in the open state. When some event occurs, the activity will be run.

All of these items can be added to your Rose model through the Detail tab of the state specification window, as shown in Figure 8.3.

To add an activity:

1. Open the specification window for the desired state.

2. Select the Detail tab.

3. Right-click on the Actions box.

4. Select Insert from the popup menu.

5. Double-click the new action.

6. Enter the action in the Actions field.

7. In the When box, select Entry Until Exit to make the new action an activity.

FIGURE 8.3:

State Specification window

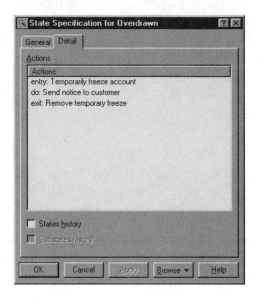

To add an entry action:

1.   Open the specification window for the desired state.

2.   Select the Detail tab.

3.   Right-click on the Actions box.

4.   Select Insert from the pop-up menu.

5.   Double-click the new action.

6.   Enter the action in the Actions field.

7.   In the When box, select On Entry.

To add an exit action:

1.   Open the specification window for the desired state.

2.   Select the Detail tab.

3.   Right-click on the Actions box.

4.   Select Insert from the pop-up menu.

5. Double-click the new action.

6. Enter the action in the Actions field.

7. In the When box, select On Exit.

To send an event:

1. Open the specification window for the desired state.

2. Select the Detail tab.

3. Right-click the Actions box.

4. Select Insert from the pop-up menu.

5. Double-click the new action.

6. Select Send Event as the type.

7. Enter the event, arguments, and target in their respective fields.

Adding Transitions

A *transition* is a movement from one state to another. The set of transitions on a diagram shows how the object moves from one state to another. On the diagram, each transition is drawn as an arrow from the originating state to the succeeding state.

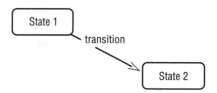

Transitions can also be reflexive. Something may happen that causes an object to transition back to the state it is currently in. Reflexive transitions are shown as an arrow starting and ending on the same state.

To add a transition:

1. Select Transition from the Toolbox toolbar.

2. Click on the state where the transition begins.

3. Drag the transition line to the state where the transition ends.

To add a reflexive transition:

1. Select Transition to Self from the Toolbox toolbar.

2. Click on the state where the reflexive transition occurs.

OR

1. Select Tools ➣ Create ➣ Loop.

2. Click on the state where the reflexive transition occurs.

OR

1. Select Transition from the Toolbox toolbar.

2. Click on the state where the reflexive transition occurs.

3. Drag the transition line outside of the state and release.

4. Drag the transition line back into the state.

To add documentation to a transition:

1. Double-click the desired transition to open the specification window.

2. Select the General tab.

3. Enter documentation in the Documentation field.

Adding Transition Details

There are various specifications you can include for each transition. These include events, arguments, guard conditions, actions, and send events. Let's look at each of these, again in the context of our ATM example. Figure 8.2 shows the State Transition diagram for an Account class.

Event

An *event* is something that occurs that causes a transition from one state to another. In the account example, the Customer Requests Closure event causes the account to move from the open state to the closed state. An event is shown on the diagram along the transition arrow.

On the diagram, an event can be drawn using an operation name or by simply using an English phrase. In the account example, the events are all given English names. If you use operations instead, the Customer Requests Closure event might be written as RequestClosure().

Events can have arguments. For example, the deposit event that moves the account from the overdrawn state to the open state might have an argument called Amount, which holds the amount of the deposit. In your Rose model, you can add arguments to events.

Most transitions will have events—the events are what cause the transition to occur in the first place. However, you can also have an automatic transition, which has no event. With an automatic transition, an object automatically moves from one state to another as soon as all the entry actions, activities, and exit actions have occurred.

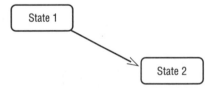

Guard Condition

A *guard condition* controls when a transition can or cannot occur. In the account example, a deposit event will move the account from the overdrawn state to the open state, but only if the account balance is greater than zero. If the balance is not greater than zero, the transition will not occur.

A guard condition is drawn along the transition line, after the event name, and enclosed in square brackets.

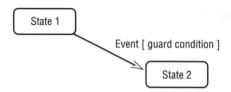

Guard conditions are optional. However, if there is more than one automatic transition out of a state, there must be mutually exclusive guard conditions on each automatic transition. This will help the reader of the diagram understand which path is automatically taken.

Action

An *action*, as we mentioned above, is a noninterruptible behavior that occurs as part of a transition. Entry and exit actions are shown inside states, because they define what happens every time an object enters or leaves a state. Most actions, however, will be drawn along the transition line, because they won't apply every time an object enters or leaves a state.

For example, when transitioning from the open state to the closed state, the action Store Date of Closure Request occurs. This is a noninterruptible behavior that occurs only on the transition from open to closed.

An action is shown along the transition line, after the event name, and preceded by a slash.

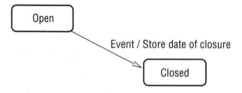

An event or action may be a behavior that occurs inside the object, or may be a message sent to another object. If an event or action is sent to another object, it is preceded by a ^ on the diagram.

State
do: ^target. Send event(arguments)

To add an event:

1. Double-click the desired transition to open the specification window.
2. Select the General tab.
3. Enter the event in the Event field.

To add arguments to an event:

1. Double-click the desired transition to open the specification window.
2. Select the General tab.
3. Enter the arguments in the Arguments field.

To add a guard condition:

1. Double-click the desired transition to open the specification window.
2. Select the Detail tab.
3. Enter the guard condition in the Condition field.

To add an action:

1. Double-click the desired transition to open the specification window.
2. Select the Detail tab.
3. Enter the action in the Action field.

To send an event:

1. Double-click the desired transition to open the specification window.
2. Select the Detail tab.
3. Enter the event in the Send Event field.
4. Enter any arguments in the Send Arguments field.
5. Enter the target in the Send Target field.

Adding Special States

There are two special states that can be added to the diagram: the start state and the stop state.

Start State

The *start state* is the state the object is in when it is first created. In our account example, a new account begins in the open state. A start state is shown on the diagram with a filled circle. A transition is drawn from the circle to the initial state.

A *start state* is mandatory: the reader of the diagram will need to know what state a new object is in. There can be only one start state on the diagram.

Stop State

The *stop state* is the state an object is in when it is destroyed. A stop state is shown on the diagram as a bull's-eye. Stop states are optional, and you can add as many stop states as you need.

To add a start state:

1. Select Start State from the toolbox toolbar.
2. Click on the State Transition diagram where the Start State should appear.

To add a stop state:

1. Select End State from the toolbox toolbar.
2. Click on the State Transition diagram where the End State should appear.

Using Nested States

To reduce clutter on your diagram, you can nest one or more states inside another. The nested states are referred to as *substates*, while the larger state is referred to as a *superstate*.

If two or more states have an identical transition, they can be grouped together into a superstate. Then, rather than maintaining two identical transitions (one for each state) the transition can be moved to the superstate. Figure 8.1 is an example of a diagram without nested states.

Figure 8.4 is the same diagram with nested states.

FIGURE 8.4:

State Transition diagram with nested states

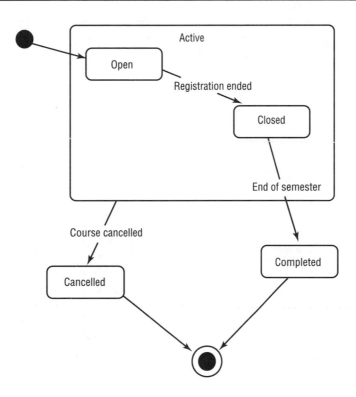

As you can see, superstates can help to reduce the clutter on a State Transition diagram.

At times, you may need the system to remember which state it was last in. If you have three states in a superstate, then leave the superstate, you may want the system to remember where you left off inside the superstate.

There are two things you can do to resolve this issue. The first is to add a start state inside the superstate. The start state will indicate where the default starting point is in the superstate. The first time the object enters that superstate, this is where the object will be.

The second is to use state history to remember where the object was. If the history option is set, an object can leave a superstate, then return and pick up right where it left off. The History option is shown with a small "*H*" in a circle at the corner of the diagram, as shown in Figure 8.5.

FIGURE 8.5:

Superstate history

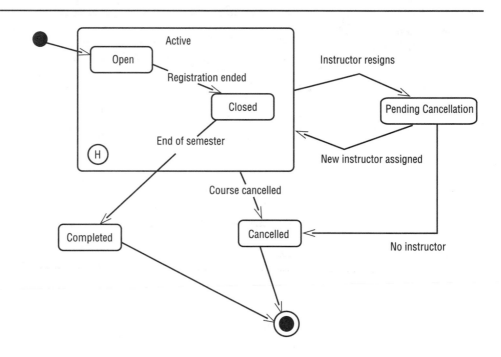

To nest a state:

1.   Select State from the Toolbox toolbar.

2.   Click on the state in which to nest to new state.

To use state history:

1. Open the specification window for the desired state.

2. Select the Detail tab.

3. Select the States History check box.

4. If you have states within states within states, you can apply the history fea-
    ture to all nested states within the superstate. To do so, select the Substates
    History check box.

Exercise

In this exercise, we will create a State Transition diagram for the Order class.

Problem Statement

In designing the Order class, Karen realized that it was a class to watch out for.
Many of the requirements varied significantly as the state of an order changed.
Pending orders behaved very differently from filled orders, for example, which
behaved differently from canceled orders.

To be sure the design was sound, she sat down with the other developers in the
group and worked out a State Transition diagram for the class. With this information, the developers had a very good sense of what it was going to take to code
the class.

Create a State Transition Diagram

Create the State Transition diagram shown in Figure 8.6 for the Order class.

FIGURE 8.6:

State Transition for the
Order class

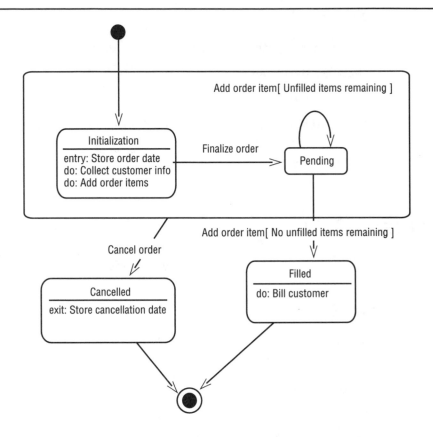

Exercise Steps:

Create the Diagram

1. Locate the Order class in the browser.

2. Right-click the class and select Open State Diagram.

Add the Start and Stop States

1. Select Start State from the toolbox.

2. Place the state on the diagram.

Continued on next page

3. Select End State from the toolbox.

4. Place the state on the diagram.

Add the Superstate

1. Select State from the toolbox.

2. Place the state on the diagram.

Add the Remaining States

1. Select State from the toolbox.

2. Place the state on the diagram.

3. Name the state **Cancelled**.

4. Select State from the toolbox.

5. Place the state on the diagram.

6. Name the state **Filled**.

7. Select State from the toolbox.

8. Place the state within the superstate.

9. Name the state **Initialization**.

10. Select State from the toolbox.

11. Place the state within the superstate.

12. Name the state **Pending**.

Add State Details

1. Double-click the Initialization state.

2. Select the Detail tab.

3. Right-click the Actions box.

4. Select Insert from the pop-up menu.

5. Double-click the new action.

6. Name the new action **Store Order Date**.

Continued on next page

7. Make sure that On Entry is selected in the When box.

8. Repeat steps 3–7 to add the following actions:

- **Collect Customer Info, Entry until Exit**

- **Add Order Items, Entry until Exit**

9. Click OK twice to close the specification.

10. Double-click the Cancelled state.

11. Repeat Steps 2–7 to add the following action:

- **Store Cancellation Date, On Exit**

12. Click OK twice to close the specification.

13. Double-click the Filled state.

14. Repeat Steps 2–7 to add the following action:

- **Bill Customer, Entry until Exit**

15. Click OK twice to close the specification.

Add Transitions

1. Select Transition from the toolbox.

2. Click the Start State.

3. Drag the transition line to the Initialization state.

4. Repeat steps 1–3 to add the following transitions:

- **Initialization to Pending**

- **Pending to Filled**

- **Superstate to Cancelled**

- **Cancelled to End State**

- **Filled to End State**

5. Select Transition to Self from the toolbox.

6. Click in the Pending state.

Add Transition Details

1. Double-click the Initialization to Pending transition to open the specification.

Continued on next page

2. In the Event field, enter **Finalize Order**.

3. Click OK to close the specification.

4. Repeat steps 1–3 to add the event **Cancel Order** to the transition between the superstate and the Cancelled state.

5. Double-click the Pending to Filled transition to open the specification.

6. In the Event field, enter **Add Order Item**.

7. Select the Detail tab.

8. In the Condition field, enter **No unfilled items remaining**.

9. Click OK to close the specification.

10.. Double-click the reflexive transition (Transition to Self) on the Pending state.

11. In the Event field, enter **Add order item**.

12. Select the Detail tab.

13. In the Condition field, enter **Unfilled items remaining**.

14. Click OK to close the specification.

Summary

In this chapter, we took a look at the State Transition diagram, another of the UML diagrams supported by Rose. Although source code is not generated from these diagrams, they can prove invaluable when examining, designing, and documenting the dynamic behavior of a class.

A State Transition diagram shows the various states in which an object can exist, how the object moves from one state to another, what happens in each state, and what happens during the transitions from one state to another. All of this information is part of the detailed design of the class. The developers can use this information when programming the class.

In Rose, you can create a State Transition diagram for a class. You can create, at most, one State Transition diagram per class, which shows the states and transitions for the class. Not every class will need a State Transition diagram—only those with significant dynamic behavior. To determine whether a class has significant dynamic behavior, you can examine the values its attributes can have, and the relationships it can have.

In the next chapter, we'll prepare for source code generation by examining the Component view of Rose. In the Component view, we'll move from the logical design to the physical design, and look at the code libraries, executable files, and other components of a system.

CHAPTER

NINE

9

Component View

- Exploring Types of Components

- Creating Components and Mapping Classes to Components

- Using Component Diagrams

We move now to the Component view of Rose. In the Component view, we'll focus on the physical organization of the system. First, we'll decide how the classes will be organized into code libraries. Then, we'll take a look at the different executable files, data link library (DLL) files, and other runtime files in the system. We won't concern ourselves yet with where the different files will be placed on the network. We'll consider these issues in the Deployment view.

What Is a Component?

A *component* is a physical module of code. Components can include both source code libraries and runtime files. For example, if you are using C++, each of your .CPP and .H files is a separate component. The .EXE file you create after the code is compiled is also a component.

Before you generate code, you map each of your files to the appropriate component(s). In C++, for example, each class is mapped to two components—one representing the .CPP file for that class and one representing the .H file. In Java, you map each class to a single component, representing the .JAVA file for that class. When you generate code, Rose will use the component information to create the appropriate code library files.

Once the components are created, they are added to a Component diagram and relationships are drawn between them. The only type of relationship between components is a dependency. A dependency suggests that one component must be compiled before another. We'll look at this in more detail shortly.

Types of Components

In Rose, you can use several different icons to represent the different types of components. We mentioned above that there are two primary types of components: source code libraries and runtime components. Within each of these two groups are a number of different icons you can use. Let's start by looking at source code library components.

Component   The component icon is used to represent a software module with a well-defined interface. In the Component specification, you specify the type of component in the Stereotype field (e.g., ActiveX, Applet, Application, DLL, and Executables, among others). See the stereotypes section below for a discussion of the different stereotypes you can use with this icon.

Subprogram Specification and Body   These icons are used to represent a subprogram's visible specification and the implementation body. A subprogram is typically a collection of subroutines. Subprograms do not contain class definitions.

Main Program   A main program is the file that contains the root of a program. In PowerBuilder, for example, this is the file that contains the application object.

Package Specification and Body   A package is the implementation of a class. A package specification is a header file, which contains function prototype information for the class. In C++, package specifications are the .H files. A package body contains the code for the operations of the class. In C++, package bodies are the .CPP files.

In Java, you use the package specification icon to represent the .JAVA files.

There are additional Component icons that are used for runtime components. Runtime components include executable files, DLL files, and tasks.

DLL file   This icon is used to represent a data link library (DLL) file.

Task Specification and Body   These icons are used to represent packages that have independent threads of control. An executable file is commonly represented as a Task Specification with a .EXE extension.

Component Diagrams

A *Component diagram* is a UML diagram that displays the components in the system and the dependencies between them. Figure 9.1 is an example of a Component diagram.

You can see from this diagram both the source code and runtime components in the system.

With this diagram, the staff responsible for compiling and deploying the system will know which code libraries exist and which executable files will be created when the code is compiled. Developers will know which code libraries exist and what the relationships are between them. The component dependencies will let those who are responsible for compiling know in which order the components need to be compiled.

FIGURE 9.1:

Component diagram

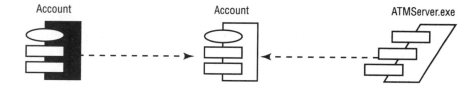

Account   Account   ATMServer.exe

Creating Component Diagrams

In Rose, you can create Deployment diagrams in the Component view. Once the diagrams are created, you can create components directly on the diagram or drag existing components from the browser to the diagram.

In the browser, Component diagrams are displayed with the following icon:

To create a Component diagram in the Component view:

1. In the browser, right-click the package to contain the Component diagram.

2. Select New ➤ Component Diagram from the pop-up menu.

3. Enter the name of the new Component diagram.

OR

1. Select Browse ➤ Component Diagram. This displays the Select Component Diagram window.

2.   Select the desired package.

3.   Select <New> from the Component Diagram box and click OK.

4.   Enter the name of the new Component Diagram and click OK.

To delete a Component diagram:

1.   In the browser, right-click the Component diagram.

2.   Select Delete from the pop-up menu.

OR

1.   Select Browse ➢ Component Diagram. This displays the Select Component Diagram window.

2.   Select the desired package.

3.   Select the component to delete.

4.   Click the Delete button.

Adding Components

Once you've created the Component diagram, the next step is to add components. In the Component Diagram toolbar, buttons are available for all the different types of icons listed above. In C++, Java, or Visual Basic projects, the most commonly used icons are the Package Specification, Package Body, and Executable icons. As we mentioned above, the Package Specification icon is used for a .H file. Either a Package Specification or a Component icon can be used for a .JAVA file, a Visual Basic project, or a DLL file. The Package Body icon is used for a .CPP file.

You can add documentation to the components as well. Documentation may include a description of the purpose of the component or a description of the class(es) in the component.

Like classes, components can be packaged together to organize them. Typically, you create one Component view package for each Logical view package. For example, if a Logical view package called Orders contained classes called Order, OrderItem, and OrderForm, the corresponding Component view package would contain the components that hold the Order, OrderItem, and OrderForm classes.

To add a component:

1. Select Component from the toolbox toolbar.
2. Click on the diagram where the new component will be placed.
3. Enter a name for the new component.

OR

1. Select Tools ➤ Create ➤ Component.
2. Click on the diagram where the new component will be placed.
3. Enter a name for the new component.

OR

1. In the browser, right-click the package to contain the component.
2. Select New ➤ Component from the pop-up menu.
3. Enter a name for the new component.

To add documentation to a component:

1. Right-click on the desired component.
2. Select Open Specification from the pop-up menu. This opens the component's specification window.
3. Select the General tab.
4. Enter documentation in the Documentation field.

OR

1. Double-click the desired component. This opens the component's specification window.
2. Select the General tab.
3. Enter documentation in the Documentation field.

OR

1. Select the desired component.

2. Select Browse ➤ Specification. This opens the component's specification window.

3. Select the General tab.

4. Enter documentation in the Documentation field.

OR

1. Select the desired component.

2. Enter documentation in the Documentation window.

To delete a component from the diagram only:

1. Select the component in the diagram.

2. Press Delete.

Note   The component has been removed from the diagram, but still exists in the browser and on other Component diagrams.

To delete a component from the model:

1. Select the component on a Component diagram.

2. Select Edit ➤ Delete from Model, or press Ctrl+D.

OR

1. Right-click the component in the browser.

2. Select Delete from the shortcut menu.

Note   Rose will remove the component from all Component diagrams, as well as from the browser.

Adding Component Details

As with other Rose model elements, there are a number of detailed specifications you can add to each component. These include:

Stereotype   The first detail is a component stereotype. The stereotype controls which icon will be used to represent the component.

The stereotypes we listed above were <none> (which uses the Component icon), subprogram specification, subprogram body, main program, package specification, package body, executable, DLL, task specification, and task body. In addition, Rose includes stereotypes for ActiveX, Applet, Application, Generic Package, and Generic Subprogram files.

You can create additional stereotypes if you'd like to represent new types of components in your particular programming language and application.

Language   In Rose, you can assign languages on a component-by-component basis. Therefore, you can generate part of your model in C++, part in Java, part in Visual Basic, and so on, provided you have the Enterprise version of Rose installed. This is a new feature that was added in Rose 98.

Rose Enterprise contains add-ins for C++, Java, Visual Basic, and Oracle8. There are many more add-ins available from various vendors to extend the capabilities of Rose. Add-ins for other languages (PowerBuilder, Forte, Visual Age Java, etc.) may be purchased as well. For a complete list of Rose Link Partners, visit the Rational Rose Web site at www.rational.com.

Declarations   In Rose, there is a place to include supplementary declarations that will be added during code generation for each component. Declarations include language-specific statements that are used to declare variables, classes, and so on. A C++ #include statement is also considered a declaration.

Classes   Before code can be generated for a class, it must be mapped to a component. This mapping helps Rose know which physical file the code for the class should be stored in.

You can map one or more classes to each component. After you have mapped a class to a component, the component name will appear in parentheses after the class name in the Logical view.

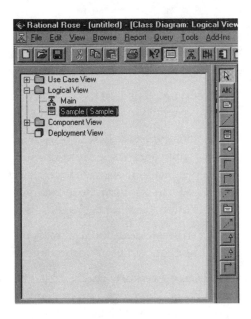

To assign a stereotype:

1. Open the desired component's standard specification window.

2. Select the General tab, as shown in Figure 9.2.

3. Enter the stereotype in the Stereotype field.

FIGURE 9.2:

Assigning a stereotype to a
component

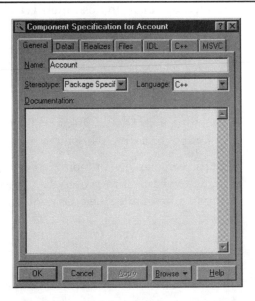

If you are using Rose 98i, and the component is a Java or CORBA component, an additional component specification *window* is provided, as shown below.

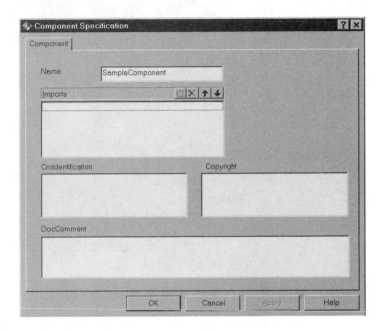

OR

1. Select the desired component.

2. Type the stereotype within the double-angle brackets: << **Name** >>.

To assign a language:

1. Open the desired component's standard specification window.

2. Select the General tab.

3. Enter the language in the Language field.

To add declarations:

1. Open the desired component's standard specification window.

2. Select the Detail tab, as shown in Figure 9.3.

3. Enter the declarations in the Declarations field.

Adding declarations to a
component

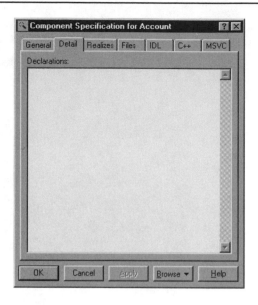

To map classes to a component:

1.   Open the desired component's standard specification window.

2.   Select the Realizes tab, as shown in Figure 9.4.

Mapping classes to a
component

3. Right-click the class to map.

4. Select Assign from the pop-up menu.

OR

1. In the browser, select the class to map.

2. Drag the class to the desired component, either in the browser or on a diagram.

Attaching Files and URLs to a Component

You can attach a file or a URL directly to a component. For example, you may want to attach the source code file to a component in your model. Or you may want to attach a testing script that will test the functionality provided by the component. Rose allows you to attach a file or URL through the browser or the component specification window.

To attach a file to a component:

1. Right-click the component in the browser or on a Component diagram.

2. Select Open Standard Specification from the shortcut menu.

3. Select the Files tab.

4. Right-click anywhere inside the white space in the Files tab.

5. Select Insert File from the shortcut menu.

6. Using the Open dialog box, find the file you wish to attach.

7. Select Open to attach the file to the component.

OR

1. Right-click the component in the browser.

2. Select New ➤ File.

3. Using the Open dialog box, find the file you wish to attach.

4. Select Open to attach the file to the component.

To attach a URL to a component:

1. Right-click the component in the browser or on a Component diagram.

2. Select Open Standard Specification from the shortcut menu.

3. Select the Files tab.

4. Right-click anywhere inside the white space in the Files tab.

5. Select Insert URL from the shortcut menu.

6. Type the name of the URL to attach.

OR

1. Right-click the component in the browser.

2. Select New ➤ URL.

3. Type the name of the URL to attach.

To open an attached file:

1. Locate the file in the browser.

2. Double-click the filename. Rose will automatically start the appropriate application and load the file.

OR

1. Right-click the file in the browser.

2. Select Open from the shortcut menu. Rose will automatically start the appropriate application and load the file.

OR

1. Right-click the component in the browser or on a Component diagram.

2. Select Open Standard Specification from the shortcut menu.

3. Select the Files tab.

4. Double-click the file you wish to open. Rose will automatically start the appropriate application and load the file.

OR

1. Right-click the component in the browser or on a Component diagram.

2. Select Open Standard Specification from the shortcut menu.

3.   Select the Files tab.

4. Right-click the file you wish to open.

5. Select Open File/URL from the shortcut menu. Rose will automatically start the appropriate application and load the file.

To open an attached URL:

1. Locate the URL in the browser.

2. Double-click the URL. Rose will automatically start your Web browser application and load the URL.

OR

1. Right-click the URL in the browser.

2. Select Open from the shortcut menu. Rose will automatically start your Web browser application and load the URL.

OR

1. Right-click the component in the browser or on a Component diagram.

2. Select Open Standard Specification from the shortcut menu.

3. Select the Files tab.

4. Double-click the URL you wish to open. Rose will automatically start your Web browser application and load the URL.

OR

1. Right-click the component in the browser or on a Component diagram.

2. Select Open Specification from the shortcut menu.

3. Select the Files tab.

4. Right-click the URL you wish to open.

5. Select Open File/URL from the shortcut menu. Rose will automatically start your Web browser application and load the URL.

To delete an attached file or URL:

1. Right-click the file or URL in the browser.

2. Select Delete from the shortcut menu.

Adding Component Dependencies

The only type of relationship that exists between components is a *component dependency*. A component dependency suggests that one component depends on another. A component dependency is drawn as a dashed arrow between the components:

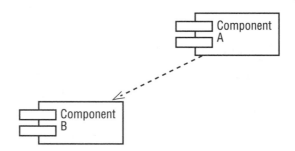

In this example, Component A depends upon Component B. In other words, there is some class in A that depends on some class in B.

These dependencies have compilation implications. In this example, because A depends on B, A cannot be compiled until B has been compiled. Someone reading this diagram will know that B should be compiled first, followed by A.

As with package dependencies, you want to avoid circular dependencies with components. If A depends on B, and B depends on A, you cannot compile either until the other has been compiled. Thus, you have to treat the two as one large component. All circular dependencies should be removed before you attempt to generate code.

The dependencies also have maintenance implications. If A depends on B, any change to B may have an impact on A. Maintenance staff can use this diagram to assess the impact of a change. The more components a single component depends on, the more likely it is to be affected by a change.

Finally, the dependencies will let you know what may or may not be easily reused. In this example, A is difficult to reuse. Because A depends on B, you cannot reuse A without also reusing B. B, on the other hand, is easy to reuse, since it does not depend on any other components. The fewer components a single component depends on, the easier it is to reuse.

To add a component dependency:

1. Select the Dependency icon from the toolbox.

2. Drag the dependency line from the Client component to the Supplier component.

OR

1. Select Tools ➤ Create ➤ Dependency.

2. Drag the dependency line from the Client component to the Supplier component.

To delete a component dependency:

1. Select the desired component dependency.

2. Press the Delete key.

OR

1. Select the desired component dependency.

2. Select Edit ➤ Delete.

Exercise

In this exercise, we will create the Component diagram for the order processing system. At this point, we've identified the classes that are needed for the Enter New Order use case. As other use cases are built, new components will be added to the diagram.

Problem Statement

With the analysis and design completed, Dan, one of the members of the deployment team, created the Component diagrams. By now, the team had decided to use C++, so he set about creating the appropriate components for each class.

Figure 9.5 shows the main Component diagram for the entire system. This main diagram focuses on the packages of components you will create.

FIGURE 9.5:

Main Component diagram for the order system

Figure 9.6 includes all of the components in the Entities package. These are the components that will contain the classes in the Entities package in the Logical view.

FIGURE 9.6:

Entities Package Component diagram

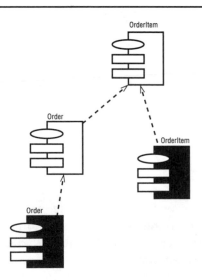

Figure 9.7 includes the components in the Control package. These components will contain the classes in the Control package in the Logical view.

FIGURE 9.7:

Control Package
Component diagram

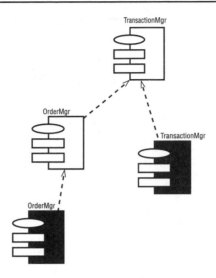

Figure 9.8 includes the components in the Boundaries package. These components will contain the classes in the Boundaries package in the Logical view.

FIGURE 9.8:

Boundaries Package
Component diagram

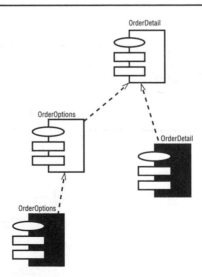

Figure 9.9 shows all of the components in the system. We've named this diagram the System Component diagram. With this one diagram, you can see all of the dependencies between all of the components in the system.

FIGURE 9.9:

System Component diagram for the order system

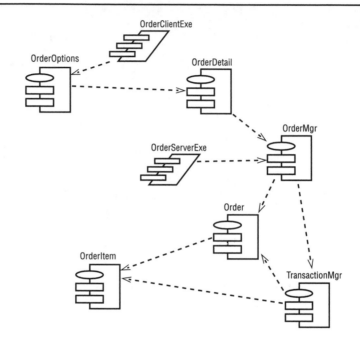

Exercise Steps:

Create the Component Packages

1. Right-click the Component view in the browser.

2. Select New ➤ Package.

3. Name the new package **Entities**.

4. Repeat steps 1–3 for packages **Boundaries** and **Control**.

Continued on next page

Add the Packages to the Main Component Diagram

1. Open the Main Component diagram by double-clicking it.

2. Drag the Entities, Boundary, and Control packages from the browser to the Main Component diagram.

Draw Package Dependencies

1. Select Dependency from the toolbox.

2. On the Main Component diagram, click on the Boundaries package.

3. Drag the dependency to the Control package.

4. Repeat steps 1–3 to add a dependency from the Control package to the Entities package.

Add the Components for the Packages and Draw Dependencies

1. Double-click the Entities package in the Main Component diagram to open the Main Component diagram for the Entities package.

2. Select Package Specification from the toolbox.

3. Place the package specification on the diagram.

4. Enter the name of the package specification as **OrderItem**.

5. Repeat steps 2–4 to add the **Order** package specification.

6. Select Package Body from the toolbox.

7. Place the package body on the diagram.

8. Enter the name of the package body as **OrderItem**.

9. Repeat steps 6–8 to add the **Order** package body.

10. Select Dependency from the toolbox.

11. Click on the OrderItem package body.

12. Drag the dependency line to the OrderItem package specification.

Continued on next page

13. Repeat steps 10–12 to add a dependency from the Order package body to the Order package specification.

14. Repeat steps 10–12 to add a dependency from the Order package specification to the OrderItem package specification.

15. Use this method to create the following components and dependencies.

For the Boundaries package:

- OrderOptions package specification
- OrderOptions package body
- OrderDetail package specification
- OrderDetail package body

Dependencies in the Boundaries package:

- OrderOptions package body to OrderOptions package specification
- OrderDetail package body to OrderDetail package specification
- OrderOptions package specification to OrderDetail package specification

For the Control package:

- OrderMgr package specification
- OrderMgr package body
- TransactionMgr package specification
- TransactionMgr package body

Dependencies in the Control package:

- OrderMgr package body to OrderMgr package specification
- TransactionMgr package body to TransactionMgr package specification
- OrderMgr package specification to TransactionMgr package specification

Create the System Component Diagram

1. Right-click the Component view in the browser.

2. Select New ➤ Component Diagram from the pop-up menu.

Continued on next page

3. Name the new diagram **System**.

4. Double-click the System Component diagram.

Place Components on the System Component Diagram

1. If needed, expand the Entities component package in the browser to open the package.

2. Click the Order package specification within the Entities component package.

3. Drag the Order package specification onto the diagram.

4. Repeat steps 2 and 3 to place the OrderItem package specification on the diagram.

5. Use this method to place the following components on the diagram.

In the Boundaries component package:

- OrderOptions package specification

- OrderDetail package specification

In the Control component package:

- OrderMgr package specification

- TransactionMgr package specification

- OrderClientExe task specification

- OrderServerExe task specification

6. Select Task Specification from the toolbox.

7. Place a Task Specification on the diagram and name it OrderClientExe.

8. Repeat steps 6 and 7 for the OrderServerExe task specification.

Add Remaining Dependencies to the System Component Diagram

The dependencies that already exist are automatically displayed on the System Component diagram after you add the components. Next, we add the remaining dependencies.

1. Select Dependency from the toolbox.

Continued on next page

2. Click the OrderDetail package specification.

3. Drag the dependency line to the OrderMgr package specification.

4. Repeat steps 1–3 to add the following dependencies:

- OrderMgr package specification to Order package specification

- TransactionMgr package specification to OrderItem package specification

- TransactionMgr package specification to Order package specification

- OrderClientExe task specification to OrderOptions package specification

- OrderServerExe task specification to OrderMgr package specification

Map classes to components

1. In the Logical view of the browser, locate the Order class in the Entities package.

2. Drag the Order class to the Order component package specification in the Component view. This maps the Order class to the Order component package specification.

3. Drag the Order class to the Order component package body in the Component view. This maps the Order class to the Order component package body.

4. Repeat steps 1-3 to map the following classes to components:

- OrderItem class to OrderItem package specification

- OrderItem class to OrderItem package body

- OrderOptions class to OrderOptions package specification

- OrderOptions class to OrderOptions package body

- OrderDetails class to OrderDetails package specification

- OrderDetails class to OrderDetails package body

- OrderMgr class to OrderMgr package specification

- OrderMgr class to OrderMgr package body

- TransactionMgr class to TransactionMgr package specification

- TransactionMgr class to TransactionMgr package body

Summary

In this chapter, we examined the Component view of Rose. The Component view is concerned with the physical structure of the system. A component is simply a file associated with the system. It may be a source code file, an executable file, or a DLL file. In Rose, there are various icons you can use to distinguish between the different types of components.

Classes are mapped to specific languages by first mapping them to components. Each component is assigned a specific language. In the Enterprise version of Rose, you can generate part of your code in one language and part in another.

Component dependencies give you information about the compilation dependencies. These relationships will let you know in what order the various components must be compiled.

In the next chapter, we'll discuss how the components are deployed on the network.

CHAPTER
TEN

Deployment View

- Creating and Using a Development Diagram

- Adding Processors

- Adding Devices

- Adding Connections

- Adding Processors

In this chapter, we'll examine the final view of Rose—the Deployment view. The Deployment view is concerned with the physical deployment of the application. This includes issues such as the network layout and the location of the components on the network. We'll also consider deployment issues here, such as: How much network bandwidth do we have? How many concurrent users do we expect? What will we do if a server goes down? And so on.

The Deployment view contains processors, devices, processes, and connections between processors and devices. All of these are diagrammed on a Deployment diagram. There is only one Deployment diagram per system, and therefore one Deployment diagram per Rose model.

Deployment Diagrams

A Deployment diagram shows all of the nodes on the network, the connections between them, and the processes that will run on each one. Figure 10.1 is an example of a Deployment diagram.

FIGURE 10.1:

Deployment diagram for the ATM system

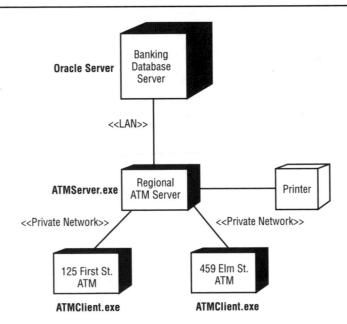

In the following sections, we'll examine each piece of this diagram.

Opening the Deployment Diagram

In Rose, the Deployment diagram is created in the Deployment view. Because there is only one diagram, it isn't shown in the browser. To access the Deployment diagram, you can double-click the words Deployment view in the browser.

To open the Deployment diagram:

1.   Double-click Deployment view in the browser.

2.   Rose will open the Deployment diagram for the model.

Adding Processors

A processor is any machine that has processing power. The servers, workstations, and other machines with processors are included in this category.

In UML, processors are displayed with this symbol:

To add a processor:

1.   Select Processor from the toolbox.

2.   Click the Deployment diagram to place the processor.

3.   Enter the name of the processor.

OR

1.   Select Tools ➤ Create ➤ Processor.

2.   Click the Deployment diagram to place the processor.

3.   Enter the name of the processor.

OR

1.   Right-click the Deployment view in the browser.

2.   Select New ➤ Processor from the pop-up menu.

3.   Enter the name of the processor.

To add documentation to a processor:

1.   Right-click the desired processor.

2.   Select Open Specification from the popup menu. This opens the processor's specification window.

3.   Select the General tab.

4.   Enter documentation in the Documentation field.

OR

1.   Double-click the desired processor. This opens the processor's specification window.

2.   Select the General tab.

3.   Enter documentation in the Documentation field.

OR

1.   Select the desired processor.

2.   Select Browse ➤ Specification. This opens the processor's specification window.

3.   Select the General tab.

4.   Enter documentation in the Documentation field.

OR

1.   Select the desired processor.

2.   Enter documentation in the documentation window.

To delete a processor from the diagram only:

1. Select the processor in the diagram.
2. Press Delete.

OR

1. Select the processor in the diagram.
2. Select Edit ➤ Delete.

NOTE   Note that the processor has been removed from the diagram, but still exists in the browser.

To delete a processor from the model:

1. Select the processor on the Deployment diagram.
2. Select Edit ➤ Delete from Model, or press Ctrl-D.

OR

1. Right-click the processor in the browser.
2. Select Delete from the shortcut menu.

NOTE   Rose will remove the processor from the Deployment diagram, as well as from the browser.

Adding Processor Details

In the processor specification, you can add information about the processor's stereotype, characteristics, and scheduling.

The stereotype, as with other model elements, is used to classify the processor. For example, you may have some Unix machines and other PC machines. You may want to define stereotypes to differentiate between the two.

A processor's characteristics are physical descriptions of the processor. For example, these could include the processor's speed or amount of memory.

The scheduling field documents the type of process scheduling used by the processor. The options are as follows:

Preemptive   Indicates that high-priority processes can preempt lower-priority processes.

Non Preemptive   Indicates that the processes have no priority. The current process executes until it is finished, at which time the next process begins.

Cyclic   Indicates the control cycles between the processes; each process is given a set amount of time to execute, and then control passes to the next process.

Executive   Indicates that there is some sort of computational algorithm that controls the scheduling.

Manual   Indicates that the processes are scheduled by the user.

To assign a stereotype:

1.   Open the desired processor's specification window.

2.   Select the General tab, as shown in Figure 10.2.

3.   Enter the stereotype in the Stereotype field.

FIGURE 10.2:

Entering a processor
stereotype

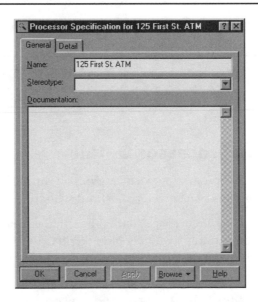

OR

1. Select the desired processor.

2. Type the stereotype within double-angle brackets: **<< Name >>**.

To add characteristics to a processor:

1. Open the desired processor's specification window.

2. Select the Detail tab, as shown in Figure 10.3.

3. Enter the characteristics in the Characteristics field.

FIGURE 10.3:

Entering processor
characteristics

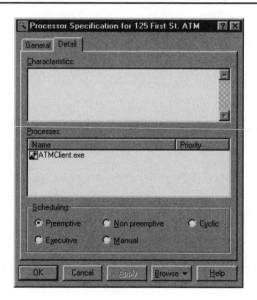

To set scheduling for a processor:

1. Open the desired processor's specification window.

2. Select the Detail tab.

3. Select one of the following for scheduling: preemptive, non-preemptive,
    cyclic, executive, or manual.

To show scheduling on the diagram:

1.   Right-click on the desired processor.

2.   Select Show Scheduling from the pop-up menu.

To show processes on the diagram:

1.   Right-click the desired processor.

2.   Select Show Processes from the pop-up menu.

Adding Devices

A device is a machine or piece of hardware without processing power. Devices include items such as dumb terminals, printers, and scanners.

In UML, devices are displayed with this symbol:

Both processors and devices can also be referred to as *nodes* on a network.

To add a device:

1.   Select Device from the toolbox.

2.   Click the Deployment diagram to place the device.

3.   Enter the name of the device.

OR

1.   Select Tools ➤ Create ➤ Device.

2.   Click on the Deployment diagram to place the device.

3.   Enter the name of the device.

OR

1. Right-click the Deployment view in the browser.

2. Select New ➤ Device from the pop-up menu.

3. Enter the name of the device.

To add documentation to a device:

1. Right-click the desired device.

2. Select Open Specification from the pop-up menu. This opens the device's specification window.

3. Select the General tab.

4. Enter documentation in the Documentation field.

OR

1. Double-click the desired device. This opens the device's specification window.

2. Select the General tab.

3. Enter documentation in the Documentation field.

OR

1. Select the desired device.

2. Select Browse ➤ Specification. This opens the device's specification window.

3. Select the General tab.

4. Enter documentation in the Documentation field.

OR

1. Select the desired device.

2. Enter documentation in the documentation window.

To delete a device from the diagram only:

1. Select the device in the diagram.

2. Press Delete.

OR

1. Select the device in the diagram.

2. Select Edit ➤ Delete.

NOTE   Note that the device has been removed from the diagram, but still exists in the browser.

To delete a device from the model:

1. Select the device on the Deployment diagram.

2. Select Edit ➤ Delete from Model, or press Ctrl+D.

OR

1. Right-click the device in the browser.

2. Select Delete from the shortcut menu.

NOTE   Rose will remove the device from the Deployment diagram, as well as from the browser.

Adding Device Details

Like processors, there are various details that can be added to a device. The first is the stereotype, which is used to classify the device. The second is the Characteristics field. As with processors, the characteristics of a device are the physical descriptions of the device.

To assign a stereotype:

1. Open the desired device's specification window.

2. Select the General tab, as shown in Figure 10.4.

3. Enter the stereotype in the Stereotype field.

FIGURE 10.4:

Entering a device
stereotype

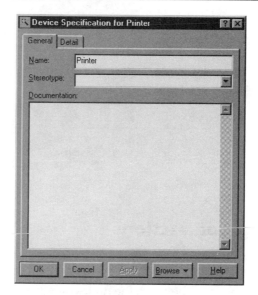

OR

1. Select the desired device.

2. Type the stereotype within double-angle brackets: **<< Name >>.**

To add characteristics to a device:

1. Open the desired device's specification window.

2. Select the Detail tab, as shown in Figure 10.5.

3. Enter the characteristics in the Characteristics field.

FIGURE 10.5:

Entering device
characteristics

Adding Connections

A connection is a physical link between two processors, two devices, or a processor and a device. Most commonly, connections represent the physical network connections between the nodes on your network. A connection can also be an Internet link between two nodes.

To add a connection:

1. Select Connection from the toolbox.

2. Click on the node to connect.

3. Drag the connection line to another node.

OR

1.   Select Tools ➤ Create ➤ Connection.

2.   Click on the node to connect.

3.   Drag the connection line to another node.

To delete a connection:

1.   Select the connection in the diagram.

2.   Press Delete.

OR

1.   Select the connection in the diagram.

2.   Select Edit ➤ Delete.

Adding Connection Details

Connections may be assigned stereotypes. Connections can also be given characteristics, which are used to provide details about the physical connection. For example, a connection might be a T1 line. This type of note would be added in the Characteristics field.

To assign a stereotype:

1.   Open the desired connection's specification window.

2.   Select the General tab, as shown in Figure 10.6.

3.   Enter the stereotype in the Stereotype field.

FIGURE 10.6:

Entering a connection
stereotype

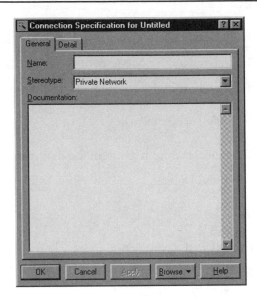

OR

1. Select the desired connection.

2. Type the stereotype within double-angle brackets: **<< Name >>.**

To add characteristics to a connection:

1. Open the desired connection's specification window.

2. Select the Detail tab, as shown in Figure 10.7.

3. Enter the characteristics in the Characteristics field.

FIGURE 10.7:

Entering connection
characteristics

Adding Processes

A process is a single thread of execution that runs on a processor. An executable file, for example, is considered a process. When adding processes to the diagram, focus only on the processes related to the system being built.

Processes can be displayed on a Deployment diagram or hidden from view. If they are displayed, they are listed directly below the processor(s) on which they are run.

Processes may be assigned a priority. If the processor on which they are run uses preemptive scheduling, the priority of the process will determine when it can run.

To add a process:

1. Right-click the desired processor in the browser.

2. Select New ➤ Process from the pop-up menu.

3. Enter the name of the new process.

OR

1. Open the desired processor's specification window.

2. Click the Detail tab.

3. Right-click in the Processes box.

4. Select Insert from the pop-up menu.

5. Enter the name of the new process.

To add documentation to a process:

1. Open the desired processor's specification window.

2. Select the Detail tab.

3. Enter documentation in the Documentation field.

OR

1. Double-click the desired process in the browser.

2. Select the Detail tab.

3. Enter documentation in the Documentation field.

OR

1. Right-click the desired process in the browser.

2. Select Open Specification from the pop-up menu.

3. Select the Detail tab.

4. Enter documentation in the Documentation field.

To add a priority to a process:

1. Open the desired processor's specification window.

2. Select the General tab, as shown in Figure 10.8.

3. Enter the priority in the priority field.

FIGURE 10.8:

Entering process
information

To delete a process:

1. Right-click the desired process in the browser.

2. Select Delete from the pop-up menu.

OR

1. Open the desired processor's specification.

2. Click on the Detail tab.

3. Right-click the desired process.

4. Select Delete from the pop-up menu.

Exercise

In this exercise, we'll create a Deployment diagram for the Order Processing
system.

Problem Statement

The project team had done quite a bit of analysis and design up to this point. The use cases, object interaction, and components were all nicely defined. However, the network management unit needed to know which components would reside on which machines. So, the team put together a Deployment diagram for the Order Processing system.

Create Deployment Diagram

Create the Deployment diagram for the Order Processing system. Your completed diagram should look like Figure 10.9.

FIGURE 10.9:

Deployment diagram for the Order Processing system

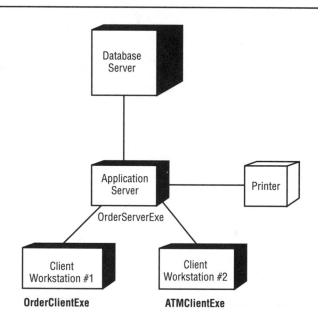

Exercise Steps:

Add the Nodes to the Deployment Diagram

1. Double-click the Deployment view in the browser to open the Deployment diagram.

2. Select Processor from the toolbox.

3. Click the diagram to place the processor.

4. Enter the processor name as **Database Server**.

5. Repeat steps 2–4 to add the following processors:

- **Application Server**

- **Client Workstation #1**

- **Client Workstation #2**

6. Select Device from the toolbox.

7. Click the diagram to place the device.

8. Enter the device name as **Printer**.

Add Connections

1. Select Connection from the toolbox.

2. Click on the Database Server processor.

3. Drag the connection line to the Application Server processor.

4. Repeat steps 1–3 to add the following connections:

- Application Server processor to Client Workstation #1 processor

- Application Server processor to Client Workstation #2 processor

- Application Server processor to Printer device.

Continued on next page

Add Processes

1. Right-click the Application Server processor in the browser.

2. Select New ➤ Process from the menu.

3. Enter the process name as **OrderServerExe**.

4. Repeat steps 1–3 to add the following processes:

- For the Client Workstation #1 processor: **OrderClientExe**

- For the Client Workstation #2 processor: **OrderClientExe**

Show the Processes

1. Right-click the Application Server process.

2. Select Show Processes from the menu.

3. Repeat steps 1 and 2 to show the processes for the following processors:

- Client Workstation #1 processor

- Client Workstation #2 processor

Summary

In this chapter, we covered the Deployment view of Rose. In the Deployment diagram, the team describes the network structure and where the various processes are run. Now, you have the information you need to:

- Define the system scope with use cases and actors and diagram the use cases and actors on a Use Case diagram.

- Analyze a problem with use cases and Use Case documentation.

- Describe the objects in the system, and the system flow, in a Sequence or Collaboration diagram.

- Create the classes needed to implement the functionality in the flow of events, and diagram the classes.

- Define and diagram the attributes, operations, and relationships of the classes.

- Examine the dynamic behavior of a class by creating a State Transition diagram.

- Perform an architectural assessment by grouping the classes into packages, and examining the relationships between the classes and the packages.

- Define and view the physical structure of the system in a Processor diagram.

- View the network structure and deployment information on a Deployment diagram.

In the next section, we'll take a close look at the code generation features of Rose. The next few chapters will discuss how to generate C++, Java, and Power-Builder code from a Rose model. We'll also look at how to define an Oracle8 schema using Rose, how to generate Data Definition Language (DDL) scripts, and how to generate Interface Definition Language (IDL) files.

CHAPTER
ELEVEN

11

Introduction to Code Generation Using Rational Rose

■ Generating code using Rational Rose

■ Checking your Rose model

■ Setting code generation properties

■ Selecting a class, component, or package

One of the most powerful features of Rational Rose is its ability to generate code that represents a model. In this chapter, we'll take a look at the fundamental steps you must take before you can generate code from your Rose model. In the next several chapters, we'll examine the detailed steps you must take to generate code in C++, Java, PowerBuilder, and Visual Basic. We'll also take a look at generating IDL, DDL, and Oracle8 schema from a Rose model.

The code generation options you have available will vary by the version of Rose you have installed. There are three different versions of Rose 98 and 98i currently available:

- Rose Modeler allows you to create a model for your system, but will not support code generation or reverse engineering.

- Rose Professional allows you to generate code in one language.

- Rose Enterprise allows you to generate code in C++, Java, Visual Basic, Oracle8 schema and other languages.

A number of Rose partner companies have developed add-ins to support code generation and reverse engineering in other languages. Check Rational's Web site, `www.rational.com`, for information about add-in products available for Rose.

Preparing for Code Generation

There are six basic steps to generating code:

1. Check the model.

2. Create the components.

3. Map the classes to the components.

4. Set the code generation properties.

5. Select a class, component, or package.

6. Generate the code.

Not all of these steps are necessary in each language. For example, you can generate C++ code without first creating components. You can create code in any language without running the Check Model step, although you may have some errors during the code generation. In the following chapters, we'll discuss the details of generating code in the various languages.

Although not all of these steps are required, we recommend completing the first five steps before generating code. The model check will help to find inconsistencies and problems in your model that you certainly wouldn't want to affect the code. The component steps serve as a way to map your logical system design to its physical implementation, and they provide you with a great deal of useful information. If you skip these steps, Rose will use the package structure in the Logical view to create components.

Step One: Check the Model

Rose includes a language-independent model check feature that you can run to ensure your model is consistent before you generate code. It's always a good idea to run this check before you attempt to generate code. It can find inconsistencies and errors in your model that might prevent code from being generated correctly.

To check your Rose model:

1.   Select Tools ➤ Check Model from the menu.

2.   Any errors that are found will be written to the log window.

Common errors include things like messages on a Sequence or Collaboration diagram that are not mapped to an operation, or objects on a Sequence or Collaboration diagram that are not mapped to a class. The following are some of the common errors and their solutions.

The message below indicates that you have an object in a Sequence or a Collaboration diagram that has not been mapped to a class.

```
Unresolved reference from use case "<Use case name>" to ClassItem with
name (Unspecified) by object <Object name>>
```

Look at the objects on your Sequence or Collaboration diagram. Each box should contain the object name, followed by a colon, followed by the class name, as follows:

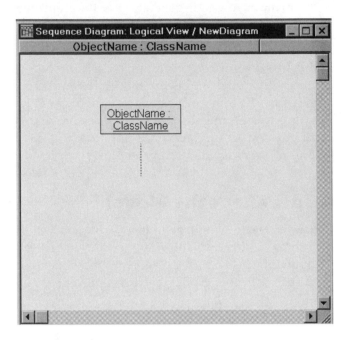

Find the object without the class name. Right-click the object and select Open Specification from the shortcut menu. In the object specification window, select the object's class using the Class drop-down list box.

The following message lets you know that you have a message on a Sequence or a Collaboration diagram that has not been mapped to an operation.

```
Unresolved reference to Operation with name <Message name> in message
<Message name> between <Class name> and <Class name> in Sequence dia-
gram <Use case name>/<Sequence diagram name>
```

Right-click the appropriate message on the diagram (the error in the L og window will let you know the name of the offending message and its Sequence or Collaboration diagram), and map the message to an operation. If necessary, create a new operation for the message.

Access Violations

The Check Model menu item will find most of the inconsistencies and problems in a model. The Access Violations menu item will find violations that occur when there is a relationship between two classes in different packages, but no relationship between the packages themselves. For example, if we have an Order class in an Entities package that has a relationship to an OrderManager class in a Control package, there must be a relationship between the Entities package and the Control package. If there is not, Rose will find an access violation.

To find access violations:

1. Select Report ➤ Show Access Violations from the menu.

2. Rose will display any access violations in a window, as shown in Figure 11.1.

FIGURE 11.1:

Access violations window

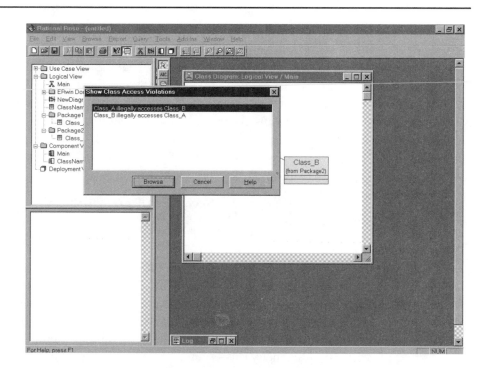

Language-Specific Check

To run a language-specific check, choose Tools ➤ Check Model. If you are using Java, you can run a Java-specific syntax check by selecting Tools ➤ Java ➤ Syntax Check. This check will find errors such as multiple public classes in a single compilation unit.

Step Two: Create Components

The second step in the code generation process is to create components to hold the classes. There are many types of components: source code files, executable files, runtime libraries, ActiveX components, and applets, to name a few. Before you generate code, you can map each of your classes to the appropriate source code component.

Once the components are created, you can add dependencies between them on a Component diagram. Dependencies between the components are the compilation dependencies in the system. (See Chapter 9 for more information about components and component dependencies.)

If you are generating C++, Java, or Visual Basic, you aren't required to complete this step in order to generate code. In Java or Visual Basic, Rose will automatically create the appropriate component for each of your classes. However, the dependencies between the classes will not be generated.

To create a component:

1. Open a Component diagram.

2. Use the Component icon on the Diagram toolbar to add a new component to the diagram.

Step Three: Map Classes to Components

Each source code component represents the source-code file for one or more classes. In C++, for example, each class is mapped to two source-code components, one representing the header file and one representing the body file. In PowerBuilder, many classes are mapped to a single component. A PowerBuilder source-code component is a PowerBuilder library (.PBL) file. In Java, each source code component represents a single .JAVA file.

The third step in the code generation process is to map each of your classes to the appropriate components. For PowerBuilder, you must map each class to a component before you can generate code. However, this is an optional step with C++, Java, or Visual Basic. Rose can generate code without it. If you are generating Java or Visual Basic code, Rose will also generate the appropriate components and map the classes for you. However, components will not be automatically created for C++, and component dependencies are not generated for any language. Therefore, it's a good idea to go ahead and complete this step regardless of the language you are using.

To map a class to a component:

1. Right-click the component on a Component diagram or in the browser.

2. Select Open Specification from the shortcut menu.

3. Select the Realizes tab.

4. On the Realizes tab, right-click the appropriate class or classes and select Assign from the shortcut menu.

5. The browser will show the component name in parentheses after the class name in the Logical view.

OR

1. Locate the class in the Logical view of the browser.

2. Drag the class to the appropriate component in the Component view.

3. The component name will appear in parentheses after the class name in the Logical view.

Step Four: Set the Code Generation Properties

There are a number of code generation options you can set for classes, attributes, components, and other model elements. These properties control how the code will be generated. Common default settings are provided in Rose.

For example, one of the code generation properties for a C++ attribute is GenerateGetOperation, which controls whether or not a Get() operation will be created for the attribute. One of the properties for a Java class is GenerateDefault-Constructor, which controls whether or not a constructor should automatically be created for the class. One of the properties for a relationship in Visual Basic is GenerateDataMember, which controls whether or not an attribute will automatically be created to support the relationship.

Each language in Rose has a number of code generation properties. In the following chapters, we'll discuss the code generation properties for each specific language. Before you generate code, it's a good idea to examine the code generation properties and make any needed changes.

To view the code generation properties, select Tools ➣ Options, then select the appropriate language tab. For example, here is the tab for the Visual Basic properties:

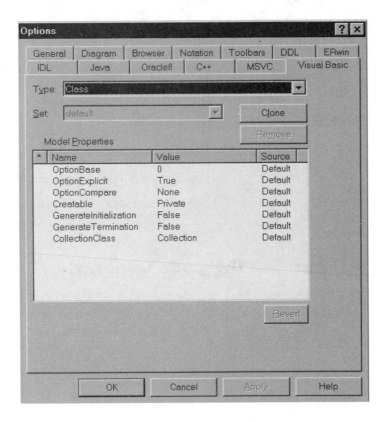

From the drop-down list box, you can select from Class, Attribute, Operation, or the other types of model elements. Each language will have different model elements available in the drop-down list box. As you select different values, different property sets will appear. We just saw the Class properties in Visual Basic. Here are the Attribute properties:

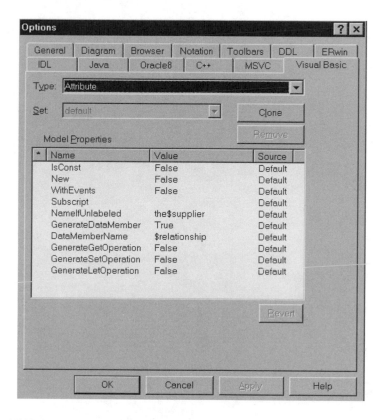

Any changes you make to a property set in the Tools ➤ Options window will affect all model elements using that set. For example, if you change the Generate DefaultConstructor class property on the Java tab, this change will affect all classes in your model that will be implemented in Java.

At times, you may want to change the code generation properties for a single class, attribute, operation, or other model element. To do so, open the specification window for the model element. Select the language tab (C++, Java, Visual Basic, or PowerBuilder) and change the properties here. Any changes you make in the specification window for a model element will only affect that model element.

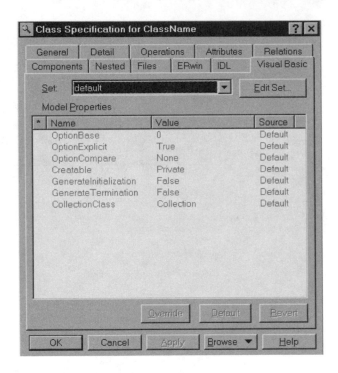

Cloning Property Sets

Rather than making changes directly to the default property sets, you can clone them and then make changes to the copy. To clone a property set, press the Clone button on Clone the Property Set window. Rose will prompt you to enter a name for the new property set.

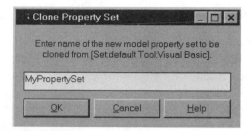

Once you've cloned a property set, it will be available by opening the Set drop-down list box on the Clone Property Set window.

You can make as many changes as you'd like to this cloned set, without affecting the original default set. We recommend leaving the default set alone and only changing cloned sets.

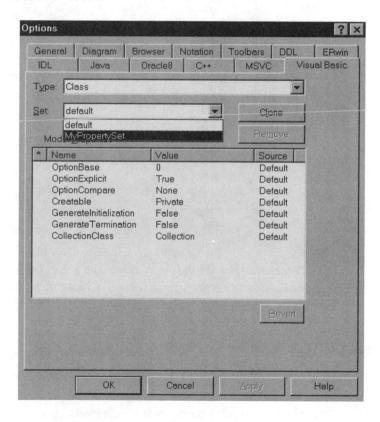

Deleting Property Sets

If you no longer need a cloned property set, you can remove it from the model
through the Tools ➤ Options window. Select the tab for the appropriate language
and then select the cloned property set in the Set drop-down list box.

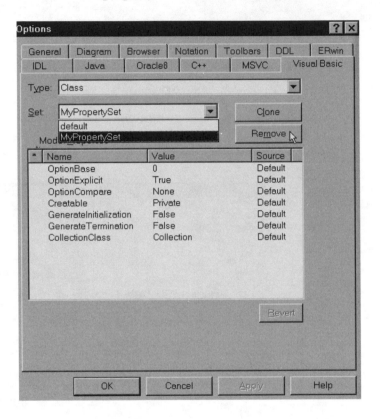

Once you've selected the appropriate set, select the Remove button. Rose will
remove that property set from the model. Note that you cannot remove the
default property set.

Step Five: Select a Class, Component, or Package

When generating code, you can generate a class at a time, a component at a
time, or an entire package at a time. Code can be generated from a diagram or
from the browser. If you generate code from a package, you can either select a
Logical view package on a Class diagram, or a Component view package on a

Component diagram. If you select a Logical view package, all of the classes in that package will be generated. If you select a Component view package, all of the components in that package will be generated.

You can also generate code for a number of classes, components, or packages at once. On a diagram, use the Ctrl key to select the classes, components, or packages you want to generate code for, then select the appropriate code generation command from the menu.

Step Six: Generate Code

If you have Rose Professional or Enterprise installed, you will have some language-specific menu options available on the Tools menu, as shown in Figure 11.2.

FIGURE 11.2:

Code generation
menu items

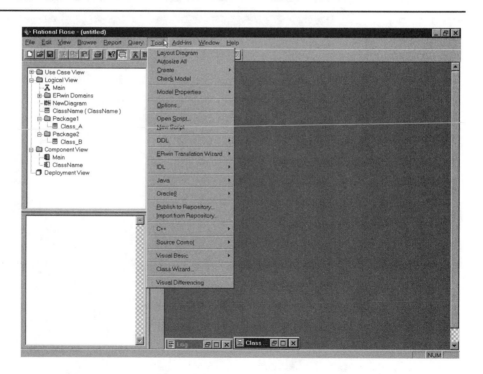

To show or hide these menu options, select the Add-Ins ➢ Add-In Manager menu option. In the Add-In Manager dialog box, as shown in Figure 11.3, use the check boxes to show or hide the options for various languages.

Once you have a class or component selected on a diagram, select the appropriate code generation option from the menu. If any errors are encountered as the code generation progresses, these errors will be noted in the log window.

What Gets Generated?

When you generate code, Rose collects information from the Logical view and the Component view of your model. Although no modeling tool can create a completed application for you, Rose will generate a great deal of skeletal code, as shown below:

FIGURE 11.3:

Add-In Manager

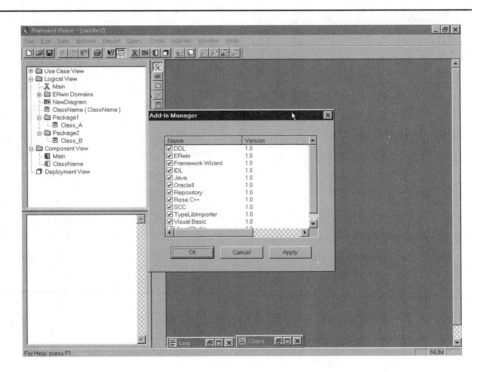

Classes   All classes in the model will be generated in the code.

Attributes   The code will include the attributes of each class, including the visibility, data type, and default value.

Operation signatures   The operations will be declared in the code, along with any parameters, the data types of the parameters, and the return type of the operation.

Relationships   Some of the relationships in your model will cause attributes to be created when you generate code.

Components   Each component will be implemented by the appropriate source code file.

Once the files have been generated, there are two steps remaining. First, the developers take the files and code each of the operations of the classes. Then, the graphical user interface is designed.

Rose is not intended to be a GUI design tool—you can use your programming language's environment to design the screens and forms. This approach helps you ensure the system you're building has a solid design. The team can review the Rose model to come to agreement on the best architecture and the best design, and then generate code from the model. Rather than having 20 different programmers designing in 20 different directions, everyone is working off the same blueprint.

When generating code, Rose will use the package structure you've set up in the Component view to create the appropriate directories. By default, the root directory it uses for code generation is the directory with the Rose application file in it. You can change the directory through the code generation properties for your language.

If you don't have components set up, Rose will use the package structure in the Logical view to set up the directory structure. Again, the default directory is the Rose directory, but you can change it through the code generation properties.

Summary

In this chapter, we presented an overview of the code generation capabilities of Rose. In the next several chapters, we'll take a look at the specific code generated in C++, Java, Visual Basic, and PowerBuilder. We'll also examine the Interface Definition Language (IDL) and the Data Definition Language (DDL) you can generate from your Rose model, and discuss how to generate Oracle8 schema.

To review, the steps for generating code are as follows:

1. Check the model.

2. Create the components.

3. Map the classes to the components.

4. Set the code generation properties.

5. Select a class, component, or package.

6. Generate the code.

C++ and Visual C++ Code Generation

- Setting C++ Code Generation Properties

- Generating C++ Code from Your Rose Model

- Mapping Rose Elements to C++ Constructs

C++ is one of the most widely used object-oriented languages in the industry. Rational Rose supports integration with C++ through its code generation and reverse engineering capabilities. In this chapter, we'll discuss how to generate C++ code from your Rational Rose model.

Rose 98 provides integration with C++; Rose 98i provides code generation for standard C++ and also provides tight integration with Microsoft's Visual C++ version 6. In this chapter, we'll discuss both the code generation procedures for standard C++ and the procedures for generating code in Visual C++.

You will need to follow these steps to generate code in standard C++:

1. Create components (optional; see Chapter 10).

2. Assign classes to components (optional; see Chapter 10).

3. Set the code generation properties (optional).

4. Select a class or component to generate on a Class or Component diagram.

5. Select Tools ➤ C++ ➤ Code Generation.

6. Select Tools ➤ C++ ➤ Browse Header or Browse Body to view the generated code.

The first step in code generation is to create components for the classes. These components are the .CPP and .H files for your code. In C++, this step is not required. If you do not have components defined, Rose will generate a .CPP and .H file for each class. However, we recommend creating components to give you the ability to control the mapping between classes and components and to model the component dependencies.

Once components have been created and the classes mapped, the next step is to set the code generation properties for your classes, components, operations, and other model elements. The code generation properties control certain aspects of the code that is generated. In this chapter, we'll discuss the code generation properties that can be set, and take a close look at how each Rose model element is implemented in the code.

If you are generating code in Visual C++ with Rose 98i, you will use a wizard. To start the wizard, select Tools ➤ Visual C++ ➤ Update Code. The Visual C++ Code Update tool will start, and a welcome screen will be displayed. Click Next to continue. Rose will display the Select Components and Classes window. Before you can generate a class in Visual C++, the class must be assigned to a component. If you have not assigned the class to a component, select the Create a VC++ Component and Assign New Classes to It (Ctrl+R) option in the wizard window. Using this option, you can create as many components as you need before you generate the code. Then select the components and/or classes in your model you wish to generate code for.

To change the code generation properties for your Visual C++ components and classes, right-click the VC++ folder on this screen. You can then edit any of the code generation properties, such as the container class, to support relationship multiplicity, whether a constructor and destructor will automatically be generated, and whether Get and Set operations or other member functions will automatically be generated. The code generation properties are discussed in greater detail in the following section, "C++ Code Generation Properties."

Once all classes have been assigned to components, you have selected the classes and/or components you wish to generate, and all code generation properties have been set, click Next to continue. A summary page will be displayed to let you know which class(es) or component(s) were generated and which errors were encountered during the code generation process.

Rose will use a lot of information from the model to generate code. For example, it will look at the multiplicity, role names, containment, and other details of each relationship. It will look at the attributes, operations, visibility, and other details of each class. From all of the information you entered using the specification windows for the various model elements, Rose will gather what it needs to generate code.

C++ Code Generation Properties

C++ code generation using Rational Rose is extremely flexible. You have full control over what gets generated and many of the details of how the generated code will look. For example, for each class you can decide whether a constructor, copy constructor, and destructor will automatically be created. For each attribute, you control the visibility, name, and whether Get and Set operations should automatically be created. For each header file, you control the filename, the copyright notice, the configuration management settings, and the #include statements in the file.

All of these things are controlled through the code generation properties. Rose provides property sets that deal with classes, attributes, operations, header files, implementation files, associations, aggregations, generalizations, packages, dependencies, subsystems, and the overall project.

You can see all of these properties by selecting Tools ➤ Options, and then selecting the C++ tab. The code generation properties in Rose 98 and 98i are slightly different. We have indicated those properties that are only available in Rose 98.

Code generation properties can be set for the entire model or for a specific model element. You can change the default code generations properties for the entire model by selecting Tools ➤ Options, then selecting the C++ tab. You can also change the default from a model element's specification, select the C++ tab, then select Edit Set. Code generation properties can be set for a single class, attribute, operation, or other model element, which will override the default setting. To do so, open the specification window for the model element, select the C++ tab, modify the property value, and press the Override button. In the following sections, we'll examine many of the more commonly used code generation properties for classes, operations, attributes, header files, implementation files, and the overall project. Later in this chapter, as we proceed through the code generated for various types of relationships and multiplicities, we'll examine some additional code generation properties.

Project Properties

The project properties are those code generation properties that apply more to the whole project than to any specific model element, such as a class or relationship.

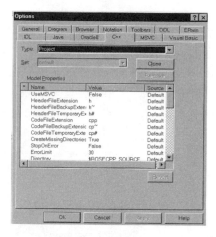

The options in this section include things like the default directory to use when generating code, the file extensions to use, and the maximum number of errors that can occur during code generation. The most commonly used project properties are listed in Table 12.1, along with their purpose and default value.

In this section and each of the following sections, we have provided tables for the most commonly used C++ properties. For a complete listing of all C++ code generation properties, consult the online help in Rose.

TABLE 12.1: Project Code Generation Properties

Property	Purpose	Default
UseMSVC	Controls whether MSVC source code is produced.	False
HeaderFileExtension	Controls the filename extension used for generated header files.	h
HeaderFileBackup-Extension	Controls the filename extension used for backup header files, if a generated file is overwriting an existing file.	h~
HeaderFileTemporary-Extension	Sets the filename extension to use for temporary files created during code generation.	h#
CodeFileBackup-Extension	Controls the filename extension used for backup implementation files, if a generated file is overwriting an existing file.	cp~

Continued on next page

TABLE 12.1: Project Code Generation Properties

Property	Purpose	Default
CodeFileExtension	Controls the filename extension used for generated implementation files.	cpp
CodeFileTemporary-Extension	Sets the filename extension to use for temporary files created during code generation.	cp#
CreateMissingDirectories	Controls whether Rose should create directories to mirror the packages when generating code.	True
StopOnError	Controls whether Rose will stop generating code if it encounters an error.	False
ErrorLimit	Sets the maximum number of errors that can occur before Rose stops generating code.	30
Directory	Sets the root directory for code generation, under which all directories and C++ files will be generated.	By default, Rose will use the directory in the pathmap with the symbol $ROSECPP_SOURCE.
PathSeparator	Sets the path separator (for example, backslash or slash) used in #include statements.	Blank
FileNameFormat	Controls the formatting of the filenames automatically generated by Rose.	128vx_b (maximum 128 characters, vowels included, case retained, underscores retained).
BooleanType	Sets the data type to be used in the code for a Boolean data type in the model.	Int
AllowTemplates	Controls whether Rose will generate templates for parameterized classes in the model.	True
AllowProtected-Inheritance	Controls whether protected derivation will be generated in the code.	False
CommentWidth	Sets the maximum number of characters in a single line of generated comments.	60
AllowExplicit-Instantiations	Controls whether explicit instantiations of parameterized classes may be generated.	False
AlwaysKeepOrphaned-Code	Controls whether orphaned code is placed in a protected region.	False

In addition, there are some project properties that deal with multiplicity in relationships. When generating code, Rose will automatically create attributes for certain types of relationships. For example, if you have a unidirectional association between class Client and class Supplier, and the multiplicity on the relationship is one-to-one, Rose will generate an attribute of type Supplier inside Client.

If the multiplicity is more than one, Rose will use a container class, such as a list, when generating the attribute. Different relationships and different multiplicities will use different container classes. The default container classes to use are set in the project's C++ code generation properties. To change the default, you can change the container class specified in these properties.

Again, the following properties provide defaults; they will only be used if the ContainerClass code generation property for the relationship has not been set. The ContainerClass property for a relationship specifies the container class that will be used when generating attributes for that specific relationship.

OneByValueContainer

OneByReferenceContainer

OptionalByValueContainer

OptionalByReferenceContainer

FixedByValueContainer

UnorderedFixedByValueContainer

FixedByReferenceContainer

UnorderedFixedByReferenceContainer

BoundedByValueContainer

UnorderedBoundedByValueContainer

BoundedByReferenceContainer

UnorderedBoundedByReferenceContainer

UnboundedByValueContainer

UnorderedUnboundedByValueContainer

UnboundedByReferenceContainer

UnorderedUnboundedByReferenceContainer

QualifiedByValueContainer

UnorderedQualifiedByValueContainer

QualifiedByReferenceContainer

UnorderedQualifiedByReferenceContainer

Class Properties

Class properties are the C++ code generation properties that apply to classes. These properties will let you change the class name, decide whether or not constructors and destructors should be created for the class, and set other class-specific properties.

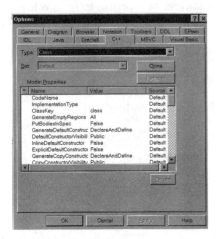

There are two places to set these properties. To set them for all classes, select Tools ➢ Options, then the C++ tab, and select Class from the drop-down list box. To set them for only one class, select the C++ tab on the class specification window and edit the properties there.

Table 12.2 lists many of the C++ class properties, their purpose, and their default value.

TABLE 12.2: Class Code Generation Properties

Property	Purpose	Default
CodeName	The name of the class in the generated code.	By default, Rose will use the class name in the model.
ImplementationType	Controls whether a class is generated using a class definition or elemental data type.	Blank
ClassKey	Controls whether the keyword class, struct, or union is used in the class definition.	Class
GenerateEmptyRegions	Controls whether empty regions are created, and whether they are preserved during round-trip engineering.	All
PutBodiesInSpec	Controls whether the class implementation is generated in the header file.	False
GenerateDefault-Constructor	Controls whether a constructor will automatically be generated for the class.	True
DefaultConstructor-Visibility	Sets the visibility (public, private, protected) of the constructor.	Public
InlineDefaultConstructor	Controls whether the default constructor is inlined.	False
ExplicitDefault-Constructor	Controls whether the explicit keyword will be used for the default constructor.	False
GenerateCopy-Constructor	Controls whether a copy constructor will automatically be generated for the class.	True
CopyConstructorVisibility	Sets the visibility (public, private, protected) of the copy constructor.	Public
InlineCopyConstructor	Controls whether the copy constructor is inlined.	False
ExplicitCopyConstructor	Controls whether the explicit keyword will be used for the copy constructor.	False
GenerateDestructor	Controls whether a destructor is automatically generated for the class.	True

TABLE 12.2 CONTINUED: Class Code Generation Properties

Property	Purpose	Default
DestructorVisibility	Sets the visibility (public, private, protected) of the destructor.	Public
DestructorKind	Controls whether the virtual keyword is used in the destructor.	Common (False)
InlineDestructor	Controls whether the destructor is inlined.	False
GenerateAssignment-Operation	Controls whether an assignment operation (=) is created and whether a skeleton definition is created.	DeclareAndDefine (operation and skeleton created)
AssignmentVisibility	Sets the visibility (public, private, protected) of the operation.	Public
AssignmentKind	Controls whether the virtual keyword will be used.	Common (False)
InlineAssignment-Operation	Controls whether the assignment operation is inlined.	False
GenerateEquality-Operations	Controls whether equality operations (== and !=) are created, and whether skeleton definitions are created.	DeclareAndDefine (operation and skeleton created)
EqualityVisibility	Sets the visibility (public, private, protected) of the operations.	Public
EqualityKind	Controls whether the virtual keyword will be used.	Common (False)
InlineEqualityOperation	Controls whether the equality operations are inlined.	False
GenerateRelational-Operations	Controls whether equality operations (<, >, <= and >=) are created.	False
RelationalVisibility	Sets the visibility (public, private, protected) of the operations.	Public
RelationalKind	Controls whether the virtual keyword will be used.	Common (False)
InlineRelational-Operations	Controls whether the relational operations are inlined.	False
GenerateStorageMgmt-Operations	Controls whether new and delete operations are created.	False

Continued on next page

TABLE 12.2 CONTINUED: Class Code Generation Properties

Property	Purpose	Default
StorageMgmtVisibility	Sets the visibility (public, private, protected) of the operations.	Public
InlineStorageMgmt-Operations	Controls whether the relational operations are inlined.	False
GenerateSubscript-Operation	Controls whether a subscript function ([]) is created.	False
SubscriptVisibility	Sets the visibility (public, private, protected) of the operation.	Public
SubscriptKind	Controls whether the virtual keyword is used in the operation.	Common (False)
SubscriptResultType	Sets the result type of the function.	Blank (Void)
InlineSubscriptOperation	Determines whether the operation is inlined.	False
GenerateDereference-Operation	Controls whether a dereference function (*) is created.	False
DereferenceVisibility	Sets the visibility (public, private, protected) of the operation.	Public
DereferenceKind	Controls whether the virtual keyword is used in the operation.	Common (False)
DereferenceResultType	Sets the result type of the function.	Blank (Void)
InlineDereference-Operation	Determines whether the operation is inlined.	False
GenerateIndirection-Operation	Controls whether an indirection function (->) is created.	False
IndirectionVisibility	Sets the visibility (public, private, protected) of the operation.	Public
IndirectionKind	Controls whether the virtual keyword is used in the operation.	Common (False)
IndirectionResultType	Sets the result type of the function.	Blank (Void)
InlineIndirection-Operation	Determines whether the operation is inlined.	False

Continued on next page

TABLE 12.2 CONTINUED: Class Code Generation Properties

Property	Purpose	Default
GenerateStream-Operations	Controls whether stream operations (<< and >>) are generated.	False
StreamVisibility	Sets the visibility (public, private, protected) of the operation.	Public
InlineStreamOperations	Determines whether the operations are inlined.	False

Attribute Properties

Attribute properties are the C++ specific properties that relate to attributes. Using these properties, you can, for example, decide whether the attribute will be generated in the code, what the attribute name should be in the generated code, and whether Get and Set operations should be created for the attribute.

There are two places to set these properties. To set them for all attributes, select Tools ➤ Options, then the C++ tab, and select Attribute from the drop-down list box. To set them for only one attribute, select the C++ tab on the attribute specification window and edit the properties there.

Table 12.3 lists the attribute properties, their purpose, and their default value.

TABLE 12.3: Attribute Code Generation Properties

Property	Purpose	Default
CodeName	Sets the attribute's name in the generated code.	Blank (uses attribute name from the model)
GenerateDataMember	Controls whether a member variable will be generated for the attribute.	True
DataMemberName	Sets the name of the member variable generated for the attribute.	By default, Rose will use the attribute name from the model.
DataMemberVisibility	Sets the visibility of the generated member variable.	Private
DataMemberMutability	Controls whether the attribute will be created with the mutable keyword, the const keyword, or neither.	Neither (Unrestricted)
DataMemberIsVolatile	Controls whether the attribute will be created with the v keyword.	False
DataMemberFieldSize	Specifies the number of bits of the generated attribute.	Blank
GenerateGetOperation	Controls whether a Get operation is created for the attribute to help other classes get to the value of the attribute.	True
GenerateSetOperation	Controls whether a Set operation is created for the attribute to help other classes set the value of the attribute.	True
GetName	Sets the name of the Get operation that is generated.	get_<attribute name>
SetName	Sets the name of the Set operation that is generated.	set_<attribute name>
GetSetKinds	Controls whether the Get and Set operations are virtual, static, abstract, friend, or none of these.	None (Common)
GetIsConst	Controls whether the Get operation uses the const keyword.	True
GetResultIsConst	Controls whether the Get operation returns a const value.	The value set in the GetIsConst property (Same_As_Function)

TABLE 12.3 CONTINUED: Attribute Code Generation Properties

Property	Purpose	Default
GetSetByReference	Controls whether the Get and Set operations pass arguments and return values by reference or by value.	By value
InlineGet	Determines whether the Get operations are inlined.	True
SetReturnsValue	Specifies whether the Set operation returns a nonvoid.	False
InlineSet	Determines whether the Set operations are inlined.	True

Operation Properties

The operation properties are the C++ code generation properties that are specific to operations. These properties will let you set the name of the operation, control whether the operation is virtual, and set other code generation specifications for each operation.

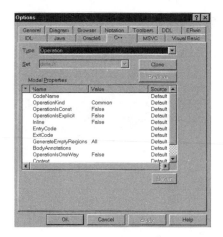

There are two places to set these properties. To set them for all operations, select Tools ➢ Options, then the C++ tab, and select Operation from the drop-down list box. To set them for only one operation, select the C++ tab on the operation specification window and edit the properties there.

Table 12.4 lists many of the operation code generation properties, their purpose, and their default value.

TABLE 12.4: Operation Code Generation Properties

Property	Purpose	Default
CodeName	Sets the name of the generated operation.	Operation name from the model
OperationKind	Controls whether the operation is virtual, static, abstract, friend, or none of these.	None (Common)
OperationIsConst	Controls whether the operation will be generated with the const keyword.	False
OperationIsExplicit	Controls whether the keyword explicit will be used when generating the operation.	False
Inline	Controls whether to inline the operation.	False
EntryCode	Used to enter code or comments that are generated along with the operation. (This code will not be placed in the protected region, which is protected during round-trip engineering.)	Empty
ExitCode	Used to enter code or comments that are generated along with the operation. (This code will not be placed in the protected region, which is protected during round-trip engineering.)	Empty
GenerateEmptyRegions	Controls whether protected regions are generated with the operation.	Always generate (All)
BodyAnnotations	Controls whether notations are generated in the implementation file for the operation's documentation, concurrency, space, time, qualifications, exceptions, pre-conditions, post-conditions, and semantics.	All are generated

Module Specification (Header File) Properties

The module specification properties are those properties that are related to the header files (.H) you will generate from Rose. These properties give you the ability to decide whether or not to generate the header file, include a copyright notice in the header file, change the header filename, or control other specifications of the header file.

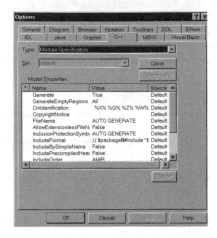

There are two places to set these properties. To set them for all header files, select Tools ➤ Options, then the C++ tab, and select Module Specification from the drop-down list box. To set them for only one file, select the C++ tab on the component specification window and edit the properties there.

Table 12.5 lists many of the code generation properties for header files, their purposes, and their default values.

TABLE 12.5: Header File Code Generation Properties

Property	Purpose	Default
Generate	Controls whether the header file will be generated	True
GenerateEmptyRegions	Controls whether protected regions will be generated	All
CmIdentification	Used to enter codes that your configuration management software can use	%X%%Q%%Z%%W%
CopyRightNotice	Used to enter a copyright in the header file	Blank
FileName	Sets the name of the header file	Component name
AllowExtensionlessFile-Name	Allows a header file to be generated without an extension	False

Continued on next page

TABLE 12.5 CONTINUED: Header File Code Generation Properties

Property	Purpose	Default
InclusionProtectionSymbol	Sets the symbol to use in preprocessor directives to prevent the header file from being included more than once	AUTO GENERATE (uses the name of the component)
IncludeFormat	Sets the syntax to use for include statements	//$package #include "$file"
IncludeBySimpleName	Determines whether include statements will contain full path names or only filenames	False (Full path)
IncludePrecompiledHeader	Determines whether the precompiled header is placed at the start of the includes	False
IncludeOrder	Sets the order of the regions of code with include statements	AMIR (Additional includes, AFX_INCLUDES for Visual C++ only, Includes, Rose-generated includes)
AdditionalIncludes	Used to enter any additional #include statements you want to see in the code	Blank
InliningStyle	Controls where definitions of inlined functions are generated (following the class definition or in the class declaration)	FollowingClass-Declaration
TypesDefined	Specifies the types defined in a module	Blank
IncludeClosure	Specifies the header files #included by the module	Blank

Module Body (Implementation File) Properties

The module body properties are those properties that are related to the implementation files (.CPP) you will generate from Rose. These properties give you the ability to decide whether or not to generate the file, include a copyright notice in the file, change the filename, or control other specifications of the implementation file.

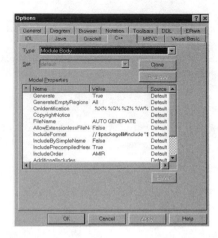

There are two places to set these properties. To set them for all implementation files, select Tools ➤ Options, then the C++ tab, and select Module Body from the drop-down list box. To set them for only one file, select the C++ tab on the component specification window and edit the properties there.

Table 12.6 lists many of the code generation properties for implementation files, their purposes, and their default values.

TABLE 12.6: Implementation File Code Generation Properties

Property	Purpose	Default
Generate	Controls whether the implementation file will be generated	True
GenerateEmptyRegions	Controls whether protected regions will be generated	All
CmIdentification	Used to enter codes that your configuration management software can use	%X%%Q%%Z%%W%
CopyRightNotice	Used to enter a copyright in the implementation file	Blank
FileName	Sets the name of the implementation file	Component name
AllowExtensionlessFileName	Allows a header file to be generated without an extension	False
IncludeFormat	Sets the syntax to use for include statements	//$package #include "$file"

Continued on next page

TABLE 12.6 CONTINUED: Implementation File Code Generation Properties

Property	Purpose	Default
IncludeBySimpleName	Determines whether include statements will contain full path names or only filenames	False (Full path)
IncludePrecompiledHeader	Determines whether the precompiled header is placed at the start of the includes	True
IncludeOrder	Sets the order of the regions of code with include statements	AMIR (Additional includes, AFX_INCLUDES for Visual C++ only, Includes, Rose-generated includes)
AdditionalIncludes	Used to enter any additional #include statements you want to see in the code	Blank
InliningStyle	Controls where definitions of inlined functions are generated (following the class definition or in the class declaration)	FollowingClassDeclaration
TypesDefined	Specifies the types defined in a module	Blank
IncludeClosure	Specifies the header files included by the module	Blank

Association Properties

Association properties are the C++ code generation properties that deal with association relationships. Using these properties, you can control the code generated for the associations. In C++, there is only one association property.

To set this property, select Tools ➤ Options, then the C++ tab, and select Association from the drop-down list box.

There is only one code generation property for associations. The NameIfUnlabeled property is used to set the name of the attribute that will be generated for the relationship if there is no role name. By default, the value the_$targetClass will be used.

Role Properties

Role properties are the C++ code generation properties that affect the code generated for relationships. There are a number of role properties that will let you set the name of the attribute that is created, set the container class to be used for the attribute, and change other specific pieces of the generated code.

As with most of the other property sets, there are two places to set these properties. To set them for all relationships, select Tools ➢ Options, then the C++ tab, and select Role from the drop-down list box. To set them for a single relationship, open the relationship specification. On the C++ tab of the relationship specification window, you can change the properties for that relationship.

Table 12.7 lists the role properties, their meanings, and their default values.

TABLE 12.7: Role Code Generation Properties

Property	Purpose	Default
CodeName	Sets the name of the relationship in the generated code.	Blank
ForwardReferenceOnly	Controls whether Rose will place a forward declaration for the supplier class of the relationship before the class definitions in the module.	False
NameIfUnlabeled	Sets the name of the attribute that will be generated, if no role name is present and DataMemberName is blank or $relationship.	the_$targetClass
GenerateDataMember	Controls whether an attribute is created for the relationship.	True
DataMemberName	Sets the name of the generated attribute.	$target
DataMemberVisibility	Sets the visibility of the generated attribute.	Implementation
DataMemberMutability	Controls whether the keyword mutable, the keyword const, or neither keyword will be generated for the attribute.	Neither keyword (Unrestricted)
DataMemberIsVolatile	Controls whether the v keyword will be used in the code.	False
DataMemberFieldSize	Specifies the number of bits of the generated attribute.	Blank
InitialValue	Sets the initial value of the generated attribute.	Blank
ContainerClass	Sets the data type of the attribute that is created for the relationship.	Blank
ContainerGet	If the relationship has a qualifier, this property is used to enter the prototype C++ expression to retrieve a specific element from the container.	$data.get(keys)
ContainerSet	If the relationship has a qualifier, this property is used to enter the prototype C++ expression to set a specific element in the container.	$data.set(keys, $value)

Continued on next page

TABLE 12.7 CONTINUED: Role Code Generation Properties

Property	Purpose	Default
QualifiedContainer	If the relationship has a qualifier, this property sets the container class that will be used to store references to the supplier class, and values for the qualifier key.	Blank
AssocClassContainer	Specifies the data type to be used when generating an attribute to support the relationship to an association class.	$supplier*
AssocClassInitialValue	Sets the initial value of the attribute generated to support the relationship to an association class.	Blank
GetSetKinds	Controls whether the Get and Set operations are virtual, static, abstract, friend, or none of these.	None (Common)
GetSetByReference	Controls whether the Get and Set operations pass arguments and return values by reference or by value.	Passed by value
GenerateGetOperation	Controls whether a Get operation is created for the attribute.	True
GetName	Sets the name of the Get operation that is generated.	get_$target
GetIsConst	Controls whether the Get operation is produced with the const keyword.	True
GetResultIsConst	Controls whether the Get operation returns a const value.	Whichever value is set in GetIsConst (Same_As_Function)
InlineGet	Controls whether Rose inlines the Get operation.	True
GenerateSetOperation	Controls whether a Set operation is created for the data member.	True
SetName	Sets the name of the Set operation that is generated.	set_$target
SetReturnsValue	Controls whether the Set operation returns a nonvoid value.	False
InlineSet	Controls whether Rose inlines the Set operation.	True
QualifiedGetSetBy-Reference	Specifies whether arguments and return values in the qualified Get and Set methods are passed by value or by reference.	Same_As_GetSet-ByReference

Continued on next page

TABLE 12.7 CONTINUED: Role Code Generation Properties

Property	Purpose	Default
GenerateQualifiedGet-Operation	Controls whether Rose generates a Get operation which will get an item from the container generated to support the relationship.	True
QualifiedGetName	Sets the name of the qualified Get operation.	get_$target
QualifiedGetIsConst	Controls whether the qualified Get operation is produced with the const keyword.	True
QualifiedGet-ResultIsConst	Controls whether the qualified Get operation returns a const value.	Whichever value is set in QualifiedGetIsConst (Same_As_Function)
InlineQualifiedGet	Controls whether Rose inlines the qualified Get operation.	True
GenerateQualifiedSet Operation	Controls whether Rose generates a Set operation that will set the value of an item in the container generated to support the relationship.	True
QualifiedSetName	Sets the name of the qualified Set operation.	get_$target
QualifiedSet-ReturnsValue	Controls whether the qualified Set operation returns a nonvoid value.	False
InlineQualifiedSet	Controls whether Rose inlines the qualified Set operation.	True
GenerateAssocClass-DataMember	Controls whether Rose creates a data member to support a relationship to an association class.	True
AssocClassDataMember-Name	Sets the name of the data member created for the relationship to an association class.	$target
AssocClassData-MemberVisibility	Sets the visibility of the data member created for the relationship to an association class.	Implementation
AssocClassDataMember-Mutability	Controls whether the keyword mutable, the keyword const, or neither keyword will be generated for the data member.	Neither keyword (Unrestricted)
AssocClassData-MemberIsVolatile	Controls whether the v keyword will be used in the code.	False

Continued on next page

TABLE 12.7 CONTINUED: Role Code Generation Properties

Property	Purpose	Default
AssocClassGetSetKinds	Controls whether the Get and Set operations are virtual, static, abstract, friend, or none of these.	None (Common)
GenerateAssocClassGet-Operation	Controls whether Rose will generate a Get function for the data member created to support the relationship to an association class.	True
AssocClassGetName	Sets the name of the Get function for the data member created to support the relationship to an association class.	get_$target
AssocClassGetIsConst	Controls whether the association class Get operation is produced with the const keyword.	True
AssocClassGet-ResultIsConst	Controls whether the association class Get operation returns a const value.	Whichever value is set in QualifiedGetIs-Const (Same_As_Function)
InlineAssocClassGet	Controls whether Rose inlines the association class Get operation.	True
GenerateAssocClassSet-Operation	Controls whether Rose will generate a Set function for the data member created to support the relationship to an association class.	True
AssocClassSetName	Sets the name of the set function for the data member created to support the relationship to an association class.	set_$target
AssocClassSet-ReturnsValue	Controls whether the association Set operation returns a nonvoid value.	False
InlineAssocClassSet	Controls whether Rose inlines the association class Set operation.	True
AssocClassForward-ReferenceOnly	Controls whether a forward declaration for the association class will appear before the definition of the association class.	True
GenerateForward-Reference (98)	Controls whether a referenced interface will be included with a #include or a forward reference.	False (#include)
IsReadOnly (98)	Controls whether the data member is read only.	False
BoundedRoleType (98)	Controls whether a sequence or array will be used in a bounded relationship.	Sequence

Aggregation (Has Relationship) Properties

Has properties are the C++ properties that deal with aggregations. Using these properties, you can control the code generated for an aggregation.

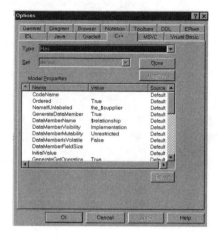

To set these properties, select Tools ➤ Options, then the C++ tab, and select Has from the drop-down list box.

Table 12.8 lists the code generation properties for aggregations, their purposes, and their default values.

TABLE 12.8: Aggregation Code Generation Properties

Property	Purpose	Default
CodeName	Sets the name of the relationship in the generated code	Blank
Ordered	Controls whether the objects on the supplier side of the relationship are ordered	True
NameIfUnlabeled	Sets the name of the attribute that will be generated, if no role name is present and DataMemberName is blank or $relationship	the_$supplier
GenerateDataMember	Controls whether an attribute is created for the relationship	True
DataMemberName	Sets the name of the generated attribute	$relationship
DataMemberVisibility	Sets the visibility of the generated attribute	Implementation

Continued on next page

TABLE 12.8 CONTINUED: Aggregation Code Generation Properties

Property	Purpose	Default
DataMember-Mutability	Controls whether the keyword mutable, the keyword const, or neither keyword will be generated for the attribute	Neither keyword (Unrestricted)
DataMemberIsVolatile	Controls whether the v keyword will be used in the code	False
DataMemberFieldSize	Specifies the number of bits of the generated attribute	Blank
InitialValue	Sets the initial value of the generated attribute	Blank
GenerateGet-Operation	Controls whether a Get operation is created for the data member	True
GenerateSetOperation	Controls whether a Set operation is created for the data member	True
GetName	Sets the name of the Get operation that is generated	get_<attribute name>
SetName	Sets the name of the Set operation that is generated	set_<attribute name>
GetSetKinds	Controls whether the Get and Set operations are virtual, static, abstract, friend, or none of these	None (Common)
ContainerClass	Sets the data type used for the generated attribute if the multiplicity is greater than one	Blank
SelectorName	Controls whether direct Set and Get functions will be created for the data member	Blank (False)
SelectorType	Specifies the type for the argument specified in the SelectorName property	Blank
GetIsConst	Controls whether the Get operation is produced with the const keyword	True
GetResultsIsConst	Controls whether the Get operation returns a const value	Whichever value is set in GetIsConst (Same_As_Function)
GetSetByReference	Controls whether the Get and Set operations pass arguments and return values by reference or by value	Passed by value

Continued on next page

TABLE 12.8 CONTINUED: Aggregation Code Generation Properties

Property	Purpose	Default
InlineGet	Controls whether Rose inlines the Get operation	True
SetReturnsValue	Controls whether the Set operation returns a nonvoid value	False
InlineSet	Controls whether Rose inlines the Set operation	True
Forward ReferenceOnly	Controls whether Rose will place a forward declaration for the supplier class of the relationship before the class definitions in the module	False
GenerateForward Reference (98)	Controls whether a referenced interface will be included with a #include or a forward reference	False (#include)
IsReadOnly (98)	Controls whether the data member is read only	False
BoundedHasRelType (98)	Controls whether a sequence or array will be used in a bounded relationship	Sequence

Dependency Properties

The dependency properties control how dependency relationships will be implemented in C++.

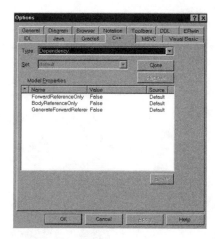

There are two places to set the dependency properties. To set the properties for all dependencies, select Tools ➣ Options, then the C++ tab, and select Dependency from the drop-down list box. To set the properties for only one dependency, select the C++ tab on the dependency specification window and edit the properties there.

Table 12.9 lists the code generation properties for dependencies.

TABLE 12.9: Dependency Code Generation Properties

Property	Purpose	Default
Forward-ReferenceOnly	Controls whether Rose will place a forward declaration for the supplier class of the relationship before the class definitions in the module	False
BodyReferenceOnly	Controls whether the forward declaration or #include statement is generated only in the module body, not in the module specification	False
GenerateForward-Reference (98)	Controls whether a referenced interface is included with a #include statement or a forward reference	#include (False)

Subsystem Properties

Subsystem properties are the properties that apply to Component view packages in your Rose model.

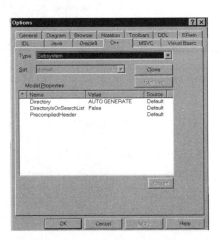

You can set the subsystem properties by selecting Tools ➤ Options, the C++ tab, and Subsystem from the drop-down list box. To set the properties for only one subsystem, select the C++ tab on the package specification window and edit the properties there.

Table 12.10 lists the code generation properties for subsystems.

TABLE 12.10: Subsystem Code Generation Properties

Property	Purpose	Default
Directory	Sets the name of the directory that will be created for the package	Package name (AUTO GENERATE)
DirectoryIsOnSearchList	Controls whether the path in a #include statement contains an absolute or a relative path	Absolute path (False)
PrecompiledHeader	Specifies a precompiled header that should be included in the generated code	Blank

Class Category Properties

Subsystem properties apply to the Component view packages in the model. The class category properties are those that apply to the Logical view packages in the model.

Table 12.11 lists the class category properties.

TABLE 12.11: Class Category Code Generation Properties

Property	Purpose	Default
IsNameSpace	Specifies whether the package is a namespace	False
Indent	Sets the number of spaces to indent if the package is a namespace	2
CodeName	Sets the name of the namespace	Blank
GenerateEmptyRegions	Sets the type of protected regions that will be generated	All

Generalization Properties

As with other relationships, you can set code generation properties for generalization (inheritance) relationships in C++. There is only one property you can set for a generalization relationship. The InstanceArguments property allows you to set the actual arguments used for a class that inherits from a parameterized class. The default value of this property is blank.

Generated Code

In the following sections, we'll take a look at the C++ code generated for a class, an attribute and operation, and for the different types of relationships between classes. In each of these sections, we'll include some sample code to give you an idea of what will be generated from your Rose model.

Rose uses the information in the specifications of the model elements when generating code. For example, it will look at the different specifications for a class (visibility, attributes, operations, and so on) when generating code for the class.

> **NOTE** The code samples in the following sections were generated using Rose 98i. The code generated with Rose 98 will be very similar, but there are minor differences between the two.

Let's begin by looking at the code generated for a typical class.

Classes

A class in your object model will become a C++ class when you generate code. Each class will generate code similar to the following:

```
Class TheClass
{
public:
    TheClass();
    ~TheClass();
};
```

However, a great deal of additional information will also be generated in the code. We'll look at a complete header and implementation file shortly. All of the attributes, operations, and relationships of the class will be reflected in the generated code. The major elements generated for each class include:

- The class name
- The class visibility
- A constructor for the class
- A destructor for the class
- Get() and Set() operations for each attribute
- Class documentation
- Attributes
- Operations
- Relationships
- Documentation

Each class in the model will generate two C++ files, a header file, and an implementation file. Each file will be named using the class name. For example, an Employee class will generate an Employee.h file and an Employee.cpp file.

When generating code, Rose will use the package structure you established in the Component view of your model to generate the appropriate directories. A directory will be created for each package in the model. Within each of the directories Rose creates there will be the .cpp and .h files for the classes in that package. If you have not created components and packages in the Component view, Rose will use the package structure in the Logical view to create the directory structure.

Much of the information in your Rose model will be used directly when generating code. For example, the attributes, operations, relationships, and class name of each class will directly affect the code generated. Other model fields, such as the documentation entered for the class, will not directly affect the code. These field values are created as comments in the generated code.

Table 12.12 lists the fields available in the Class Specification window and notes which of these fields will directly affect the code generated.

TABLE 12.12: Effect of Class Specifications on Generated Code

Fields	Affect on Code
Name	Name in model will become class name
Type	Directly affects the type of class created
Stereotype	Comment
Export Control	Directly affects the class visibility
Documentation	Comment
Cardinality	Comment
Space	Comment
Persistence	Comment in generated code, but affects whether DDL can be generated for the class
Concurrency	Comment
Abstract	Creates an abstract class
Formal Arguments	Formal arguments are included in the code for a parameterized class
Operations	Generated in code
Attributes	Generated in code
Relationships	Generated in code

Let's look at the code generated for the following class:

Generated Header File

The following code is the header file that was generated for this class. We'll examine this header file one section at a time to look in detail at what Rose generates for a class. Before we do, however, let's discuss the annotations that Rose inserts into the source code. Rose adds these annotations so that code can be modified and regenerated (round-trip engineering) without overwriting these changes. A typical section of the code will look something like this:

```
//## begin name%123456789000.codesection preserve=yes
//## end name%123456789000.codesection
```

The 12-digit string of numbers and letters (in this example, %123456789000) is a unique identifier Rose assigns to the various code sections. The preserve= (no/yes) tells Rose to either re-evaluate this section or to leave it as is when regenerating the source code. These identifiers help ensure that neither your model nor your code is damaged when you do round-trip engineering. For example, after you generate code, you add implementation code by inserting lines between the //## begin and //## end statements. If you reverse engineer the code back into Rose, make changes to the model, and regenerate the code, Rose will not overwrite or erase the programming you just completed.

The header file for the class displayed above is:

```
//## begin module%37267F000276.cm preserve=no
//    %X% %Q% %Z% %W%
//## end module%37267F000276.cm

//## begin module%37267F000276.cp preserve=no
//## end module%37267F000276.cp

//## Module: Sampleclass%37267F000276; Package specification
//## Subsystem: <Top Level>
//## Source file: C:\Program Files\Rational\Rose 98i\C++\source\➡
Sampleclass.h

#ifndef Sampleclass_h
#define Sampleclass_h 1

//## begin module%37267F000276.additionalIncludes preserve=no
//## end module%37267F000276.additionalIncludes
```

```
//## begin module%37267F000276.includes preserve=yes
//## end module%37267F000276.includes

//## begin module%37267F000276.declarations preserve=no
//## end module%37267F000276.declarations

//## begin module%37267F000276.additionalDeclarations preserve=yes
//## end module%37267F000276.additionalDeclarations


//## begin SampleClass%37267EF301B8.preface preserve=yes
//## end SampleClass%37267EF301B8.preface

//## Class: SampleClass%37267EF301B8
//## Category: <Top Level>
//## Persistence: Transient
//## Cardinality/Multiplicity: n

class SampleClass
{
  //## begin SampleClass%37267EF301B8.initialDeclarations preserve=yes
  //## end SampleClass%37267EF301B8.initialDeclarations

  public:
    //## Constructors (generated)
      SampleClass();

      SampleClass(const SampleClass &right);

    //## Destructor (generated)
      ~SampleClass();

    //## Assignment Operation (generated)
      const SampleClass & operator=(const SampleClass &right);

    //## Equality Operations (generated)
      int operator==(const SampleClass &right) const;

      int operator!=(const SampleClass &right) const;

    // Additional Public Declarations
      //## begin SampleClass%37267EF301B8.public preserve=yes
      //## end SampleClass%37267EF301B8.public
```

```
  protected:
    // Additional Protected Declarations
      //## begin SampleClass%37267EF301B8.protected preserve=yes
      //## end SampleClass%37267EF301B8.protected

  private:
    // Additional Private Declarations
      //## begin SampleClass%37267EF301B8.private preserve=yes
      //## end SampleClass%37267EF301B8.private

  private: //## implementation
    // Additional Implementation Declarations
      //## begin SampleClass%37267EF301B8.implementation preserve=yes
      //## end SampleClass%37267EF301B8.implementation

};

//## begin SampleClass%37267EF301B8.postscript preserve=yes
//## end SampleClass%37267EF301B8.postscript

// Class SampleClass

//## begin module%37267F000276.epilog preserve=yes
//## end module%37267F000276.epilog


#endif
```

As you can see, Rose generates a class with the same name as the class in the model. Let's examine each piece of this file, one at a time.

Configuration Management Section

The configuration management section is provided to support integration with your configuration management software. It includes the following lines:

```
//## begin module%37267F000276.cm preserve=no
//    %X% %Q% %Z% %W%
//## end module%37267F000276.cm
```

This section of the header includes information about your configuration management settings. To change the configuration management settings, select Tools ➤ Options from the menu. In the C++ tab, select Module Specification from the drop-down list box in the Type field to display the module specification code generation properties. You can change the value of the CmIdentification property to a string that your configuration management software will recognize.

Some sample values you can place in this setting include:

- $date, which inserts the date the code was generated

- $time, which inserts the time the code was generated

- $module, which inserts the component name

- $file, which inserts the component's file

Copyright Notice Section

The copyright notice section can be used to incorporate a copyright notice into your code. It includes the following two lines:

```
//## begin module%37267F000276.cp preserve=no
//## end module%37267F000276.cp
```

By default, there is no copyright notice generated for your code. If, however, you'd like to add a copyright, you can change the code generation properties. Select Tools ➤ Options from the menu, then select the C++ tab. Select Module Specification from the drop-down list box to display the module specification code generation properties. Change the CopyrightNotice field to include any copyright information. If information is entered, it will be generated, along with the above two lines, in the header file.

Some sample values you can place in this setting include:

- $date, which inserts the date the code was generated

- $time, which inserts the time the code was generated

- $module, which inserts the component name

- $file, which inserts the component's file

The copyright notice is placed between the //## begin and //## end statements to protect it during round-trip engineering.

Module Section

The module section contains some basic information about the component being generated. The module section includes the following lines:

```
//## Module: Sampleclass%37267F000276; Package specification
//## Subsystem: <Top Level>
//## Source file: C:\Program Files\Rational\Rose 98i\C++\source\➡
   Sampleclass.h
```

This section includes comments that describe what module (i.e., component) the class is in. In this case, as you can see in the first line, the class SampleClass was contained inside a package specification called SampleClass.

The second line lets you know what Logical view package the class is contained in. In this case, the class was not placed inside a Logical view package, so its subsystem is <Top Level>.

The third line lists the location of the header file itself. The format depends on the module specification's property setting.

Preprocessor Directives Section

The preprocessor directives include the following lines:

```
#ifndef Sampleclass_h
#define Sampleclass_h 1
```

These lines are inserted into the code to prevent the header file from being included more than once. The format depends on the module specification's property setting.

Includes Sections

There are two includes sections generated in the code. The first is used for any includes statements you specified in the model using the code generation properties. The second is where programmers manually add include statements into the source code. The #include statements are inserted between the protected code region marked by the annotations, //## begin and //## end. When you perform round-trip engineering, Rose will protect the #include statements between these lines.

```
//## begin module%37267F000276.additionalIncludes preserve=no
//## end module%37267F000276.additionalIncludes
```

In this section, Rose will insert any additional #include statements you'd like to add to your code. To add a new #include statement, select Tools ➤ Options from the menu, and then the C++ tab. Select Module Specification from the drop-down list box, then type any additional includes in the AdditionalIncludes field. The names you type in this field must be a list, and each name must be in the format "name" or <name>.

```
//## begin module%37267F000276.includes preserve=yes
//## end module%37267F000276.includes
```

This section is provided in order for you to manually enter any #include statements into the source code.

Declarations Sections

The declarations sections are provided to insert any declarations into your code. Once code has been generated, you can insert declarations between the //## begin and //## end statements to be sure the declarations are not affected if you do round-trip engineering.

```
//## begin module%37267F000276.declarations preserve=no
//## end module%37267F000276.declarations

//## begin module%37267F000276.additionalDeclarations preserve=yes
//## end module%37267F000276.additionalDeclarations
```

Class Definition Section

This section contains information about the class itself, including the class name, its Logical view and Component view packages, its persistence, and its cardinality. The first line in this section includes the class name. The second line, Category, lists the Logical view package the class is in. If the class is not in a Logical view package, <Top Level> is shown. When generating code with Rose 98 rather than 98i, a Subsystem line is added. The Subsystem line lists the Component view package the class is in. Again, if the component for a class is not in a Component view package, <Top Level> will be listed. The Cardinality/Multiplicity line is intended to show how many instances of the class you expect to have in memory at a given time.

In the class definition, the default constructor, copy constructor, and destructor will be included. To prevent these from generating, or to change the generation options, change the C++ code generation options for the class. Open the class specification window, then select the C++ tab.

You can change GenerateDefaultConstructor, DefaultConstructorVisibility, InlineDefaultConstructor, and ExplicitDefaultConstructor properties to control whether the default constructor is created, the visibility of the constructor, whether the constructor will be generated inline, and whether the constructor should be an explicit constructor.

Change the GenerateCopyConstructor, CopyConstructorVisibility, InlineCopy-Constructor, and ExplicitCopyConstructor properties to control whether the copy constructor is created, the visibility of the constructor, whether the constructor will be generated inline, and whether the constructor should be an explicit constructor.

Change the GenerateDestructor, DestructorVisibility, DestructorKind, and InlineDestructor properties to control whether the destructor is created, the visibility of the destructor, whether the destructor is virtual, and whether the destructor should be an explicit constructor.

By default, Rose will generate an assignment operation and an equality operation. To prevent these from generating, or to change the generation properties, change the GenerateAssignmentOperation, AssignmentVisibility, Assignment-Kind, InlineAssignmentOperation, GenerateEqualityOperations, Equality-Visibility, EqualityKind, and InlineEqualityOperations code generation properties for the class.

If you have public attributes or operations for the class, these declarations will also appear under the public section of this file.

In the protected, private, and private implementation sections, Rose will include declarations for your protected, private, and implementation attributes and operations, respectively.

```
class SampleClass
{
  //## begin SampleClass%37267EF301B8.initialDeclarations preserve=yes
  //## end SampleClass%37267EF301B8.initialDeclarations

  public:
    //## Constructors (generated)
      SampleClass();

      SampleClass(const SampleClass &right);

    //## Destructor (generated)
      ~SampleClass();
```

```
    //## Assignment Operation (generated)
      const SampleClass & operator=(const SampleClass &right);

    //## Equality Operations (generated)
      int operator==(const SampleClass &right) const;

      int operator!=(const SampleClass &right) const;

    // Additional Public Declarations
      //## begin SampleClass%37267EF301B8.public preserve=yes
      //## end SampleClass%37267EF301B8.public

  protected:
    // Additional Protected Declarations
      //## begin SampleClass%37267EF301B8.protected preserve=yes
      //## end SampleClass%37267EF301B8.protected

  private:
    // Additional Private Declarations
      //## begin SampleClass%37267EF301B8.private preserve=yes
      //## end SampleClass%37267EF301B8.private

  private: //## implementation
    // Additional Implementation Declarations
      //## begin SampleClass%37267EF301B8.implementation preserve=yes
      //## end SampleClass%37267EF301B8.implementation

};

//## begin SampleClass%37267EF301B8.postscript preserve=yes
//## end SampleClass%37267EF301B8.postscript

// Class SampleClass

//## begin module%37267F000276.epilog preserve=yes
//## end module%37267F000276.epilog

#endif
```

If you entered any documentation for the class using the documentation window or the documentation area of the class specification window, this documentation will be included as a comment in the code.

Generated Implementation File

The other file generated by Rose is an implementation file, with the default extension ".CPP." The following is the implementation file generated along with the header file we just examined.

```
//## begin module%37267F0103AC.cm preserve=no
//     %X% %Q% %Z% %W%
//## end module%37267F0103AC.cm

//## begin module%37267F0103AC.cp preserve=no
//## end module%37267F0103AC.cp

//## Module: Sampleclass%37267F0103AC; Package body
//## Subsystem: <Top Level>
//## Source file: C:\Program Files\Rational\Rose 98i\C++\source\➡
Sampleclass.cpp

//## begin module%37267F0103AC.additionalIncludes preserve=no
//## end module%37267F0103AC.additionalIncludes

//## begin module%37267F0103AC.includes preserve=yes
//## end module%37267F0103AC.includes

// Sampleclass
#include "Sampleclass.h"
//## begin module%37267F0103AC.declarations preserve=no
//## end module%37267F0103AC.declarations

//## begin module%37267F0103AC.additionalDeclarations preserve=yes
//## end module%37267F0103AC.additionalDeclarations


// Class SampleClass

SampleClass::SampleClass()
  //## begin SampleClass::SampleClass%.hasinit preserve=no
  //## end SampleClass::SampleClass%.hasinit
  //## begin SampleClass::SampleClass%.initialization preserve=yes
  //## end SampleClass::SampleClass%.initialization
{
  //## begin SampleClass::SampleClass%.body preserve=yes
  //## end SampleClass::SampleClass%.body
}
```

```
SampleClass::SampleClass(const SampleClass &right)
  //## begin SampleClass::SampleClass%copy.hasinit preserve=no
  //## end SampleClass::SampleClass%copy.hasinit
  //## begin SampleClass::SampleClass%copy.initialization preserve=yes
  //## end SampleClass::SampleClass%copy.initialization
{
  //## begin SampleClass::SampleClass%copy.body preserve=yes
  //## end SampleClass::SampleClass%copy.body
}


SampleClass::~SampleClass()
{
  //## begin SampleClass::~SampleClass%.body preserve=yes
  //## end SampleClass::~SampleClass%.body
}


const SampleClass & SampleClass::operator=(const SampleClass &right)
{
  //## begin SampleClass::operator=%.body preserve=yes
  //## end SampleClass::operator=%.body
}


int SampleClass::operator==(const SampleClass &right) const
{
  //## begin SampleClass::operator==%.body preserve=yes
  //## end SampleClass::operator==%.body
}

int SampleClass::operator!=(const SampleClass &right) const
{
  //## begin SampleClass::operator!=%.body preserve=yes
  //## end SampleClass::operator!=%.body
}


// Additional Declarations
  //## begin SampleClass%37267EF301B8.declarations preserve=yes
  //## end SampleClass%37267EF301B8.declarations
```

```
//## begin module%37267F0103AC.epilog preserve=yes
//## end module%37267F0103AC.epilog
```

As we did with the header file, let's examine each piece of the implementation file.

Configuration Management Section

As in the header file, the configuration management section is provided in the implementation file to support integration with your configuration management software. It includes the following lines:

```
//## begin module%37267F0103AC.cm preserve=no
//    %X% %Q% %Z% %W%
//## end module%37267F0103AC.cm
```

This section of the file includes information about your configuration management settings. The properties on the second line are the default configuration management settings.

As with the header file, you can change the configuration management settings for the implementation file. To change these settings, select Tools ➢ Options from the menu. In the C++ tab, select Module Body from the drop-down list box to display the module body code generation properties. You can use the CmIdentification property to change the default values on this second line. Using this property, set the change management settings to a string that your configuration management software will recognize.

Some sample values you can place in this setting include:

- $date, which inserts the date the code was generated

- $time, which inserts the time the code was generated

- $module, which inserts the component name

- $file, which inserts the component's file

Copyright Notice Section

You can insert a copyright notice into the implementation file. As in a header file, the copyright notice section can be used to incorporate a copyright notice into the implementation file. It includes the following two lines:

```
//## begin module%37267F0103AC.cp preserve=no
//## end module%37267F0103AC.cp
```

To add a copyright notice, select Tools ➤ Options from the menu, then select the C++ tab. Select Module Body from the drop-down list box to display the module body code generation properties. Change the CopyrightNotice field to include any copyright information. If information is entered, it will be generated, along with the above two lines, in the implementation file.

Some sample values you can place in this setting include:

- $date, which inserts the date the code was generated

- $time, which inserts the time the code was generated

- $module, which inserts the component name

- $file, which inserts the component's file

The copyright notice is placed between the //## begin and //## end statements to protect it during round-trip engineering.

Module Section

The module section contains some basic information about the implementation file being generated. The module section includes the following lines:

```
//## Module: Sampleclass%37267F0103AC; Package body
//## Subsystem: <Top Level>
//## Source file: C:\Program Files\Rational\Rose 98i\C++\source\➥
Sampleclass.cpp
```

This section includes comments that describe which module (i.e., component) the class is in. In this case, as you can see in the first line, the class SampleClass was contained inside a component called SampleClass.

The second line lets you know which Logical view package the class is contained in. In this case, the class was not placed inside a Logical view package, so its subsystem is <Top Level>.

The third line lists the location of the implementation file itself.

Includes Sections

The implementation file, like the header file, contains two includes sections. One is used for includes statements you specified using the code generation properties. The second is used after code is generated to manually add #include statements. The #include statements are inserted between the //## begin and //## end lines, in the protected code region. When you perform round-trip engineering, Rose will protect the #include statements between these lines.

```
//## begin module%37267F0103AC.additionalIncludes preserve=no
//## end module%37267F0103AC.additionalIncludes
```

In this section, Rose will insert any additional #include statements you'd like to add to your code. To add a new #include statement, select Tools ➤ Options from the menu, and then the C++ tab. Select Module Body from the drop-down list box, then type any additional includes in the AdditionalIncludes field. The names you type in this field must be a list, and each name must be in the format "name" or <name>.

```
//## begin module%37267F0103AC.includes preserve=yes
//## end module%37267F0103AC.includes
```

This section is provided in order for you to enter any #include statements. At the bottom of the includes section, Rose will insert a #include statement for the header file for the class. In this example, the following two lines were generated:

```
// Sampleclass
#include "Sampleclass.h"
```

Declarations Sections

The declarations sections are provided to insert any declarations into your code. Once code has been generated, you can insert declarations between the //## begin and //## end statements to be sure the declarations are not affected if you do round-trip engineering.

```
//## begin module%37267F0103AC.declarations preserve=no
//## end module%37267F0103AC.declarations

//## begin module%37267F0103AC.additionalDeclarations preserve=yes
//## end module%37267F0103AC.additionalDeclarations
```

Class Definition Section

This section contains the implementation code for the class. Rose will include code for the default constructor, copy constructor, and destructor. As with the header file, you can change whether the constructor, copy constructor, and destructor are generated, and set the generation properties. To do so, change the code generation properties in the C++ tab of the Component Specification window. Table 12.13 shows the properties that will affect the constructor, destructor, and copy constructor.

TABLE 12.13: Constructor, Copy Constructor, and Destructor Properties

Property	Purpose	Default
GenerateDefaultConstructor	Controls whether the default constructor will be generated	True (Declare-AndDefine)
DefaultConstructorVisibility	Sets the visibility of the default constructor	Public
InlineDefaultConstructor	Determines whether the default constructor is inline	False
ExplicitDefaultConstructor	Determines whether the default constructor is explicit	False
GenerateCopyConstructor	Controls whether the copy constructor will be generated	True (Declare-AndDefine)
CopyConstructorVisibility	Sets the visibility of the copy constructor	Public
InlineCopyConstructor	Determines whether the copy constructor is inline	False
ExplicitCopyConstructor	Determines whether the copy constructor is explicit	False
GenerateDestructor	Controls whether the destructor will be generated	True
DestructorVisibility	Sets the visibility of the destructor	Public
DestructorKind	Determines whether the destructor is virtual	Not virtual (Common)
InlineDestructor	Determines whether the destructor is inline	False

The code generated in the class definition section is listed below:

```
// Class SampleClass

SampleClass::SampleClass()
  //## begin SampleClass::SampleClass%.hasinit preserve=no
  //## end SampleClass::SampleClass%.hasinit
  //## begin SampleClass::SampleClass%.initialization preserve=yes
  //## end SampleClass::SampleClass%.initialization
{
  //## begin SampleClass::SampleClass%.body preserve=yes
  //## end SampleClass::SampleClass%.body
}

SampleClass::SampleClass(const SampleClass &right)
  //## begin SampleClass::SampleClass%copy.hasinit preserve=no
  //## end SampleClass::SampleClass%copy.hasinit
  //## begin SampleClass::SampleClass%copy.initialization preserve=yes
  //## end SampleClass::SampleClass%copy.initialization
{
  //## begin SampleClass::SampleClass%copy.body preserve=yes
  //## end SampleClass::SampleClass%copy.body
}


SampleClass::~SampleClass()
{
  //## begin SampleClass::~SampleClass%.body preserve=yes
  //## end SampleClass::~SampleClass%.body
}


const SampleClass & SampleClass::operator=(const SampleClass &right)
{
  //## begin SampleClass::operator=%.body preserve=yes
  //## end SampleClass::operator=%.body
}


int SampleClass::operator==(const SampleClass &right) const
{
  //## begin SampleClass::operator==%.body preserve=yes
  //## end SampleClass::operator==%.body
}
```

```
int SampleClass::operator!=(const SampleClass &right) const
{
  //## begin SampleClass::operator!=%.body preserve=yes
  //## end SampleClass::operator!=%.body
}


// Additional Declarations
  //## begin SampleClass%37267EF301B8.declarations preserve=yes
  //## end SampleClass%37267EF301B8.declarations

//## begin module%37267F0103AC.epilog preserve=yes
//## end module%37267F0103AC.epilog
```

Attributes

Aside from the class itself, Rose will generate the attributes for the class. For each attribute, Rose will include:

- Visibility
- Data type
- Default value
- Get operation
- Set operation

For a given attribute, Rose will generate code similar to the following:

```
Class TheClass
{
public:
    int PublicAttribute;
    int GetPublicAttribute();
    int GetProtectedAttribute();
    int GetPrivateAttribute();
void set_PublicAttribute (int value);
void set_ProtectedAttribute (int value);
void set_PrivateAttribute (int value);
```

```
protected:
    int ProtectedAttribute;

private:
    int PrivateAttribute;
};
```

However, a great deal more, including comments and Rose identifiers, will be generated in a full header and implementation file. Let's look in detail at the code generated for the following class:

There are three sections of code generated in the header file for the attribute in the above class. The first is as follows:

```
private:
    //## Get and Set Operations for Class Attributes (generated)

        //## Attribute: ID%372684250050
        const int get_ID () const;
        void set_ID (int value);
```

The above section includes declarations for the Get and Set operations that are automatically generated for the attribute. You can set whether Get and Set operations should be generated for the attribute by changing the code generation properties for the attribute. The code generation properties listed in Table 12.14 will affect the Get and Set operations.

TABLE 12.14: Properties Affecting Get and Set Operations

Property	Purpose	Default
GenerateGetOperation	Controls whether the Get operation is generated	True
GenerateSetOperation	Controls whether the Set operation is generated	True
GetName	Sets the name of the Get operation	get_<attribute name>
SetName	Sets the name of the Set operation	set_<attribute name>
GetSetKinds	Controls whether the Get and Set operations are virtual, static, abstract, friend, or none of these	None (Common)
GetIsConst	Controls whether the Get operation is produced with the const keyword	True
GetResultsIsConst	Controls whether the Get operation returns a const value	Whichever value is set in GetIsConst (Same_As_Function)
GetSetByReference	Controls whether the Get and Set operations pass arguments and return values by reference or by value	Passed by value (False)
InlineGet	Controls whether Rose inlines the Get operation	True
SetReturnsValue	Controls whether the Set operation returns a non-void value	False
InlineSet	Controls whether Rose inlines the Set operation	True

The second section of code produced in the header file for an attribute is the following:

```
private: //## implementation
    // Data Members for Class Attributes

    //## begin SampleClass::ID%372684250050.attr preserve=no
    private: int {U}
    int ID;
    //## end SampleClass::ID%372684250050.attr
```

This section declares each of the attributes. In this case, we have a private attribute called ID, which is an integer. The attribute is therefore listed in the "private:" section of the code. The code is generated between the //## begin and //## end statements to protect it during round-trip engineering.

The third section of code generated in the header file includes the code for the Get and Set operations. The Get operation returns the value of the attribute, and the Set operation sets the value of the attribute.

```
//## Get and Set Operations for Class Attributes (inline)

inline const int SampleClass::get_ID () const
{
  //## begin SampleClass::get_ID%372684250050.get preserve=no
  return ID;
  //## end SampleClass::get_ID%372684250050.get
}

inline void SampleClass::set_ID (int value)
{
  //## begin SampleClass::set_ID%372684250050.set preserve=no
  ID = value;
  //## end SampleClass::set_ID%372684250050.set
}
```

In the implementation file, there are two sections of code that include information about the attribute: the constructor and the copy constructor. In these constructors, Rose will include the logic to set the default value of the attribute, if you have specified a default value. In our example, the default value of the ID attribute is zero, so the following lines are generated:

```
SampleClass::SampleClass()
  //## begin SampleClass::SampleClass%.hasinit preserve=no
    : ID(0)
  //## end SampleClass::SampleClass%.hasinit
  //## begin SampleClass::SampleClass%.initialization preserve=yes
  //## end SampleClass::SampleClass%.initialization
{
  //## begin SampleClass::SampleClass%.body preserve=yes
  //## end SampleClass::SampleClass%.body
}
```

```
SampleClass::SampleClass(const SampleClass &right)
  //## begin SampleClass::SampleClass%copy.hasinit preserve=no
    : ID(0)
  //## end SampleClass::SampleClass%copy.hasinit
  //## begin SampleClass::SampleClass%copy.initialization preserve=yes
  //## end SampleClass::SampleClass%copy.initialization
{
  //## begin SampleClass::SampleClass%copy.body preserve=yes
  //## end SampleClass::SampleClass%copy.body
}
```

Operations

Rose generates code for each of the operations in the class. For each operation, the generated code includes the operation name, the parameters, the parameter data types, and the return type. Each operation will generate code similar to the following:

```
Class TheClass
{
public:
void PublicOperation();

protected:
void ProtectedOperation();

private:
void PrivateOperation();
};
```

Again, however, there is more detail generated than what's shown above. Here, we'll examine the code generated for the following class:

In the header file, Rose will generate the signature for the operation:

```
class SampleClass
{
  //## begin SampleClass%3726867600AA.initialDeclarations preserve=yes
  //## end SampleClass%3726867600AA.initialDeclarations

  public:
    //## Constructors (generated)
      SampleClass();

      SampleClass(const SampleClass &right);

    //## Destructor (generated)
      ~SampleClass();

    //## Assignment Operation (generated)
      const SampleClass & operator=(const SampleClass &right);

    //## Equality Operations (generated)
      int operator==(const SampleClass &right) const;

      int operator!=(const SampleClass &right) const;


    //## Other Operations (specified)
    //## Operation: DoSomething%3726869500FA

    //    This is documentation entered into the documentation
    //    window for the DoSomething operation.

      int DoSomething (int Parameter1);
```

As you can see, the full operation signature is generated in the code. Any documentation you entered for the operation is also generated, as a comment in the code. If you enter information for the operation protocol, qualifications, exceptions, time, space, preconditions, semantics, or postconditions, this information will also appear in the header file, as you can see in the code on the following page.

```
      //## Other Operations (specified)
  "   //## Operation: DoSomething%3726869500FA; This is the operation
      protocol, used to describe in what order operations can run.
      // This is documentation entered into the documentation
      //   window for the DoSomething operation.
  "   //## Qualification: This is the operation qualification, which
      includes language-dependent qualifications.
  "   //## Exceptions: Exceptions
  "   //## Time Complexity: This is the operation time, which speci-
      fies how long the operation is expected to take.
  "   //## Space Complexity: This is the operation size, which quan-
      tifies how much memory the operation is expected to take.
  "   //## Preconditions:
      //   These are the preconditions, which include conditions
      //   that must be true before the operation can run.
  "   //## Semantics:
      //   These are the operation semantics, which describe, in
      //   pseudocode, what the operation will do.
  "   //## Postconditions:
      //   These are the postconditions, which include conditions
      //   that must be true after the operation runs.
      int DoSomething (int Parameter1) throw (Exceptions);
```

Rose will also generate code for the operation in the implementation file. We just examined the header file for the SampleClass class; now, let's take a look at the implementation file for this class.

In the implementation file, Rose inserts the following lines for each operation you define:

```
//## Other Operations (implementation)
int SampleClass::DoSomething (int Parameter1)
{
  //## begin SampleClass::DoSomething%3726869500FA.body preserve=yes
  //## end SampleClass::DoSomething%3726869500FA.body
}
```

Once you have generated the code, you insert the implementation code for each operation between the //## begin and //## end statements in the implementation file. By placing the code in the protected code region, you protect it during round-trip engineering.

If you enter exception information for the operation, using the Exceptions field on the Detail tab of the Operation Specification window, these exceptions are included in the code, as shown on the following page.

```
//## Other Operations (implementation)
int SampleClass::DoSomething (int Parameter1) throw (Exceptions)
{
  //## begin SampleClass::DoSomething%3726869500FA.body preserve=yes
  //## end SampleClass::DoSomething%3726869500FA.body
}
```

As with other model elements, you can control the code generated for an operation by modifying its code generation properties. For example, you can create virtual functions by modifying the OperationKind property. The code generation properties for operations are listed above, but we list them again in Table 12.15 for your reference.

TABLE 12.15: Operation Code Generation Properties

Property	Purpose	Default
CodeName	Sets the name of the generated operation.	Operation name from the model
OperationKind	Controls whether the operation is virtual, static, abstract, friend, or none of these.	None (Common)
OperationIsConst	Controls whether the operation will be generated with the const keyword.	False
OperationIsExplicit	Controls whether the keyword explicit will be used when generating the operation.	False
Inline	Controls whether to inline the operation.	False
EntryCode	Used to enter code or comments that are generated along with the operation (this code will not be placed in the protected region, which is protected during round-trip engineering).	Empty
ExitCode	Used to enter code or comments that are generated along with the operation (this code will not be placed in the protected region, which is protected during round-trip engineering).	Empty
GenerateEmpty-Regions	Controls whether protected regions are generated with the operation.	All (Always generate)
BodyAnnotations	Controls whether notations are generated in the implementation file for the operation's documentation, concurrency, space, time, qualifications, exceptions, pre-conditions, post-conditions, and semantics.	All are generated

Bi-directional Associations

To support bi-directional associations, Rose will generate attributes in the code. Each of the classes in the relationship will contain an attribute to support the association.

The code generation properties we will examine in this section are:

- DataMemberVisibility role property

- GenerateGetOperation role property

- GenerateSetOperation role property

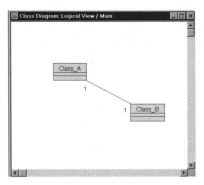

The code generated for the two classes shown above will resemble something like this:

```
Class Class_A
{
public:
   Class_A();
   ~Class_A();
private:
   Class_B *the_Class_B;
};
```

and

```
Class Class_B
{
public:
```

```
   Class_B();
   ~Class_B();
 private:
   Class_A *the_Class_A;
 };
```

As you can see, Rose will automatically generate attributes on both sides of the bi-directional association relationship. With the the_Class_B attribute, Class_A can easily access Class_B. Using the the_Class_A attribute, Class_B can easily access Class_A.

Let's examine in detail the code generated for the two classes shown above. The association will be reflected in the header files for both Class_A and Class_B. The header file for Class_A is shown below. We'll take a look at each of the marked lines.

```
//## begin module%3726883A0212.cm preserve=no
//    %X% %Q% %Z% %W%
//## end module%3726883A0212.cm


//## begin module%3726883A0212.cp preserve=no
//## end module%3726883A0212.cp


//## Module: Class_A%3726883A0212; Pseudo Package specification
//## Source file: C:\Program Files\Rational\Rose 98i\C++\source\➥
Class_A.h

#ifndef Class_A_h
#define Class_A_h 1

//## begin module%3726883A0212.additionalIncludes preserve=no
//## end module%3726883A0212.additionalIncludes


//## begin module%3726883A0212.includes preserve=yes
//## end module%3726883A0212.includes
```

➜   `// Class_B`
➜   `#include "Class_B.h"`
```
//## begin module%3726883A0212.additionalDeclarations preserve=yes
//## end module%3726883A0212.additionalDeclarations
```

```
//## begin Class_A%3726883A0212.preface preserve=yes
//## end Class_A%3726883A0212.preface

//## Class: Class_A%3726883A0212
//## Category: <Top Level>
//## Persistence: Transient
//## Cardinality/Multiplicity: n

class Class_A
{
  //## begin Class_A%3726883A0212.initialDeclarations preserve=yes
  //## end Class_A%3726883A0212.initialDeclarations

  public:
    //## Constructors (generated)
      Class_A();

      Class_A(const Class_A &right);

    //## Destructor (generated)
      ~Class_A();

    //## Assignment Operation (generated)
      const Class_A & operator=(const Class_A &right);

    //## Equality Operations (generated)
      int operator==(const Class_A &right) const;

      int operator!=(const Class_A &right) const;

    //## Get and Set Operations for Associations (generated)

        //## Association: <unnamed>%3726887C02D0
        //## Role: Class_A::<the_Class_B>%3726887D0032
        const Class_B * get_the_Class_B () const;
        void set_the_Class_B (Class_B * value);

      // Additional Public Declarations
        //## begin Class_A%3726883A0212.public preserve=yes
        //## end Class_A%3726883A0212.public
```

```
        protected:
          // Additional Protected Declarations
            //## begin Class_A%3726883A0212.protected preserve=yes
            //## end Class_A%3726883A0212.protected

        private:
          // Additional Private Declarations
            //## begin Class_A%3726883A0212.private preserve=yes
            //## end Class_A%3726883A0212.private

        private: //## implementation
          // Data Members for Associations

→           //## Association: <unnamed>%3726887C02D0
→           //## begin Class_A::<the_Class_B>%3726887D0032.role preserve=no→
            public: Class_B {1 -> 1RHN}
→           Class_B *the_Class_B;
→           //## end Class_A::<the_Class_B>%3726887D0032.role

          // Additional Implementation Declarations
            //## begin Class_A%3726883A0212.implementation preserve=yes
            //## end Class_A%3726883A0212.implementation

    };

    //## begin Class_A%3726883A0212.postscript preserve=yes
    //## end Class_A%3726883A0212.postscript

    // Class Class_A

→     //## Get and Set Operations for Associations (inline)
→
→     inline const Class_B * Class_A::get_the_Class_B () const
→         {
→       //## begin Class_A::get_the_Class_B%3726887D0032.get preserve=no
→     return the_Class_B;
→       //## end Class_A::get_the_Class_B%3726887D0032.get
→     }
→
→     inline void Class_A::set_the_Class_B (Class_B * value)
```

```
→      {
→        //## begin Class_A::set_the_Class_B%3726887D0032.set preserve=no
→        the_Class_B = value;
→        //## end Class_A::set_the_Class_B%3726887D0032.set
→      }

       //## begin module%3726883A0212.epilog preserve=yes
       //## end module%3726883A0212.epilog


       #endif
```

The first two marked lines

```
// Class_B
#include "Class_B.h"
```

are generated to ensure that the header file for Class_B is included. This sets up
the relationship between Class_A and Class_B, so that Class_A knows that
Class_B exists. Although we will not examine the full header file for Class_B here,
it will include very similar lines:

```
// Class_A
#include "Class_A.h"
```

The second set of marked lines

```
//## Association: <unnamed>%3726887C02D0
      //## Role: Class_A::<the_Class_B>%3726887D0032
      const Class_B * get_the_Class_B () const;
      void set_the_Class_B (Class_B * value);
```

includes the declarations for the Get andSet operations generated for Class_B.
When you generate code, as we will see shortly, Rose will place an attribute
called the_Class_B inside Class_A. Because a Get and Set operation is generated
for each attribute, and an association creates an attribute, a Get and Set operation
will be created for the association's attribute.

The third set of marked lines

```
//## Association: <unnamed>%3726887C02D0
      //## begin Class_A::<the_Class_B>%3726887D0032.role preserve=no
public: Class_B {1 -> 1RHN}
      Class_B *the_Class_B;
      //## end Class_A::<the_Class_B>%3726887D0032.role
```

creates the attribute, the_Class_B, which we discussed a moment ago. For each association, Rose will generate the appropriate attributes. By default, the attribute is named the_<class name>. To change the name of the attribute, set a role name on the association. Rose will use the role name to generate the attribute name. Each generated attribute will have private visibility, by default. To change the visibility, open the Association Specification window. Select either the C++ A or C++ B tab, and change the DataMemberVisibility property.

Finally, the fourth set of lines contains the code for the Get and Set operations of the the_Class_B attribute:

```
//## Get and Set Operations for Associations (inline)

inline const Class_B * Class_A::get_the_Class_B () const
{
  //## begin Class_A::get_the_Class_B%3726887D0032.get preserve=no
  return the_Class_B;
  //## end Class_A::get_the_Class_B%3726887D0032.get
}

inline void Class_A::set_the_Class_B (Class_B * value)
{
  //## begin Class_A::set_the_Class_B%3726887D0032.set preserve=no
  the_Class_B = value;
  //## end Class_A::set_the_Class_B%3726887D0032.set
}
```

You can control whether these operations are created by changing the GenerateGetOperation and GenerateSetOperation code generation properties. In the association specification window, select either C++ A or C++ B to view the code generation properties that apply to each end of the relationship. Change the GenerateGetOperation or GenerateSetOperation properties to control whether the Get and Set operations will be created.

Note that this association had a multiplicity of one-to-one. See below for a discussion of how other multiplicity settings will affect code generation.

Unidirectional Associations

As with bi-directional associations, Rose will generate attributes to support unidirectional associations. However, with a unidirectional association, an attribute is only generated at one end of the relationship.

The code generation properties we will examine in this section are:

- DataMemberVisibility role property

- GenerateGetOperation role property

- GenerateSetOperation role property

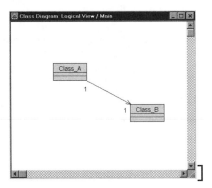

For the Class_A and Class_B classes above, code similar to the following would be created:

```
Class Class_A
{
public:
```

```
    Class_A();
    ~Class_A();
 private:
    Class_B *the_Class_B;
 };
```

and

```
Class Class_B
{
public:
    Class_B();
    ~Class_B();
};
```

As you can see, Rose will only generate a private attribute for the relationship at one end of the association. Specifically, it will generate an attribute in the Client class, but not in the Supplier class.

The code generated in the Supplier class includes all of the header and implementation file lines discussed in the previous section about bi-directional associations. With a bi-directional association, each class is given a new attribute and the code discussed in the previous section is included in both classes. With a unidirectional association, the code is included only in the Client class.

Again, note that the multiplicity here is one-to-one. Let's take a look at how code is affected when the multiplicity settings are changed.

Associations with a Multiplicity of One to Many

In a one-to-one relationship, Rose can simply create the appropriate attributes to support the association. With a one-to-many relationship, however, one class must contain a set of the other class. The code generation properties we will examine in this section are:

- UnorderedUnboundedByReferenceContainer project property
- ContainerClass role property

To begin, let's look at an example.

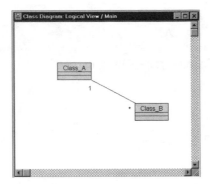

In this case, we've got a one-to-many relationship. As we saw above, Class_B can simply generate an attribute that is a pointer to Class_A. However, a simple pointer attribute in the Class_A class won't be enough. Instead, the attribute generated in Class_A must use some sort of container class as its data type. This container class could be a list, set, or any other container class you wish to use.

Rose will generate code similar to the following for this example:

```
Class Class_A
{
public:
    Class_A();
    ~Class_A();
private:
    UnboundedSetByReference<Class_B> the_Class_B;
};
```

and

```
Class Class_B
{
public:
    Class_B();
    ~Class_B();
private:
    Class_A *the_Class_A;
};
```

As you can see, Class_B includes a simple pointer to Class_A, as we saw above. However, a container class was used in Class_A when generating the Class_B attribute.

Rose does not provide you with an implementation-level container class by default. Instead, it will generate code, as it did above, with UnboundedSetByReference as the container class. It is left up to you to put a valid container class in the C++ code generation properties.

To change the container class, there are three properties you can set: two that are global defaults, and one that is specific to the relationship.

To set the container class for all of your one-to-many relationships, select Tools ➤ Options from the menu. On the C++ tab, select Project from the drop-down list box. Change the value in the UnorderedUnboundedByReferenceContainer property to set the container class.

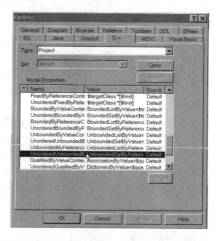

Or, to change the container class for only one relationship, open the relationship specifications and select the C++ A or C++ B tab. Change the ContainerClass property to reflect the container class you wish to use.

When generating code, Rose will first check the ContainerClass property for the relationship. If there is something in this property, this is the container class that will be used. If the ContainerClass property is empty, Rose will check the UnorderedUnboundedByReferenceContainer property.

The third property you can set is the ContainerClass property from the Tools ➢ Options screen. On the C++ tab of this screen, select Role from the drop-down list box. Changing the ContainerClass property here is the equivalent of changing the ContainerClass property in the Association Specification window of all relationships.

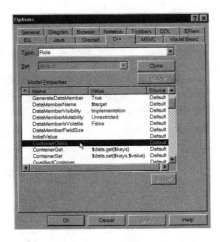

The following are portions of the code in the header file for Class_A that were produced as a result of its bi-directional, one-to-many relationship with Class_B. Four things were inserted into the header file: the #include statement for Class_B, the attribute the_Class_B, and the Get and Set operations for this attribute.

```
// Class_B
#include "Class_B.h"

//## Get and Set Operations for Associations (generated)

        //## Association: <unnamed>%3726887C02D0
        //## Role: Class_A::<the_Class_B>%3726887D0032
        const UnboundedSetByReference<Class_B> get_the_Class_B () const;
        void set_the_Class_B (UnboundedSetByReference<Class_B> value);

private: //## implementation
    // Data Members for Associations
```

```
//## Association: <unnamed>%3726887C02D0
//## begin Class_A::<the_Class_B>%3726887D0032.role preserve=no
public: Class_B {1 -> nRHN}
UnboundedSetByReference<Class_B> the_Class_B;
//## end Class_A::<the_Class_B>%3726887D0032.role


//## Get and Set Operations for Associations (inline)

inline const UnboundedSetByReference<Class_B>
   Class_A::get_the_Class_B () const
{
  //## begin Class_A::get_the_Class_B%3726887D0032.get preserve=no
  return the_Class_B;
  //## end Class_A::get_the_Class_B%3726887D0032.get
}

inline void Class_A::set_the_Class_B
   (UnboundedSetByReference<Class_B> value)
{
  //## begin Class_A::set_the_Class_B%3726887D0032.set preserve=no
  the_Class_B = value;
  //## end Class_A::set_the_Class_B%3726887D0032.set
}
```

In the header file for Class_B, we can see that a pointer to Class_A was included as an attribute, and Get and Set operations were created for this attribute. Because a container class is not needed for the attribute in Class_B, the code generated for Class_B is exactly the same as we described in the previous sections on bi-directional associations and unidirectional associations. The portions of the Class_B header file that deal with Class_A are:

```
// Class_A
#include "Class_A.h"



//## Get and Set Operations for Associations (generated)

    //## Association: <unnamed>%3726887C02D0
    //## Role: Class_B::<the_Class_A>%3726887D0064
    const Class_A * get_the_Class_A () const;
    void set_the_Class_A (Class_A * value);
```

```
private: //## implementation
   // Data Members for Associations

      //## Association: <unnamed>%3726887C02D0
      //## begin Class_B::<the_Class_A>%3726887D0064.role preserve=no
      public: Class_A {n -> 1RHN}
      Class_A *the_Class_A;
      //## end Class_B::<the_Class_A>%3726887D0064.role

//## Get and Set Operations for Associations (inline)

inline const Class_A * Class_B::get_the_Class_A () const
{
  //## begin Class_B::get_the_Class_A%3726887D0064.get preserve=no
  return the_Class_A;
  //## end Class_B::get_the_Class_A%3726887D0064.get
}

inline void Class_B::set_the_Class_A (Class_A * value)
{
  //## begin Class_B::set_the_Class_A%3726887D0064.set preserve=no
  the_Class_A = value;
  //## end Class_B::set_the_Class_A%3726887D0064.set
}
```

Again, note that Class_B contains a simple pointer to Class_A, rather than using a container class.

Associations with a Multiplicity of Many to Many

The code generated here is similar to that created for a one-to-many relationship. However, here Rose will generate container classes on both ends of the relationship.

The code generation properties we will examine in this section include:

- UnorderedUnboundedByReferenceContainer project property
- ContainerClass role property

Let's look at the code generated for the following relationship:

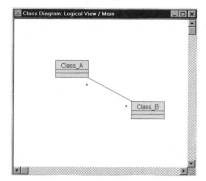

In this situation, container classes are used at both ends of the relationship. The code that is generated will look something like the following:

```
Class Class_A
{
public:
   Class_A();
   ~Class_A();
private:
    UnboundedSetByReference<Class_B> the_Class_B;
};
```

and

```
Class Class_B
{
public:
   Class_B();
   ~Class_B();
private:
    UnboundedSetByReference<Class_A> the_Class_A;
};
```

Again, however, this is a simplified picture of the generated code. Rose will also insert comments for you, and several sections of the header file will be affected. The specific code for Class_A will look exactly like the example from the previous section, "Associations with a Multiplicity of One to Many." The difference here is that now a container class will also be used to create an attribute in Class_B.

The following are the four sections inserted into the header file of Class_B to support the relationship.

```
// Class_A
#include "Class_A.h"


//## Get and Set Operations for Associations (generated)

        //## Association: <unnamed>%3726887C02D0
        //## Role: Class_B::<the_Class_A>%3726887D0064
        const UnboundedSetByReference<Class_A> get_the_Class_A () const;
        void set_the_Class_A (UnboundedSetByReference<Class_A> value);

private: //## implementation
    // Data Members for Associations

        //## Association: <unnamed>%3726887C02D0
        //## begin Class_B::<the_Class_A>%3726887D0064.role preserve=no
        public: Class_A {n -> nRHN}
        UnboundedSetByReference<Class_A> the_Class_A;
        //## end Class_B::<the_Class_A>%3726887D0064.role

//## Get and Set Operations for Associations (inline)

inline const UnboundedSetByReference<Class_A>
    Class_B::get_the_Class_A () const
{
  //## begin Class_B::get_the_Class_A%3726887D0064.get preserve=no
  return the_Class_A;
  //## end Class_B::get_the_Class_A%3726887D0064.get
}

inline void Class_B::set_the_Class_A
    (UnboundedSetByReference<Class_A> value)
{
  //## begin Class_B::set_the_Class_A%3726887D0064.set preserve=no
  the_Class_A = value;
  //## end Class_B::set_the_Class_A%3726887D0064.set
}
```

As with one-to-many associations, you can change the container class used in many-to-many associations by modifying the UnorderedUnboundedByReferenceContainer or the ContainerClass property.

The ContainerClass property can be found by opening the specification window for the association and choosing either the C++ A or the C++ B tab, whichever end of the relationship you wish to modify. On the tab, change the ContainerClass property to include the specific container class you wish to use. Changing this property here will only affect the current relationship.

To change the container class for all relationships, change either the Unordered-UnboundedByReferenceContainer project property, or the ContainerClass property from the options screen. Select Tools ➤ Options, then select the C++ tab. Select Project from the drop-down list box and change the UnorderedUnbounded-ByReferenceContainer property. Or, select Role from the drop-down list box, and change the ContainerClass property.

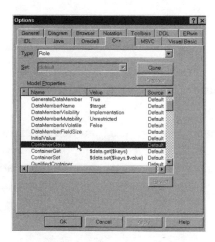

If there is something in the ContainerClass property, Rose will use that value to generate code. If the ContainerClass property is empty, it will look at the UnorderedUnboundedByReferenceContainer property.

Associations with Bounded Multiplicity

So far, we've examined one-to-one relationships, one-to-many relationships, and many-to-many relationships. A relationship with "many" at one end is referred to as an unbounded relationship. Now, let's look at a bounded relationship.

The code generation properties we will be discussing here are:

- ContainerClass role property
- BoundedByReferenceContainer project property
- FixedByReferenceContainer project property

An example of a bounded relationship is shown below:

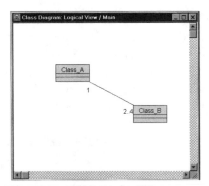

In this example, each instance of Class_A is related to two through four instances of Class_B.

There are two types of bounded relationships we will examine here: bounded associations and fixed associations. Bounded associations are those with a multiplicity range, such as 2..4 in the example above. Fixed associations are those with a single number in the multiplicity. For example, a one-to-four relationship is a fixed relationship.

With these relationships, as with "many" relationships, Rose uses a container class when creating the attributes. In Class_B, a simple pointer to Class_A can be generated. However, in Class_A, some sort of container class must be used.

Let's start with bounded associations. A simplified version of the code generated for Class_A and Class_B above is shown below:

```
Class Class_A
{
public:
   Class_A();
   ~Class_A();
private:
    BoundedSetByReference<Class_B> the_Class_B;
};
```

and

```
Class Class_B
{
public:
   Class_B();
   ~Class_B();
private:
    Class_A *the_Class_A;
};
```

Let's look at the detailed code that is actually created for this relationship. Class_B, as we mentioned above, will simply have a pointer to Class_A. The code generated here is the same as was described in the unidirectional and bi-directional associations sections. The header file will include the following sections:

```
// Class_A
#include "Class_A.h"

//## Get and Set Operations for Associations (generated)

     //## Association: <unnamed>%3726887C02D0
     //## Role: Class_B::<the_Class_A>%3726887D0064
     const Class_A * get_the_Class_A () const;
     void set_the_Class_A (Class_A * value);
```

```
private: //## implementation
    // Data Members for Associations

        //## Association: <unnamed>%3726887C02D0
        //## begin Class_B::<the_Class_A>%3726887D0064.role preserve=no
        public: Class_A {2..4 -> 1RHN}
        Class_A *the_Class_A;
        //## end Class_B::<the_Class_A>%3726887D0064.role


//## Get and Set Operations for Associations (inline)

inline const Class_A * Class_B::get_the_Class_A () const
{
  //## begin Class_B::get_the_Class_A%3726887D0064.get preserve=no
  return the_Class_A;
  //## end Class_B::get_the_Class_A%3726887D0064.get
}

inline void Class_B::set_the_Class_A (Class_A * value)
{
  //## begin Class_B::set_the_Class_A%3726887D0064.set preserve=no
  the_Class_A = value;
  //## end Class_B::set_the_Class_A%3726887D0064.set
}
```

In Class_A, a container class is used for the Class_B attribute. The sections of code in the header file of Class_A that refer to Class_B are shown below:

```
// Class_B
#include "Class_B.h"


//## Get and Set Operations for Associations (generated)

        //## Association: <unnamed>%3726887C02D0
        //## Role: Class_A::<the_Class_B>%3726887D0032
        const BoundedSetByReference<Class_B,4> get_the_Class_B () const;
        void set_the_Class_B (BoundedSetByReference<Class_B,4> value);

private: //## implementation
    // Data Members for Associations
```

```
//## Association: <unnamed>%3726887C02D0
//## begin Class_A::<the_Class_B>%3726887D0032.role preserve=no
public: Class_B {1 -> 2..4RHN}
BoundedSetByReference<Class_B,4> the_Class_B;
//## end Class_A::<the_Class_B>%3726887D0032.role

//## Get and Set Operations for Associations (inline)

inline const BoundedSetByReference<Class_B,4>
  Class_A::get_the_Class_B () const
{
  //## begin Class_A::get_the_Class_B%3726887D0032.get preserve=no
  return the_Class_B;
  //## end Class_A::get_the_Class_B%3726887D0032.get
}

inline void Class_A::set_the_Class_B
  (BoundedSetByReference<Class_B,4> value)
{
  //## begin Class_A::set_the_Class_B%3726887D0032.set preserve=no
  the_Class_B = value;
  //## end Class_A::set_the_Class_B%3726887D0032.set
}
```

Notice that by default, Rose uses a BoundedSetByReference container class. As before, it is left up to you to enter a valid container class to use in these relationships. The container class can be set in three places.

First, you can set the container class for one specific relationship by opening the association specifications, selecting the C++ A or C++ B tab, and changing the ContainerClass property.

To set the container class for all association relationships, select Tools ➤ Options, then the C++ tab. Select Role from the drop-down list box, and change the value of the ContainerClass property.

To set the container class for all bounded association relationships, select Tools ➤ Options, then the C++ tab. Select Project from the drop-down list box, and change the value of the BoundedByReferenceContainer property.

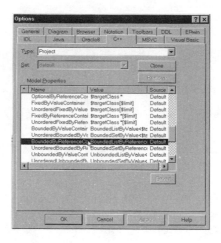

When generating code, Rose will first check the ContainerClass property in the relationship. If this property is empty, the ContainerClass property of the Role property set will be used. If this is also empty, the BoundedByReferenceContainer property will be used.

Now, let's examine fixed relationships. Assume the relationship between Class_A and Class_B is one-to-four, as shown below.

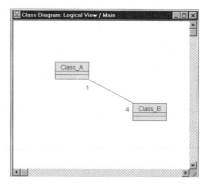

The code in the header file for Class_A still must use a container class for the Class_B attribute. Here, Rose will use an array, by default.

```
private: //## implementation
    // Data Members for Associations

    //## Association: <unnamed>%3726887C02D0
    //## begin Class_A::<the_Class_B>%3726887D0032.role preserve=no
    public: Class_B {1 -> 4RHN}
```

→
```
        Class_B *the_Class_B[4];
        //## end Class_A::<the_Class_B>%3726887D0032.role
```

As before, there are a few different ways to change the default. The first, which will only affect the current relationship, is to change the ContainerClass property on the C++ tab of the relationship specifications.

The second approach is to change the ContainerClass property through the Tools ➤ Options menu. Select the C++ tab, then select Role. Changing this property will affect all association relationships.

Finally, you can change the FixedByReferenceContainer project property. Select Tools ➤ Options, then select the C++ tab. Choose Project from the drop-down list box, and change the value of the FixedByReferenceContainer property.

Reflexive Associations

A reflexive association is treated much the same as an association between two classes.

For the following situation:

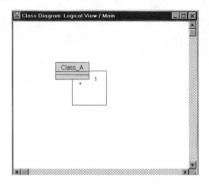

code similar to this is generated:

```
class Class_A
{
public:
    Class_A();
    ~Class_A();
Private:
    UnboundedSetByReference<Class_A> Class_A;
};
```

As with a regular association, an attribute is created inside the class to support the relationship. If the multiplicity is one, a simple attribute is created. If the multiplicity is more than one, a container class is used, as in the above example.

The following are portions of the header file created for the relationship shown above.

```
//## Get and Set Operations for Associations (generated)

        //## Association: <unnamed>%37268D26001E
        //## Role: Class_A::<the_Class_A>%37268D2701CD
        const Class_A * get_the_Class_A () const;
        void set_the_Class_A (Class_A * value);

        //## Association: <unnamed>%37268D26001E
        //## Role: Class_A::<the_Class_A>%37268D2701CC
        const UnboundedSetByReference<Class_A> get_the_Class_A () const;
        void set_the_Class_A (UnboundedSetByReference<Class_A> value);
```

```
private: //## implementation
    // Data Members for Associations

        //## Association: <unnamed>%37268D26001E
        //## begin Class_A::<the_Class_A>%37268D2701CD.role preserve=no
        public: Class_A {n -> 1RHN}
        Class_A *the_Class_A;
        //## end Class_A::<the_Class_A>%37268D2701CD.role

        //## Association: <unnamed>%37268D26001E
        //## begin Class_A::<the_Class_A>%37268D2701CC.role preserve=no
        public: Class_A {1 -> nRHN}
        UnboundedSetByReference<Class_A> the_Class_A;
        //## end Class_A::<the_Class_A>%37268D2701CC.role

//## Get and Set Operations for Associations (inline)

inline const Class_A * Class_A::get_the_Class_A () const
{
  //## begin Class_A::get_the_Class_A%37268D2701CD.get preserve=no
  return the_Class_A;
  //## end Class_A::get_the_Class_A%37268D2701CD.get
}

inline void Class_A::set_the_Class_A (Class_A * value)
{
  //## begin Class_A::set_the_Class_A%37268D2701CD.set preserve=no
  the_Class_A = value;
  //## end Class_A::set_the_Class_A%37268D2701CD.set
}

inline const UnboundedSetByReference<Class_A> Class_A::get_the_Class_A
   () const
{
  //## begin Class_A::get_the_Class_A%37268D2701CC.get preserve=no
  return the_Class_A;
  //## end Class_A::get_the_Class_A%37268D2701CC.get
}

inline void Class_A::set_the_Class_A
   (UnboundedSetByReference<Class_A> value)
{
```

```
    //## begin Class_A::set_the_Class_A%37268D2701CC.set preserve=no
    the_Class_A = value;
    //## end Class_A::set_the_Class_A%37268D2701CC.set
}
```

As you can see, the code generated here is very similar to the code generated in a typical one-to-many relationship. In this situation, Class_A contains an attribute of type Class_A.

By-Value Aggregations (Composition Relationships)

There are two types of aggregation relationships: by-value and by-reference. In a by-value relationship, one class contains another. In a by-reference relationship, one class contains a reference to another.

The code generation properties we will be examining here are:

- ContainerClass role property
- FixedByValueContainer project property
- UnorderedBoundedByValueContainer project property

Let's start by examining by-value aggregations, which are also known as composition relationships. In the UML, a composition is shown using the following symbol:

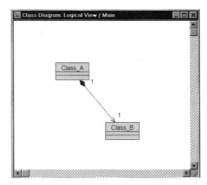

As with association relationships, Rose will generate attributes when code is generated for an aggregation. In our example above, Class_B is an attribute inside Class_A. A simplified version of the generated code would look like this:

```
Class Class_A
{
public:
    Class_A();
    ~Class_A();
private:
    Class_B the_Class_B;
};
```

and

```
Class Class_B
{
public:
    Class_B();
    ~Class_B();
};
```

Let's look at the actual code that was generated for this relationship. Inside Class_A, an attribute was created for Class_B.

```
private: //## implementation
    // Data Members for Associations

    //## Association: <unnamed>%37268F970050
    //## begin Class_A::<the_Class_B>%37268F970316.role preserve=no
public: Class_B {1 -> 1VHN}
    Class_B the_Class_B;
    //## end Class_A::<the_Class_B>%37268F970316.role
```

If the multiplicity of the relationship is greater than one, Rose will use a container class when creating the relationship. Let's take a look at this relationship now:

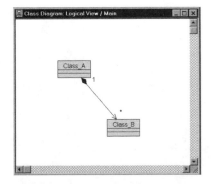

The following is from the header file for Class_A.

```
private: //## implementation
    // Data Members for Associations

    //## Association: <unnamed>%37268F970050
    //## begin Class_A::<the_Class_B>%37268F970316.role preserve=no
public: Class_B {1 -> nVHN}
    UnboundedSetByValue<Class_B> the_Class_B;
    //## end Class_A::<the_Class_B>%37268F970316.role
```

In this case, Rose uses UnboundedSetByValue as the default container class. Had the multiplicity been fixed (for example, a one-to-four relationship), Rose would have used an array instead. Had the multiplicity been bounded (for example, a 1 to 2..4 relationship), Rose would have used a BoundedSetByValue container. To change the container class that is used, change the ContainerClass property of the relationship.

To change the container class for all fixed aggregations, change the FixedByValueContainer project property. To change the container class for all bounded aggregations, change the UnorderedBoundedByValueContainer project property.

By-Reference Aggregations

The code generated for a by-reference aggregation is very similar to the code generated for a by-value aggregation. However, with a by-reference aggregation, the attributes that are created are pointers.

The code generation properties we will be examining here are:

- ContainerClass role property

- FixedByReferenceContainer project property

- UnorderedBoundedByReferenceContainer project property

For example, let's look at the by-reference version of the relationship we just examined:

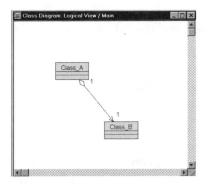

Here again, we have a one-to-one relationship, but this time the aggregation is by-reference. The following is a simplified version of the code that's generated:

```
Class Class_A
{
public:
   Class_A();
   ~Class_A();
private:
     Class_B *the_Class_B;
};
```

as is

```
Class Class_B
{
public:
   Class_B();
   ~Class_B();
};
```

The code generated in the header file of Class_A includes the following:

```
private: //## implementation
    // Data Members for Associations

     //## Association: <unnamed>%37268F970050
     //## begin Class_A::<the_Class_B>%37268F970316.role preserve=no
public: Class_B {1 -> 1RHN}
    Class_B *the_Class_B;
     //## end Class_A::<the_Class_B>%37268F970316.role
```

Here, there is a pointer created as an attribute inside Class_A. As with other relationships, if the multiplicity is more than one, a container class is used. Had the multiplicity been fixed (for example, a one–to-four relationship), an array would have been used:

```
Class_B *the_Class_B[4];
```

Had the multiplicity been bounded (for example, a 1 to 2..4 relationship), Rose would have used "BoundedSetByReference" as the container class:

```
BoundedSetByReference<Class_B,4> the_Class_B;
```

To change the container class for the relationship, you can change the Container-Class property in the C++ tab of the relationship specification window.

To change the container class for all fixed by-reference aggregations, change the FixedByReference project property. To change the container class for all bounded by-reference aggregations, change the UnorderedBoundedByReference project property.

Dependency Relationships

With a dependency relationship, no attributes are created. If there is a dependency between Class_A and Class_B:

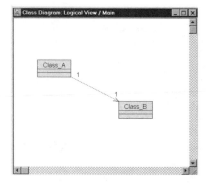

No attributes will be created in either Class_A or Class_B. The code that is generated will look something like the following:

```
Class Class_A
{
public:
    Class_A();
    ~Class_A();
};
```

and

```
Class Class_B
{
public:
    Class_B();
    ~Class_B();
};
```

Rose will only place two references to Class_B inside of Class_A. One will be a reference to Class_B.h, and the other is merely a comment, letting you know that a dependency exists. These two sections of the Class_A header file appear as follows:

```
// Class_B
#include "Class_B.h"
```

and

```
//## Uses: <unnamed>%372690CD02E4;Class_B {1 -> 1}
```

Generalization Relationships

A generalization relationship in the UML becomes an inheritance relationship in C++. In your Rose model, an inheritance relationship is shown as follows:

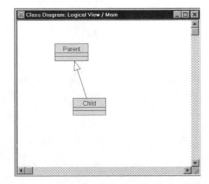

For this type of relationship, Rose will generate something that looks like this:

```
Class Parent
{
public:
   Parent();
   ~Parent();
};
```

and

```
Class Child : public Parent
{
public:
   Child();
   ~Child();
};
```

Let's look at the actual code that is generated. In the code for the parent class, there is no mention of the child class. This helps keep the parent generic; many classes can inherit from it without affecting its code.

In the child class, the code is generated to support its inheritance from the parent class. The class declaration will look like this:

```
class Child : public Parent  //## Inherits: <unnamed>%3729546E0028
{
  //## begin Child%37295469024E.initialDeclarations preserve=yes
  //## end Child%37295469024E.initialDeclarations

  public:
    //## Constructors (generated)
      Child();

      Child(const Child &right);

    //## Destructor (generated)
      ~Child();

    //## Assignment Operation (generated)
      const Child & operator=(const Child &right);
```

```
        //## Equality Operations (generated)
          int operator==(const Child &right) const;

          int operator!=(const Child &right) const;

        // Additional Public Declarations
          //## begin Child%37295469024E.public preserve=yes
          //## end Child%37295469024E.public

    protected:
        // Additional Protected Declarations
          //## begin Child%37295469024E.protected preserve=yes
          //## end Child%37295469024E.protected

    private:
        // Additional Private Declarations
          //## begin Child%37295469024E.private preserve=yes
          //## end Child%37295469024E.private

    private: //## implementation
        // Additional Implementation Declarations
          //## begin Child%37295469024E.implementation preserve=yes
          //## end Child%37295469024E.implementation

    };
```

Rose will also create a #include line in the child, to include the header file of the parent. In this example, the inheritance relationship was implemented with public inheritance. To use protected inheritance instead, open the relationship specifications. On the General tab, set the relationship's visibility to protected. Rose will generate a child class that looks like this:

```
class Child : protected Parent  //## Inherits:
<unnamed>%3729546E0028
```

However, this will only work if the project's AllowProtectedInheritance C++ property is True. Select Tools ➤ Options, then the C++ tab. Select Project from the drop-down list box, and be sure AllowProtectedInheritance is set to True.

To use virtual inheritance, open the relationship specifications. On the General tab, select Virtual inheritance.

When Rose generates code for virtual inheritance, the child class will look like this:

```
class Child : virtual public Parent //## Inherits:
```

Parameterized Classes

When generating parameterized classes, Rose will create a template class in C++. For example, with the following class:

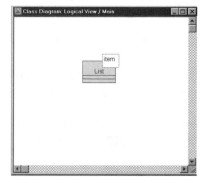

Rose generates a template class called List. The header file for this class is shown below. Any formal arguments you create for the class will also be included in the header file. To add a formal argument, open the class specifications and select the Detail tab. Near the bottom of the tab, insert the argument in the Formal Arguments area.

```
//## begin module%372955190050.cm preserve=no
//    %X% %Q% %Z% %W%
//## end module%372955190050.cm
```

```
//## begin module%372955190050.cp preserve=no
//## end module%372955190050.cp

//## Module: List%372955190050; Pseudo Package specification
//## Source file: C:\Program Files\Rational\Rose 98i\C++\source\List.h

#ifndef List_h
#define List_h 1

//## begin module%372955190050.additionalIncludes preserve=no
//## end module%372955190050.additionalIncludes

//## begin module%372955190050.includes preserve=yes
//## end module%372955190050.includes

//## begin module%372955190050.additionalDeclarations preserve=yes
//## end module%372955190050.additionalDeclarations


//## begin List%372955190050.preface preserve=yes
//## end List%372955190050.preface

//## Class: List%372955190050; Parameterized Class Utility
//## Category: <Top Level>
//## Persistence: Transient
//## Cardinality/Multiplicity: n

template <int Item>
class List
{
  //## begin List%372955190050.initialDeclarations preserve=yes
  //## end List%372955190050.initialDeclarations

  public:
    // Additional Public Declarations
      //## begin List%372955190050.public preserve=yes
      //## end List%372955190050.public

  protected:
    // Additional Protected Declarations
      //## begin List%372955190050.protected preserve=yes
      //## end List%372955190050.protected
```

```
private:
  // Additional Private Declarations
    //## begin List%372955190050.private preserve=yes
    //## end List%372955190050.private

private: //## implementation
  // Additional Implementation Declarations
    //## begin List%372955190050.implementation preserve=yes
    //## end List%372955190050.implementation

};

//## begin List%372955190050.postscript preserve=yes
//## end List%372955190050.postscript

// Parameterized Class Utility List

//## begin module%372955190050.epilog preserve=yes
//## end module%372955190050.epilog


#endif
```

Example of Generated C++

Throughout the book, we have been working with an ATM example application. In this section, we have generated the skeletal C++ code for the ATM example. For reference, the component models are shown in Figures 12.1 and 12.2.

For the ATM Client Component, we set the language of all components to C++. Then, we selected both the ATMServer and ATMClient packages in the Main Component diagram. Then, we selected Tools ➤ C++ ➤ Code Generation. The code that was generated for each component is included on the CD.

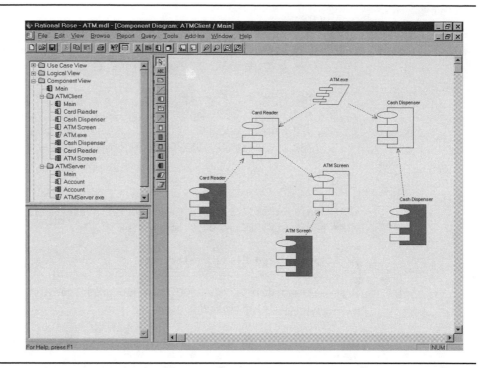

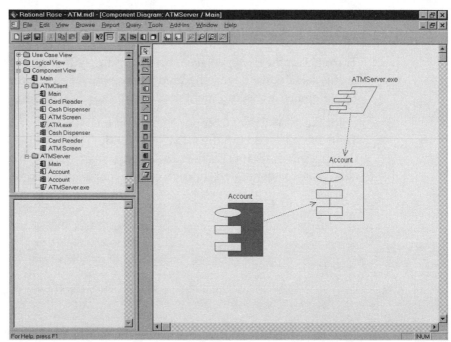

Exercise

In Chapters 3–10, we completed a model for an Order Entry system. Now, we are going to generate C++ code for the Order Entry system. We will use the System Component diagram shown in Figure 12.3. To generate the code, we need to perform the steps shown below. The code for this exercise is included on the CD.

FIGURE 12.3:

System Component diagram for the Order Entry System

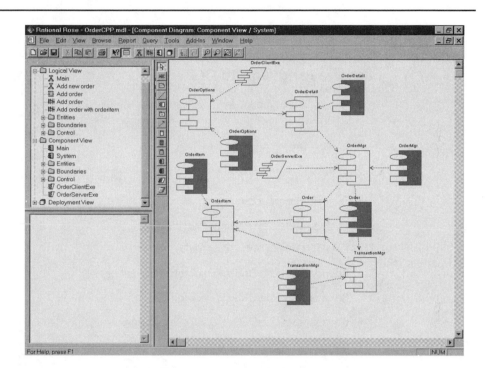

Exercise Steps:

Add Package Bodies to the System Component Diagram

1. Open the System Component diagram.

2. Select the Entities: Order Package body from the browser.

Continued on next page

3. Drag the Order Package body to the System Component diagram.

4. Repeat Steps 2–3 for the following components:

- Entities: OrderItem Package Body
- Boundaries: OrderOptions Package Body
- Boundaries: OrderDetail Package Body
- Control: TransactionMgr Package Body
- Control: OrderMgr Package Body

Set the Language to C++

1. Open the Component Specification for the Order component (package specification) within the Entities component package.

2. Select the language as C++.

3. Repeat Steps 1–2 for the following components:

- Entities: Order Package Body
- Entities: OrderItem Package Specification
- Entities: OrderItem Package Body
- Boundaries: OrderOptions Package Specification
- Boundaries: OrderOptions Package Body
- Boundaries: OrderDetail Package Specification
- Boundaries: OrderDetail Package Body
- Control: TransactionMgr Package Specification
- Control: TransactionMgr Package Body
- Control: OrderMgr Package Specification
- Control: OrderMgr Package Body
- OrderClientExe Task Specification
- OrderServerExe Task Specification

Continued on next page

Generate C++ Code

1. Open the System Component diagram.

2. Select all objects on the System Component diagram.

3. Select Tools ➤ C++ ➤ Code Generation from the menu.

Summary

In this chapter, we took a look at how various Rose model elements are implemented in C++. Using the code generation properties for classes, packages, attributes, operations, associations, aggregations, and other model elements, you have a great deal of control over what gets generated.

Again, the steps needed to generate code are:

1. Create components.

2. Assign classes to components.

3. Set the code generation properties.

4. Select a class or component to generate on a Class or Component diagram.

5. Select Tools ➤ C++ ➤ Code Generation.

6. Select Tools ➤ C++ ➤ Browse Header or Browse Body to view the generated code.

CHAPTER

THIRTEEN

13

Java Code Generation

■ Setting Java Code Generation Properties

■ Generating Java Code from Your Rose Model

■ Mapping Rose Elements to Java Constructs

In this chapter, we'll discuss how to generate Java code from your Rational Rose model. We'll discuss the code generation properties that can be set for Java and take a close look at how each Rose model element is implemented in the code.

To generate code, you'll need to follow these steps:

1. Create the components (see Chapter 10).

2. Assign classes to the components (see Chapter 10).

3. Set the code generation properties.

4. Select a class or component to generate on a Class or Component diagram.

5. Select Tools ➤ Java ➤ Code Generation.

6. Select Tools ➤ Java ➤ Browse Java Source to view the generated code.

Rose will take a lot of information from the model to generate code. For example, it will look at the multiplicity, role names, containment, and other details of each relationship. It will look at the attributes, operations, visibility, and other details of each class. From all of the information you entered using the specification windows for the various model elements, Rose will gather what it needs to generate code.

Java Code Generation Properties

The Java code generation properties can be set in two places. The defaults are set using the Tools ➤ Options menu item and then selecting the Java tab, as shown in Figure 13.1. You can set properties for the following items:

- Attributes
- Classes
- Module bodies
- Module specifications
- Operations
- Projects
- Roles

We'll discuss using these various properties throughout this chapter. We'll begin with a brief description of the available code generation properties, then cover projects, modules, classes, attributes, operations, and roles. Finally, we'll take you step-by-step through the Java code generation of the ATM system, and then give you an exercise to generate Java from the Order Entry model.

FIGURE 13.1:

Java code generation properties window

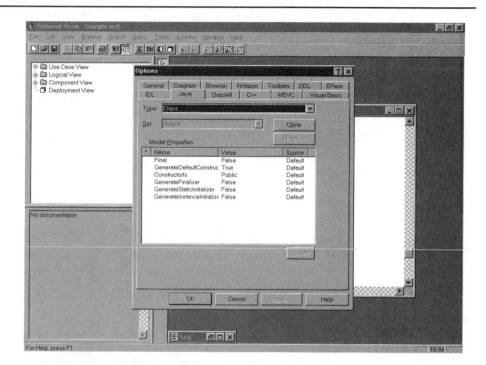

Project Properties

The project properties affect all aspects of Java code generation in Rose. Here, we provide a listing of the properties and their common settings.

The project properties are code generation properties that apply more to the whole project than to any specific model element, such as a class or relationship. The options in this section include things like the default directory to use when generating code, the file extensions to use, and whether or not to stop generation if an error occurs. Each of the project properties is listed in Table 13.1, along with their purpose and default value.

In this and subsequent code generation property tables, we list the most commonly used properties. The property sets vary slightly between Rose 98 and Rose 98i.

TABLE 13.1: Java Project Properties

Property	Purpose	Default
CreateMissingDirectories	If true, creates any directories that are required if they do not exist.	By default, Rose will create missing directories.
StopOnError	If true, Rose will stop code generation at the first error.	By default, code generation will stop on an error.
Editor (98i)	Select the editor to use while browsing code.	The default is Rose's built-in editor.
VM (98i)	Select the version of the Java Virtual Machine (Sun or Microsoft).	The default VM is Sun.
ClassPath (98i)	Specifies the directory where code will be generated.	By default, code is generated in the current directory.
Directory (98)	Specifies the directory where code will be generated.	By default, code is generated in the current directory.
UsePrefixes	If true, Rose will add user-defined prefixes to the variable names.	By default, Rose will append a prefix of "the" to instance and class variables. If true, Rose will add the user-defined prefixes to the variable names.
InstanceVariablePrefix	If UsePrefixes is true, then this prefix will be added to all instance variables.	The default instance variable prefix, if used, is m_.
ClassVariablePrefix	If UsePrefixes is true, then this prefix will be added to all class variables.	The default class variable prefix, if used, is 's_.
DefaultAttributeDataType	If no type is selected for an attribute, this type will be used.	The default attribute data type is integer.
DefaultOperation-ReturnType	If no return type is selected for an operation, this type will be used.	The default operation return type is void.

When generating code, Rose will automatically create attributes for certain types of relationships. For example, if you have a unidirectional association between class Client and class Supplier, and the multiplicity on the relationship is one-to-one, Rose will generate an attribute of type Supplier inside the Client.

Class Properties

In this section, we discuss the Java code generation properties that apply to classes. These properties will let you change the class name, decide whether or not constructors should be created for the class, and set other class-specific properties.

There are two places to set these properties. To set them for all classes, select Tools ➤ Options, then the Java tab, and select Class from the drop-down list box. To set them for only one class, select the Java tab on the class specification window and edit the properties there.

Table 13.2 lists the Java class properties, their purpose, and their default value.

TABLE 13.2: Java Class Properties

Property	Purpose	Default
Final	Includes the final modifier in the generated code.	By default, a final modifier will not be included.
Static (98i)	Declares a nested Java class as static and that only one instance of the class can exist.	False.
GenerateDefaultConstructor	Controls whether a constructor will automatically be generated for the class.	By default, a constructor will be generated.
ConstructorIs	Sets the visibility (public, private, protected) of the constructor.	The default setting is public.
GenerateFinalizer	Includes a finalizer in the class.	By default, a finalizer is not included.
GenerateStaticInitializer	Includes a static initializer in the class.	By default, a static initializer is not included.
GenerateInstance Initializer	Includes an instance initializer in the class.	By default, an instance initializer is not included.

Attribute Properties

In this section, we cover the Java code generation properties that relate to attributes. Using these properties, you can, for example, decide whether the attribute will be generated in the code.

There are two places to set these properties. To set them for all attributes, select Tools ➤ Options, then the Java tab, and select Attribute from the drop-down list box. To set them for only one attribute, select the Java tab on the attribute specification window and edit the properties there.

Table 13.3 lists the attribute properties, their purpose, and their default value.

TABLE 13.3: Java Attribute Properties

Property	Purpose	Default
GenerateDataMember (98)	Controls whether a member variable will be generated for the attribute.	By default, each attribute will be generated.
Final	Includes a final modifier in the attribute.	By default, a final modifier is not included.
Transient	Includes a transient modifier in the attribute.	By default, a transient modifier is not included.
Volatile	Includes a volatile modifier in the attribute.	By default, a volatile modifier is not included.
PropertyType (98i)	Specifies the property type for a Java bean.	Not a property.
IndividualChangeMgt (98i)	Specifies whether or not the Java bean gets its own registration mechanism.	False.
Read/Write (98i)	Sets whether or not Rose will generate a Get and/or a Set method.	Read & Write.

Operation Properties

Next we discuss the Java code generation properties that are specific to operations. These properties will let you, for example, control whether the operation is abstract or not.

There are two places to set these properties. To set them for all operations, select Tools ➢ Options, then the Java tab, and select Operation from the drop-down list box. To set them for only one operation, select the Java tab on the operation specification window, and edit the properties there.

Table 13.4 lists the operation code generation properties, their purpose, and their default value.

TABLE 13.4: Java Operation Properties

Property	Purpose	Default
Abstract	Includes an abstract modifier in the operation.	By default, an abstract modifier is not included.
Static	Includes a static modifier in the operation.	By default, a static modifier is not included.
Final	Includes a final modifier in the operation.	By default, a final modifier is not included.
Native	Includes a native modifier in the operation.	By default, a native modifier is not included.
Synchronized	Includes a synchronized modifier in the operation.	By default, a synchronized modifier is not included.

Module Properties

The module specification and body properties are those properties that are related to the files you will generate from Rose. These properties give you the ability to decide, for example, whether or not to include a copyright notice in the file.

There are two places to set these properties. To set them for all header files, select Tools ➤ Options, then the Java tab, and select Module Specification from the drop-down list box. To set them for only one file, select the Java tab on the component specification window and edit the properties there.

Table 13.5 lists the code generation properties for module specifications, their purposes, and their default values.

In Rose 98i, the CMIdentification and CopyrightNotice property values are also displayed in fields in the component specification window for Java components. The default property values are provided in the component specification fields.

TABLE 13.5: Java Module Specification Properties

Property	Purpose	Default
Generate (98)	If true, a module specification will generate code.	By default, a module specification generates code.
CMIdentification	Specifies a user-defined configuration management identification string.	By default, the user-defined configuration management identification string is blank.
CopyrightNotice	Specifies a user-defined copyright string to include in the code as a comment.	By default, the copyright notice is blank.
AdditionalImports (98)	Specifies any additional import statements to include the generated code.	By default, no additional imports are included in the code.

Role Properties

Role properties are the Java code generation properties that affect the code generated for relationships. Using these properties, you can set the container class to be used for the attribute and change other specifics of the generated code for a role.

As with most of the other property sets, there are two places to set these properties. To set them for all relationships, select Tools ➤ Options, then the Java tab, and select Role from the drop-down list box. To set them for a single relationship, open the relationship specification. On the Java tab of the relationship specification window, you can change the properties for that relationship.

Table 13.6 lists the role properties, their purpose, and their default value.

TABLE 13.6: Java Role Properties

Property	Purpose	Default
GenerateDataMember (98)	Controls whether or not an attribute is created for the relationship.	True.
ContainerClass	Specifies the container class to use if the relationship's multiplicity is greater than one.	By default, an array is used.
InitialValue	Specifies the default value for the attribute.	By default, no initial value is used.
Final	Includes a final modifier in the attribute.	By default, a final modifier is not included.
Transient	Includes a transient modifier in the attribute.	By default, a transient modifier is not included.
Volatile	Includes a volatile modifier in the attribute.	By default, a volatile modifier is not included.
PropertyType (98i)	Specifies the property type for a Java bean.	Not a property.
IndividualChangeMgt (98i)	Specifies whether or not the Java bean gets its own registration mechanism.	False.
Read/Write (98i)	Sets whether or not Rose will generate a Get and/or a Set method.	Read & Write.

Generated Code

In the following sections, we'll take a look at the Java code generated for a class, attribute, and operation, and for the different types of relationships between classes. In each of these sections, we'll include some sample code to give you an idea of what will be generated from your Rose model.

Rose uses the information in the specifications of the model elements when generating code. For example, it will look at the different specifications for a class (visibility, attributes, operations, and so on) when generating code for the class.

Let's begin by looking at the code generated for a typical class.

Classes

A class in your object model will become a Java class when you generate code. All of the attributes, operations, and relationships of the class will be reflected in the generated code. The major elements generated for each class include:

- The class name
- The class visibility
- A constructor for the class
- Class documentation
- Attributes
- Operations
- Relationships

Without a component mapping, each class in the model will generate one file with the .java extension. Each file will be named using the class name. For example, an Employee class will generate an `Employee.java` file.

Much of the information in your Rose model will be used directly when generating code. For example, the attributes, operations, relationships, and class name of each class will directly affect the code generated. Other model properties, such as the documentation entered for the class, will not directly affect the code. These properties are created as comments in the generated code.

Table 13.7 lists the properties available in the class specification window (standard specification window in Rose 98i), and notes which of these properties will directly affect the code generated.

TABLE 13.7: Effect of Class Specifications on Generated Code

Property	Effect on Code
Name	Name in model will become class name.
Type	Directly affects the type of class created.
Stereotype	Comment.
Export Control	Directly affects the class visibility.
Documentation	Comment.
Persistence	Affects whether DDL can be generated for the class.
Abstract	Creates an abstract class.
Formal Arguments	Formal arguments are included in the code for a parameterized class.
Operations	Generated in code.
Attributes	Generated in code.
Relationships	Generated in code.

Let's look at the code generated for the class shown on the next page. The following code is the Java file that was generated for this class.

```java
// Source file: SampleClass.java

/*
Copyright Notice
*/

/**
   SampleClass documentation
 */

public class SampleClass {
   public SampleClass() {
     }
}
```

By default, Rose generates a class declaration with a public constructor. This is in sharp contrast to the C++ code that Rose generates. Operator assignments, copy constructors, destructors, gets, and sets are not generated for Java. However, Rose will generate a modifier for abstract classes.

Copyright Notice Section

The copyright notice section includes the following:

```
/*
Copyright Notice
*/
```

By default, there is no copyright notice generated for your code. If, however, you'd like to add a copyright notice to all files, you can change the code genera-tion properties. Select Tools ➤ Options from the menu, then select the Java tab. Select Module Specification from the drop-down list box to display the module specification code generation properties. Change the CopyrightNotice field to include any copyright information. If information is entered, it will be generated.

You can override the default for a specific component by changing the value in the Copyright field in the component specification window or in the CopyrightNotice property on the Java tab of the component's standard specification window.

Attributes

Aside from the class itself, Rose will generate the attributes for the class. For each attribute, Rose will include information about the attribute visibility, data type, and default value in the code. Let's look at the code generated for the following class.

```
// Source file: SampleClass.java

/*
Copyright Notice
*/

/**
   SampleClass documentation
 */
public class SampleClass {
    private int ID;

    public SampleClass() {
    }
}
```

As you can see, the code includes the attribute visibility, data type, and default value. There are only a few properties for attributes. You can prevent an attribute from generating, or apply the final, transient, or volatile modifiers to the attribute. The table of attribute properties has been reproduced here for your convenience.

Property	Purpose	Default
GenerateDataMember	Controls whether a member variable will be generated for the attribute.	By default, each attribute will be generated.
Final	Includes a final modifier in the attribute.	By default, a final modifier is not included.

| Transient | Includes a transient modifier in the attribute. | By default, a tran - sient modifier is not included. |
| Volatile | Includes a volatile modifier in the attribute. | By default, a volatile modifier is not included. |

To prevent an attribute from generating, change the GenerateDataMember code generation property for the attribute. In the attribute specification window, select the Java tab. Change the GenerateDataMember property to False.

To apply one of the modifiers, such as the transient modifier to an attribute, set the appropriate property to true. In this case, you set the transient property to true and the attribute generates with the modifier, as in the following code:

```
// Source file: SampleClass.java

/*
Copyright Notice
*/

/**
    SampleClass documentation
 */
public class SampleClass {
    private transient int ID;

    SampleClass() {
    }
}
```

The visibility options affect the generated attribute. In the above example, and as default, attributes are given private visibility. If you set an attribute to pro-tected or public, the following code is an example of what you will get:

```
// Source file: SampleClass.java

/*
Copyright Notice
*/
```

```
/**
   SampleClass documentation
 */
public class SampleClass {
➜     private int ID;
➜     public String Name;
➜     protected String SSN;

      SampleClass() {
      }
}
```

Operations

Rose generates each of the operations in the class. For each operation, the generated code includes the operation name, the parameters, the parameter data types, and the return type. Here, we'll examine the code generated for the following class:

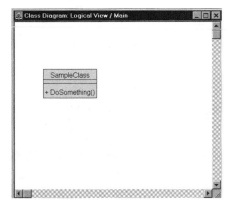

```
//Source file: SampleClass.java
```

```
/**
   SampleClass documentation
 */
public class SampleClass {
      private transient int ID;
      public String Name;
      protected String SSN;
```

```java
    public SampleClass() {}

    /**
        DoSomething documentation
        @roseuid 372E31F800BF
        */
    public int DoSomething(int Parameter1) {}
}
```

As you can see, the full operation signature is generated in the code. Any documentation you entered for the operation is also generated as a comment in the code.

Rose generates skeletal code for operations. That is, the operation signature is generated. Once you have generated the code, you insert the implementation code for each operation between the { and } delimiters of the operation. This protects the code during round-trip engineering.

If you enter exception information for the operation, using the Exceptions field on the Detail tab of the operation specification window, these exceptions are included in the code, as shown here:

```java
//Source file: SampleClass.java


/**
    SampleClass documentation
  */
public class SampleClass {
    private transient int ID;
    public String Name;
    protected String SSN;

    public SampleClass() {}

    /**
        DoSomething documentation
        @roseuid 372E31F800BF
      */
    public int DoSomething(int Parameter1) throws Exception {}
}
```

As with other model elements, you can control the code generated for an operation by modifying its code generation properties. The code generation properties for operations are listed in Table 13.4, but we list them again here for your reference.

Property	Purpose	Default
Abstract	Includes an abstract modifier in the attribute.	By default, an abstract modifier is not included.
Static	Includes a static modifier in the attribute.	By default, a static modifier is not included.
Final	Includes a final modifier in the attribute.	By default, a final modifier is not included.
Native	Includes a native modifier in the attribute.	By default, a native modifier is not included.
Synchronized	Includes a synchronized modifier in the attribute.	By default, a synchronized modifier is not included.

Bi-Directional Associations

To support bi-directional associations, Rose will generate attributes in the code. Each of the classes in the relationship will contain an attribute to support the association. By default, Rose 98i names the roles by appending "the" to the class name.

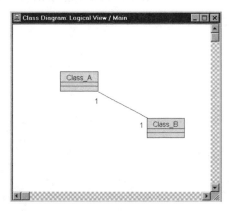

Code for Class A:

```
//Source file: Class_A.java


public class Class_A {
public Class_B theClass_B;

public Class_A() {}
}
```

Code for Class B:

```
//Source file: Class_B.java


public class Class_B {
public Class_A theClass_A;

public Class_B() {}
}
```

As you can see, Rose will automatically generate attributes on both sides of the bi-directional association relationship. With the theClass_B attribute, Class A can easily access Class B. Using the theClass_A attribute, Class B can easily access Class A. If you want to use different names for the attributes instead of the Class_A and theClass_B, you can set role names for the association. These names will be used instead, as in the following code:

Code for Class A:

```
//Source file: Class_A.java


public class Class_A {
public Class_B Supplier_to_A;

public Class_A() {}
}
```

Code for Class B:

```
//Source file: Class_B.java


public class Class_B {
public Class_A Supplier_to_B;

public Class_B() {}
}
```

Rose will use the role name to generate the attribute name. By default, each generated attribute will have public visibility. To change the visibility, open the association specification window. Select either the Role A General or Role B General tab, and change the export control property.

Note that this association had a multiplicity of one to one. See below for a discussion of how other multiplicity settings will affect code generation.

Each of the generated attributes has public visibility. If you add role names to the association, these role names will be used to name the attributes. Otherwise, the generated attributes will have the prefix from the project property InstanceVariablePrefix. By default in Rose 98, this is m_, followed by the class name. In Rose 98i, the default is "the" followed by the class name. For example, the Employee.

In addition to specifying visibility, you can specify initial values for the generated attributes. Open the desired association's specification, then select the Java A or Java B tab. Modify the InitialValue property to contain the initial value for the generated attribute.

Note that this association had a multiplicity of one to one. See below for a discussion of how other multiplicity settings will affect code generation.

Unidirectional Associations

As with bi-directional associations, Rose will generate attributes to support unidirectional associations. However, with a unidirectional association, an attribute is only generated at one end of the relationship.

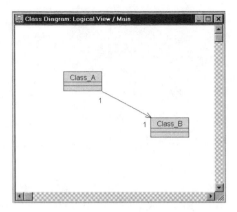

For the A and B classes above, code similar to the following would be created:

Code for Class A:

```
//Source file: Class_A.java


public class Class_A {
    public Class_B theClass_B;

    public Class_A() {}
    }
```

Code for Class B:

```
//Source file: Class_B.java


public class Class_B {

    public Class_B() {}
}
```

As you can see, Rose will only generate an attribute for the relationship at one end of the association. Specifically, it will generate an attribute in the Client class, but not in the Supplier class.

The code generated in the Supplier class is the same as discussed in the previous section about bi-directional associations. With a bi-directional association, each class is given a new attribute, and the code discussed in the previous section is included in both classes. With a unidirectional association, the code is included only in the Client class.

Again, note that the multiplicity here is one to one. Let's take a look at how code is affected when the multiplicity settings are changed.

Associations with a Multiplicity of One to Many

In a one-to-one relationship, Rose can simply create the appropriate attributes to support the association. With a one-to-many relationship, however, one class must contain a set of the other class. Let's look at an example.

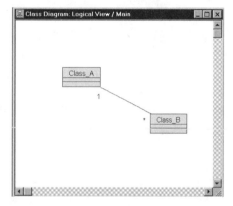

In this case, we've got a one-to-many relationship. The code generated for this relationship is shown below:

Code for Class A:

```
//Source file: Class_A.java


public class Class_A {
public Class_B theClass_B[];

public Class_A() {}
}
```

Code for Class B:

```
//Source file: Class_B.java


public class Class_B {
   public Class_A theClass_A;

   public Class_B() {}
}
```

Here, Class B simply contains an attribute of type A because the multiplicity states that there is one instance of A for each instance of B. However, the multiplicity also states that there are many instances of B for each instance of A. Therefore, an array of B objects is created inside A.

If you don't want to use an array, you can change the code generation properties to use a different container class. In the Java tab of the association specification window, set the ContainerClass code generation property to the name of the container class you'd rather use. For example, the following code is generated for the above association, but with the container class as type Container.

Code for Class A:

```
// Source file: A.java

public class Class_A {
      public Container theClass_B;

      public Class_A() {
      }
}
```

Associations with a Multiplicity of Many to Many

The code generated here is similar to that created for a one-to-many relationship. However, here Rose will generate arrays on both ends of the relationship. Let's look at the code generated for the following relationship.

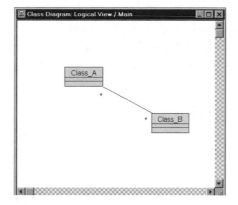

Code for Class A:

```
//Source file: Class_A.java


public class Class_A {
        public Class_B theClass_B[];

        public Class_A() {}
}
```

Code for Class B:

```
//Source file: Class_B.java


public class Class_B {
        public Class_A theClass_A[];

        public Class_B() {}
}
```

In this situation, arrays are created at both ends of the relationship. An array is used by default, but as we mentioned above, you can change the container class that is used. To do so, use the relationship specification window for the association. On the Java A or Java B tab, change the ContainerClass property. Set this property to the name of the container class you wish to use.

To change the container class for all many-to-many association relationships, choose Tools ➤ Options from the menu. On the Java tab, select Role from the drop-down list box. Change the value of the ContainerClass code generation property to the container class you wish to use.

Reflexive Associations

A reflexive association is treated much the same as an association between two classes. Let's look at the code generated for the following situation:

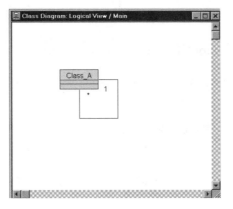

```
//Source file: Class_A.java


public class Class_A {
        public Class_A theClass_A[];

    public Class_A() {}
}
```

As with a regular association, an attribute is created inside the class to support the relationship. If the multiplicity is one, a simple attribute is created. If the multiplicity is more than one, an array is created as an attribute, as above.

Aggregations

There are two types of aggregation relationships: by-value and by-reference. With a by-value relationship, one class contains another. With a by-reference relationship, one class contains a reference to another. Code generated for either type of aggregation in Java is the same.

The code generation property we will be examining here is the ContainerClass role property.

Let's start by examining by-value aggregations, which are also known as composition relationships. In UML, a composition is shown using the symbol shown on the next page.

As with association relationships, Rose will generate attributes when code is generated for an aggregation. In our example above, Class B is an attribute inside Class A. The generated code would look like this:

Class A:

```
//Source file: Class_A.java


public class Class_A {
     public Class_B theClass_B;

     public Class_A() {}
}
```

Class B:

```
//Source file: Class_B.java


public class Class_B {

     public Class_B() {}
}
```

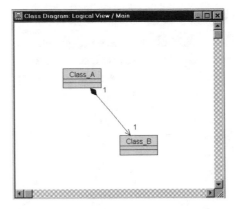

If the multiplicity of the relationship is greater than one, Rose will use a container class when creating the relationship. Let's take a look at this relationship now:

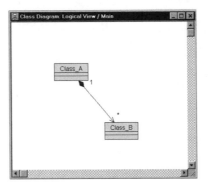

Class A:

```
//Source file: Class_A.java

import java.awt.Container;

public class Class_A {
    public Container theClass_B;

public Class_A() {}
}
```

Class B:

```
//Source file: Class_B.java


public class Class_B {

    public Class_B() {}
}
```

Rose uses the value in the ContainerClass property when the multiplicity of the relationship is greater than one. If the ContainerClass contains no value, then Rose will use an array to contain the multiple objects.

Dependency Relationships

With a dependency relationship, no attributes are created. If there is a dependency between Class A and Class B, no attributes will be created in either Class A or Class B.

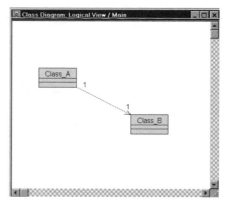

The code that is generated will look something like the following:

```
//Source file: Class_A.java


public class Class_A {

    public Class_A() {}
}
```

and

```
//Source file: Class_B.java


public class Class_B {

    public Class_B() {}
}
```

Rose will place no references to Class B inside of Class A. The dependency relationship does not generate any code for the relationship.

Generalization Relationships

A generalization relationship in UML becomes an inheritance relationship in Java. In your Rose model, an inheritance relationship is shown as follows:

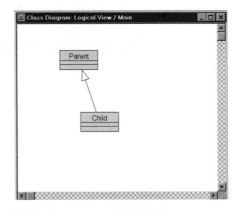

For this type of relationship, Rose will generate something that looks like this:

```
//Source file: Parent.java


public class Parent {

    public Parent() {}
}
```

and

```
//Source file: C:/Program Files/Rational/Rose
   98i/java/source/Child.java


public class Child extends Parent {

   public Child() {}
}
```

In the code for the parent class, there is no mention of the child class. This helps keep the parent generic; many classes can inherit from it without affecting its code. In the child class, the code is generated to support its inheritance from the parent class. The class declaration will look like this:

```
Public class Child extends Parent
```

Example of Generated Java

Throughout the book, we have been working with an ATM example application. In this section, we have generated the skeletal Java code for the ATM example. For reference, the component models are shown in Figures 13.2 and 13.3.

For the ATM Client Component, we set the language of all components to Java. Next, we selected both the ATMServer and ATMClient packages in the Main Component diagram. Then, we selected Tools ➤ Java ➤ Generate Java. The code that was generated for each component is included on the CD.

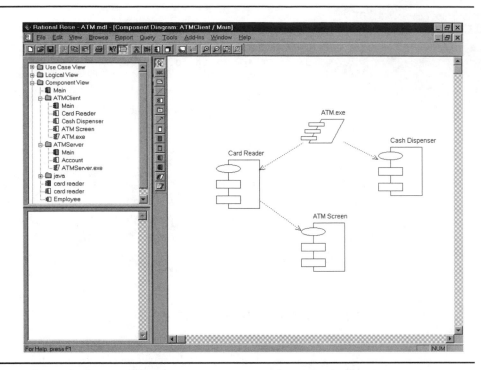

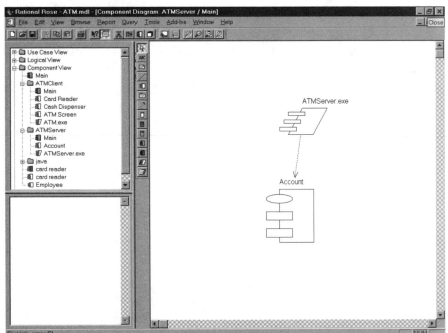

Exercise

In Chapters 3 through 10, we completed a model for an Order Entry system. Now, we are going to generate Java code for the Order Entry system. We will use the System component diagram shown in Figure 13.4. To generate the code, we need to perform the steps shown below. The code for this exercise is included on the CD.

FIGURE 13.4:

System Component diagram for the Order Entry system

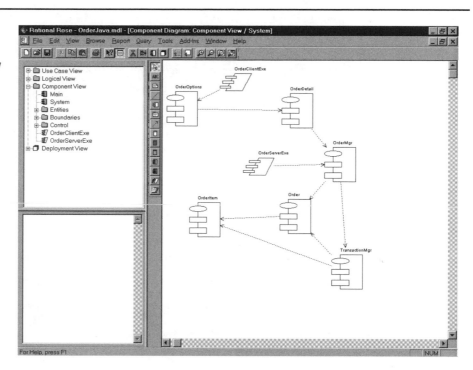

Exercise Steps:

Remove the Package Bodies

1. In the exercise for Chapter 9, we created a package specification and package body for each class. Since the package bodies are not used in Java, the first step is to delete them from the model.

Continued on next page

2. Open the System Component specification.

3. Select the OrderOptions package body.

4. Press Ctrl+D to delete the package body.

5. Repeat steps 3 and 4 for the following components:

   - `OrderDetail package body`

   - `OrderMgr package body`

   - `Order package body`

   - `OrderItem package body`

   - `TransactionMgr package body`

Set the Language to Java

1. Open the component specification for the Order component (package specification) within the Entities component package.

2. Select Java as the language.

3. Repeat Steps 1 and 2 for the following components:

   - `Entities: OrderItem Package Specification`

   - `Boundaries: OrderOptions Package Specification`

   - `Boundaries: OrderDetail Package Specification`

   - `Control: TransactionMgr Package Specification`

   - `Control: OrderMgr Package Specification`

   - `OrderClientExe Task Specification`

   - `OrderServerExe Task Specification`

Import Java Data Types

1. The model file we are using needs to include the Java data types in order to generate Java. These types have been included in the Data Types directory on the CD. Open the Main Class diagram.

2. Select File ➤ Import from the menu. Import the file **Data Types\Java Classes.ptl** from the CD.

Continued on next page

3. Open the Main Component diagram.

4. Select File ➤ Import from the menu. Import the file `Data Types\Java Components.ptl` from the CD.

Set Java Data Types

1. Since Java data types are named slightly differently than the C++ data types we have been using, we now need to set the data types of all attributes and operations to valid Java data types. NOTE: If you have completed the exercises to this point, all you will need to do is change the Date data type to `java.util.Date`.

2. Open the Add Order Class diagram.

3. Set the data types of attributes, operations, and arguments to appear as in Figure 13.5.

FIGURE 13.5:

Java data types for the Order Entry classes

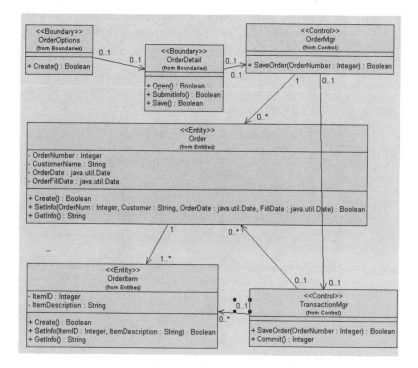

Continued on next page

Generate Java

1. Open the System Component diagram.

2. Select all objects on the diagram.

3. Select Tools ➢ Java ➢ Generate Java from the menu. The generated Java should look like the exercise code for this chapter on the accompanying CD-ROM.

Summary

In this chapter, we took a look at how various Rose model elements are implemented in Java. Using the code generation properties for classes, packages, attributes, operations, associations, aggregations, and other model elements, you have a great deal of control over what gets generated.

Again, these are the steps you'll need to follow to generate code:

1. Create components.

2. Assign classes to components.

3. Set the code generation properties.

4. Select a class or component to generate on a Class or Component diagram.

5. Select Tools ➢ Java ➢ Code Generation.

6. Select Tools ➢ Java ➢ Browse Java Source to view the generated code.

CHAPTER

FOURTEEN

Visual Basic Code Generation

- Setting Visual Basic Code Generation Properties

- Generating Visual Basic Code from Your Rose Model

- Mapping Rose Elements to Visual Basic Constructs

In this chapter, we'll discuss how to generate Visual Basic code from your Rational Rose model.

To generate code, you will need to follow these steps:

1. Create components (see Chapter 10).

2. Assign classes to components (see Chapter 10).

3. Set the code generation properties.

4. Select a class or component to generate on a Class or Component diagram.

5. Select Tools ➤ Visual Basic ➤ Update Code (or Code Generation) to begin the Code Generation Wizard.

6. Select Tools ➤ Visual Basic ➤ Browse Visual Basic Source to view the generated code.

We'll discuss the code generation properties that can be set, and take a close look at how each Rose model element is implemented in the code.

Rose will use a lot of information in the model to generate code. For example, it will look at the multiplicity, role names, containment, and other details of each relationship. It will look at the attributes, operations, visibility, and other details of each class. From all of the information you entered using the specification windows for the various model elements, Rose will gather what it needs to generate code.

Visual Basic Code Generation Properties

Visual Basic code generation using Rational Rose is extremely flexible. You have full control over what gets generated, and over many of the details of how the generated code will look. For example, for each class, you can decide if initialization and termination routines will automatically be created. For each attribute, you control the visibility, name, and whether Get and Set operations should automatically be created. For each module, you control the filename. For each generalization, you control if the implements delegation is used.

All of these things are controlled through the code generation properties. Rose provides property sets that deal with classes, attributes, operations, module specifications, associations, and generalizations.

You can see all of these properties by selecting Tools ➤ Options, then selecting the Visual Basic tab.

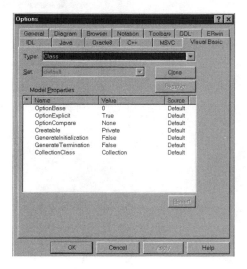

Anything you change using this window will set the default for all classes, attributes, operations, and so on.

You can also set the code generation properties for a single class, attribute, operation, or other model element. To do so, open the specification window for the model element, and select the Visual Basic tab. On this tab, you can change the properties that apply to that particular type of model element.

In the following sections, we'll examine many of the more commonly used code generation properties for classes, operations, attributes, and modules. Later in this chapter, as we go through the code generated for various types of relationships and multiplicities, we'll examine some additional code generation properties.

Class Properties

Class properties are the Visual Basic code generation properties that apply to classes. These properties will let you change the class name, decide whether or not initialization and termination routines should be created for the class, and set other class-specific properties.

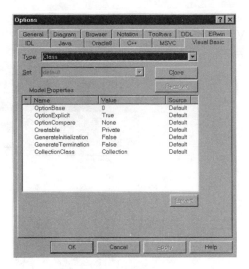

There are two places to set these properties. To set them for all classes, select Tools ➤ Options, then the Visual Basic tab, and select Class from the drop-down list box. To set them for only one class, select the Visual Basic tab on the class specification window and edit the properties there.

Table 14.1 lists many of the Visual Basic class properties, their purpose, and their default value.

TABLE 14.1: Class Code Generation Properties

Property	Purpose	Default
Update Code (98i)	Specifies if code can be updated for the class	True
Update Model (98i)	Specifies if the model can be updated for the class	True
OptionBase	Sets the base identifier for arrays (usually 0 or 1)	(none)
OptionExplicit	Controls whether variable names must be explicitly declared	True
OptionCompare	Controls the method by which string comparisons are made	(none)
Instancing	Determines how classes are exposed to other applications	Private
Creatable (98)	Controls the instantiation of the class by other modules	Private
GenerateInitialization (98)	Controls the generation of an initialization routine for the class	False
GenerateTermination (98)	Controls the generation of a termination routine for the class	False
CollectionClass (98)	Sets the object type for collections in the class	Collection

Attribute Properties

Attribute properties are the Visual Basic specific properties that relate to attributes. Using these properties, you can, for example, decide whether the attribute will be generated in the code, what the attribute name should be in the generated code, and whether Get, Set, or Let operations should be created for the attribute.

There are two places to set these properties. To set them for all attributes, select Tools ➢ Options, then the Visual Basic tab, and select Attribute from the drop-down list box. To set them for only one attribute, select the Visual Basic tab on the attribute specification window, and edit the properties there.

Table 14.2 lists the attribute properties, their purpose, and their default value.

TABLE 14.2: Attribute Code Generation Properties

Property	Purpose	Default
IsConst (98)	Controls if the attribute is constant	False
New	Controls if the attribute is generated with a new modifier	False
WithEvents	Controls if the attribute is generated with the With Events modifier	False
Subscript (98i)	Specifies the array subscript for an attribute	Empty
NameIfUnlabeled (98)	Sets the name of the attribute, if it is not labeled	The$supplier
GenerateDataMember (98)	Controls whether or not the attribute is generated	True
DataMemberName (98)	Specifies the name of the data member	Attribute name from the model
GenerateGetOperation (98)	Controls if a Get operation is generated for the attribute	False
GenerateSetOperation (98)	Controls if a Set operation is generated for the attribute	False
GenerateLetOperation (98)	Controls if a Let operation is generated for the attribute	False

Operation Properties

The operation properties are the Visual Basic code generation properties that are specific to operations. These properties will let you set the name of the operation, control whether the operation is static, and set other code generation specifications for each operation.

There are two places to set these properties. To set them for all operations, select Tools ➤ Options, then the Visual Basic tab, and select Operation from the drop-down list box. To set them for only one operation, select the Visual Basic tab on the operation specification window and edit the properties there.

Table 14.3 lists many of the operation code generation properties, their purpose, and their default value.

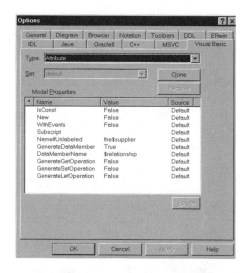

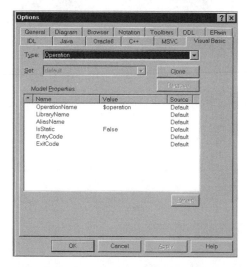

TABLE 14.3: Operation Code Generation Properties

Property	Purpose	Default
OperationName (98)	Sets the name of the generated operation.	Operation name from the model
LibraryName	Sets the name of library in which to generate the operation.	Empty
AliasName	Sets the name of an operation alias.	Empty
IsStatic	Controls if the operation is static.	False
ReplaceExistingBody (98i)	Specifies whether to overwrite existing body code with the default body code.	False
EntryCode	Used to enter code or comments that are generated along with the operation. (This code will not be placed in the protected region, which is protected during round-trip engineering.)	Empty
ExitCode	Used to enter code or comments that are generated along with the operation. (This code will not be placed in the protected region, which is protected during round-trip engineering.)	Empty
DefualtBody	If ReplaceExistingBody is true, specifies the default text (code and comments) to include in the body.	Empty

Module Specification Properties

The module specification properties are related to the project files you will generate from Rose. There is only one property, the project filename.

There are two places to set these properties. To set them for all header files, select Tools ➢ Options, then the Visual Basic tab, and select Module Specification from the drop-down list box. To set them for only one file, select the Visual Basic tab on the component specification window, and edit the properties there.

Table 14.4 lists many of the code generation properties for header files, their purpose, and their default value.

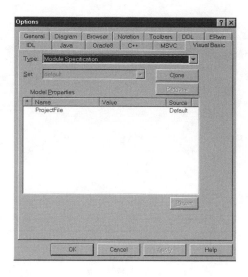

TABLE 14.4: Module Specification Code Generation Properties

Property	Purpose	Default
ProjectFile	Sets the name of the project file	<Set using the Code Generation Wizard>
UpdateCode (98i)	Specifies if code can be generated for this component	True
UpdateModel (98i)	Specifies if the model can be updated for this component	True
ImportReferences (98i)	Specifies whether to import ActiveX components	True
QuickImport (98i)	Specifies whether to import only ActiveX interface classes or all classes including methods and operations	True

Role Properties

Role properties are the Visual Basic code generation properties that affect the code generated for relationships. There are a number of role properties, which will let you set the name of the attribute that is created, control the generation of Get, Set, and Let operations, and change other specific pieces of the generated code.

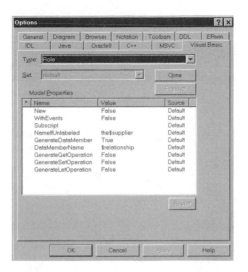

There are two places to set these properties. To set them for all associations, select Tools ➤ Options, then the Visual Basic tab, and select Role from the drop-down list box. To set them for only one operation, select the Visual Basic tab on the association specification window, and edit the properties there.

Table 14.5 lists the code generation property for roles.

TABLE 14.5: Role Code Generation Properties

Property	Purpose	Default
UpdateCode (98i)	Specifies if code can be generated for this role	True
New	Controls if the association is generated with a new modifier	False
WithEvents	Controls if the association is generated with the With Events modifier	False
Fullname (98i)	Specifies whether to use the full name of the referenced class in the property declaration	False
Subscript (98i)	Specifies the array subscript for an attribute	Empty
NameIfUnlabeled (98)	Sets the name of the association, if it is not labeled	The $supplier
GenerateData Member (98)	Controls whether or not the attribute for the association is generated	True

Continued on next page

TABLE 14.5 CONTINUED: Role Code Generation Properties

Property	Purpose	Default
DataMemberName (98)	Specifies the name of the data member	Attribute name from the model
GenerateGet Operation (98)	Controls if a Get operation is generated for the association	False
GenerateSet Operation (98)	Controls if a Set operation is generated for the association	False
GenerateLet Operation (98)	Controls if a Let operation is generated for the association	False

Generalization Properties

Generalization properties are the Visual Basic code generation properties that affect the code generated for generalization relationships. As Visual Basic does not support inheritance, there is only one property for generalization relationships, using the implements delegation.

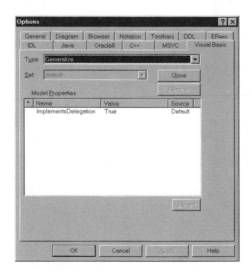

There are two places to set these properties. To set them for all generalizations, select Tools ➤ Options, then the Visual Basic tab, and select Generalize from the drop-down list box. To set them for only one operation, select the Visual Basic tab on the generalization specification window, and edit the properties there. The only code generation property for generalizations is the ImplementsDelegation property, which controls if the generalization is realized by an implements delegation. By default, this property is true.

Using the Code Generation Wizard in Rose 98

After you have created classes and associations in the Rose model, you can use a Code Generation Wizard to generate the Visual Basic code. To begin this process, select the objects to generate, then select Tools ➤ Visual Basic ➤ Generate Code from the menu.

FIGURE 14.1:

Code Generation Wizard

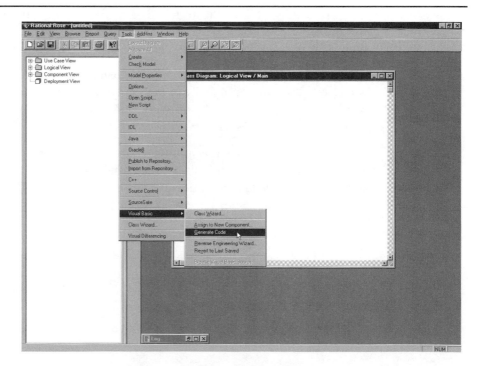

If you have not assigned the objects to components yet, you will see a window like the one in Figure 14.2. Select the type of Visual Basic project to use, then click OK. Note that you can assign classes to new components directly by selecting the class, then selecting Tools ➤ Visual Basic ➤ Assign to New Component from the menu.

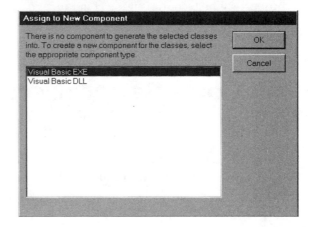

The Code Generation Wizard will display a welcome window, as shown in Figure 14.3. If you do not wish to see the welcome window again, click the check box marked *Don't show this page in the future*. Click Next to continue.

Next, you will be asked to select classes using the window in Figure 14.4. You can select classes automatically or manually. Automatic selection will synchronize all classes in the model with the Visual Basic project. With manual selection, you specify which classes to generate or update. Click Next to continue.

The wizard will now show a preview of all classes to be generated or updated. This preview is displayed in Figure 14.5. Select a class and click on the Preview button to preview the generation properties for that class. If you do not wish to preview any classes, click Next.

FIGURE 14.3:

Code Generation Wizard Welcome window

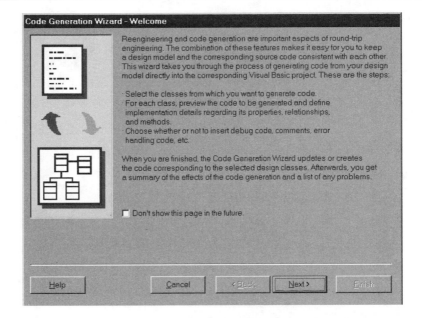

FIGURE 14.4:

Selecting classes to be generated

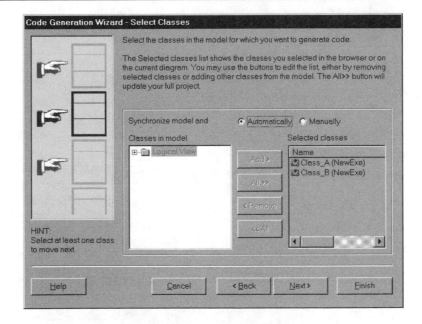

Previewing classes to be generated

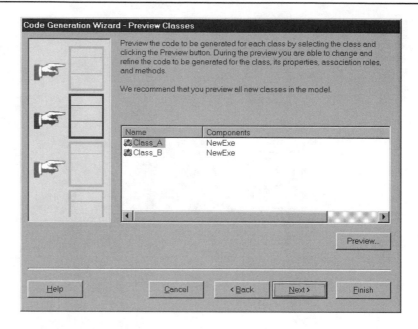

If you preview a class, the first preview window, Class Options, is displayed, as shown in Figure 14.6. From this window, you can set the instancing and collection class properties. Click Next to continue.

FIGURE 14.6:

Setting class generation options

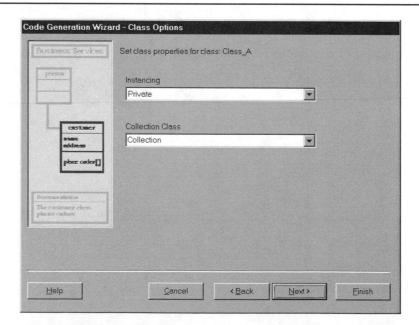

The Property Options window is displayed, as in Figure 14.7. Select an attribute and modify any of the attribute code generation properties below:

- Generate Variable
- Constant
- New
- WithEvents
- Array bounds
- Property Get
- Property Set
- Property Let

In addition, you can see a preview of the declaration statement. When you are satisfied with all attribute properties, click Next to continue.

FIGURE 14.7:

Setting property options

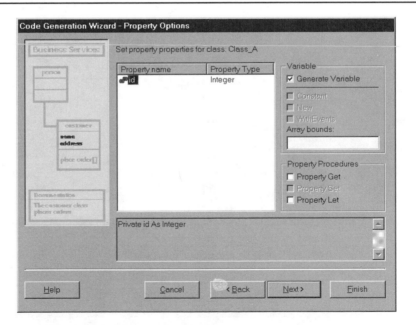

The Role Options window shown in Figure 14.8 will be displayed. Use this window to set code generation properties for associations in the same manner as you used the Property Options window to set code generation properties for attributes. Click Next to continue.

The Method Options window will be displayed. Figure 14.9 depicts this window. Any operations in the class will be shown. You can set the following code generation properties for the selected operation:

- Method Type

- Static

- DLL Library Name (DLL Component Type only)

- DLL Alias Name (DLL Component Type only)

In addition, you can see a preview of the declaration statement. When you are satisfied with all operation properties, click Finish to continue. When you have returned to the preview window, preview any other classes you desire, then click Next to continue. This completes the preview of the class.

FIGURE 14.8:

Setting role options

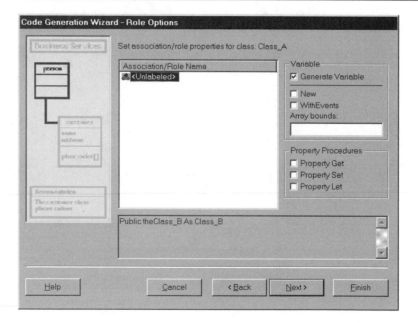

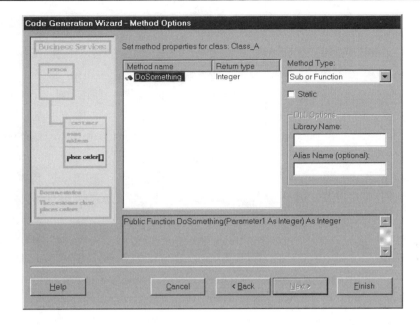

Next, the General Options window is displayed. From this window (Figure 14.10), you can set generation properties for the whole project. You can set the following properties here:

- Include debug code

- Include Err.Raise in all generated methods

- Include comments

- Generate new collection classes

When you are satisfied with the general options that are selected, click Next to continue.

FIGURE 14.10:

Setting general options

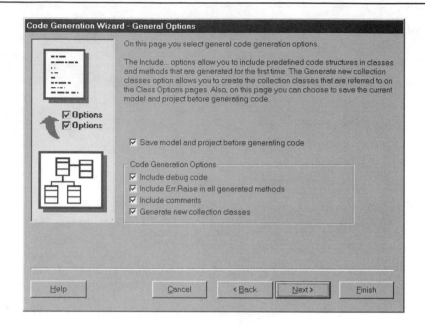

Lastly, the Finish window will be shown, as in Figure 14.11. Review the generation information, then click Finish to generate the code.

FIGURE 14.11:

Code Generation Wizard
Finish window

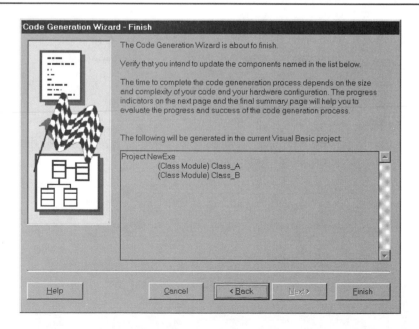

Using the Code Generation Wizard in Rose 98i

After you have created classes and associations in the Rose model, you can use a Code Generation Wizard to generate the Visual Basic code. To begin this process, select the objects to generate, then select Tools ➤ Visual Basic ➤ Update Code from the menu. You will see the screen shown in Figure 14.12.

The Visual Basic components in the model will appear as "Click next to continue." in Figure 14.13. If there are no Visual Basic components, create a new component by selecting the Visual Basic language and clicking Create a Visual Basic Component and Assign New Classes to It or pressing Ctrl+R.

FIGURE 14.12:

Code Update Tool Welcome screen

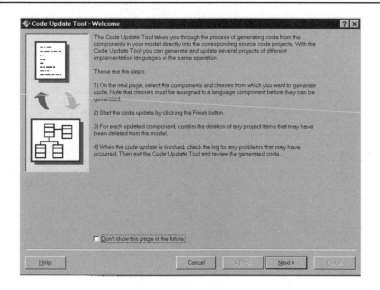

FIGURE 14.13:

Select components and
classes

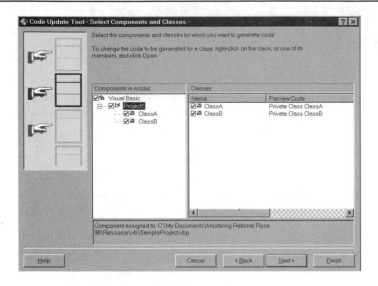

Check the box next to the components or classes you wish to update. Right-click and select Open to view the properties for the object. Right-click on the Visual Basic item to view the Visual Basic properties as shown in Figure 14.14.

FIGURE 14.14:

Visual Basic properties

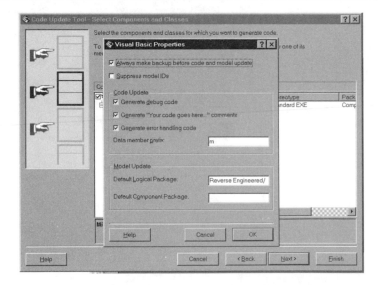

From this window, you can change many of the code generation properties for the whole model. For example, you can set the prefix to be used for data members.

Right-click on a component to assign classes to the component or to view the Visual Basic component properties as shown in Figure 14.15. For example, you can set the project file and component stereotype from this window. A component must have a project file and stereotype for code generation to function properly.

To assign classes, right-click on a component and select Assign Classes from the menu. The Component Assignment tool displayed in Figure 14.16 will be displayed. Click on an unassigned class and drag it to a component to assign.

FIGURE 14.15:

Visual Basic component properties

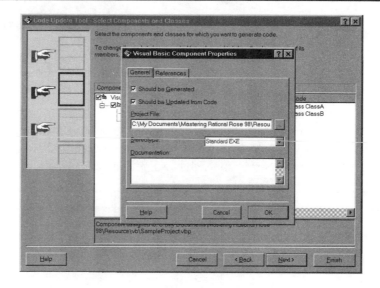

FIGURE 14.16:

Component
Assignment tool

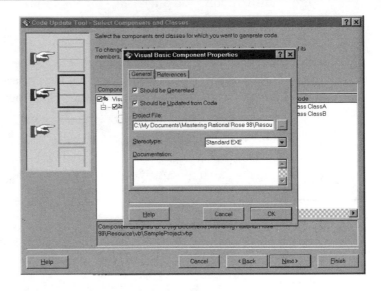

From the Select Components and Classes window, right-click on a class or class member (attribute or operation) to open the Model Assistant, as shown in Figure 14.17. The Model Assistant allows you to view and change the code generation properties for each class, property, and method.

FIGURE 14.17:

Model Assistant window

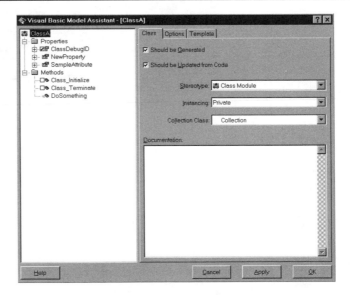

Expanding an attribute will display the Get, Set, and Let properties for the attribute. Check the box to generate the Get, Set, or Let property. Click on the Get, Set, or Let property to change the options for that property, as shown in Figure 14.18.

Click on the name of the attribute itself to display the data member properties for the attribute, as shown in Figure 14.19. Using these properties, you can set the attribute's access level, data type, and other code generation properties.

FIGURE 14.18:

Get Property options for SampleAttribute

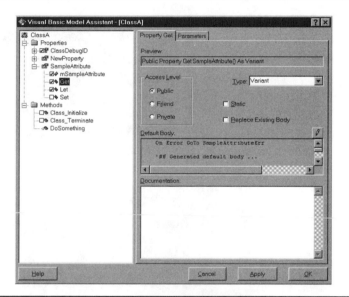

FIGURE 14.19:

Data Member properties for m_SampleAttribute

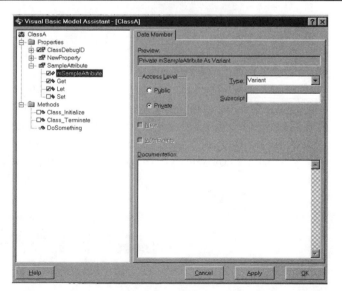

When you are finished inspecting and/or modifying the code generation properties in the Model Assistant, click OK to close it. Then, click Next to finish the code generation and Figure 14.20 will be displayed. This window explains the process. Click Finish to begin the code update.

When the code update is completed, a summary of the update will be displayed, as in Figure 14.21. Click Close to close the summary and return to the model.

FIGURE 14.20:

Code Update Tool Finish
window

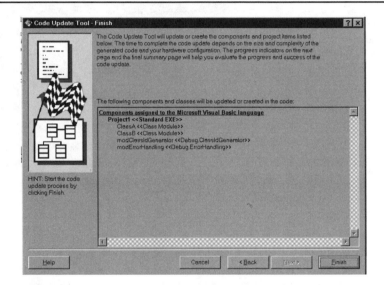

Generated Code

In the following sections, we'll take a look at the Visual Basic code generated for a class, an attribute and operation, and for the different types of relationships between classes. In each of these sections, we include some sample code to give you an idea of what will be generated from your Rose model.

FIGURE 14.21:

Code Update summary

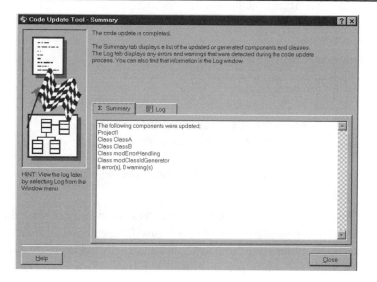

Rose uses the information in the specifications of the model elements when generating code. For example, it will look at the different specifications for a class (visibility, attributes, operations, and so on) when generating code for the class.

Let's begin by looking at the code generated for a typical class.

Classes

A class in your object model will become a Visual Basic class when you generate code. Each class will generate code similar to the following:

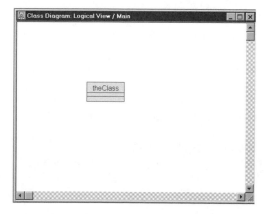

Class Module: theClass

```
Option Explicit

 '##ModelId=372E96CF00AA
Public mlClassDebugID As Long

 '##ModelId=372E96CF0079
Public Property Get ClassDebugID() As Variant
    On Error GoTo ClassDebugIDErr

        Call RaiseError(MyUnhandledError, "ClassDebugID Property")
End Property
```

The module theClass contains the generated code for the class. If this is a new project, the following two files will also be created. The modClassIDGenerator module contains one function to select the next class debug ID. The modErrorHandler class contains a simple error-handling routine. These two files will only be created once per project, whereas a separate module file similar to theClass will be created for each class you generate.

Module: modClassIDGenerator

```
Option Explicit

 'Class ID generator
 '##ModelId=372E96F60226
Public Function GetNextClassDebugID() As Long
    Static lClassDebugID As Long
    lClassDebugID = lClassDebugID + 1
    GetNextClassDebugID = lClassDebugID
End Function
```

Module: modErrorHandler

```
Option Explicit

 '##ModelId=372E96F603B0
Public Const MyObjectError1 = 1000

 '##ModelId=372E96F603B1
Public Const MyObjectError2 = 1010
```

```
'##ModelId=372E96F603B2
Public Const MyObjectErrorN = 1234

'##ModelId=372E96F603B3
Public Const MyUnhandledError = 9999

'There are a number of methods for retrieving the error
'message.  The following method uses a resource file to
'retrieve strings indexed by the error number you are
'raising.
'##ModelId=372E96F603AD
Public Sub RaiseError(ErrorNumber As Long, Source As String)
     Dim strErrorText As String

     strErrorText = GetErrorTextFromResource(ErrorNumber)

     'raise an error back to the client
     Err.Raise vbObjectError + ErrorNumber, Source, strErrorText
End Sub

' This function will retrieve an error description from a resource
' file (.RES).  The ErrorNum is the index of the string
' in the resource file.  Called by RaiseError
'##ModelId=372E96F60370
Private Function GetErrorTextFromResource(ErrorNum As Long) As String
     On Error GoTo GetErrorTextFromResourceError
     Dim strMsg As String

     ' get the string from a resource file
     GetErrorTextFromResource = LoadResString(ErrorNum)

     Exit Function
GetErrorTextFromResourceError:
     If Err.Number <> 0 Then
          GetErrorTextFromResource = "An unknown error has occurred!"
     End If
End Function'
```

This example shows what is generated by default for a class. However, a great deal of additional information can also be generated in the code. We'll look at a more complete example shortly. All of the attributes, operations, and relationships of the class will be reflected in the generated code. The major elements generated for each class include:

- The class name
- An initialize routine for the class
- A terminate routine for the class
- Get, Set, and Let operations for each attribute
- Class documentation
- Attributes
- Operations
- Relationships
- Documentation

Each class in the model will generate one Visual Basic class module file. Each file will be named using the class name. For example, an Employee class will generate an Employee class module file.

When generating code, Rose will use the package structure you established in the Component view of your model to generate the appropriate directories. A directory will be created for each package in the model. Within each of the directories Rose creates will be the module files for the classes in that package. If you have not created components and packages in the Component view, Rose will use the package structure in the Logical view to create the directory structure.

Much of the information in your Rose model will be used directly when generating code. For example, the attributes, operations, relationships, and class name of each class will directly affect the code generated. Other model properties, such as the documentation entered for the class, will not directly affect the code. These properties are created as comments in the generated code.

Table 14.6 lists the properties available in the class specification window, and notes which of these properties will directly affect the code generated.

TABLE 14.6: Effect of Class Specifications on Generated Code

Property	Effect on Code
Name	Name in model will become class name
Type	Directly affects the type of class created
Stereotype	Directly affects the type of module file created (Class Module, MDI Form, etc.)
Export Control	Does not affect generation
Documentation	Comment
Cardinality	Does not affect generation
Space	Does not affect generation
Persistence	Does not affect Visual Basic code generation, but does affect whether DDL can be generated for the class
Concurrency	Does not affect generation
Abstract	Does not affect generation
Formal Arguments	Formal arguments are included in the code for a parameterized class
Operations	Generated in code
Attributes	Generated in code
Relationships	Generated in code

Attributes

Aside from the class itself, Rose will generate the attributes for the class. For each attribute, Rose will include:

- Visibility (public or private only; protected visibility is not allowed)
- Data type
- Default value
- Get operation

- Set operation

- Let operation

For a given attribute, Rose will generate code similar to the following:

```
'##ModelId=3734B0F6006E
Private mPrivateAttribute As integer

'##ModelId=3734B10D0118
Public Property Get PrivateAttribute() As integer
    On Error GoTo PrivateAttributeErr

    '## Generated default body ...
    Let PrivateAttribute = mPrivateAttribute

    Exit Property
PrivateAttributeErr:
    Call RaiseError(MyUnhandledError, "PrivateAttribute Property Get")
End Property

'##ModelId=3734B10D011B
Public Property Let PrivateAttribute(ByVal vNewValue As integer)
    On Error GoTo PrivateAttributeErr

    '## Generated default body ...
    Set mPrivateAttribute = vNewValue

    Exit Property
PrivateAttributeErr:
    Call RaiseError(MyUnhandledError, "PrivateAttribute Property Set")
End Property
```

In this code, the attributes are created with property Get and Let statements.

Let's look at the code generated for the following class:

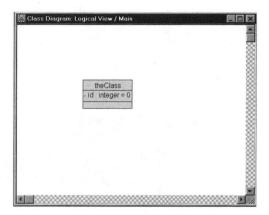

The first code generated for an attribute is the declaration, shown below:

```
'##ModelId=3734B22F023A
Private mid As Integer
```

By default, this is all that will be generated. However, if you have configured the Visual Basic options to generate Get, Set, or Let operations, they will be generated, as shown here:

```
'##ModelId=3734B27F0174
Public Property Let id(ByVal vNewValue As Integer)
    On Error GoTo idErr

    '## Generated default body ...
    mid = vNewValue

    Exit Property
idErr:
    Call RaiseError(MyUnhandledError, "id Property Let")
End Property

'##ModelId=3734B27F0173
Public Property Get id() As Integer
    On Error GoTo idErr

    '## Generated default body ...
    id = mid
```

```
        Exit Property
    idErr:
        Call RaiseError(MyUnhandledError, "id Property Get")
    End Property
```

In addition, the Rose model will be updated to include the new operations, as in Figure 14.22.

FIGURE 14.22:

Sample class after VB code generation

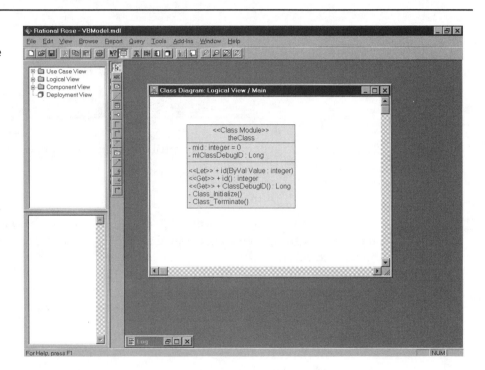

You can set the code generation properties to generate Get, Set, or Let operations, and change other aspects of the code using the properties shown above in Table 14.2.

Operations

Rose generates code for each of the operations in the class. For each operation, the generated code includes the operation name, the parameters, the parameter data types, and the return type. Each operation will generate code similar to the following:

```
'##ModelId=3734B41B005A
Private Sub PrivateOperation()
    On Error GoTo PrivateOperationErr

    '## Your code goes here ...

    Exit Sub
PrivateOperationErr:
    Call RaiseError(MyUnhandledError, "PrivateOperation Sub")
End Sub

'##ModelId=3734B3FA001E
Friend Sub ProtectedOperation()
    On Error GoTo ProtectedOperationErr

    '## Your code goes here ...

    Exit Sub
ProtectedOperationErr:
    Call RaiseError(MyUnhandledError, "ProtectedOperation Sub")
End Sub

'##ModelId=3734B3DE0190
Public Sub PublicOperation()
    On Error GoTo PublicOperationErr

    '## Your code goes here ...

    Exit Sub
PublicOperationErr:
    Call RaiseError(MyUnhandledError, "PublicOperation Sub")
End Sub
```

In this example, the operations had no arguments or return types. In the following example, the operation has an argument and a return type:

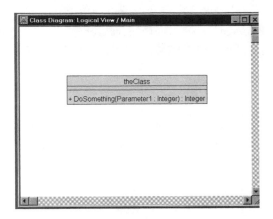

```
'Operation documentation
'##ModelId=3734B4850366
Public Function DoSomething(Parameter1 As Integer) As Integer
    On Error GoTo DoSomethingErr

    '## Your code goes here ...

    Exit Function
DoSomethingErr:
    Call RaiseError(MyUnhandledError, "DoSomething Function")
End Function
```

As you can see, the full operation signature is generated in the code. Any documentation you entered for the operation is also generated as a comment in the code. If you enter information for the operation protocol, qualifications, exceptions, time, space, preconditions, semantics, or post-conditions, this information will not be included in the generated code.

Once you have generated the code, you insert the implementation code for each operation at the *Your Code Goes Here...* line. By placing the code in this protected code region, you protect it during round-trip engineering.

As with other model elements, you can control the code generated for an operation by modifying its code generation properties. For example, you can create static functions by modifying the Is property. The code generation properties for operations are listed above, in Table 14.3, for your reference.

Bi-directional Associations

To support bi-directional associations, Rose will generate attributes in the code. Each of the classes in the relationship will contain an attribute to support the association.

The code generation properties we will examine in this section are:

- DataMemberName role property
- GenerateGetOperation role property
- GenerateSetOperation role property
- GenerateLetOperation role property

The code generated for the association in the two classes shown below will resemble something like this:

Class_A:

```
'##ModelId=3734B5B70244
Public NewProperty As Class_B
```

and Class_B:

```
'##ModelId=3734B5B70280
Public NewProperty As Class_A
```

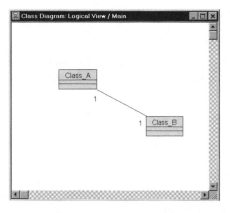

As you can see, Rose will automatically generate attributes on both sides of the bi-directional association relationship. With the NewProperty attribute, Class_A can easily access Class_B. Using the NewProperty attribute, Class_B can easily access Class_A. If you supply no role names, the default (and less useful) New-Property will be used. If you supply a role name, that role name will be used as the attribute name.

Let's examine the code generated for the two classes shown above. The association will be reflected in the class module files for both Class_A and Class_B. The class module file for Class_A is shown below. Here, we checked the Get and Set property options in the Model Assistant. In Rose 98, use the GenerateGetOperation and GenerateSetOperation code generation properties.

Class_A:

```
'##ModelId=3734B5B70244
Private mNewProperty As Class_B

'##ModelId=3734B6F10099
Public Property Set NewProperty(ByVal vNewValue As Class_B)
    On Error GoTo NewPropertyErr

    '## Generated default body ...
    Set mNewProperty = vNewValue

    Exit Property
NewPropertyErr:
    Call RaiseError(MyUnhandledError, "NewProperty Property Set")
End Property

'##ModelId=3734B6F10096
Public Property Get NewProperty() As Class_B
    On Error GoTo NewPropertyErr

    '## Generated default body ...
    Set NewProperty = mNewProperty

    Exit Property
NewPropertyErr:
    Call RaiseError(MyUnhandledError, "NewProperty Property Get")
End Property
```

and Class_B:

```
'##ModelId=3734B5B70280
Private mNewProperty As Class_A

'##ModelId=3734B6FD00F5
Public Property Set NewProperty(ByVal vNewValue As Class_A)
    On Error GoTo NewPropertyErr

    '## Generated default body ...
    Set mNewProperty = vNewValue

    Exit Property
NewPropertyErr:
    Call RaiseError(MyUnhandledError, "NewProperty Property Set")
End Property

'##ModelId=3734B6FD00F2
Public Property Get NewProperty() As Class_A
    On Error GoTo NewPropertyErr

    '## Generated default body ...
    Set NewProperty = mNewProperty

    Exit Property
NewPropertyErr:
    Call RaiseError(MyUnhandledError, "NewProperty Property Get")
End Property
```

When you generate code, Rose will place an attribute called mNewProperty inside Class_A. Because a Get and Set operation is generated for each attribute, and an association creates an attribute, a Get and Set operation can be created for the association's attribute. By default, the attribute is named mNewProperty. To change the name of the attribute, set a role name on the association. Rose will use the role name to generate the attribute name. Each generated attribute will have private visibility by default. To change the visibility, open the association specification window. Select either the Role A General or Role B General tab, and change the Export Control.

The remaining lines contain the code for the Get and Set operations. You can control whether these operations are created by checking the Get and Set operations in the Model Assistant. In Rose 98, change the GenerateGetOperation and GenerateSetOperation code generation properties. In the association specification window, select either Visual Basic A or Visual Basic B to view the code generation properties that apply to each end of the relationship. Change the GenerateGetOperation or GenerateSetOperation properties to control whether the Get and Set operations will be created.

Note that this association had a multiplicity of one to one. See below for a discussion of how other multiplicity settings will affect code generation.

Unidirectional Associations

As with bi-directional associations, Rose will generate attributes to support unidirectional associations. However, with a unidirectional association, an attribute is only generated at one end of the relationship.

The code generation properties we will examine in this section are:

- DataMemberName role property
- GenerateGetOperation role property
- GenerateSetOperation role property
- GenerateLetOperation role property

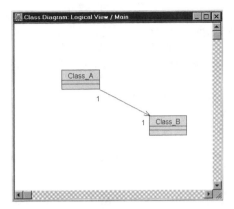

For the Class_A and Class_B classes above, code similar to the following would be created:

Class_A:

```
'##ModelId=3734B85400FA
Private mNewProperty As Class_B

'##ModelId=3734B8B40284
Public Property Set NewProperty(ByVal vNewValue As Class_B)
    On Error GoTo NewPropertyErr

    '## Generated default body ...
    Set mNewProperty = vNewValue

    Exit Property
NewPropertyErr:
    Call RaiseError(MyUnhandledError, "NewProperty Property Set")
End Property

'##ModelId=3734B8B40281
Public Property Get NewProperty() As Class_B
    On Error GoTo NewPropertyErr

    '## Generated default body ...
    Set NewProperty = mNewProperty
```

```
    Exit Property
NewPropertyErr:
    Call RaiseError(MyUnhandledError, "NewProperty Property Get")
End Property
```

And no code would be generated in Class_B for the association, since it is unidirectional.

As you can see, Rose will only generate a private attribute for the relationship at one end of the association. Specifically, it will generate an attribute in the Client class, but not in the Supplier class.

The code generated in the Supplier class includes all of the code lines discussed in the previous section about classes. With a bi-directional association, each class is given a new attribute, and the code discussed in the previous section is included in both classes. With a unidirectional association, the code is included only in the Client class.

Again, note that the multiplicity here is one to one. Let's take a look at how code is affected when the multiplicity settings are changed.

Associations with a Multiplicity of One to Many

In a one-to-one relationship, Rose can simply create the appropriate attributes to support the association. With a one-to-many relationship, however, one class must contain a set of the other class. The code generation property we will examine in this section is the Subscript role property.

To begin, let's look at an example.

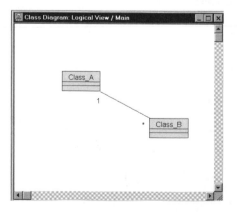

In this case, we've got a one-to-many relationship. As we saw above, Class_B can simply generate an attribute that is a pointer to Class_A. However, a simple pointer attribute in the Class_A class won't be enough. Instead, the attribute generated in Class_A must use a sort of container class or an array as its data type. Rose will generate code similar to the following for this example:

Class_A:

```
'##ModelId=3734BA5C037A
Private mNewProperty As Collection

'##ModelId=3734BA8703BA
Public Property Set NewProperty(ByVal vNewValue As Collection)
    On Error GoTo NewPropertyErr

    '## Generated default body ...
    Set mNewProperty = vNewValue

    Exit Property
NewPropertyErr:
    Call RaiseError(MyUnhandledError, "NewProperty Property Set")
End Property

'##ModelId=3734BA8703B7
Public Property Get NewProperty() As Collection
    On Error GoTo NewPropertyErr

    '## Generated default body ...
    Set NewProperty = mNewProperty

    Exit Property
NewPropertyErr:
    Call RaiseError(MyUnhandledError, "NewProperty Property Get")
End Property
```

and Class_B:

```
'##ModelId=36C6433603B6
Private mNewProperty As Class_A
```

As you can see, Class_B includes a simple reference to Class_A, as we saw above. However, a container class was used in Class_A when generating the Class_B attribute.

Rose provides you with the Collection type as a container class. If you would rather, you can use an array by specifying the Subscript role property. In the class module file for Class_B, we can see that a reference to Class_A was included as an attribute, and Get and Set operations were created for this attribute. Because a container class is not needed for the attribute in Class_B, the code generated for Class_B is exactly the same as we described in the previous sections, "Bi-directional Associations" and "Unidirectional Associations." However, the code for Class_A includes the Get and Set operations, both of which need to be completed after code generation. Since the container class is being used, Rose cannot create useful default code for Get and Set operations. You must complete the code to meet your needs.

Associations with a Multiplicity of Many to Many

The code generated here is similar to that created for a one-to-many relationship. However, here Rose will generate container classes on both ends of the relationship.

The code generation properties we will examine in this section include:

- ContainerClass role property
- Subscript role property

Let's look at the code generated for the following relationship:

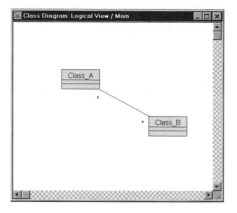

In this situation, container classes are used at both ends of the relationship. The code that is generated will look something like the following:

Class_A:

```
'##ModelId=3734BA5C037A
Private mNewProperty As Collection

'##ModelId=3734BA8703BA
Public Property Set NewProperty(ByVal vNewValue As Collection)
    On Error GoTo NewPropertyErr

    '## Generated default body ...
    Set mNewProperty = vNewValue

    Exit Property
NewPropertyErr:
    Call RaiseError(MyUnhandledError, "NewProperty Property Set")
End Property

'##ModelId=3734BA8703B7
Public Property Get NewProperty() As Collection
    On Error GoTo NewPropertyErr

    '## Generated default body ...
    Set NewProperty = mNewProperty

    Exit Property
NewPropertyErr:
    Call RaiseError(MyUnhandledError, "NewProperty Property Get")
End Property
```

and Class_B:

```
'##ModelId=3734BA5C037B
Private mNewProperty As Collection

'##ModelId=3734BBF303B1
Public Property Set NewProperty(ByVal vNewValue As Collection)
    On Error GoTo NewPropertyErr

    '## Generated default body ...
    Set mNewProperty = vNewValue
```

```
    Exit Property
NewPropertyErr:
    Call RaiseError(MyUnhandledError, "NewProperty Property Set")
End Property

'##ModelId=3734BBF303AE
Public Property Get NewProperty() As Collection
    On Error GoTo NewPropertyErr

    '## Generated default body ...
    Set NewProperty = mNewProperty

    Exit Property
NewPropertyErr:
    Call RaiseError(MyUnhandledError, "NewProperty Property Get")
End Property
```

The specific code for Class_A will look exactly like the example from the previous section, "Associations with a Multiplicity of One to Many." The difference here is that now a container class will also be used to create an attribute in Class_B.

As with one-to-many associations, you can use an array by specifying the Subscript role property. You will also need to change the code for Get and Set operations.

Reflexive Associations

A reflexive association is treated much the same as an association between two classes. For the following situation, code similar to the following is generated:

```
'##ModelId=3734BA5C037A
Private mNewProperty As Class_A

'##ModelId=3734BCA9001E
Public NewProperty2 As Collection

'##ModelId=3734BA8703BA
Public Property Set NewProperty(ByVal vNewValue As Class_A)
    On Error GoTo NewPropertyErr

    '## Generated default body ...
    Set mNewProperty = vNewValue
```

```
    Exit Property
NewPropertyErr:
    Call RaiseError(MyUnhandledError, "NewProperty Property Set")
End Property

'##ModelId=3734BA8703B7
Public Property Get NewProperty() As Class_A
    On Error GoTo NewPropertyErr

    '## Generated default body ...
    Set NewProperty = mNewProperty

    Exit Property
NewPropertyErr:
    Call RaiseError(MyUnhandledError, "NewProperty Property Get")
End Property
```

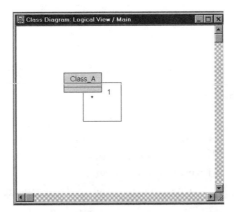

As with a regular association, an attribute is created inside the class to support the relationship. If the multiplicity is one, a simple attribute is created. If the multiplicity is more than one, a container class is used.

As you can see, the code generated here is very similar to the code generated in a typical one-to-many relationship. In this situation, Class_A contains an attribute of type Class_A.

By-value Aggregations (Composition Relationships)

There are two types of aggregation relationships: by-value and by-reference. With a by-value relationship, one class contains another. With a by-reference relationship, one class contains a reference to another.

The code generation property we will be examining here is the ContainerClass role property.

Let's start by examining by-value aggregations, which are also known as composition relationships. In UML, a composition is shown using the following symbol:

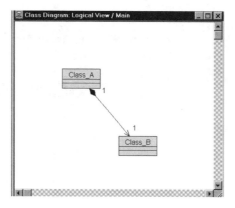

As with association relationships, Rose will generate attributes when code is generated for an aggregation. In our example above, Class_B is an attribute inside Class_A. A simplified version of the generated code would look like this:

Class_A:

```
'##ModelId=3734BEF00234
Private mNewProperty as Class_B

'##ModelId=3734BEF00235
Public Property Set NewProperty(ByVal vNewValue As Class_B)
    On Error GoTo NewPropertyErr

    '## Generated default body ...
    Set mNewProperty = vNewValue
```

```
    Exit Property
NewPropertyErr:
    Call RaiseError(MyUnhandledError, "NewProperty Property Set")
End Property

'##ModelId=3734BEF00232
Public Property Get NewProperty() As Class_B
    On Error GoTo NewPropertyErr

    '## Generated default body ...
    Set NewProperty = mNewProperty

    Exit Property
NewPropertyErr:
    Call RaiseError(MyUnhandledError, "NewProperty Property Get")
End Property
```

and Class_B:

```
'##ModelId=3734B5B70280
Private mNewProperty As Class_A

'##ModelId=3734B6FD00F5
Public Property Set NewProperty(ByVal vNewValue As Class_A)
    On Error GoTo NewPropertyErr

    '## Generated default body ...
    Set mNewProperty = vNewValue

    Exit Property
NewPropertyErr:
    Call RaiseError(MyUnhandledError, "NewProperty Property Set")
End Property

'##ModelId=3734BA8703B7
Public Property Get NewProperty() As Class_A
    On Error GoTo NewPropertyErr

    '## Generated default body ...
    Set NewProperty = mNewProperty

    Exit Property
NewPropertyErr:
    Call RaiseError(MyUnhandledError, "NewProperty Property Get")
End Property
```

It is interesting to note that there is no code difference between an aggregation and an association in Visual Basic.

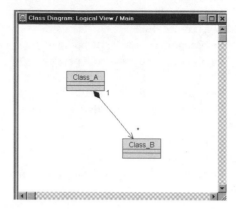

If the multiplicity of the relationship is greater than one, Rose will use a container class when creating the relationship.

By-reference Aggregations

The code generated in Visual Basic for a by-reference aggregation is the same as the code generated for a by-value aggregation. The code generation property we will be examining here is the ContainerClass role property.

For example, let's look at the by-reference version of the relationship we just examined:

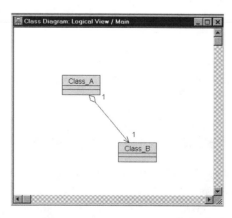

Here again, we have a one-to-one relationship, but this time the aggregation is by-reference. The following is a simplified version of the code that's generated:

Class_A:

```
'##ModelId=3734BEF00234
Private mNewProperty as Class_B

'##ModelId=3734BEF00235
Public Property Set NewProperty(ByVal vNewValue As Class_B)
    On Error GoTo NewPropertyErr

    '## Generated default body ...
    Set mNewProperty = vNewValue

    Exit Property
NewPropertyErr:
    Call RaiseError(MyUnhandledError, "NewProperty Property Set")
End Property

'##ModelId=3734BEF00232
Public Property Get NewProperty() As Class_B
    On Error GoTo NewPropertyErr

    '## Generated default body ...
    Set NewProperty = mNewProperty

    Exit Property
NewPropertyErr:
    Call RaiseError(MyUnhandledError, "NewProperty Property Get")
End Property
```

and Class_B:

```
'##ModelId=3734B5B70280
Private mNewProperty As Class_A

'##ModelId=3734B6FD00F5
Public Property Set NewProperty(ByVal vNewValue As Class_A)
    On Error GoTo NewPropertyErr

    '## Generated default body ...
    Set mNewProperty = vNewValue
```

```
      Exit Property
NewPropertyErr:
    Call RaiseError(MyUnhandledError, "NewProperty Property Set")
End Property

'##ModelId=3734BA8703B7
Public Property Get NewProperty() As Class_A
    On Error GoTo NewPropertyErr

    '## Generated default body ...
    Set NewProperty = mNewProperty

    Exit Property
NewPropertyErr:
    Call RaiseError(MyUnhandledError, "NewProperty Property Get")
End Property
```

It is interesting to note that there is no difference between the code generated for a by-value and by-reference association. As with other relationships, if the multiplicity is more than one, a container class is used.

Dependency Relationships

With a dependency relationship, no attributes are created. If there is a dependency between Class_A and Class_B:

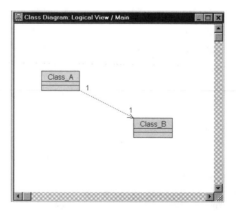

no attributes will be created in either Class_A or Class_B. The code that is generated will look something like the following:

Class_A:

```
Option Explicit

'##ModelId=3734C4EC0067
Private mlClassDebugID As Long

'##ModelId=3734C4EC0066
Public Property Get ClassDebugID() As Variant
    On Error GoTo ClassDebugIDErr

    ClassDebugID = mlClassDebugID

    Exit Property
ClassDebugIDErr:
    Call RaiseError(MyUnhandledError, "ClassDebugID Property")
End Property
```

and Class_B:

```
Option Explicit

'##ModelId=3734C51D005A
Public mlClassDebugID As Long

'##ModelId=3734C51C03D4
Public Property Get ClassDebugID() As Variant
    On Error GoTo ClassDebugIDErr

    ClassDebugID = mlClassDebugID

    Exit Property
ClassDebugIDErr:
    Call RaiseError(MyUnhandledError, "ClassDebugID Property")
End Property
```

Rose will place no references to Class_B inside of Class_A.

Generalization Relationships

A generalization relationship in UML becomes an inheritance relationship in object-oriented languages. However, Visual Basic does not support inheritance. Instead, a generalization can become an implements delegation in Visual Basic. In your Rose model, an inheritance relationship is shown as follows:

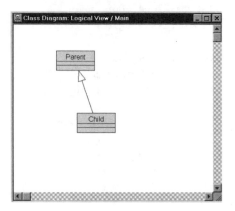

For this type of relationship, Rose will generate something that looks like this:

Parent:

```
Option Explicit

'##ModelId=3734C5A40028
Public mlClassDebugID As Long

'##ModelId=3734C5A303DE
Public Property Get ClassDebugID() As Variant
    On Error GoTo ClassDebugIDErr

    ClassDebugID = mlClassDebugID

    Exit Property
ClassDebugIDErr:
    Call RaiseError(MyUnhandledError, "ClassDebugID Property")
End Property
```

and Child:

```
Option Explicit
```

```
'##ModelId=3734C577003C
Implements Parent

'##ModelId=3734C586014A
Private mParentObject As New Parent

'##ModelId=3734C58601BF
Private mlClassDebugID As Long

'##ModelId=3734C58601BE
Public Property Get ClassDebugID() As Variant
    On Error GoTo ClassDebugIDErr

    ClassDebugID = mlClassDebugID

    Exit Property
ClassDebugIDErr:
    Call RaiseError(MyUnhandledError, "ClassDebugID Property")
End Property
```

Looking at the code that was generated, there is no mention of the child class in the parent class. This helps keep the parent generic; many classes can inherit from it without affecting its code.

In the child class, the code is generated to implement the functionality of the parent in the child. The implements delegation will look like this:

```
Implements Parent
```

In addition, the child class will include an instance of the parent, as shown here:

```
'##ModelId=36C66A3F00A0
Private mParentObject As New Parent
```

Parameterized Classes

Parameterized classes cannot be generated in Visual Basic.

Example of Generated Visual Basic Code

Throughout the book, we have been working with an ATM example application. In this section, we have generated the skeletal Visual Basic code for the ATM example. For reference, the component models are shown in Figure 14.23.

For the ATM system, we set the language of the ATM.exe and ATMServer.exe components to Visual Basic. Next, we set the stereotype of both components to Visual Basic EXE. Then, we set the stereotype of all classes to Class Module. We selected both the ATMServer.exe and ATM.exe components in the Main Component diagram. Then, we selected Tools ➤ Visual Basic ➤ Generate Code. The code that was generated for each component can be found on this book's CD-ROM.

FIGURE 14.23:

ATM component model

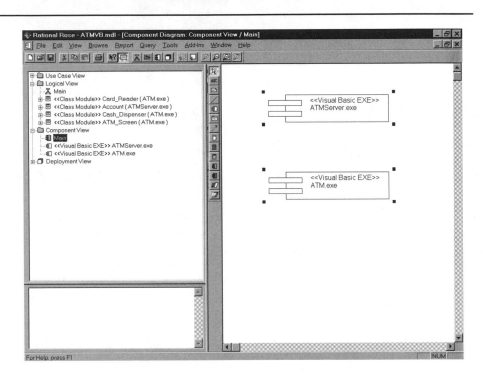

Exercise

In Chapters 3 through 10, we completed a model for an Order Entry system. Now, we are going to generate Visual Basic code for the Order Entry system. We will use the Component diagram shown in Figure 14.24. To generate the code, we need to perform the steps shown below. The code for these exercises is included on the CD.

FIGURE 14.24:

Component diagram for the
Order Entry system

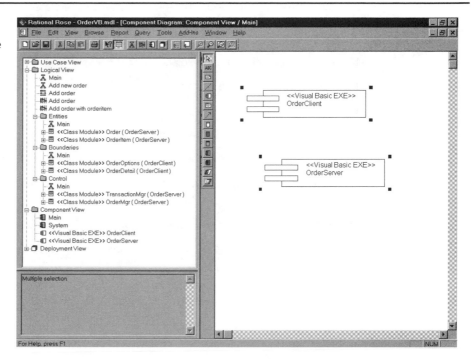

Exercise Steps:

Set the Language to Visual Basic

1. Open the Main Component diagram.

2. Create a new component called **OrderClient**.

3. Create a new component called **OrderServer**.

4. Open the component specification window for OrderClient.

5. Set the language to Visual Basic.

6. Click the Apply button.

7. Set the stereotype of the OrderClient component to Standard EXE.

8. Repeat steps 4 through 7 for the OrderServer component.

Continued on next page

9. In Chapter 9, we created one component for each class. Visual Basic does not require this, so we delete the additional components. Open the System Component diagram.

10. Select all components on the diagram.

11. Press Ctrl+D to delete all components on the diagram.

12. Open the Main Component diagram.

13. Select the Boundaries, Entities, and Control packages.

14. Press Ctrl+D to delete the packages and all components contained in them.

15. In the browser, drag and drop the OrderDetail class onto the OrderClient component.

16. Repeat step 15 for the OrderOptions class.

17. In the browser, drag and drop the Order class onto the OrderServer component.

18. Repeat step 17 for the following classes:

    - OrderItem
    - TransactionMgr
    - OrderMgr

19. Open the class specification for the OrderDetail class.

20. Set the stereotype to Class Module.

21. Repeat steps 19 through 20 for the following classes:

    - OrderOptions
    - OrderItem
    - Order
    - TransactionMgr
    - OrderMgr

Set Role Names

1. Open the Add Order Class diagram.

2. Open the properties for the association between OrderDetail and OrderOptions.

Continued on next page

3. Set the Role A Name to **theOrderDetail.**

4. Set the Role B Name to **theOrderOptions**.

5. Click OK to close the properties window.

6. Repeat steps 2 through 5 for all associations, using the *the* followed by the name of the class for each role name.

Generate Visual Basic

1. Select Tools ➤ Visual Basic ➤ Update Code from the menu.

2. Using the wizard, generate code for all classes in these two components. The generated code is shown on the accompanying CD-ROM.

Summary

In this chapter, we took a look at how various Rose model elements are implemented in Visual Basic. Using the code generation properties for classes, packages, attributes, operations, associations, aggregations, and other model elements, you have a great deal of control over what gets generated.

Again, the steps needed to generate code are as follows:

- Create components.

- Assign classes to components.

- Set the code generation properties.

- Select a class or component to generate on a Class or Component diagram.

- Select Tools ➤ Visual Basic ➤ Update Code to start the Code Generation Wizard.

- Select Tools ➤ Visual Basic ➤ Browse Source Code to view the generated code.

CHAPTER

FIFTEEN

PowerBuilder Code Generation

- Setting PowerBuilder code generation properties

- Generating Visual Basic code form your Rose model

- Mapping Rose elements to PowerBuilder constructs

- Inheriting classes from classes in PB System Classes or PB Enumerated Types

PowerBuilder is available as a language add-in option for Rose. If you have the PowerBuilder add-in, you can generate and reverse engineer PowerBuilder code. In this chapter, we'll discuss how to generate PowerBuilder code from your Rational Rose model. While installing the PowerBuilder add-in, you can select either PowerBuilder version 5, 6, or 6.5. The examples in this chapter use Power-Builder 6.5. However, the steps and procedures for code generation are exactly the same for the other versions of PowerBuilder.

You'll notice after you install the PowerBuilder add-in that you will have two packages of classes available in the Logical view: PB System Classes and PB Enumerated Types.

The steps needed to generate PowerBuilder code from your model are very similar to the steps needed to generate C++, Java, or Visual Basic code. There are, however, a few differences. Specifically, when using PowerBuilder, all of your classes and attributes must have a stereotype. A second restriction is that all classes must be inherited from a recognized PowerBuilder class in PB System Classes or PB Enumerated Types. These two restrictions help Rose determine what type of PowerBuilder object (window, nonvisual object, etc.) to generate for each class.

You will need to follow these steps to generate PowerBuilder code:

1. Create a main component.

2. Create additional components.

3. Assign classes to components.

4. Set the code generation properties.

5. Assign stereotypes to classes.

6. Inherit classes from a class in PB System Classes or PB Enumerated Types.

7. Select a class or component to generate on a Class or Component diagram.

8. Select Tools ➤ PowerBuilder ➤ Code Generation.

The first step is to create components to hold the classes. In PowerBuilder, you can map many classes to each component. Each of the components will become a PowerBuilder library (PBL) file.

There are two types of components to use for PowerBuilder. The first is a Main Program:

This PBL will hold the application object. To set the name of the application object, create a class with the stereotype of application and associate that class with the component. The second type of component you will use is a Subprogram Specification.

These components are the PBL files that do not contain an application object. All of your classes should be mapped either to the Main Program component or one of the Subprogram Specification components. The component mapping will control which PBL file the class will be generated in.

The next step is to set the code generation properties. In this chapter, we'll examine the PowerBuilder code generation properties, and take a look at the code that is generated from Rose.

Before you can generate code, each class must have the appropriate stereotype set. The PowerBuilder add-in uses the stereotype settings to decide which type of object (window, user object, application, and so on) to create in PowerBuilder. Every class, attribute, and operation must have a stereotype set. Table 15.1 lists the PowerBuilder stereotypes.

TABLE 15.1: PowerBuilder Stereotypes

Stereotype	Applies to Model Element	PowerBuilder Type
Application	Class	Application object
Menu	Class	PowerBuilder menu
Structure	Class	PowerBuilder structure
System Class	Class	PowerBuilder system class
User Defined Object	Class	User object
Window	Class	Window

Continued on next page

TABLE 15.1 CONTINUED: PowerBuilder Stereotypes

Stereotype	Applies to Model Element	PowerBuilder Type
Control	Attribute	PowerBuilder control (button, text box, etc.)
Field	Attribute	Structure element
Property	Attribute	PowerBuilder object property
Variable	Attribute	Instance variable
EventExtend	Operation	Event extended from ancestor
EventOverride	Operation	Event that overrides ancestor
EventOverrideInternal	Operation	Event that overrides ancestor, and is not visible in PowerBuilder (create and destroy, for example)
Function	Operation	PowerBuilder function
Subroutine	Operation	PowerBuilder subroutine
UserEvent	Operation	User-defined event

After each class, attribute, and operation has a stereotype, the final step is to be sure all classes have been inherited from a class in PB System Classes or PB Enumerated Types. The inheritance relationships will let the PowerBuilder add-in know what type of PowerBuilder object to create. For example, to create a nonvisual user object, inherit a class from the Nonvisualobject class in PB System Classes.

The question of how to deal with datawindows arises frequently. The best way to take care of datawindows is to use PowerBuilder to create them, and then to reverse engineer them back into Rose. Rose will not generate data window objects.

PowerBuilder Code Generation Properties

As with the other languages, the PowerBuilder code that is generated from a Rose model is controlled by a number of code generation property sets. For PowerBuilder, Rose includes property sets that pertain to attributes, a module body, or a module specification.

You can view and set all of these properties by selecting Tools ≻ Options, then selecting the PowerBuilder tab.

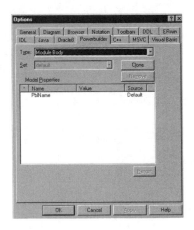

Anything you change using this window will set the default for all attributes, Module Body components, or Module Specification components.

You can also set the code generation properties for a single attribute, Module Specification component, or Module Body component. To do so, open the specification window for the model element and select the PowerBuilder tab. On this tab, you can change the properties that apply to that particular element. In the following sections, we'll examine the PowerBuilder code generation properties.

Attribute Properties

Each attribute in a class will generate as an instance variable in PowerBuilder. Using the attribute properties, you can control whether the instance variable is a constant. There is only one code generation property for PowerBuilder attributes.

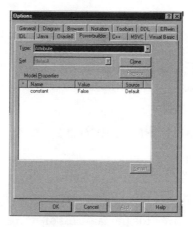

There are two places to set the value of this property. To set it for all attributes, select Tools ➤ Options, then the PowerBuilder tab, and select Attribute from the drop-down list box. To set it for only one attribute, select the PowerBuilder tab on the attribute specification window and edit the property there.

Module Specification Properties

The module specification properties are related to the Module Specification components in your Rose model. In PowerBuilder, you create Module specification components using the Subprogram Specification icon.

Each of these Subprogram Specification components represents a different PBL file in your PowerBuilder application. You can set the properties for all components by selecting Tools ➤ Options, then the PowerBuilder tab, and then Module Specification from the drop-down list box.

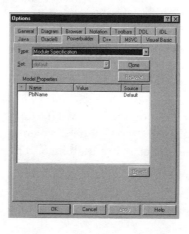

To set them for only one file, select the PowerBuilder tab on the component specification window and edit the properties there. As with attributes, there is only one code generation property for a PowerBuilder Subprogram Specification. The PBLName property sets the filename of the PBL file to be generated. By default, the filename is the same as the component name.

Module Body Properties

In PowerBuilder, a Module Body is a component that will contain the application object. It is created or shown on a Component diagram using the Main Program icon.

Using the code generation properties, you can set the name of the generated PBL file. To set the filename for all Main Program components, select Tools ➤ Options, then the PowerBuilder tab, and select Module Body from the drop-down list box. To set the filename for only one file, select the PowerBuilder tab on the component specification window and edit the properties there.

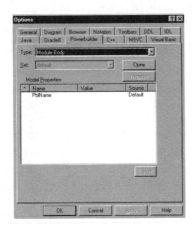

Generated Code

In the next several sections, we'll examine the PowerBuilder code that is generated for different types of model elements. We'll begin by looking at the generation of a single class in isolation, and then examine how the PowerBuilder add-in generates code for the different types of UML relationships.

Each class in your Rose model will generate a single class in PowerBuilder. In general, each of the attributes of the class will become an instance variable in

PowerBuilder, and each of the operations will become a function. There are, however, different types of attributes and operations you can create using different stereotypes in your Rose model. In the following sections, we'll discuss how the different stereotypes will affect the generated code.

Classes

There are several different types of classes you can generate: application objects, menus, structures, system classes, user-defined objects, and windows. The type of class you generate is set by changing the stereotype in the class specification window:

Creating NonVisual Objects

Let's start by examining the most common type of class, the user-defined object. We have a single class, called SampleUserDefinedObject, with a single attribute and a single operation.

The class has a stereotype, as does its attribute and its operation. However, we can't generate code from this class until all of the steps listed above are complete. The class is first mapped to a component, which will control what PBL file the class will be generated in. Figure 15.1 shows a Main Program component, called SamplePB, and the class mapped to this component.

FIGURE 15.1:

Mapping a PowerBuilder class to a component

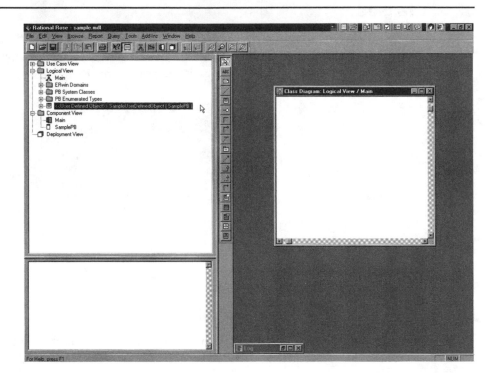

The final step before code generation can begin is to inherit this class from one of the recognized PowerBuilder classes. In this example, to create a nonvisual PowerBuilder object, we inherited the class from the nonvisualobject class in the PB System Classes package, as shown in Figure 15.2.

Many of your Entity classes, Control classes, Utility classes, and Helper classes will be implemented as nonvisual PowerBuilder objects. The Boundary classes in your model will frequently be implemented as PowerBuilder window objects. In this case, because we generated a nonvisual object, a nonvisual PowerBuilder object was created in the code, as shown in Figure 15.3.

FIGURE 15.2:

Inheriting a class from a known PowerBuilder class

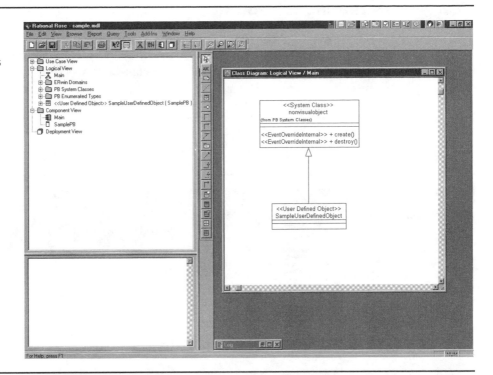

FIGURE 15.3:

Nonvisual PowerBuilder object

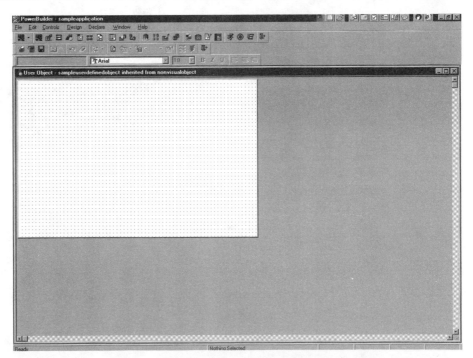

Creating Windows

Another commonly used PowerBuilder stereotype is the Window. In Rose, you can assign the stereotype Window to a class in order to generate a PowerBuilder window from it. The attributes of the class will become instance variables of the window and the operations will become functions or events.

To generate a window, first set the stereotype of the class to Window. Then, inherit the class from the Window class in PB System Classes. Your Class diagram should look similar to the one in Figure 15.4.

FIGURE 15.4:

Generating a PowerBuilder window

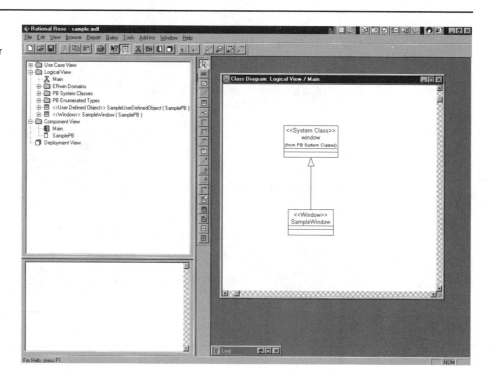

Once the code generation has finished, you will have a Window object in your PowerBuilder file. For the window shown above, Figure 15.5 shows the window that was created in PowerBuilder.

FIGURE 15.5:

Generated PowerBuilder window

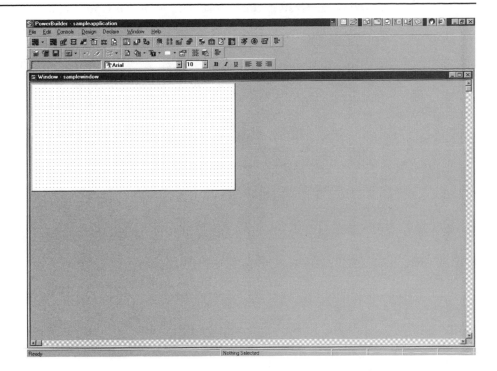

Creating Application Objects

Each PowerBuilder application must have an application object. In Rose, you can create an application object through a stereotyped class. Select the class you wish to generate as an application object and set its stereotype to Application.

When code is generated, the class will be created as a PowerBuilder application object.

Attributes

The attributes in your classes will be generated as instance variables, shared variables, or fields. Fields are generated only for structures. Other types of classes will include instance variables or shared variables.

When generating code, Rose will use the attribute's name, stereotype, data type, and default value. All of this information will be included in the Power-Builder code.

The visibility of the attribute will be reflected in the generated code. Power-Builder will directly support public, private, and protected attributes. Figure 15.6 shows the attributes that are created for the following class:

If an attribute is static in the Rose model, it will be generated as a shared variable.

Operations

Each operation in a class can be implemented as a PowerBuilder function or event. The operation stereotype will determine how the operation is implemented. Table 15.2 lists the possible stereotypes for an operation.

FIGURE 15.6:

Attributes in Power–Builder code

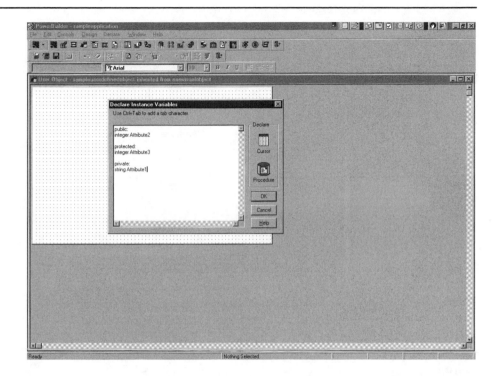

TABLE 15.2: Operation Stereotypes

Stereotype	Applies to Model Element	PowerBuilder Type
EventExtend	Operation	Event extended from ancestor
EventOverride	Operation	Event that overrides ancestor
EventOverrideInternal	Operation	Event that overrides ancestor and is not visible in PowerBuilder (create and destroy, for example)
Function	Operation	PowerBuilder function
Subroutine	Operation	PowerBuilder subroutine
UserEvent	Operation	User-defined event

As an example, let's look at the code generated for a user event. The following class has an operation with a stereotype of EventExtend:

As you can see in Figure 15.7, Rose generates a user event to support the operation.

FIGURE 15.7:

Generated user event

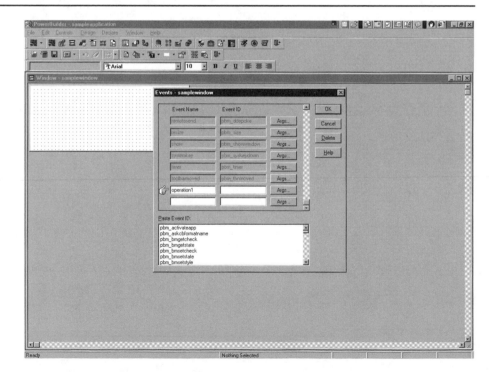

If the stereotype of an operation is set to function or subroutine, there is an additional step to complete before you generate code. In the documentation window for the operation, enter a PowerBuilder return statement, such as **Return 0**. The statement you enter must be valid PowerBuilder syntax, and the data type of the return value should be the same as the operation's return type. When the code is generated, the return statement will be generated inside the function.

Bi-directional Associations

In a bi-directional association, Rose will generate attributes to support the relationship. Each class in the relationship will have a new attribute, referring to the other class.

For example, let's look at the following relationship:

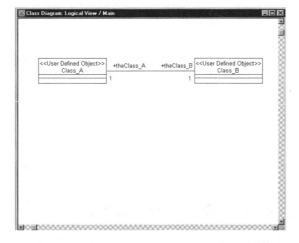

In this case, each of these two classes will get a new attribute when you generate code. If role names were set for the relationship, the role name will be used as the attribute name. In the above example, the following is the attribute generated for Class_A. Figure 15.8 shows the instance variable created for a bi-directional association.

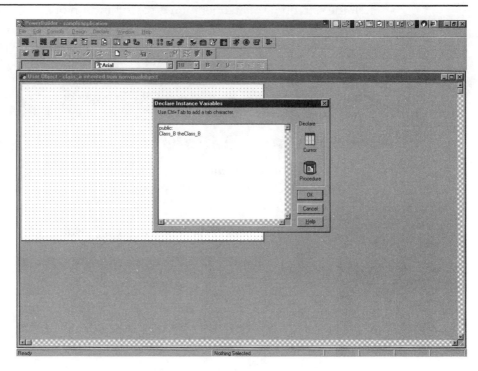

Association names, qualifiers, and constraints are useful as information in your Rose model, but they do not affect the generated code.

Unidirectional Associations

Unidirectional associations are generated exactly as bi-directional associations are, with the exception that an attribute is created on only one side of the relationship. In the following example, an attribute is generated inside Class_A, but not in Class_B.

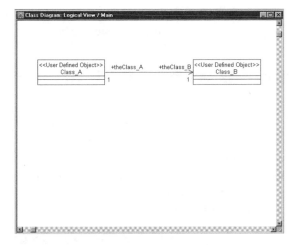

Figure 15.9 shows the attribute generated for Class_A. Notice that it is exactly the same as the attribute generated for Class_A in a bi-directional relationship.

FIGURE 15.9:

Unidirectional association
in PowerBuilder

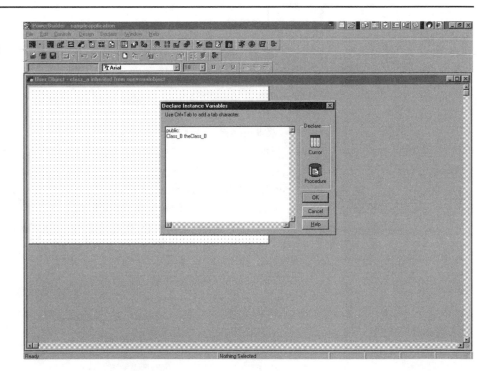

The relationships we've looked at so far have been one-to-one relationships. Now, let's examine how multiplicity affects the relationships.

Associations with a Multiplicity of One to Many

In a one-to-many relationships, Rose will generate the appropriate attributes, as it does in a one-to-one relationship. If the relationship is bi-directional, attributes will be created at both ends. If the relationship is unidirectional, an attribute will only be created at one end. The difference with a one-to-many relationship is that the attribute created to support the many sides of the relationship must be some sort of a container class. For PowerBuilder, Rose uses an array as the container class. Let's look at an example.

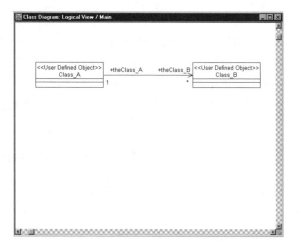

In this example, an attribute is created inside Class_A. Because the multiplicity is one to many, an array is used as the attribute type. Figure 15.10 shows the instance variable generated inside Class_A to support the relationship.

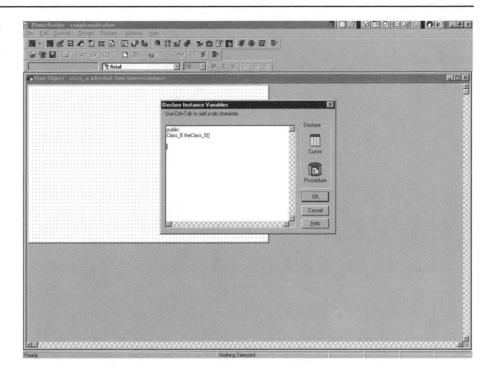

FIGURE 15.10:

One-to-many associations in PowerBuilder

Associations with a Multiplicity of Many to Many

In a many-to-many relationship, the attributes at both ends of the relationship use a container class. In the example above, if the multiplicity had been many to many, both Class_A and Class_B would have an array as an instance variable.

Figure 15.11 shows the instance variable created in Class_A.

Figure 15.12 shows the instance variable created in Class_B.

FIGURE 15.11:

Many-to-many
association—Class A

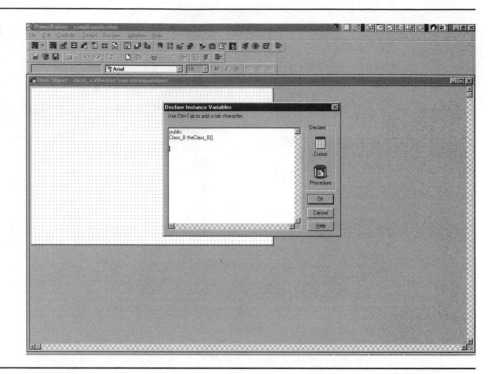

FIGURE 15.12:

Many-to-many
association—Class B

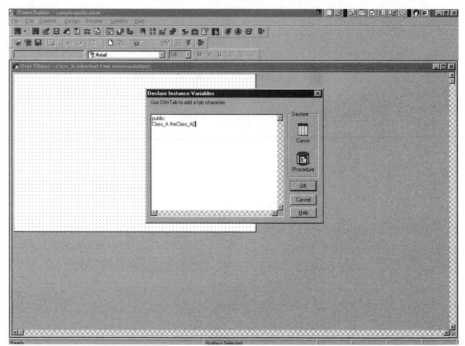

Reflexive Associations

In a reflexive association, an instance variable is created, just as it is in a regular association. If Class_A has a reflexive relationship, it will have an instance variable of type Class_A. Let's look at the code in the following example:

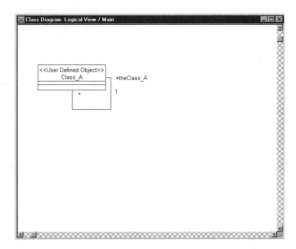

The above example shows the instance variable that is created to support the relationship.

Aggregations

In PowerBuilder, there is no distinction between an association and an aggregation. Bi-directional aggregations are implemented as we discussed above for bi-directional associations. Unidirectional aggregations are also implemented as we described above, in the section dealing with unidirectional associations.

Although it does not carry any meaning in PowerBuilder, an aggregation is a meaningful and useful modeling tool in Rose. Aggregations are frequently used in Rose to model the relationships between a window and the controls on it. Each of the controls can be shown as a separate class, which is connected via an aggregation to the window.

FIGURE 15.13:

Implementation of a reflexive association in Power-Builder

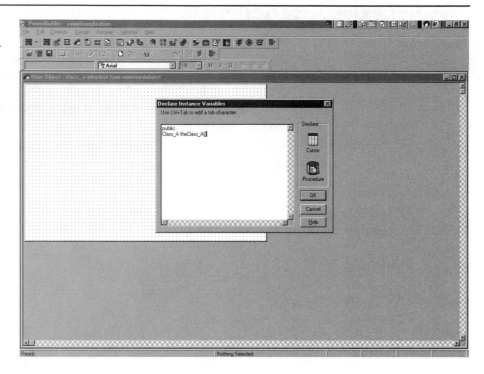

Dependency Relationships

Dependency relationships do not generate attributes. When you generate Power-Builder code for a dependency, neither class will receive an instance variable to support the relationship.

Generalization Relationships

PowerBuilder directly supports the concept of inheritance. Any generalization relationships in your Rose model will be implemented as inheritance relationships in PowerBuilder.

All of your classes should be inherited from something before you generate code. At the root of your inheritance structure should be the recognized Power-Builder classes in PB System Classes or PB Enumerated Types. All classes in your model should be inherited from one of these.

Let's take a look at an example.

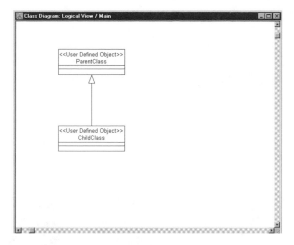

In this example, the ChildClass class is inherited from the ParentClass class. Both of these classes are nonvisual PowerBuilder objects. As you can see in Figure 15.14, Rose will generate the inheritance relationship in the code.

FIGURE 15.14:

Generalization relationship in PowerBuilder code

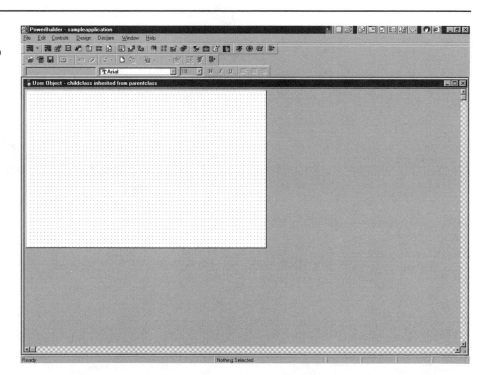

Example of Generated PowerBuilder

Throughout the book, we have been working with an ATM example application. In this section, we have generated the skeletal PowerBuilder code for the ATM example. For reference, the component models are shown in Figures 15.15 and 15.16.

For the ATM system, we set the language of all components to PowerBuilder. Next, we selected both the ATMServer and ATMClient components in the Main Component diagram. Then, we selected Tools ➤ PowerBuilder ➤ Code Generation.

FIGURE 15.15:

ATM client component model

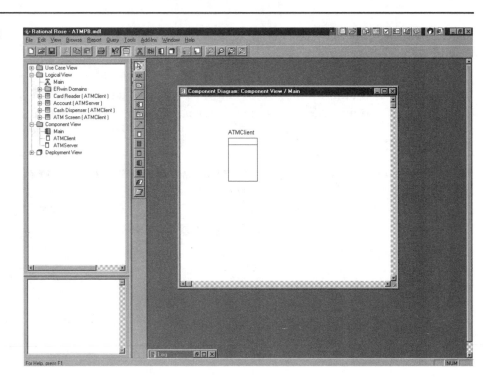

The following classes were generated in PowerBuilder. Figure 15.17 shows the PowerBuilder library painter, after all of the classes were generated.

FIGURE 15.16:

ATM server component
model

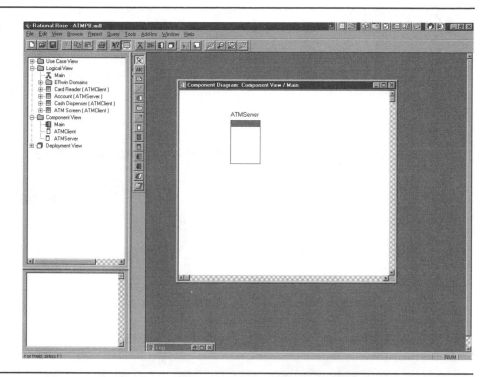

FIGURE 15.17:

Generated code for ATM
example

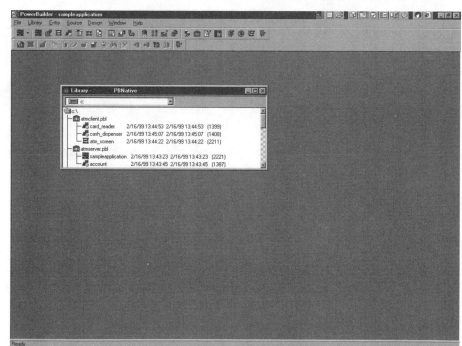

Exercise

In Chapters 3 through 10, we completed a model for an order entry system. Now, we are going to generate PowerBuilder code for the order entry system. We will use the Component diagram shown in Figure 15.18. To generate the code, we need to perform the steps shown below.

FIGURE 15.18:

Component diagram for the order entry system

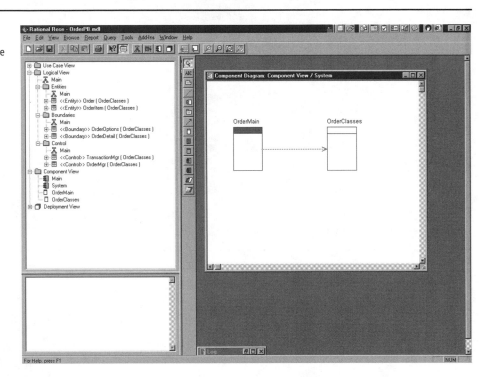

Exercise Steps:

Set the Language to PowerBuilder

1.   Open the System Component diagram.

In Chapter 9, we created one component for each class. PowerBuilder does not require this, so we delete the additional components.

2.   Select all components on the diagram.

3.   Press Ctrl+D to delete all components on the diagram.

4.   Open the Main Component diagram.

5.   Select the Boundaries, Entities, and Control packages.

6.   Press Ctrl+D to delete the packages and all components contained in them.

7.   Create a new Main Program component, called OrderMain.

8.   Open the component specification window for OrderMain.

9.   Set the language to PowerBuilder.

10. In the browser, drag and drop the OrderItem class onto the OrderMain component.

11. Repeat step 10 for the following classes:

- Order

- OrderOptions

- OrderDetail

- TransactionMgr

- OrderMgr

Set Data Types

Open the Add Order Class diagram. In previous chapters, we used the Boolean datatype. Because this is not a recognized PowerBuilder type, we will need to modify it before generating code.

Generate PowerBuilder

1.   Select the OrderMain and OrderClasses components.

2.   Select Tools ➢ PowerBuilder ➢ Code Generation from the menu.

3.   Start PowerBuilder and open the application in `OrderMain.pbl`. The PowerBuilder library painter should look like Figure 15.19.

FIGURE 15.19:

PowerBuilder code for the order entry system

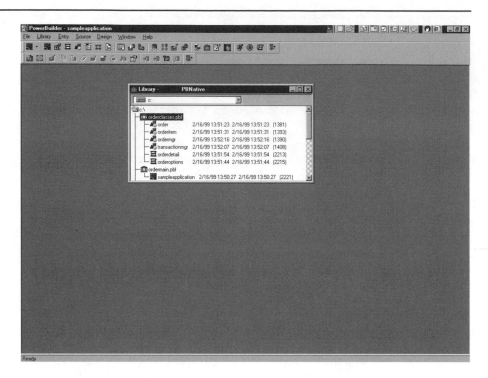

Summary

In this chapter, we examined the PowerBuilder code that is generated from classes, attributes, and operations in a Rose model. To create PowerBuilder code, follow these steps:

1. Create a main component.

2. Create additional components.

3. Assign classes to components.

4. Set the code generation properties.

5. Assign stereotypes to classes.

6. Inherit classes from a class in PB System Classes or PB Enumerated Types.

7. Select a class or component to generate on a Class or Component diagram.

8. Select Tools ➤ PowerBuilder ➤ Code Generation.

When generating code, Rose will use the components, classes, attributes, and operations from your Rose model. Stereotypes are particularly important in PowerBuilder generation; it is the stereotypes that help Rose determine which type of PowerBuilder object to create. Unlike code generation in other languages, PowerBuilder requires you to inherit all of your classes and assign stereotypes to all classes, attributes, and operations before you can generate code.

CHAPTER

SIXTEEN

16

CORBA/IDL Code Generation

- Setting IDL Code Generation Properties

- Generating IDL Code from Your Rose Model

- Mapping Rose Elements to IDL Constructs

In this chapter, we'll discuss how to generate Interface Design Language (CORBA/IDL) code from your Rational Rose model.

To generate CORBA/IDL from your model, you'll need to follow these steps:

1. Set the CORBA (98i) or IDL (98) code generation properties.

2. Select the class(es) or component(s) to generate on a Class or Component diagram.

3. Select Tools ➤ CORBA ➤ Generate CORBA (98i).

4. Select Tools ➤ IDL ➤ Generate IDL (98).

We'll also discuss the various CORBA/IDL code generation properties for classes, attributes, operations, and other model elements, and examine the CORBA/IDL that is generated from these various model elements. There are several different types of CORBA/IDL you can generate from Rose: an interface, a TypeDef, an enumeration, a const, an exception, a struct, or a union. We'll examine how each of these different types is generated.

CORBA/IDL Code Generation Properties

The CORBA/IDL that is generated from your Rose model is controlled by a series of code generation property sets. Rose includes a property set for attributes, classes, dependencies, aggregations, module bodies, module specifications, operations, associations, subsystems, and for the overall project.

In Rose 98i, all of the CORBA/IDL options are noted on the menus as CORBA. In Rose 98, these options are noted as IDL. For simplicity, we will show the menu items here as CORBA. For Rose 98, just substitute IDL in the menu item.

You can view and set all of these properties by selecting Tools ➤ Options, then selecting the CORBA tab.

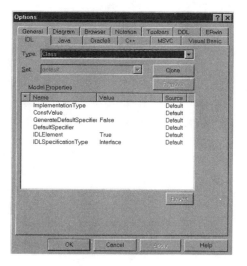

Anything you change using this window will set the default for all classes, attributes, operations, and so on.

You can also set the code generation properties for a single class, attribute, operation, or other model element. To do so, open the specification window for the model element and select the CORBA tab. On this tab, you can change the properties that apply to that particular type of model element. In the following sections, we'll examine the CORBA code generation properties.

Project Properties

Project properties are the CORBA code generation properties that apply more to the whole project than to any specific model element, such as a class or relationship.

The options in this section include things like the default directory to use when generating code and the maximum number of errors that can occur during code generation. Each of the project properties are listed in Table 16.1, along with their purpose and default value.

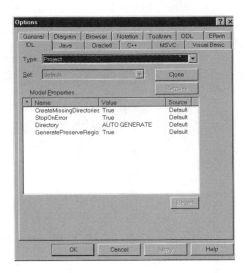

TABLE 16.1: Project CORBA Generation Properties

Property	Purpose	Default
CreateMissing-Directories	Controls whether Rose should create directories to mirror the packages when generating code.	True
Editor (98i)	Controls which editor to use to view and edit CORBA files.	BuiltIn (Uses a built-in CORBA editor)
IncludePath (98i)	Path used to resolve the location of .IDL files during code generation and reverse engineering.	Empty
StopOnError	Controls whether Rose will stop generating code if it encounters an error.	True
Directory (98)	Sets the root directory for code generation, under which all directories and CORBA files will be generated.	By default, Rose will use the directory in the pathmap with the symbol $ROSECPP_ SOURCE.
GeneratePreserve-Regions (98)	Controls whether preserve regions, which protect code during round-trip engineering, should be included in the generated CORBA.	True

Class Properties

Class properties are the CORBA code generation properties that apply to classes. These properties will let you control whether IDL code should be generated for a class, determine the CORBA type, and set other class-specific properties.

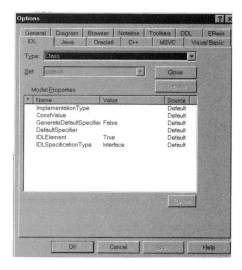

There are two places to set these properties. To set them for all classes, select Tools ➤ Options, then the CORBA tab, and select Class from the drop-down list box. To set them for only one class, select the CORBA tab on the class specification window, and edit the properties there.

Table 16.2 lists many of the CORBA class properties, their purposes, and their default values.

TABLE 16.2: Class CORBA/IDL Generation Properties

Property	Purpose	Default
ArrayDimensions (98i)	Sets the dimensions of the array used in the class definition if the class is a TypeDef.	Empty
ImplementationType	This value has different uses based on the class's stereotype. If CORBAConstant, then the value indicates the data type of the constant. If CORBATypeDef, then the value indicates the data type. If CORBAUnion, then the value is equivalent to the switch type.	Empty

Continued on next page

TABLE 16.2 CONTINUED: Class CORBA/IDL Generation Properties

Property	Purpose	
ConstValue	If a CORBA constant is being generated, controls the value of the constant.	Blank
GenerateDefault-Specifier (98)	If a union is being generated, controls whether a default case is generated.	False
DefaultSpecifier (98)	If a union is being generated, and GenerateDefault Specifier is set to True, sets the label of the default case.	Blank
IDLElement (98)	Controls whether CORBA should be generated from the class.	True
IDLSpecificationType (98)	Controls the CORBA type (Interface, TypeDef, Enumeration, Const, Exception, Struct, Union).	Interface

You can set some of these properties from the class specification window in Rose 98i. Double-click on a CORBA class and the following window will appear:

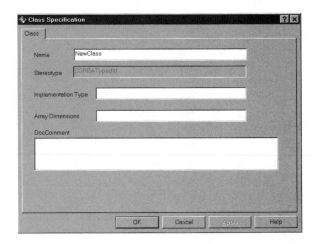

From here, you can change the documentation, implementation type, and array size options.

Attribute Properties

Attribute properties are the CORBA-specific properties that relate to attributes. Using these properties, you can control what is generated for each attribute in the model.

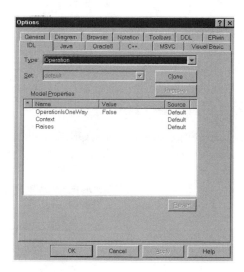

There are two places to set these properties. To set them for all attributes, select Tools ➤ Options, then the CORBA tab, and select Attribute from the drop-down list box. To set them for only one attribute, select the CORBA tab on the attribute specification window, and edit the properties there.

Table 16.3 lists the attribute properties, their purposes, and their default values.

TABLE 16.3: Attribute CORBA Generation Properties

Property	Purpose	Default
ArrayDimensions	Sets the array dimensions used for an exception, struct, or union when the BoundedRoletype association property is set to Array	Blank
CaseSpecifier	Sets the label of the case statement of a union	Blank
IsReadOnly	Controls whether the generated attribute is read only	False

Continued on next page

TABLE 16.3 CONTINUED: Attribute CORBA Generation Properties

Property	Purpose	Default
Order	Sets the order of generated attributes and roles	Blank
IsConst (98)	Controls whether the generated attribute is constant	False
ConstValue (98)	If IsConst is True, sets the value of the attribute	Blank

Operation Properties

Operation properties are the CORBA code generation properties that are specific to operations.

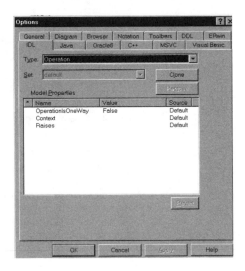

There are two places to set these properties. To set them for all operations, select Tools ➤ Options, then the CORBA tab, and select Operation from the drop-down list box. To set them for only one operation, select the CORBA tab on the operation specification window, and edit the properties there.

Table 16.4 lists the operation code generation properties, their purposes, and their default values.

TABLE 16.4: Operation CORBA Generation Properties

Property	Purpose	Default
OperationIsOneWay	Controls whether the one-way keyword will be generated for the operation	False
Context	Includes a context statement for the operation	Blank
Raises (98)	Includes a raises statement for the operation	Blank

Module Specification Properties

Module specification properties are the properties that are related to the module specification components in your Rose model.

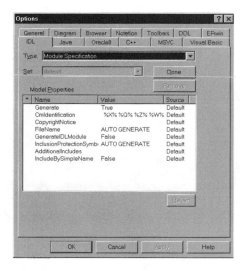

There are two places to set these properties. To set them for all header files, select Tools ➤ Options, then the CORBA tab, and select Module Specification from the drop-down list box. To set them for only one file, select the CORBA tab on the component specification window and edit the properties there.

Table 16.5 lists the code generation properties for module specifications, their purposes, and their default values.

TABLE 16.5: Module Specification CORBA Generation Properties

Property	Purpose	Default
AdditionalIncludes	Used to enter any additional #include statements you want to see in the code	Blank
CmIdentification	Used to enter codes that your configuration management software can use	%X%%Q%%Z%%W%
CopyrightNotice	Used to enter a copyright in the file	Blank
InclusionProtectionSymbol	Sets the symbol that will be used to prevent a file from being included more than once	Auto Generate
Generate (98)	Controls whether the module specification will be generated	True
FileName (98)	Sets the name of the file	Component name (Auto Generate)
GenerateIDLModule (98)	Determines whether an IDL module is generated	False
IncludeBySimpleName (98)	Controls whether the include statements will use the path or just the filename	Path (False)

You can change some of the CORBA generation properties in Rose 98i from the component specification window. Double-click on a CORBA component in a Component diagram. The following window will be displayed:

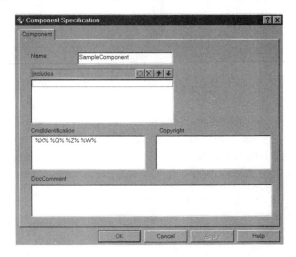

From this window, you can include interfaces or change various code generation options, such as the documentation, change management identification, and copyright.

Module Body Properties

Module body properties are the properties that are related to the module body components in your Rose model.

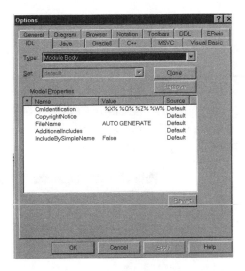

There are two places to set these properties. To set them for all module body files, select Tools ➢ Options, then the CORBA tab, and select Module Body from the drop-down list box. To set them for only one file, select the CORBA tab on the component specification window and edit the properties there.

Table 16.6 lists many of the code generation properties for module bodies, their purposes, and their default values.

TABLE 16.6: Module Body CORBA Generation Properties

Property	Purpose	Default
AdditionalIncludes	Used to enter any additional #include statements you want to see in the code	Blank
CmIdentification	Used to enter codes that your configuration management software can use	%X%%Q%%Z%%W%

Continued on next page

TABLE 16.6 CONTINUED: Module Body CORBA Generation Properties

Property	Purpose	Default
CopyrightNotice	Used to enter a copyright in the file	Blank
InclusionProtection Symbol (98i)	Sets the symbol that will be used to prevent a file from being included more than once	Auto Generate
FileName (98)	Sets the name of the file	Component name
IncludeBySimpleName (98)	Controls whether the include statements will use the path or just the filename	Path (False)

You can change some of the CORBA generation properties in Rose 98i from the component specification window. Double-click on a CORBA component in a Component diagram. The following window will be displayed:

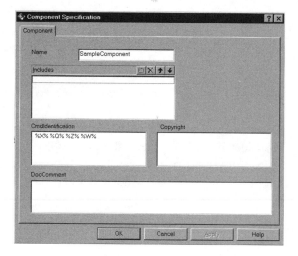

From this window, you can include interfaces or change various code generation options, such as the documentation, change management identification, and copyright.

Association (Role) Properties

Role properties are the CORBA properties that deal with associations. Using these properties, you can control the code generated for the associations.

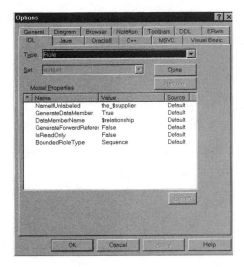

There are two places to set these properties. To set them for all associations, select Tools ➤ Options, then the CORBA tab, and select Role from the drop-down list box. To set them for only one association, select the CORBA tab on the association specification window, and edit the properties there.

Table 16.7 lists the code generation properties for associations, their purposes, and their default values.

TABLE 16.7: Association CORBA Generation Properties

Property	Purpose	Default
ArrayDimensions (98i)	Sets the array dimensions used for an exception, struct, or union when the BoundedRoletype association property is set to Array	Blank
CaseSpecifier (98i)	Sets the label of the case statement of a union.	Blank
GenerateForwardReference	Controls whether a referenced interface is included with a #include statement or a forward reference.	#include (False)
IsReadOnly	Controls whether the generated attribute is read only.	False
Order (98i)	Sets the order of attributes and roles generated.	Blank
BoundedRoleType	If the relationship multiplicity is greater than one, controls whether an array or sequence is used for the generated attribute.	Sequence

Continued on next page

TABLE 16.7 CONTINUED: Association CORBA Generation Properties

Property	Purpose	Default
NameIfUnlabeled (98)	Sets the name of the attribute that will be generated, if no role name is present and DataMemberName is blank or $relationship.	the_$supplier
GenerateDataMember (98)	Controls whether an attribute is created for the relationship.	True
DataMemberName (98)	Sets the name of the generated attribute.	$relationship

Aggregation (Has Relationship) Properties (98)

Has properties are the CORBA properties that deal with aggregations. Using these properties, you can control the code generated for an aggregation. These properties are only available in Rose 98; Rose 98i does not use them.

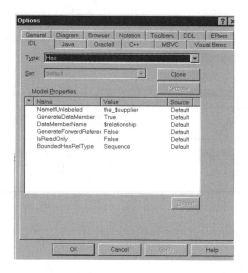

There are two places to set these properties. To set them for all aggregations, select Tools ➢ Options, then the IDL tab, and select Has from the drop-down list box. To set them for only one aggregation, select the IDL tab on the aggregation specification window, and edit the properties there.

Table 16.8 lists the code generation properties for aggregations, their purposes, and their default values.

TABLE 16.8: Aggregation IDL Generation Properties

Property	Purpose	Default
NameIfUnlabeled	Sets the name of the attribute that will be generated, if no role name is present and DataMemberName is blank or $relationship.	the_$supplier
GenerateDataMember	Controls whether an attribute is created for the relationship.	True
DataMemberName	Sets the name of the generated attribute.	$relationship
GenerateForwardReference	Controls whether a referenced interface is included with a #include statement or a forward reference.	#include (False)
IsReadOnly	Controls whether the generated attribute is read only.	False
BoundedHasRelType	If the relationship multiplicity is greater than one, controls whether an array or sequence is used for the generated attribute.	Sequence

Dependency Properties

The dependency properties are the CORBA properties that control how dependency relationships are generated.

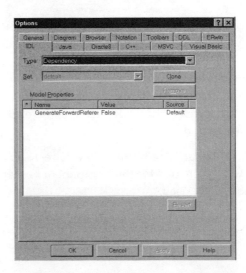

There are two places to set the dependency property. To set the property for all dependencies, select Tools ➢ Options, then the CORBA tab, and select Dependency from the drop-down list box. To set the property for only one dependency, select the CORBA tab on the dependency specification window, and edit the properties there. There is only one dependency property, GenerateForwardReference, which controls whether a referenced interface is included with a #include statement or a forward reference. By default, a #include statement is used.

Subsystem Properties (98)

Subsystem IDL properties are the properties that apply to Component view packages in your Rose model. There is only one subsystem property, Directory. Subsystem properties are only available in Rose 98.

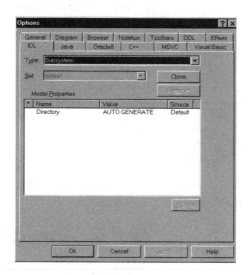

You can set the subsystem property by selecting Tools ➢ Options, the CORBA tab, and Subsystem from the drop-down list box. To set the property for only one subsystem, select the CORBA tab on the package specification window and edit the property there.

The only subsystem property is Directory, which sets the name of the directory that will be created for the Component view package. By default, the package name will be used.

Generated Code

In the following sections, we'll examine the CORBA that is generated from the various types of model elements. Rose will use the information you entered in the specification windows for the various model elements when generating the CORBA/IDL.

Let's begin by looking at the code generated for a typical class.

Classes

A class in your object model will generate a single IDL file. The file that is generated will look something like the following:

```
Interface TheClass
{
};
```

However, a great deal of additional information, such as configuration management statements, copyright notices, and include statements, will also be generated in the code. We'll look at a complete file shortly. All of the attributes, operations, and relationships of the class will be reflected in the generated code. The major elements generated for each class include:

- Class name
- Attributes
- Operations
- Relationships
- Documentation

When generating code, Rose will use the package structure you established in the Component view of your model to generate the appropriate directories. A directory will be created for each package in the model. Within each of the directories Rose creates will be the files for the classes in that package. If you have not created components and packages in the Component view, Rose will use the package structure in the Logical view to create the directory structure.

Much of the information in your Rose model will be used directly when generating code. For example, the attributes, operations, relationships, and class name of each class will directly affect the code generated. Other model properties, such as the documentation entered for the class, will not directly affect the code. These properties are created as comments in the generated code.

Table 16.9 lists the properties available in the class specification window, and notes which of these properties will directly affect the IDL generated.

TABLE 16.9: Effect of Class Specifications on IDL

Property	Affect on Code
Name	Name in model will become class name
Type	No effect
Stereotype	No effect
Export Control	No effect
Documentation	Comment
Cardinality	No effect
Space	No effect
Persistence	No effect
Concurrency	No effect
Abstract	No effect
Formal Arguments	No effect
Operations	Generated in code
Attributes	Generated in code
Relationships	Generated in code

Let's look at the code generated for the following class.

The following IDL file was generated for this class:

```
//Source file: c:/program files/rational/rose 98i/corba/SampleClass.idl

#ifndef __SAMPLECLASS_DEFINED
#define __SAMPLECLASS_DEFINED

/* CmIdentification
  %X% %Q% %Z% %W% */

#include "IncludedClass.idl".[this is default.]

interface SampleClass {
};

#endif
```

Let's examine each piece of this file, one at a time.

Module Section

The module section contains some basic information about the class being generated. It includes the following line:

```
//Source file: c:/program files/rational/rose 98i/corba/SampleClass.idl
```

This section includes comments that describe what class is being generated, and where the IDL file is located.

Configuration Management Section

The configuration management section is provided to support integration with your configuration management software. It includes the following lines:

```
/* CmIdentification
  %X% %Q% %Z% %W% */
```

This section of the file includes information about your configuration management settings. The properties on the second line (%X% %Q% %Z% %W%) are the default configuration management settings. To change the configuration management settings, select Tools ➤ Options from the menu. In the CORBA tab, select Module Specification from the drop-down list box to display the module specification code generation properties. You can use the CmIdentification property to change the default values on this second line. Using this property, set the change management settings to a string that your configuration management software will recognize.

Some sample values you can place in this setting include:

- $date, which inserts the date the code was generated

- $time, which inserts the time the code was generated

- $module, which inserts the component name

- $file, which inserts the component's file

Preprocessor Directives Section

The preprocessor directives include the following lines:

```
#ifndef __SAMPLECLASS_DEFINED
#define __SAMPLECLASS_DEFINED
```

These lines are inserted into the code to prevent the file from being included more than once.

Includes Section

The includes section is the area of the generated code with any entries you added in the AdditionalIncludes code generation property for the component, and any entries you added in the Includes section of the specification window for the component.

The includes section for the SampleClass is as follows:

```
#include "IncludedClass.idl"
```

In this example, only one other class, called IncludedClass, was included.

Class Definition Section

This section contains information about the class itself, including the class name, its attributes, its operations, and its relationships. For the class above, the definition section includes the following:

```
interface SampleClass {
};
```

If you entered any documentation for the class using the documentation window or the documentation area of the class specification window, this documentation will be included as a comment in the code.

Code Generated for Different Types of CORBA/IDL

By default, Rose will generate an interface for each class. However, you have other generation options, including TypeDef, enumeration, and const. You can set the generation option by modifying the CORBASpecificationType class property.

Let's examine the code generated for the following class, with each of the different CORBA/IDL specification type options.

TypeDef Generation

If the class stereotype is set to CORBATypeDef, an interface will not be generated for the class. Instead, a TypeDef will be created. In the Implementation Type property on the class specification window, enter the definition which this Type-Def will be aliasing. The code generated for the SampleClass class looks like this:

```
//Source file: c:/program files/rational/rose 98i/corba/SampleClass.idl

#ifndef __SAMPLECLASS_DEFINED
#define __SAMPLECLASS_DEFINED

/* CmIdentification
   %X% %Q% %Z% %W% */

#include "IncludedClass.idl"

typedef int SampleClass;
#endif
```

→

Enumeration Generation

The second CORBA type you can generate is an enumeration. If you select this option, Rose will use the key word enum in the generated file. Here is the code generated for the class above, but this time the stereotype was set to CORBAEnum.

```
//Source file: c:/program files/rational/rose 98i/corba/SampleClass.idl

#ifndef __SAMPLECLASS_DEFINED
#define __SAMPLECLASS_DEFINED

/* CmIdentification
   %X% %Q% %Z% %W% */

#include "IncludedClass.idl"

enum SampleClass {
  Attribute1,
  Attribute2
};

#endif
```

→

Constant Generation

The third CORBA type you can generate is a constant. In this case, Rose will include the key word const in the generated IDL. To generate a constant, set the class stereotype to CORBAConstant. In the class specification window in Rose 98i, set the Implementation Type field to the data type you wish to use, and the Constant Value field to the value of the constant. In Rose 98, set the Implementation-Type class property to the data type you wish to use and the ConstValue property to the value of the constant.

The following is the file generated for SampleClass.

```
//Source file: c:/program files/rational/rose 98i/corba/SampleClass.idl

#ifndef __SAMPLECLASS_DEFINED
#define __SAMPLECLASS_DEFINED

/* CmIdentification
  %X% %Q% %Z% %W% */

#include "IncludedClass.idl"

const int SampleClass = 4;

#endif
```

Exception Generation

The fourth CORBA type you can generate is an exception. If the class stereotype is set to CORBAException, Rose will include the key word exception in the code. Here is the file generated for SampleClass:

```
//Source file: c:/program files/rational/rose 98i/corba/SampleClass.idl


#ifndef __SAMPLECLASS_DEFINED
#define __SAMPLECLASS_DEFINED


/* CmIdentification
  %X% %Q% %Z% %W% */

#include "IncludedClass.idl"

exception SampleClass {
   string Attribute1;
   string Attribute2;
};

#endif
```

Structure Generation

Another CORBA type you can generate is a structure. Rose will include the struct key word in the generated file if the stereotype of the class is set to CORBAStruct. The attributes of the class will appear as data members in the generated file. The code generated for SampleClass is:

```
//Source file: c:/program files/rational/rose 98i/corba/SampleClass.idl

#ifndef __SAMPLECLASS_DEFINED
#define __SAMPLECLASS_DEFINED

/* CmIdentification
  %X% %Q% %Z% %W% */

#include "IncludedClass.idl"
```

```
→        struct SampleClass {
→        string Attribute1;
→        string Attribute2;
→        };
```

```
#endif
```

Union Generation

Finally, you can generate a union in CORBA by setting the class stereotype to CORBAUnion. The code generated would look like this:

```
//Source file: c:/program files/rational/rose 98i/corba/SampleClass.idl

#ifndef __SAMPLECLASS_DEFINED
#define __SAMPLECLASS_DEFINED

/* CmIdentification
  %X% %Q% %Z% %W% */

#include "IncludedClass.idl"

union SampleClass switch(int) {
   case 1: string Attribute1;
   case 2: string Attribute2;
};

#endif
```

Before you can generate code, each of the attributes must have a case specifier. Open the specification window for each of the attributes, and enter a value in the Case Specifier property. The values you enter will control the case statements generated in the code. In the above example, the case specifier for Attribute1 was 1, and the specifier for Attribute2 was 2.

Attributes

As you may have noticed in the examples above, attributes are generated in the code along with the class. This isn't true for all CORBA types, however. In this section, we'll examine the code generated for attributes for each of the types: interface, TypeDef, enumeration, constant, exception, structure, and union. For each of these types, we'll take a look at what is generated for the following class:

Attributes Generated for an Interface

In an interface, all of the attributes of the class will appear in the generated code. For each attribute, Rose will include:

- Data type
- Documentation

This is the interface that is generated for the SampleClass class:

```
//Source file: c:/program files/rational/rose 98i/corba/SampleClass.idl

#ifndef __SAMPLECLASS_DEFINED
#define __SAMPLECLASS_DEFINED

/* CmIdentification
   %X% %Q% %Z% %W% */

#include "IncludedClass.idl"

interface SampleClass {
    attribute string Attribute1;
    attribute string Attribute2;
};

#endif
```

Attributes Generated for a TypeDef

If the class stereotype is set to CORBATTypeDef, attributes do not appear in the generated code.

Attributes Generated for an Enumeration

With an enumeration, Rose will place the attributes in the generated code. However, Rose will ignore the data types, default values, and other specifications of the attribute. Here is the enumeration that was generated for the SampleClass class:

```
//Source file: c:/program files/rational/rose 98i/corba/SampleClass.idl

#ifndef __SAMPLECLASS_DEFINED
#define __SAMPLECLASS_DEFINED

/* CmIdentification
   %X% %Q% %Z% %W% */

#include "IncludedClass.idl"

enum SampleClass {
Attribute1,
Attribute2
};

#endif
```

Attributes Generated for a Constant

If the class stereotype is set to CORBAConstant, attributes do not appear in the generated code.

Attributes Generated for an Exception

If the class stereotype is set to CORBAException, all of the attributes of the class will be included in the code. For each attribute, the code will include:

➜   Data type

➜   Documentation

For example, here is the code generated when CORBASpecificationType is set to exception for SampleClass:

```
//Source file: c:/program files/rational/rose 98i/corba/SampleClass.idl

#ifndef __SAMPLECLASS_DEFINED
#define __SAMPLECLASS_DEFINED

/* CmIdentification
  %X% %Q% %Z% %W% */

#include "IncludedClass.idl"

exception SampleClass {
    string Attribute1;
    string Attribute2;
};

#endif
```

Attributes Generated for a Structure

If the class stereotype is set to CORBAStruct, all of the attributes of the class will be included in the code. For each attribute, the code will include: Data type

➜   Documentation

For example, here is the code generated when CORBASpecificationType is set to struct for SampleClass:

```
//Source file: c:/program files/rational/rose 98i/corba/SampleClass.idl

#ifndef __SAMPLECLASS_DEFINED
#define __SAMPLECLASS_DEFINED

/* CmIdentification
  %X% %Q% %Z% %W% */

#include "IncludedClass.idl"

struct SampleClass {
string Attribute1;
string Attribute2;
};

#endif
```

Attributes Generated for a Union

If the class stereotype is set to CORBAUnion, the attributes of the class will appear as case statements in the union. For example, here is the code generated for SampleClass:

```
//Source file: c:/program files/rational/rose 98i/corba/SampleClass.idl

#ifndef __SAMPLECLASS_DEFINED
#define __SAMPLECLASS_DEFINED

/* CmIdentification
   %X% %Q% %Z% %W% */

#include "IncludedClass.idl"

union SampleClass switch(int) {
    case 1: string Attribute1;
    case 2: string Attribute2;
};

#endif
```

The values used in the case statements are set by the values you entered in the Case Specifier field in each attribute's specification window.

Operations

The operations you defined in your Rose model will appear in the generated IDL. Like attributes, though, operations are only included for certain CORBA types. In this section, we'll take a look at the code generated for operations of the following class:

We'll examine how the code is generated as the value in the CORBASpecificationType property changes.

Operations Generated for an Interface

With an interface, all of the operations for the class will appear in the generated code, along with their parameters, parameter data types, and return type. For the SampleClass class, the following interface was generated:

```
//Source file: c:/program files/rational/rose 98i/corba/SampleClass.idl

#ifndef __SAMPLECLASS_DEFINED
#define __SAMPLECLASS_DEFINED

/* CmIdentification
   %X% %Q% %Z% %W% */

#include "IncludedClass.idl"

interface SampleClass {
    /*
    @roseuid 3738DE2901AE */
    string Operation1 ();

};

#endif
```

Operations Generated for Other CORBA/IDL Types

Operations are only shown in the generated IDL for interfaces. If the class stereotype is a TypeDef, enumeration, const, exception, struct, or union, operations will not be generated in the code.

Bi-Directional Associations

To support bi-directional associations, Rose will generate attributes in the code. Each of the classes in the relationship will contain an attribute to support the association. The names of the generated attributes will be controlled by the role names on the association relationship. You must enter role names before you can generate code.

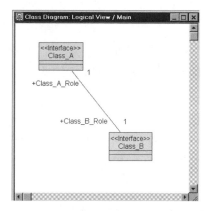

The code generated for the two classes shown above will resemble something like this:

```
Interface Class_A
{
attribute Class_B Class_B_Role;
};
```

and

```
Interface Class_B
{
attribute Class_A Class_A_Role;
};
```

As you can see, Rose will automatically generate attributes on both sides of the bi-directional association relationship. With the Class_B_Role attribute, Class_A can easily access Class_B. Using the Class_A_Role attribute, Class_B can easily access Class_A.

The full code generated for Class_A is:

```
//Source file: c:/program files/rational/rose 98i/corba/Class_A.idl

#ifndef __CLASS_A_DEFINED
#define __CLASS_A_DEFINED

/* CmIdentification
  %X% %Q% %Z% %W% */
```

➡️
```
#include "Class_B.idl"

interface Class_A {
```
➡️
```
    attribute Class_B Class_B_Role;
};

#endif
```

As you can see, Class_A now includes an attribute of type Class_B. Class_B will also include an attribute of type Class_A. These two attributes support the relationship between Class_A and Class_B.

Bi-Directional Associations Generated for a TypeDef

If the stereotype for Class_A is set to CORBATTypeDef, a Class_B attribute will not be included in the code for Class_A. However, a #include statement will be added to the code in Class_A, as follows:

```
#include "Class_B.idl"
```

Bi-Directional Associations Generated for an Enumeration

If the stereotype of Class_A is set to CORBAEnum, an include statement for Class_B.IDL will be included in the code. However, no attribute will be generated in Class_A. The code for Class_A looks like this:

```
//Source file: c:/program files/rational/rose 98i/corba/Class_A.idl

#ifndef __CLASS_A_DEFINED
#define __CLASS_A_DEFINED

/* CmIdentification
   %X% %Q% %Z% %W% */
```
➡️
```
#include "Class_B.idl"

enum Class_A {
};

#endif
```

Bi-Directional Associations Generated for a Constant

If Class_A is a constant, it will have an include statement for Class_B, but will not have an attribute that supports the relationship. Here is the code generated for Class_A:

```
//Source file: c:/program files/rational/rose 98i/corba/Class_A.idl

#ifndef __CLASS_A_DEFINED
#define __CLASS_A_DEFINED

/* CmIdentification
  %X% %Q% %Z% %W% */

#include "Class_B.idl"

const int Class_A = 4;

#endif
```

Bi-Directional Associations Generated for an Exception

If Class_A is an exception, an attribute of type Class_B will be generated inside it. Here is the code generated for Class_A:

```
//Source file: c:/program files/rational/rose 98i/corba/Class_A.idl

#ifndef __CLASS_A_DEFINED
#define __CLASS_A_DEFINED

/* CmIdentification
  %X% %Q% %Z% %W% */

#include "Class_B.idl"

exception Class_A {
Class_B Class_B_Role;
};

#endif
```

Bi-Directional Associations Generated for a Structure

If the stereotype of Class_A is CORBAStruct, an attribute will be created inside Class_A when you generate the IDL.

The code for Class_A is as follows:

```
//Source file: c:/program files/rational/rose 98i/corba/Class_A.idl

#ifndef __CLASS_A_DEFINED
#define __CLASS_A_DEFINED

/* CmIdentification
   %X% %Q% %Z% %W% */

#include "Class_B.idl"

struct Class_A {
    Class_B Class_B_Role;
};

#endif
```

Bi-Directional Associations Generated for a Union

If the CORBASpecificationType property for Class_A is set to union, the generated code will have an include statement for Class_B, but will not have a generated attribute for Class_B inside Class_A. Here is the code generated for Class_A:

```
//Source file: c:/program files/rational/rose 98i/corba/Class_A.idl

#ifndef __CLASS_A_DEFINED
#define __CLASS_A_DEFINED

/* CmIdentification
   %X% %Q% %Z% %W% */

#include "Class_B.idl"

union Class_A switch(int) {
    case 2: string Attribute2;
    case 1: string Attribute1;
```

→
```
       case 3: Class_B Class_B_Role;
  };

  #endif
```

Note that the attribute generated from the association needs a case specifier, as do the other attributes of Class_A. The case specifier can be set using the Case-Specifier role code generation property for the relationship.

Unidirectional Associations

As with bi-directional associations, Rose will generate attributes to support unidirectional associations. However, with a unidirectional association, an attribute is only generated at one end of the relationship.

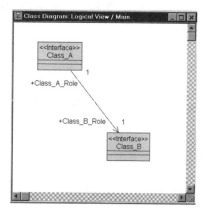

For the Class_A and Class_B classes above, code similar to the following would be created:

```
Interface Class_A
{
   attribute Class_B Class_B_Role;
};
```

and

```
Interface Class_B
{
};
```

As you can see, Rose will only generate a private attribute for the relationship at one end of the association. Specifically, it will generate an attribute in the Client class, but not in the Supplier class.

For each of the other CORBA types (TypeDef, enumeration, const, exception, struct, or union), Rose will generate code as shown in the bi-directional associations section above. The only difference with a unidirectional association is that the attribute will only be created on one side of the relationship.

Again, note that the multiplicity here is one to one. Let's take a look at how code is affected when the multiplicity settings are changed.

Associations with a Multiplicity of One to Many

In a one-to-one relationship, Rose can simply create the appropriate attributes to support the association. With a one-to-many relationship, however, one class must contain a set of the other class.

To begin, let's look at an example.

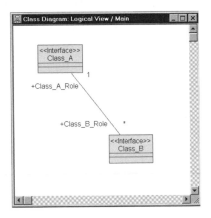

In this case, we've got a one-to-many relationship. As we saw above, Class_B can simply generate an attribute that is a pointer to Class_A. However, a simple pointer attribute in the Class_A class won't be enough. Instead, the attribute generated in Class_A must use some sort of container class as its data type. In IDL, there are two container classes you can use: a sequence or an array. By default, Rose will use a sequence.

Rose will generate code similar to the following for this example:

```
Interface Class_A
{
typedef sequence <Class_B> Class_B_Role_def;
attribute Class_B_Role_def Class_B_Role;
};
```

and

```
Interface Class_B
{
    attribute Class_A Class_A_Role;

};
```

As you can see, Class_B includes a simple pointer to Class_A, as we saw above. However, a container class was used in Class_A when generating the Class_B attribute.

The full code generated for Class_A is:

```
//Source file: c:/program files/rational/rose 98i/corba/Class_A.idl

#ifndef __CLASS_A_DEFINED
#define __CLASS_A_DEFINED

/* CmIdentification
  %X% %Q% %Z% %W% */

#include "Class_B.idl"

interface Class_A {
typedef sequence <Class_B> Class_B_Role_def;

attribute Class_B_Role_def Class_B_Role;
};

#endif
```

Again, Rose will use a sequence as the default container class. To use an array instead, open the relationship specification. On the CORBA A or CORBA B tab, change the BoundedRoleType property to Array. To use an array for all relationships with a multiplicity greater than one, select Tools ➤ Options from the menu. On the CORBA tab, select Role from the drop-down list box. Change the value in the BoundedRoleType property to Array.

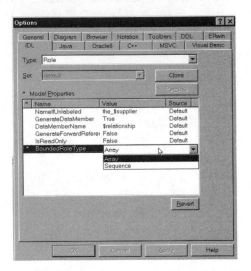

One-to-Many Associations Generated for a TypeDef

If the stereotype of Class_A is CORBATypeDef, a #include statement will be added to the code, but an attribute will not be generated in Class_A to support the relationship with Class_B. The code generated for Class_A is as follows:

```
//Source file: c:/program files/rational/rose 98i/corba/Class_A.idl

#ifndef __CLASS_A_DEFINED
#define __CLASS_A_DEFINED

/* CmIdentification
   %X% %Q% %Z% %W% */

#include "Class_B.idl"

typedef int Class_A;

#endif
```

One-to-Many Associations Generated for an Enumeration

As with a TypeDef, Rose will not generate attributes to support the relationship if Class_A is an enumeration. There will, however, be a #include statement in the code generated for Class_A. The code for Class_A is as follows:

```
//Source file: c:/program files/rational/rose 98i/corba/Class_A.idl

#ifndef __CLASS_A_DEFINED
#define __CLASS_A_DEFINED

/* CmIdentification
  %X% %Q% %Z% %W% */

#include "Class_B.idl"

enum Class_A {
};

#endif
```

One-to-Many Associations Generated for a Constant

If Class_A is a constant, it will have a #include statement for Class_B, but will not have an attribute for the relationship. The code for Class_A is shown below:

```
//Source file: c:/program files/rational/rose 98i/corba/Class_A.idl

#ifndef __CLASS_A_DEFINED
#define __CLASS_A_DEFINED

/* CmIdentification
  %X% %Q% %Z% %W% */

#include "Class_B.idl"

const int Class_A = 4;

#endif
```

One-to-Many Associations Generated for an Exception

If Class_A is an exception, an attribute will be created inside it to support the relationship to Class_B. In a one-to-many relationship, Rose will use a container class when generating this attribute. By default, as with one-to-many relationships between interfaces, Rose will use a sequence as a container. You can change the container class to use an array by changing the BoundedRoleType role property to Array.

The following code is generated for Class_A when its stereotype is set to CORBAException and Class_A has a one-to-many relationship with Class_B.

```
//Source file: c:/program files/rational/rose 98i/corba/Class_A.idl

#ifndef __CLASS_A_DEFINED
#define __CLASS_A_DEFINED

/* CmIdentification
   %X% %Q% %Z% %W% */

#include "Class_B.idl"

exception Class_A {
sequence <Class_B> Class_B_Role;
};

#endif
```

One-to-Many Associations Generated for a Structure

When the stereotype of Class_A is set to CORBAStruct, and Class_A has a one-to-many relationship with Class_B, an attribute will be created in Class_A to support that relationship. As with the other one-to-many relationships, Rose will use a container class when creating the attribute. By default, a structure is used. To use an array instead, change the BoundedRoleType role property.

The following is the code generated for Class_A:

```
//Source file: c:/program files/rational/rose 98i/corba/Class_A.idl

#ifndef __CLASS_A_DEFINED
#define __CLASS_A_DEFINED
```

```
     /* CmIdentification
       %X% %Q% %Z% %W% */

➜    #include "Class_B.idl"

     struct Class_A {
➜    sequence <Class_B> Class_B_Role;
     };

     #endif
```

One-to-Many Associations Generated for a Union

If Class_A is a union, both a #include statement and an attribute will be generated in Class_A to support the relationship with Class_B. The code for Class_A is as follows:

```
//Source file: c:/program files/rational/rose 98i/corba/Class_A.idl

#ifndef __CLASS_A_DEFINED
#define __CLASS_A_DEFINED

/* CmIdentification
  %X% %Q% %Z% %W% */

#include "Class_B.idl"

union Class_A switch(int) {
case 1: string Attribute1;
   case 2: string Attribute2;
   case 3: sequence <Class_B> Class_B_Role;
};

#endif
```

The ➜ arrows point to the `#include "Class_B.idl"` line and the `union Class_A switch(int) {` / `case 1: string Attribute1;` lines.

Associations with a Multiplicity of Many-to-Many

The code generated here is similar to that created for a one-to-many relationship. However, here Rose will generate container classes on both ends of the relationship.

Let's look at the code generated for the following relationship:

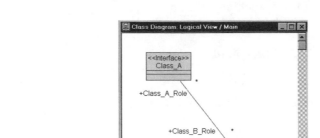

In this situation, container classes are used at both ends of the relationship. The code that is generated will look something like the following:

```
Interface Class_A
{
    typedef sequence <Class_B> Class_B_Role_def;
attribute Class_B_Role_def Class_B_Role;

};
```

and

```
Interface Class_B
{
typedef sequence <Class_A> Class_A_Role_def;
    attribute Class_A_Role_def Class_A_Role;

};
```

The complete code generated for Class_A will look exactly as it did in the previous section. The difference is that now the code for Class_B will also include an attribute with a container type. The code generated for Class_B is:

```
//Source file: c:/program files/rational/rose 98i/corba/Class_B.idl

#ifndef __CLASS_B_DEFINED
#define __CLASS_B_DEFINED
```

```
/* CmIdentification
   %X% %Q% %Z% %W% */
```

→
```
#include "Class_A.idl"
interface Class_B {
```
→
```
    typedef sequence <Class_A> Class_A_Role_def;
```
→
```
    attribute Class_A_Role_def Class_A_Role;
};
```

```
#endif
```

Many-to-Many Associations Generated for Other CORBA Types

The code generated for a many-to-many relationship with other CORBA types will look exactly like the code we examined in the previous section. The only difference is that Class_B will now contain an attribute of type Class_A.

Associations with Bounded Multiplicity

An association with bounded multiplicity is one that has a range of numbers at one end of the relationship. For example, the following relationship has bounded multiplicity:

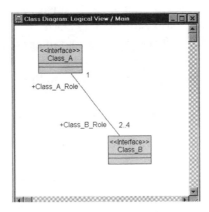

In this example, each instance of Class_A is related to two through four instances of Class_B.

The two types of bounded relationships we will examine are bounded associations and fixed associations. Bounded associations have a multiplicity range, like 2..4. Fixed associations have a single number in the multiplicity. For example, a multiplicty of 4 is fixed. As with one-to-many and many-to-many relationships, Rose uses container classes when generating the attributes. By default, Rose will use a sequence, but you can change the container to an array as well.

For the example above, Rose will generate something like this:

```
Interface Class_A
{
    typedef sequence <Class_B, 4> Class_B_Role_def;
attribute Class_B_Role_def Class_B_Role;

};
```

and

```
Interface Class_B
{
attribute Class_A Class_A_Role;

};
```

By default, a sequence is used as a container class in bounded relationships. However, you can use an array instead by selecting the CORBA A or CORBA B tab of the relationship specification, then changing the BoundedRoleType property to Array. To change the container class for all bounded relationships, select Tools ➤ Options from the menu. On the CORBA tab, select Role from the drop-down list box. Change the value in the BoundedRoleType property to Array.

Bounded Associations Generated for an Exception

If Class_A is an exception, the code generated will include an attribute to support the relationship to Class_B. In this case, a simplified version of the generated code will look something like this:

```
Exception Class_A
{
sequence <Class_B, 4> Class_B_Role;
};
```

As with other relationships where the multiplicity is greater than one, Rose will use a sequence as the default container class. To use an array, change the BoundedRoleType property to Array.

Bounded Associations Generated for a Structure

The code generated for a structure will include an attribute to support the relationship between Class_A and Class_B. A simplified version of the code is as follows:

```
Struct Class_A
{
sequence <Class_B, 4> Class_B_Role;
};
```

Again, a sequence is the default container. To use an array instead, you can change the BoundedRoleType role property to Array.

Bounded Associations Generated for a Union

If Class_A is a union, and has a bounded association with Class_B, an attribute will be created in Class_A to support the relationship. By default, the container used in this attribute is a sequence. Here, we have a sequence of length 4.

```
union Class_A switch(int) {
   case 3: sequence <Class_B, 4> Class_B_Role;
};
```

Bounded Associations Generated for Other CORBA/IDL Types

If types other than interface, exception, structure, or union are used, no attributes will be generated to support the relationship. However, #include statements will be placed in both Class_A and Class_B.

Reflexive Associations

A reflexive association is treated much the same as an association between two classes. For the following situation

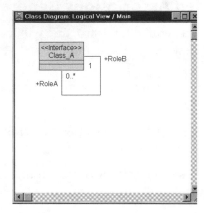

code similar to this is generated:

```
Interface Class_A
{

    typedef sequence <Class_A> RoleA_def;
    attribute Class_A RoleB;
attribute RoleA_def RoleA;
};
```

The first two lines support the 0..* end of the relationship. They include a container class that will support this multiplicity. The third line supports the end of the relationship with a multiplicity of one.

The full code generated for Class_A is:

```
//Source file: c:/program files/rational/rose 98i/corba/Class_A.idl

#ifndef __CLASS_A_DEFINED
#define __CLASS_A_DEFINED

/* CmIdentification
   %X% %Q% %Z% %W% */
```

```
interface Class_A {
→       typedef sequence <Class_A> RoleA_def;

→       attribute Class_A RoleB;
→       attribute RoleA_def RoleA;
    };

    #endif
```

Reflexive Associations Generated for an Exception

If Class_A is stereotyped as an exception, only one attribute will be generated for the relationship. In this example, an attribute was generated to support the *one* end of the one-to-many relationship. The code for Class_A is shown below:

```
//Source file: c:/program files/rational/rose 98i/corba/Class_A.idl

#ifndef __CLASS_A_DEFINED
#define __CLASS_A_DEFINED

/* CmIdentification
  %X% %Q% %Z% %W% */

exception Class_A {
→       Class_A RoleB;
    };

    #endif
```

Reflexive Associations Generated for a Structure

If Class_A is a structure, an attribute will be created inside of it to support the reflexive relationship. If the relationship looks like the previous reflexive association, then the following code will be generated:

```
//Source file: c:/program files/rational/rose 98i/corba/Class_A.idl

#ifndef __CLASS_A_DEFINED
#define __CLASS_A_DEFINED

/* CmIdentification
```

```
    %X% %Q% %Z% %W% */

struct Class_A {
    Class_A RoleB;
};

#endif
```

Reflexive Associations Generated for a Union

If Class_A is a union, a single attribute will be created inside the class to support the reflexive relationship. The following code is generated for Class_A:

```
//Source file: c:/program files/rational/rose 98i/corba/Class_A.idl

#ifndef __CLASS_A_DEFINED
#define __CLASS_A_DEFINED

/* CmIdentification
  %X% %Q% %Z% %W% */

union Class_A switch(int) {
    case 1: Class_A RoleB;
};

#endif
```

Reflexive Associations Generated for Other CORBA/IDL Types

Because attributes are not generated for a TypeDef, enumeration, or constant, reflexive associations with these types will not be reflected in the code.

Aggregations

When generating CORBA/IDL, associations and aggregations are treated the same. All of the considerations we've discussed so far (the multiplicity, whether the relationship is unidirectional or bi-directional, and whether the relationship is reflexive) apply the same to aggregations as they did to associations. This is true for any of the CORBA types (interface, TypeDef, enumeration, constant, exception, structure, or union).

For information about how unidirectional aggregations, aggregations with various multiplicity indicators, and reflexive aggregations are generated, please see the corresponding sections on associations.

Dependency Relationships

With a dependency relationship, no attributes are created. If there is a dependency between Class_A and Class_B no attributes will be created in either Class_A or Class_B.

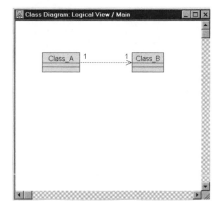

The code that is generated will look something like the following:

```
Interface Class_A
{
};
```

and

```
Interface Class_B
{
};
```

Rose will only place one reference to Class_B inside of Class_A—an include statement for Class_B.IDL. Class_A will not be referenced in Class_B at all.

Because no attributes are generated for a dependency, an attribute will not be created for any of the CORBA types (interface, TypeDef, enumeration, constant, exception, structure, or union).

Generalization Relationships

A generalization relationship in UML becomes an inheritance relationship in IDL. In your Rose model, an inheritance relationship is shown as follows:

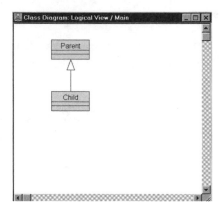

For this type of relationship, Rose will generate something that looks like this:

```
Interface Parent
{
};
```

and

```
Interface Child : Parent
{
};
```

Let's look at the actual code that is generated. In the code for the parent class, there is no mention of the child class. This helps keep the Parent generic; many classes can inherit from it without affecting its code.

In the child class, the code is generated to support its inheritance from the parent class. The code for the child class is:

```
//Source file: c:/program files/rational/rose 98i/corba/Child.idl

#ifndef __CHILD_DEFINED
#define __CHILD_DEFINED
```

```
/* CmIdentification
  %X% %Q% %Z% %W% */
```

➡
```
#include "Parent.idl"
```

➡
```
interface Child : Parent {
};
```

```
#endif
```

Generalizations Generated for a TypeDef

If the child class is a TypeDef, a #include statement will appear in the generated code for the parent, but an inheritance relationship will not be shown in the code. The IDL for the child class is:

```
//Source file: c:/program files/rational/rose 98i/corba/Child.idl

#ifndef __CHILD_DEFINED
#define __CHILD_DEFINED

/* CmIdentification
  %X% %Q% %Z% %W% */

#include "Parent.idl"

typedef  Child;

#endif
```

Generalizations Generated for an Enumeration

The same is true for an enumeration. Although a #include statement is generated, the inheritance relationship itself is not represented in the code. In this case, the generated code looks like this:

```
//Source file: c:/program files/rational/rose 98i/corba/Child.idl

#ifndef __CHILD_DEFINED
#define __CHILD_DEFINED
```

```
/* CmIdentification
   %X% %Q% %Z% %W% */

#include "Parent.idl"

enum Child {
};

#endif
```

Generalizations Generated for a Constant

As with a TypeDef or enumeration, a generalization relationship will not be directly implemented in code with a constant. A #include statement will be generated to reference the parent. The code for this example looks like this:

```
//Source file: c:/program files/rational/rose 98i/corba/Child.idl

#ifndef __CHILD_DEFINED
#define __CHILD_DEFINED

/* CmIdentification
   %X% %Q% %Z% %W% */

#include "Parent.idl"

const  Child = ;

#endif
```

Generalizations Generated for an Exception

Inheritance is not supported with an exception. Therefore, as in the other cases, a #include statement will be generated, but the generalization itself will not be reflected in the code. The IDL for this situation looks like this:

```
//Source file: c:/program files/rational/rose 98i/corba/Child.idl

#ifndef __CHILD_DEFINED
#define __CHILD_DEFINED
```

```
/* CmIdentification
   %X% %Q% %Z% %W% */

#include "Parent.idl"

exception Child {
};

#endif
```

Generalizations Generated for a Structure

As with the other CORBA types, inheritance is not supported with a structure. A #include statement will be included to reference the parent, but the inheritance relationship will not be reflected in the code. The IDL generated for a generalization with a structure is as follows:

```
//Source file: c:/program files/rational/rose 98i/corba/Child.idl

#ifndef __CHILD_DEFINED
#define __CHILD_DEFINED

/* CmIdentification
   %X% %Q% %Z% %W% */

#include "Parent.idl"

struct Child {
};

#endif
```

Generalizations Generated for a Union

A generalization with a union is much the same as a generalization with all other CORBA types except interface. Because generalizations are not supported with a union, they will not appear in the generated code. The only reference to the parent in the generated code is a #include statement. The code looks like this:

```
//Source file: c:/program files/rational/rose 98i/corba/Child.idl
```

```
#ifndef __CHILD_DEFINED
#define __CHILD_DEFINED

/* CmIdentification
   %X% %Q% %Z% %W% */

#include "Parent.idl"

union Child switch() {
};

#endif
```

Example of Generated CORBA/IDL

In previous chapters, we generated code for the ATM example in various languages. In this example, we will generate IDL for the Account class in the ATM example.

The CORBA generated for the Account class is included on the CD.

Exercise

In Chapters 3–10, we completed a model for an Order Entry system. Now, we are going to generate IDL code for some of the classes in the Order Entry system. We will generate IDL for the Order class, the OrderItem class, the TransactionMgr class, and the OrderMgr class. To generate the IDL, we need to perform the steps shown below. The code for this exercise is included on the CD.

Exercise Steps:

Set CORBA Stereotypes

1. Open the Add Order Class diagram.

2. Open the class standard specification window for the Order class.

Continued on next page

3. Set the stereotype of the Order class to Interface.

4. Repeat steps 2 and 3 for the OrderItem, TransactionMgr, and OrderMgr classes.

Set Role Names

1. For each relationship on the diagram, open the relationship specification window. Create role names at both ends of the relationship.

Create Components

1. In Chapter 9, we created components assuming C++ as a default language. Now, we need to set up CORBA components. A first step is to remove the old components we no longer need.

2. Open the Main Component diagram.

3. Select all items on the diagram and press Ctrl+D to delete them.

4. Using the Component toolbar button, create four new components: Order, OrderItem, TransactionMgr, and OrderMgr.

5. Open the specification window for the Order component.

6. Set the language of the component to CORBA.

7. In the browser, drag the Order class from the Logical view to the Order component in the Component view.

8. Repeat steps 5–7 to map the OrderItem, TransactionMgr, and OrderMgr classes to the appropriate components and to set the language for all components to CORBA.

Set Directory to Generate Code

1. Select Tools ➤ CORBA ➤ Project Specification.

2. Select the New toolbar button in the Directories field to add the directory to generate code.

Set CORBA Data Types

1. Open the specification window for the OrderNumber attribute of the Order class.

2. Select the "…" button next to the Type field on the specification window.

3. Select the + next to CORBA Types in the hierarchy.

Continued on next page

4. Select Long from the list of classes.

5. Repeat steps 1–4 for all attributes in the Order, OrderItem, OrderMgr, and TransactionMgr classes to map each attribute to the appropriate CORBA type.

6. Open the specification window for the SetInfo operation of the Order class.

7. Select the "…" button next to the Return field on the specification window.

8. Select the + next to CORBA Types in the hierarchy.

9. Select boolean from the list of classes.

10. Double-click the Integer OrderNum argument from the list of arguments.

11. On this specification window, click the + next to CORBA Types in the hierarchy, and select long from the list of classes.

12. Repeat steps 6–11 for all operations and arguments in the Order, OrderItem, OrderMgr, and TransactionMgr classes.

Generate CORBA/IDL

1. Open the Add New Order Class diagram.

2. Select the Order, OrderItem, TransactionMgr, and OrderMgr classes.

3. Select Tools ➤ CORBA ➤ Generate CORBA. When prompted, map the components to the directory you added in the project specification window above. The code that is generated is shown on the CD.

Summary

In this chapter, we examined how the different types of elements in your Rose model are generated in CORBA /IDL. We looked at the different code generation properties for classes, packages, attributes, operations, associations, aggregations, and other model elements, and discussed how these properties affect the generated code.

Again, the steps needed to generate code are:

1. Set the CORBA/IDL code generation properties.

2. Select the class(es) or component(s) to generate on a Class or Component diagram.

3. Select Tools ➤ CORBA ➤ Generate CORBA.

Once these steps are complete, you will have CORBA/IDL files that were generated from your model.

DDL Code Generation

- Setting the Persistency of Classes

- Setting the DDL Code Generation Properties

- Generating DDL from Your Rose Model

If you have a class in your model that you'd like to create as a table in your database, Rose can create the Structured Query Language (SQL) statement for the table. Each of the attributes in the class will become a field in the database table. Through the code generation properties, you can set the data type, length, and other details for each of the fields. In this chapter, we'll discuss how to generate Database Definition Language (DDL) code from your Rational Rose model.

You'll need to follow these steps to generate DDL from your model:

1. Set the persistency of classes.

2. Set the DDL code generation properties.

3. Select the class(es) to generate on a Class diagram.

4. Select Tools ➢ DDL ➢ Generate Code.

By default, Rose will not generate DDL for all of your classes. Many of your classes, such as your control classes or boundary classes, are not meant to translate into database tables. Your entity classes will be the ones that will become tables.

The first step, then, is to mark the classes for which you'd like to generate DDL. In Rose, all classes that are marked persistent can be used to generate DDL. To mark a class as persistent, open its class specification window. On the Detail tab, select the Persistent radio button, as shown at right.

Once the appropriate classes have been marked as persistent, you can set their DDL generation properties and generate the DDL for them. In this chapter, we'll discuss the various DDL code generation properties for attributes or for the project. Because operations and other model elements are not reflected in the DDL, there are no DDL generation properties for these elements.

DDL Code Generation Properties

As with the other languages, the DDL that is generated from a Rose model is controlled by a set of properties. In Rose, there are DDL property sets for the project and for attributes. You can view and set these properties by selecting Tools ➣ Options, and then selecting the DDL tab.

Anything you change using this window will set the default for all attributes or for the entire project. You can set the DDL generation properties for a single attribute by opening its attribute specification window and selecting the DDL tab. Any changes you make here will only affect the one attribute.

Project Properties

The project properties are those DDL code generation properties that affect the entire project.

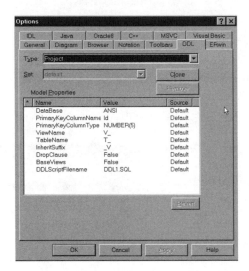

With these properties, you can set the default database to be used, the default primary key name, the prefix for a view, the prefix for a table, and other universal database settings. Each of the project properties are listed in Table 17.1, along with their purpose and default value.

TABLE 17.1: Project DDL Generation Properties

Property	Purpose	Default
Directory (98i)	Sets the default directory to generate DDL.	Current directory
DataBase	Sets the default database (ANSI, Oracle, SQL Server, Sybase, Watcom) to use.	ANSI
PrimaryKeyColumnName	If you do not explicitly set one of the attributes in a class to be the primary key, Rose will create a primary key for you. The primary key will be named <class name>, followed by the value of this property.	Id
PrimaryKeyColumnType	If you do not explicitly set one of the attributes in a class to be the primary key, Rose will create a primary key for you. This property controls the data type of the generated primary key.	NUMBER(5)

Continued on next page

TABLE 17.1 CONTINUED: Project DDL Generation Properties

Property	Purpose	Default
ViewName	Sets the prefix to be used on all generated views.	V_
TableName	Sets the prefix to be used on all generated tables.	T_
InheritSuffix	Sets the suffix to be used for views that were created for inheritance mapping.	_V
DropClause	Controls whether a DROP TABLE statement will be run before each CREATE TABLE statement.	False
BaseViews	Controls whether a view is generated for the table.	False
DDLScriptFilename	Sets the filename of the DDL script that is generated.	DDL1.SQL

Attribute Properties

The second DDL property set is the attribute property set. With these properties, you can control the default data type for each field, the default length of each field, and whether or not NULL values will be allowed.

There are two places to set these properties. To set them for all attributes, select Tools ➤ Options, then the DDL tab, and select Attribute from the drop-down list box. To set them for only one attribute, select the DDL tab on the attribute specification window and edit the properties there.

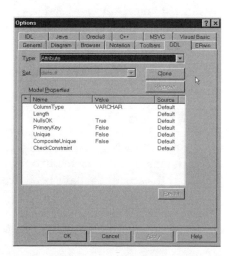

Table 17.2 lists the DDL attribute properties, their purpose, and their default value.

TABLE 17.2: Attribute DDL Generation Properties

Property	Purpose	Default
ColumnType	Sets the data type of the field generated for the attribute.	VARCHAR
Length	Sets the length of the field generated for the attribute.	Blank
NullsOK	Controls whether NULL values will be allowed in the field.	True
PrimaryKey	Controls whether or not the field is the primary key, or part of the primary key.	False
Unique	Controls whether unique values are required for each record.	False
CompositeUnique	Controls whether the field is part of a concatenated key for the table.	False
CheckConstraint	Sets the constraint check for the field.	Blank

Generated Code

In the simplest scenario, Rose will generate a single database table for each class you've marked as persistent. However, if there are relationships between the persistent classes, the generated DDL becomes a little more complex. Rose will automatically insert foreign keys and create views to support the relationships. In the following sections, we'll examine the DDL that is generated for a simple class and for the different types of relationships between classes.

Let's begin by looking at the DDL generated for a single class.

Classes and Attributes

If a class has been marked persistent, an SQL script can be generated for it that will create a database table. Each attribute in the class will become a field in the table. If none of the attributes have been explicitly marked as the primary key,

Rose will create a primary key for you, using the table name and the default prefix Id. Let's look at the DDL created for this class:

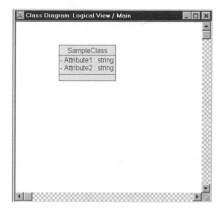

```
CREATE TABLE T_SampleClass(
    Attribute1 VARCHAR,
    Attribute2 VARCHAR,
    SampleClassId NUMBER(5),
    PRIMARY KEY(SampleClassId))
```

In this case, none of the DDL generation properties were changed; the default values were used. The above SQL is the ANSI SQL that was created for the class.

As you generate DDL, Rose will ask whether to use ANSI, Oracle, SQL Server, Sybase, or Watcom.

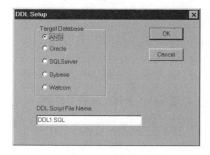

Had we used Oracle in the above example, the generated DDL would have looked like this:

```
CREATE TABLE T_SampleClass(
    Attribute1 VARCHAR(),
```

```
    Attribute2 VARCHAR(),
    SampleClassId NUMBER(5),
    PRIMARY KEY(SampleClassId));
```

Using SQL server, the generated DDL would have been:

```
CREATE TABLE T_SampleClass(
    Attribute1 VARCHAR(),
    Attribute2 VARCHAR(),
    SampleClassId NUMBER(5),
    PRIMARY KEY(SampleClassId))
go
```

With Sybase, the generated DDL would have looked like this:

```
CREATE TABLE T_SampleClass(
    Attribute1 VARCHAR(),
    Attribute2 VARCHAR(),
    SampleClassId NUMBER(5),
    PRIMARY KEY(SampleClassId))
go
```

Finally, with Watcom, the generated DDL would have been:

```
CREATE TABLE T_SampleClass(
    Attribute1 VARCHAR(),
    Attribute2 VARCHAR(),
    SampleClassId NUMBER(5),
    PRIMARY KEY(SampleClassId));
```

As you can see, the DDL that is generated looks very similar between databases, but Rose will use whatever syntax the selected database expects. Once the SQL statements have been generated from Rose, you can simply execute them against your database.

Changing the Table Name

By default, Rose will use T_, followed by the class name, as the name of the generated table. To change the default table prefix, select Tools ➤ Options, then the DDL tab. Select Project from the drop-down list box, and change the value of the TableName property.

Setting the Primary Key

If you do not explicitly set one or more of the attributes to become the primary key, Rose will automatically create one for you. By default, the name of the primary key will be <class name>, followed by Id. In the example above, the primary key of the SampleClass class became SampleClassId. To change the suffix used, select Tools ➤ Options, then the DDL tab. Select Project from the drop-down list box and change the value of the PrimaryKeyColumnName property.

By default, the data type of the primary key will be NUMBER(5). To change the data type, select Tools ➤ Options, then the DDL tab. Select Project from the drop-down list box and change the value of the PrimaryKeyColumnType property.

If you want to set one of the attributes of the class as the primary key, open the specification window for that attribute. Select the DDL tab and change the PrimaryKey property to True.

To create a composite primary key, set the PrimaryKey property of two or more attributes to true. For example, if both attributes in the SampleClass class were set to be primary keys, a composite key is created.

```
CREATE TABLE T_SampleClass(
    Attribute1 VARCHAR(),
    Attribute2 VARCHAR(),
    PRIMARY KEY(Attribute1,Attribute2))
```

Changing the Data Type or Length of a Field

The default data type for each field is VARCHAR. However, you can change the default data type or change the data type for only one field. To change the default for all fields, select Tools ➤ Options, then the DDL tab. Change the ColumnType attribute property to change the default.

To change the data type for a single attribute, first open the attribute specification window. On the DDL tab, change the value of the ColumnType property.

Controlling Whether NULL Values Can Be Used in a Field

To control whether or not a field can have NULL values, you can change the NullsOK property of an attribute. By default, all fields can have NULL values. If you change the NullsOK property for an attribute to False, Rose will add a NOT NULL clause to the generated code. For example, here we changed the NullsOK property to False for the Attribute1 attribute:

```
CREATE TABLE T_SampleClass(
    Attribute1 VARCHAR() NOT NULL,
    Attribute2 VARCHAR(),
    PRIMARY KEY(Attribute1))
```

Bi-Directional Associations

If there is a bi-directional association between two classes, Rose will include the relationship in the generated DDL by including foreign keys. Each of the two tables will have a foreign key, referencing the primary key of the other table. For example, let's look at the DDL generated for this relationship:

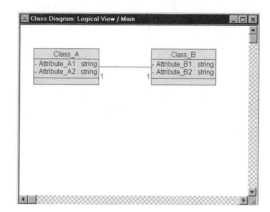

The DDL generated for the two classes shown above is:

```
CREATE TABLE T_Class_A(
    Attribute_A1 VARCHAR(),
    Attribute_A2 VARCHAR(),
    Class_BId NUMBER(5) REFERENCES T_Class_B(Class_BId),
    Class_AId NUMBER(5),
    PRIMARY KEY(Class_AId))
```

```
CREATE TABLE T_Class_B(
    Attribute_B1 VARCHAR(),
    Attribute_B2 VARCHAR(),
    Class_AId NUMBER(5) REFERENCES T_Class_A(Class_AId),
    Class_BId NUMBER(5),
    PRIMARY KEY(Class_BId))
```

As you can see, both T_Class_A and T_Class_B have foreign keys that reference the other.

Changing the Foreign Key Names

By default, Rose will use the primary key names as foreign keys in other tables. For example, the primary key of T_Class_A is Class_AId. Therefore, Class_AId is used as the name of the foreign key in T_Class_B.

To change the foreign key name, add an association name to the relationship between the two classes. Rose will use this association name as the foreign key name. In our example, this is the DDL that is generated if the association between Class_A and Class_B is called AssociationName:

```
CREATE TABLE T_Class_A(
    Attribute_A1 VARCHAR(),
    Attribute_A2 VARCHAR(),
➜   AssociationName NUMBER(5) REFERENCES T_Class_B(Class_BId),
    Class_AId NUMBER(5),
    PRIMARY KEY(Class_AId))


CREATE TABLE T_Class_B(
    Attribute_B1 VARCHAR(),
    Attribute_B2 VARCHAR(),
➜   AssociationName NUMBER(5) REFERENCES T_Class_A(Class_AId),
    Class_BId NUMBER(5),
    PRIMARY KEY(Class_BId))
```

As you can see, Rose now uses the name of the association when creating foreign keys in these two tables.

Creating Indexes

To create an index for a table, there should be a qualifier on the relationship. For example, say we want to create an index for Attribute_A1 in Class_A and for Attribute_B1 in Class_B. We can add the qualifiers as follows:

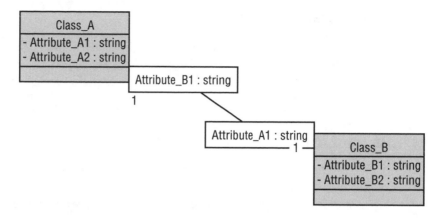

In the DDL that is generated, we will now have an index in each table. T_Class_A will have an index on the Attribute_A1 field and T_Class_B will have an index on the Attribute_B1 field. This is the DDL that was generated:

```
CREATE TABLE T_Class_A(
    Attribute_A1 VARCHAR(),
    Attribute_A2 VARCHAR(),
    Class_BId NUMBER(5) REFERENCES T_Class_B(Class_BId),
    Class_AId NUMBER(5),
    PRIMARY KEY(Class_AId))

    CREATE INDEX Class_A_1 ON T_Class_A(Attribute_A1)


CREATE TABLE T_Class_B(
    Attribute_B1 VARCHAR(),
    Attribute_B2 VARCHAR(),
    Class_AId NUMBER(5) REFERENCES T_Class_A(Class_AId),
    Class_BId NUMBER(5),
    PRIMARY KEY(Class_BId))

    CREATE INDEX Class_B_1 ON T_Class_B(Attribute_B1)
```

Association Multiplicity

When generating DDL, Rose only examines the navigability of the relationship. The multiplicity of the association isn't taken into account and won't affect the generated DDL. Therefore, a one-to-one, one-to-many, or many-to-many relationship will all be generated the same way.

Unidirectional Associations

The DDL generated for a unidirectional association is very similar to that generated for a bi-directional association. However, with a unidirectional association, a foreign key will only be placed at one end of the relationship. Let's look at the DDL generated for the unidirectional association.

In this example, a foreign key will be created for the T_Class_A table, but not for the T_Class_B table. The following is the DDL that was generated for this relationship:

```
CREATE TABLE T_Class_A(
    Attribute_A1 VARCHAR(),
    Attribute_A2 VARCHAR(),
➔   Class_BId NUMBER(5) REFERENCES T_Class_B(Class_BId),
    Class_AId NUMBER(5),
    PRIMARY KEY(Class_AId))


CREATE TABLE T_Class_B(
    Attribute_B1 VARCHAR(),
    Attribute_B2 VARCHAR(),
    Class_BId NUMBER(5),
    PRIMARY KEY(Class_BId))
```

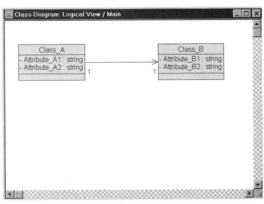

Association Multiplicity

As with bi-directional relationships, Rose ignores the multiplicity when generating DDL for unidirectional relationships. A one-to-one, one-to-many, or many-to-many relationship will all be generated the same way.

Reflexive Associations

With a reflexive association, Rose will place a foreign key in the class that references the primary key of the class. As with regular associations, Rose will ignore the relationship multiplicity when generating code.

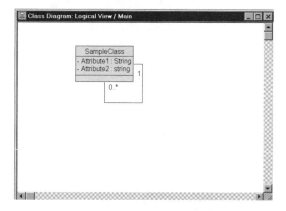

The following is the DDL generated for the above class:

```
CREATE TABLE T_SampleClass(
    Attribute1 VARCHAR() NOT NULL,
    Attribute2 VARCHAR(),
    Attribute1 VARCHAR() NOT NULL,
    FOREIGN KEY (Attribute1) REFERENCES T_SampleClass,
    PRIMARY KEY(Attribute1))
```

As you can see, there is a foreign key inside T_SampleClass that references Attribute1, which is the primary key of T_SampleClass.

Aggregations

The DDL generated for an aggregation will depend a little bit on which database you are using. If you generate the DDL using ANSI, SQL Server, or Sybase, an aggregation will be generated exactly the same as an association.

If you are using Oracle or Watcom, Rose will add an ON DELETE CASCADE clause to the generated DDL.

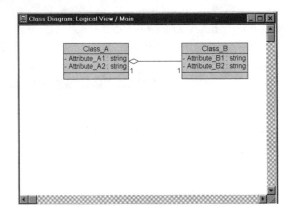

For the above example, this is the Oracle DDL that is generated:

```
CREATE TABLE T_Class_A(
     Attribute_A1 VARCHAR(),
     Attribute_A2 VARCHAR(),
     Class_BId NUMBER(5) REFERENCES T_Class_B(Class_BId) ON DELETE CASCADE,
     Class_AId NUMBER(5),
     PRIMARY KEY(Class_AId));

CREATE TABLE T_Class_B(
     Attribute_B1 VARCHAR(),
     Attribute_B2 VARCHAR(),
     Class_AId NUMBER(5) REFERENCES T_Class_A(Class_AId),
     Class_BId NUMBER(5),
     PRIMARY KEY(Class_BId));
```

Dependency Relationships

If there is a dependency relationship between two classes, Rose will generate DDL as if there were no relationship at all between the two classes. Each table is generated and no foreign keys are added to support the dependency relationship.

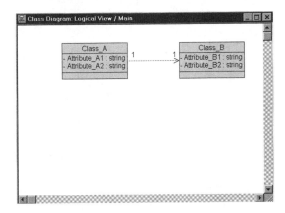

The following is the DDL that is generated for the above relationship:

```
CREATE TABLE T_Class_A(
    Attribute_A1 VARCHAR(),
    Attribute_A2 VARCHAR(),
    Class_AId NUMBER(5),
    PRIMARY KEY(Class_AId))

CREATE TABLE T_Class_B(
    Attribute_B1 VARCHAR(),
    Attribute_B2 VARCHAR(),
    Class_BId NUMBER(5),
    PRIMARY KEY(Class_BId))
```

Generalization Relationships

Because relational databases don't directly support inheritance, Rose will create views to support any generalization relationships in the model. In a parent-child relationship, Rose will first create tables for the parent and the child. A view will also be created to support the inheritance relationship. Let's look at the DDL that is generated for the following relationship:

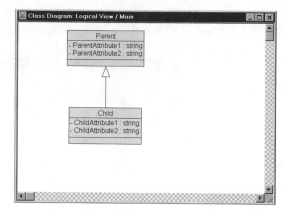

In this example, two tables will be created, one for the child and one for the parent. In addition, a view will be created that will mimic the inheritance relationship between them.

```
CREATE TABLE T_Parent(
    ParentAttribute1 VARCHAR(),
    ParentAttribute2 VARCHAR(),
    PRIMARY KEY(ParentAttribute1))


CREATE TABLE T_Child(
    ChildAttribute1 VARCHAR(),
    ChildAttribute2 VARCHAR(),
    ParentAttribute1 VARCHAR(),
    PRIMARY KEY(ParentAttribute1),
    FOREIGN KEY (ParentAttribute1) REFERENCES T_Parent
)



CREATE VIEW Child_V(
    ChildAttribute1,
    ChildAttribute2,
    ParentAttribute1,
    ParentAttribute2)
    AS SELECT
    T_Child.ChildAttribute1,
```

```
T_Child.ChildAttribute2,
T_Parent.ParentAttribute1,
T_Parent.ParentAttribute2
FROM T_Child,T_Parent
WHERE T_Child.ParentAttribute1=T_Parent.ParentAttribute1
```

When generating DDL for inheritance relationships, you cannot use a Rose-generated primary key for the parent class. You must set the PrimaryKey DDL property for one of the parent's attributes to True.

Example of Generated DDL

In the previous chapters, we generated code for the ATM example in various languages. In this example, we will generate DDL for the Account class in the ATM example.

The following is the ANSI SQL generated for the Account class. As you can see, each attribute of the class became a field in the generated table. Rose also generated a primary key, AccountId, for the table.

```
CREATE TABLE T_Account(
    Account Number VARCHAR(),
    PIN VARCHAR(),
    Balance VARCHAR(),
    AccountId NUMBER(5),
    PRIMARY KEY(AccountId))
```

Exercise

In this exercise, we will generate DDL for the Order and OrderItem classes in the Order Entry system. To generate the DDL, we need to perform the steps shown below.

Exercise Steps:

Mark Classes as Persistent

1. Open the Add New Order class diagram.

2. Select the Order class.

Continued on next page

3. Open the class specification window and select the Detail tab.

4. Check the Persistent check box and close the specification window.

5. Repeat steps 2-4 for the OrderItem class.

Set DDL properties

1. Open the specification window for the OrderNumber attribute of the Order class.

2. Select the DDL tab.

3. Change the ColumnType property to NUMBER.

4. Change the Length property to 3.

5. Change the PrimaryKey property to True and close the specification window.

6. Repeat steps 1-5 to make the ItemID attribute of the OrderItem class a primary key with type NUMBER and length 5.

Generate IDL

1. Select the Order and OrderItem classes on the Class diagram.

2. Select Tools ➤ DDL ➤ Generate Code. Select ANSI as the database type. The code that is generated should look like the following:

```
CREATE TABLE T_OrderItem(
    ItemID NUMBER(5),
    ItemDescription VARCHAR(),
    PRIMARY KEY(ItemID))


CREATE TABLE T_Order(
    OrderNumber NUMBER(3),
    CustomerName VARCHAR(),
    OrderDate VARCHAR(),
    OrderFillDate VARCHAR(),
    ItemID NUMBER(5),
    FOREIGN KEY (ItemID) REFERENCES T_OrderItem,
    PRIMARY KEY(OrderNumber))
```

Summary

In this chapter, we examined how DDL is generated from your Rose model. In Rose, you can mark a class as persistent if you want to generate DDL for it. You must follow these steps to generate DDL:

1. Set the persistency of classes.

2. Set the DDL code generation properties.

3. Select the class(es) to generate on a class diagram.

4. Select Tools ➤ DDL ➤ Generate Code.

Oracle8 Schema Generation

- Generating tables, views, stored procedures, triggers, and other Oracle8 elements with the Data Type Creation Wizard in Rose

- Setting the Oracle8 property sets for the project, class, attributes, and roles

- Generating an Oracle8 schema from your Rose model

Through its integration with Oracle8, Rose can help you to generate tables, views, stored procedures, triggers, and other Oracle8 elements. The Oracle8 integration is a wizard-driven, easy-to-use link between Rational Rose and Oracle.

Oracle8 is available in the Enterprise version of Rose. It has both forward and reverse engineering capabilities, allowing you to create new databases or examine existing ones. This latter capability is especially helpful in re-engineering efforts, where existing code and databases must be examined.

In this chapter, we'll examine the forward engineering feature of Rose. We'll look at the code generation properties for Oracle8, and discuss how different Rose elements are implemented in Oracle8.

Oracle8 Code Generation Properties

As with the other languages, the DDL that is generated from a Rose model to create an Oracle8 database is controlled by a set of properties. In Rose, there are Oracle8 property sets for the project, class, attributes, operations, module specifications, and roles. You can view and set these properties by selecting Tools ➤ Options, then selecting the Oracle8 tab.

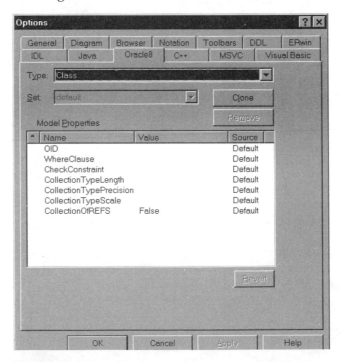

Anything you change using this window will set the default for all objects. You can set the Oracle8 generation properties for a single attribute, class, or role by opening its specification window and selecting the Oracle tab.

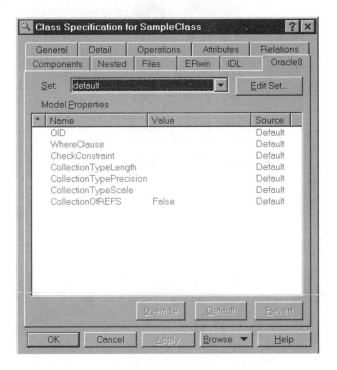

Project Properties

The project properties are those code generation properties that apply more to the whole project than to any specific model element, such as a class or relationship.

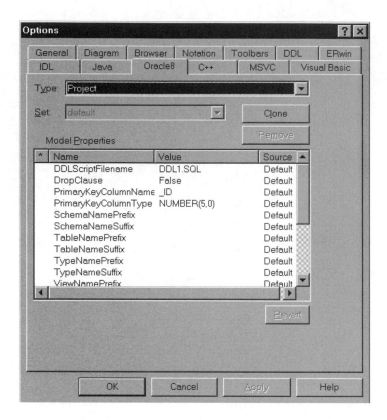

The options in this section include things like the default filename to use when generating code, the suffixes for primary key columns, schemas, tables, and more. Each of the project properties are listed in Table 18.1, along with their purpose and default value.

TABLE 18.1: Project Code Generation Properties

Property	Purpose	Default
DDLScriptFileName	Sets the default filename of the script generated from Rose	DDL1.SQL
DropClause	Controls whether a DROP statement will be run for each Oracle entity	False
PrimaryKeyColumnName	Sets the suffix to be used when generating primary keys	_ID

Continued on next page

TABLE 18.1: CONTINUED Project Code Generation Properties

Property	Purpose	Default
PrimaryKeyColumnType	Sets the default data type for primary keys	NUMBER(5,0)
SchemaNamePrefix	Sets the prefix to add to the beginning of a component name for generated schema	Blank
SchemaNameSuffix	Sets the suffix to add to the end of a component name for generated schema	Blank
TypeNamePrefix	Sets the prefix to add to the beginning of a class name for generated Object	Blank
TypeNameSuffix	Sets the suffix to add to the end of a class name for generated Object	Blank
TableNamePrefix	Sets the prefix to add to the beginning of a class name for generated tables	Blank
TableNameSuffix	Sets the suffix to add to the end of a class name for generated tables	Blank
ViewNamePrefix	Sets the prefix to add to the beginning of a class name for generated views	Blank
ViewNameSuffix	Sets the suffix to add to the end of a class name for generated views	Blank
VARRAYNamePrefix	Sets the prefix to add to the beginning of a class name for generated VARRAYs	Blank
VARRAYNameSuffix	Sets the suffix to add to the end of a class name for generated VARRAYs	Blank
NestedTableNamePrefix	Sets the prefix to add to the beginning of a class name for generated Nested tables	Blank
NestedTableNameSuffix	Sets the suffix to add to the end of a class name for generated Nested tables	Blank
ObjectTableNamePrefix	Sets the prefix to add to the beginning of a class name for generated Object tables	Blank
ObjectTableNameSuffix	Sets the suffix to add to the end of a class name for generated Object tables	Blank

Class Properties

Class properties are the Oracle8 code generation properties that apply to classes. These properties will let you set collection types and where clauses.

There are two places to set these properties. To set them for all classes, select Tools ➢ Options, then the Oracle8 tab, and select Class from the drop-down list box. To set them for only one class, select the Oracle8 tab on the class specification window and edit the properties there.

Table 18.2 lists the Oracle8 class properties, their purpose, and their default value.

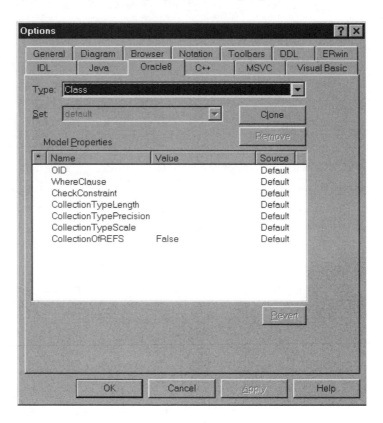

TABLE 18.2: Class Code Generation Properties

Property	Purpose	Default
OID	Sets the object ID	Blank
WhereClause	Sets the filter criteria	Blank
CheckConstraint	Sets a check constraint	Blank

Continued on next page

TABLE 18.2 CONTINUED: Class Code Generation Properties

Property	Purpose	Default
CollectionTypeLength	Sets the length of the values in a scalar VARRAY	Blank
CollectionTypePrecision	Sets the precision of the values in a scalar VARRAY	Blank
CollectionTypeScale	Sets the size of a scalar VARRAY	Blank
CollectionOfREFS	Indicates whether the type is a collection of REFs to other objects	False

Attribute Properties

Attribute properties are the Oracle8 properties that relate to attributes. Using these properties, you can, for example, decide if the attribute will be unique, set the attribute to the primary key, or set constraints.

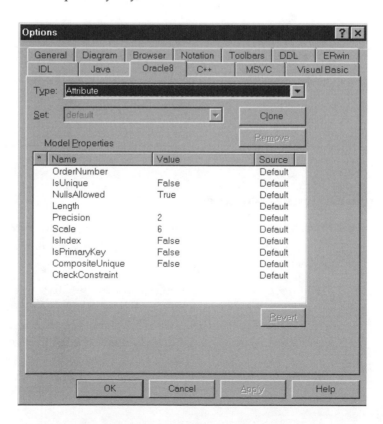

There are two places to set these properties. To set them for all attributes, select Tools ➤ Options, then the Oracle8 tab, and select Attribute from the drop-down list box. To set them for only one attribute, select the Oracle8 tab on the attribute specification window, and edit the properties there.

Table 18.3 lists the attribute properties, their purpose, and their default value.

TABLE 18.3: Attribute Code Generation Properties

Property	Purpose	Default
OrderNumber	Sets the column order of the attribute	Blank
IsUnique	Determines whether values in the field must be unique	False
NullsAllowed	Determines whether NULL values are allowed in the field	True
Length	Sets the field length	Blank
Precision	Sets the precision to be used for NUMBER fields	2
Scale	Length of a NUMBER type	6
IsIndex	Determines whether the attribute is part of an index	False
IsPrimaryKey	Determines whether the attribute is the primary key	False
CompositeUnique	Determines whether the attribute is a part of a composite key	False
CheckConstraint	Sets a check constraint	Blank

Operation Properties

The operation properties are the Oracle8 code generation properties that are specific to operations. These properties will let you determine the kind of method to generate.

There are two places to set these properties. To set them for all operations, select Tools ➤ Options, then the Oracle8 tab, and select Operation from the drop-down list box. To set them for only one operation, select the Oracle8 tab on the operation specification window, and edit the properties there.

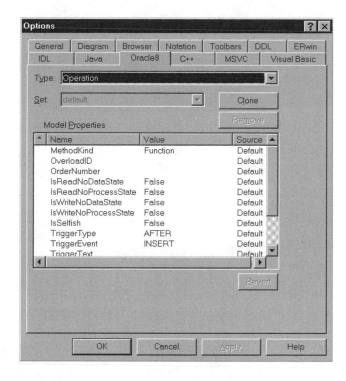

Table 18.4 lists many of the operation code generation properties, their purpose, and their default value.

TABLE 18.4: Operation Code Generation Properties

Property	Purpose	Default
MethodKind	Determines whether the operation is a Map Method, Order Method, Function, Procedure, Operator, Constructor, Destructor, Trigger, or Calculated Column	Function
OrderNumber	If the column is a calculated view column, specifies the order number in the view	Blank

Continued on next page

TABLE 18.4: CONTINUED Operation Code Generation Properties

Property	Purpose	Default
TriggerType	Sets the type of trigger to create (BEFORE or AFTER)	AFTER
TriggerEvent	Sets the event to start the trigger (INSERT, DELETE, UPDATE)	INSERT
TriggerText	Sets the procedural text of the trigger	Blank
TriggerForEach	Controls the trigger fires for each row or statement	ROW

Module Specification Properties

The module specification properties are those properties that are related to the schemas you will generate from Rose. These properties give you the ability to decide whether or not to generate the schema.

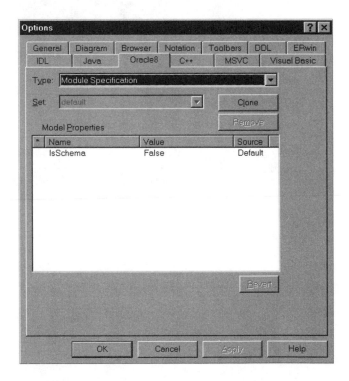

There are two places to set these properties. To set them for all components, select Tools ➤ Options, then the Oracle8 tab, and select Module Specification from the drop-down list box. To set them for only one component, select the Oracle8 tab on the component specification window and edit the properties there.

The only code generation property for an Oracle8 module is called IsSchema, and controls whether the component represents an Oracle8 schema. The default value for this property is False.

Role Properties

Role properties are the Oracle8 code generation properties that affect relationships. There is one role property, which will let you set the order number of the attribute that is generated for the relationship.

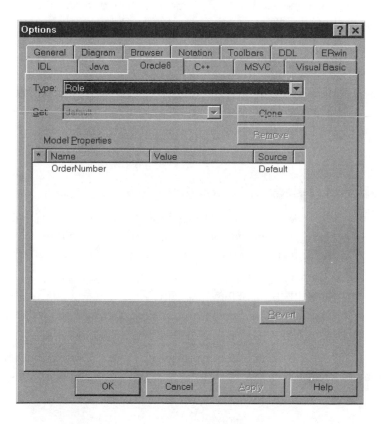

As with most of the other property sets, there are two places to set these properties. To set them for all relationships, select Tools ➤ Options, then the Oracle8 tab, and select Role from the drop-down list box. To set them for a single relationship, open the relationship specification. On the Oracle8 tab of the relationship specification window, you can change the properties for that relationship.

There is only one code generation property for relationships in Oracle8. The OrderNumber property sets the column order number of the attribute that is generated for the relationship. By default, this field is blank.

Creating Oracle8 Objects

The generated code for Oracle8 will be different than that for the other languages. In Oracle8, you generate a schema, Relational tables, Object types, and views. In Rose, there is a Data Type Creation Wizard to help you create each of these different Oracle8 constructs. We recommend using the wizard to create Oracle8 objects. It is possible to create the objects directly in Rose, but extremely difficult. Using the wizard, all of the code generation properties will be set for you. If you directly create the objects in Rose, you will need to set all of these properties manually. In the following sections, we will look at how to create Oracle8 constructs with the Data Type Creation Wizard.

Object Types

An Object type is an Oracle8 construct that contains information (attributes) and behavior (methods). Just as you group information and the behavior that acts on that information into a class, you group these items into an Object type.

In Rose, Object types are shown as classes with a stereotype of ObjectType. Each attribute of the class will be implemented as an attribute of the generated Object type, and the operations will be implemented as methods. We'll look at attributes and operations more closely in the following sections.

To create an Object type, select Tools ➤ Oracle8 ➤ Data Type Creation Wizard. On the window that appears, select ObjectType, as shown in Figure 18.1.

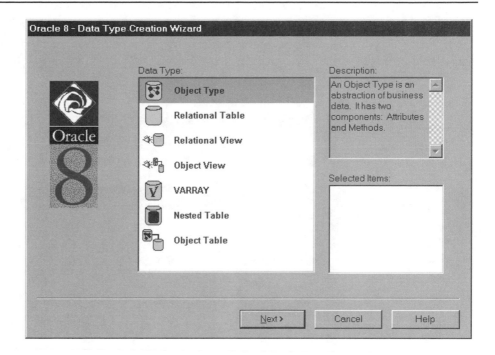

Once you've selected Object Type, click the Next button. On the Data Type Description screen, enter the name of the new Object type, the schema (component) for the Object type, the package that will contain the type, and the Class diagram the type will be shown on. If you'd like, you can also enter documentation at the bottom of the window. The Data Type Description screen is shown in Figure 18.2.

Click Next and the Define Attribute window will open, as shown in Figure 18.3. You can either select from existing attributes, or create new attributes for the Object type.

FIGURE 18.2:

Data Type Description screen

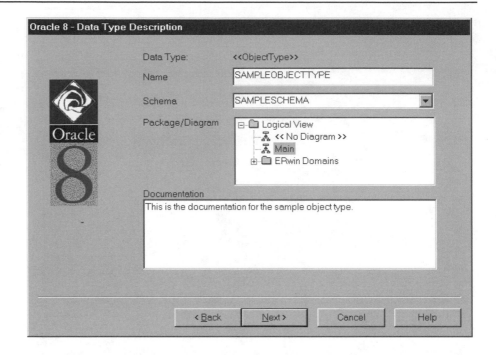

FIGURE 18.3:

Define Attribute window

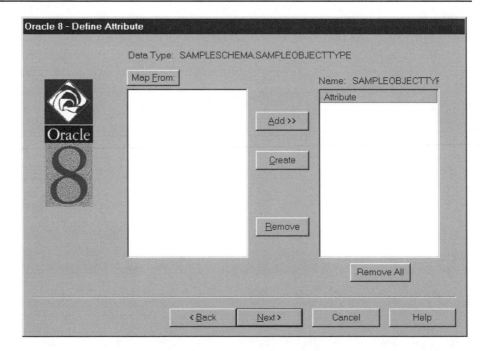

To select from existing attributes, select the Map From button. If you selected some Object types or tables before you started the wizard, they will already be displayed in the Map From box. Select from the items in the box, or add a new attribute. To add a new attribute, select the Create button. The Create/Edit Attribute window will appear, as shown in Figure 18.4.

FIGURE 18.4:

Create/Edit Attribute window

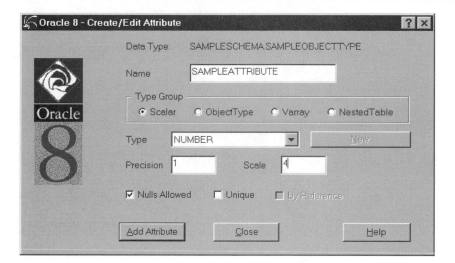

In this window, enter the name, type, precision, length, and other details of the new attribute. When you have finished, click the Add Attribute button. When you have added all of the attributes, click the Close button.

The next screen you will see is the Define Operations screen, as shown in Figure 18.5.

FIGURE 18.5:

Define Operations window

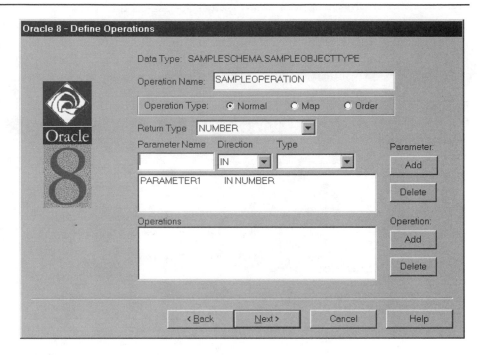

To create an operation, first type in the operation name and select the operation type. In the Return Type drop-down list box, select the type of information to be returned from the operation.

If the operation will have parameters, enter the parameter name, direction, and type. Click the Add button to add the parameter.

When all parameters have been added, click the Add button to add the operation. Add any additional operations using the same procedure. When done, click the Next button.

FIGURE 18.6:

Ordering window

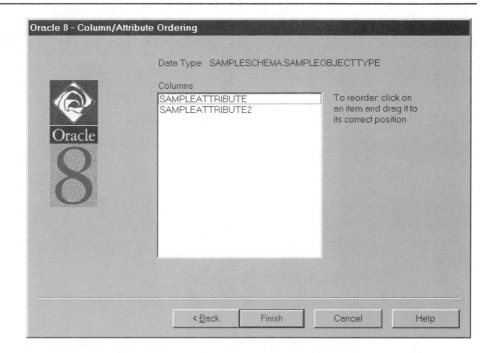

FIGURE 18.6:

Ordering window

Next, you are given the opportunity to change the order of the attributes. In the Ordering window, as shown in Figure 18.6, you will see a list of all attributes you created for this Object type. To reorder the attributes, drag the attribute to the new location. When the order is correct, click the Finish button.

Note that the Ordering window is a separate wizard for Oracle8. After you have created a data type, you can run the ordering wizard by selecting Tools ➢ Oracle8 ➢ Ordering Wizard.

Rose will create a class for you with the stereotype of ObjectType, as shown in Figure 18.7. All of the attributes and operations you defined using the wizard will be included in this class.

FIGURE 18.7:

SampleObjectType class

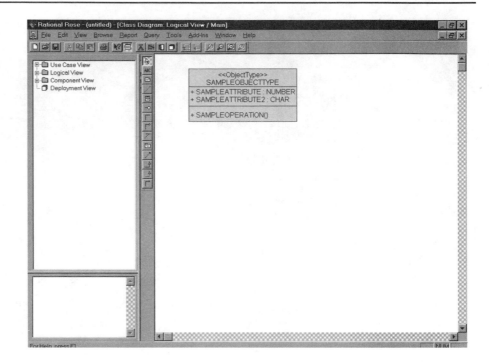

Relational Table

A Relational table is similar to an Object type in Oracle8, except that it contains no methods. In addition, Relational tables can have indexes and keys.

In Rose, Relational tables are shown as classes with a stereotype of Relational-Table. Each attribute of the class will be implemented as an attribute of the generated Relational table.

To create a relational table, select Tools ➤ Oracle8 ➤ Data Type Creation Wizard. On the window that appears, select Relational Table, as shown in Figure 18.8.

Creating a Relational table

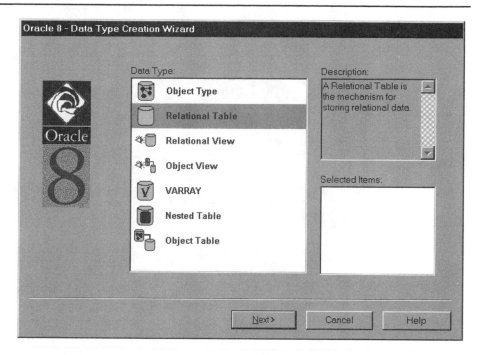

Once you've selected Relational Table, click the Next button. On the Data Type Description screen, enter the name of the new Relational table, the schema (component) for the Relational table, the package that will contain the table, and the Class diagram the table will be shown on. If you'd like, you can also enter documentation at the bottom of the window. The Data Type Description screen is shown in Figure 18.9.

On the Define Column window, as shown in Figure 18.10, you can either select from existing attributes or create new columns (attributes) for the Relational table.

FIGURE 18.9:

Data Type Description
screen

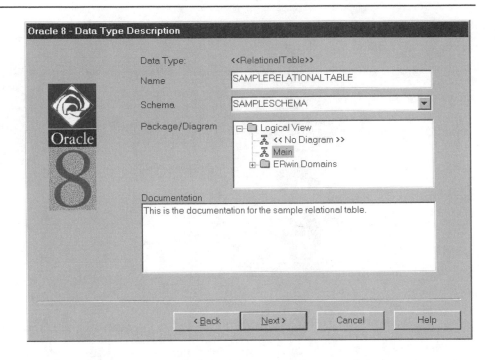

FIGURE 18.10:

Define Column window

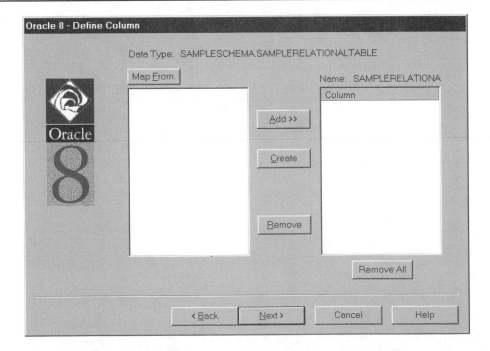

To select from existing attributes, select the Map From button. If you selected some Relational tables before you started the wizard, they will already be displayed in the Map From box. Select from the items in the box, or add a new column. To add a new column, select the Create button. The Create/Edit Column window will appear, as shown in Figure 18.11.

FIGURE 18.11:

Create/Edit Column window

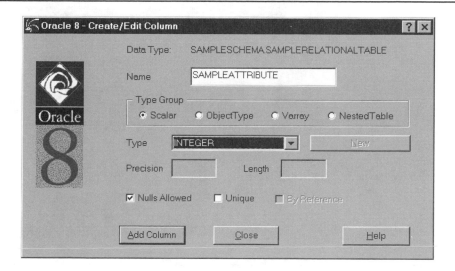

In this window, enter the name, type, precision, length, and other details of the new attribute. When you have finished, click the Add Column button. When you have added all of the columns, click the Close button.

The next screen you will see is the Indices screen, as shown in Figure 18.12.

To create an index, first enter the index name. In the Columns list box, select the column(s) you want to include in the index and press the Add button. If you want to make the index the primary index, select the Primary Key check box. Press Create Index to create the new index. It will appear in the Indices list box at the bottom of the screen. Create another index by entering the index name, or press Next if you've created all the indices for this table.

The next screen you will see is the Foreign Keys window, as shown in Figure 18.13. In this window, you can create one or more foreign keys for the table. To begin, enter a foreign key name in the FK (Foreign Key) Name drop-down list box. In the Tables list box, select the table whose primary key will become the foreign key of the current table. As you select tables from this list box, their primary

FIGURE 18.12:

Indices window

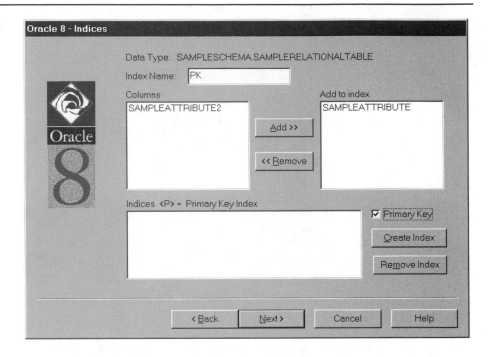

FIGURE 18.13:

Foreign Keys window

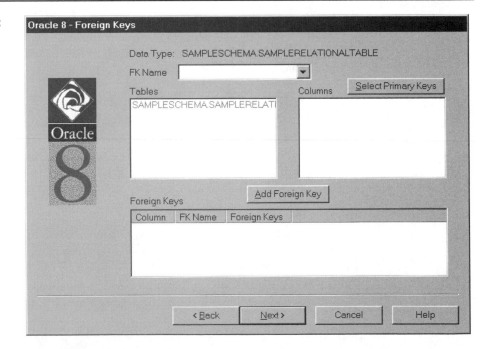

keys will be displayed in the Columns list box. When you have found the appropriate column, select it in the Columns list box and press the Add Foreign Key button. The new foreign key will be displayed in the Foreign Keys list box toward the bottom of the screen. To add another foreign key, enter another foreign key name in the FK Name drop-down list box, and repeat the steps we've just discussed. When you have added all of the foreign keys, click the Next button.

Note that the Foreign Keys window is a separate wizard for Oracle8. After you have created a data type, you can run the foreign keys wizard by selecting Tools ➢ Oracle8 ➢ Edit Foreign Keys.

Next you are given the opportunity to change the order of the columns. In the Ordering window, as shown in Figure 18.14, you will see a list of all columns you created for this Relational table. To reorder the columns, select the column to move and drag it to the new location. When the order is correct, click the Finish button.

FIGURE 18.14:

Ordering window

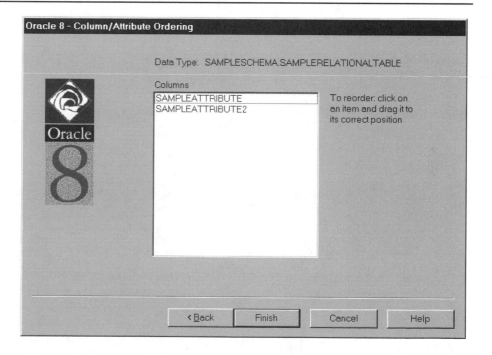

Note that the Ordering window is a separate wizard for Oracle8. After you have created a data type, you can run the ordering wizard by selecting Tools ➢ Oracle8 ➢ Ordering Wizard.

Rose will create a class for you with the stereotype of RelationalTable, as shown in Figure 18.15. All of the columns you defined using the wizard will be included in this class.

FIGURE 18.15:

SampleRelationalTable
class

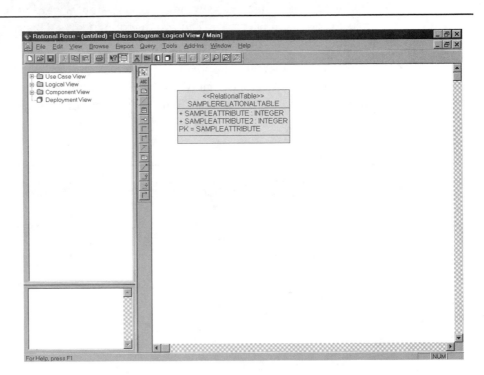

If you created foreign keys for this table, Rose will include this information in the model by adding the appropriate associations and qualifiers. Each foreign key will become an association between two tables. Qualifiers will be added to the associations to let you know which attributes participate in this relationship. Rose will put an association name on the relationship, using the foreign key name, and will give the association the stereotype <<FK>>. An example of this is shown in Figure 18.16.

FIGURE 18.16:

Foreign Key on a Class
diagram

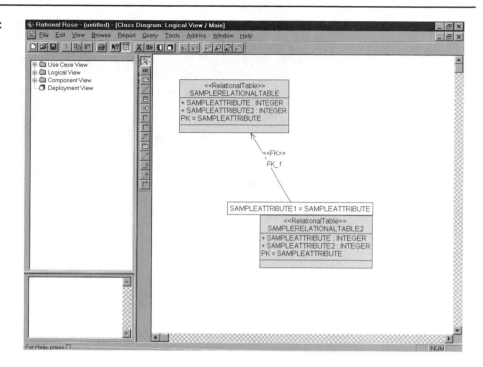

Relational View

A Relational view is a virtual table that takes its information from multiple tables. In Rose, Relational views are shown as classes with a stereotype of Relational-View. Each attribute of the class will be implemented as an attribute of the generated Relational view.

To create a Relational view, select Tools ➢ Oracle8 ➢ Data Type Creation Wizard. On the window that appears, select Relational View, as shown in Figure 18.17.

Once you've selected Relational View, click the Next button. On the Data Type Description screen, enter the name of the new Relational view, the schema ➢ component) for it, the package that will contain it, and the Class diagram it will be shown on. If you'd like, you can also enter documentation at the bottom of the window. The Data Type Description screen is shown in Figure 18.18.

FIGURE 18.17:

Creating a Relational view

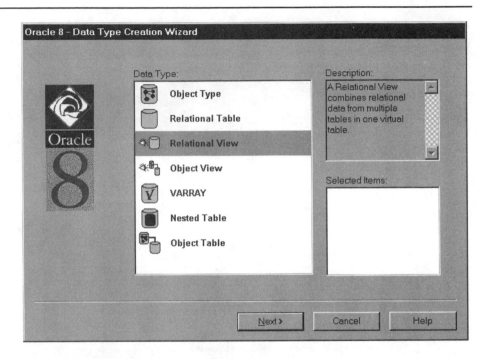

FIGURE 18.18:

Data Type Description screen

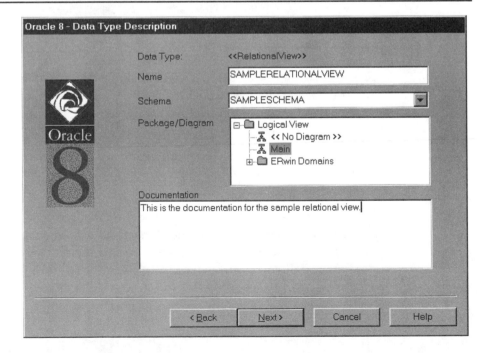

On the Define Column window, as shown in Figure 18.19, you can either select from existing attributes, or create new attributes for the Relational view.

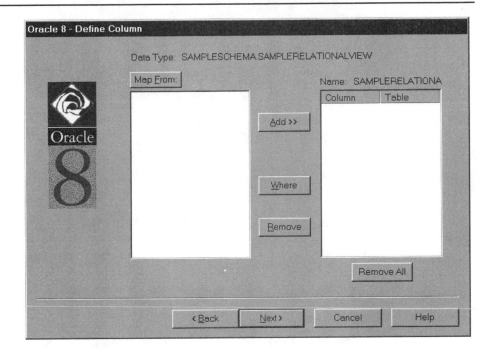

To select from existing columns, select the Map From button. If you selected some Relational tables or views before you started the wizard, they will already be displayed in the Map From box. Select from the items in the box, or add a new column. Selecting a table in the Map From box will add all of that table's columns to the view. To remove a column from the view, select the column and click the Remove button.

To enter a where clause for the view, click the Where button. Enter the where clause in the Where Clause window, shown in Figure 18.20.

FIGURE 18.20:

Define Where Clause
window

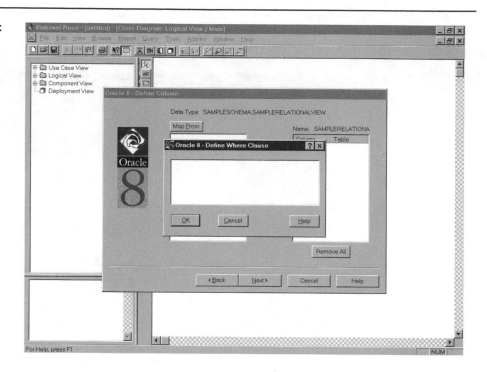

Next you are given the opportunity to change the order of the columns. In the Ordering window, as shown in Figure 18.21, you will see a list of all columns you created for this Relational view. To reorder the columns, select the column to move and drag it to the new location. When the order is correct, click the Finish button.

Note that the Ordering window is a separate wizard for Oracle8. After you have created a data type, you can run the ordering wizard by selecting Tools ➢ Oracle8 ➢ Ordering Wizard.

FIGURE 18.21:

Ordering window

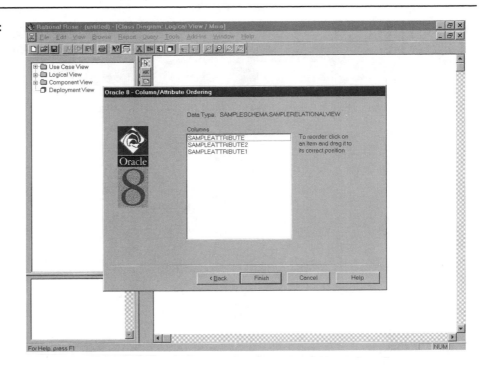

Rose will create a class for you with the stereotype of RelationalView, as shown in Figure 18.22. All of the columns you defined using the wizard will be included in this class. In addition, Rose will create a dependency from the view to each table in the view.

Object View

An Object view is a virtual object that takes its information from multiple tables. In Rose, Object views are shown as classes with a stereotype of Objectview. Each attribute of the class will be implemented as an attribute of the generated Object view.

To create an Object view, select Tools ➤ Oracle8 ➤ Data Type Creation Wizard. On the window that appears, select Object View, as shown in Figure 18.23.

FIGURE 18.22:

SampleRelationalView class

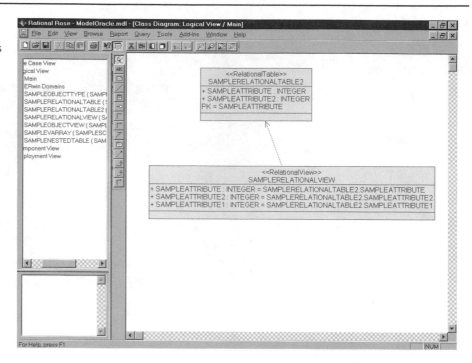

FIGURE 18.23:

Creating an Object view

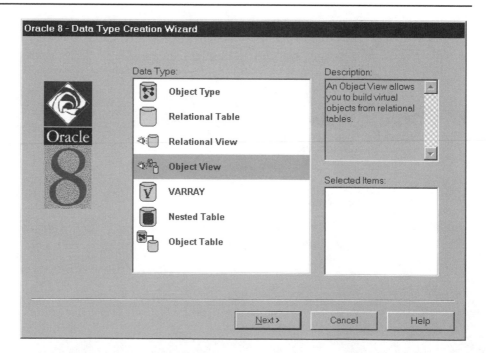

Once you've selected Object View, click the Next button. On the Data Type Description screen, enter the name of the new Object view, the schema (component) for the Object view, the package that will contain the view, and the Class diagram the view will be shown on. If you'd like, you can also enter documentation at the bottom of the window. The Data Type Description screen is shown in Figure 18.24.

FIGURE 18.24:

Data Type Description screen

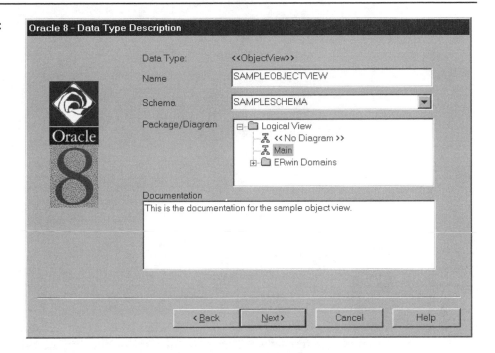

Next, the Type Selection window in Figure 18.25 will appear. Either select an existing Object type or click the New ObjectType button to create a new Object type.

FIGURE 18.25:

Object Type Selection
window

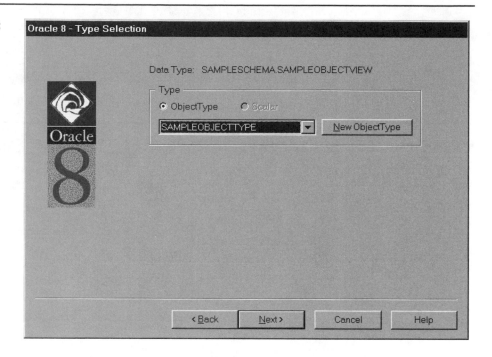

The attributes from the selected Object type will appear on the Object View
Map window, as in Figure 18.26. Click the Map To button to display a list of
tables and views from which attributes can be mapped. Select the desired tables
or views and click OK. Select the attribute in the Object view and the appropriate
attribute in the Map To list box, then click Map. When all attributes have been
mapped, enter a where clause for the view by clicking the Where button. Enter
the where clause in the Where Clause window, shown in Figure 18.27. When all
attributes have been mapped and a where clause has been entered (if needed),
click the Next button to continue.

FIGURE 18.26:

Object View Map window

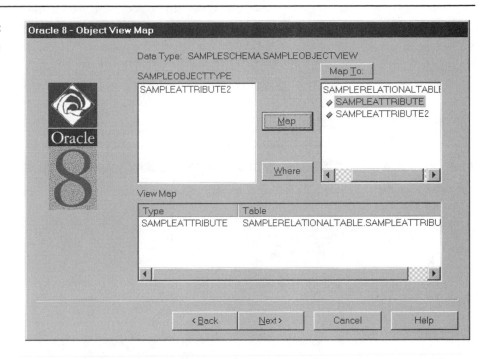

FIGURE 18.27:

Entering a Where clause

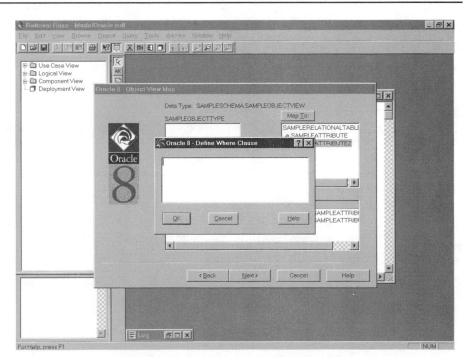

In the next window, you create an object identifier for the view, which is similar to a primary key. Select the attributes to be in the object identifier from the Attributes list box. Click the Add button to add those attributes to the object identifier. Click the Finish button when you are done.

Rose will create a class for you with the stereotype of ObjectView, as shown in Figure 18.28. Rose will create a dependency from the Object view to each table in the Object view.

FIGURE 18.28:

SampleObjectView class

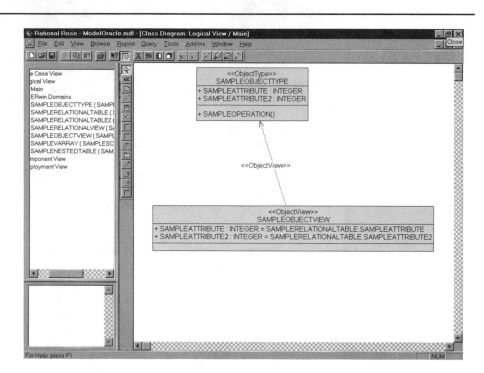

VARRAYs

A VARRAY is a container object in Oracle8. It is an array of Object types or scalars such as number, character, or date. A VARRAY is shown as a class with a stereotype of VARRAY.

To create a VARRAY, select Tools ➣ Oracle8 ➣ Data Type Creation Wizard. On the window that appears, select VARRAY, as shown in Figure 18.29.

FIGURE 18.29:

Creating a VARRAY

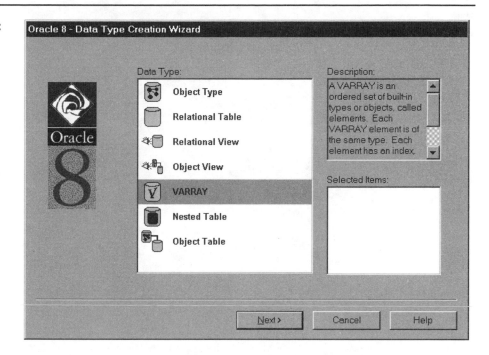

Once you've selected VARRAY, click the Next button. On the Data Type Description screen, enter the name of the new VARRAY, the schema (component) for the VARRAY, the package that will contain the VARRAY, and the Class diagram the VARRAY will be shown on. If you'd like, you can also enter documentation at the bottom of the window. The Data Type Description screen is shown in Figure 18.30. When you are done, click the Next button.

FIGURE 18.30:

Data Type Description
screen

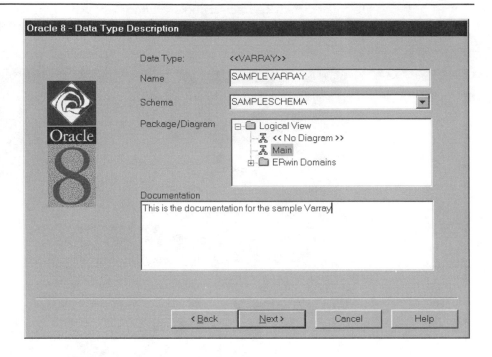

The Type Selection window will be displayed, as shown in Figure 18.31. Select the type for the VARRAY, either an Object type or scalar. If needed, enter the precision and length, or scale. Last, enter the cardinality, or size, of the VARRAY. Click Finish when you are done.

Rose will create a class for you with the stereotype of VARRAY, as shown in Figure 18.32. Rose will create a dependency from the VARRAY to the specified Object type.

Nested Tables

A Nested table is an object that appears as a column in a table. It can be of any Object type or scalar such as number, character, or date. A Nested table is shown as a class with a stereotype of NestedTable.

FIGURE 18.31:

Type Selection window

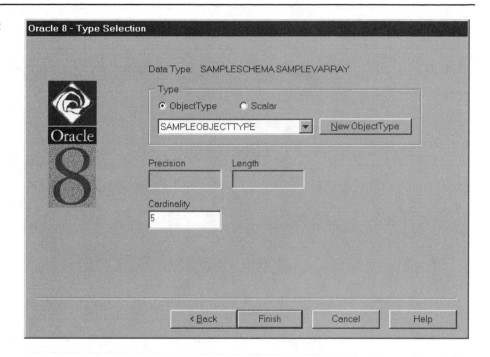

FIGURE 18.32:

SampleVARRAY class

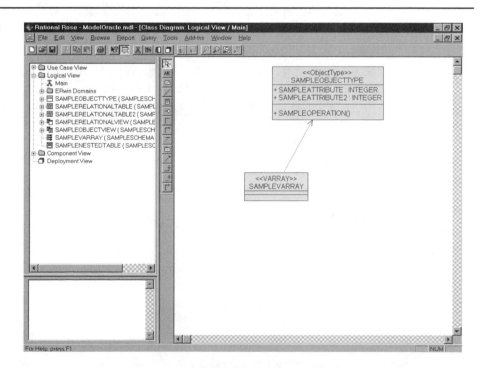

To create a Nested table, select Tools ➤ Oracle8 ➤ Data Type Creation Wizard. On the window that appears, select Nested Table, as shown in Figure 18.33.

FIGURE 18.33:

Creating a Nested table

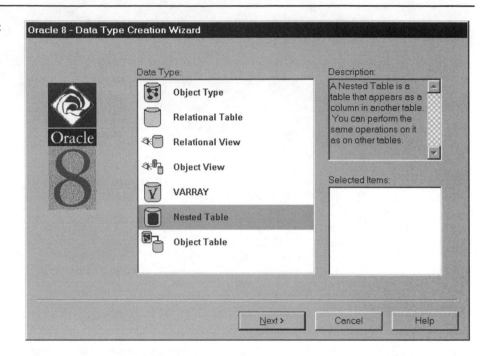

Once you've selected Nested Table, click the Next button. On the Data Type Description screen, enter the name of the new Nested table, the schema (component) for it, the package that will contain it, and the Class diagram it will be shown on. If you'd like, you can also enter documentation at the bottom of the window. The Data Type Description screen is shown in Figure 18.34. When you are done, click the Next button.

FIGURE 18.34:

Data Type Description
screen

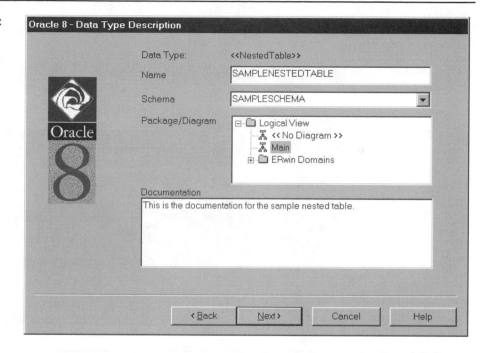

The Type Selection window will be displayed, as shown in Figure 18.35. Select the type for the Nested table, either an Object type or scalar. If needed, enter the precision and length, or scale. Click Finish when you are done.

Rose will create a class for you with the stereotype of NestedTable, as shown in Figure 18.36. Rose will create a dependency from the Nested table to the specified Object type.

FIGURE 18.35:

Type Selection window

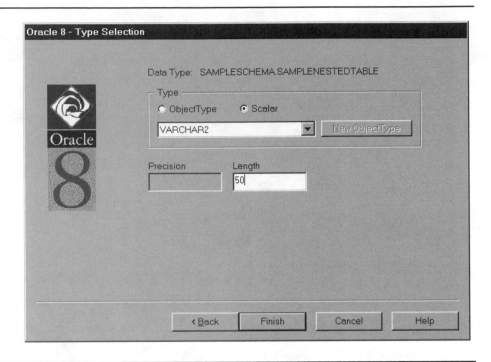

FIGURE 18.36:

SampleNestedTable class

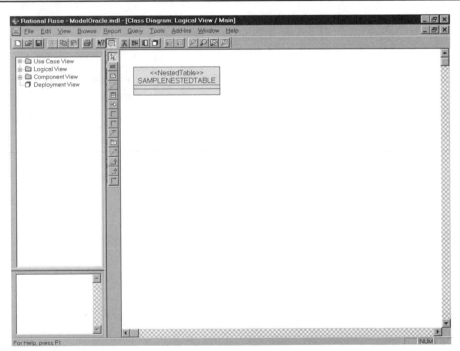

Object Table

An Object table is a collection of Object types. It can be of any Object type you have specified in the schema. An Object table is shown as a class with a stereotype of ObjectTable.

To create an Object table, select Tools ➤ Oracle8 ➤ Data Type Creation Wizard. On the window that appears, select Object Table, as shown in Figure 18.37.

FIGURE 18.37:

Creating an Object table

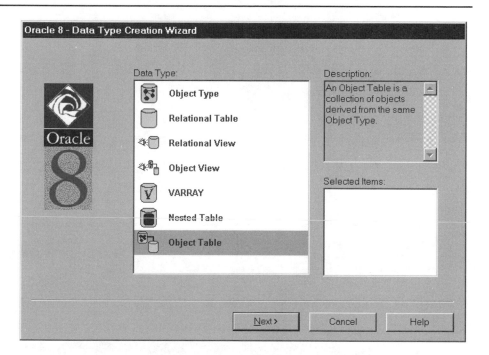

Once you've selected Object Table, click the Next button. On the Data Type Description screen, enter the name of the new Object table, the schema (component) for the Object table, the package that will contain the Object table, and the Class diagram the Object table will be shown on. If you'd like, you can also enter documentation at the bottom of the window. The Data Type Description screen is shown in Figure 18.38. When you are done, click the Next button.

The Type Selection window will be displayed, as shown in Figure 18.39. Select the type for the Object table. Click Finish when you are done.

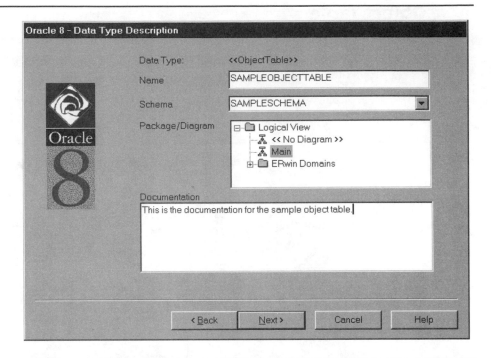

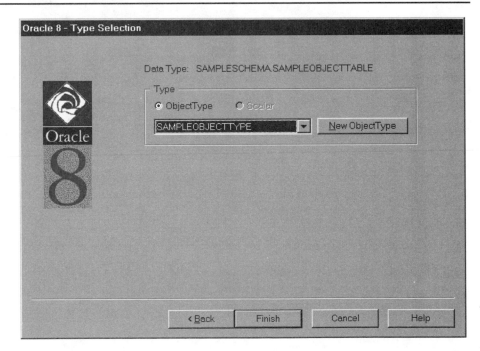

Rose will create a class for you with the stereotype of ObjectTable, as shown in Figure 18.40. Rose will create a dependency from the Object table to the specified Object type.

FIGURE 18.40:

SampleObjectTable class

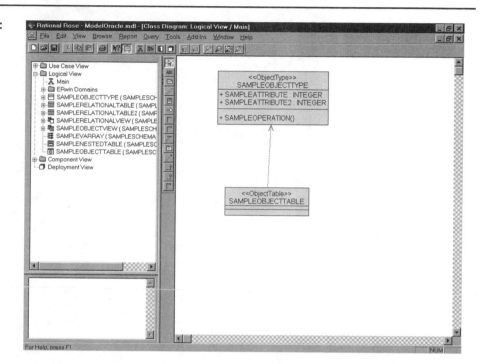

Generated Code

After creating the Oracle8 data types, you can generate the statements necessary to create the database schema. Before generating the statements, you can also run a syntax check to see if any errors will prevent successful generation. To do this, select the objects to check and then Tools ➤ Oracle8 ➤ Syntax Checker from the menu.

To generate the statements to create the tables, views, and objects, select the objects to generate, then Tools ➤ Oracle8 ➤ Schema Generation from the menu. The Schema Generation window will be displayed, as in Figure 18.41.

FIGURE 18.41:

Schema Generation
window

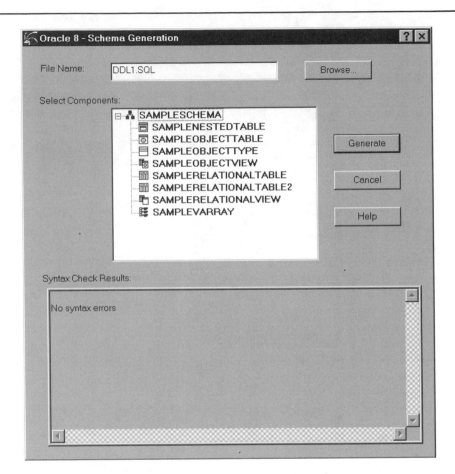

Here you can specify the filename for the statements and choose the schemas and objects to generate. Objects to be generated appear in bold. To deselect an object, click it. The object's name will become unbold. Click Generate to generate the statements. The DDL Execution window will appear. The top half of the window will show any errors during execution. The bottom half displays the statements to be executed. At this point, you can execute the statements by pressing the Execute button, if the Oracle8 client software is installed and you can connect to an Oracle8 database.

Summary

In this chapter, we took a look at how various Rose model elements are implemented in Oracle8. Using the Data Type Creation Wizard, you can create Object types, Relational tables, Relational views, Object views, VARRAYs, Nested tables, and Object tables. You can then generate the DDL necessary to create these objects in an Oracle8 database and execute the DDL to create the objects, if desired.

In the next chapter, we'll present an overview of reverse engineering using Rational Rose. Over the next several chapters, we'll discuss how to generate a Rose model from C++, Java, Visual Basic, and PowerBuilder code. We'll also look at how to reverse engineer an Oracle8 schema.

CHAPTER
NINETEEN

Introduction to Reverse Engineering Using Rational Rose

■ Reverse engineering your code to see the organization and architecture of an existing system

Reverse engineering is the ability to take information from source code and create or update a Rose model. Through their integration to C++, Java, Visual Basic, and many other languages, Rose 98 and 98i support reverse engineering code into a UML model. One of the challenges with Information Technology projects is keeping the object model consistent with the code. As requirements change, it can be tempting to change the code directly, rather than changing the model and then generating the changed code from the model. Reverse engineering helps us keep the model synchronized with the code.

In the following chapters, we'll discuss the details of reverse engineering code from various languages into Rose. In the reverse engineering process, Rose will read components, packages, classes, relationships, attributes, and operations from the code. Once this information is in a Rose model, you can make any needed changes, and then regenerate the code through the forward engineering features of Rose.

The options you will have available will depend on the version of Rose you are using.

- Rose Modeler will not include any reverse engineering functionality.

- Rose Professional includes reverse engineering capabilities for one language.

- Rose Enterprise includes C++, Visual C++ (in 98i), Visual Basic, and Java reverse engineering, as well as Oracle8 schema reverse engineering.

- Rose Add-ins will give you reverse engineering capabilities in other languages, such as PowerBuilder or Forte, to name a few.

Model Elements Created During Reverse Engineering

During the reverse engineering process, Rose will collect information about:

- Classes
- Attributes

- Operations

- Relationships

- Packages

- Components

Using this information, Rose will create or update an object model. Depending upon the language you are reverse engineering, you can create a new Rose model or update the current Rose model.

Let's begin by examining classes, attributes, and operations. If you have a source-code file that contains a class, the reverse engineering process will create a corresponding class in your Rose model. Each of the attributes and operations of the class will appear as attributes and operations of the new class in the Rose model. Along with the attribute and operation names, Rose pulls in information about their visibility, data types, and default values.

For example, when reverse engineering the following Java class, Rose will produce the model shown in Figure 19.1.

```java
// Source file: SampleClass.java

public class SampleClass {
    public double PublicAttribute;
    private int PrivateAttribute = 1;
    protected int ProtectedAttribute;

    SampleClass() {
    }

    public int PublicOperation(Double Parameter1) {
    }

    public int PrivateOperation() {
    }

    protected Double ProtectedOperation(int Parameter1, Double➥
Parameter2) {
    }
}
```

FIGURE 19.1:

Reverse engineering a Java
class

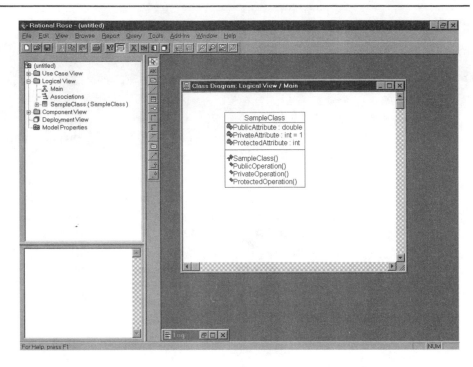

If you originally created the classes using Rose, and made some changes to the
classes in the code, these changes will be reflected in the model during the reverse
engineering process. For example, if you deleted an operation in the code, the
operation will be deleted from the model during reverse engineering. If you
added an attribute or operation directly into the code, this new attribute or operation will be added to the model during reverse engineering.

In addition to classes, Rose will collect information about the relationships in
the code. If one class contains an attribute whose data type is another class, Rose
will create a relationship between the two classes. For example, given the following two Java classes, Rose will create an association relationship between them, as
shown in Figure 19.2.

```
// Source file: Class_A.java

package javaclasses;

import java.javaclasses.Class_B;
```

```
public class Class_A {
    public Class_B m_Class_B;

    Class_A() {
    }
}

// Source file: Class_B.java

package javaclasses;

public class Class_B {

    Class_B() {
    }
}
```

FIGURE 19.2:

Reverse engineering an association relationship

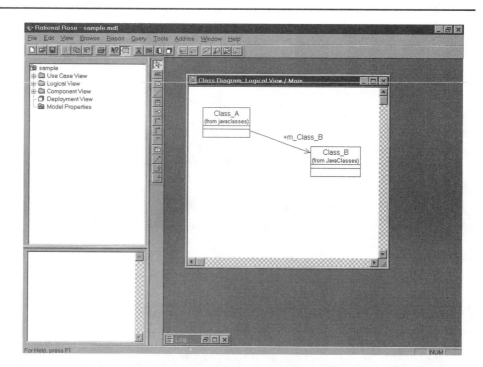

Inheritance relationships are also generated in the Rose model. Rose will create generalization relationships to support any inheritance in the code. If you have packages of foundation classes in your model, such as the JDK or PowerBuilder system types, Rose will add generalization relationships between the reverse-engineered classes and the base classes. For example, Figure 19.3 shows the results of reverse engineering two PowerBuilder windows, one of which inherits from the other. Both of them also inherit from the PowerBuilder base class, Window.

FIGURE 19.3:

Reverse engineering a generalization relationship

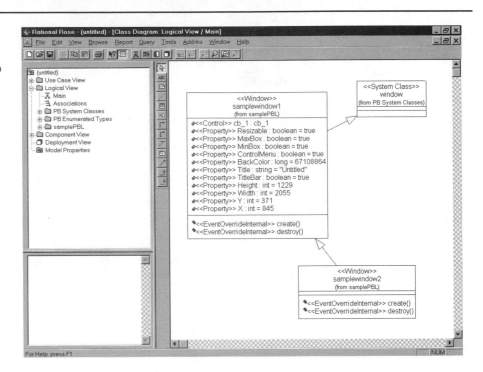

The components in the code will also be represented in Rose after the reverse engineering process. Each language deals with components a little bit differently. We'll discuss the reverse engineering of components in the following chapters.

Round-Trip Engineering

When you generate code using Rose, there are identification numbers placed in the generated code. For example, you may see a line like this in the code:

```
@roseuid 36730C530302
```

These strings of numbers and letters are used to help identify the classes, operations, and other model elements in the code and to synchronize the code with your Rose model.

In addition to the ID numbers, Rose generates protected regions in the code during the code generation process. Any code you write in these protected regions will be safe during round-trip engineering.

For example, let's look at a portion of C++ code that was generated by Rose:

```
void SampleClass::DoSomething ()
{
  //## begin SampleClass::DoSomething%36EAB3DB03AC.body preserve=yes
⇒  // – Code for the operation goes here –

  //## end SampleClass::DoSomething%36EAB3DB03AC.body
}
```

When the developers write code for this class, they code the DoSomething operation in the space between the //begin and //end statements, in a protected region. If this class is reverse engineered, changes are made, and it is then regenerated, the code of the DoSomething operation will remain safe.

Summary

In this chapter, we examined reverse engineering at a high level. By reverse engineering your code, you can see the organization and architecture of an existing system. You can also view, at a very detailed level, the specifications of your classes.

Rose provides reverse engineering capabilities for several languages, including C++, Java, and Visual Basic. Add-ins are also available for PowerBuilder, Forte, and other object-oriented languages. Please refer to Rational's Web site, www.Rational.com, for a complete list of the add-ins available for Rose.

In the following chapters, we'll take a detailed look at reverse engineering code in C++, Java, Visual Basic, and PowerBuilder, as well as reverse engineering an Oracle8 schema.

Reverse Engineering with C++ and Visual C++

- Starting the C++ Analyzer application and creating a new project

- Setting the project caption, directory list, and extension list

- Selecting a base project and files to reverse engineer

- Analyzing the files, setting the export options, and exporting to Rose

- Reverse engineering Visual C++ with the Reverse Engineering Wizard

- Mapping between C++ constructs and the Rose model

There is a tremendous amount of C++ code in the industry right now. While Rose supports the idea of creating a model from scratch, many projects involve a re-engineering effort with existing code. To support these types of projects, Rose includes a reverse engineering feature for C++.

Once you have used reverse engineering to view your existing code as a Rose model, you can make any needed changes and regenerate the code using the forward engineering features of Rose. This round-trip engineering support will help you keep your model and your source code in sync.

One of the features that is available in Rose 98i is a tight integration with Microsoft's Visual C++, Version 6. In Rose, you can reverse engineer Visual C++ code into your model.

Steps in Reverse Engineering C++

In this section, we'll go through each of the steps needed to reverse engineer your C++ code. We'll begin by starting the C++ Analyzer application, which is packaged with Rose and provides the C++ reverse engineering capabilities.

Like C++ code generation, C++ reverse engineering is very customizable. The Analyzer application has a series of options, which you can use to decide what gets reverse engineered and how the different C++ constructs will appear in the generated model.

Step One: Start the C++ Analyzer Application

As we mentioned above, reverse engineering with C++ is done through an application that is external to Rose. Using this application, you can select the files to reverse engineer, set the reverse engineering properties, and generate a Rose model.

To begin, select Tools ➢ C++ ➢ Reverse Engineering. The C++ Analyzer application will start, as shown in Figure 20.1.

FIGURE 20.1:

Starting the C++ Analyzer

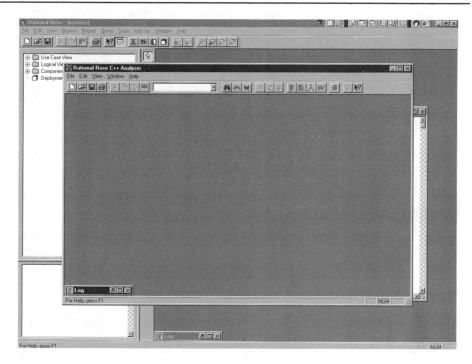

Step Two: Create a New Project

Once the C++ Analyzer has started, the next step is to create a new Analyzer project. A project is an Analyzer file that contains the list of files that you plan to reverse engineer, as well as all of the reverse engineering properties.

Select File ➢ New, and a new project will be created in the Analyzer, as shown in Figure 20.2.

Step Three: Set the Project Caption

The project's caption is a short description of the purpose of the project. If you enter a project caption, and later use this project as a base project for another one, the caption will be displayed in the base list. See below for a discussion of the base list.

A caption is optional. To set it, select the Caption button on the Project window. You can then use the Caption window, as shown in Figure 20.3, to enter the project's caption.

FIGURE 20.2:

New C++ Analyzer project

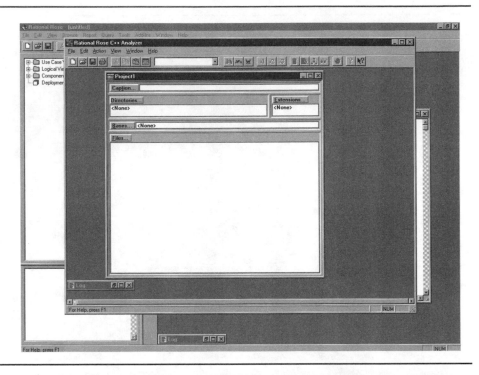

FIGURE 20.3:

Setting the project caption

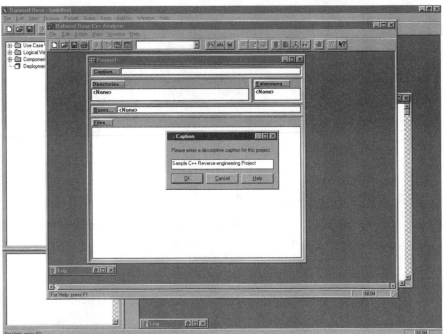

Step Four: Set the Directory List

This is an optional step. When you select files in step 7, the directory list will automatically be populated. However, you can modify this list either before or after you select files, if you'd like.

The directory list specifies the directories that contain the C++ files that you wish to reverse engineer. Using the Directories button on the project window, as shown in Figure 20.4, you can select directories to add to this list.

FIGURE 20.4:

Accessing the directory list

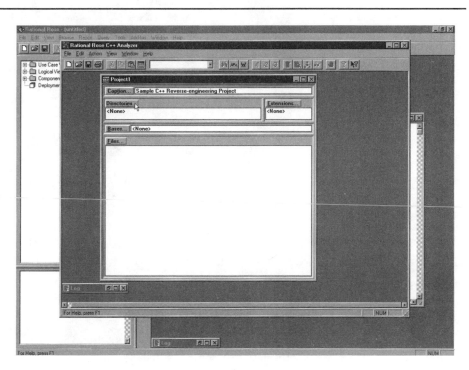

Once you've selected this button, the Project Directory List window will appear, as shown in Figure 20.5.

FIGURE 20.5:

Adding directories to the directory list

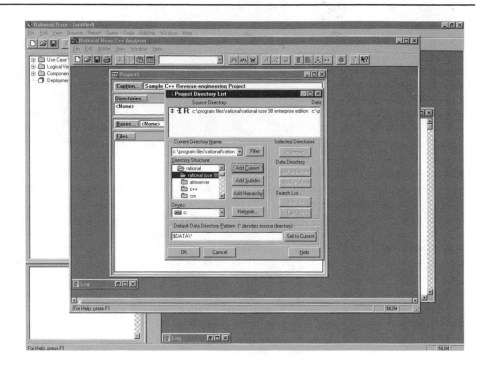

Select the directory you wish to add using the treeview in the Directory Structure list box. Press the Add Current button to add this directory; the Add Subdirs button to add this directory and its immediate subdirectories; or the Add Hierarchy button to add this directory, all subdirectories, and the entire hierarchy below the subdirectories.

Three icons are displayed next to each directory. The first can be used to move the directory higher or lower in the list. To move a directory, use this icon to drag and drop it up or down the list. The repositioning icon looks like this:

The second icon controls whether or not this directory will be searched when resolving #include statements. By default, the directory will be searched. If the directory will be searched, the following icon will appear:

Otherwise, this icon will appear:

The third icon controls whether code can be generated for items in this directory. After the reverse engineering has completed, you can make changes to the classes that were in the directory and regenerate the code for these classes. However, there may be times when you would not want to regenerate the code (i.e., for third-party libraries or other code for which you do not own the right to modify). Using the Code Regeneration icon, you can determine whether or not you will be able to regenerate the code in the future. If you want to be able to regenerate the code, the icon will look like this:

R

Otherwise, the icon will look like this:

Ɍ

Step Five: Set the Extension List

This is an optional step. When you select files in step 7, the list will automatically be filled in with the extensions of these files. You can, however, set up this list first, if you'd like.

The extension list is a list of the file extensions of the source files you wish to reverse engineer, as well as the file extensions of any header files that are #included in the source files you wish to reverse engineer. The Extension List window is shown in Figure 20.6.

FIGURE 20.6:

Setting the extension list

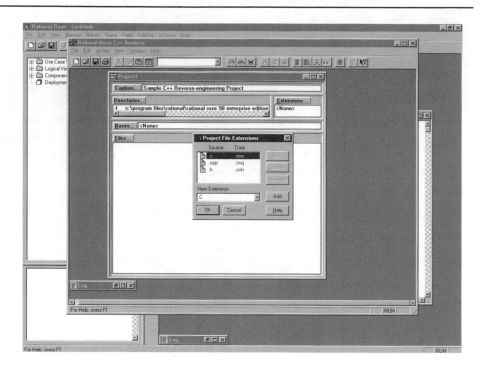

The extensions you add to this list will be the default filter used when selecting files to reverse engineer in step 7. For example, if you add .CPP to the extension list, .CPP will be the default filter when selecting files.

Step Six: Select Base Projects

A base project is a C++ Analyzer project file that contains information about base classes that are being used. For example, you may have an Analyzer project that holds information about some C++ foundation classes your organization created. Each of your company's projects uses these foundation classes as a base. The Analyzer project that holds the path names, filenames, and other information about these foundation classes becomes a base project for the current project.

The advantages of base projects include reuse and consistency. They help you reuse components across various projects, and thus help ensure that your projects are consistent.

The base project window is shown in Figure 20.7.

FIGURE 20.7:

Selecting a base project

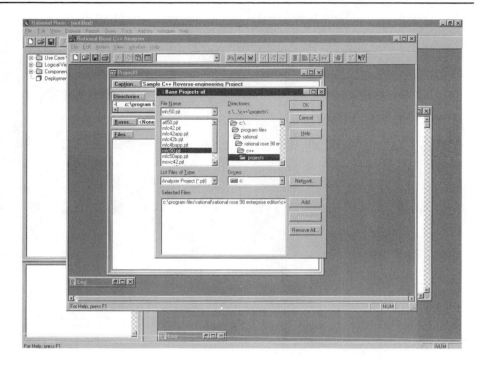

Base projects are optional when reverse engineering. To add a base project, locate the path and filename using the Directories and Filename fields and click the Add button to add it to the list. On the project window, the base project and its caption will display.

Step Seven: Select Files to Reverse Engineer

In this step, you identify all of the C++ files you wish to reverse engineer. To begin, select the Files button on the project window. The project files window will appear, as shown in Figure 20.8.

Using the Directory Structure treeview, select the directory that contains the files you wish to reverse engineer. By default, all .H, .HH, .HPP, .HXX, .CPP, .CXX, .CC, and .C files in that directory will be displayed in the Files Not in List (Filtered) list box. If you have placed values in the extension list, these extensions will be used instead of .H, .HH, .HPP, .HXX, .CPP, .CXX, .CC, and .C.

FIGURE 20.8:

Selecting files to reverse engineer

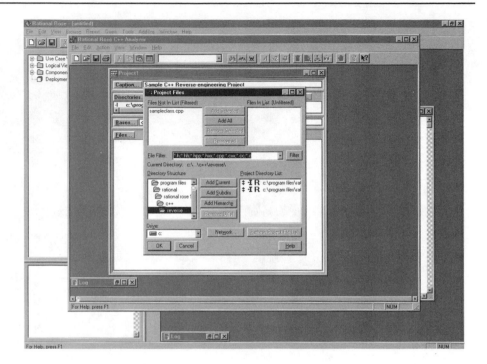

To select a file, first select it in the Files Not In List (Filtered) list box. Click the Add Selected button to move it into the Files In List (Filtered) list box or the Add All button to move all files into the list.

Repeat this process, selecting directories and files, until the Files In List (Filtered) list box includes all of the files you wish to reverse engineer. Press OK and the selected files will now be listed in the project window.

Step Eight: Analyze the Files

During the analysis step, design information will be extracted from all of the source-code files you selected in step 7. If errors are encountered, they will be written to the log window.

To analyze the files, first select them in the Files list box. To select all files, press Ctrl+A. Select Action ➤ Analyze or press F3 to start the analysis. As the files are being parsed and examined, the progress and any errors will be noted in the log.

The number of errors in each file will also be displayed in the Files list box. To view the errors for a file, check the log or double-click the file in the Files list box. The errors for that file will be displayed, as shown in Figure 20.9.

FIGURE 20.9:

Viewing errors in file analysis

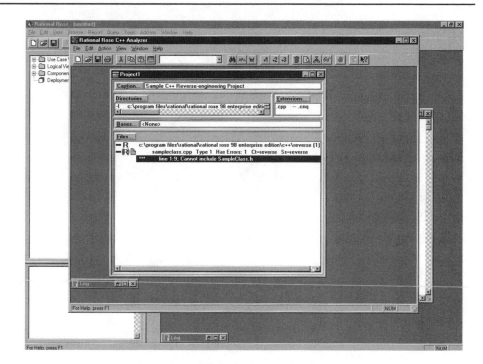

Step Nine: Set Export Options

Now that the code has been analyzed, this information can be used to create a Rose model. Just as there are a number of options to generate code from a Rose model, there are a number of reverse engineering options in the C++ Analyzer. To view and set these options, select Edit ➤ Export Options, or press Ctrl+R. The export options window is shown in Figure 20.10.

FIGURE 20.10:

Setting the export options

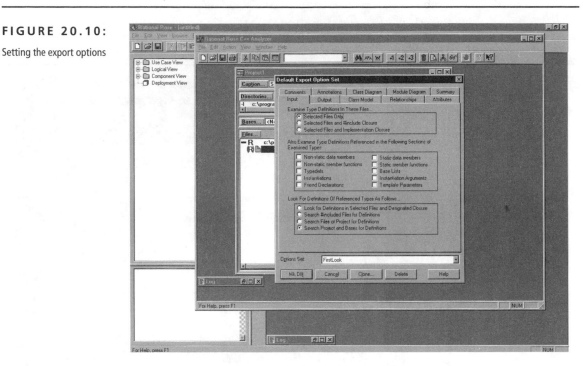

Before we examine the properties provided here, let's take a moment to discuss the three basic option sets that come with the C++ Analyzer. In the Options Set drop-down list box at the bottom of the export options screen, you can select FirstLook, RoundTrip, or DetailedAnalysis. If you select FirstLook, the default properties on the tabs in this window will be set to provide a higher-level look at the source code. If you select DetailedAnalysis, a more in-depth examination will be performed. Finally, if you select RoundTrip, the properties will be set to support round-trip engineering (reverse engineering existing code into a Rose model and forward engineering model changes into the code).

On the Input tab, you can set options that will determine what will be examined. The first set of radio buttons, labeled Examine Type Definitions In These Files, is used to set the files that will be examined. The options are:

Selected Files Only   Examines only the files in the Files list.

Selected Files And #include Closure   Examines the files in the list, as well as any files in #include directives (and files in #include directives of the #include directive files).

Selected Files And Implementation Closure   Examines the files in the list, any files in #include directives, and the implementation files associated with the files in the #include directives. Like the previous option, this option is recursive (files in #include directives of the #include directive files will be included).

The next set of options, Also Examine Type Definitions Referenced in the Following Sections of Examined Types, allows you to decide whether typedefs, static data members, and other C++ constructs will be included in the reverse engineering process.

Finally, you can set the search criteria for class definitions using the Look For Definitions Of Referenced Types As Follows check boxes.

On the Output tab, you control the Rose output settings, such as the model filename; whether UML, OMT, or Booch should be used as the notation; and whether Class diagrams should be created. The Output tab is shown in Figure 20.11.

FIGURE 20.11:

Setting the output options

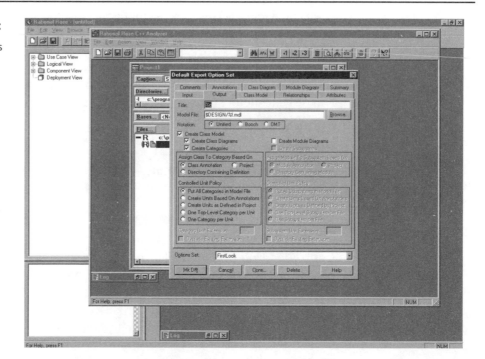

Other options on this window include:

Title Sets the title to use on the generated diagrams, with the following symbols:

%c The name of the project caption

%d The simple name of the directory that contains the project

%e The full name of the directory that contains the project

%f The simple name generated from the selected File List entries

If a single file is selected, the resulting name is the simple name of the selected file. If multiple files are selected, and every selected file is assigned to the same category, then the resulting name is the name of the category. Otherwise, the resulting name is the name of the project.

%p Replaced by the project name

Create Class Model Allows the generation of classes into the reverse-engineered model. The above symbols can also be used.

Create Class Diagrams Determines whether or not Class diagrams are generated in the Rose model.

Create Categories Determines whether or not Logical view packages will be generated.

Create Module Diagrams Controls whether or not Component diagrams will be created.

Create Subsystems Determines whether or not Component view packages will be created.

Assign Class To Category Based On Determines how the classes will be grouped into packages.

Controlled Unit Policy Determines whether or not the Logical view packages will be set up as controlled units in Rose.

Assign Module To Subsystem Based On Determines how components will be grouped into packages.

Controlled Unit Policy Determines whether or not the Component view packages will be set up as controlled units in Rose.

On the Class Model tab, you can set the properties that control which classes, templates, template instantiations, TypeDefs, and enumerations will be generated. These are fine-tuning options you can set before you generate the model. The Class Model tab is shown in Figure 20.12.

FIGURE 20.12:

Setting the class options

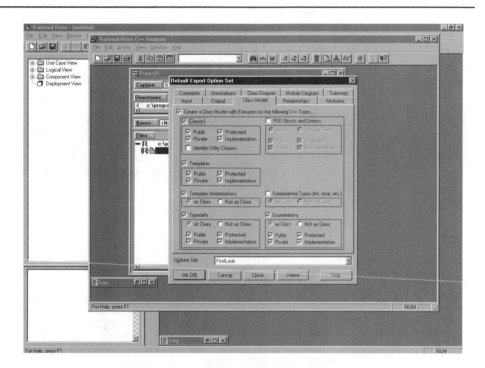

The options on this tab are:

Create a Class Model With Elements For The Following C++ Types
Controls whether classes, TypeDefs, and the other C++ constructs will be generated in the model

Classes   Controls whether classes are generated as classes in the model

Templates   Controls whether templates are generated as classes in the model

Template Instantiations   Controls whether template instantiations are generated as classes in the model

Typedefs   Controls whether TypeDefs are generated as classes in the model

POD Structs And Unions   Controls whether structures and unions are generated as classes in the model

Fundamental Types (int, char, etc.)   Controls whether fundamental types are generated as classes in the model

Enumerations   Controls whether enumerations are generated as classes in the model

The Relationships tab is used to control how relationships are generated in the Rose model. The Relationships tab is shown in Figure 20.13.

FIGURE 20.13:

Setting the relationship options

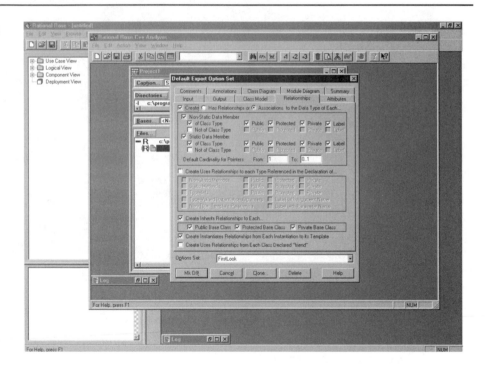

The options on this tab are:

Create   Determines whether data members will be modeled as relationships

Has Relationships or Associations   Controls whether associations or aggregations will be created

Non-Static Data Member   Controls whether nonstatic C++ data members are represented in the generated model

Static Data Member   Controls whether static C++ data members are represented in the generated model

Create Uses Relationships To Each Type Referenced In The Declaration of   Controls when uses relationships are created in the model for various types of constructs

Create Inherits Relationships To Each   Controls the generalization relationships that will be created in the model

Create Instantiates Relationships From Each Instantiation To Its Template   Controls whether instantiates relationships will be created in the model

Create Uses Relationships From Each Class Declared "friend"   Controls whether relationships will be set up between classes with friend visibility

The Attributes tab controls how attributes and operations are generated in the Rose model. The tab is shown in Figure 20.14.

FIGURE 20.14:

Setting the attribute options

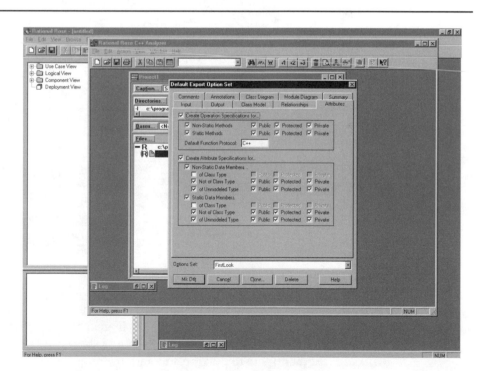

The properties you can set using this tab include the following:

Create Operation Specifications For   Controls the C++ constructs that will generate operations in the Rose model

Create Attribute Specifications For   Controls the C++ constructs that will generate attributes in the Rose model

The Comments tab, as shown in Figure 20.15, lets you specify where in the code the comments lie. With this information, the C++ Analyzer can pull the comments into the documentation window of Rose. In the Rose model, you can use the documentation window to view the comments for various model elements.

FIGURE 20.15:

Setting comments options

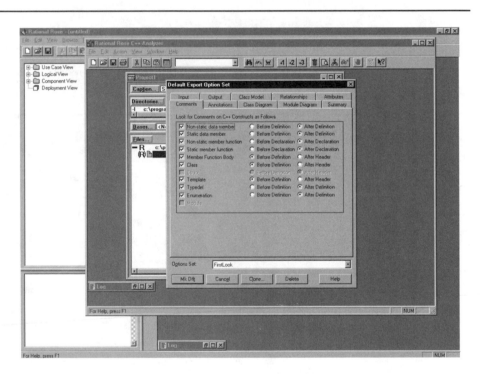

The Annotations tab controls whether annotation information is pulled into the documentation window of Rose for various model elements. Annotations are the comments and identifiers that Rose places in generated code to support round-trip engineering. Using the Annotations tab, as shown in Figure 20.16, you can decide whether or not to pull the annotations for operations, relationships, data members, and other code elements into the Rose model, and where they should be located.

FIGURE 20.16:

Setting annotations options

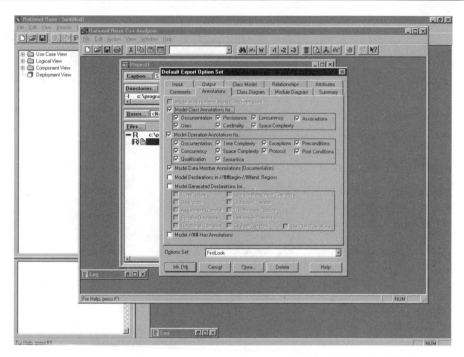

The Class Diagrams tab controls whether or not Class diagrams will be generated and also controls what will be displayed on these diagrams. The Class Diagrams tab is shown in Figure 20.17.

The options that are available on this tab include:

Create Class Diagrams   Controls whether or not Class diagrams will be generated

Draw Categories   Controls whether packages will be included on the Class diagrams

Diagram Name   Sets the name of the generated Class diagram

Draw Model Elements Derived From The Following Constructs   Controls which elements (classes, TypeDefs, enumerations, etc.) will be displayed on the Class diagram

Draw Relationships Derived From Type References In The Following Constructs   Controls whether relationships derived from member variables and other constructs should be displayed on the Class diagram

FIGURE 20.17:

Setting Class diagram
options

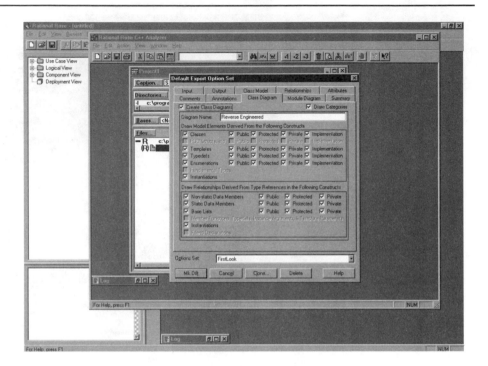

The Module Diagram tab is used to control the options that relate to the Component diagram that can be generated during the reverse engineering process. The Module Diagram tab is shown in Figure 20.18.

The options available on this tab include:

Create Module Diagrams   Controls whether or not a Component diagram will be generated.

Diagram Name   Sets the name of the generated Component diagram.

Derive Module Names From Annotations   Controls whether component names are contained in the annotations that were added during the original code generation from Rose or whether the component names should be derived from the filenames.

Draw Visibility Relationships For   Controls whether relationships for #include directives and other C++ constructs should be labeled on the Component diagram. If so, this section also gives you a place to enter the label to use for the construct.

Draw Subsystems Controls whether Component view packages appear on the diagram.

Setting Component view diagram options

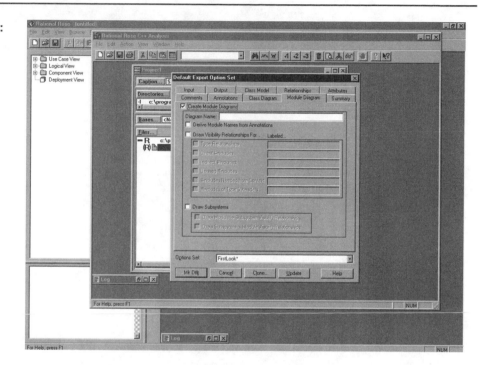

Finally, the Summary tab will show you the values of the options in all of the other tabs. The Summary tab is shown in Figure 20.19.

Step Ten: Export to Rose

Your final step is to export the analyzed files to a Rose model. To do so, Select Action ➤ Export to Rose, or press F8. The Export To Rose dialog box will appear, as shown in Figure 20.20.

This dialog box will allow you to set the name of the generated Rose model, the caption of the project, and the options set to use. It will also give you an overview of the options by listing them in the Summary Of Options area. To generate the model, click OK on this window. If a model with the specified filename already exists, the Analyzer will ask whether to overwrite it.

FIGURE 20.19:

Viewing a summary of the reverse engineering

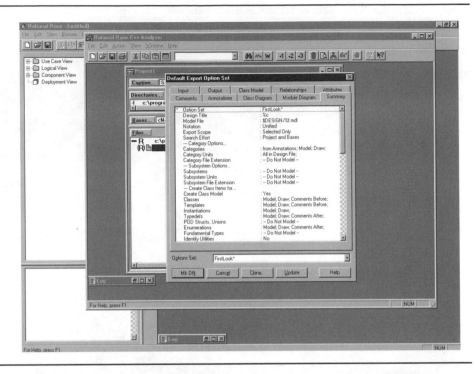

FIGURE 20.20:

Exporting a project to Rose

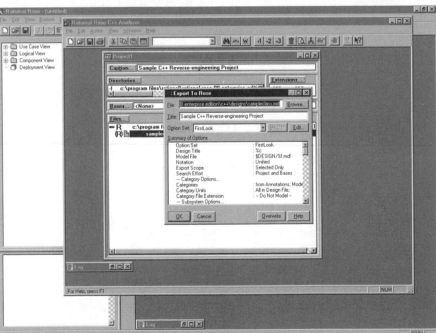

Steps in Reverse Engineering Visual C++

In this section, we'll examine the steps needed to reverse engineer your Visual C++ code into a Rose model. There are two possibilities for the reverse engineering process: creating a new model from your Visual C++ code and updating an existing model.

Step One: Begin the Reverse Engineering Wizard

The reverse engineering of Visual C++ code is wizard-driven. The wizard will walk you through all of the steps needed to reverse engineer your code. To begin the wizard, select Tools ➤ Visual C++ ➤ Update Model from Code.

The Model Update Tool Welcome screen will appear, as shown in Figure 20.21.

FIGURE 20.21:

Visual C++ Model Update Tool Welcome screen

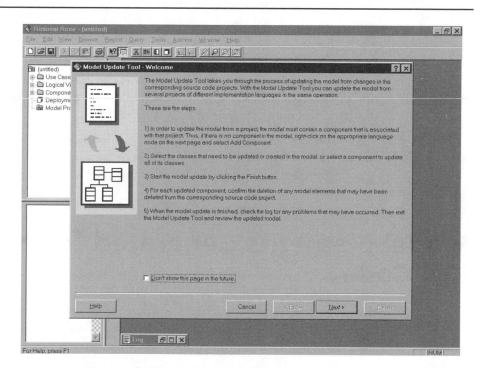

Step Two: Select the Project(s) to Reverse Engineer

Once you've started the wizard, the next screen you will see is the Select Components and Classes window. A component must exist in the Rose model and be associated with a VC++ project. If no components exist, then you can create a component by right-clicking the language node and selecting Add Component. If components exist, then select the classes or components you wish to reverse engineer. Some of the components may have question marks next to them. These are incomplete components that you cannot reverse engineer.

Once you have selected all of the classes and/or components you wish to reverse engineer, click Next to continue.

Step Three: Review and Finish

In this step, you can view the classes and components you plan to reverse engineer. If you want to make any changes, select Back to go back to the Select Components and Classes window. Otherwise, select Finish to reverse engineer the selected components and classes into your Rose model.

As you reverse engineer, any new classes that are in the code but not in the model will be added to the Rose model. Likewise, any changes to the classes in the code will now be reflected in the model.

When the reverse engineering process has finished, the results will be displayed on the summary page. Any errors or warnings from the reverse engineering process will be displayed, along with a list of what was reverse engineered.

Model Elements Generated from C++ Code

In this section, we'll examine how various pieces of C++ code appear in the generated Rose model. Specifically, we'll look at classes, data members, member functions, friend declarations, and class templates.

When reverse engineering, the Analyzer will use both the information in the code and the selections you made in the reverse engineering options screen. These options will determine what, specifically, will be created for each C++ construct.

Classes

Each class in your C++ code will be represented as a class in the model. By default, the class will also appear on a generated Class diagram and a package will be created for the class.

Let's look at the model generated when reverse engineering the following C++ header file: \reverse\SampleClass.h

```
class SampleClass {
    int a, b, c;
protected:
    int d, e, f;
};
```

In the reverse engineering process, the Analyzer parses this file and determines which classes, attributes, operations, and other model elements should be created. Figure 20.22 shows the model that was generated for the above class.

FIGURE 20.22:

Reverse engineering a class

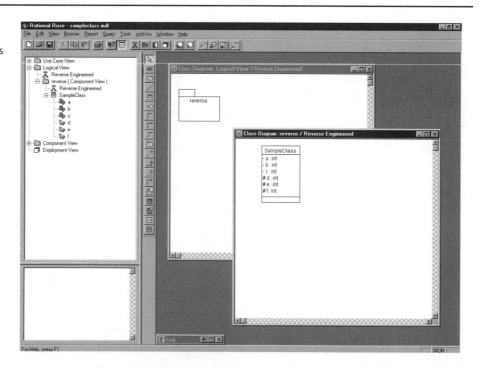

The elements that are generated in the model include:

- The class itself, which is created in the Logical view.

- Attributes and operations of the class, which we'll discuss in the following sections.

- A Logical view package that contains the class. The name of this package will be the name of the directory that contained the source code. In this example, the `sampleclass.cpp` file was contained in a directory called `reverse`.

- A Class diagram that shows the reverse engineered classes. By default, the name of this diagram will be Reverse Engineered. You can change the diagram name by changing the reverse engineering properties in the C++ Analyzer.

- A Package diagram that shows the packages of classes that were reverse engineered. The default name of this diagram is Reverse Engineered, but you can change it using the reverse engineering properties.

Data Members

Each of the data members in the class will be represented as either an attribute or a relationship in the generated model. If the data type of the data member is another class in the model, as in the following, it will appear as an aggregation relationship. If the data type is not represented as another class in the model, the data member will appear as an attribute.

```
#include Class_B.h

class Class_A {
    int x;
    Class_B the_class_b;
};

class Class_B {
    int a, b, c;
};
```

Figure 20.23 shows the model that was generated when reverse engineering the above two classes. As you can see, the data members a, b, and c in Class_B were generated as attributes, because the class int was not in the model. However, the data member the_Class_b, which was contained in Class_A, appeared as an aggregation by-value relationship. If the the_Class_B data member of Class_A had been a pointer to Class_B, the relationship generated would have been a by-reference relationship.

If a data member is marked static in the code, it will also be marked static in the generated Rose model.

FIGURE 20.23:

Reverse engineering data members

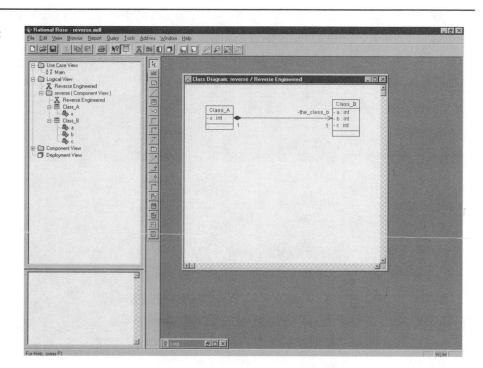

Member Functions

Member functions are generated as operations in the Rose model. If an argument or return type of a function uses another class in the model as a data type, the appropriate relationships will also be generated, as they were for data members.

In the following example, the Analyzer will generate a class called Sample-Class, which will include a protected operation called foo. Figure 20.24 shows the model that was generated from this class.

```
class SampleClass {
   int a, b, c;
protected:
   int d, e, f;
   int foo (int parameter1) { };
};
```

FIGURE 20.24:

Reverse engineering
member functions

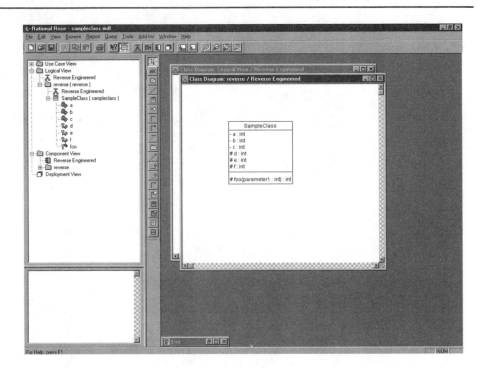

Class Friend Declarations

A friend declaration in your C++ code will generate as a dependency in the Rose model.

In the following example, a dependency relationship will be created between Class_B and Class_A to support the friend declaration. Figure 20.25 shows the model that was created for these two classes.

```
#include Class_B.h

class Class_A {
   int x;
   friend Class_B;

};

class Class_B {
   int a, b, c;
};
```

FIGURE 20.25:

Reverse engineering friend
declarations

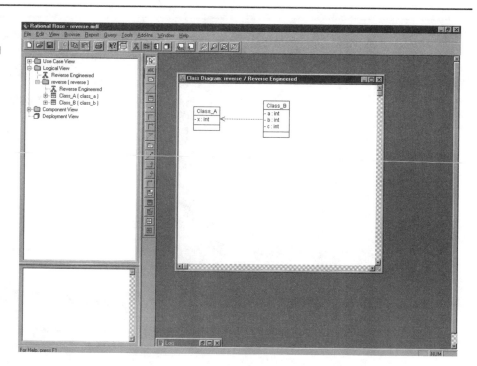

Class Templates

A class template in your C++ code will appear as a parameterized class in the
Rose model. Below, we have some sample code for a Stack class. In the Rose
model, this will appear as a parameterized class, with a dependency relationship
to the Item class.

```
template<class Item> class Stack {
   Item *theitem;
   int size;
public:
   Stack (int size);
   ~Stack();
   void push (const Item&);
   Item& Pop();
};
```

Figure 20.26 shows the Rose model that was created. As you can see, there was a dependency relationship created between the Stack class and the Item class.

FIGURE 20.26:

Reverse engineering a class template

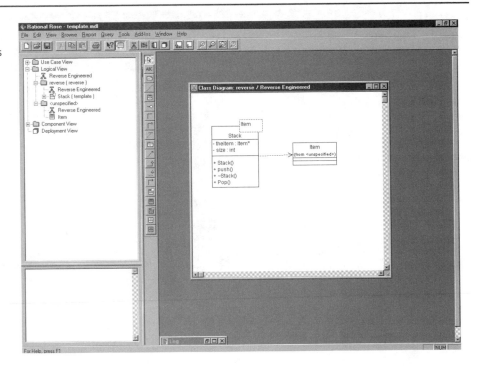

Derived Classes

An inheritance relationship in the C++ code will be modeled using a generalization relationship in Rose. The Analyzer will reverse engineer both the ancestor and the descendant classes, and will place them on a Class diagram.

Let's examine the model created for the following classes:

```cpp
class Parentclass {
    int a, b, c;

};
#include Parentclass.h

class Childclass : public Parentclass {
    int x, y, z;

};
```

Figure 20.27 shows the Rose model that was generated for the above code. As you can see, the inheritance relationship in the code was generated in the object model as well.

FIGURE 20.27:

Reverse engineering a derived class

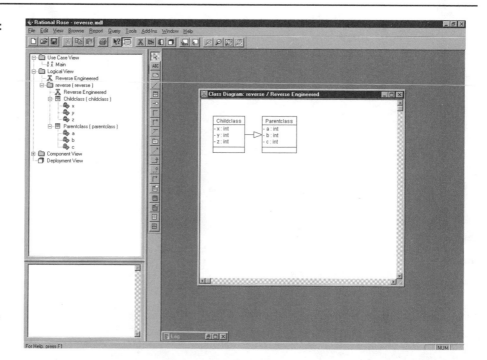

Summary

In this chapter, we examined how C++ code can be reverse engineered into Rose. By following the steps that were outlined in this chapter, you can examine the architecture of an existing C++ application.

Once the files have been reverse engineered into Rose, you can make any needed changes to the model. For example, you may be re-engineering or re-architecting an existing application. The reverse engineering capabilities will help you see the structure of the existing code. You can then make any needed changes and regenerate the code through the forward engineering capabilities of Rose. Because Rose supports round-trip engineering, it will not overwrite the work you've already put into the code.

Reverse Engineering
with Java

- Importing the Java Developer's Kit in Rose 98

- Selecting files to reverse engineer

- Reverse engineering Java code intro your Rose mode

- Mapping between Java constructs and the Rose model

In this chapter, we'll take a look at how to reverse engineer Java code into Rose. We'll first discuss the steps involved in reverse engineering, and then take a close look at specifically what gets pulled into Rose.

Before you reverse engineer, you may want to load the Java Developer's Kit (JDK) into your Rose model. This will make the fundamental Java classes and data types available to the other classes in your model. In Rose 98, you can load the JDK by selecting Tools ➤ Java ➤ Import JDK 1.1X. In Rose 98i, you can use the Framework wizard to import the JDK framework. After you've completed this step, the Java classes will be available in a Java package in the Logical view. Figure 21.1 shows the browser as it will appear after importing the JDK.

FIGURE 21.1:

Importing the JDK in Rose 98

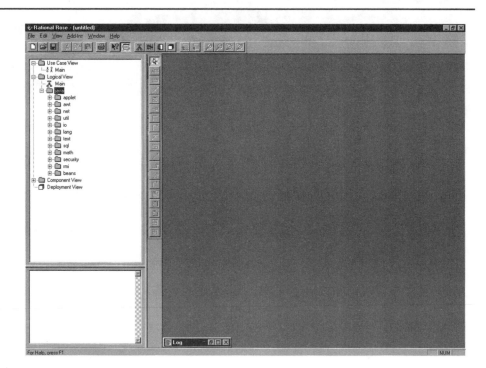

Steps in Reverse Engineering

In this section, we'll go through each of the steps needed to reverse engineer Java code. The information in your code will be imported directly into the Rose model that is currently open.

1. To begin the process, select Tools ➤ Java ➤ Reverse Engineer Java. Rose will display the Java Reverse Engineering window, as shown in Figure 21.2. Using this window, you can select the files you want to reverse engineer. If you instead see a message that the CLASSPATH environment variable is not set, there is another step that you must take first. Create an environment variable called CLASSPATH, and set this variable to the directory or directories where the Java class files are stored.

FIGURE 21.2:

Java Reverse Engineer window

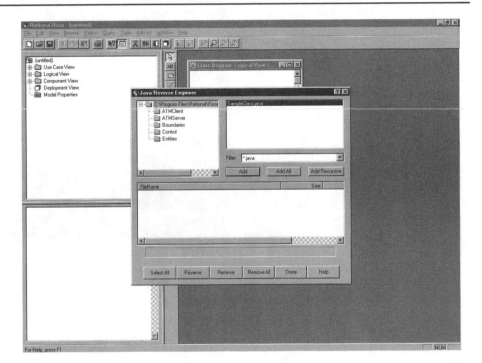

2. From the directory tree structure, select the directory that contains the files you want to reverse engineer. As you change directories, the available files will appear in the list box in the upper-right area of the window, as we saw in Figure 21.2.

3. Select the files you wish to reverse engineer and press the Add button. The files will now appear in the lower section of the window, as shown in Figure 21.3.

FIGURE 21.3:

Selecting files to reverse engineer

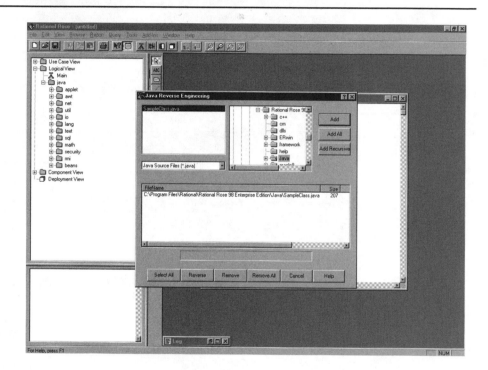

4. Once all needed files have been added to the bottom section of the windows, click to select the files you wish to reverse engineer (or press the Select All button to reverse engineer them all), and click the Reverse button. If there are any errors, they will be written to the log window.

Model Elements Generated from Java Code

In this section, we'll discuss the model elements that are generated from the various constructs in Java. For example, we'll see how a class in a .JAVA file maps to a class in your Rose model.

First, however, let's take a quick look at the mapping between Java constructs and the Rose model. Table 21.1 shows how various types of Java code will be generated in Rose.

TABLE 21.1: Java to Rose Mapping

Java Construct	Rose Notation
Class	Class
Method	Operation
Attribute	Attributes and relationships
Interface	Class with interface stereotype
Package	Package
Inheritance Relationship	Generalization

Classes

Let's begin by looking at classes. Each class in your Java code will be represented as a class in the model. The class will be created in a Logical view package, and a corresponding component will be created in a Component view package. Let's look at the model generated when reverse engineering this class:

```
// Source file: JavaClasses/SampleClass.java

package JavaClasses;

public class SampleClass {
```

```
        private int attribute1;

        SampleClass() {
        }

        public int operation1() {
        }
    }
```

In this example, Rose will create a class called SampleClass, which will have one attribute and two operations. Figure 21.4 shows the Rose model that was created for this class.

FIGURE 21.4:

Reverse engineering a class

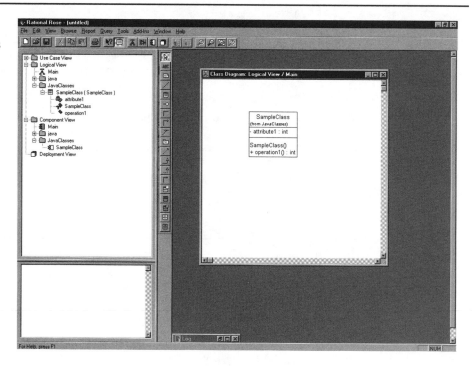

The elements that are generated in the model include:

- The class itself, which is created in the Logical view.

- Attributes and operations of the class, which we'll discuss in the following sections.

- A Logical view package that contains the class. This package will get its name from the package statement in the source-code file.

- A component in the Component view for the class.

- A Component view package for the component.

Attributes

Each of the attributes in the source code will be represented as either an attribute or a relationship in the generated model. If the data type of the data member is another class in the model, it will appear as an association relationship. If the data type is not represented as another class in the model, the data member will appear as an attribute.

Let's look at two examples of attributes. One will be generated as an attribute and the other as an association relationship.

```
// Source file: JavaClasses/Class_A.java

package JavaClasses;

import java.javaclasses.class_B;

public class Class_A {
    private int attribute1;
    public Class_B the_Class_B;

    Class_A() {
    }
}

// Source file: JavaClasses/Class_B.java

package JavaClasses;

public class Class_B {
    private int attribute2;

    Class_B() {
     }
}
```

As you can see in Figure 21.5, both of the classes were generated in the Rose model. In Class_A, the attribute1 attribute was simply created as an attribute in the generated class, along with information about its visibility and data type. However, the the_Class_B attribute was generated as a relationship between Class_A and Class_B.

FIGURE 21.5:

Reverse engineering attributes and association relationships

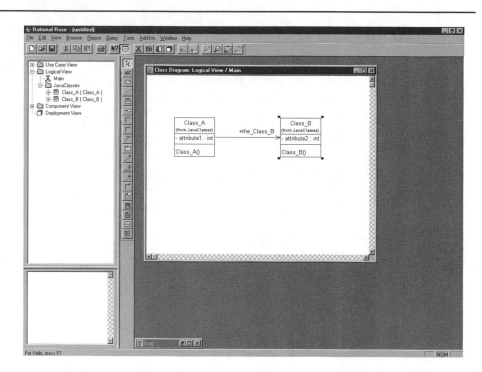

In this example, there was a simple, one-to-one relationship between Class_A and Class_B. When reverse engineering Java code, Rose will examine the multiplicity and add it to the relationship. Let's take another look at the previous example, but this time with a multiplicity greater than one. We'll examine the model created for these two classes:

```
// Source file: JavaClasses/Class_A.java

package JavaClasses;

import java.javaclasses.class_B;
```

```
public class Class_A {
    private int attribute1;
    public Class_B the_Class_B[];

      Class_A() {
    }
}

// Source file: JavaClasses/Class_B.java

package JavaClasses;

public class Class_B {
    private int attribute2;

    Class_B() {
    }
}
```

Figure 21.6 shows the Rose model that was generated for these two classes.

FIGURE 21.6:

Reverse engineering
relationships with a
multiplicity greater
than one

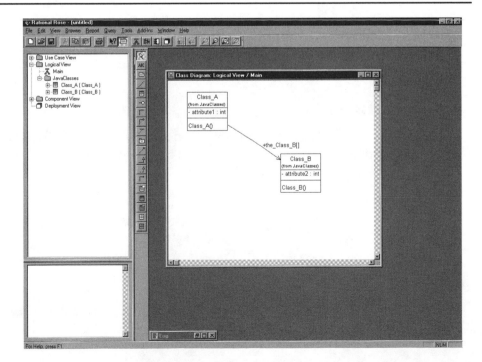

Methods

Just as each of the attributes in the code are read in, each of the methods in the code will be included in the Rose model. The method name, visibility, parameters, parameter data types, and return type will all be examined by Rose and included in the generated model. Let's examine the model created for the following Java class:

```
// Source file: JavaClasses/SampleClass.java

package JavaClasses;

public class SampleClass {
    private int attribute1;
    private int attribute2;

    SampleClass() {
    }

    public int operation1(int parameter1) {
    }
}
```

As you can see in Figure 21.7, the constructor and the operation1 method are both reverse engineered into the Rose model.

Interfaces

An interface in Java will be pulled into the Rose model as a class with a stereotype of interface. For example, let's look at the model generated for the following interface:

```
// Source file: SampleInterface.java

public interface SampleInterface {

    public int operation1();
}
```

In this example, the interface SampleInterface is generated as a class in the Rose model. Figure 21.8 shows the class that is generated.

FIGURE 21.7:

Reverse engineering a Java
constructor and method

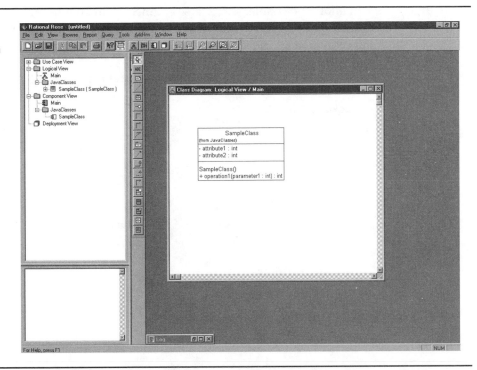

FIGURE 21.8:

Reverse engineering
interfaces

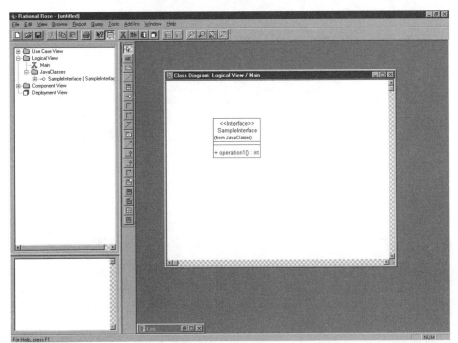

In another example, we reverse engineer both an interface and a class that implements that interface. Let's look at the model that is generated for the following two classes:

```java
// Source file: JavaClasses/SampleInterface.java

package JavaClasses;

public interface SampleInterface {

    public int operation1();
}

// Source file: JavaClasses/SampleClass.java


package JavaClasses;

import java.javaclasses.sampleinterface;

public class SampleClass implements SampleInterface{


    SampleClass() {
    }


    public int operation1() {
    }
}
```

The model that was generated from these two classes is shown in Figure 21.9.

FIGURE 21.9:

Reverse engineering an interface and class

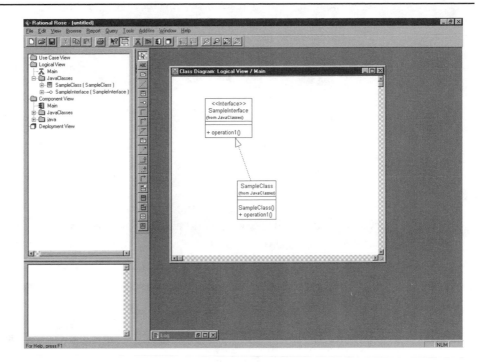

As you can see, Rose will place a realizes relationship between the class and the interface. Because the Java portion of Rose understands the concept of an interface, you can also regenerate each of these classes, after making any needed changes.

Inheritance Relationships

An inheritance relationship in your Java source code will be modeled using a generalization relationship in Rose, as shown below.

```
// Source file: JavaClasses/Parentclass.java

package JavaClasses;

public class Parentclass {
    private int attribute1;

    Parentclass() {
    }
}
```

```
// Source file: JavaClasses/Childclass.java

package JavaClasses;

import java.javaclasses.parentclass;

public class Childclass extends Parentclass {
    private int attribute2;

    Childclass() {
    }
}
```

Figure 21.10 shows the Rose model that was generated for the above code. As you can see, both the parent and child classes were generated in the Rose model. In addition, a generalization relationship was added between these two classes.

FIGURE 21.10:

Reverse engineering inheritance relationships

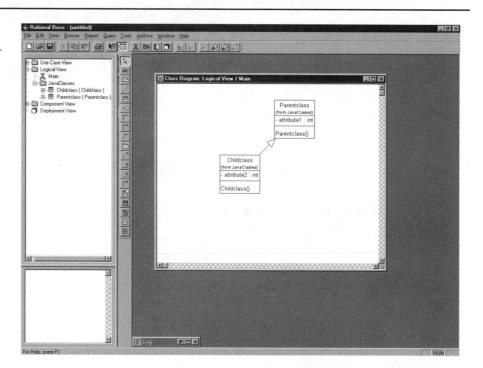

Summary

In this chapter, we discussed the reverse engineering process for Java code and examined the mapping from Java to UML. By reverse engineering existing code, you can get a detailed understanding of the structure of an existing system. The forward and reverse engineering capabilities of Rose can help you be sure the model and the code remain consistent.

In the next chapter, we'll take a look at how you can reverse engineer existing Visual Basic code. Rose provides a wizard-driven reverse engineering process for Visual Basic that will help you take an existing VB application and generate a model for it. Once you have the model, you can examine the architecture of your VB application, make changes to the model, and regenerate VB code from Rose.

CHAPTER
TWENTY-TWO

Reverse Engineering with Visual Basic

- Reverse engineering Visual Basic code using the Framework Wizard

- Selecting components and classes to reverse engineer

- Understanding how each type of Visual Basic construct is represented in the Rose model

22

Using Rose, you can reverse engineer information from a Visual Basic project into a UML model. You can then view the architecture of your existing system, make any changes to the model, and regenerate code if necessary.

As part of the reverse engineering process, Rose brings in information about Visual Basic classes, attributes, operations, and other constructs. Once the reverse engineering process is complete, you will have:

- Classes
- Class diagrams
- Packages
- Components
- Attributes
- Operations
- Association relationships
- Aggregation relationships
- Generalization relationships

The Visual Basic reverse engineering process is wizard-driven. Rose includes a Model Update tool that automates much of the reverse engineering. In this chapter, we'll walk through the wizard and discuss how to reverse engineer Visual Basic code.

Steps in Reverse Engineering

To reverse engineer Visual Basic code, begin by using the Framework Wizard to import the Visual Basic types, such as label and text, for the appropriate version into the Rose model. To start the wizard, select Tools ➢ Visual Basic ➢ Update Model from Code. You will see the welcome screen shown in Figure 22.1.

FIGURE 22.1:

The Model Update Wizard Welcome screen

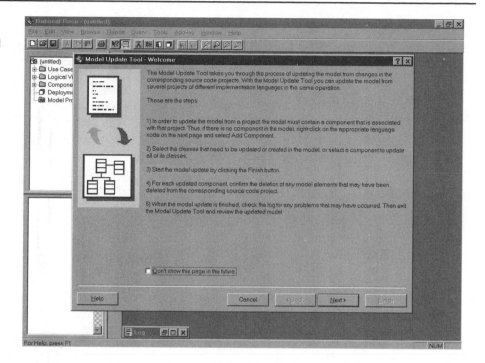

Next, select the Visual Basic components and classes to use. If the model does not contain a Visual Basic component, you can create one by selecting the Add Component button shown in Figure 22.2. If you create a new component, the Visual Basic project will be reverse engineered into it. If you select an existing component, the wizard will synchronize the model to reflect any changes in the code.

After selecting the components and classes to update, the wizard will present the finish screen shown in Figure 22.3. This screen will list the classes and components to be updated and provides a final confirmation before the operation begins. Click Finish to reverse engineer the project.

FIGURE 22.2:

Selecting components and classes to reverse engineer

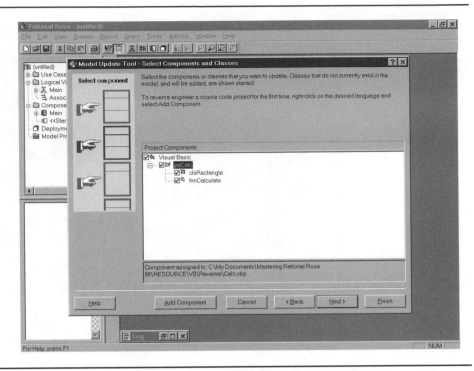

FIGURE 22.3:

The Model Update Wizard Finish screen

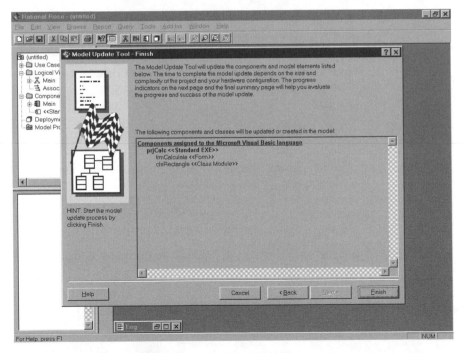

After the reverse engineering is complete, the summary screen in Figure 22.4 will be displayed. The summary gives a record of which components were reverse engineered. Click Close to close the summary and complete the process.

FIGURE 22.4:

Reverse Engineer Model Update Tool Summary screen

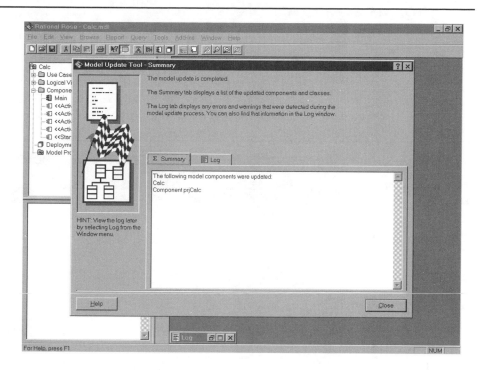

Model Elements Generated from Visual Basic Code

We've looked at the steps needed to reverse engineer Visual Basic code into Rational Rose; now, we'll examine how each type of Visual Basic construct is represented in the Rose model.

Most of the Visual Basic elements will be reverse engineered as stereotyped classes. Forms, for example, will be reverse engineered as classes with the stereotype Form. Other Visual Basic constructs will be reverse engineered as interfaces.

The controls on the form will be reverse engineered as interfaces called CommandButton, TextBox, etc. In this section, we'll look at some of these examples.

Forms and Controls

A Visual Basic form will be reverse engineered as a class with a stereotype of Form. All of the variables on the form will be represented as attributes in the class. Information about the variable's data type, default value, and visibility will also be included in the Rose model.

Figure 22.5 shows a Visual Basic form, called frmCalculate.

FIGURE 22.5:

frmCalculate Visual Basic form

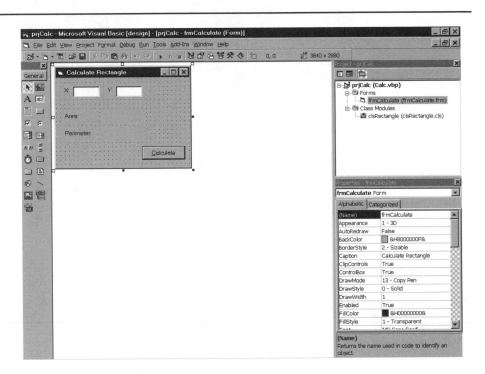

Figure 22.6 shows the results of reverse engineering this form into Rose. As you can see, all of the methods of the form were created as operations in Rose. All variables and contained controls on the form will be displayed as association relationships. In this example, our form had a single variable, M_rectangle, of type clsRectangle. When the code was reverse engineered, the variable was modeled

as an association relationship between the frmCalculate class and the clsRectangle class. The name of the association is the same as the name of the variable; in this case, the association is named M_rectangle.

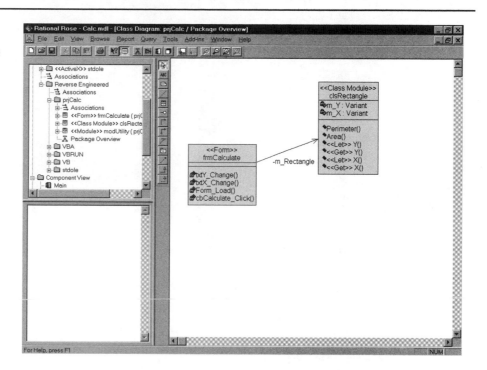

The controls on the form will also be reverse engineered. In the example above, there were nine controls: four labels for the X, Y, Area, and Parameter fields; four text boxes for the X, Y, Area, and Parameter fields; and one command button. Each of the types of controls (command buttons, labels, etc.) is displayed as an interface on the diagram. To show that the control has been placed on the form, Rose uses an aggregation relationship, as shown in Figure 22.7. The role name in the aggregation relationship will be taken from the name of the control on the form. For example, our command button was named cbCalculate in Visual Basic, so the role name cbCalculate is used in Rose. The stereotype of the aggregation relationship will be ContainedControl for all contained controls.

FIGURE 22.7:

Controls on a form in a
Rose model

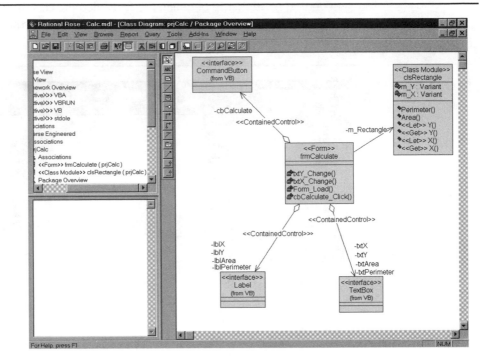

Class Modules

When you reverse engineer a Visual Basic class module, it will be represented in
the Rose model as a class with the stereotype of Class Module. Any methods or
events associated with the class module will be shown as stereotyped operations.
Any variables in the class module will be shown as association relationships to
other classes. Figure 22.8 shows a Visual Basic class module, clsRectangle.

FIGURE 22.8:

Sample Visual Basic class module

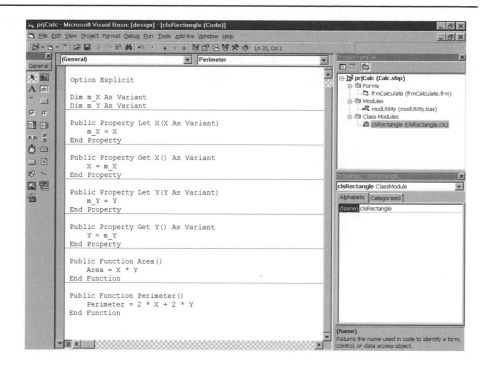

When this class module was reverse engineered, information about its attributes, operations, and relationships was also reverse engineered. Figure 22.9 shows this class in the Rose model. As you can see in this example, Rose will use the Set, Let, and Get keywords to assign a stereotype of Set, Let, or Get to the appropriate operations.

When reverse engineering, Rose will examine the comments directly preceding a model element in the code. For example, when reverse engineering a property, Rose will use the comments directly preceding the property declaration. Any comments that are read by the reverse engineering process will be placed in the Documentation window for the appropriate model element.

FIGURE 22.9:

Class Module in a Rose model

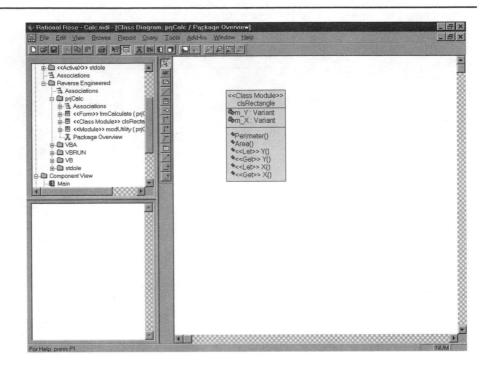

Modules

In Rose, all operations must be contained within a class. Therefore, Visual Basic modules are imported into Rose using a Utility class. Utility classes contain collections of related operations, and can be used to house global variables and functions.

Each module will be represented in Rose as a class with a stereotype of Module. Figure 22.10 shows an example of a module that was reverse engineered into Rose.

FIGURE 22.10:

Visual Basic module in
Rose model

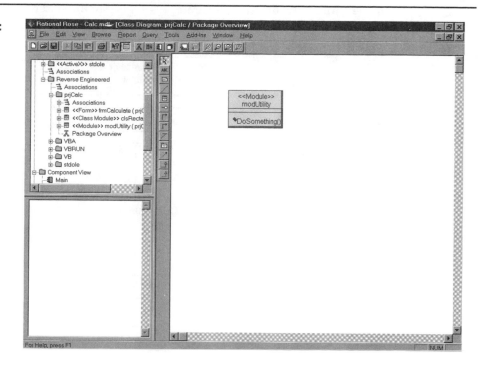

Implements Statements

The implements statement in Visual Basic is a partial implementation of inheritance. Therefore, the implements statement will become a generalization in the model. For example, the declaration of child class implements parent below:

```
Option Base 0
Option Explicit
•    Implements Parent


Private mParentObject As New Parent
```

The following diagram illustrates how this parent-child relationship is modeled in Rose. A generalization is modeled to show the use of the implements statement.

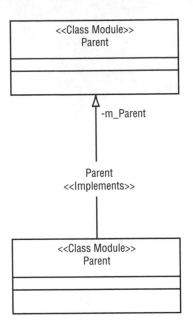

Summary

In this chapter, we examined the steps required to reverse engineer a Visual Basic project into your Rose model. Most objects will translate directly into a stereo-typed class in Rose. In addition, Rose will capture information about the variables, functions, and relationships in the code. You can then change the model and forward engineer the changes back into the Visual Basic project.

In the next chapter, we'll examine the reverse engineering process for Power-Builder. As with C++, Java, and Visual Basic, Rose can generate a UML model from existing code in PowerBuilder. Each of the windows, datawindows, and other PowerBuilder objects will be modeled as a class. In the next chapter, we'll take a look at this process in detail.

Reverse Engineering with PowerBuilder

■ Select files and classes to reverse engineer

■ Reverse engineering Rose model elements from various PowerBuilder constructs

■ Reverse engineering information about the attributes, operations, and relationships of each class

The PowerBuilder Link for Rational Rose includes both code generation and reverse engineering functionality. With code generation, you can create some skeletal code for a new system or some modified code for an existing system. Using the reverse engineering functionality, you can analyze the structure of an existing PowerBuilder system.

The add-in supports reverse engineering of PowerBuilder 5, 6, and 6 code. After the reverse engineering is complete, you will have:

- Classes

- Class diagrams

- Packages

- Components

- Attributes

- Operations

- Association relationships

- Aggregation relationships

- Generalization relationships

In this chapter, we'll examine the model that is created when you reverse engineer PowerBuilder code. The PowerBuilder add-in includes many stereotypes; each PowerBuilder construct has a corresponding stereotype in Rose. Table 23.1 lists the PowerBuilder stereotypes and the corresponding Rose stereotypes.

TABLE 23.1: PowerBuilder Stereotypes

Stereotype	Applies to Model Element	PowerBuilder Type
Application	Class	Application object
Menu	Class	PowerBuilder menu
Structure	Class	PowerBuilder structure
System Class	Class	PowerBuilder system class
User Defined Object	Class	User object

Continued on next page

TABLE 23.1 CONTINUED: PowerBuilder Stereotypes

Stereotype	Applies to Model Element	PowerBuilder Type
Window	Class	Window
Control	Attribute	PowerBuilder control (button, text box, etc.)
Field	Attribute	Structure element
Property	Attribute	PowerBuilder object property
Variable	Attribute	Instance variable
EventExtend	Operation	Event extended from ancestor
EventOverride	Operation	Event that overrides ancestor
EventOverrideInternal	Operation	Event that overrides ancestor and is not visible in PowerBuilder (create and destroy, for example)
Function	Operation	PowerBuilder function
Subroutine	Operation	PowerBuilder subroutine
UserEvent	Operation	User-defined event

Using these stereotypes, you can model the various PowerBuilder constructs in Rose. Table 23.2 lists the PowerBuilder entities and how each is represented in the Rose model.

TABLE 23.2: PowerBuilder to UML Mapping

PowerBuilder Element	Rose Element
Class	Stereotyped class
PBL	Component (Subprogram Specification or Main Program)
Application Object	Class with <<Application>> stereotype
Window	Class with <<Window>> stereotype
Nonvisual User Object	Class with <<User Defined Object>> stereotype

Continued on next page

TABLE 23.2 CONTINUED: PowerBuilder to UML Mapping

PowerBuilder Element	Rose Element
Menu	Class with <<Menu>> stereotype
Control (button, datawindow control, etc.)	Class with <<Control>> stereotype
Datawindow	Class with <<Data Window>> stereotype
Global Function	Class with <<Function>> stereotype
Query	Class with <<Query>> stereotype
Structure	Class with <<Structure>> stereotype
Shared Variable	Attribute or association with static flag set to True
Non-shared Variable	Attribute or association with static flag set to False
Window or User Object Function	Attribute with <<Function>> stereotype
Event	Operation with <<EventOverride>> or <<EventOverrideInternal>> stereotype
User Event	Operation with <<EventUser>> stereotype

Steps in Reverse Engineering

Many PowerBuilder elements, such as windows and Nonvisual User objects, can be created in Rose and forward engineered into PowerBuilder. However, there are certain PowerBuilder constructs, such as datawindows and menus, that are easier to create in PowerBuilder and then reverse engineer into Rose. Using both the forward and reverse engineering features, you can be sure your model and code stay consistent.

In this section, we'll examine the specific steps needed to reverse engineer your PowerBuilder code. Using the wizard, you can select the PowerBuilder library (.PBL) files you wish to reverse engineer and the specific PowerBuilder classes you want to pull into Rose.

To begin, select Tools ➤ PowerBuilder ➤ Reverse Engineer. The Rose Power-Builder Link dialog box will appear, as shown in Figure 23.1.

FIGURE 23.1:

PowerBuilder Analyzer
window

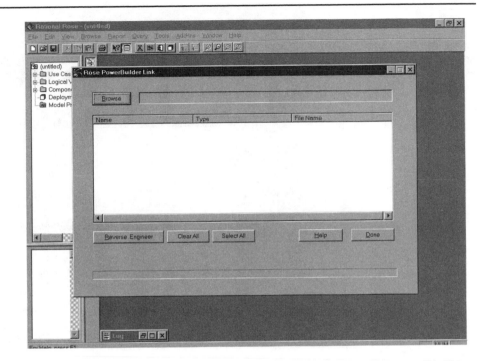

Using this dialog box, you can select the .PBL files and objects to reverse engi-neer. Click the Browse button to select a .PBL file. Once you've chosen a .PBL file, the PowerBuilder classes in that file will appear in the Rose Power Builder Link window, as shown in Figure 23.2.

Click the Browse button again and continue to select .PBL files until all classes you wish to reverse engineer are visible in the Rose PowerBuilder Link.

In the list box, select the class(es) you wish to reverse engineer, or press the Select All button to select all of the classes. Click Analyze to reverse engineer the classes. If any errors occurr, they will be written to the log window.

Model Elements Generated from PowerBuilder Code

In this section, we'll take a look at the Rose model elements that are created from various PowerBuilder constructs, including windows, datawindows, and Nonvi-sual User objects.

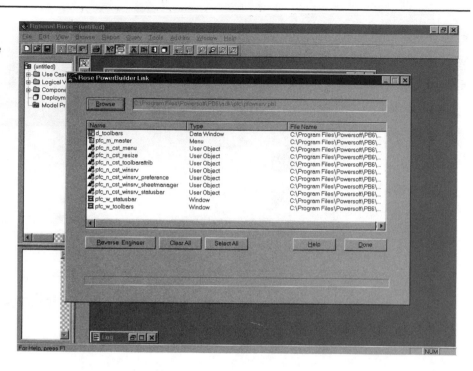

Most PowerBuilder elements are reverse engineered as stereotyped classes. See
Table 23.1 for a listing of the PowerBuilder stereotypes. In addition to the classes,
Rose will reverse engineer information about the attributes, operations, and rela-
tionships of each class.

Application Object

A PowerBuilder Application object is represented in Rose as a class with a stereotype of <<Application>>. Rose will use the name of the PowerBuilder Application object to name the Application class in the model.

Each of the Application object's instance variables will appear in the class, with
the stereotype of <<Variable>>. For example, the transaction objects sqlca and
sqlsa will appear as stereotyped attributes. Each of the Application object's functions and events will appear as stereotyped operations. Figure 23.3 shows the
Rose class that was generated for an Application object.

FIGURE 23.3:

Reverse engineering an
Application object

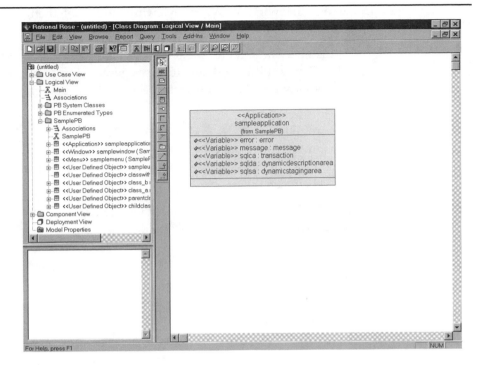

A typical PowerBuilder Application object will have five attributes: sqlca,
sqlda, sqlsa, an error attribute, and a message attribute. Each of these will be
reverse engineered as public attributes. The create and destroy functions of the
application object will be reverse engineered as public operations. The first several lines of these two functions will be displayed in the documentation window.

Nonvisual User Objects

A Nonvisual User object, like an Application object, will appear as a stereotyped
class in Rose. The stereotype for Nonvisual User objects is <<User Defined
Object>>.

Any User object functions or events for the Nonvisual User object will be
represented as stereotyped operations in Rose. For example, the constructor, create, and destroy methods are all represented as operations. When reverse engineering operations, Rose will place the first several lines of the operation into the

Documentation window. When reviewing the model, then, you can see what the operation will do by looking at the documentation window.

Any instance variables for the User object are represented as stereotyped attributes. The PowerBuilder link will reverse engineer information about the attribute name, visibility, and data type. Instance variables are given the stereotype <<Variable>>.

Aside from the attributes and operations, Rose includes information about the relationships a Nonvisual User object participates in. For example, if the object was inherited from another Nonvisual User object, a generalization relationship is created between them.

Figure 23.4 shows the Rose class that was generated by reverse engineering a Nonvisual User object from PowerBuilder.

Windows

A PowerBuilder window is pulled into Rose as a class with a stereotype of <<Window>>. When forward engineering, Rose will use the <<Window>> stereotype to create a window in PowerBuilder.

Each of the instance variables on the window will be generated as an attribute with a stereotype of <<Variable>>. Rose will include the attribute's name, data type, and visibility.

Each of the window's properties will be reverse engineered as an attribute with the stereotype of <<Property>>. For example, the Height, Width, X position, Y position, and Title window properties in PowerBuilder are included as attributes in Rose, along with their visibility, data types, and default values.

The window's events will appear as operations with the stereotype of <<EventOverride>> or <<EventOverrideInternal>>. User events for the window will appear as operations with a stereotype of <<UserEvent>>. The operations' parameters, parameter data types, and return types will also be included in the model. The first several lines of the operation will appear in the documentation window, as shown in Figure 23.5.

FIGURE 23.4:

Reverse engineering a
Nonvisual User object

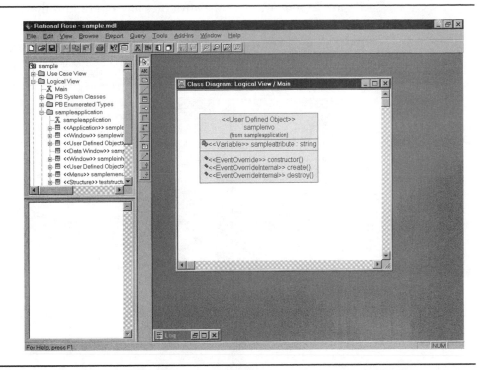

FIGURE 23.5:

Documentation window for
an operation

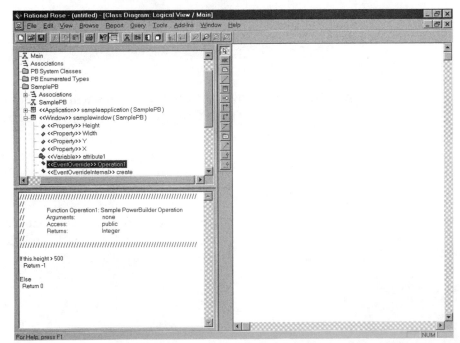

Figure 23.6 shows all of the attributes and operations that were generated by reverse engineering a single window. As you can see, all of the instance variables, window functions, and events were pulled into Rose, along with visibility, data type, and default value information.

FIGURE 23.6:

Reverse engineering a window

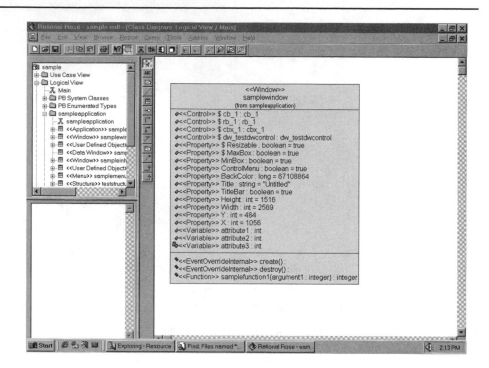

Any controls that are placed on the window will also appear as attributes. For example, if a window has a Command button cb_1, it will have an attribute, $cb_1, of type cb_1. The cb_1 class can also be shown on a Class diagram. It will appear as a class with a stereotype of <<Control>>, and will have attributes corresponding to the properties of a Command button. For example, it will have attributes called Text, TextSize, Height, Width, X, Y, and TabOrder. Each of these properties will have visibility, data types, and default values set. Figure 23.7 shows the window we just examined, along with the controls that were placed on that window. As you can see, Rose uses an aggregation relationship to model the connection between a window and its controls.

FIGURE 23.7:

Relationship between a
control and a window

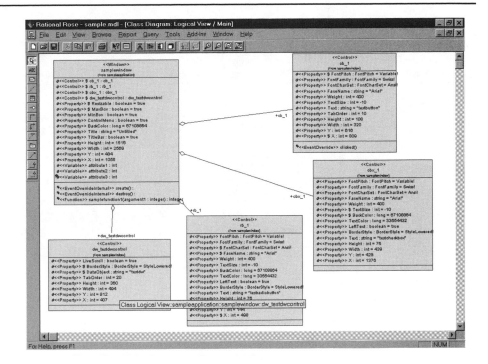

Attributes

Any instance variables that were declared in a PowerBuilder class will appear as
attributes or relationships in the Rose model. Simple data types, such as int or
boolean, are represented as attributes. More complex data types, such as Command buttons, are shown both as an attribute and as a relationship to a class. For
example, the Command button will appear as an attribute cb_1, as well as an
association to a Command Button class.

The reverse engineering process creates the attribute, along with its data type,
visibility, and default value. Shared variables appear as static attributes in Rose,
marked with a $ before the attribute name.

Figure 23.8 shows the attributes that were created by reverse engineering the
instance variables in a Nonvisual User object.

FIGURE 23.8:

Reverse engineering an instance variable. (Select the attribute in the class to display the documentation.)

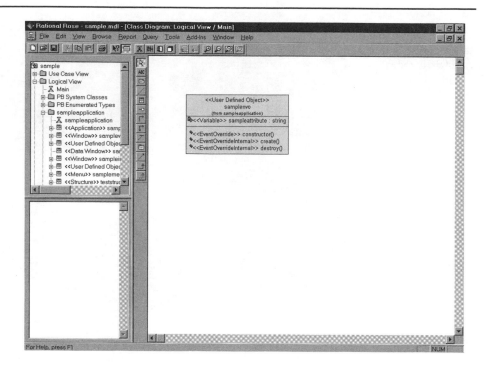

Operations

Like attributes, operations can be reverse engineered from PowerBuilder code. Each object function or event within a PowerBuilder class is represented in Rose with an operation. For example, a PowerBuilder window will have functions called create and destroy, both of which will be reverse engineered into Rose.

When reverse engineering, Rose will pull in information about the operation's name, parameters, parameter data types, return type, and visibility. All of this information will be automatically created in the operation. In addition, Rose will take the first several lines of the operation and place this information in the documentation window. You can then use the documentation window to quickly see what the operation will do.

Figure 23.9 shows the operations that were reverse engineered from a Non-visual User object.

FIGURE 23.9:

Reverse engineering a function or event. (Select an operation in the class to display the documentation.)

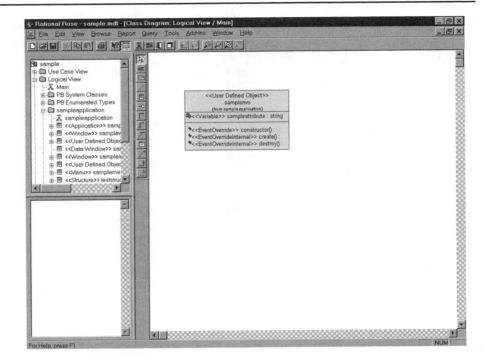

Datawindows

The Rose PowerBuilder link does not support forward engineering of datawindows. The Datawindow objects must be created in PowerBuilder and then reverse engineered into Rose.

When a datawindow is reverse engineered, it will appear as a class with a stereotype of <<Data Window>>. Figure 23.10 shows a PowerBuilder datawindow that was reverse engineered.

FIGURE 23.10:

Reverse engineering a datawindow

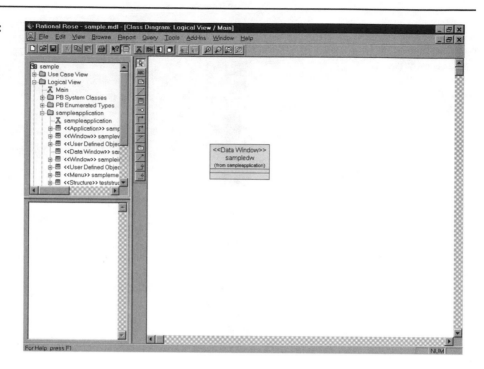

Structures

A PowerBuilder structure object will appear in Rose as a class with a stereotype of <<Structure>>. Each of the fields in the structure will appear as an attribute with a stereotype of <<Variable>>. As with other attributes, Rose will include information about the attribute name, visibility, data type, and default value.

Figure 23.11 shows a PowerBuilder structure that was reverse engineered into Rose.

FIGURE 23.11:

Reverse engineering a structure

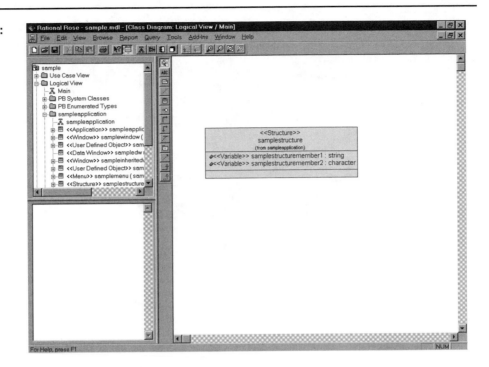

Menus

Each PowerBuilder menu will be represented in the model as a series of classes. The menu itself will appear as a class. Each submenu (File, Edit, Window, Help, etc.) will appear as a separate class, linked with an aggregation to the menu class. Finally, each separate menu item will appear as a class.

The stereotype of the menu class will be <<Menu>>. Submenus and menu items will appear as classes with stereotypes of <<Control>>. Figure 23.12 shows how a PowerBuilder menu, called samplemenu, with a single menu item, m_samplemenuitem, is represented in Rose.

FIGURE 23.12:

Reverse engineering
a menu

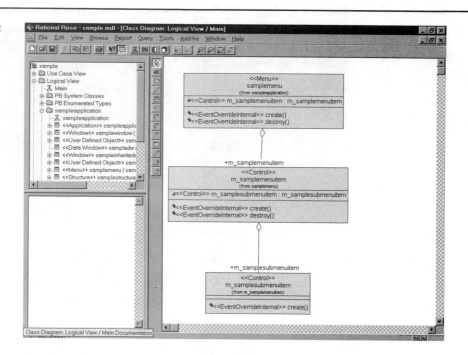

As you can see, Rose includes aggregation relationships to describe the connection between the menu and the menu items. Each of the menu's functions will appear as a stereotyped operation in Rose. Information about the function's name, parameters, parameter data types, and return type will also be included, and the first several lines of the function will appear in the documentation window. Each event of the menu, submenu, or menu item will also appear as a stereotyped operation.

Each instance variable will appear as a stereotyped attribute. As with other attributes, Rose will include information about the attribute's name, data type, default value, and visibility.

Inheritance Relationships

As you reverse engineer your code, any inheritance relationships from PowerBuilder will also be reverse engineered. These relationships will be represented by generalization relationships in the model. For example, Figure 23.13 shows an inheritance relationship between two windows.

FIGURE 23.13:

Reverse engineering an inheritance relationship

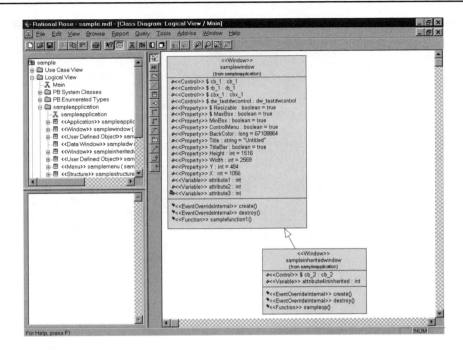

The reverse engineering process will also establish generalization relationships between the classes you reverse engineer and the base PowerBuilder classes in the PB System Classes or PB Enumerated Types packages. For example, both of the windows above are inherited from the base class Window. Figure 23.14 shows the inheritance structure for these three classes.

Association Relationships

When you generate code, the association relationships are generated by creating instance variables in the classes. Therefore, many of the instance variables in PowerBuilder will be represented as association relationships in Rose.

For example, assume a window, my_window, has an instance variable of type my_nvo, and my_nvo is a Nonvisual User object in the PowerBuilder code. When the window and Nonvisual User object are pulled into Rose, an association relationship will be set up between them. It will be a unidirectional association, from the my_window class to the my_nvo class. Figure 23.15 shows the results of reverse engineering these two classes.

FIGURE 23.14:

Inheriting classes from base
PowerBuilder classes

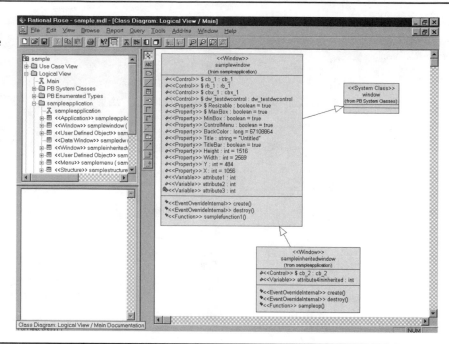

FIGURE 23.15:

Reverse engineering an
association relationship

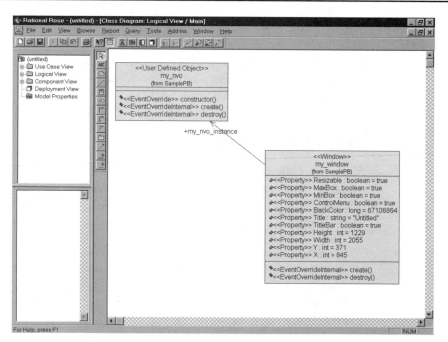

Summary

In this chapter, we examined the steps required to reverse engineer PowerBuilder code into your Rose model. Most PowerBuilder objects will translate directly into a stereotyped class in Rose. In addition, Rose will capture information about the instance variables, functions, events, and relationships in the PowerBuilder code.

We examined how several types of PowerBuilder objects will be represented in the model. Table 23.3 is a summary of the conversion.

TABLE 23.3: PowerBuilder Objects in Rose

PowerBuilder Element	Rose Element
Application Object	Class with <<Application>> stereotype
Nonvisual User Object	Class with <<User Defined Object>> stereotype
Window	Class with <<Window>> stereotype
Instance Variable	Attribute or Association
Function	Operation
Event	Operation
Datawindow	Class with <<Data Window>> stereotype
Structure	Class with <<Structure>> stereotype
Menu	Class with <<Menu>> stereotype
Menu Item	Class with <<Control>> stereotype
Inheritance Relationship	Generalization

CHAPTER

TWENTY-FOUR

24

Reverse Engineering with Oracle8

- Using the Schema Analyzer in Rose to reverse engineer Oracle8 Object types, Relational tables, Relational views, Object views, VARRAYS, Nested tables, and Object tables

- Reverse engineering generalizations

Using Rose, you can create an object model by reverse engineering an Oracle8 schema. In this chapter, we will look at how the Oracle8 elements are reverse engineered into Rose model elements. Using the Schema Analyzer in Rose, you can reverse engineer the following Oracle8 elements from a schema:

- Object types

- Relational tables

- Relational views

- Object views

- VARRAYS

- Nested tables

- Object tables

Each of these constructs are modeled as classes with the above named stereotypes. In addition, generalizations and foreign key relationships can also be reverse engineered.

Steps in Oracle8 Reverse Engineering

To begin the reverse engineering process, select Tools ➤ Oracle8 ➤ Analyze Schema. Rose will prompt you for the name of the schema you would like to reverse engineer, as shown in Figure 24.1. Enter the name of the schema and click OK to continue.

When prompted, enter the name of the database server, your user ID, and your password, as shown in Figure 24.2. Rose will establish communication with the server to finish the reverse engineering process.

Rose will create a new component in the Component view for the Oracle8 schema. Any Relational tables, Object tables, Object views, or other elements in your schema will generate stereotyped classes in Rose.

FIGURE 24.1:

Oracle8 Schema Analyzer

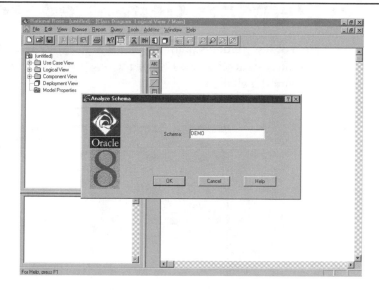

FIGURE 24.2:

Oracle8 Database Connect
dialog box

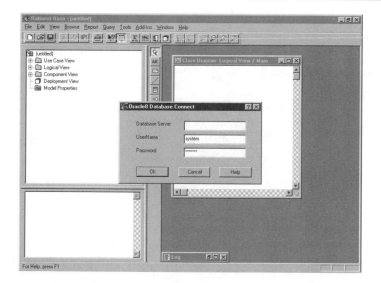

Model Elements Generated from Oracle8

Each of the elements of an Oracle8 schema will generate a stereotyped class in Rose. In this section, we'll examine how each Oracle8 element is mapped to a Rose model element.

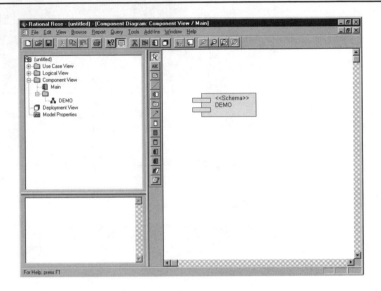

Let's start with the schema itself. In Rose, an Oracle8 schema is represented by a component with the stereotype <<Schema>>. When you reverse engineer a schema, Rose will automatically place a new component in the Component view to support the schema, as shown in Figure 24.3.

Each of the Relational tables in the schema will be shown in Rose as a class with a stereotype of <<Relational Table>>. The Product table is shown in Figure 24.4 as an example.

Each of the fields in the database table will be shown as an attribute of the Relational table class. The data type of the Database field will be used as the data type of the attribute. Indexes for the table are modeled as attributes within the Relational table class. Index attributes will have an IsIndex property set to True. Triggers on the table are reverse engineered as operations with package/ implementation visibility. In the details for the attribute, Rose will include the field specifications. For example, if NULL values are not allowed in the field, the NullsAllowed property will be set to False.

FIGURE 24.4:

Product relational table

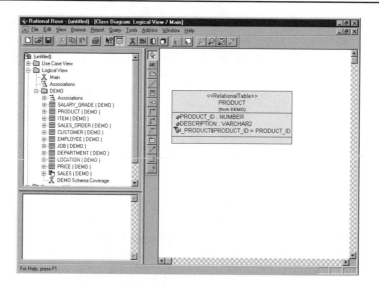

If the table included a foreign key, Rose would model this as an association relationship between the table and the foreign table along with the appropriate qualifier. The association would be given the stereotype of FK.

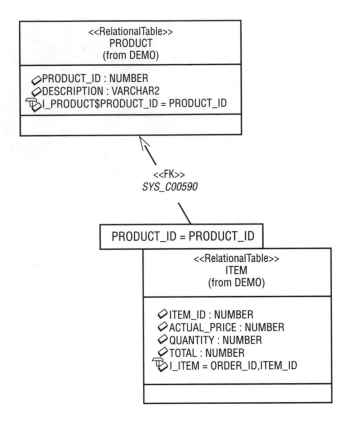

Each of the Relational views in the schema is modeled as a class with a stereotype of RelationalView. As with Relational tables, each of the fields in the Relational view is modeled as an attribute. Computed columns are modeled as methods in the class. Figure 24.5 shows a Relational view reverse engineered from Oracle8.

For an object type in the Oracle8 schema, the Object type will be modeled as a class with a stereotype of ObjectType. The Object type's fields are modeled as attributes and the functions and procedures are modeled as operations. A sample reverse-engineered Object type is shown in Figure 24.6.

FIGURE 24.5:

Sales Relational view

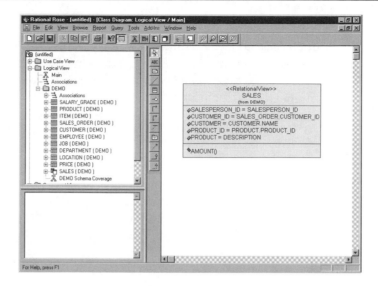

FIGURE 24.6:

Sample Object type

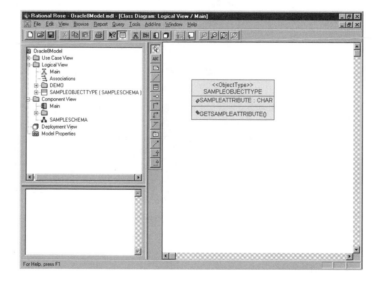

Summary

In this chapter, we examined how the various Oracle8 schema elements are reverse engineered into a Rational Rose model. Each element reverse engineers as a class in the Rose model with the appropriate stereotype. Once you have reverse engineered your Oracle8 schema, you can make modifications and then use the Schema Generator to forward engineer those changes into Oracle8.

INDEX

Note to the reader: Throughout this index **boldfaced** page numbers indicate primary discussions of a topic. *Italicized* page numbers indicate illustrations and tables.

Q

W

What's on the CD-ROM

The CD contains a variety of sample code and Unified Modeling Language (UML) models drawn from the book. These are designed to help you learn UML and Rational Rose. Throughout the book, two ongoing examples (an ATM example and an Order Processing example) are used to demonstrate the various modeling capabilities of Rose. By looking through the sample models on the CD-ROM, you can get a sense of how your object model may look as a project progresses.

The CD contains the following:

- Rose models in various stages of completion for the ATM example. Each model represents how the ATM system design might look at the end of a chapter. Models are provided in both Rose 98 and Rose 98i formats.

- Rose models in various stages of completion for the Order Processing example. Each model represents how the Order Processing system design looks after an exercise in the book. As with the ATM example, models are provided in both Rose 98 and Rose 98i formats.

- Code generated in C++, Java, Visual Basic, PowerBuilder, and IDL for the ATM and Order Processing examples.

- A sample of the HTML version of a Rose model that can be generated with the new Web Publisher feature available in Rose 98i.

- Sample Rose scripts.

- The file OrderFlow.doc, which is used in the exercise for Chapter 3.

- A trial version of METEX PowerBuilder Link, which is necessary to generate the PowerBuilder code.

- A link to the Rational Web site, http://www.rational.com/products/rose/tryit/, where you can download a trial version of the Rose software.

To view and edit the Rose models, you will need an installation of either Rose 98 or Rose 98i. To generate C++, Java, or Visual Basic code from these models, you will need Rose Enterprise Edition (containing all three languages), or Rose Professional Edition for C++, Java, or Visual Basic.